The Folk Arts and Crafts of New England

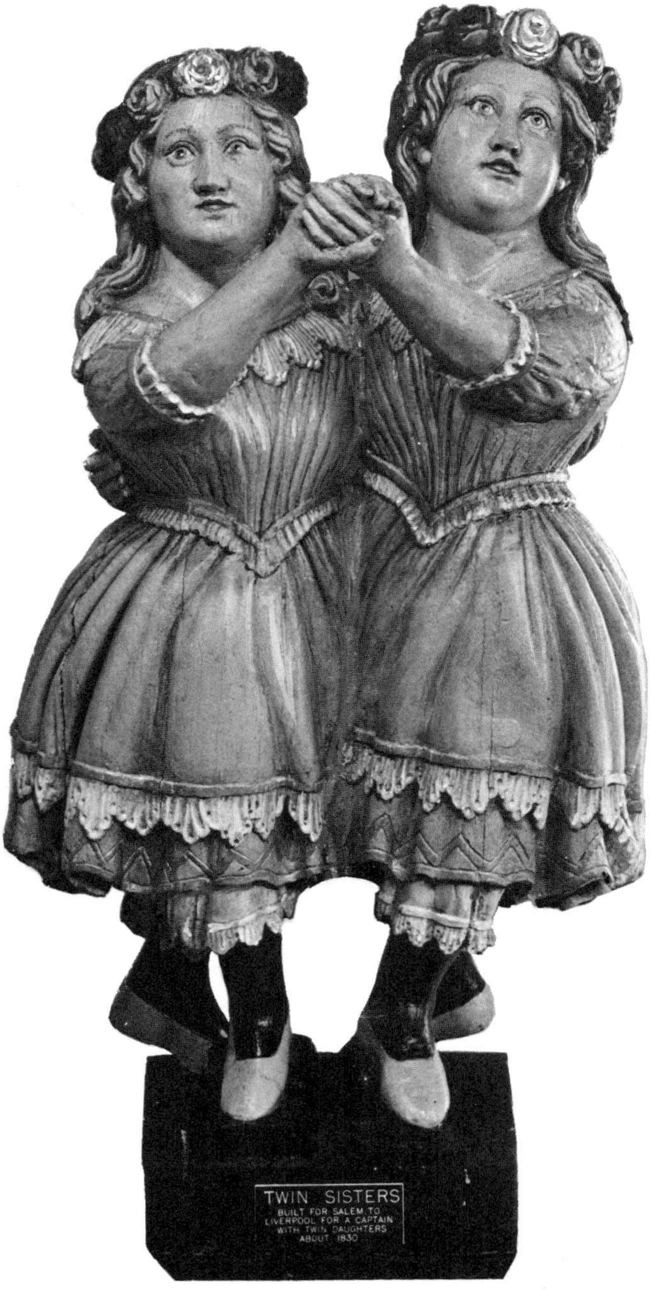

A distinctly uncommon type of figurehead carved about 1840, these two dancing children are believed to have been the daughters of a shipowner in the Salem—Newburyport area. The Twin Sisters, a fairly recent acquisition at the Mystic Seaport Museum, Mystic, Connecticut, have become one of the favorite subjects for comment. Their costumes are blue and white and wreaths of pink roses serve to accentuate their golden hair. *Photo Louis S. Martel; courtesy Mystic Seaport.*

By
Priscilla
Sawyer
Lord
and
Daniel J.
Foley

The Folk Arts and Crafts of New England

Updated Edition

CHILTON BOOK COMPANY
Radnor, Pennsylvania

Published in Radnor, PA by Chilton Book Company and simultaneously in Don Mills, Ontario, Canada, by Thomas Nelson & Sons, Ltd.

Designed by William E. Frost
Manufactured in the United States of America
Library of Congress Catalog Card Number 75-18530

To E. L. L. and E. S. S.

Also by Priscilla Sawyer Lord and Daniel J. Foley: *Easter Garland*

Acknowledgments

To the following individuals and organizations we are deeply grateful for assistance with the varied details relative to research, the preparation of the manuscript, and the selection of illustrations. Patient families, friends, and associates who have contributed most graciously in countless ways remain anonymous by choice but were ever willing to do their bit to smooth the way while this book was in the making.

Mr. J. Sanger Attwill
Mr. Richard Carter Barret
Mrs. James Bailey
Miss Ruth Bean
Mrs. Pauline Blanchard
Miss Caroline Branley
Mr. M. V. Brewington
Mrs. John B. Breymann III
John Carter Company
Mr. Samuel Chamberlain
Mrs. Homer R. Cilley
Crane Paper Company
Mr. Abbott Lowell Cummings
Mr. George Cushing, Jr.
Mr. and Mrs. Edwin R. Dayton
Mr. Ernest G. Dodge
Mrs. Peg Doore
Mrs. Sterling Emerson
Mr. and Mrs. Dean Fales
Miss Catherine Fennelly
Mr. Edward Flanagan
Mr. George Frankovich
Mr. Joseph W. P. Frost
Mrs. William W. Gallagher
Miss Helen Hagar
Miss Bessom Harris
Mr. William Henry Harrison
Mrs. Donald Hunt
Miss C. Sally Low
Mr. John Leavitt
Mr. Wilfred Marchand
Mr. Haydn Mason
Massachusetts Horticultural Society
Mr. and Mrs. Richard Merrill
Mrs. Priscilla H. Lowry Middlemass
Mrs. James A. O'Shea, Jr.
Mrs. Gerald Papin
Miss Dorothy Pasco
Mr. C. K. Perrin
Mrs. Charles Potter
Mrs. Amelia M. Rawding
Mrs. Robert Reardon
Mr. Gordon Robertson
Salem Public Library
Saugus Ironworks Restoration

Mrs. Frank H. Sawyer
Mr. Malcolm Sawyer
Mrs. Helena C. Schmidt
Mrs. Philip C. F. Smith
Mrs. Martha Genung Stearns
Mrs. A. Ralph Stephan
Miss Ruth Swain
Mrs. Lura Woodside Watkins
Mrs. Elsie Wright

Abbot Public Library, Marblehead, Massachusetts
Abby Aldrich Rockefeller Folk Art Museum, Williamsburg, Virginia
Bennington Museum, Bennington, Vermont
Boston Public Library, Boston, Massachusetts
Brick Museum, Kennebunk, Maine
Currier Art Gallery, Manchester, New Hampshire
Essex Institute, Salem, Massachusetts
Fruitlands Museum, Harvard, Massachusetts
Henry Francis Dupont Winterthur Museum, Winterthur, Delaware
Massachusetts Horticultural Society
Mystic Seaport, Mystic, Connecticut
Museum of Fine Arts, Boston, Massachusetts
Old Sturbridge Village, Sturbridge, Massachusetts
Peabody Museum, Salem, Massachusetts
Plimoth Plantation, Plymouth, Massachusetts
Salem Public Library, Salem, Massachusetts
Sandwich Glass Museum and Historical Society, Sandwich, Massachusetts
Saugus Iron Works Restoration, Saugus, Massachusetts
Shelburne Museum, Shelburne, Vermont
Wadsworth Athenaeum, Hartford, Connecticut
Women's Educational Industrial Union, Boston, Massachusetts

To the Devin-Adair Co., New York, for permission to quote from *Thoreau's Guide to Cape Cod,* Alexander B. Adams, Editor, 1962.

To Henry Holt and Co., New York, for permission to quote from *The Yankees of Connecticut* by W. Storrs Lee, 1957.

To Houghton, Mifflin Co., Boston, for permission to quote from *American Painting—First Flowers of Our Wilderness* by James Thomas Flexner, 1947.

Finally, to Alice Morse Earle who pioneered in researching the arts and crafts of New England, more than fifty years ago, we owe an immense debt of gratitude.

PRISCILLA SAWYER LORD • DANIEL J. FOLEY

Contents

Introduction

A keen awareness of the achievements of early America pervades every level of our present-day society which is obviously motivated by a genuine and highly sincere desire to know and to learn what has made the New World "tick." And not the least important phase of this growing interest is the attention being focused on the arts and crafts which have molded and modeled our historic background. The accomplishments of every era are revealed in the artifacts that have been preserved, and the rich heritage of the preceding three centuries which is ours exists primarily because of the hand skills of our forebears. From them emerged our present technological achievements. In colonial times and well into the nineteenth century, the vast majority of men lived and achieved whatever measure of success was theirs by virtue of one or several skills. In these, they were aided and abetted by their womenfolk whose deft hands seemed capable of almost any task, however tedious or demanding, thus releasing the men for more important work. Each and every skill involved the use of their hands—human instruments of power, strength and creative ability. Gradually, mechanization has removed the need for handwork in many crafts, but not all by any means. There still remain many processes in which handwork is in constant demand. The making of furniture, the cutting of diamonds, the etching of crystal, the production of fabrics—to mention only a few—require hand skills not matched presently even by the most advanced machinery, nor are they likely to be.

Machinery and automation have in reality inspired a renaissance of interest in the arts and crafts as is seen in the growth of craft centers throughout the country and shops catering to the needs of enthusiasts. Exhibitions sponsored by leading museums, galleries, and art associations indicate that there will be no dearth of handmade heirlooms for future generations to enjoy. This revival meets a vital need for the often unfulfilled creative urge with which each of us is endowed. Marion Downer has expressed this perfectly in *The Story of Design*,

> "Whatever we look at with delight,
> Whatever we see that gives us pleasure,
> though we may think we have forgotten it the next day—will influence us all our lives."

Since this renaissance of interest in hand skills is of more than casual significance, we hark back to its origin in America on Christmas Day at Plymouth in the year 1620. The felling of timber, the cutting of thatch, the making of mortar, the whir of the saw, the steady pounding of the carpenter's hammer—these and sundry other essential operations attested to the fact that "no man rested." Nor was there a pair of hands among the women and children that did not fashion something useful or assist in its making. Were it not for the fact that they were well skilled in the everyday arts and crafts, the early settlers at Plimoth Plantation and settlements at Salem, Boston, and elsewhere along the New England coast would have failed miserably. Courage, determination, and fortitude, bolstered by the inherent skill of their hands, established the firm foundation of colonial life in New England.

At every turn, necessity became the mother of invention, and the rhythm of dextrous motion as it warmed their chilled bodies gave assurance to their firm convictions and resolute actions. Whatever measure of success they were to have was to be wrought by the labor of their hands—strong, sturdy, and knowing. Hands that could grasp and hold a tool, shape a peg,, guide an adz, twist, turn, and remain steady—hands that seemed never to tire, never to waver—hands that were willing, warm, and flexible. These attributes together with their indomitable courage were their prime source of strength aganist the ever present adversity of the untamed wilderness. In an era when everything needed for survival had to be made, every available pair of hands had to be employed.

The urge to build, to make, to mold, to select, to bring order (even to the simplest task) was a part of their being. True, conditions in the New World were vastly different from the life in villages and towns in England. In the *Index of American Design* Holger Cahill wrote: "The hands that made the first two hundred years of this country's material culture expressed something more than the untutored creative and instinct and the rude vigor of a frontier civilization." They built and they created in an ancient tradition, supported by the accumulated experience of centuries.

Even the most cursory survey of early architecture, furnishings, and the utensils needed for everyday living reveals the inventiveness and creative skill of the makers. It has often been said that many of the early craftsmen who usually were proficient in several or many skills were Jacks-of-all-trades. Yet, the term is hardly appropriate or even accurate since the implication that they were master of none of their skills is indeed an erroneous concept. With the exception of those artisans who lived in the principal seaport towns where they were able to earn a livelihood as specialists, the large majority were farmer-craftsmen who by necessity had to be able to perform a number of tasks well. For example, at the beginning of the eighteenth century, it was said that the majority of Connecticut farmers bought little except salt, nails, rum, sugar, tea, and coffee. Most countrymen and their families at the time dressed in homespun and made their own shoes, breeches, hats, and stockings.

As the colonies grew in numbers, people from every part of Europe brought their combined knowledge and their individual skills and fused them with what was already established. Thus, in spinning and weaving, in the needle arts, rugmaking, building, carving, painting, and all the other arts and skills, the essence of many cultures is reflected. With it all is blended some of the fascinating techniques of the various tribes of American Indians.

Appreciation of any art or craft practiced by a skilled artisan is heightened and enriched as we come to know something of how it was wrought. While it may not be essential to commit to memory the various steps involved or even to retain the web of detail that surrounds the making of an object, it is nonetheless a broadening experience to have some sort of vignette for a setting. Then the quilted quilt, the carved figurehead, the silver chafing dish, the bit of polished wampum takes on a new kind of meaning. For more than three centuries, New Englanders by inheritance and by adoption have been making useful and decorative objects of every conceivable kind and description, and the tradition remains unbroken. Men, women and children too, continue to find ways to use their hands. The urge to create cannot be stifled or subdued, since no other outlet is more rewarding and satisfying than working with one's hands. It is more than therapy—it is a natural expression of well being and fulfillment. The labor involved and the effort required seem insignificant when the object itself is used, enjoyed, and admired.

In Bright and Shining Colors

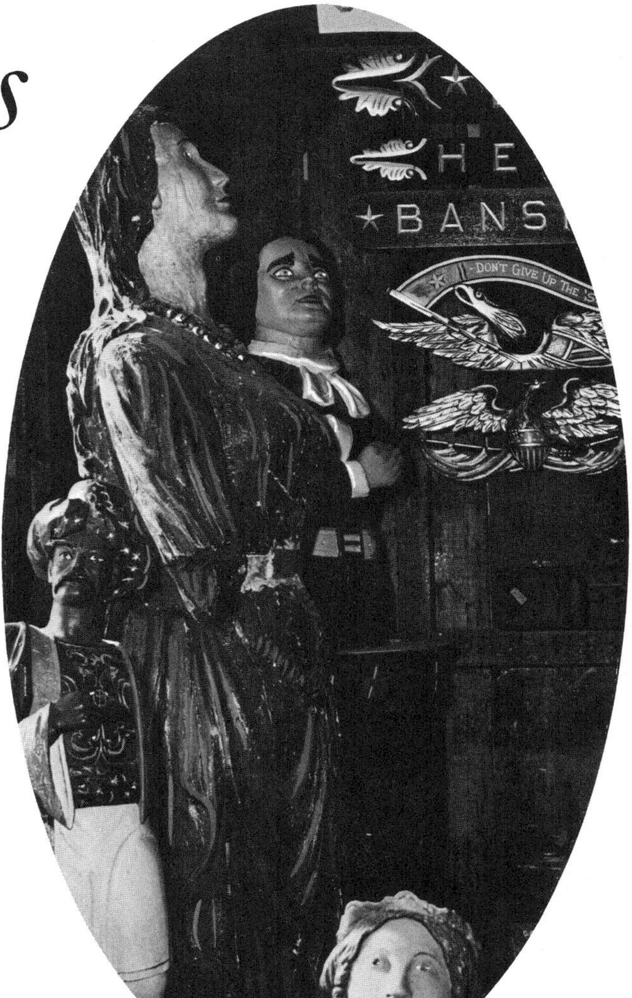

In seaport towns, the shipcarver's shop was the favorite haunt of sea captains, sailors, and small boys who were lured by the array of wood sculpture being made or repaired. Here yarns were swapped as the carver and his apprentices chiseled away or wielded their paint brushes. *Photo Louis S. Martel: courtesy Mystic Seaport*

The arts and crafts of New England which first flowered in the wilderness emerged from the inherent skill, energy, and ingenuity of a people who championed the kind of freedom that would allow them a choice as to how they would live as well as how they would worship. Commerce as well as conscience motivated them and a spirit of adventure was intermingled with these desires.

However limited their concept of the wilderness was, they knew full well when they set sail from the mother country that they were facing a new and strange land, untamed, uncivilized, and unsettled. No sooner had they set foot on the rock-bound coast of New England than they were compelled to prepare for survival. Nature's first law spurred them on to use every ounce of their strength and resourcefulness. Brickmaking for chimneys, pottery-making for cooking and eating, weaving for bodily comfort, wood-turning for housing, stone cutting for burial markers together with the village forge and such fireside industries as candlemaking, spinning, and weaving—all were basic to survival.

That the potter's art, the needlewoman's stitching, the woodcarver's modeling, and the stonecutter's chiseling were enhanced by a subtle and sensitive feeling for beauty was due largely to the skill in craftsmanship and the experience gained in the Old World. These stalwart folk knew intimately the beauty of natural forms. They were familiar with ancient symbols and they loved color. Furthermore, they took notable pride in creating these objects. Equally important was their memory of the work which they had done at home where not only their achievements but those of others reflected the latest in design and fashion. The great Elizabethan Age had produced an abundance of skilled craftsmen as a result of commerce with other nations and had brought to England top quality handwork from many countries.

Natural talents were perfected by that ancient method of training—apprenticeship where men learned an art or a craft from a master. This teacher held the title "master craftsman" in a particular skill because he had proven himself by perfecting the techniques he had learned. During a man's term as an apprentice, it helped to learn every phase of the craft which he had chosen. The work was arduous, the workday was a long one, the training period lasted three to seven years. When an apprentice became a journeyman he had acquired, in addition to a fairly broad knowledge of the techniques of his craft, the three R's. He knew well that it would take time, practice, diligent application, and long years of experience to become a master craftsman. When he achieved that status, he had truly earned it.

Skills were not acquired in ten easy lessons and there were no adult education courses. When children pursued the craft of their forebears, often the combined know-how of several generations was reflected in the finished product. This often gave to a signboard, a silver teapot, a carved chest, or whatever, a stamp of individuality and distinction—a quality which at once made it unique. Even though many handcrafted articles were of necessity produced in quantity, as with pottery where a kind of mass-production technique was needed to meet a specific demand, the maker left his mark on it. Seldom were two of anything exactly alike.

Elizabeth I, whom some of the early settlers remembered and all had heard about, having ruled England for forty-five years, from 1558 to 1603, made her influence felt in every phase of English life. Her manner of living, the trappings of her court, the very elegance of her dress—all went "hand in glove" with the shrewdness of the rule she imposed. She inspired potters as well as poets, playwrights as well as plunderers to do her bidding. At a time when it was considered unbecoming for a woman to display any degree of mental competence, she challenged her subjects, and foreign rulers as well, with a keen and calculating mind.

As the unwed matriarch of an empire in the building, Elizabeth had few peers in all English history. Despite their achievements, James I (1603-1625), who succeeded her, and Charles I (1625-1649) lacked the color, the verve, the daring courage and the indomitable spirit of Elizabeth I. Charles I and his consort, Henrietta Maria, emulated Elizabeth's taste for elegant dress, and in portraying them Van Dyck put a stamp of approval on their style. In a day when printing was costly and the illustrations used were woodcuts or engravings, much of the detail about modes and manners and changing styles was circulated by word of mouth.

Elizabeth the queen was, by no standard based on fair judgment, a beauty in any sense of the word. She was slender and rather gaunt in

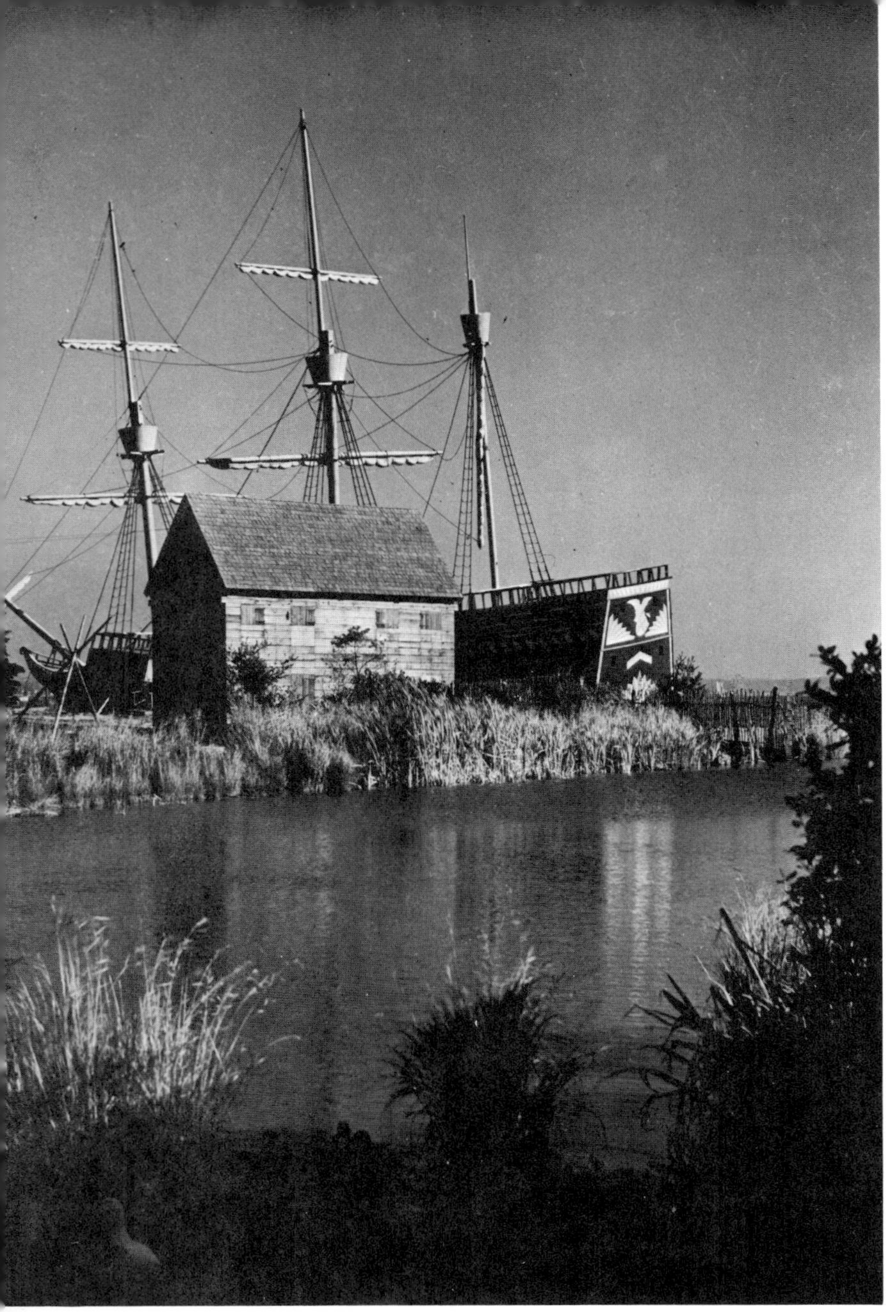

Pioneer Village, Salem, Massachusetts, a restoration erected in 1930 to commemorate the three-hundredth anniversary of the founding of the Massachusetts Bay Colony. Above is the gate house to the village and a replica of the ship *Arbella* as it appeared in 1630. *Photo courtesy Samuel Chamberlain*

appearance with a thin, oblong face and small, peering eyes; she was exceedingly plain. To compensate for these inherited characteristics, she knew full well the importance and effect of fine clothes. She was obviously partial to bright colors. Many a needlewoman worked unendingly to plainstitch and to embroider, to cut and to fit the garments she wore. Bedecked and bejeweled, she moved in her own imperious way amid the glitter and glory of her court. Though the Puritans held this ostentation in disdain, the women knew well all the details of her frills and fancies, her preferences in fabrics, colors, and jewels. They knew, too, that Sir Walter Raleigh wore a jeweled belt and gold chains. Tawny yellow, russet, ginger-lyne, and deer color as well as shades of scarlet (the grain colors) marked the color preferences of the day. Then, as now, everyone who could sought to imitate, in whatever modest fashion they might, their illustrious queen. And the memory of her fabulous way of life lingered, long, long after her death.

One and all, the Puritans frowned on extravagance in any form, but as Samuel Eliot Morison shows so clearly in *Builders of the Bay Colony,* "they appreciated comeliness, whether in a ship, a house, or a woman; and they loved bright-colored paint on ships and houses—But not on women. . . . Captain Endicott tricked out the trim of his great house at Salem with scarlet paint, hung carved bargeboards under the eaves, and lived there well and generously. Puritan costume was distinguished from court costume by comparative plainness and absence of lace and spangle, rather than by color. Only the ministers followed the ancient sacerdotal tradition in wearing black." There were "sad colored" clothes of russet, gray, green and dark blue, and for working clothes men wore leather and undyed homespun woolens; but on great occasions the Puritan might be gaudy. Governor Bellingham wears a scarlet cloak in his portrait, painted in 1641. A snatch of inventories in the Essex County probate records, for 1636-1644, yields a purple cloth suit, doublet, and hose; a green doublet, a long blue coat with silver buttons; blue, black, red and green waistcoats; purple and russet gowns; aprons of green and tawny; blue and red petticoats; plain and embroidered women's caps of various bright colors."

The settlers who came to Massachusetts Bay were of two distinct groups. In contrast to the Puritans who came to Salem and Boston, the Pilgrims who settled Plymouth counted among their number many men of low station, mostly artisans, led, to be sure, by men of competence, skill, and learning. The Puritan colonizers, on the other hand, embraced such professions as religion, trade, medicine, and not a few were well versed in the arts and sciences, together with all types of skilled artisans. These included carpenters, joiners, glassmakers, goldsmiths, weavers, as well as potters, blacksmiths, braziers, and many others. In great part, they represented men of the middle class; some had been large landholders and included even those of noble birth, like Lady Arbella and her husband Isaac Johnson, who arrived in 1630. Their heritage was rich and varied and reflected the fashion and mode of living of post-Elizabethan England.

Thus, in the New World, *color,* in one form or another, from whatever displayed it or wherever obtainable, was a much more conspicuous feature of everyday life than is commonly believed. References are constantly made to the "sad colors" of the early garments which the women and children wore, but this was based on necessity—the lack of dyes to produce the brighter colors they preferred. Yet the long black cloaks which the men wore were lined with red. The magic of color is spelled out clearly and boldly in old records and letters, journals, and inventories as witness the descriptions of "mingled colours" in the "ruggs" dating from the 1630's, as described in Chapter 10. True, these were brought from "home," and even those acquired a little later were imported until such time as dyes were available.

The popular concept of the Puritan was that of a stern personality—staunch, stalwart, and forbidding—one who shunned color in any form and the ostentation associated with it as well. Actually, the men often outdid the women in wearing bright colors. William Brewster owned a violet cloth coat, black silk stockings, and a doublet; Bradford's wardrobe indicated anything but austerity in the bright colors of his clothes. Forgotten or overlooked is the fact that in the New England in which they lived it was not always November. Nor did the pallid sun always shine through a steel blue sky casting its pewter hue on the fields covered with drab-brown and sand-colored grass. If they wore "sad colors" at first (and they did), we know why.

Nathaniel Hawthorne painted the picture of Puritan dreariness and gloom in his somber romances—all done in tones of mouse-colored grays, grim black, and chaste white and, occasionally, lurid scarlets. No one should have known better than he that the Puritans not only knew but used and loved color. They were no haters of beauty, but so it seemed to those of succeeding generations. Hawthorne's roots had been deeply imbedded in Puritan soil for generations. It may well be that to convey his ideas and to delineate characters, he used these colors symbolically. In any event, the picture he painted has been imprinted indelibly in the popular mind, establishing itself as an ill-begotten myth.

"The belief that the Puritan home was soberly colorless is part of the New England myth; seldom has color run such riot through American rooms. A modern chest of drawers must be plain so that it will not distract attention from the entire decor. Since the conception of planning a chamber as a unified whole had not yet developed, the medieval chest suffered from no such restriction. A smooth expanse of wood made early American fingers itch for carving tool or paintbrush. If a Colonial was not in the mood to draw a design, he could at least disguise the surface to make it look like something else. The Metropolitan Museum of Art has a table whose top was painted to imitate marble, while its base masquerades as tortoise shell." This, from James T. Flexner, author of *American Paintings, First Flowers of our Wilderness,*

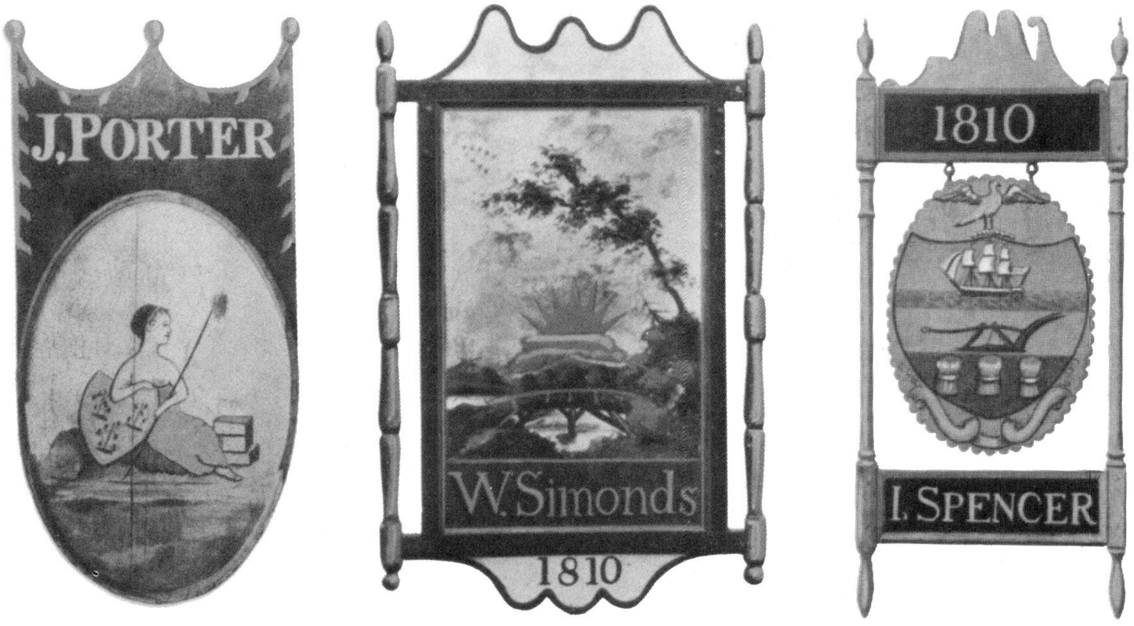

Tavern and trade signs were thoughtfully designed, solidly constructed, and painted in bright colors. Gold leaf often made them glisten in the sun.

who further emphasizes the taste and leanings of the Puritan woman.

"The settler's wife was likely to abet his hatred for plain surfaces by making Turkey-work rugs to throw over the tables, gaily colored cushions for the chairs, and embroidered hangings to further brighten the painted walls. Add copper pans and pewter jugs polished and ranged carefully for display; add spinning wheels and cobblers' tools; add a brood of twelve children playing and working in the kitchen, and you have not a still life of a Puritan in a peaked hat, but a picture of vigorous and hearty living."

The Puritans brought with them from England a tradition of design that had been an integral part of the culture of their fold for numberless generations. That pigment was applied to walls and furniture, that shapes were sometimes worked in textiles rather than on canvas, does not change the fact that the seventeenth-century settler was familiar with the application of color to achieve a decorative effect."

Anyone who has ever stood in the middle of a seventeenth-century room can recall that, even in the subdued glow of candlelight, such a setting reveals itself with all the muted richness of tone found in an old tapestry. Highlights and shadows (on walls, ceilings, and floor) enhance the atmosphere. Even a casual glance at the incised surfaces of a carved chest or the serpentine turnings on an ancient armchair shows us that they, too, are not without their share of color—light and dark. Then as now, add linseed oil—or that natural kind from the rubbing of many hands on the arms of the chair—and the highlights of the polished surface literally shine, accentuating the varied tones of the wood. The reds, blues, and soft mustards in the "mingled colourd" rugs on the bed, table or chest become all the more apparent in the sunlight when seen against the pumpkin-yellow glow of the mellow pine paneling. The silvery tones of gleaming pewter, the warmer sheen of copper and brass and the almost vermilion brilliance of the redware add lustre to the setting. Even the master's scarlet-lined cloak, hung on a peg near the door, lends a vibrant note.

"Here is good living for those who love good fires," wrote the Reverend Francis Higginson in his *New-England's Plantation*. And George Francis Dow adds: ". . . under the spell of the glowing flames, the bare, whitewashed walls, the brown timbers and floor boards of the ceiling, the dress of pewter, and the simple furnishings of the room, enriched by the shadows, became a place full of cheer—a place where privation and homesickness might be forgotten in the glow of the bright firelight. On cold nights the short bench inside the fireplace was a chosen place and the settle, a long seat made of board with a high back to keep off the draft, was drawn before the fire and here sat the older members of the family."

In the daylight hours, the play of sunlight filtering in through the small-paned leaded windows (and through the open "batten" door in warm weather) varying in its intensity with the passing of each hour, causes the colors to soften or become more vivid. The magic of color is everywhere reflected, changeless in its value, yet everchanging to the eye as this or that object is encompassed in nature's brightest spotlight. Time and constant exposure to the sun's bright rays soften these tints and shades, sprung in one form or another from the earth. And, with age, the results are and were all the more subtle in their varied blending.

To be sure, not every family in the colonies had a house as well furnished and equipped as that of Henry Dunster, president of Harvard College from 1640 to 1654. But, when he died in 1660, his estate included the following items and, significantly enough, color was considered sufficiently important to be included in the inventory. Nothing drab or somber here: "Eleven feather beds or Downs, all well furnished. One had phlox and cherry curtains ingrain with a Deep silk Fringe on the Vallance and a smaller on the Curtain, and a coverlet made of Red Kersey and barred with green lace round the sides and two down the middle. Also there apertained to that bed an outlining the quilt, also another a blew serge suit, very rich and costly curtains and valances laced and fringed, and a blew rug to the bed. Also a Greene suite in the same manner, also another Red wrought suite with a stoole and all things complete. Also a Canopy bed with curtains, a chest of Drawers, of which one of that chest was full with linnen, a Damask Suite, several Diaper Suites, a fine yellow Rug, with a starr and with abundance of Flaxen Linnen for common use. In another part of the Chest of Drawers tapes and tafetys for screen and shades. A paire of candle-sticks of sorts, A great brasse pot, Brasse of all sorts useful for a family, Pewter of several sorts. Plate of all sorts great and small, 29 spoons, A very fair salt with 3 knobs on top of it, 3 silver pitchers of lesser sort, A great silver tankard, 4 mugs to stand on a table, quite fine; 6 porringers. 1 small, 3 great bowles; 4 mugs and a pot, Silver grater with cover. 6 plain trenchers, Plate. Also Blanketts, Coverletts and Rugs." In the very same year that Henry Dunster died, John Hull, a leading Boston merchant, was importing from England such stuff as "hats of various shapes and color, blue duffels and red penistones, red and yellow flannels, red galant cloth and blue ditto; red and blue worsted stockings." Obviously the colonists liked red!

Let there be no mistaken notion that the colonialist of the seventeenth century disliked color or shied away from it. Notwithstanding the fact that when time ran out for the "elder" or some other loved one, the cold gray and dull brown of the winged skulls on the gravestones and the gloomy black crepe, too, hung heavy; yet in life, every fleeting moment of it, the Puritan lived, breathed, worked, and played in the midst of bright and shining colors.

Even in winter, New England had its sparkling color. Along the coast from Eastport to Block Island and inland, as well, the winter sun sets (as in the 1700's) on many a day in an

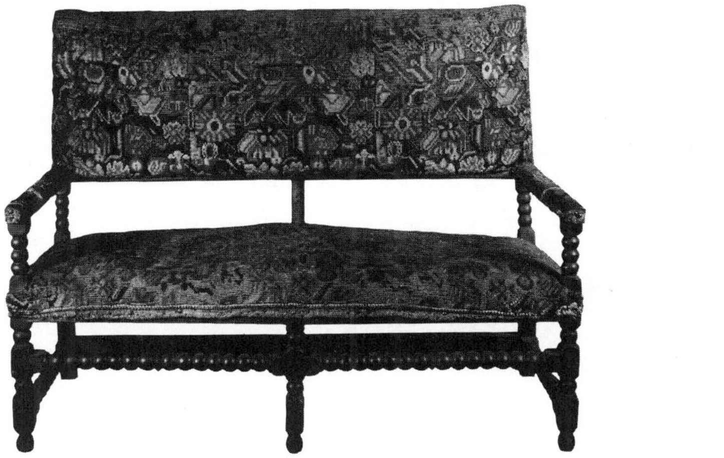

Among the treasures brought to the colonies by the Huguenots was a settee covered in needlepoint. Owned by a family that settled in Salem in 1685, it remains as one of the highly prized pieces of seventeenth-century furniture in the Essex Institute. *Photo courtesy Essex Institute*

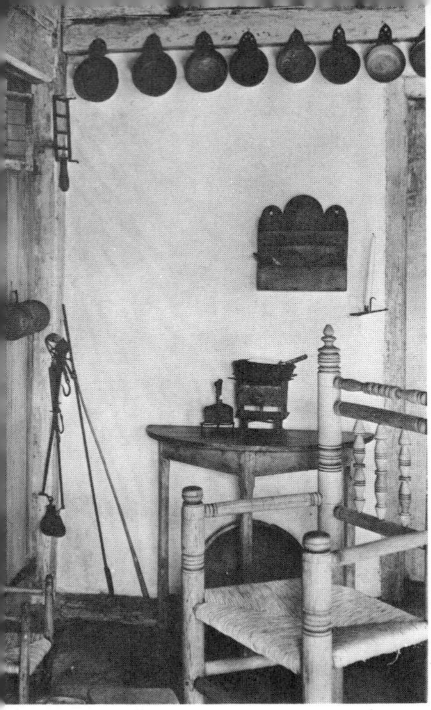

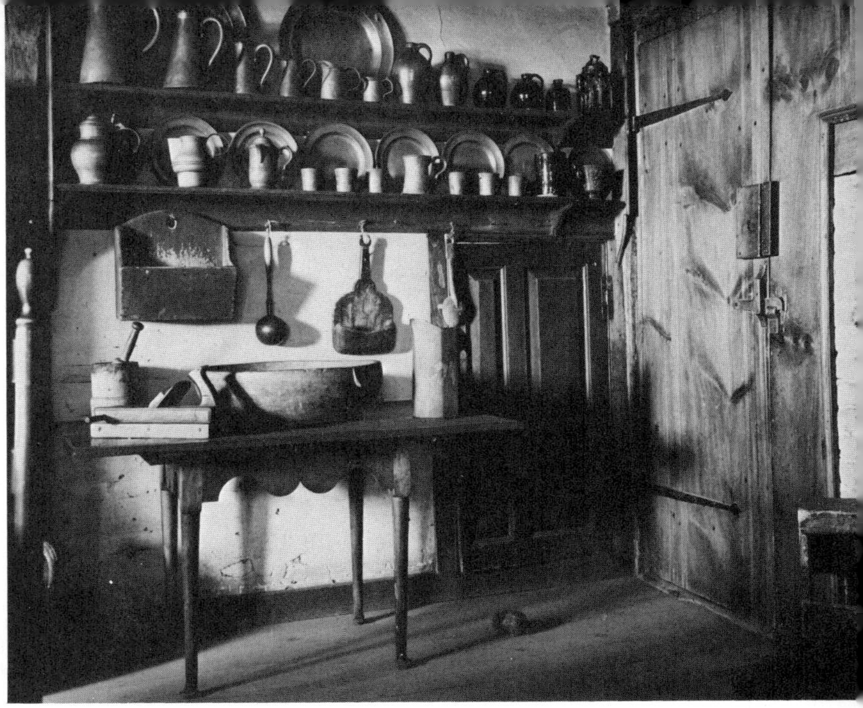

(*Above, left*) In an era when closets and cupboards were few, utensils of tin, iron, and wood were kept near at hand. Old Haskell House (*c.*1652), West Gloucester, Massachusetts. (*Above, right*). Color galore is to be found in the kitchen (also the living room) of the John Ward House (1682) in Salem, Massachusetts, where pewter, copper, redware, and dark brown glazed pottery are arranged on the shelves. The table, with its duck-foot legs and generous curves, has all the mellow richness of old pine. *Photos courtesy Samuel Chamberlain*

unforgettable blaze of glory and, though fleeting in its everchanging beauty, the sunset, then as now, evokes many a psalm of praise. Again, the sun playing on the water, by the sea or on an inland lake or stream, makes it gleam and sparkle as if jewels were being scattered on its glassy surface.

When spring came, in all its burgeoning fullness, there was color galore—the color of trees, shrubs, flowers. These the colonials loved, for their dedication to gardening was inherent. Hawthorne expressed it this way: "There is not a softer trait to be found in the character of those stern men than that they should have been sensible of those flower-roots clinging among the fibres of their rugged hearts, and felt the necessity of bringing them over sea, and making them hereditary in the new land."

On the seventy-second day of John Winthrop's tedious voyage across the wide ocean, there came flying as to the Ark, a dove; and there came also a "pleasant and sweet air" to the weary passengers on board the *Arbella* and her fellow transports "a smell of the shore like the smell of a garden"; and four days later the *Arbella* came to anchor.

> "With hearts revived in conceit new Lands
> and Trees they spy,
> Scenting the Caedars and sweet fern from
> heat's reflection dry,"

wrote one colonist of that arrival, in his *Good Newes from Newe England.*

Fair and beautiful before these ship-weary souls lay the picturesque rocks, the green shores of the Land of Promise, sweet as they are today with summer incense from the cedars and sweet fern; radiant with the ephemeral, the paradisiacal glory of a New England day in June, rare and perfect . . . "sweet single roses and strawberries"—daisies—buttercups.

Many of the earliest dooryard gardens planted along the Atlantic seaboard faced on the ocean or on some inlet from the sea. Enclosed by fences of wattle, rough pickets, or simple rail construction, these little plots were filled with herbs, culinary and medicinal, and favorite flowers of the Old World. Continually, they provided a nostalgic link with gardens left behind across the sea. These flower patches beyond the threshold were something to behold. Here were the blues—light and dark in larkspur (lark's heels, too, they called it); brilliant and sparkling in the starry blooms of borage and the bell-shaped rampion; richer still when the blue flags waved their banners. Orange and gold and touches of russet literally shone in the French marigolds, the calendulas, the tansy, the dyer's-weed (genista), and the showy elecampane. There was the soft pink of hyssop and bouncing Bet; the lavender and purple of fra-

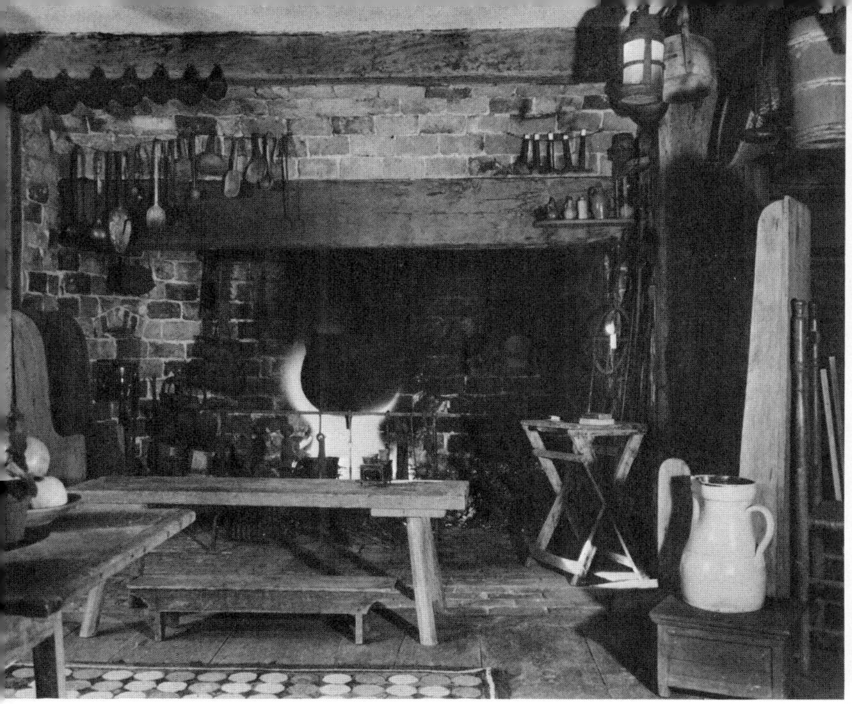

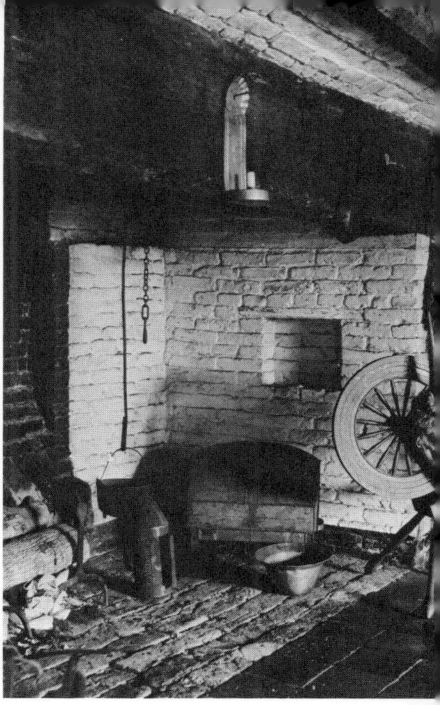

(*Above, left*) Beauport, at Gloucester, has been aptly called the most fascinating house in America. Henry Davis Sleeper built a little cottage on Eastern Point and into it poured his love for furnishings, objects of art, and household utensils that to him reflected use and beauty as made by men and women of earlier generations. (*Above, right*) The muted red tiles in the hearth are nearly twice the size of the bricks used within the fireplace of the Abraham Browne House (1663), Watertown, Massachusetts. *Photo courtesy Samuel Chamberlain*

grant thyme. On and on the riot ran—color by the door. So, too, the everchanging landscape—around and behind them—in its myriad tints and shades!

John Josselyn, writing in the mid-seventeenth century, reminds us that not all the roots and seed brought to the New World flourished. For some, the ground in winter was too damp; for others the severe cold was more than they could stand, but this did not deter the sturdy Englishwomen who tended them, or dampen their ardor. They soon found ways to combat the weather, even winter gales and heavy snow. Their love of gardens was inborn.

On June 26, 1629, the Reverend Higginson wrote in his journal: "Friday a foggy morning, but after clear, and wind calms . . . The sea was abundantly stored with rockweed and yellow flowers, like gilliflowers. By noon we were within three leagues of Cape Ann; and as we sailed along the coasts, we saw every hill and dale and every island full of gay woods and high trees. The nearer we came to the shore, the more flowers in abundance, sometimes joined in sheets nine or ten yards long, which we supposed to be brought from the low meadows by the tide. Now what with fine woods and green trees by land, these yellow flowers painting the sea, made us all desirous to see our new paradise of New-England . . ."

The brilliant attire in which the maples, oaks, and sassafras decked themselves in autumn was an experience new to the pioneers. They had not known such spectacular pageants of fall color at home. True, some trees and shrubs of the English countryside change color as summer wanes, but generally the effects are much more subdued than what they witnessed in the new land. The golden days of October and early November were indeed an inspiration for these homesick settlers, ill equipped to face the rigors of the wilderness, but determined to establish themselves and their way of life. Somehow, they survived and flourished and those "flower-roots clinging among the fibres of their rugged hearts" actually took root in the virgin soil of Colonial America. Thomas Morton, a contemporary of Bradford and Winthrop expressed himself thus: "I did not think that in all the known world it could be parallel'd for so many goodly groves of trees, dainty fine round rising hillucks, delicate faire large plains, sweet crystall fountaines, and cleare running streams that twine in fine meanders through the meads, making so sweet a mumering noise to heare as would even fill the senses with delight a sleepe, so pleasantly doe they glide upon the pebble stones, jetting most jocundly where they doe meete and hand in hand runne downe to Neptune's Court, to pay yearely tribute which they owe him as soveraigne Lord of all springs."

Furthermore, the story of color as reflected in the clothing, furnishings, and homes of colonial New England in the eighteenth century and its even greater influence in the life of the new-country citizen from the Revolution on is here in the pages of this book. The end product of every art and skill practiced was bound up with color in one way or another. Bright colors continued to play a vital part in the lives of the colonials. Not only were floors painted and decorated, but walls were similarly treated. Panels in doors and over mantels often held scenic effects. Except in a few isolated instances, highly ornamental stenciling and fresco work (long since concealed by layers of wallpaper and numerous coats of paint) have unfortunately disappeared. The same is true of furniture, which, once painted, has in many cases been restored to its prime natural finish. Clocks, mirrors, picture frames, boxes for storing all sorts of objects, trays, in fact every type and kind of article went through the "painting stage" from 1750 on. Hangings and valances for beds as well as spreads, coverlets, curtains, rugs, cushions, chairs, and sofas—all these—lent more than a little touch of color. The itinerant painter (or limner as he was sometimes called,) with his likenesses and "land-skips," like so many of his compatriots at the time, was a traveling artist, one of that great roving band of craftsmen who hawked as they walked and tricked out many a creditable job for New England parlors.

In some houses, prior to 1700, plain whitewashed walls were enhanced or accentuated by the use of dark red or black borders. Here and there mention is made of interior painting on walls, woodwork, and shutters, but little is known about it. Nor can it be expected that evidence is likely to be uncovered because of the numerous coats of paint applied in many houses over the years. (However, scraping paint to determine original color can be a most fascinating avocation.)

Nina Fletcher Little, having researched this field in a most thorough and scholarly way, has reported her findings in *American Decorative Wall Painting*. Because linseed oil was not easily obtainable and pigments were expensive, the story of painting and decorating houses, both inside and out, begins about 1725. The new trend resulted in a wide variety

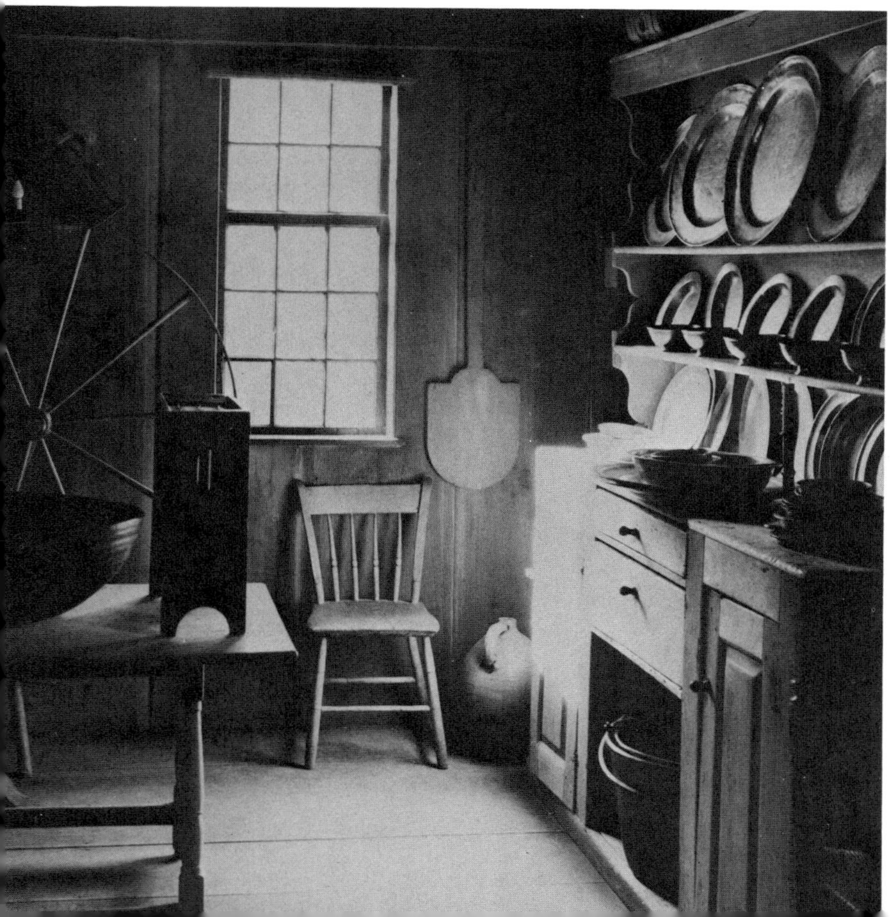

Sudbury's Wayside Inn (1686), for more than two hundred and fifty years known variously as Hoew's Tavern and Red Horse Tavern, and one of the best loved hostelries in all New England, inspired Longfellow's "Tales of a Wayside Inn." Few establishments today link the past and the present with so warm and gracious a spirit of continuity, providing rest and refreshment, as in the era when first it opened. Additions, improvements, and furnishings that "grew" with the house over the years tell a vivid story of the development of the New England way of life. Most of all, the old kitchen literally shines with the soft natural colors of gleaming pewter, ancient woodenware, and time-aged paneling and floor boards. *Photos courtesy Samuel Chamberlain*

of expression on the part of the itinerant craftsmen who plied their trade throughout New England. Mrs. Little sums it up in this manner: "The influence of the traveling decorator on the early homes of rural America can hardly be over-estimated. It was the itinerant painter who, for a modest sum, could provide the woodwork and walls of the simplest interior with patterns and color. What a house might lack in the way of fine paneling, or wall hangings, could be simulated by the use of paint, if cleverly applied by an ingenious country craftsman. Paneled wainscot could be imitated to enrich a plain plaster wall; painted door casings could be supplied to 'dress up' a wood-sheathed entry; gold-framed pictures could be 'hung' in the best parlor; and wallpaper could be so artfully reproduced that the owner might enjoy at least a visual effect of luxury." These decorators were men of many skills and, aside from apprentice training they had received, they continued to learn by doing. In addition, they acquired more than a little knowledge of changing fashion from some of the houses where they were employed. In the days prior to the Revolution and long afterward, the sea captains were bringing home all sorts of strange furniture, china, and fabrics. Already, there were those who collected things, curious and rare, brought from ports like Zanzibar, Canton, Mocha, and Manila. Like the sea captains whose trade was greatly diversified, these artists could do plain or fancy work in all branches of the trade. In 1785 Abraham Delanoy of New Haven advertised in the *Connecticut Journal:* "Likenesses painted on canvas, carriages painted, ornamented, gilt and varnished. Signs of all kinds. Plain house and ship painting carried on . . . Paints mixt at short notice." In the *Connecticut Courant* in 1801 Luther Allen of Enfield announced: "Portrait painting in oil of all sizes from busts to full figures. Painting with pastels or crayons, miniature painting, hair work, etc." For the ornamental trade he did "carriage painting embellished with gildings and drawings, sign painting, lettering with gold leaf, and smalting."

There were other ways of advertising as well as in the columns of newspapers. In South Waterford, Maine, there lived a craftsman who was never spoken of except as "the striper." He was an excellent painter particularly good on wheel spokes which he usually decorated in red, white and blue, a painstaking and exacting task.

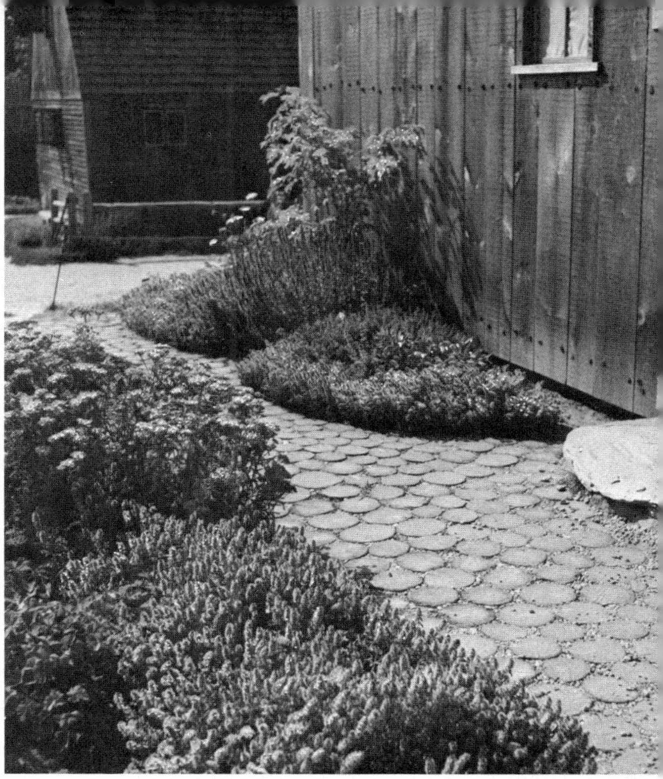

The flower patches that bloom in the dooryards at Plimoth Plantation, reminiscent of those planted in the seventeenth century, are filled with the color and fragrance of thyme, rosemary, sage, chives, pot marigolds, hyssop, lovage, an elderberry bush or two, and many other old favorites. For centuries Englishwomen had been dedicated gardeners and they soon turned their hands to the bare ground near their new homes to recapture something of the joy derived from green things growing. *Photo George Taloumis*

From his performance he was dubbed "the striper." Whenever anyone passed his handsomely painted house or stopped to look at his latest wheel-painting job it was referred to as "an advertising job"; all who saw it wanted the same.

In passing it should be mentioned that new and shining colors apparently were more widely used and more highly regarded even on the exteriors of buildings than is generally realized. Reference to Governor Endicott's "fayre" house in seventeenth-century Salem has been made previously. Among the records of the First Congregational Church at Kittery Point, Maine, may be found a bill for painting the church in 1730; the colors used were pink and blue and the signatures of Gerrish and Pepperell attest to the fact that the bill was paid. This is contrary to a notion long held that a Puritan church, especially one with a steeple or bell tower, was not appropriately painted unless the edifice was gleaming white. A search through old records undoubtedly would reveal other equally interesting examples of color as used on public buildings.

In Pomfret, Connecticut, in 1762, it was voted that "the new meeting-house be colored on the outside of an orange color—the doors and bottom boards of a chocolate color—the windows, jets (cornices), corner boards and weather boards, colored white." These contrasting hues seem to have met with considerable favor since five years later, 1767, the villagers of Thompson, Connecticut, voted to paint their new house of worship "the same as Pomfret." In 1797, Timothy Dwight, that keen-eyed observer and recorder, remarked that only a small number of the houses in Dover, New Hampshire, were painted with a "dull disagreeable colour," while those of Suffield in his own state of Connecticut were "painted white [the common colour of houses in New England]; and in the midst of lots universally covered with a rich verdure, and adorned with flourishing orchards, exhibit a scene uncommonly cheerful."

A book published in 1801, *Paints and receipts for wooden work,* gave the following instructions "for laying on of your coloring, for outdore work it must be mixt with linsid oil, but for indore work it may be mixed with Strong Beer or Milk." Spanish Brown, a dull dark red,

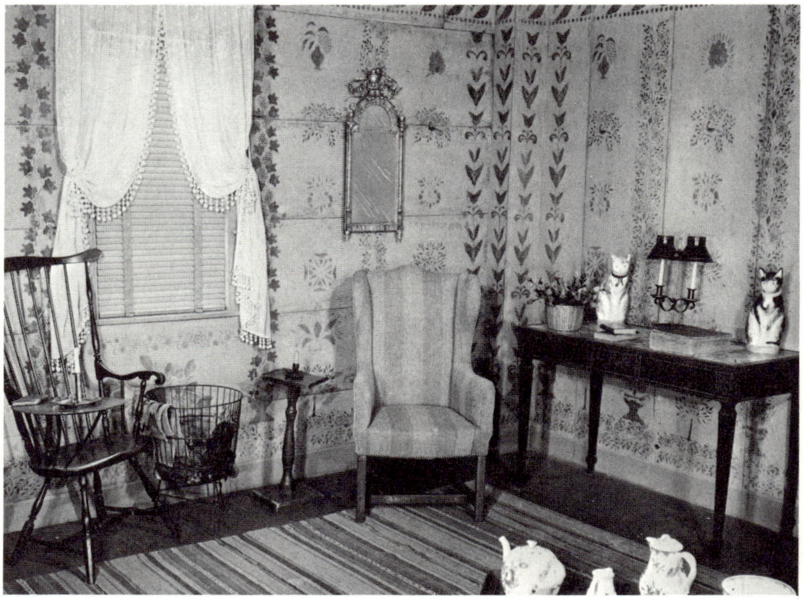

When wallpaper was too costly for homeowners of modest income, stenciling was used for decorative effects. Conventionalized motifs based on leaf and flower patterns were popular; borders accentuated windows, doorframes, ceilings, and baseboards. The effect created comes into sharp focus when the sun, shining through the parlor windows of the Stencil House (1790), at Vermont's Shelburne Museum, enlivens the varied green tones. *Photos E. J. Mengis: courtesy Shelburne Museum*

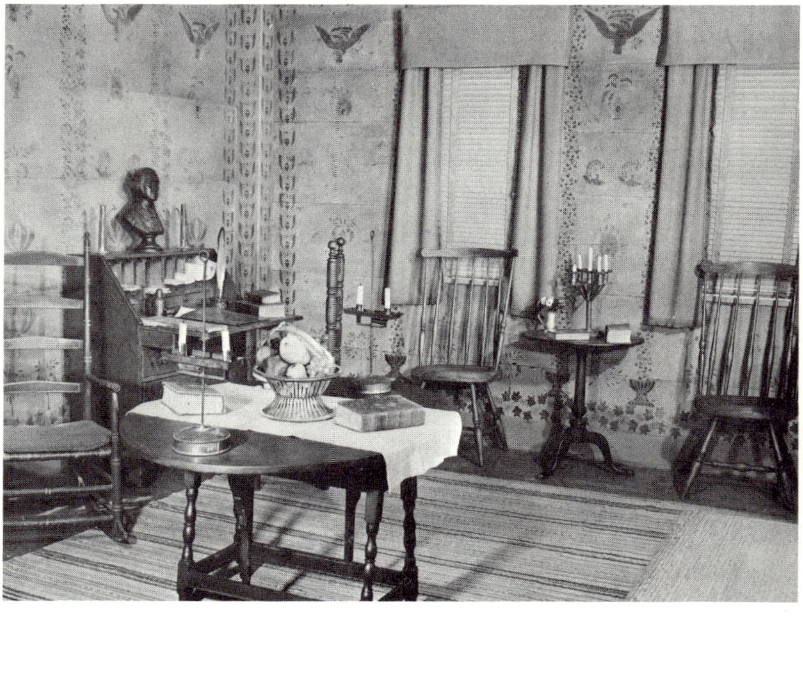

The American eagle had its place on the stenciled walls of many a New England house. Wide wallboards are a feature of this and other rooms in the Stencil House at the Shelburne Museum. The wall decorations, predominantly blue green and muted red, applied in the early 1800's, are believed to have been the work of Moses Eaton or some other itinerant artist who was familiar with Eaton's designs. Furnishings throughout the house, even to the smallest detail, reflect the discriminating taste of Mrs. J. Watson Webb. Curiously enough, the simple weatherbeaten exterior of this farmhouse reveals nothing of the warmth and rare charm of the interior.

of a horseflesh color, "was often used both on the walls and roofs of houses."

The itinerant artist who came to "take" likenesses usually mixed his own pigments, especially if he had been apprenticed to a sign, coach, or house painter in his younger days. Consequently, when he was asked what this or that color was and where it came from, he could tell some strange stories, but, however weird they sounded, they were true. The powdered colors were sold in the bladders of small animals. By pricking the bladder with a bone tack, a small amount was released and mixed in linseed oil; then the tack served as a stopper. Esther Forbes has given us a vivid picture of these curious containers in *Rainbow on the Road.* "Even as the size of the bird determined the size of the brush, the size of the animal whose bladder served as container determined the amount of color bought. The biggest bladder used was that of a rabbit. If you wanted more, instead of going into sheep or swine bladders, you bought two rabbitsful. This was about an ounce. A rat's bladder was smaller. These were commonest but other animals served. A mouse's bladder was the smallest unit."

Children especially always wanted to know where the colors came from and what they were called. There was verdigris to produce a lovely blue or green; vermilion came from quicksilver, sulphur, and red lead; paris green, with its vinegary smell, was poisonous. Others were "burnt terra di Sienna," brazilwood, logwood, gamboge, Chinese red, and cochineal from insects. One of the paints used for backgrounds was "Mummy" obtained by grinding up the remains of the ancient Egyptians "with their spices and tarred wrappings and people who'd been dead way back in the Old Testament days." But the strangest tale of all concerned the account given of King's yellow which came from the mountains of Persia where a natural vein of sulphide of arsenic had been found. This was the stuff that the Borgias used to eradicate their enemies. Even in handling it and grinding it, there was great danger. This was poison too, dangerous and deadly.

How the small boys laughed, and their sisters, too, as the limners reeled off the romantic story of where their pigments came from. Colors made good talk. Perhaps as the "yarn" was being told, mother or father, looking over the shoulder of the painter, took a notion to have another head taken while the limner had his brushes out and his paints were still wet and shiny on the palette.

The rigorous climate of New England was obviously conducive to the development of home industry, reflecting an extensive variety in skill and accomplishment. A small room attached to the house or a separate building for a shop served the needs of most craftsmen who worked alone or employed one or two apprentices. These "beehives" of industry that remain (original or restored) may be seen on the grounds of historical societies or in various historical sites such as Sturbridge Village, Mystic Seaport, The Shelburne Museum, and others. (Colonial Williamsburg has probably the most complete group of craftsmen's shops, all operating continuously.)

A goodly number of craftsmen, especially in small or isolated towns, practiced several skills, usually related, although not always as in the case of a man possessed of diversified talent. It became a common practice to speak of such a person as a Jack-of-all-trades ("and master of none") but such was not the case. Necessity demanded diversity of skill. In 1771, Captain Judah Woodruff of Farmington, Connecticut, not only designed and built a church in his community, but carved the pulpit and sounding board with his own hands. Men of ability, versatile and competent, were numerous, and they have left their monuments in the work which they have wrought.

Colonial life developed its own patterns, but did so despite the efforts of the conservatives who were eager to preserve the *status quo,* not invent; to control, not release; to preserve a past rather than create a future. Here is the point of view of one New Englander. "It's more noble to be employed in serving and supplying the necessities of others, than merely in pleasing the fancy of any. The plow-man that raiseth grain, is more serviceable to mankind than the painter who draws only to please the eye. The carpenter who builds a good house to defend us from Wind and Weather is more serviceable than the curious Carver, who employs his Art to please the Fancy." First things come first!!! Nonetheless, the opportunity was afforded for "the painter who draws only to please the eye" and "the curious Carver who employs his Art to please the Fancy." First things did come first and the Colonialist's love of beauty in form, color, and texture followed, including all those bright and shining colors.

Spinning, Weaving, and Dyeing

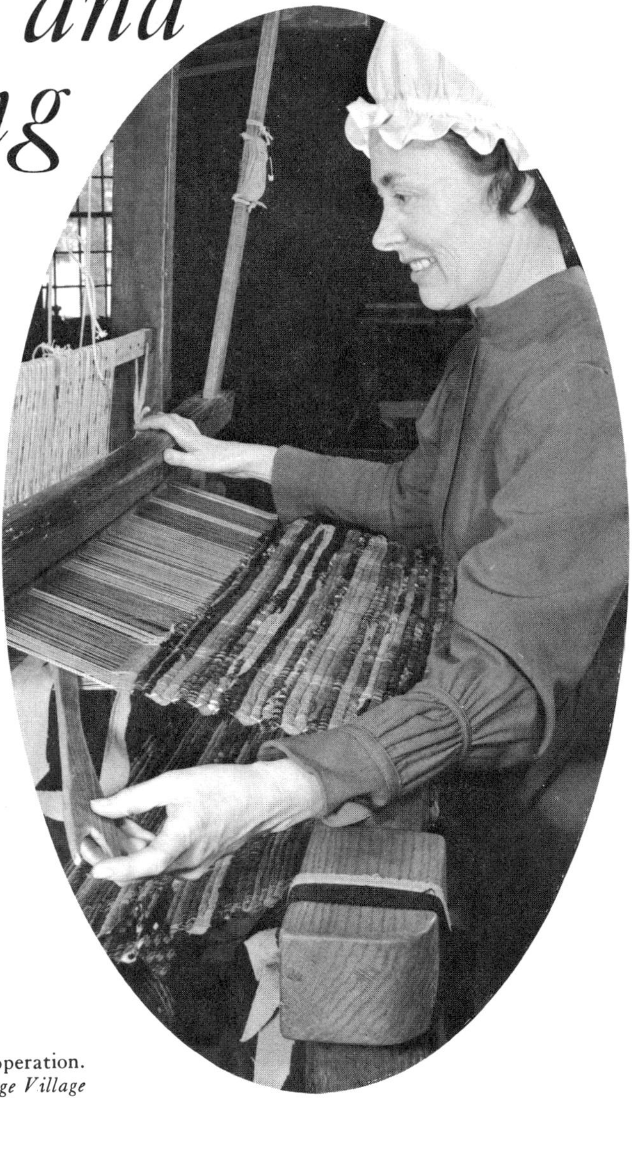

A spinning wheel in operation.
Photo courtesy Old Sturbridge Village

The role of the pioneer woman, the Pilgrim mother, has been greatly overlooked and her contribution to the almost superhuman task of making the first settlement in New England a successful colony has been neglected to a considerable degree. True, there have been notable sculptural memorials erected to her memory, executed with heroic skill, but only those who see them are reminded of her greatness. To her goes the credit for the cultural well-being of the small community and to her go the plaudits for preserving the courage of those about her. No sympathy should be wasted on her for coming here to the wilderness; she wanted to come. Rather there should be praise of her for accomplishing all she achieved in fostering, establishing, and maintaining a homelike atmosphere.

While the men were felling trees, and hewing timbers, trying to tame the wilderness by clearing land, planting and plowing, their women tackled equally arduous tasks. Between stints of cooking coarse and strange foodstuffs in open fireplaces, bearing, caring for and teaching the children, they attended to the wants of their husbands, comforted the sick, administered to the dying. Even so, they found time to daub mud on the walls of their dwellings, making the boards weatherproof; to sweep the earthen floors, over and over again; to put branches between the cracks in the walls; to bank the foundations of the houses with branches; to provide the lighting, and countless other necessary utilities. When the first crops ripened and the first raw materials became available for home manufacture, they gathered and spun the hemp and wove it into cloth. All this they accomplished and more, too, as revealed in the record of their diversified arts and crafts.

The housekeeping guide of that day was Thomas Tusser's *Book of Housewifery* and it was he who warned that the flax should be sown in May. By 1640 every householder was compelled to sow flax because it was not plentiful.

> "Good flax and good hemp to have of her own
> In May a good huswife will see it be sown,
> And afterwards trim it to serve at a need,
> The fimble to spin, the carl for her seed."

Very quickly it was July and the hemp was ripe.

> "Wife pluck from thy seed hemp the fimble hemp clean.
> This looketh more yellow, the other more green.
>
> "Use th' one for thy spinning, leave Michell th' other
> For sho thread and hatter, for rope and such other.
>
> Now pluck up thy flax for the maidens to spin,
> But first see it dried and trimly got in."

From the writers of that day we learn that the housewife gathered the plants, not by cutting them off, but by pulling them up by the roots where they laid flat a day and a night, spread out on the ground. The stalks were then tied into bundles and stacked upright until the time came to water the flax or the hemp, or both. This was done by running water (having been lugged from its source) over the flax. (The odor of rotting flax is most offensive.) The sodden mass was placed in water which had been troughed off by boards. Then, the top was covered with boards and weighted down so that the flax was thoroughly immersed. About four days later the bundles were removed and denuded of their rotted leaves and filth; they were then set upright in the sun by the side of the house or whatever lean-to they could be placed against to dry thoroughly. A brake (ancient name for the tool used) made of wood was then applied to the flax with heavy blows to separate the woody parts from the fibres to remove "the hexe from the rind." This process was repeated a second time. (It had to be accomplished in clear sunny weather, else the flax would not break well.)

The fibres were gathered into large bundles to be swingled and scraped with a wooden swingle knife, shaped like a dagger. This step was essential to remove the hard "bun" in the centre. Then, the refuse was beaten a second time, and from it was gathered what was called "swingle-tree hurds" from which very coarse cloth like bagging could be spun and woven. However, if it were to be spun at home, it went through a second swingling. These carefully swingled strikes were bunched up in great rolls and set in a chimney corner to dry thoroughly. After this process, the flax was ready to be beetled or hammered. The roll was placed in a wooden trough and pounded with a heavy pestle-shaped beetle till soft; the roll was opened

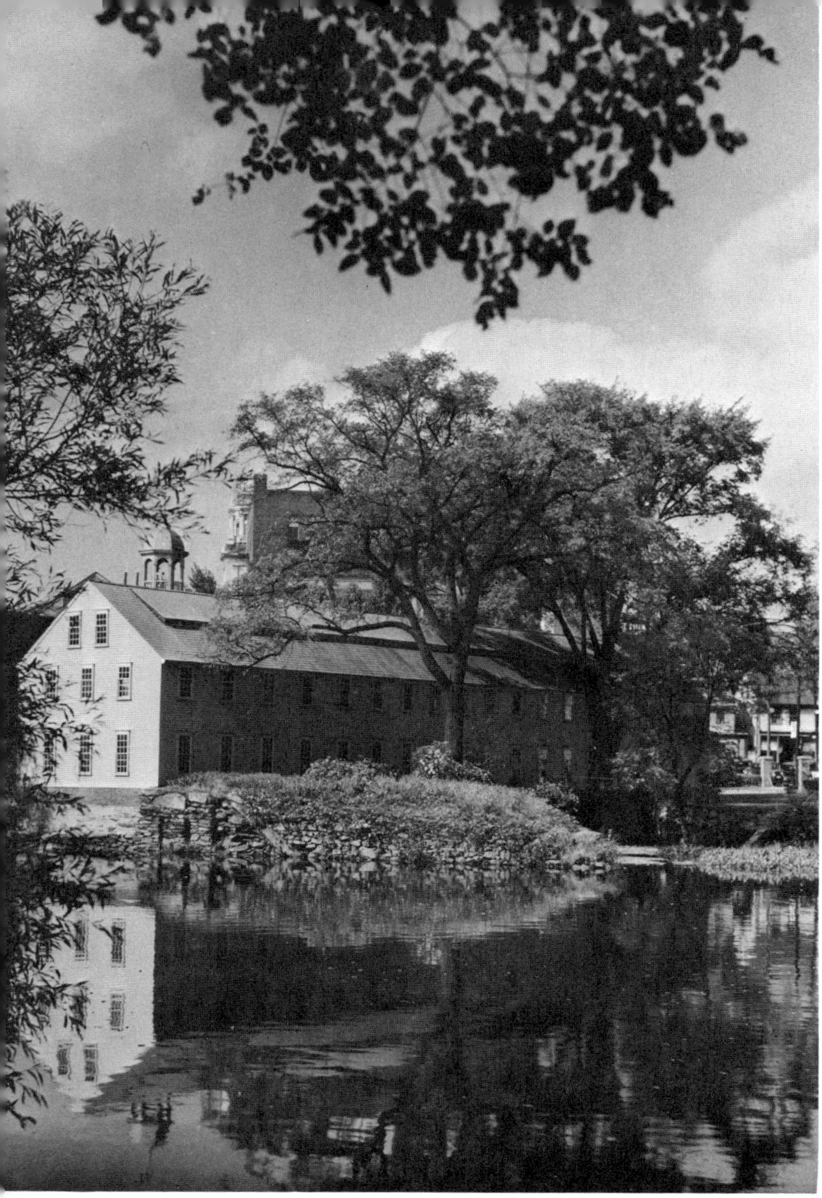

Old Slater Mill, Blackstone River, Pawtucket, Rhode Island. The industrial revolution came to Rhode Island when a young Englishman, Samuel Slater, with the backing of Moses Brown, established at Pawtucket in 1790 the first successful water-powered cotton mill in America. Slater had been employed by the firm of Strutt & Arkwright, makers of the famous Arkwright machines in England, and had a thorough knowledge of their construction. From memory he built a series of these machines, on which were produced the first cotton thread successfully spun by use of water power in America. The present "mill," constructed in 1793 at the falls in Pawtucket, still contains pieces of the original machinery designed by Slater. *Photo courtesy Samuel Chamberlain*

and slowly beaten again. Next came the heckling or hatcheling, dusty, dirty, tiring work. The heckle was a comb-like instrument which cleaned and straightened the fibers. Heckling was done thrice; first with a coarse, wide-toothed comb, then with finer ones. The hurds of this process was also carefully saved and spun.

The flax was then ready to be spun into thread or linen yarn by rock or wheel. By the former, which was the old classic distaff, a finer thread could be made; the latter was swifter. From the spindles or spools, the thread was reeled off upon reels two feet long; then made into skeins or lays of eighty threads. Twenty lays were called a knot or slipping. Would it not seem that the housewife had already spent all the time and labor on her flax that could be endured? Worse was to come. (Would a field of flax ever seem that beautiful blue again that is the gardener's delight to see?) The slippings of thread were laid in warm water for four days. The water had to be changed each day, and the slippings wrung out carefully and frequently by hand. Finally they were washed in the brook till the water that ran over and through them was clear.

The next step was bucking (named from the bucking-tub in which the process was carried on). A layer of wood ashes was placed in the bottom of the tub, with a layer of slippings of thread; this procedure was followed until the tub was filled. Then, it was covered with a cloth. A peck or two of ashes was placed on it and water poured over it, producing lye. The slippings remained overnight in the lye. The following morning another exhausting process known as "driving a buck of yarn" was required. The linen yarn had to be basted with hot lye and beaten, over and over again, for four hours. For a week after, it lay in water which was constantly changed. At long last came the grand seething—beating, rinsing, washing, and drying. When it was thoroughly scoured and whitened, the slippings were wound in round balls, ready for weaving. (There were other processes of bleaching the yarn, a trifle less tedious, including one with warm water and bran—but that was considered a *shiftless* method.)

The linen thread was often woven into cloth, usually away from home, at a weaver's shop; but wherever the web was made, it was not, even then, considered finished. Once again it was subjected to the process of bucking and drying. Loops were sewed on the selvage edges (the edge finished off to prevent raveling); stakes were driven into the turf; the web was spread between them, drawn tightly and kept in the sun for weeks. It had to be kept slightly wet all this time, but not too wet because it would mildew. (How welcome the news must have been in 1628 when it was announced that a pair of sheets was to be furnished to each Massachusetts Bay colonist.) After spinning became fashionable and flax was raised in abundance, homespun sheets were made in large quantities, and owned by all respectable householders. "Twenty and one pair" was no unusual number to appear in an inventory.

On July 23, 1630, John Winthrop wrote from New England to his wife in England (she planned to join him and did). "Remember to come well furnished with linnen, woolen, some more bedding, brasse, leather bottels, drinkinge horner &c; ley my sonne provide 12 axes of severall sorts of the Braintree Smithe, or some other prime workman, whatever they coste, & some Augers great & smale, & many other necessaryes which I cant now thinke of, as candles, sope, & store of beife suett, &c. once againe farewell, my deare wife . . ."

In 1775, Lyman Beecher, father of Harriet Beecher Stowe, wrote in North Guilford, Connecticut, "Flax-pulling was hard enough to break your back the first day, the second lighter, the third easy enough. We had about three days' pulling for Uncle Benton and me, boy and man then we rotted it, beat it and bleached it. I knew my business about flax . . . Flax in summer, wool in winter for spinning—woman's work is never done."

Wool was produced on many farms and the women of the family were not only capable of but were expected to take the wool as it came from the sheep and use "every last bit" of it even the tag locks. Then follow the cleansing, carding, and spinning of it into yarn and weaving it into cloth, from which the clothes of the family were cut and made. Carding was done with hand cards and the carded rolls were spun into yarn upon the hand wheel. A good day's yield was five skeins. The yarn was woven into cloth on a hand-loom which was so large that it occupied a great deal of room. Not every family possessed a loom, but there were weavers in every locality. The yarn which went lengthwise of the cloth had to be drawn into the harness by hand; that which went the opposite way came from the shuttle. The yarn in the shuttle was wound upon short quills, pieces of elder three inches long; the quills were wound on a wheel called a "quill wheel" which made a great deal of noise when in operation. This work was usually done by children or some helper, while the woman of the house was weaving.

In 1640 it is recorded that William Rix, a Massachusetts weaver, built a house with the object of setting up his own loom in it. Wool, cotton, and hemp were taken to him to be spun and woven into simple cloth just as corn or wheat was taken to the grist mill to be ground into coarse flour. Other professional weavers followed suit and soon the industry began to grow so fast that the colonial government appointed inspectors to fix prices on spinning and weaving.

When the spun yarn was to be knitted, it was generally colored before using. The dye pot was of earthenware and had its place in the chimney corner just inside the fireplace. It was covered with a piece of board or plank on which the children often sat. The dye was made of indigo dissolved in chamber-lye (urine). Into this the yarn was placed and remained until it was colored. (This made for an odorous yarn!)

Governor Winthrop wrote in 1631 to his son in England: "If you could bring two or three hundred sheepskins and lambskins, with the wool on, dyed red, it would be a good commodity here; and the coarsest woolen cloth (so it be not flocks) and of sad colours, and some red; . . . store of coarse linen."

The first known textile factory was established in 1638 near Ipswich, Massachusetts, by Ezekiel Rogers, the minister-leader of a group of twenty weaving families who had migrated from York, England. They wove wool mostly, though later flax and cotton were included. It was about this time that the colonists realized that they must conserve and increase their wool supply. It was even urged in public proclamations that anyone known to be coming to the colonies be asked to bring lambs with them.

Coupled with all of this strenuous work there was an attempt at social activities. There were flaxing parties when the flax had to be gathered, although there are few accounts of these. Then, too, there were spinning parties for the ladies, as recorded by the Reverend Samuel Deane, "Spinning Day," in his diary for May 1, 1788. The account appeared in the Cumberland, Maine, *Gazette,* May 8, 1788.

"On the 1st instant, assembled at the house of the Reverend Samuel Deane, of this towne, more than one hundred of the fair sex, married and single ladies, most of whom were skilled in the important art of spinning. An emulous industry was never more apparent than in this beautiful assembly. The majority of fair hands gave motion to not less than sixty wheels. Many were occupied in preparing the materials, besides those who attended to the entertainment of the rest—provision for which was mostly presented by the guests themselves, or sent in by other generous promotors of the exhibition, as were also the materials for the work. Near the close of the day Mrs. Deane was presented by the company with two hundred and thirty-six seven knotted skeins of excellent cotton and linen yarn, the work of the day, excepting about a dozen skeins which some of the company brought in ready spun. Some had spun six, and many not less than five skeins apiece. She takes this opportunity to returning thanks to each, which the hurry of the day rendered impracticable at the time. To conclude, and crown the day, a numerous band of the best singers attended in the evening, and performed an agreeable variety of excellent pieces in psalmody.

A handwoven cloth covers the table in the kitchen of the John Ward House (1684), Salem, Massachusetts. Spoons, knives (no forks), woodenware, and pottery mugs complete the setting. The array of pewter and the early bottles on the dresser as well as the extensive collection of seventeenth-century kitchen utensils and furnishings bespeak the work of craftsmen in various fields. *Photo courtesy Essex Institute*

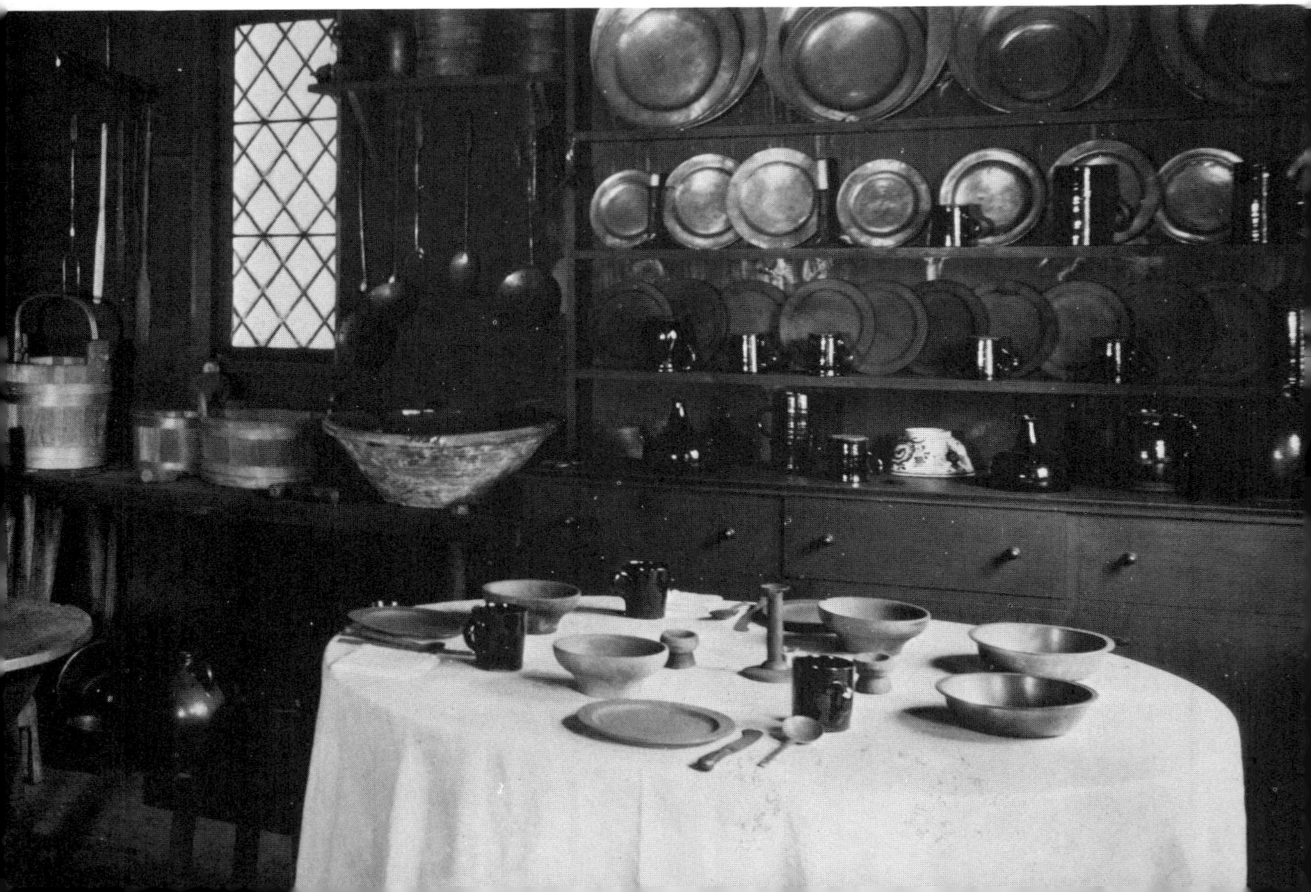

'The price of a virtuous woman is far above rubies. . . . She layeth her hands to the spindle, and her hands hold the distaff.' "

The art of spinning is no longer widely practiced but any one interested in the crafts of colonial days may journey to Maine or to Vermont for there still remain a few families who spin their own yarns. A visit to Old Sturbridge Village in Sturbridge, Massachusetts, is most rewarding since all the processes of preparing the wool—carding, spinning, and weaving—are demonstrated in complete detail, in an atmosphere that is historically appropriate and accurately portrayed.

Hand Weaving

The whack! whack! whack! of the hand-looms heard today in a weaver's room is the same monotonous thud that resounded in the ears of our forebears in the seventeenth century. Nor has the process changed in many centuries. Hand-looms were used in Egypt, centuries before the Christian era. In present-day weaving only the types of design are new, as are the textures of the woven materials and the greater durability of the threads and yarns.

Looms were not found in every early American household, but wherever they were used, they were conspicuous for their size, dominating the room. Usually they were relegated to the ell of the house, to the garrett or to the shed loft, used as a weaving room. (Benjamin Franklin had such a room added to his dwelling.) The loom is probably the most absolute bequest of antiquity which we have inherited—unchanged, in domestic use for several thousand years. Thus, the small hand-loom (or table-loom) and its larger counterpart, the "historic machine," are among the comparatively few mechanical devices that have survived modern technology. The art of weaving belongs in the front ranks of truly ancient crafts with that of the potter's wheel. While women did most of the weaving, men were sometimes proficient at it. Every town had its professional weavers and, among all artisans, they maintained high respect. Apprentices to the trade were numerous. The traveling weaver, like other itinerant tradesmen of the day, was a welcome news-monger; the weaver who "took in" weaving was often a stationary gossip, for by the precise nature of his work and its monotonous routine, he became a good listener. He "knew the measure" of every man of consequence in the area in which he worked. What is even more to the point, the women confided in him with many a secret.

Today, the loom, as of old, consists of a frame of four square timber posts, approximately seven feet high, set about as far apart as a four-poster bed, and connected at top and bottom by portions of the frame. The yarn-beam, about six inches in diameter, is located at the back of the loom. Around it are wound the warp threads, those which stretch the length of the loom to the cloth-beam located in front. The cloth-beam is usually about ten inches in diameter and the cloth is wound around it as the weaving progresses. When a piece is to be set, a large number of shuttles and spools are filled in advance and placed in a row, one above the other, in a spool-holder. The warping-bars are entirely detached from the loom and are neatly wound with warp-threads and then set in the loom. The warp thread is then drawn in with a warping-needle through the eye of the harness, or heddle. The heddle is a row of twines, cords, or wires called leashes, which are stretched vertically between two horizontal bars or rods, placed about a foot apart. One rod is suspended by a pulley at the top of the loom; to the lower rod the foot-treadle is hitched.

In the middle of each length of twine or wire is the loop or eye, through which a warp thread is passed. Then threads are next drawn through the interspaces between two dents of the reed, which is accomplished by the use of a wire hook (two warp threads are drawn in each space). The reed is a row of short, very thin parallel strips of metal, like comb-teeth; these are fixed closely at both ends in two long, strong, parallel bars of wood, set two (or more) inches apart. Usually, there are fifty or sixty of these teeth to one inch for weaving fine linen. The reed is placed in a groove on the lower edge of a heavy lathe. This batten hangs by two side bars and swings from an axle at the top of the loom. As the heavy batten swings on its axle, the reed forces with a sharp blow every newly placed thread of the weft (or woof) into its proper place, close to the previously woven part of the texture. This operation causes the heavy whack, whack sound heard in hand-weaving. It is on the accurate poise of the batten that the evenness of the completed woof largely

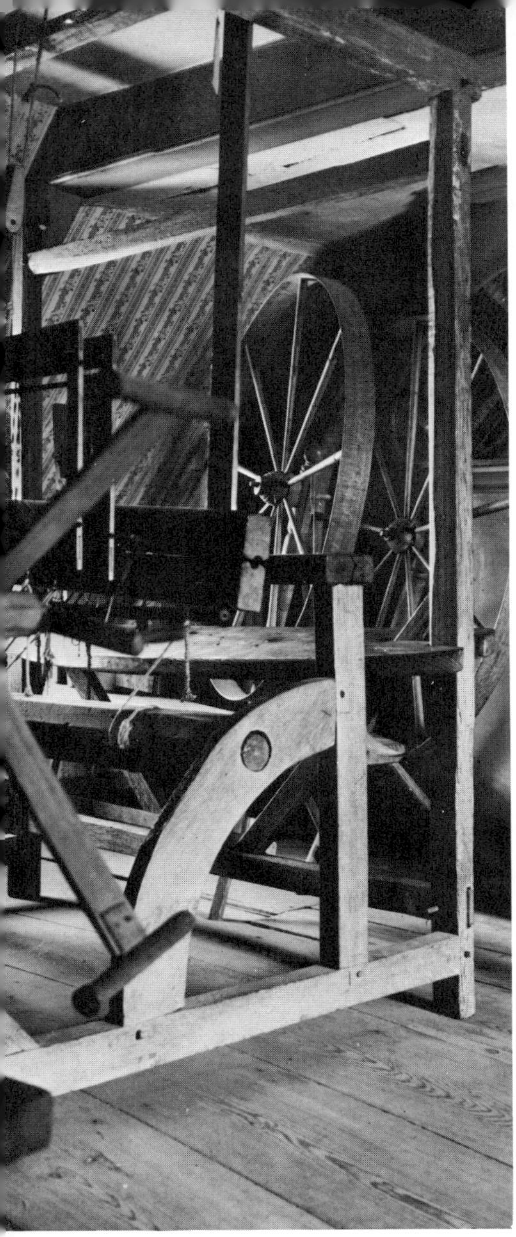

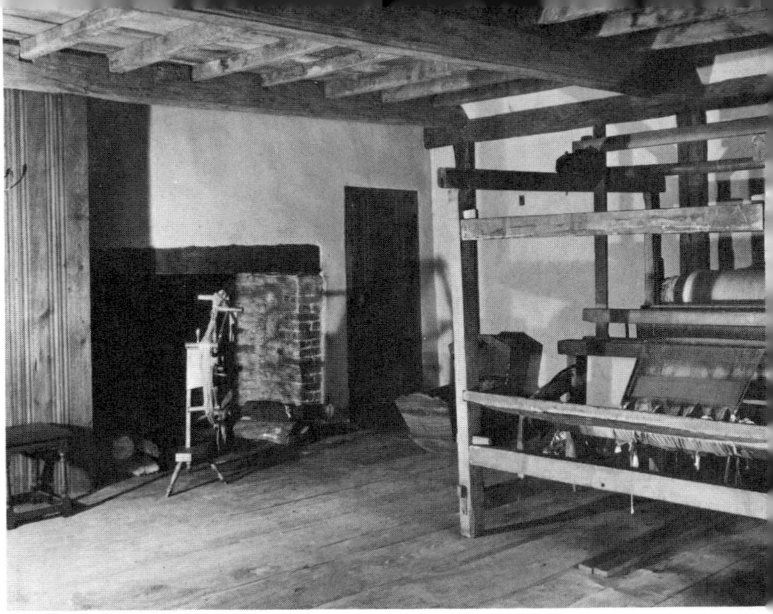

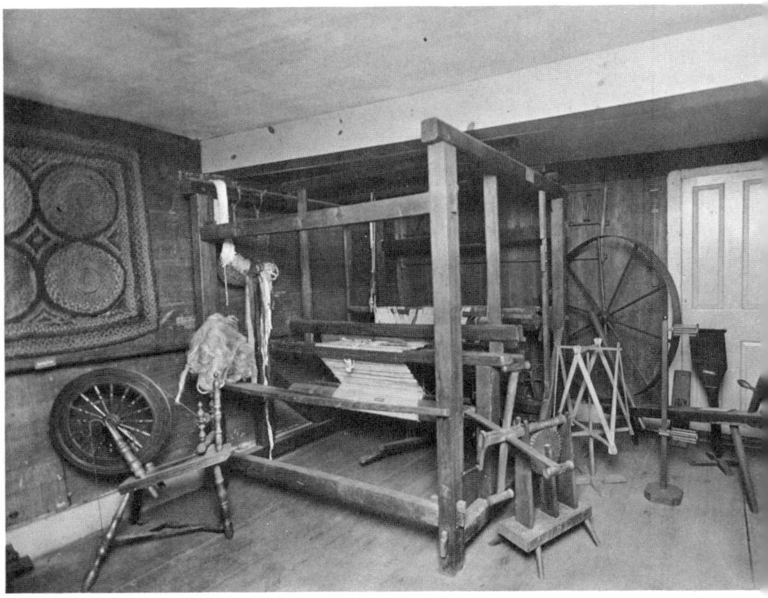

(*Left*) At the Hancock-Clarke House (1734) in Lexington, the loom was set up in the attic under the low gambrel roof and, when not in use, there was space there for storing the spinning wheels. *Photo courtesy Samuel Chamberlain*

(*Above, right*) An old loom installed in the east chamber of the Witch House at Salem is in good working condition. In front of the fireplace is an early yarn reel of the period (late 1600's) and a cradle conveniently placed. The house is so named because one of the judges involved in the witchcraft trials of 1692 lived here. *Photo courtesy Samuel Chamberlain*

(*Bottom, right*) The spinning and weaving in the John Ward House (1684), Salem, Massachusetts, show the implements necessary for these home industries. *Photo courtesy Essex Institute*

depends. (The crosswise threads in weaving are known as the woof.)

With his foot on the treadle, the weaver sits on a narrow, high bench. Three motions are used in hand-weaving. First, by the action of one foot-treadle, a single harness or heddle, is depressed from the level of the entire expanse of warp-threads. Room is created by this primary motion for the shuttle which by the second motion, is thrown from one side of the loom to the other by the weaver's hand, going over every alternate thread. With the third motion, the batten crowds the weft-thread into place. Then the motion of the other foot-treadle forces down the remaining warp threads which pass through the second set of harnesses, the shuttle is thrown back through this shed and on and on.

As is true of any description of a method, a clear understanding of "how to" is best obtained by watching a hand-loom in action. There are countless weavers and guilds in New England, and almost every town has its skilled hand weaver. To watch the fascinating procedure of hand-woven cloth (commonly referred to as homespun) as it literally "grows" before your eyes is a most rewarding experience.

Today, the infinite variety of weave patterns and textures that are possible in the hands of the skilled weaver lend a note of individuality wherever they are used. When John Kay of Lancashire developed a flying shuttle, his invention enabled a weaver to produce a much greater width than had been possible previously, and the colonists were quick to adopt it. In Beverly, Massachusetts, the first factory in New England for weaving cotton goods was opened about 1787, established by John Cabot, a name of as much prominence then as now. At Providence, Rhode Island, a famous cotton manufactory was that of Brown and Almy; their machinery was built by Samuel Slater, another outstanding Rhode Island name connected with the weaving industry of the past.

After the Revolution, manufactories in New England increased rapidly. One of the most noted was that of the Hartford Woolen Manufactory which furnished the inaugural suit for the first president of the United States. Mr. Washington wrote the following letter to his friend General Henry Knox.

> Mt. Vernon, Jany 29th, 1789
>
> My dear Sir,
>
> Having learnt from an Advertisement in the New York Daily Advertiser, that there were superfine American Broadcloths to be sold at No. 44 in Water Street; I have ventured to trouble you with the commission of purchasing enough to make me a suit of clothes.—As to the colour, I shall leave it altogether to your taste; only observing, that, if the dye should not appear to be well fixed, & clear, or if the cloth should not really be very fine, then (in my judgement) some colour mixed in grain might be preferable to an indifferent (stained) dye.—I shall have occasion to trouble you for nothing but the cloth, & twist to make the button-holes.—If these articles can be procured & forwarded, in a package by the stage, in any short time your attention will be greatly acknowledged. —Mrs. Washington would be equally thankfull to you for purchasing for her as much of what is called (in the Advertisement) powder smoke as will make her a riding habit. —If the *choice* of these cloths should have been disposed of in New York—quere could they be had from Hartford in Connecticut, where I perceive a manufactory of them is established.—
>
> With every sentiment of sincere friendship
> I am always, affectionately
> Yrs
>
> G. Washington

Silk, too, for a time was woven in Connecticut and there is one record of Connecticut silk, grown, woven, and made in that state that should be mentioned. It was the gown worn by President Stiles for commencement at Yale in the year 1789.

One of the noted weavers of recent times, in fact he was called "the last weaver in the early American tradition" was W. H. H. Rose (1839-1913), known as "Weaver Rose" who made beautiful coverlets in old, old designs such as "Sunrise," "Bonaparte's March" and others. His coverlets became collectors' items as soon as they came from his loom.

Dyeing

The education gleaned in the wilderness by those who first arrived was a far reaching one. Together with the testing of all her other skills and her resourcefulness the housewife was challenged in the field of chemistry. It was her duty not only to supply all the materials which her family wore, but also to color, by dyeing, the musty-yellow, dingy looking skeins of yarn and flax. Since she had no packet of tints or dyes, she had to rely upon the indigenous plants for her source of dye supplies. Her sole aid was indigo which reached our shores almost as quickly as she did; for a mordant (a substance that fixes color) she had to use what was at hand. With surprising speed, she soon learned that by spinning together one-third white lamb's wool, one-third black sheep's wool and one-third wool dyed in indigo, she could produce a soft gray. It was easy on the eyes, would not show the dirt quickly and was a serviceable color. Unconsciously she created for herself a "sad" color known as Puritan gray. In many instances, the colors used, were *not* the Pilgrim's choice; rather they were what nature and the lack of trading imposed upon them. It is pleasant to recall that the Pilgrim gentlemen wore black capes *lined* with *scarlet* which they brought with them. They must have presented a dramatically colorful sight, those two, the courageous Pilgrim wife in her "subtle" gray and the Pilgrim husband in his scarlet-lined black cape!

The early dyer noted and listed that:

pokeberry boiled with alum	=	crimson
petals of the iris	=	violet juice
goldenrod pressed of its juice, mixed with indigo and added alum	=	a beautiful green

For producing the basic colors she relied on the plants:

red: alder, bloodroot, cedar, cranberry, elm, grape, hemlock, maple, sorrel, sumac
yellow: alder, barberry, goldenrod, hickory, marsh-marigold, sunflower, touch-me-not
black: alder, poison ivy, sumac, walnut
orange: alder, bittersweet, touch-me-not
green: ash, mint, yellow adder's-tongue
purple: blueberry, elderberry, huckleberry
brown: grape, larkspur, oak, spruce bark, sycamore, toadflax

She discovered that some plants such as the alder would make more than one color. In most cases this depended on the length of time that the goods were boiled in the dye or the strength of the concoction. The modern dyer will have to experiment with this, as did her forebear. However, this list was "prepared" by one of those early homemakers. From another old listing we find this for "natural dyes": barks, roots, leaves, flowers, berries and nuts. Indigo, logwood, fustic, cutch, butternut, sumac, madder, brazilwood, quercitron, sunflower, peachwood, canwood, Persian berries, turmeric, mustard, saffron, henna, and cudbear. (The blossom of the hollyhock to color wine!)

From old diaries, we learn that the Indians used the bloodroot to color their faces and the slimy green algae from stagnant water to make a green stain on their bodies. The early dyer in search of colorings used what was native. For her blue she used baptisia, the false indigo which gave off a faded blue. How she longed for red, bright blue, and, somewhat strangely, for purple—all strong colors. For all of the colors she concocted there had to be a mordant. She used "drip lye" made at home from wood ashes (also used for making soap and for bleaching), and as a mordant for some colors, chamber-lye (urine) was easily procurable, but its use was offensive. One home-dyer's notes read as follows: "Butternut bark made a beautiful brown; a certain moss made a tan brown. Alder bark made a seal brown. Birch bark a gunmetal gray. Yellow-root, barberry bark and sassafras made yellow. It always took two things to make green, also laurel and hickory bark."

Martha Genung Stearns, who is so versed in herbs and their usage, writes "black was one of the hardest colors to set: mercury or poison ivy made a pretty good black. Elderberries and purple flag gave lavender. To set color in cloth copperas, alum, salt and sometimes rusty nails were used. Every family had a dye-pot, most commonly used for indigo. After the spinning of the yarn or thread was finished the housewife was busy getting the dye prepared. All the family knew that chamber-lye should be saved for this. The indigo and yarn were put into the earthen pot full of chamber-lye and allowed to stand for a long time, after which it did not need to be 'set.' The odor was offensive, and sometimes sweet-fern, flagroot or hardwood ashes were used to offset the odor." The earthen floors of the homes were frequently strewn with herbs to aid the olfactory sense. The following advertisements must have received considerable attention when they appeared:

> Linen Printer—The Printer hereof Prints, Linens, Callicoes, Silks, &c. in good Figures, very lively and durable Colours, and without the offensive smells which commonly attends the Linnens Printed here. *Boston Gazette,* Apr. 18/25, 1720 (sup).

A homely saying "dyed in the wool" showed a process of much skill.

> Dyer. Alexander Fleming, Dyer lately from Great Britain, has set up Business in Boston, in a House of Mr. Arthur's near Dr. Gardner's in Marlborough Street, on the same side of the Way, who can Dye all sorts of Colours, after the best Manner and Cheapest Rate, viz. Scarletts, Crimsons, Pinks, Purples, Straws, Wine Colours, Sea-Greens, Saxon ditto, common Blues, shearing, dressing and watering of clothes. Also he can dye linnen Yarn either red, blue, green, yellow or cloth Colours, and all Colours on silks and cleaning Cloths. *Boston Gazette,* May 14, 1754.

The above shows the pallette of embroidery hues and the crewel yarns available. This must have delighted the colonial needlewoman.

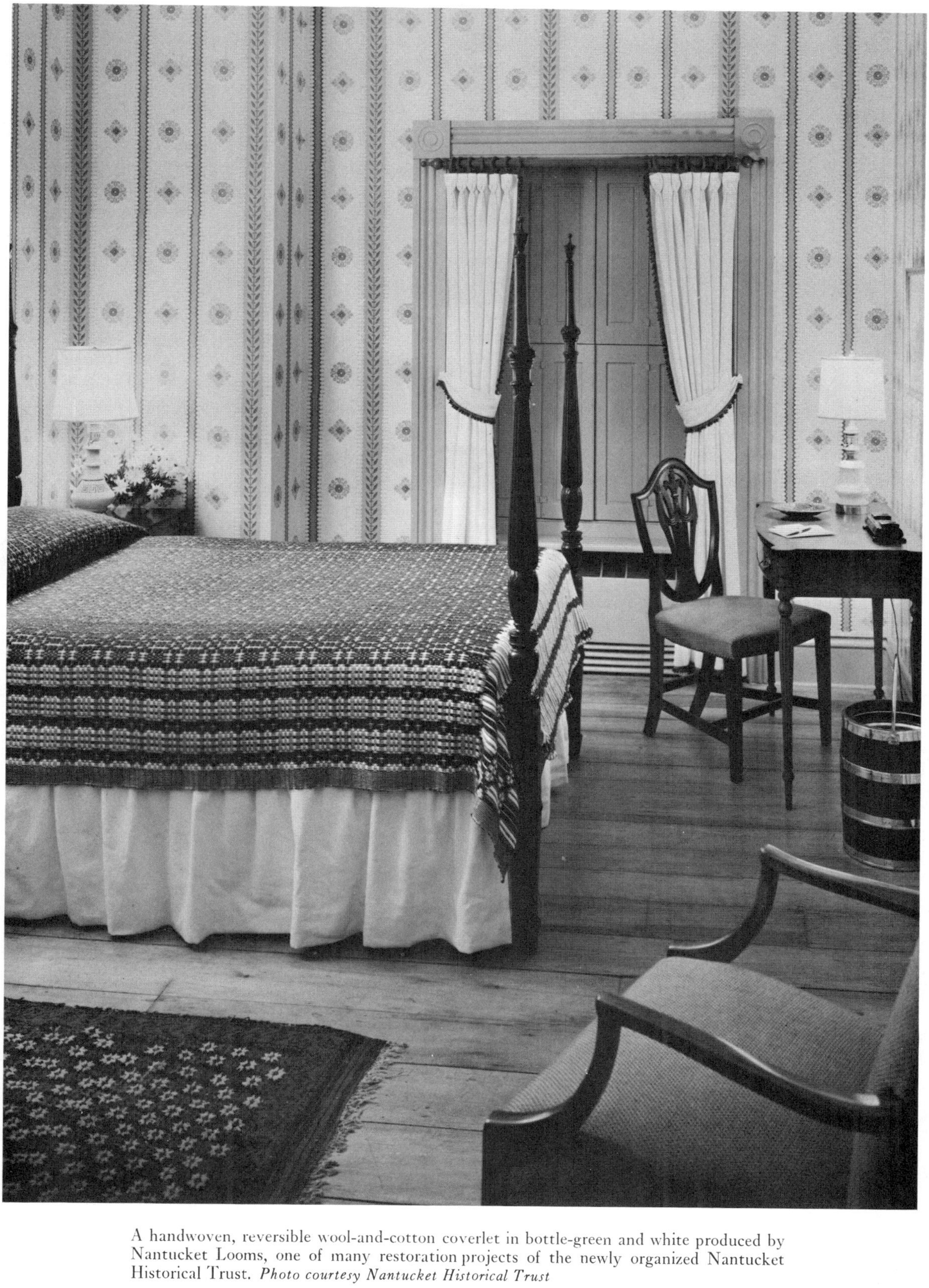

A handwoven, reversible wool-and-cotton coverlet in bottle-green and white produced by Nantucket Looms, one of many restoration projects of the newly organized Nantucket Historical Trust. *Photo courtesy Nantucket Historical Trust*

Indigo played such an important part in the dyeing attempts of the early settler that its Americanization should be noted here. The housewife in New England could get her indigo supply from abroad since ships went frequently to and from Boston to the mother country, but colonists in remote areas could not. In the south, indigo was destined to be the second greatest plantation crop of the Carolinas. The indigo plant which originated in India was introduced at an early date into the West Indies. George Lucas, while he was governor of Antigua, found it on that island before the middle of the eighteenth century. Realizing that his daughter, Eliza, back home on the family plantation in South Carolina (pleasantly situated on Wappoo Creek), had more than a passing interest in horticulture, he sent her some indigo seeds. In the early spring of 1741 Eliza planted the seeds. When she was successful in growing them, Governor Lucas sent over more seed by a Mr. Cromwell who was to prepare the plantation for indigo cultivation.

The indigo flourished, but fearing that his own industry on Antigua might be ruined, Cromwell threw lime in the vat that watered the plants, thus ruining the crop. Then, he left. Eliza, however, had avidly observed the care he had given the crop, and by emulating his practices she became successful in her venture. So grateful was her father for her perseverance and success that he gave her all the indigo on his plantation as a wedding gift when she became Mrs. Charles Pinckney. They experimented, too, with the native, wild indigo which gave a better yield and better color, but was far less profitable than planting the imported seed. Soon Mrs. Pinckney was exporting indigo and making her name known in horticultural circles across the world. It was this same Eliza Lucas Pinckney who became the mother of Charles Cotesworth Pinckney of "Millions for defence but not one cent for tribute" fame, so the people of New England knew her on both scores.

The garden at Harlow Old Fort House shows what early settlers used for coloring textiles. At this fort house in Plymouth, the Plymouth Antiquarian Society has experimented with the dyeing possibilities of native material. This work is part of its program for exploring and demonstrating the way the Plymouth colony housewife met the needs of her family. At Plimoth Plantation, Massachusetts (a restoration of the Plymouth settlement as it probably appeared about 1627), there is also an experimental garden filled with native dyestuffs which is well worth a visit.

Of necessity, the women of early colonial times produced their dyes from the materials which they found growing in the fields, pastures, and garden plots. Huge brass or copper kettles for dyeing were part of each household's outfitting. Those who learned to dye might have the delightful experience of discovering something new, as did an Indian basket-maker who found in the purple iris a dye almost as deep in color as that of its blossoms.

Had life improved in almost two hundred years? There were some perceptible changes as an extract from Mr. Goodrich's *Recollections of a Lifetime* indicates. Samuel Griswold Goodrich (1793-1860) of Ridgefield, Connecticut, was a literary figure of some prominence even before 1827 when he began to write children's books under the name of "Peter Parley." The success of Peter Parley almost surpassed belief for even in England the mere mention of his name would sell a book. There were about twenty-eight titles in his list. Goodrich, or Parley, writes:

> There was, of course, no baker in Ridgefield, each family not only made its own bread, cakes, and pies, but their own soap, candles, butter, cheese, and the like. The fabrication of cloth, linen, and woolen was no less a domestic operation. Cotton—that is raw cotton—was then wholly unknown among us at the North, except as a mere curiosity, produced somewhere in the tropics; but whether it grew on a plant, or an animal, was not clearly settled in the public mind.
>
> We raised our own flax, rotted it, hackled it, dressed it and spun it. The little wheel, turned by the foot, had its place, and was as familiar as if it had been a member of the family. How often have I seen my mother, and my grandmother, too, sit down to it—though this, as I remember, was for the purpose of spinning some finer kind of thread—the burden of the spinning being done by a neighbor of ours, Sally St. John. . .
>
> The wool was also spun in the family, partly by my sisters, and partly by Molly Gregory, daughter of our neighbor, the town carpenter. . . In her solitary operations aloft, I have often heard her send forth from the attic windows, the droning hum of her wheel, with fitful snatches of a hymn.

The eagle design in this early handwoven coverlet remains a popular motif for various kinds of fabric.

The knitting of stockings was performed by the female part of the family in the evening, and especially at tea parties. . .

The weaving of cloth-linen, as well as woolen—was performed by an itinerant workman, who came to the house, put up his loom, and threw his shuttle, till the season's work was done. The linen was bleached, and made up by the family; the woolen cloth was sent to the fuller to be dyed and dressed. Twice a year, that is, in the Spring and Autumn, the tailor came to the home and fabricated the semi-annual stitch of clothes for the male members—this being called 'whipping the cat.'

Carpets were then only known in a few families and were confined to the keeping-room and parlor. They were all home-made: the warp consisting of woolen yarn and the woof of lists and old woolen cloth, cut into strips, and sewed together at the ends. Coverlids generally consisted of quilts, made of pieces of waste calico elaborately sewed together in octagons, and quilted in rectangles, giving the whole a gay and rich appearance. This process of quilting generally brought together the women of the neighborhood, married and single and a great time they had of it—what with tea, talk, and stitching. In the evening, the beaux were admitted, so that a quilting was a real festival, not unfrequently getting young people into entanglements which matrimony alone could unravel.

Even dyeing blue a portion of the wool, so as to make linsey-woolsey for short-gowns, aprons and blue-mixed stockings—vital necessities in those days—was a domestic operation. During the autumn a dye-tub in the chimney corner—thus placed so as to be cherished by the genial heat—was as familiar to all thrifty houses, as the Bible or the back-log. It was covered with a board, and formed a cosy seat in the wide-mouthed fireplace, especially of a chill evening.

When the night had waned, and the family had retired, it frequently became the anxious seat of the lover, who was permitted to carry on his courtship, the object of his addresses sitting demurely in the corner. Some of the first families in Connecticut, I suspect, could their full annals be written, would find their foundations to have been laid in these chimney-corner courtships.

(Thus exposed to daily life—the dye-tub could have—probably, often *was* tipped over!)

Wood and the Golden Age of Carving

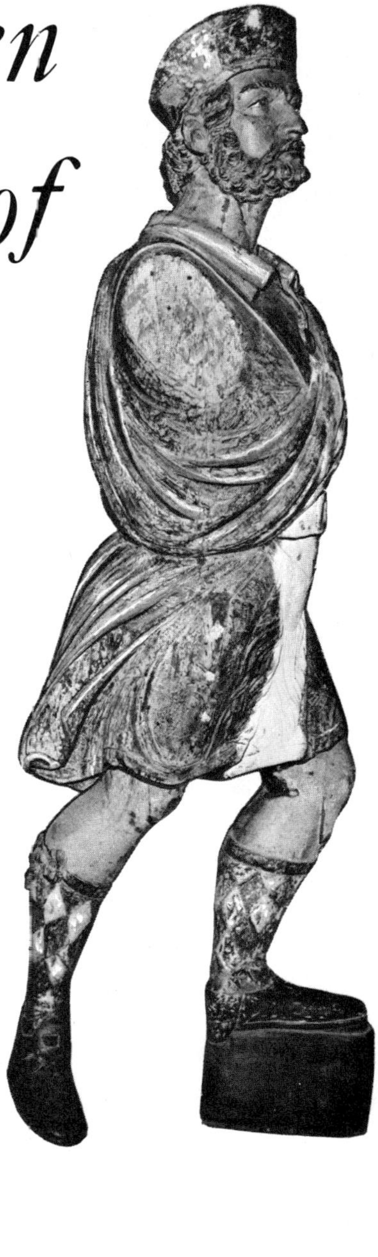

Many museums have unidentified figureheads which have been preserved under extraordinary circumstances and acquired under conditions equally astonishing. In tracking down origins, Mystic's curator, E. A. Stackpole, was struck by Herman Melville's description of the Highlander which appears in his book *Redburn*. "He was a gallant six-footer of a Highlander in full figure, with bright tartans, bare knees, barred leggings, and blue bonnet, and the most vermillion of cheeks. He was game to his wooden marrow, and stood up to it through thick and thin; one foot a little advanced, and his right arm stretched forward, daring on the waves. In a gale of wind it was glorious to watch him standing at his post like a hero, plunging up and down the watery highlands and lowlands, as the ship went foaming on her way. . . ." Could this be the figure that Melville described?

Photo Louis S. Martel: courtesy Mystic Seaport

Wood to build houses, furniture and ships; wood to provide turpentine, pitch, and tar; wood to make barrels, piggins, and noggins; wood for burning, whittling, and carving ("No better in the world I thinke" as the Reverend Francis Higginson expressed it) was one of the great natural assets of the wilderness utilized by the early settlers in the very first craft which they practiced. From *New England Plantation* written by Higginson and published in London in 1630, we also have a list of the woodworking tools which he declared essential. The first generation, at least, of colonial life may be considered the age of wood since practically every house and vehicle and practically every utensil and tool in the colonies was made in whole or in part of wood. Actually, for a hundred years, wood was king. Allen H. Eaton explained this is *Handicrafts of New England*: "'From wood piles to ball bearings' is not merely a figure of speech, but rather a true indication of the wide range in the art of woodshaping to be found in New England. An ingenious potter, . . . unable to buy ball bearings needed to make his kick wheel run smoothly, made them from hard close-grained wood."

Since wood of all kinds was in plentiful supply, both hard- and soft-grained kinds could be obtained for the cutting. Skill in the use and adaptation of wood ranged from the simple but precise method of piling logs for burning so that they would dry properly to the skillful turning of tool handles, making them easy, comfortable, and efficient to use. One has only to look at the construction of an early seventeenth-century house to see the spirit with which it was fashioned; the turnings, the paneling and what little ornamentation was used on the newel posts and baluster were executed by housewrights of more than ordinary skill. Through the apprentice system, a master taught his young trainees what he in turn had been taught by his master. Thus, the craft of building houses, as with other trades, passed from one generation to another. For the most part, the early houses had two rooms on each floor surrounding a huge central chimney. After the turn of the eighteenth century, an occasional house made of brick might be found in a Massachusetts town; stone was used to some extent even at an early date in Rhode Island and Connecticut and in the eighteenth century in Vermont. The typical dwelling of the seventeenth century is exemplified by the Parson Capen house in Topsfield, Massachusetts; in all New England perhaps no other house of this period has been photographed more frequently.

The tricks of the trade were innumerable, and a knowledge and understanding of wood was one of the marks of a good craftsman. A story is told of Benjamin Powers of Lyndon, Vermont, whose father called him "a square peg in a round hole." This expression is often used in the wrong manner for, when green and dry wood were joined by knowing craftsmen, age welded the two in such a manner as to make their own "glue"—a fact which all competent woodworkers know. Eric Sloane noted this in *Lore of the Woodworker:* "In later years, when he (Powers) became a chair-maker, he hammered green squared dowels into wet round holes in such a satisfactory manner that the joints today are stronger than the rest of the chairs." And Sloane also reminds us: "Today furniture is often made from just one kind of wood. In the old days, when people knew wood better, a simple rocking chair might contain as many as seven kinds of wood. The hard woods were used for pegging, with still harder wood to peg the pegs; soft wood cradled the load and springy woods carried the weight. Old chairs creak during weather changes, and as the early craftsman knew, wood "breathes" with the weather, warping, contracting or expanding with each change of humidity and temperature. The art is to match woods which react in opposite manners and thereby keep joints tight. So the creaking you often hear in an ancient house during weather changes is the natural movement of healthy wood as one piece settles comfortably against the other."

People who own old houses in New England point with pride to the wooden pegs used to hold the beams together and marvel at the firmness of the construction. Metal was scarce in the early days, but wooden pegs or trunnels (tree nails) contracted and expanded with the timbers they held in place. "Wood breathes, you know," as they say in New England.

Woodenware or Treen

Despite the breakaway from the mother country, the colonists were quick to emulate England's every mood in the manner of dress

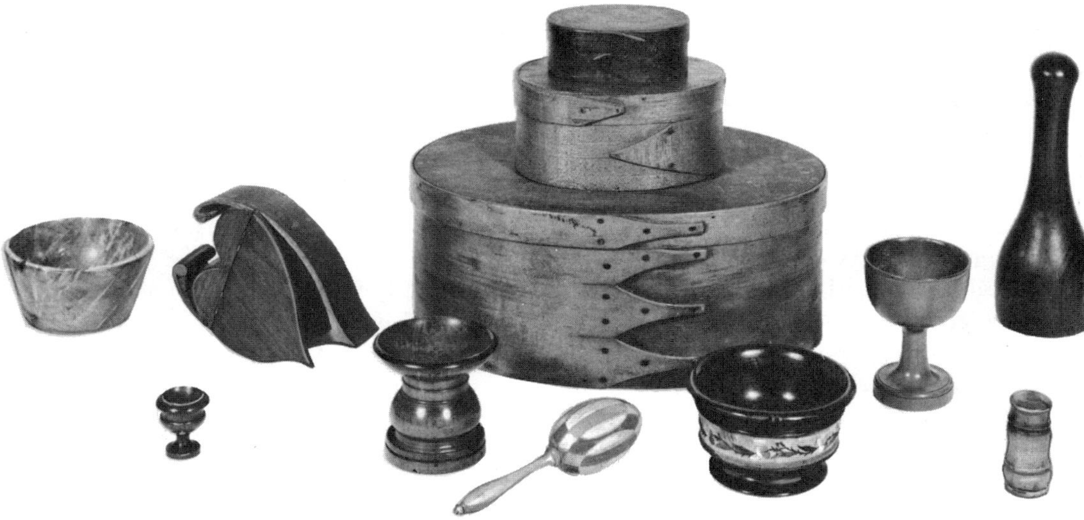

A collection of woodenware which includes: bowls, a heart-shaped box, a sander, a darning egg, a potato masher. Lower right: a pocket inkwell of boxwood, carried by a Civil War soldier. The three Shaker boxes are examples of more than average skill in the use wood. *Photo Richard Merrill: courtesy Miss Helen Hagar*

and house decoration. Woodenware had served many a useful purpose at home and for several generations was the mainstay of the larder and the table in New England. The earliest ware was plain but, as at home, the colonists were soon applying the art of carving to both small and large wooden pieces. Bits of beautiful carving appeared on small bowls, spoons, chalices, and on furniture as well. Carving displays to good advantage the grains of the various kinds of wood, also the skill of the carver. Mary E. Waller in her novel *The Wood Carver of 'Lympus* delineates a tale about a wood-carver in Vermont who was skilled in the art of *treen* even though neither he nor his customers knew it by that name. Treen is defined as "made of tree; of or belonging to, obtained or made from a tree or trees-1670." This definition is sufficiently broad to cover furniture, joinery, old-time ships, road vehicles, and many things not generally included in this term. In other words, the term "treen" usually described the miscellanea of small wooden objects found in daily domestic or farm use and in the trades and professions.

Edward H. Pento in his book *Treen, or Small Woodenware,* registers the fact that "whilst fitness for purpose was originally the first qualification of treen, beauty of form and love of craftsmanship were rarely overlooked and great care was taken in selecting suitable timber to provide shape, colour, grain and ornament."

Love tokens made in earlier centuries told a graphic story. Many a sailor carved a beautiful stay busk or knitting sheath while on a long voyage. These stay busks were so elaborately carved that the recipient usually wore it outside her belt so that all might see and admire it. Some were so large that the girl must have wondered about her friend's observations! Knitting sheaths were also displayed with equal care for here was an art as intricate as scrimshaw, only practiced and perpetuated in wood. These objects occupied the carver for hours and when one remembers that they were made with a mere pocketknife, on a pitching ship after a long twelve-hour work day, and with only the dim light of candle or rush light, their art becomes elevated! After the seventeenth century, the cabinetmaker began to incorporate this type of carving in his furniture.

With the advent of pewter, copper, and earthenware, the kitchen appointments were less and less made of wood so that woodenware disappeared from the kitchen. However, the interest in and demand for it will never fade for too many collectors are truly fascinated with beautifully carved, small wooden figures and pieces.

Ship Figureheads

Wood reached its pinnacle in an artistic way in New England during the Golden Age of shipcarving which lasted for more than a century from 1750 until the days prior to the Civil War, but its halcyon period extended to 1840 when American ships sailed to every known port in the world as well as to some that were not even charted. Shipcarvers were notably proud of their figureheads and some of them had an almost lifelike quality. Even when great man or somebody's loved one was the subject, there was often a bit of whimsey in the facial expression. On the whole, the approach was on the heroic side as far as size was concerned. Figureheads were not mere decoration in their origin. Rather, they were symbols. Those fastened to the bows of primitive craft in the days when the Phoenician traders and the Egyptians sailed the seas were beasts and birds and images of men and women as well. The Greeks, too, the Romans, and the Vikings held fast to the tradition with their sea serpents, gods, and goddesses. Figureheads served as guardians of vessels to appease the gods; as guiding eyes to find the way; perhaps as mother symbols to comfort the crew on long voyages. In the late Middle Ages, saints were sometimes carved as figureheads.

Mariners held them in high regard from the common seaman to the captain of the ship. After 1726, British ships were allowed free choice of figureheads in place of the traditional lion.

It was the custom when a ship was being built for the owner to seek out a shipcarver to make a figurehead. The craftsman designed it, carved it, and set it in place, sometimes with a bit of ceremony and always with a goodly number of onlookers. Every carver had his cronies and seamen were always dropping in as were children. Carving of a new figure for a vessel in Salem or Portsmouth, Boston or New Bedford, Mystic or Nantucket always made for a good deal of conversation. Like moss, legend began to grow with the first strike of the carver's chisel. When a ship was declared unfit for use, the figurehead would be repainted and used elsewhere, perhaps with a much changed appearance. E. O. Christensen has related in *Early American Wood Carving:* "The construction of the figurehead usually took several blocks of

"Ship's figureheads were lovely ladies who went to sea with grim clipper captains and salty sailors and lived happily beneath the ship's slender bowsprit. When a Cape Cod deepsea captain walked his quarterdeck on sunny days, he could see a coquettish curl tossed back over bare white shoulders, and glimpse a gown of blue and gold. At night when the moon was high, he could watch the lovely lady turn to silver over the shining water. When his ship was tossed in the fury of Atlantic storms, he saw his lady plunge beneath the waves to rise sea-drenched but still gallantly fighting an angry Neptune with her woman's wiles to protect the seamen that she loved." From *Ships' Figureheads from Old Cape Cod. Photo Louis S. Martel: courtesy Mystic Seaport*

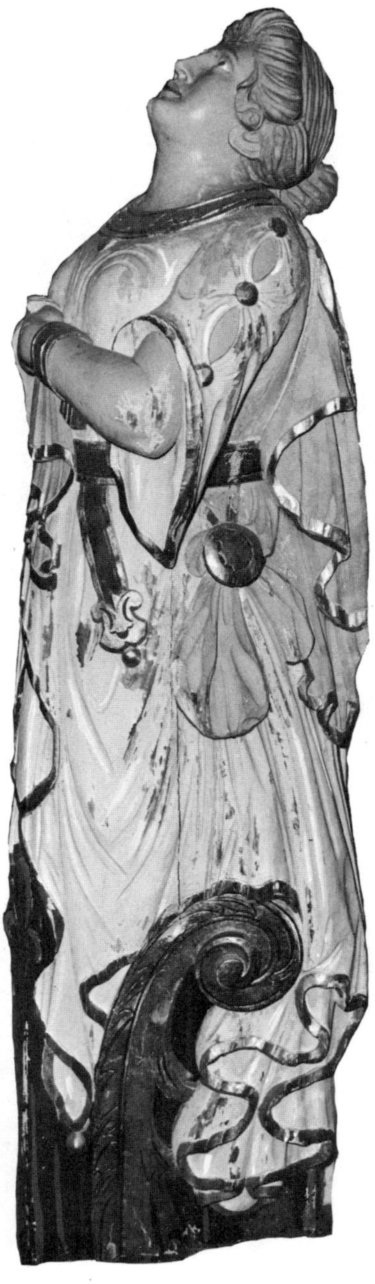

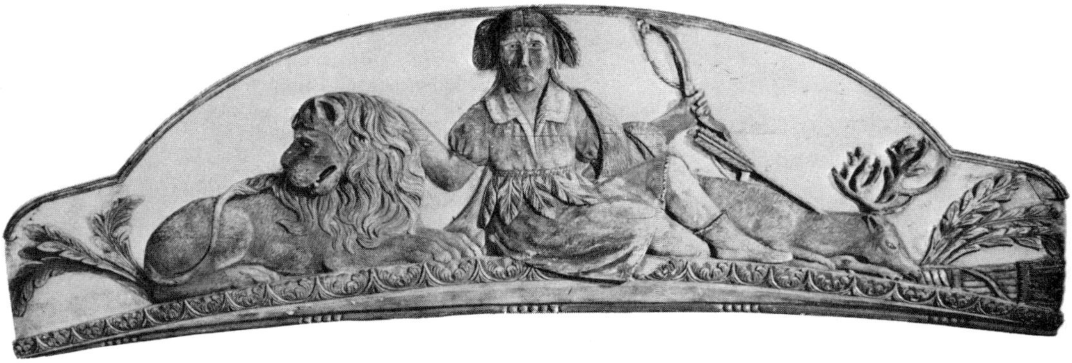

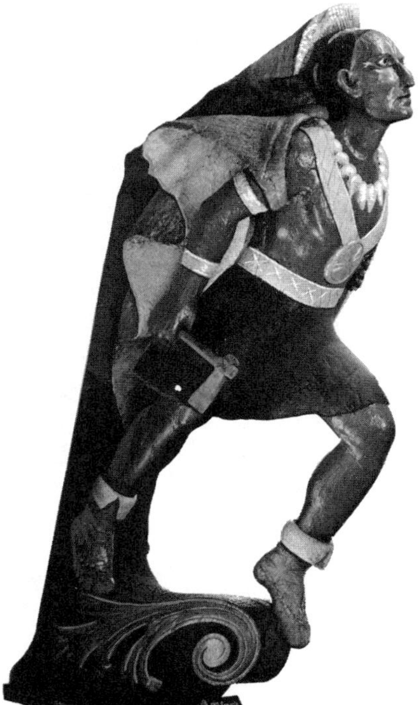

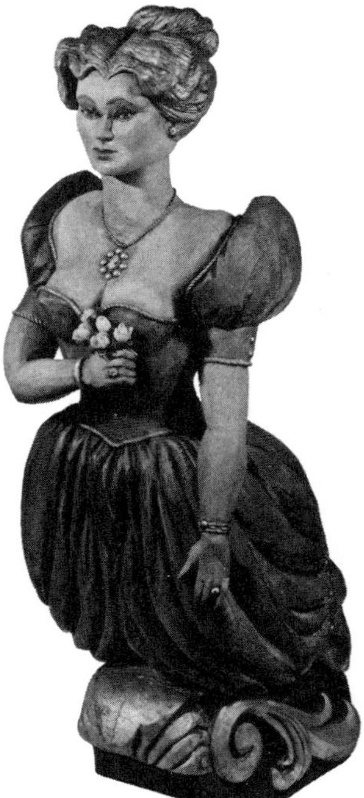

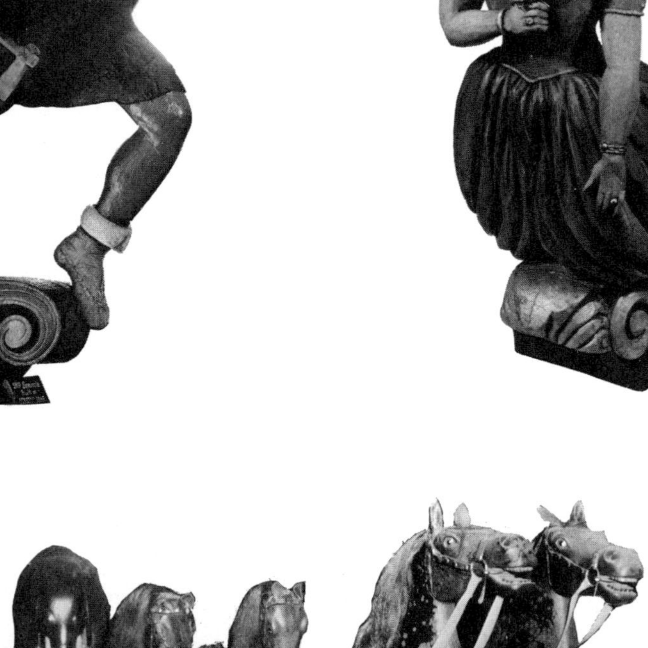

(*Top*) Stern carving from the ship *American Indian* built about 1785 in Plymouth, Massachusetts. *Photo courtesy Shelburne Museum*

(*Center, left*) "Of the hundreds of ships launched from the yards along the Mystic River this is the only figurehead which has returned to become a part of the collection at Mystic Seaport. Of fierce visage, with a shark's tooth necklace around his throat, a tomahawk clasped in his right hand and a knife in his left, the Seminole forcibly impresses as a true representative of the American Indian." Edouard A. Stackpole, Curator of the Marine Historical Association, who wrote these words, is justly proud of this seven-foot heroic figure carved in 1865. After the ship *Seminole* was dismantled in 1904 in Australia, the figurehead was placed in the Adelaide Museum. Eventually officials at Mystic learned of its whereabouts and succeeded in acquiring it for their ever-growing collection. *Photo Louis S. Martel: courtesy Mystic Seaport*

(*Center, right*) A man of many talents in many fields, Robert Perrin of Boston has a summer studio at Nantucket where "Nancy Tucket" is on display. Perrin carved this figurehead of balsa wood. *Courtesy Robert Perrin*

(*Bottom*) Five generations of children traveled from a wide area in Massachusetts to romp on the merry-go-round at Salem Willows. Commonly referred to as the "flying horses," this collection of superbly carved wooden carrousel figures mounted on a revolving wooden platform was one of the earliest to be erected in New England. Built in 1876 by Joseph Brown, it became widely known and remained as a noted landmark of this woodcarver's skill for seventy-five years. When the building and the collection were dismantled, the figures were acquired and taken to Macy's Department Store in New York City. *Photo Courtesy Essex Institute*

wood doweled together; arms were made separately and attached. To avoid splintering, the carving was with the grain of the wood, and details had to be adjusted to the grain . . . An outstretched arm was sometimes made detachable—for protection during storms."

Carving a life-size figure from wood was no task for a boy. It required consummate skill and every master carver had his apprentices. Once the figure was rough hewn, it had to be finished with patience and care. When completed, the carving had to be painted and, in some cases, gilded and then set in place.

When the American eagle became the official insignia of the new country, patriotic symbols of various kinds like Liberty and Columbia along with the eagle gave new inspiration to the figurehead carver. American folk art was aborning. Effigies of Washington, Jefferson, Alexander Hamilton, to mention only a few, gave the wood sculptor a new and wider field for expression. The lion, the dolphin, and the dragon were forgotten. Men, women, and children joined the ever-growing list of new subjects for carving. Indian chiefs and squaws were more expertly executed than the cigar store Indians used as trade signs from the 1840's on. While the image at the prow actually served no practical purpose, no ship worthy of the name was without one. Sailors even had their own superstitions about them. But whatever place these held, it was the pride of the owner that was significant. He wanted his ship to have all the import and stature of an ambassador, for America was still a young country and prestige in the trading ports of the world was vital.

Since a ship is always spoken of as *she*, it was only appropriate that female figures should predominate. After all, a ship was a man's province and the only reminder of the loved ones he had left behind was in a carving of a beautiful woman. These figures were usually life size or slightly smaller; some were heroic. It is truly difficult for anyone visiting a museum today to visualize the effect of one of these noble figures proudly displayed on the prow of a ship. Each was designed to be seen from several angles—most memorably and effectively in silhouette. As ship styles changed, so did the figures. What they signified to the sailors and to the captain on many a long voyage was something very personal and intimate. Longfellow has caught something of this mood in "The Building of the Ship":

> And at the bows an image stood,
> By a cunning artist carved in wood,
> . . . On many a dreary and misty night,
> 'T will be seen by the rays of the signal light,
> Speeding along through the rain and the dark,
> Like a ghost in its snow-white sark,
> The pilot of some phantom bark
> Guiding the vessel, in its flight
> By a path none other knows aright!

The fierce pride that stemmed from the long struggle for independence was evident in the work of the shipcarvers. To create their own style of craftsmanship seems to have been one of their most determined aims. That they achieved it is evident in the examples that remain. What some of the great figureheads looked like that proclaimed the supremacy of the new democracy in the "far away" foreign ports we can only surmise. Nor were the shipcarvers alone in their pride of performance. The work of the cabinetmakers, the silversmiths, the shipbuilders, the

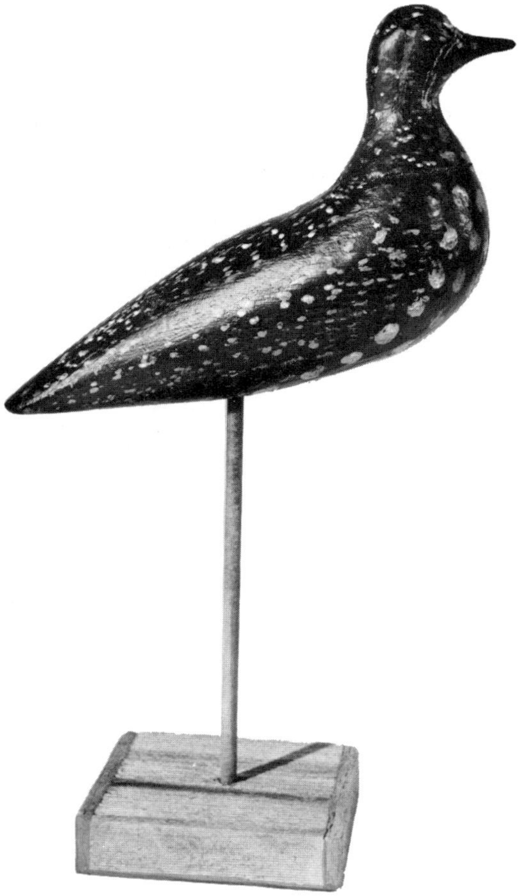

The collection of decoys at Dorset House, Shelburne Museum, is considered the most complete of its kind. *Courtesy Shelburne Museum*

carpenter-architects, and others all attest to this same kind of achievement. The shipcarver's trade was a good one since there was an abundance of work in the heyday of the Atlantic seaport towns. In *American Figureheads and Their Carvers* Pauline A. Pinckney has recorded: "Nearly every coast town along the Atlantic at some time boasted a thriving shipyard, and whether large or small, with few exceptions, supported a wood carver who did most of the carving for the community. Many of these local carvers were craftsmen of considerable skill, and it was exceptional for an owner to call in one of the more famous craftsmen from one of the larger shipbuilding centers to do the work on his vessel. When work on ship ornaments was not available the ship carver turned his hand to mantels, doorways, and other architectural carving. It was not until late in the nineteenth century, when shipbuilding in America had subsided to an extent that it could no longer supply enough work for the many skilled carvers, that these craftsmen turned to producing cigarstore Indians and ornaments and figures for the elaborate circus wagons as a source of income."

The pattern had been so well set in shipcarving that by the time large numbers of artisans arrived from various countries in Europe, an American style and technique had been set and so it remained.

Ships, the best of them, are subject to the vicissitudes of gales and heavy seas; storms have wrought havoc with many a stout vessel within a few years of its building. As a result, hundreds of figureheads have been lost when ships were wrecked, only to be washed up on the shore of some distant land long after the tragedies occurred. It is said that natives of more than one South Seas island, upon finding a Yankee figurehead, set it up as an idol and worshipped it. Other factors, too, have contributed to the fact that no example of seventeenth-century shipcarver's art survives. For that matter, a goodly number of outstanding productions of the eighteenth and nineteenth century suffered the same fate. Most of these that remain are in museums or private collections.

Decoys

Carving decoys out of pine and cedar is one of the unusual wood crafts of an earlier era that brings into sharp focus our extraordinary heritage from the Indians of this continent. Their life so intimately linked them with the habits of birds and beasts that they were able to manifest exceptional skill and aptitude with the materials which nature abundantly supplied.

The various types of decoys, including those made of wood, used along the Eastern Seaboard for the past few centuries can be traced back to various tribes of American Indians who were using them to lure ducks more than a thousand years ago. Today, the neatly carved wooden effigies hold great fascination not only for the duck hunter but for the discerning woodcarver and decorator as well. The word decoy, we are told, is a contraction from the Dutch term *Endekooy* meaning a duck cage or trap of the kind used in the days before firearms were common. It is comparatively recent in usage.

A replica of a canvasback duck created ten centuries ago by an Indian of the Tule Eater's tribe in the Southwest was ingenious in every way. Fashioned out of reeds and flat

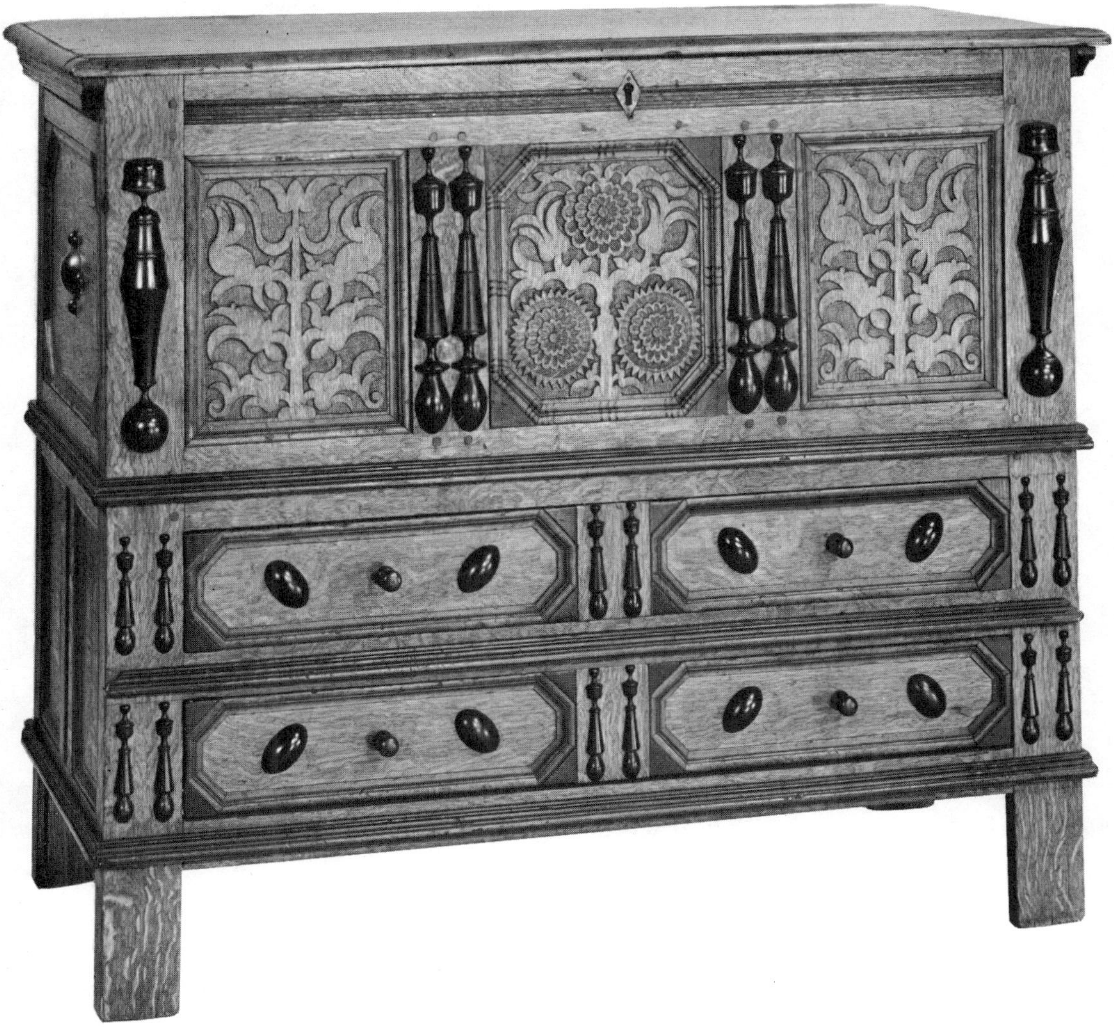

This two-drawer sunflower chest is an outstanding example of the top quality furniture made by Connecticut Valley craftsmen in the seventeenth century. *Photo courtesy the Wadsworth Athenaeum*

Saddlebox decoration for the steamboat *Mount Washington. Photo courtesy Shelburne Museum*

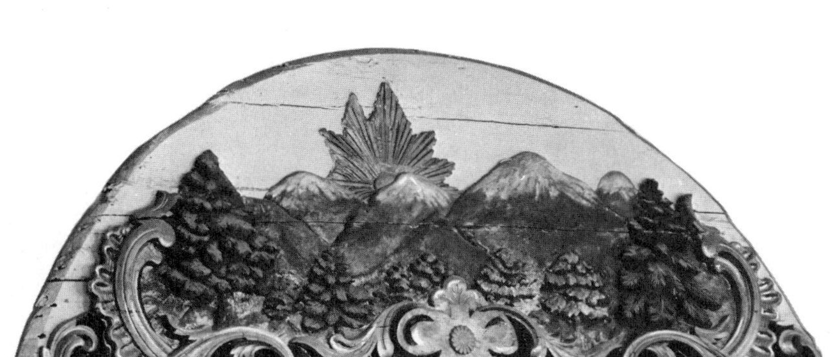

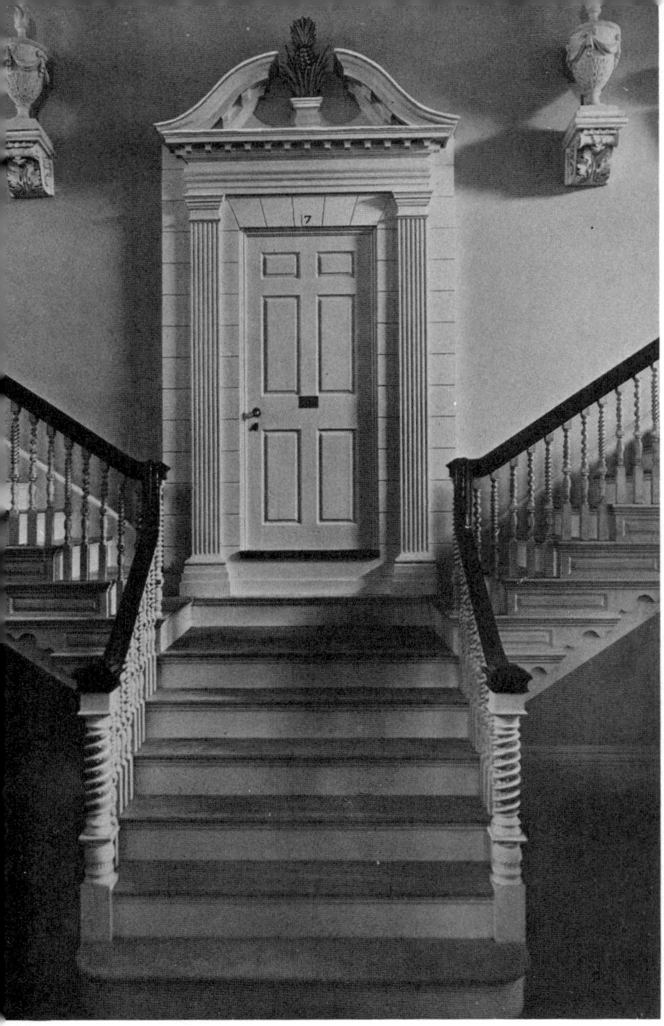

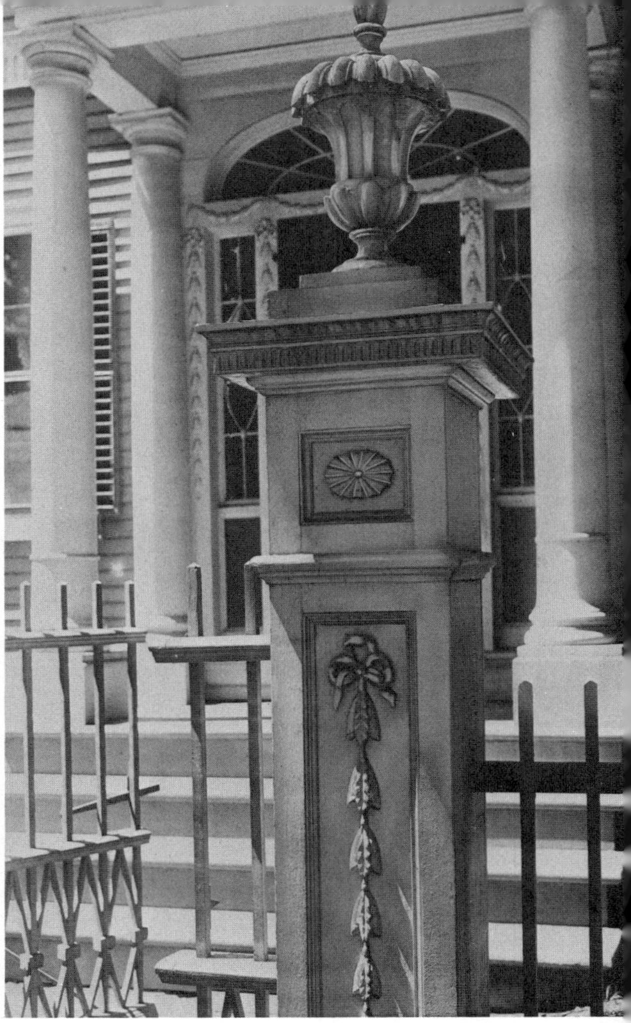

(*Above, left*) Salem's Essex Institute is rich in notable examples of woodcarving. The "pineapple" doorway was formerly the entrance to the home of Captain Thomas Poynton, built about 1740. The staircase belonged in the Hubon house on nearby Charter Street, while the urns on brackets flanking the doorway formerly topped the fence posts of the Aaron Waite house, designed by Samuel McIntire.

(*Above, right*) Entrance to the Cook-Oliver House, Federal Street, Salem, Massachusetts, designed by Samuel McIntire. The numerous monuments to McIntire's skill are far greater in number than the biographical details of this noted woodcarver. From the accounts of his death we have these appraisals. "Mr. McIntire was originally bred to the occupation of a housewright, but his vigorous mind soon passed the ordinary limits of his profession, and aspired to . . . architecture, in which he had advanced with a steady and sure step far beyond most of his countrymen . . . His native town is enriched with many memorials in this art. . . ." *Salem Gazette,* February 12, 1811. "His industry, usefulness and consistent virtue gave him an uncommon share of the affections of all who knew him. By his own well directed energies he became one of the best of men." *Essex Register,* February 9, 1811. *Both photos courtesy Essex Institute*

rushes, the head and breast were colored and feathers were used to give it a realistic appearance. (It may well be considered the inspiration for the popular wooden models made from the nineteenth century on.) The Indians also formed mock birds by setting small stones on large ones to lure wild fowl; they made birds out of mud as well, and stuffed frames with grass, floating them on the water. Heads and bodies of dead birds, strategically placed, were another approach.

From the late seventeenth century, these various devices were used in New England and elsewhere in America to lure wild fowl. For those living in the wilderness and in sparsely settled country, the search for food was a constant one and wild duck was good eating. However, the usual methods employed proved tedious and time consuming since new lures had to be made constantly. As a result, duck hunters and whittlers took to carving wooden birds. First they used white cedar until it became scarce, then they resorted to pine. Because of their general shape and appearance, these early wooden birds were referred to as "blocks" or "stools," adopting the name from the European custom of fastening a live pigeon to a movable pole or perch (stool) as a lure to other pigeons. When shooting scoter or eider ducks along the Atlantic Coast, these lures were strung out in a long line with the gunner's boat at one end, and were referred to as "tollers," from the ancient custom of calling or tolling the death knell.

D. S. Webster and William Kehoe in *Decoys at Shelburne Museum* point out that the blocks, stools, and tollers first made were decidedly primitive. "Early whittlers apparently worked on the assumption that any slight resemblance to actual wildfowl was sufficient, especially in fall when migrants from the northern breeding grounds were young. For this roughhewn work they were paid accordingly; at best from twenty to fifty cents for each block. Yet stool making soon became a recognized profession, and a demanding one for its practitioners.

"In the 1840's and 1850's the carvers began to make their blocks more closely resemble actual birds, with painted plumage, and to personalize their decoys. Definite regional types were developed because of local conditions. . . ."

In the years following the Civil War, the demand for decoys grew to such an extent that they were produced on a commercial basis. Realistic in appearance, pleasing in design and elaborately painted, decoys were sold by the dozen at prices ranging from $2.50 to $12.00, but they were not popular in New England. Novelties including a rubber decoy, one that honked, and a tip-up type appeared. Materials other than wood were used extensively in these lures.

During the Gay Nineties and the early part of this century, wild-fowl shooting was not only a popular sport but a business as well; wild fowl were in great demand in the markets. Our native birds were being exploited to such an extent that in 1913 and again in 1918 Congress passed laws limiting the number of wild ducks that could be shot in a single day, as well as defining the extent of the hunting season.

Hunters were often decoy makers as well, for who better knew the fine points needed to make a good decoy? Today, the decoys of the past century are widely sought by collectors and decorators. Undoubtedly, the nation's best known collector was Joel Barber who presented his collection to the Shelburne Museum at Shelburne, Vermont. In addition he has left a fascinating account in *Wild Fowl Decoys* first published in 1932 and still available.

Methods of carving decoys by hand are essentially those used in Civil War days. The steps involved as outlined by Webster and Kehoe in the following paragraph are described and illustrated in *Decoys at Shelburne Museum.*

"The carving consists of four major steps, body making, headmaking, assembling, and painting, and the operation of rigging—the attaching of the body weight or ballast and of the anchor and fastening. (The kinds of weights and anchors used are almost without number, varying from region to region, from carver to carver.) If these steps appear simple, this is what Joel Barber in his *Wild Fowl Decoys* aptly termed 'a misleading simplicity.' For there have never been but relatively few carvers who have had both the talent for carving and the profound, seemingly instinctive knowledge of wildfowl necessary for making the almost perfect decoy."

For the inspiration and pleasure of all who enjoy these appealing examples of the woodcarver's art, the Shelburne Museum's Dorset House is the greatest treasure house in all New England. Not one but several outstanding collections are housed there, totaling more than one thousand specimens, the largest and best rounded of its kind in this country.

Candle-lighting Time

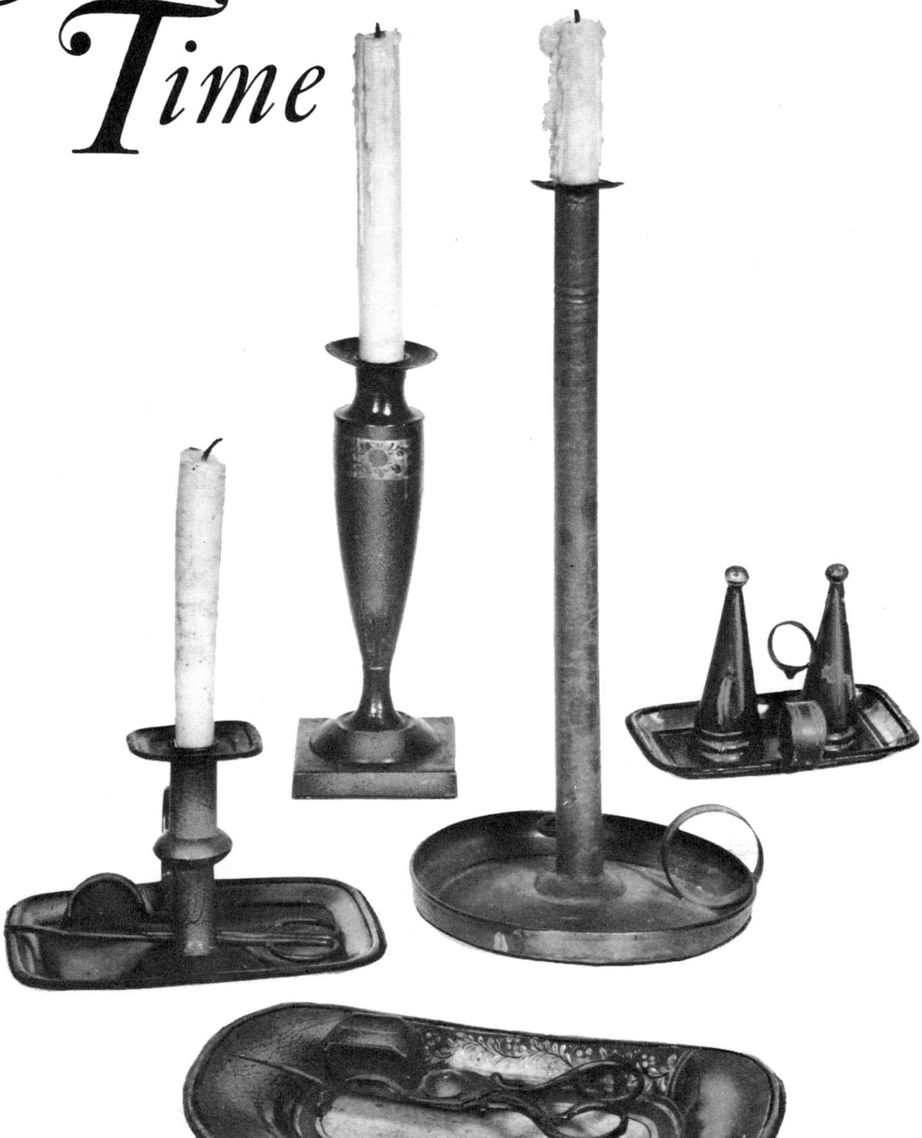

The casual reader delving into colonial history rarely notes or takes the time to think about the strain that the Puritans placed on their eyes. Mention of blindness, failing sight, or eye diseases seldom is found. Surely, all of these afflictions must have plagued the early settler to some degree.

One of the first commodities that the housewife of necessity had to supply for the household was some means of lighting; the flames that danced high in the fireplace were not adequate. Yet, the hearth fire, all-important for many reasons, was the first source of light. The torch was the second, and equally poor, method of lighting. Grasping a faggot from the fire, one could walk about with it, but it was an almost-sure way of starting a fire. A great number of torches were used. In *Early Lighting in New England,* Helen Brigham Hebard has dedescribed a few: "The torches improvised . . . range from strips of blubber, fat bodies of birds and fish, to dried tree limbs or pine knots." Splint lights made of slivers of resinous wood were used, the pitch oozing from them and spilling on the floor. Also thin strips from eight to ten inches long were cut from the heart of the fat pitch pine. Describing this "candlewood," the Reverend Francis Higginson of Salem, wrote in 1633: "They are such candles as the Indians commonly used which may serve as a shift among poore folk, but I cannot commend it for singular good, because it droppeth a pitchy kind of substance where it stands." All of these makeshift lighting devices smoked and were odorous. Again, the Reverend Higginson recorded his observations: "Though New England has no tallow to make candles of, yet by abundance of fish thereof it can afford oil for lamps." These shallow lamps made of wrought iron were known as grease and Betty lamps; they sputtered and fumed, smoked, and smelled.

Meadow rushes also served for lighting as well as the dried heads of the cattail rush. The meadow rush was gathered, trimmed, and peeled, leaving only a thin supporting strip of green skin. The porous white pith of the rush, after drying, was drawn through the fat of the household, then burned—a real incendiary wand! With what gratefulness the Puritan and the Pilgrim women must have looked upon the bayberry when they discovered its wonderful use—*candles!*

That rhyming countryman, Thomas Tusser, ever mindful of the endless tasks of the housewife, did not fail to enjoin candlemaking:

> Wife make thine owne candle.
> Provide for thy tallow ere frost commeth in,
> and make thine own candle ere Winter begin.

Candle-dipping was the great autumnal task of the seventeenth and eighteenth century housewife; it was a monotonous and tedious duty. Preparations were under way by dawn and a roaring fire in the fireplace blazed high under two kettles, hung on trammels from the lug-pole. The kettles were filled with water (brought in laboriously from outside by the housewife) and melted tallow, the hard fat gathered painstakingly from the slaughtered farm animals. At the end of the great kitchen, or in an adjoining, cooler room, two long poles were set parallel to one another, supported on stools. Across the poles, at regular intervals like the rounds of a ladder, the shorter candlerods were laid. To each candlerod was attached a dozen or more candlewicks, of loosely spun tow, sometimes dipped in saltpeter. The wicks, carefully straightened, were dipped time after time into the melted tallow, and grew so slowly that the process seemed never-ending. Since the tallow needed constant replenishing, two kettles were needed. One kettle at a time was swung off the trammel and used until the tallow began to harden; then it was melted again. This process was repeated through the day.

It was ever a matter of great concern to the housewife to have a plentiful stock of symmetrical white candles. Wax candles were also made in molds. Beeswax was used, too, for candlemaking and consequently many a family had a beehive in the yard.

The loveliest of all the Colonial candles were those made from the bayberry. The instinct of adaptability made the settlers of New England promptly turn to the products of the new land as substitutes for the familiar staples of Old England. Along with the pungent red cedar and the aromatic sweet fern that skirt the New England coast is found a still spicier perfume, that of the bayberry bush, whose leaves and fruit give forth a pure, clean scent.

These dense, woody shrubs bear a profusion of tiny, green-gray, spicy, wax-coated berries, which, the earliest colonists quickly learned, yielded an inflammable wax that would

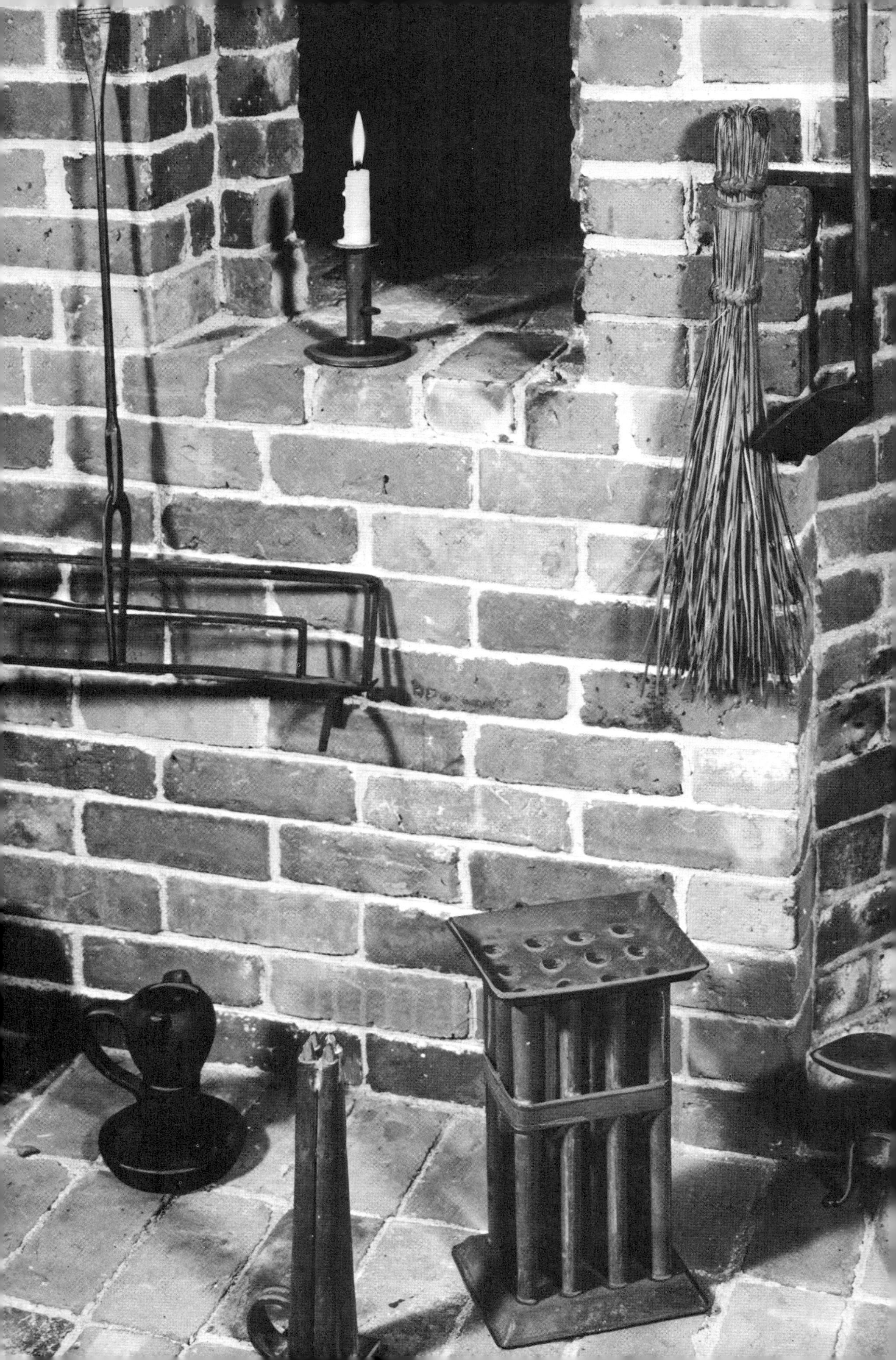

replace and supplement their lack of tallow. They named the plant "candleberry." Berries were gathered in the autumn. The method of preparing this wax was simple and it has not changed over the years. The berries were dumped into a kettle with hot water and boiled. Resolved in this manner the fat melted out, floated to the top of the water and was skimmed off into a vessel. The skimming process continued until no tallow remained. When it had congealed, it resembled common tallow or wax, except for its muddy green color. With a second melting and refining it acquired a pleasing transparent green. Bayberry candles did not bend easily nor did they melt in summer as with candles of common tallow. They burned slower and more evenly, did not smoke, and gave off an agreeable fragrance when they were extinguished.

Bayberry was not only a useful home product, but an important article of traffic, advertised frequently in the newspapers. In 1712 John Winthrop, Jr., received the following letter from Thomas Lechmere: "I am now to beg one favour of you,—that you secure for me all the bayberry wax you can possibly put your hands on. You must take a care they do not put too much tallow among it, being a custom and cheat they have got."

On a visit to Cape Cod in 1849, Henry David Thoreau wrote: "Bayberries are still common on the Cape, as they are through much of New England. The pewter molds in which bayberry candles were made can still be unearthed from time to time in antique shops, though they are becoming scarcer by the year."

Continuing on his ramble, he recorded his observations:

"Our way to the high sand-bank . . . led, as usual, through patches of bayberry bushes, which straggled into the sand. This, next to the shrub-oak, was perhaps the most common shrub thereabouts. I was much attracted by its odiferous leaves and small gray berries which are clustered about the short twigs, just below the last year's growth. I know of but two bushes in Concord, and they, being staminate plants, do not bear fruit. The berries gave it a venerable appearance, and they smelled quite spicy, like small confectionery."

Ever aware of the importance of plants and their medicinal, culinary, and household uses, he recalled: "Robert Beverly in his 'History of Virginia,' published in 1705, states that:

"At the mouth of their rivers, and all along upon the sea and bay, and near many of their creeks and swamps, grows the myrtle, bearing a berry, of which they make a hard, brittle wax, of a curious green color, which by refining becomes almost transparent. Of this they make candles, which are never greasy to the touch nor melt with lying in the hottest weather; neither does the snuff of these ever offend the smell, like that of a tallow candle; but, instead of being disagreeable, if an accident puts a candle out, it yields a pleasant fragrancy to all that are in the room; insomuch that nice people often put them out on purpose to have the incense of the expiring snuff. The melting of these berries is said to have been first found out by a surgeon in New England, who performed wonderful things with a salve made of them.' "

Little wonder that twentieth century readers find refreshment of spirit and a pleasant kind of stimulus in Thoreau's writings. He held fast to the simple way of life, reflected it in his work and actions, and frequently recorded even the minutiae observed on his journeys, as witness these comments: "From the abundance of berries still hanging on the bushes, we judged that the inhabitants did not generally collect them for tallow, though we had seen a piece in the house we had just left. I have since made some tallow myself. Holding a basket beneath the bare twigs in April, I rubbed them together between my hands and thus gathered about a quart in twenty minutes, to which were added enough to make three pints, and I might have gathered them much faster with a suitable rake and a large shallow basket. They have little prominences like those of an orange all creased in tallow, which also fills the interstices down to the stone. The oily part rose to the top, making it look like a savory black broth, which smelled much like balm or other herb tea. You let it cool, then skim off the tallow from the surface,

Candlemolds and grease lamps on the hearth at the Richard Derby House, Salem, Massachusetts. Left to right: pottery grease lamp, two candle molds, wrought iron grease lamp.
Photo Richard Merrill: courtesy Salem Maritime National Historic Site

melt this again and strain it. I got about a quarter of a pound weight from my three pints, and more yet remained within the berries. A small portion cooled in the form of small flattish hemispheres, like crystallizations, the size of a kernel of corn-nuggets I called them as I picked them out from amid the berries. Loudon says, that 'cultivated trees are said to yield more wax than those that are found wild.' If you get any pitch on your hands in the pinewoods you have only to rub some of these berries between your hands to start it off."

As previously mentioned, the making and use of the pungent bayberry candle continues to this day. As popular now as centuries ago, Mabel K. Baker makes candles in the same manner as the Pilgrim housewife. On each box produced by the Colonial Candle Company of Cape Cod, one finds her rhyming legend:

Light ye all the candles
And burn them brightly too
If burned to the socket
They'll bring wealth to the pocket
And joy through the year to you.

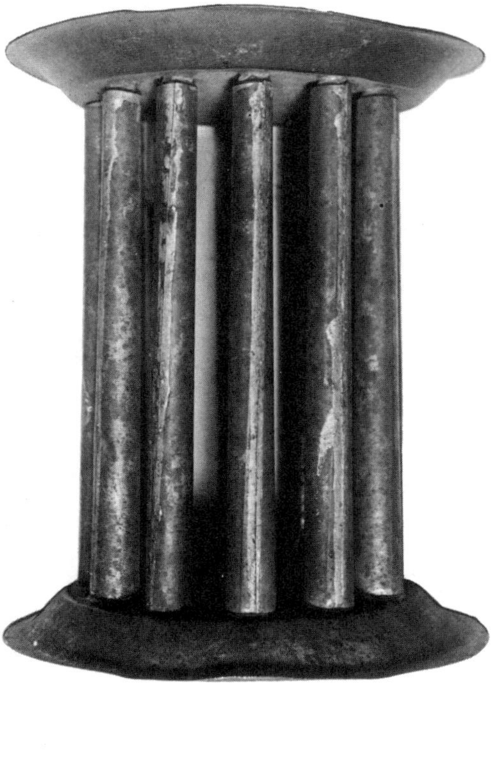

Tin candlemold, an uncommon circular type for making twelve candles. *Photo courtesy Essex Institute*

A bayberry iron waxer was found in every colonial kitchen. It consisted of two pieces of cloth sewed together and filled with ripened bayberries. These little bayberry ironing aids were handed down from generation to generation, still maintaining their effectiveness in keeping the iron well waxed. Today they, too, are still made and may be found in many a New England gift shop.

The growth of the whaling trade and the consequent use of spermaceti increased the facilities for, and the possibilities of, house illumination. In 1686 Governor Andros petitioned for a commission for a voyage after "Sperma-Coeti Whales" but not till the middle of the following century did spermaceti become in common enough use to bring forth notices such as this, in the *Boston Independent Advertiser* of January 1749:

Sperma-Ceti Candles, exceeding all others for Beauty of Sweetness of Scent when Extinguished and Duration being more than double with Tallow Candles of Equal Size and Dimension of Flame near 4 times more. Emitting a Soft easy Expanding Light, bringing the object close to the Sight rather than causing the Eye to trace after them, as all Tallow Candles do, from a Constant Dimnes which they produce. One of these Candles serves the use and purpose of 3 Tallow Candles, and upon the whole are much pleasanter & cheaper.

These candles were placed in candle-beams—rude chandeliers made with wooden arms and strips of tin with cups or sockets to support the candles; also in sliding stands, and in sconces, sometimes called prongs or candle-arms. The latter not only appeared in the inventories of all genteel folk, but decorated the walls of all genteel parlors.

In 1731, the General Assembly of Rhode Island had established a bounty for whale oil and whalebone. The earliest Rhode Island whaling vessel known by name was Benjamin Thurston's *Pelican.* The following year, this vessel benefited from the provisions of the act when it brought to Newport one hundred and fourteen barrels of oil and eight hundred pieces of whalebone. By the time of the Revolution, Rhode Island had about fifty vessels from Newport, Providence, Bristol, and Warren engaged in the trade.

The "head matter" of the giant sperm whales was used in the manufacture of spermaceti candles, which provided excellent light and

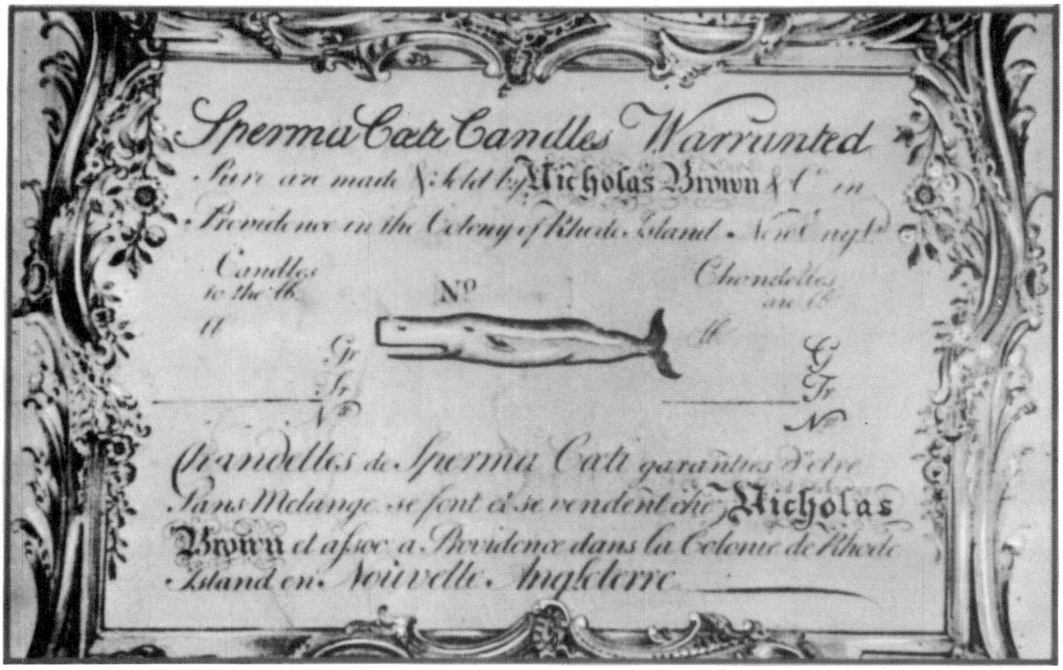

Label used on boxes of spermaceti candles made in Rhode Island.

merchants early became interested in their manufacture. In 1761 under the leadership of the Browns of Providence, a group of candle manufacturers from Newport, Boston, and Providence established the United Company of Spermaceti Chandlers to control the industry. This was the first such trust agreement in America and was a large and successful enterprise until the Revolution when the whalers were driven from the seas. A revival came in the period from 1820 to 1840. Nearly five hundred whaling voyages were made, some into the Pacific. From the middle of the nineteenth century to the present day activity is confined to the area around Narragansett Bay and the waters of the nearby Atlantic. Made in the same manner as tallow and wax candles, spermaceti candles continue to be part of the livelihood of Nantucket.

Candlemaking has become a new kind of interest for young and old alike and, each year, at Christmastime people throughout New England make their own Yuletide candles. To help at other seasons of the year, there has been placed upon the do-it-yourself market, a package of "Instant Candles."

The Potter's Wheel

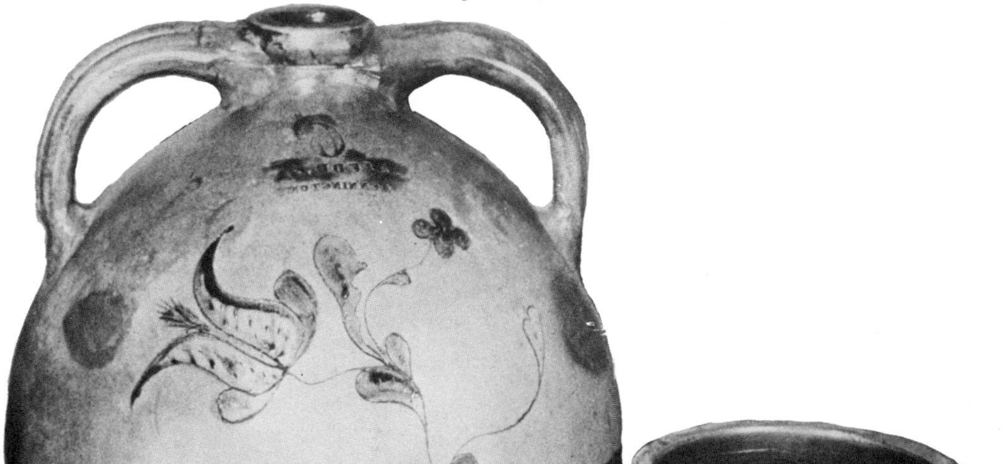

Assorted early stoneware made by Captain John Norton, of Bennington, Vermont.
Photo Richard Carter Barrett: courtesy Bennington Museum

The intrinsic beauty of pottery lies in the eye of the beholder who sees not only the finished piece but also watches the actual process at the potter's wheel. This, the oldest of the handcrafts still practiced in New England, is truly an ancient art, dating back to the beginning of time. Potters were among the craftsmen in the earliest ships to arrive in the New Land, but little or nothing remains of their work which began with the making of bricks and basic kitchen utensils. Pottery is fragile in comparison to wood or metal and since it was cheap, broken or cracked pieces were continually replaced. As one observer noted, in describing the craft of the potter, "hands of delicate strength" are needed.

The potters who first practiced their craft in New England were exposed to the most primitive conditions. Little opportunity was afforded for any conscious artistry since they were hard put to produce household articles for everyday living. Clay was plentiful in the seaport settlement at Salem where the first New England pottery was started. In 1629, the Reverend Higginson recorded, "we are setting a brick-kill on worke to make Bricke and Tyle for the making of our houses." Using the same red clay, they made pots, milk pans, mugs, plates, and similar articles of what we call redware or brownware. Lura Woodside Watkins has described it with these words: "Simple though New England redware may be, it is nevertheless sturdy and vigorous in form and it has a charm that is difficult to define. Lustrous glazes, soft colors, and shapes of good proportion combine to make a virile, handsome ware. Earthy by its very nature, with its suggestion of soil, leaves, and trees, it captures the essence of the early potter's environment. That its beauty is largely accidental makes it no less lovable: its variations are like the changes of Nature herself, never ending, ever yielding fresh enjoyment. It is truly an expression of simple people —men almost without conscious thought of art. Like them their pottery is strong, direct, stripped of pretense and foolish ornamentation. It was created to fill a demand, and incidentally, to please those who came to buy."

The word pottery used in an all-inclusive way refers to all items made of clay from the common building brick to the finest Oriental porcelain. On the other hand, the term pottery is commonly used, in a specialized sense, with reference to all of the common or coarse types of ware, excluding those of fine quality such as porcelain, stoneware, faïence, and others of fine quality. The potter's art is known as ceramics.

Porcelain, "the aristocrat of the art," is distinguished by the whiteness and fineness of its body—comparable to white marble used in statuary. It is thin, translucent, or nearly so, with sharp edges and hard in substance; this quality varies according to the "paste" or clay mixture used. Actually, there are three distinct kinds of porcelain. Hard paste, referred to as true or natural porcelain, is composed of China clay (kaolin clay) and China stone (feldspar), both materials being found in natural earth deposits. Porcelain made of these materials is extremely hard (producing a metallic ring when struck), nonporous with a fine glazed surface and cold in its whiteness. Much Chinese porcelain is of this type.

Soft-paste porcelain is referred to as artificial or glassy, since a glass-forming composition is used in place of China stone. It is soft in substance, yielding to a file or knife; its color is creamy white, with a more translucent quality than true or hard-paste porcelain. Bone porcelain (bone China) contains both China stone and China clay to which bone ash has been added. In hardness, whiteness, and translucence, it stands halfway between the other two types.

Stoneware (often classified as porcelain) is hard in substance, is more often gray or pale yellowish brown in color than white and the sharp edges may be translucent. Parian ware commonly used in making figures, Ironstone China (a trade name), the products of Josiah Wedgwood's famous English pottery, jasper and basalt, are stoneware, and other widely used stone jugs, drain pipes, and other widely used objects for everyday living also belong in this category.

Earthenware is a term in common use and includes all other pottery other than porcelain and stoneware. In contrast to porcelain, it is made from the more common types of clay, is porous unless glazed and is opaque. Majolica, lusterware, faïence, Delft, Rockingham, Bennington, and other kinds all fall into the category of earthenware.

Unlike sculpture which exists only for its intrinsic beauty of form and line, pottery embodies the elements of use and beauty.

Nearly everyone uses pottery in some form in everyday life. Even in its most primitive forms, there is the charm and appeal of the material, its color, texture, form, and the endless variety of decorative motifs often used for adornment. The stamp of individuality in each piece of handmade pottery to a large extent reflects something of the maker's feeling and personality. This, the oldest art in the world, still remains essentially a pure handcraft. As George H. Opdike once remarked, "The simple process of shaping a pot by human hands as it turns on a wheel remains exactly the same as it was in prehistoric time. Even in shapes that cannot be fashioned on a wheel but are pressed or cast in a mould—such as a squarish pot—their finishing, glazing and decorating are almost entirely handwork."

The art and the technique used in making pottery have not changed materially over the centuries. Today, methods of firing have been greatly simplified and other requirements of the process have evolved, but the background of early pottery-making in New England would have been lost had it not been for Lura Woodside Watkins. Her search began more than thirty years ago as a result of a casual chat with an antique dealer in Ashfield, Massachusetts, near Northampton. Ashfield was a center for craftsmen from the 1770's until the beginning of the Civil War. Curiosity prompted Mrs. Watkins to make some excavations on the site of an old pottery. Then she pursued town and family records, account books, and printed lists of wares and began to unearth a fascinating story which led her to the nearby town of Whately. From this modest beginning she proceeded to track down the story of pottery-making in all parts of New England. Unraveling the story involved considerable travel, the tracing of deeds, checking town directories and tax lists, interviewing descendents of the potters, examining extant examples of pottery, excavating and digging in shard piles, making measurements, composing colors, and literally piecing together fragments or visualizing and ascertaining sizes of pottery objects. This kind of sleuthing has strong appeal for those whose curiosity and interest are sufficiently great and well-directed to do the required research. Mrs. Watkins has told her story in a most engaging manner in *Early New England Potters and Their Wares*.

More than seven hundred men plied the individual potter's trade in New England from the 1620's to the year 1900, producing all sorts

Miss Katharine L. Alden, a descendant of John and Priscilla Alden, teaches pottery-making at Sparrow House, Plymouth, Massachusetts. As did early New England potters, she uses local clay and processes it herself. Below and opposite are flower pots made by Miss Alden, based on examples, *circa* 1800. *Photos Richard Merrill*

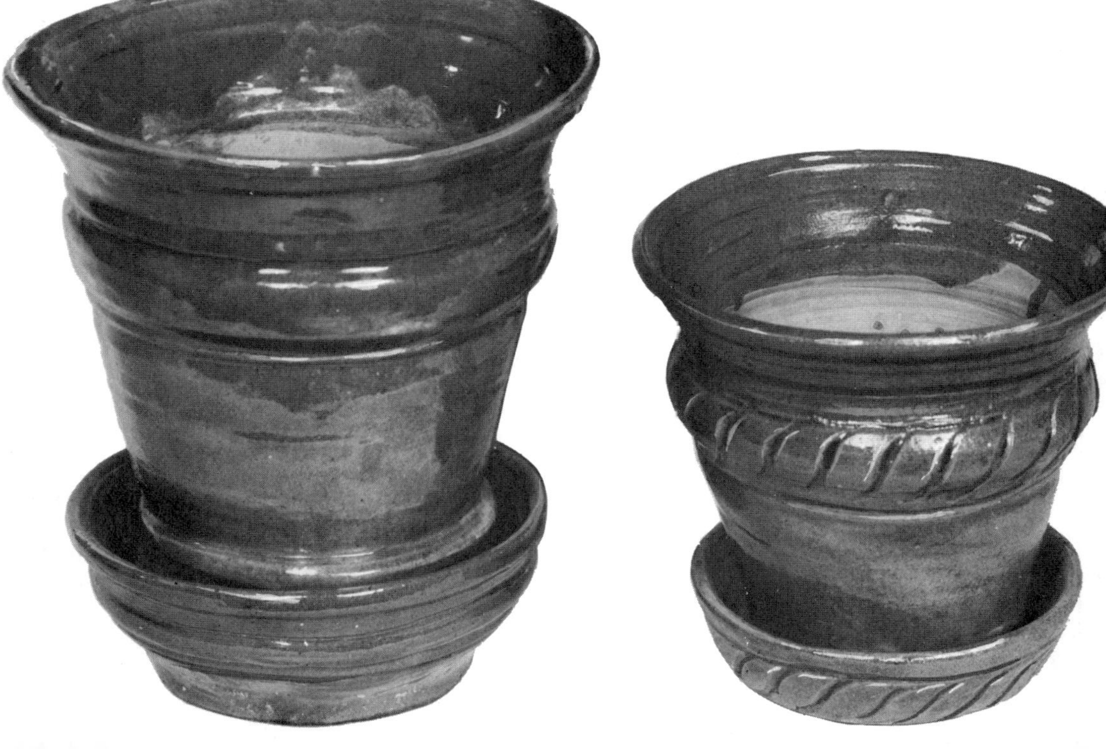

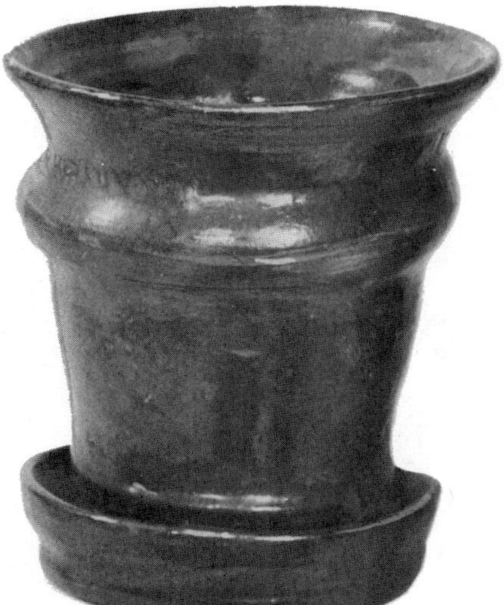

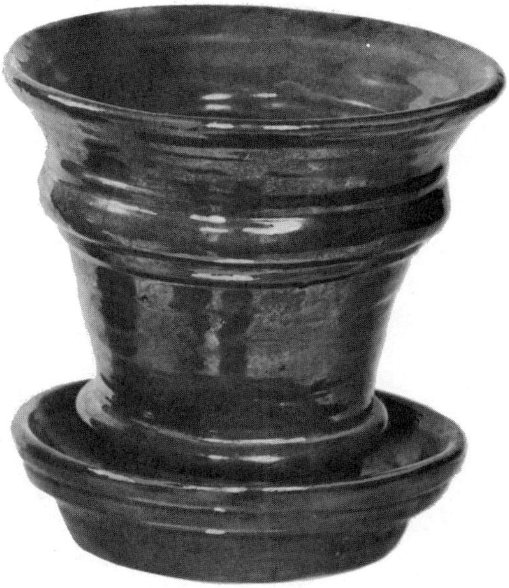

of containers for household use. This was an earthy craft. Raw materials were easy to obtain and the equipment needed required no great outlay of money. The potter not only dug his own clay, but washed and cleaned it as well, using, at first, a small mill of the type for grinding grain. The pug mill which followed was a tublike affair with a revolving upright shaft in the center to which blades were attached for grinding the clay. From the shaft or post, a long beam or "sweep" extended at right angles and to this a horse was hitched. As it walked round and round, the blades turned and the lumpy clay, with water added, was reduced to a soupy mud. The potter further worked this mixture, removing all the impurities.

The potter's wheel was his only machine, an invention of such ancient origin that no one seems to know when it was first made. His oven or kiln where the pieces were fired, a few homemade tools made of wood and wire, and molds used for "slip" casting were all that he required. Slip is a mixture of clay and water having the consistency of thick cream. Clay that has been shaped in its desired form (before firing) is referred to as the clay state. After the first firing and before glazing, it is called biscuit. Once covered with a coat of glazing and fired a second time, the piece was referred to as being glazed. Decoration—in which color was used—was applied either before or after glazing. The glazing process usually made the ware watertight.

Connecticut became the leading state in New England in the production of pottery in the nineteenth century. Stoneware of various kinds was the principal output. New Hampshire also had many potteries including that of Peter Clark of Lyndeboro established in 1775. There were others at Exeter, New Durham, Moultonboro, Keene, and Nashua.

Massachusetts where pottery-making first began in New England had its share. Daniel Boyley of Newburyport operated from 1764 to 1795. Examples of his ware, both complete and restored, form a part of the collection at the Smithsonian Institution. John Parker of Charlestown was active in the eighteenth century. The Paige Pottery in South Danvers (now Peabody), the Hewes Pottery in Cambridge, the Dedham Pottery, and the Dorchester Pottery were noted for a variety of specialities as well as the usual line of pots.

John Norton, a Connecticut Yankee from Goshen, served honorably as a captain in the Revolution, then migrated to Vermont in 1793. He established the first pottery at Bennington which remained in the family for a hundred years. Meanwhile, Norton's grandson Julius became associated with Fenton and Hall. This firm dissolved and Fenton went into a partner-

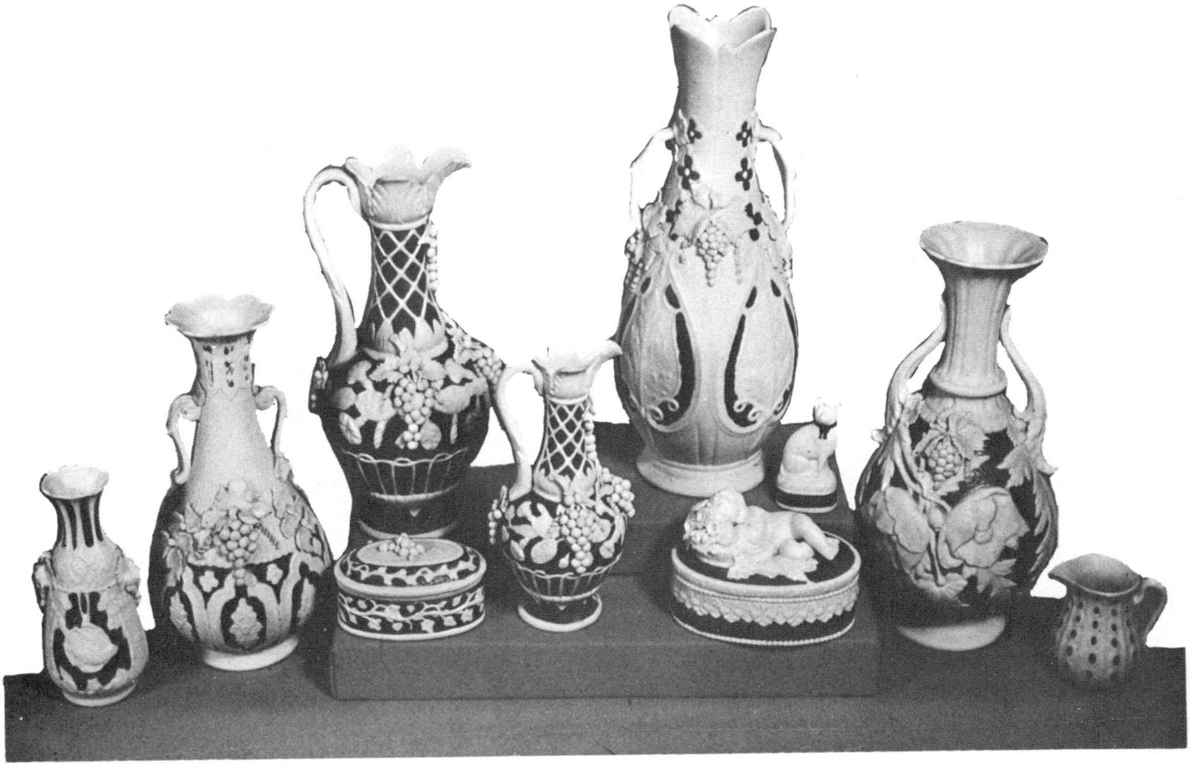

Examples of ceramic wares made in Bennington, Vermont, during the nineteenth century, now on display at the Bennington Museum. *Photo courtesy Richard Carter Barret*

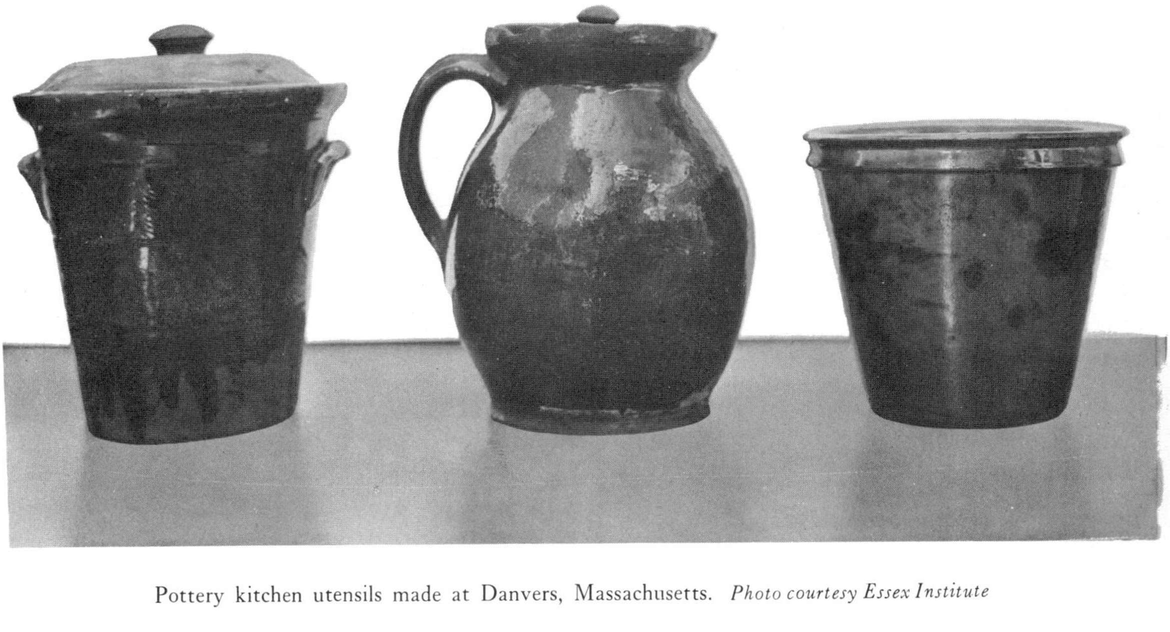

Pottery kitchen utensils made at Danvers, Massachusetts. *Photo courtesy Essex Institute*

ship with Lyman, later known as the United States Pottery Company. The story of Bennington pottery and porcelain like that of Deming Jarves and the Sandwich Glassworks is one of the fascinating episodes of American history. Christopher Webber Fenton was an extraordinary individual who had a passion for experimenting but was not distinguished as a businessman. The output of this firm was prodigious and varied as revealed by the outstanding collection at the Bennington Museum. The photograph in this chapter conveys more vividly than words the beauty and appeal of this famous New England pottery and porcelain.

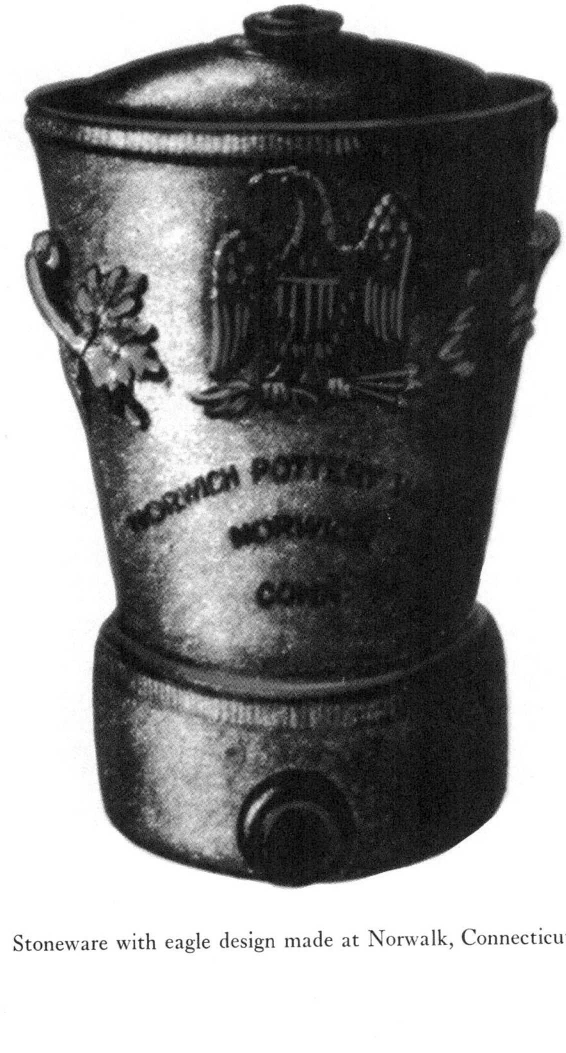

Stoneware with eagle design made at Norwalk, Connecticut.

Needles and Stitches

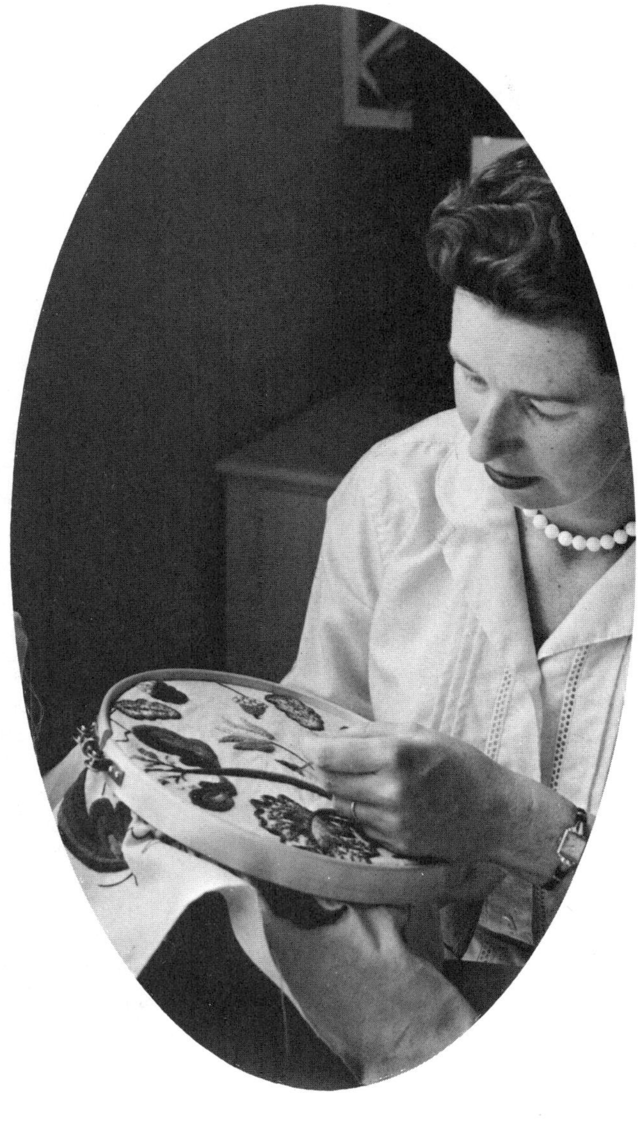

Mrs. Richard Swain of Nantucket, chairwoman of Nantucket Needlewomen, finishing a piece of crewelwork embroidery. On the hoop stand is a new design, ready to be worked. Needlework classes are a part of the crafts program sponsored by the Nantucket Historical Trust. *Photo courtesy Nantucket Historical Trust*

Ladies' handwork with the needle may be described as "seeing American history through the eye of a needle." The characteristic stitches and combinations of them portray for us the many facets of our country's growing phases, its achievements and its conquests. Thus, no book concerned with the arts and crafts of a region can neglect this womanly art.

Embroidery

Embroidery, one of the most typical forms of needlework became exceedingly popular in the eighteenth century and continued to appeal to women of all ages on every level. One housewife stated that she had "twice as many fire-skreens as chimneys," so filled with industry were her daughters. By way of defining terms, embroidery is the decorating of a material by working patterns in thread or yarn onto a carefully selected base.

A prime example of the growing phase is to be found in the embroidery known as Deerfield Embroidery. A visit to Old Deerfield Village in Massachusetts is a rewarding one for here may be seen the charming blue and white embroideries of eighteenth-century origin. In 1895 there was a unique revival in Deerfield of the old embroideries spearheaded by Margaret Whiting and Ellen Miller, both of Colonial descent, illustrators of a fine wild flower book, *Wild Flowers of Northeastern States.* Possessing a wide knowledge of flowers and an equally broad understanding of needlework, they reintroduced the white and blue embroideries of the past, and formed the Deerfield Blue and White Society. They kept faithfully to the indigo dye pot and the designs of old. This society that embroidered together was one of the earliest associated groups of craft workers brought together in a single enterprise in America. Their efforts and the record of it have been preserved in Deerfield and their society flourished until 1925. Again there is a reawakened interest in this truly New England type of embroidery.

In 1716, the Boston Schoolmaster taught "Young Gentle Women, Children all sorts of Fine Works as Feather works, Filigree, and Painting on Glass, Embroidering a new Way, Turkey-work for Handkerchiefs, fine new Fashion purses, flourishing and plain Work." We find a Newport dame teaching "Sewing Marking, Queen Stitch and Knitting," and a Boston shopkeeper taking children and young ladies to board and be taught "Dresden Embroidery on Gauze, Tent Stitch and all Sorts of Colour'd Work." Crewels, embroidery, silks, and chenilles appear frequently in early newspapers. Many of the fruits of these careful lessons of Colonial childhood remain to us; quaint samplers, bed hangings, petticoats and pockets, and frail lace veils and scarfs.

Talent was abundant and diversified and it was the desire of parents that girls be taught numerous accomplishments, even such trivia as the cutting of escutcheons, painting on velvet and quilt-piecing in a hundred different and difficult designs. The making of paper flowers was ambitiously called "papyrotamia" and was one of the required skills. They also learned to make bone lace with pillows and bobbins.

The following items which appeared in two mid-eighteenth century newspapers, read throughout New England, indicate the versatility of the teachers. "Needlework and Millinary.—This is to give Notice. That at the House of Mr. George Brownell, late School Master in Hanover, Street, Boston, are all sorts of millinary works done; making up Dresses, and flowering of muslin, making of fur-below'd Scarffe, and Quilting, and cutting of Gentlewomens Hair in the newest Fashion; and also young Gentlewomen and Children taught all sorts of fine Works, as Feather-Work, Filegre and Painting on Glass, Embroidering a new way, Turkey-Work for Handkerchiefs two ways, fine new Fashion Purses, flourishing in plain Work, and Dancing cheaper than ever was taught in Boston, Brocaded-Work for Handkerchiefs and short Aprons upon Muslin, artificial Flowers work'd with a Needle."

What was proper for young ladies of the era has been more precisely defined and described in the newspaper advertisements than even in the letters and diaries of the period. Teachers had no other means of giving notice of their abilities.

Embroidery.—Taught by Eleanor M'Gilvaine, opposite the Governor's, Dresden painting on Glass, Shell Work, Tent Stitch, and Other Works proper for Young Ladies. [*Boston Evening Post,* March 27, 1758.]

Embroidery is usually considered a feminine occupation, yet, both soldiers and sailors have turned their hands to it on occasion and have produced some distinctly characteristic work, usually in the form of love tokens. The long voyages on sailing ships provided plenty of leisure for such work, as did rest periods in camp and hospital. One of their chief specialties during the nineteenth century was the fat, betasseled pincushion. Some are heart-shaped and all lavishly decorated with buttons, beads, pinheads.

Mourning Pieces

Frequently seen in both museums and private collections and familiar to the descendants of old New England families are the elaborately embroidered mourning pieces. Of them, Alice Morse Earle has written: "These are seldom more than a century old (that would make the date 1788 on). On them weeping willows and urns, tombs and mourning figures, names of departed friends with dates of their deaths, and epitaphs were worked with vast skill, and were so much admired and were such delightful home decoration that it is no unusual thing to find these elaborate *memento mori* with empty spaces for names and dates, waiting for some one to die, and still unfilled, unfinished, blankly commemorative of no one, while the industrious embroiderer has long since gone to the tomb she so deftly and eagerly pictured, and her name, too, is forgotten."

A little pond or symbolic lake of tears, the weeping willow tree, with its drooping leaves, the distant church steeple, the funerary monument, the mourning figures—the romanticism thus engendered by these designs, creating as they did an introspective and sorrowful atmosphere, made a perfect and very popular mourning picture. An unusual mourning picture, embroidered with silk and chenille painted portraits, a memorial to three persons, worked in 1807 by Elizabeth K. Bennet, Connecticut, may be seen in the Connecticut Historical Society in Hartford.

A recently acquired embroidered memorial picture, displayed at Salem's Essex Institute, has been described in detail by Huldah M. Smith. It was made in "an oval design painted and stitched on a rectangular piece of imported satin which has been backed with canvas. The edges at top and bottom have regularly spaced holes which originally served as attachment points for the embroidery frame on which the work was stretched. The needlework is covered with glass, the four corners of which have been painted black on the reverse, each corner containing a stylized gold flower, and the whole rectangular form is enclosed within a moulded and gilded wood frame. The edges of the embroidery are tacked to the wooden panel which closes the back of the frame, on which is pasted the label of the maker of the latter . . . The design shows a young woman seated at left under a weeping willow tree, wearing a brown Empire style dress with a darker brown cloak across her knees. She holds a green handkerchief and the end of a garland of roses which is festooned from the classical urn on top of the funery monument. Her left elbow rests on the tomb, and her cheek rests on her hand. The monument is drawn and painted on the satin and forms the center of the composition. At the right is a linden tree, with four smaller trees in the distance. The face and arms of the mourner are lightly drawn in India ink, and the hair is painted brown. The foreground, painted in bluish and brownish tones, contrasts with the palely tinted sky. The embroidered section consist of parts of the ground at right and left done in satin-stitch, as is the costume of the seated figure, both tree trunks done in a flat straight stitching resembling encroaching satin-stitch, and the leaves of the linden tree embroidered in bullion knots, presenting a fine and almost moss-like texture. On the center of the tomb is appliqued a rectangular section of satin on which is printed

> Affectionately inscribed to the memory of
> Mrs. Sarah B., Wife of Mr. Jona Ingalls
> OBIT. Oct. 24th A.D. 1816, Aged 53.
>
> Her heart was gentle, and serene her mind;
> Her morals pure, in all her actions just,
> As a consort dear, and a mother kind
> As such she lies, lamented in the dust."

Georgiana Brown Harbeson in the Introduction to *American Needlework* says: "Embroidery is a personal art and the poetry of the needle. In its highest sense it is an art medium comparable to painting." Not only the mourning pictures, but the Deerfield embroidery, featuring the flowers of meadow and swamp and other favorite motifs, stitched by deft hands, bring to mind the growth and development of New England and the rest of America in a most pleasing and memorable way.

First Things First: Samplers and Knitting

A feeling of true accomplishment must have been the mother's emotion when she arrived at the time when she, herself, could create something of loveliness for her dwelling. Her soul must have sung with joy when the task at hand was that of teaching her own daughters to count carefully the threads of the linen she had woven; then using the crewels she had spun and dyed, showing them how to cross-stitch in the careful measure of counting threads, both ways, so that the stitches would achieve a geometric pattern. Not only was she teaching her child that vitally important and necessary craft of sewing, she was also teaching her child to read! While she was supervising all this activity, with her own fingers she rapidly knitted the socks, the mittens, and all other garments necessary for her family's wardrobe. This knitting skill she passed on to both the girls and boys in her family.

SAMPLERS

Loara Standish is my name
Lord guide my hart that
  I may do thy will
Also fill my hands with such
  convenient skill
As may conduce to virtue
  devoid of shame
And I will give glory to
  thy name.

Thus Loara, daughter of Miles Standish, military captain of Plymouth Colony, stitched her simple prayer on one of the earliest pieces of decorative needlework made in New England. She was born in 1623 and died in 1656, but the sampler she made still hangs in the Pilgrim Museum at Plymouth. In all probability the Pilgrims brought with them two or three samplers, but the patterns, worked with mathematical precision in simple cross-stitch, within tiny squares, were firmly imprinted in the minds of the needlewomen, since there was no room for pattern books in their scanty baggage. Samplers served as the horn books for mothers to use in instructing their children, and each girl in the family had her daily "stint" of working on her sampler. While she labored arduously away at it, sewing each stitch with meticulous care, she was learning her A.B.C.'s, her spelling, and quotations from the Bible as well. Those hours of needlework were the true reward of self-discipline, the satisfaction of work well done.

In the Miles and Abigail Fleetwood sampler (1654) we find this observation:

In prosperity friends will be plenty
but in adversity not one in twenty.

Homely philosophy often crept into stitchery and the embroidered mottos of the Victorian era were in some ways reminiscent of the samplers of an earlier day.

Most girls in America, and certainly every girl in New England between the years 1620 and 1860 made a sampler. She made it precisely for what the name implies, to serve as a sample for the numerals, letters, emblems, and decorative borders that she would utilize in later handiwork. She cross-stitched animals, birds, trees, flowers, often revealing her own imaginative concept of how they looked. The colors she chose were usually soft, the delicate shades of yellow, pale gold, brown, green, blue, rose, and subdued red. Most of the wools came from the skeins her mother made for crewel work. (It was not until Martha Washington's

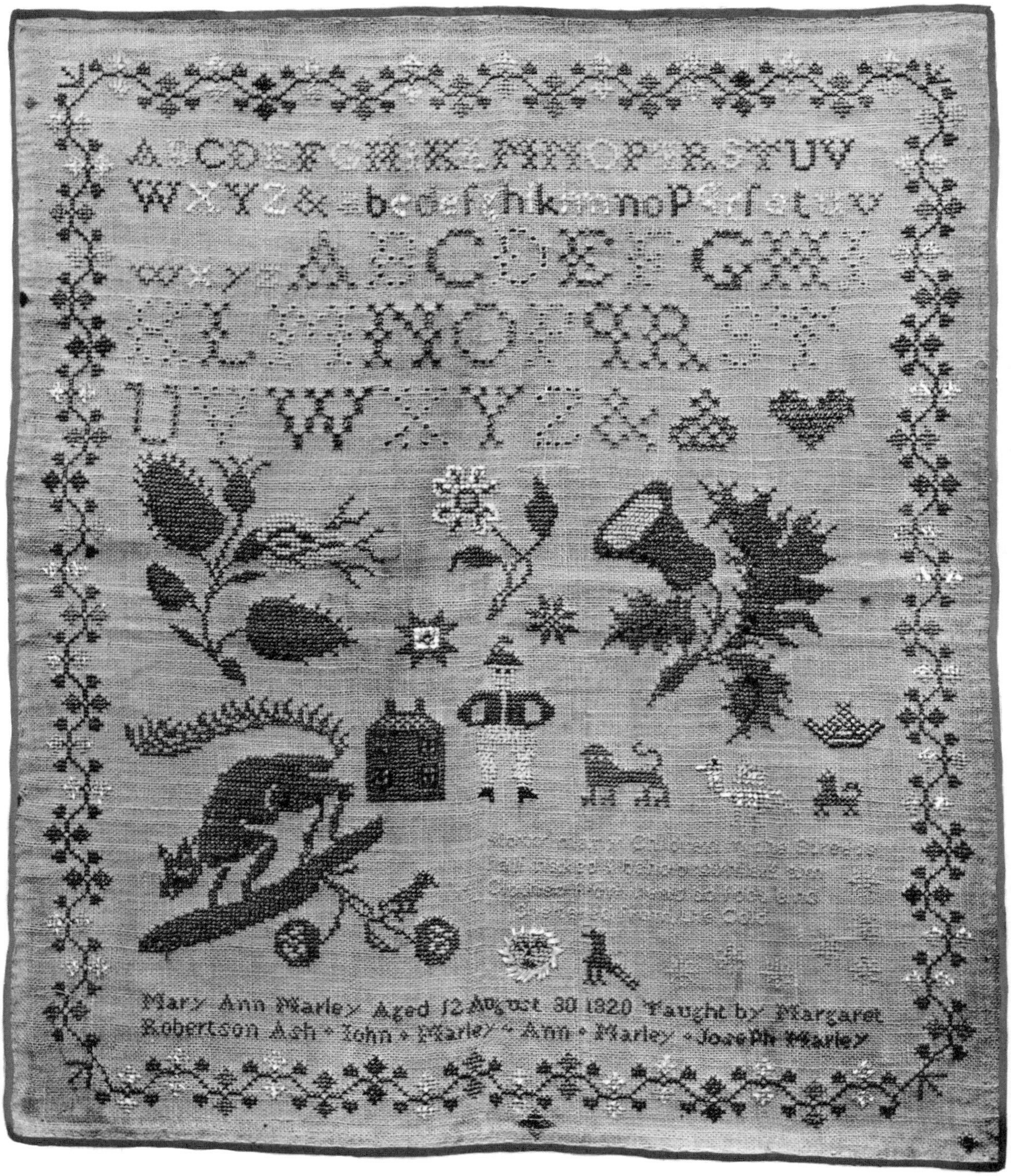

Mary Ann Marley recorded her teacher's name on her sampler, those of her brothers and sister, and a motto as well. *Photo courtesy Essex Institute*

time that silk was used and even then not extensively.)

In *Boys and Girls of Colonial Days,* Carolyn Sherwin Bailey tells the story of Patience Arnold's sampler which was completed under difficulty. One afternoon in the early 1770's, Patience was busying herself with her needlework, tediously counting the threads to embroider her name. The motto, "A Soft Answer Turneth Away Wrath" had been completed and so too the rest of the cross-stitches in the design. All that remained to be added, were the fourteen letters that would record the maker's name. The day was a warm one in Lexington, but there was no possible excuse to get outdoors to play until the little eight-year-old had finished her day's stint, and she knew it. Before carrying the newly made curds to a neighbor, her mother had admonished Patience to "give the key to the barn to no one, for the barn houses your father's constantly growing store of powder and shot, which we are likely to need before long."

The embroidering was progressing slowly, when suddenly she heard a strange noise and suddenly a long broad shadow fell across her work. In her excitement, Patience almost jingled the key which was in her pocket. The shadow was that of a British officer who with his men had attempted to ransack the barn. To the officer's demand for the key, Patience replied softly in her squeaky childlike way that she could not give the key to the "kind sir." Quick as a flash she had slipped it from her pocket into the hand that held her sampler as she worked the "e" in Patience. After searching the house, the British soldiers left disgruntled, misled and deceived, all because a little girl had learned her "lesson" well—"A Soft Answer Turneth Away Wrath." As for the embroidered letters of her own name which she had completed nervously during those terrifying moments, they were crooked and untrue, but they did spell out Patience Arnold.

More than twenty-five hundred examples of samplers made before the end of the eighteenth century have been catalogued. A sizeable number of these bear the name of the school where they were worked and frequently they contain the name of the teacher and her school. Miss Sarah Pierce's School was at Litchfield, Connecticut; Miss Polly Balch's Seminary, in Providence (1785); Sarah Knight, School Dame, lived on Ivers Lane in Salem (1792); Mrs. Rowson's Academy, famous in its day, was conducted in Boston (1812); Madame Mansfield, school mistress, had her dame school in Salem (1791). When a young girl stitched a sampler under the tutelage of a dame school, she was required to rip out and do over any portion of her stitchery that was not perfect. When the stern voice of authority did not please the young ladies, they sometimes vented their feelings in their handiwork as revealed by one who obvi-

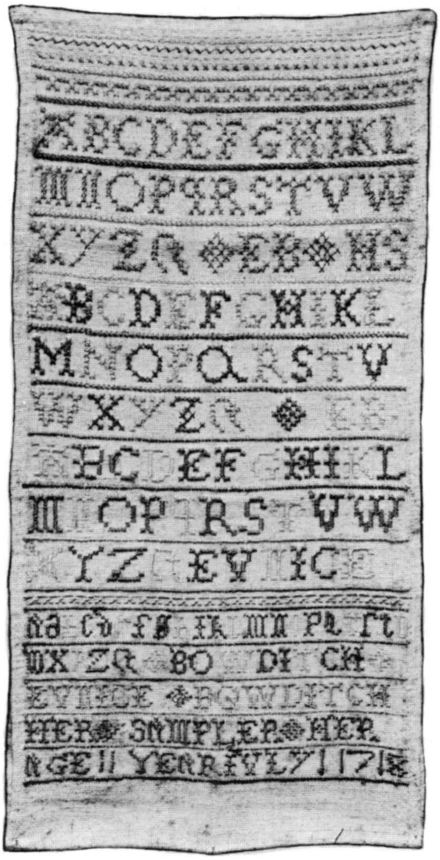

Eunice Bowditch was eleven years old when she made this sampler in 1718. *Photo courtesy Essex Institute*

ously did not cherish harsh treatment for she ended her quotation with the words: "And Hated every bit of it."

Not every colonial maiden stitched an elaborate design on her sampler. A beautifully handwoven bureau scarf in an intricate "M and O" pattern, made from flax spun and woven by a Lexington girl, indicates that she too must have rebelled at sampler-making since her plain but handsome square sampler contains only a small border, the alphabet in small and capital letters, the numbers and her name, neatly cross-stitched Dolly Hartwell Reed, aged nine, 1803. Some children completed their first piece of embroidery at the tender age of six.

Many samplers made nearly two centuries ago are cherished heirlooms in New England families and are not described in print. Little Nancy Myric, who was eight years old in 1789, worked the following: "Teach us to live that I May Dread my grace as little as my bed. Teach me to die so I may Rightfully Rise at the Last Day." Another "philosophy" one stitched by Polly Thompson Symme, aged ten in 1790, read:

Delight in Virtues way,
And you will meet Praise,
The Grass is Green,
The Rose is Red,
Here is my name when I am dead.

The material upon which a sampler was stitched was generally made from materials woven at home—a homespun linen or muslin. These woven surfaces changed in size as time went on, for the early looms were but eight or nine inches in width and therefore produced narrow swatches of material. Thus, the early samplers were long and narrow. As improvements occurred in weaving, the size changed from oblong shapes to those more nearly square.

Designs changed too, and became highly pictorial, evolving into the elaborate memorial pattern so prevalent from the early 1800's on, maps embroidered on linen also came to be fashionable. Thus the practice sheets of cross-stitch techniques evolved into decorative needlework suited to modern decor. And so it remains today. Favorite subjects of the nineteenth-century samplers were military campaigns, historical events, family portraits, hobbies, and family interests, all serving the function for which they were created—conversation pieces. (Even today,

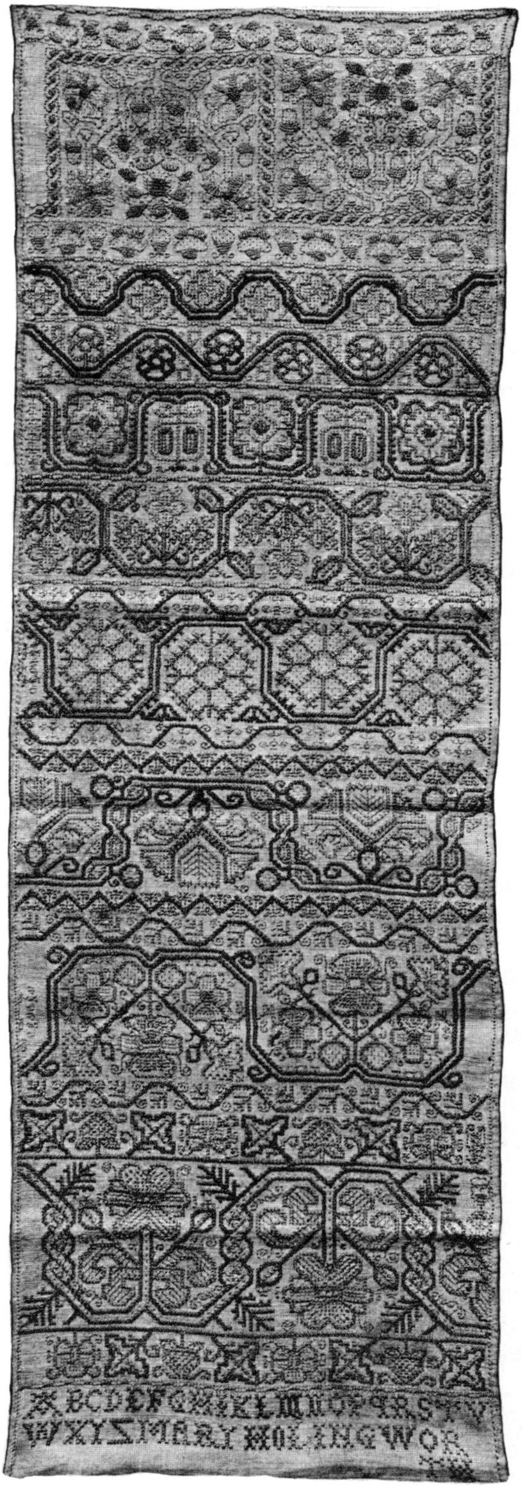

Mary Holingworth's sampler showed considerable variety in design. *Photo courtesy Essex Institute*

samplers are dated and signed by their designer; these modern samplers are wrought by women, and no longer by little girls.)

KNITTING

From time immemorial man has known how to weave and to knit for these were the only two crafts that he could employ to make the cloth with which to clothe himself.

Long before little Puritan girls were taught to spin or make samplers, they were taught to use knitting needles with their tiny hands. Boys, too, were taught this very necessary craft, for they had to knit their own suspenders; this was not a disgrace, nor was it a feminine art—for knitting was, from the very beginning, a manly art.

Both boys and girls were sent to dame schools where the girls, although not instructed in book-learning, were taught all the housewifely arts—to spin, to weave, and to knit. Even very young girls could knit coarse socks for shopkeepers. When they had become proficient at knitting they could make fine socks with elaborate stitches, the fox-and-geese pattern or the even more popular herringbone stitch. Socks knitted in these designs brought a pretty penny. In colonial days girls of four could knit mittens, in fact the female members of a household knitted dozens of pairs in a year.

The story is told that the brother of Nancy Peabody, of Shelburne, New Hampshire, came home one night and said he had lost his mittens while chopping in the woods. Nancy ran to a bundle of wool in the garret, carded and spun a big hank of yarn that very night. It was soaked and scoured the next morning, and in twenty-four hours from the time her brother announced his loss, he had a fine new pair of mittens.

Like our own arithmetic numbers, knitting is Arabic. Sitting on his donkey's back as he led the long, slow caravans of loaded camels, the ancient Arab trader plied his art of knitting as he traveled across India or to Egypt. He must have taught his craft to the Egyptians of ancient times, for in recent excavations a knitted piece has been dug up—the same stitches were found on it that grow from knitting needles today.

From those earliest days until the eighteen-hundreds knitting had been man's work. In the early half of the seventeenth century in Holland boy-apprentices had to serve six years to learn to knit; this comprised three years of serving and learning and the last three in traveling and studying the patterns and methods of other shops and copying others' designs. After this training, to become a master knitter, the journeyman had to create and make the following:

1. A carpet about five feet square, of his own design using animals, birds, flowers, foliage —all in their natural color.
2. A beret.
3. A woolen shirt.
4. A pair of hose with Spanish clocks (a forerunner of our argyle socks).

Of course, women copied their men and learned to knit "on the side" though they were never permitted to become a part of the monopolies—never allowed to join a guild. Mrs. William Lee of Calverton, England, outdid her husband is knitting so completely that he gave up knitting and turned to inventing, and to his credit he produced the first knitting machine (in the 1600's) which enabled his wife to knit faster!

To prove their knitting ability women knitted samplers, long table-like runners of various stitches—then cross-stitched their names and the date in one of the corners. Today, these are treasured heirlooms. In fact it has been said that if a woman knew all the stitches and patterns of knitting there would be little else she did not know!

From Lucy Larcom's writings (she lived in Beverly, Massachusetts) comes this comment: "Among other domestic traditions of the old time was the saying that every girl must have a pillow-case full of stockings of her own knitting before she married. I began to knit my own stockings when I was six or seven years old and kept on, until home made stockings went out of fashion."

There is a fascinating legend that the Roman soldiers cast lots for Christ's seamless garment because it was knitted. They could not divide it without raveling and destroying it, so the lucky soldier received the entire garment.

Men's interest in knitting was always in evidence and we read that Lady Pepperell, a gentlewoman of Boston, Massachusetts, and Kittery, Maine, was admonished by her father at her marriage, "never to work one moment after Saturday sunset; never to lay down her knitting except in the middle of the needle." Knitting has been the "pickup" work of many a White House first lady, and it especially was the hobby of Grace Goodhue Coolidge, a native Vermonter and the wife of the thirtieth president, Calvin Coolidge. Mrs. Coolidge and her knitting were so inseparable that when Emil Fuchs painted her portrait he posed her knitting on a period sofa in her private sitting room in the White House. Mrs. Coolidge's maternal grandmother had knitted a beautiful, lacy, raised-leaf bedspread; not only was Mrs. Coolidge proud of that heirloom but she shared the pattern of it with other knitting enthusiasts and began to make a copy of it herself. Knitting has never ceased to hold a fascination for those who can use its stitches, as popular and as necessary to the way of life now as it was in the beginning of time. Knitting has an assured future for it is one of the appealing home arts; beneficial, too, for it keeps the knitter's fingers flexible.

Lacemaking

Lacemaking was never an industry in the colonies; it was an elegant accomplishment. Pillow lace was made, and the stitches were taught in families of wealth; a guinea a stitch was charged by some teachers. The making of bobbin lace, however, was not a continuous adventure. Since the bobbin lacemakers came to these shores for freedom, it can be safely assumed that they wished to and did retain their British Isles customers and exported practically all of their bobbin lace "back home" in exchange for monies and threads.

We find many substantiations for the belief that all the laces made in Ipswich, Massachusetts, were exported, and that the few laces that were used by the colonial gentleman here were ordered from England; perhaps the very laces made in Ipswich were to cross the water once again to be worn in style in America. Alice Morse Earle in her *Home Life in Colonial Days* writes: "Many letters still exist written by prominent citizens of Colonial times ordering clothing, chiefly from Europe, rich laces, silk materials, velvet, and fine cloth of light and gay colors abound."

An order for purchases sent to a London agent by Washington in 1761 contains a full list of garments for both his stepchildren. At that ordering "Miss Custis" was six years old; among the twenty items, "Ruffles and Tuckers, to be 'laced.'" Sir William Pepperell of Kittery, Maine, ordered, in 1737, equally costly and formal clothing from England for his little daughter to disport at Piscataquay.

A letter of the day tells of seeing the youthful daughter of Governor William Tryon of New York sitting stiffly in a chair, in broad lace collar, with heavy dress, never playing, running, or even walking.

Going back to the preceding century we find that in 1634 the Massachusetts General Court passed restricting sumptuary laws. These laws forbade the purchase of woolen, silk, or linen garments with silver, gold, silk, or thread lace on them. Two years later a narrow binding of lace was permitted on linen garments. (This was not a "crocheted edge" for crocheting was to come two centuries after.) In Salem in 1652, a man was "presented" (called to the court) for "excess in bootes, ribonds, gould and silver lace."

In the 1670's Connecticut called to its aid in repressing extravagant dress, the economic power of taxation by ordering that whoever wore gold or silver lace, gold or silver buttons, silk ribbons, silk scarfs, or bone lace worth over three shillings a yard, should be taxed as worth one hundred fifty pounds.

The art of making pillow lace has been kept alive by some Ipswich decendants so that, on "Ipswich Days" in summer, one may see this skill in action.

More than forty thousand yards of pillow or bobbin lace were made by the women and girls of Ipswich, Massachusetts, in the year 1790. This was a prodigious amount of yardage for the period, but lace was in high fashion in England and on the Continent at the time.

Lacemaking was a home industry, carried on by women and girls and considered one of the "fine arts" to be taught all young ladies along with the stitches for making samplers and other pieces of needlework. As early as 1692, Sidney Perley reminds us in his *History of Ipswich:* "silk and thread lace of an elegant and lasting texture were manufactured in large quantities by women and children and sold for use and exporting."

The pillow for making lace is a simple device, a circular baseboard stuffed to form a cushion, round, ovoid, or cylindrical. When in use, it is held upon the knees. A strip of parch-

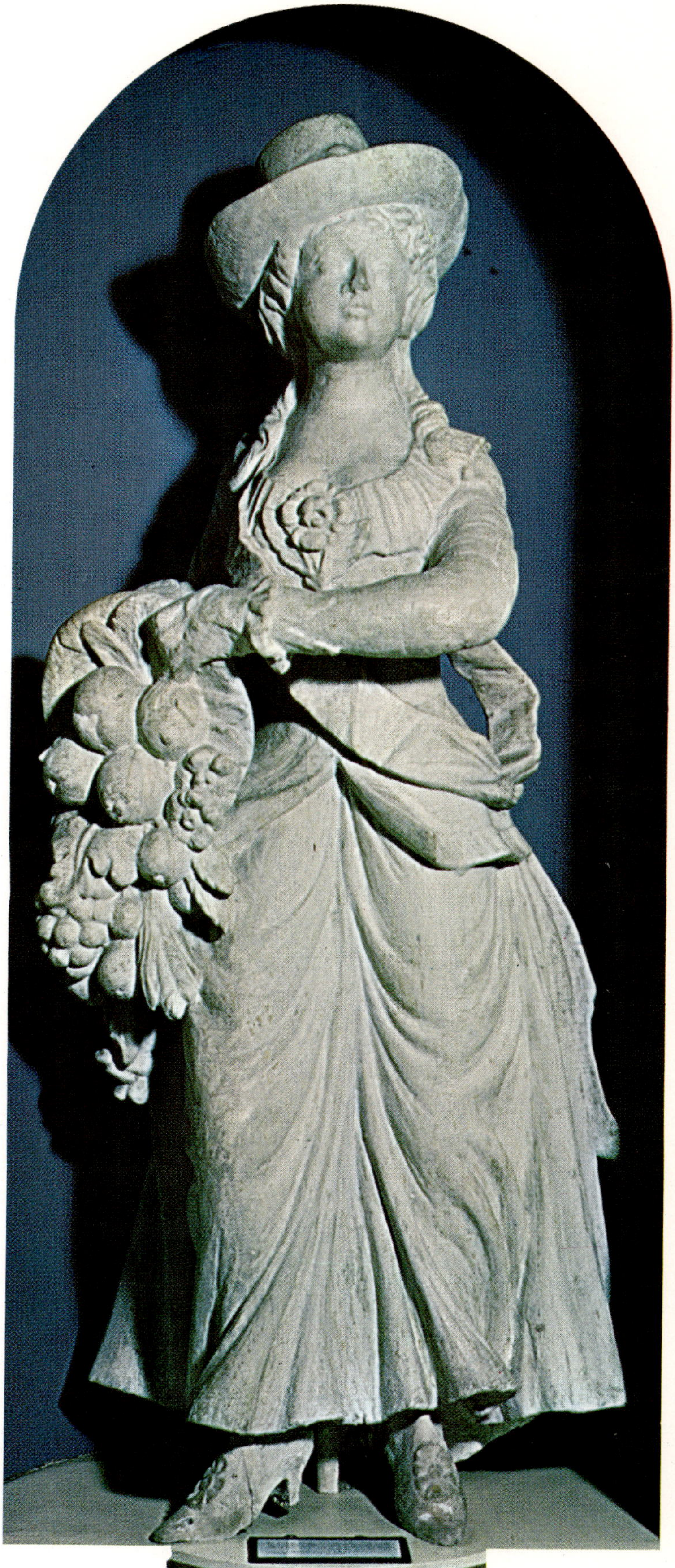

Figure of Plenty (now called Pomona), one of four garden ornaments carved by John and Simeon Skillins for Elias Hasket Derby's teahouse. Now on display at the Peabody Museum, Salem, Massachusetts. *Photo Richard Merrill; Courtesy, Peabody Museum*

(*This page, below*) The long table in Hall Tavern Dining Room, Deerfield, Massachusetts, replete with an array of woodenware (treen), horn spoons, and cups of ample size. A tin candelabra is suspended from the ceiling while pewter candlesticks are used on the table. The ironmonger's skill is shown in the equipment at the fireplace, and a superbly carved court cupboard adds an air of elegance to this pine-paneled room. *Photo Samuel Chamberlain*

(*Opposite page, above*) Mary Avery of North Andover made this bed rug in 1722. She hooked wool on loosely woven linen and made her floral and heart design in dark brown, blue, beige, and green. *Photo Richard Merrill; Courtesy, Essex Institute*

(*Opposite page, below left*) Blue and amethyst window. *Photo Haydn Mason; Courtesy, Sandwich Glass Museum and Historical Society*

(*Opposite page, below right*) Green and canary window. *Photo Haydn Mason; Courtesy, Sandwich Glass Museum and Historical Society*

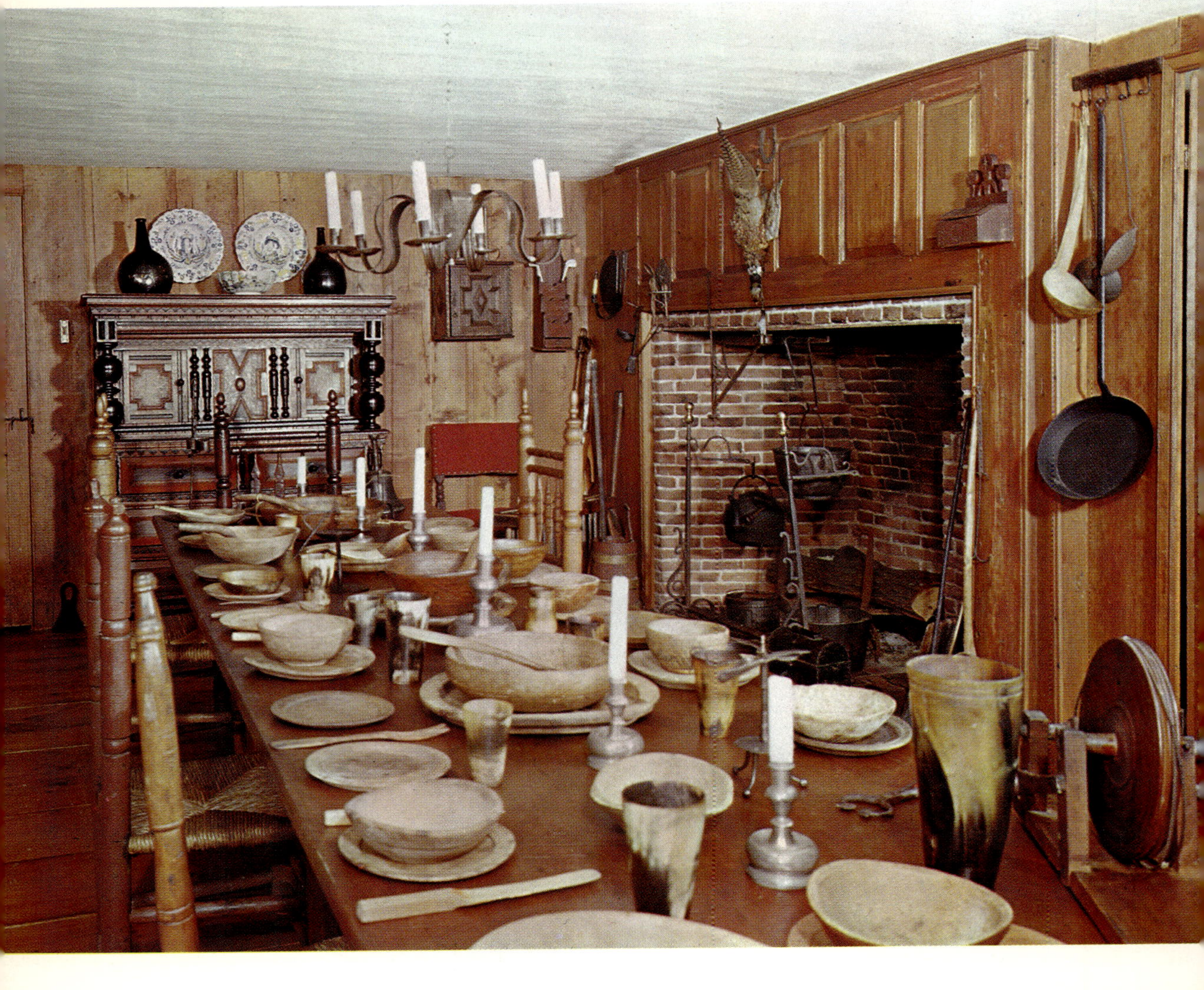

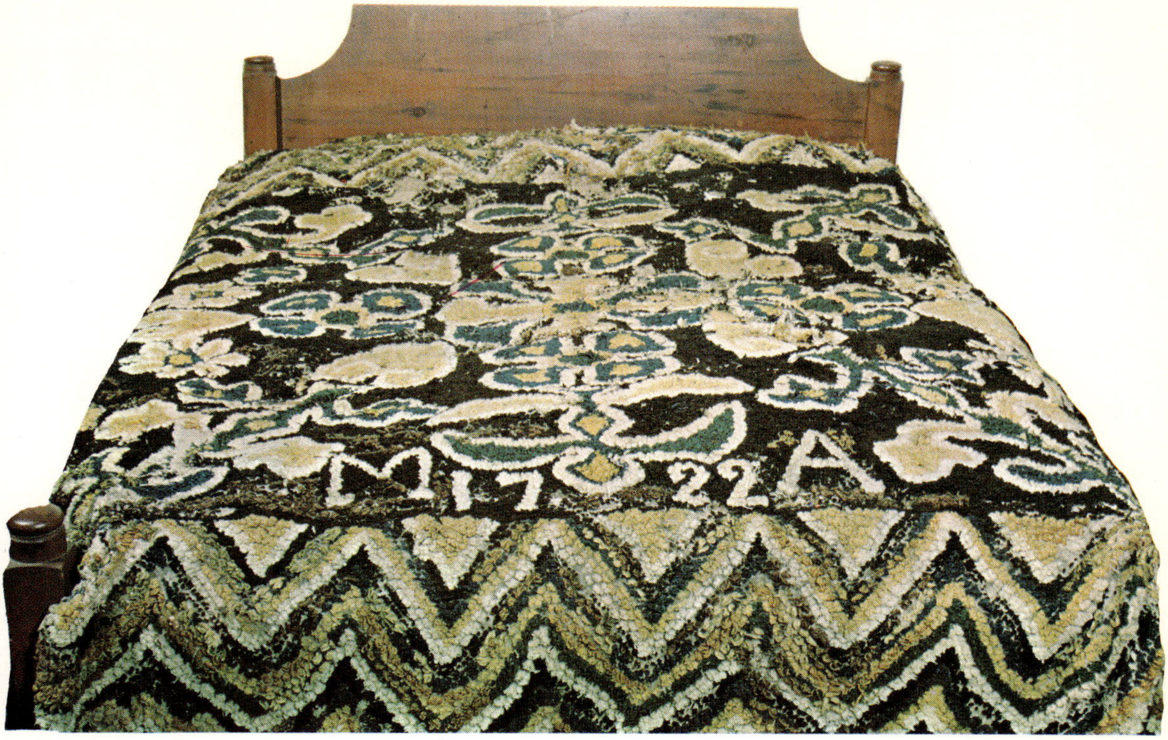
M 17 22 A

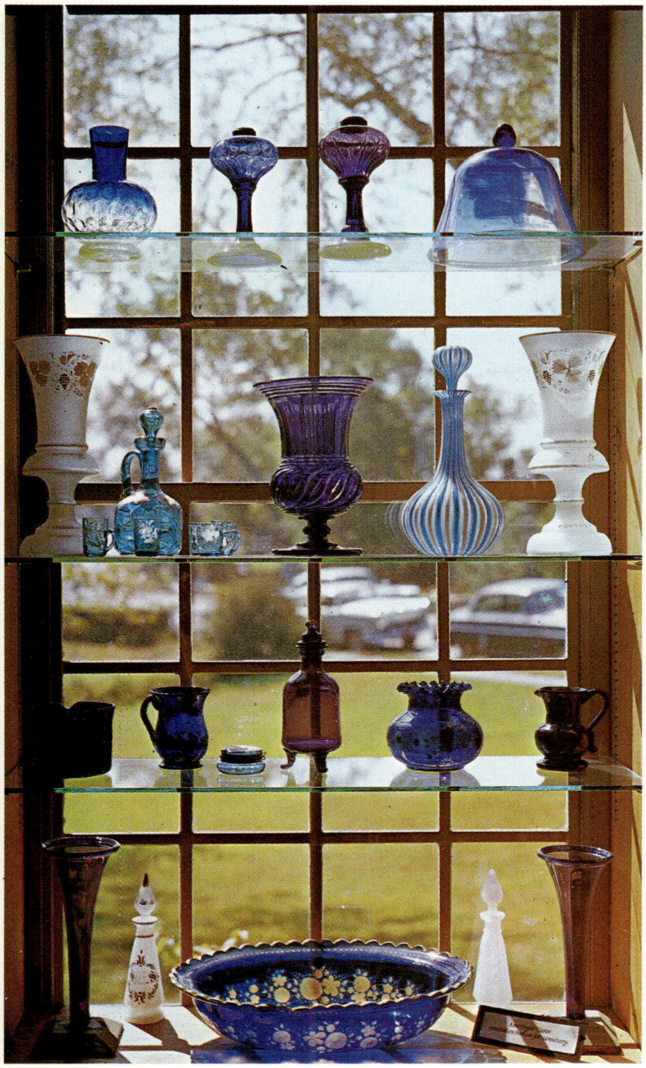

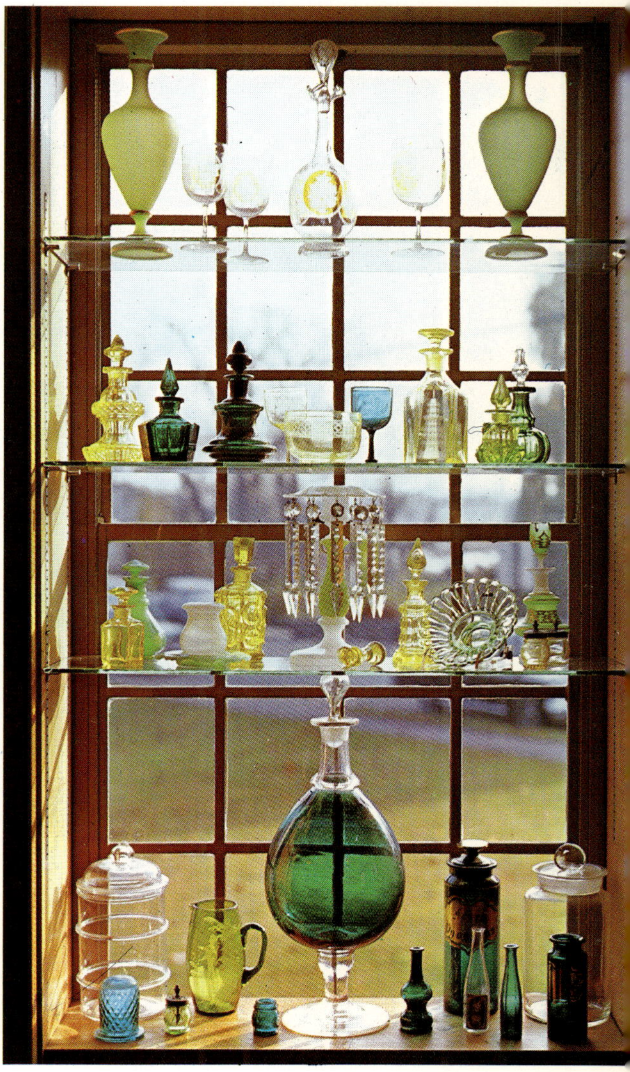

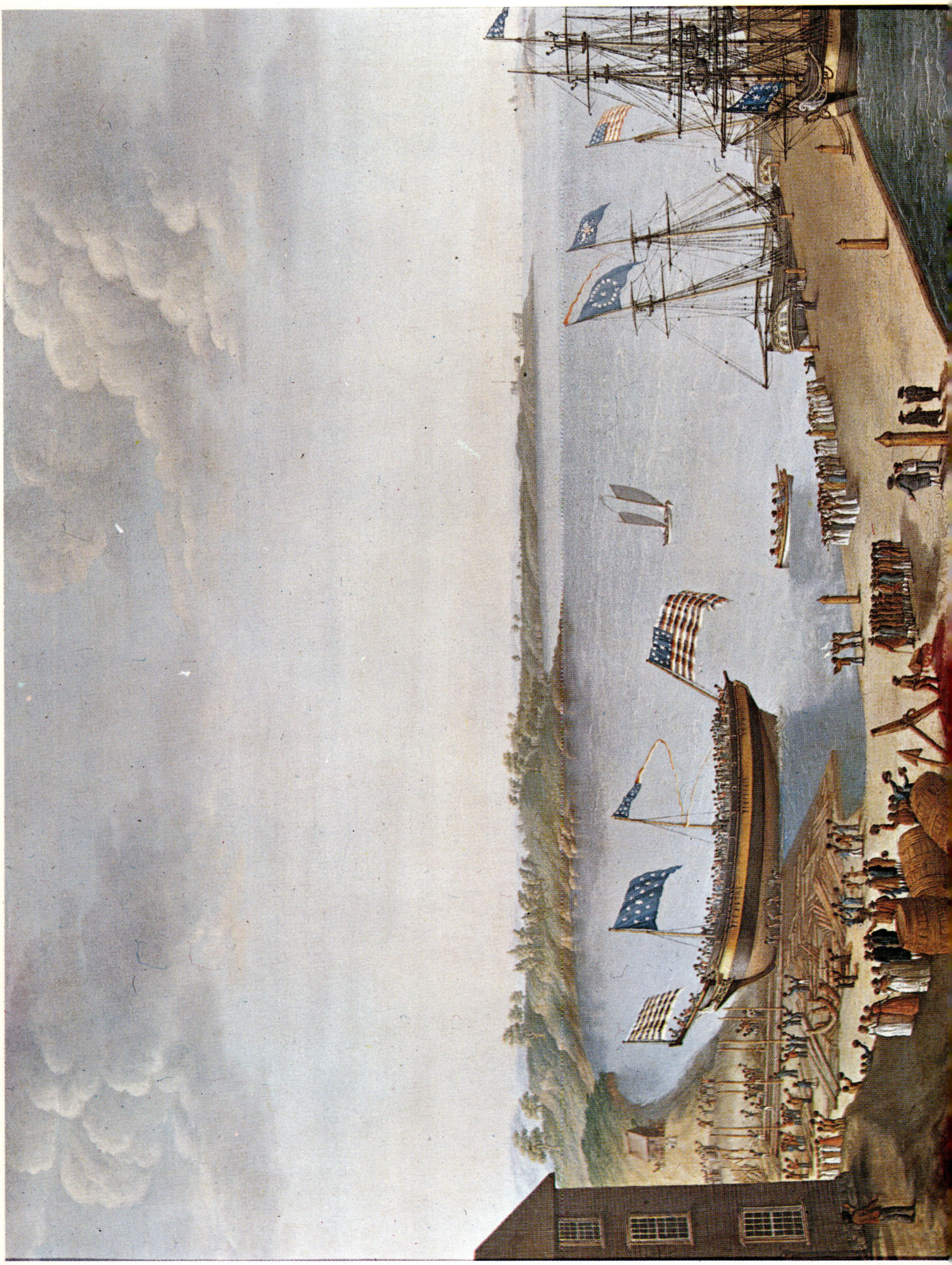

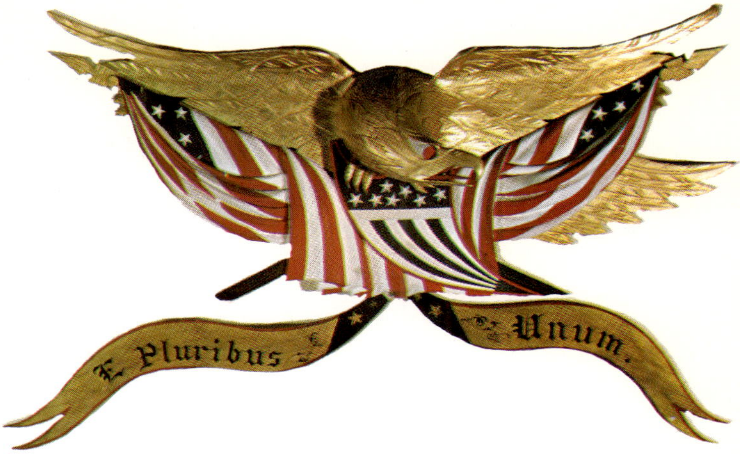

Our national emblem as carved by John Haley Bellamy, displayed at the Peabody Museum, Salem, Massachusetts. *Photo Richard Merrill; Courtesy, Peabody Museum*

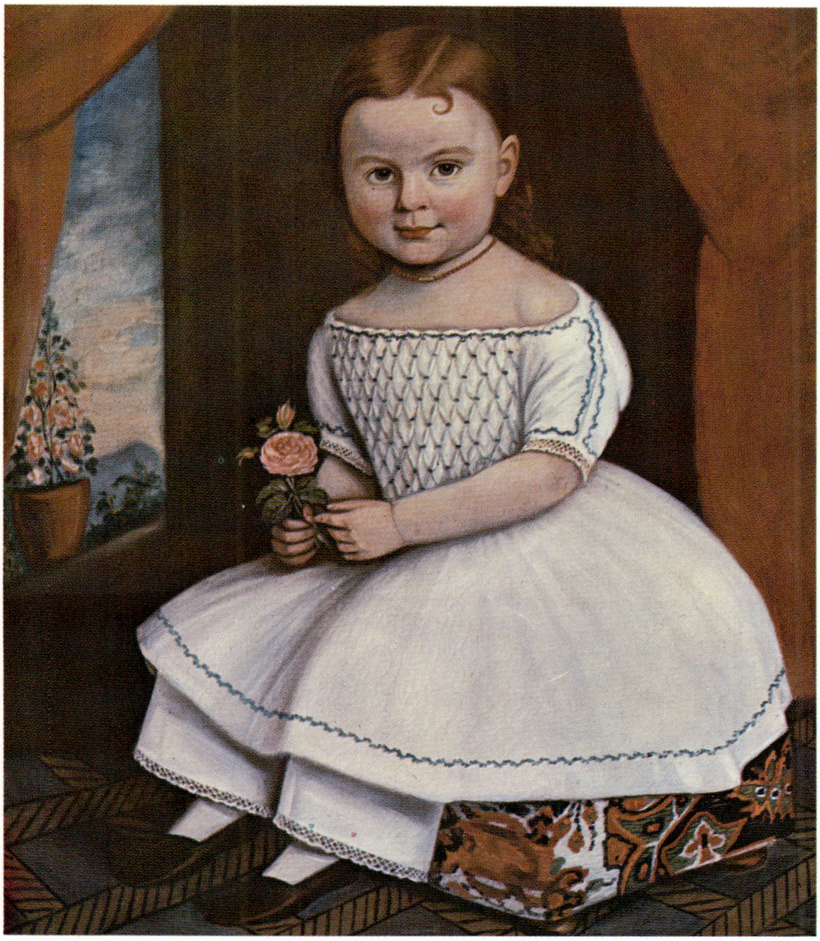

Girl with a Rose, artist unknown, is one of an impressive collection of American primitives assembled by Clara Endicott Sears for the Fruitlands Museum, which she founded, at Harvard, Massachusetts. *Photo George Cushing; Courtesy, Fruitlands Museum*

(*Opposite page*) The launching of the ship "Fame" in Salem Harbor in 1802 as painted in oil on canvas by George Ropes is one of the earliest landscape views of this famous shipping port recorded by a local artist. *Photo Richard Merrill; Courtesy, Essex Institute*

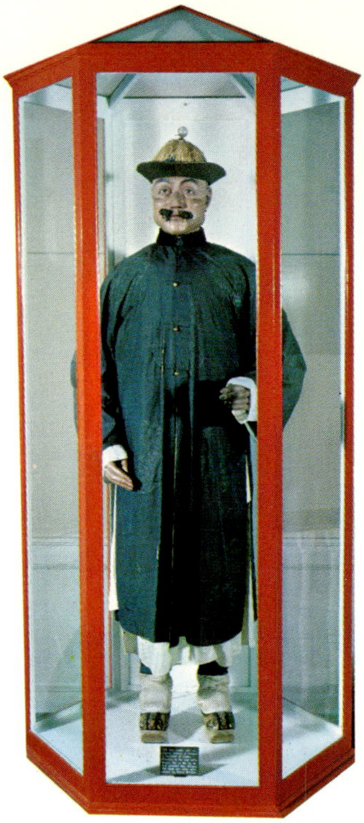

Chinese Mandarin, head and hands carved by Samuel McIntire. *Photo Richard Merrill; Courtesy, Peabody Museum*

The Vaughan collection of toys and dolls, displayed at Salem's Essex Institute, contains a wide variety of children's playthings. Some are of New England origin and others made in Europe and distant parts of the world served as models for local toymakers. *Photo Richard Merrill; Courtesy, Essex Institute*

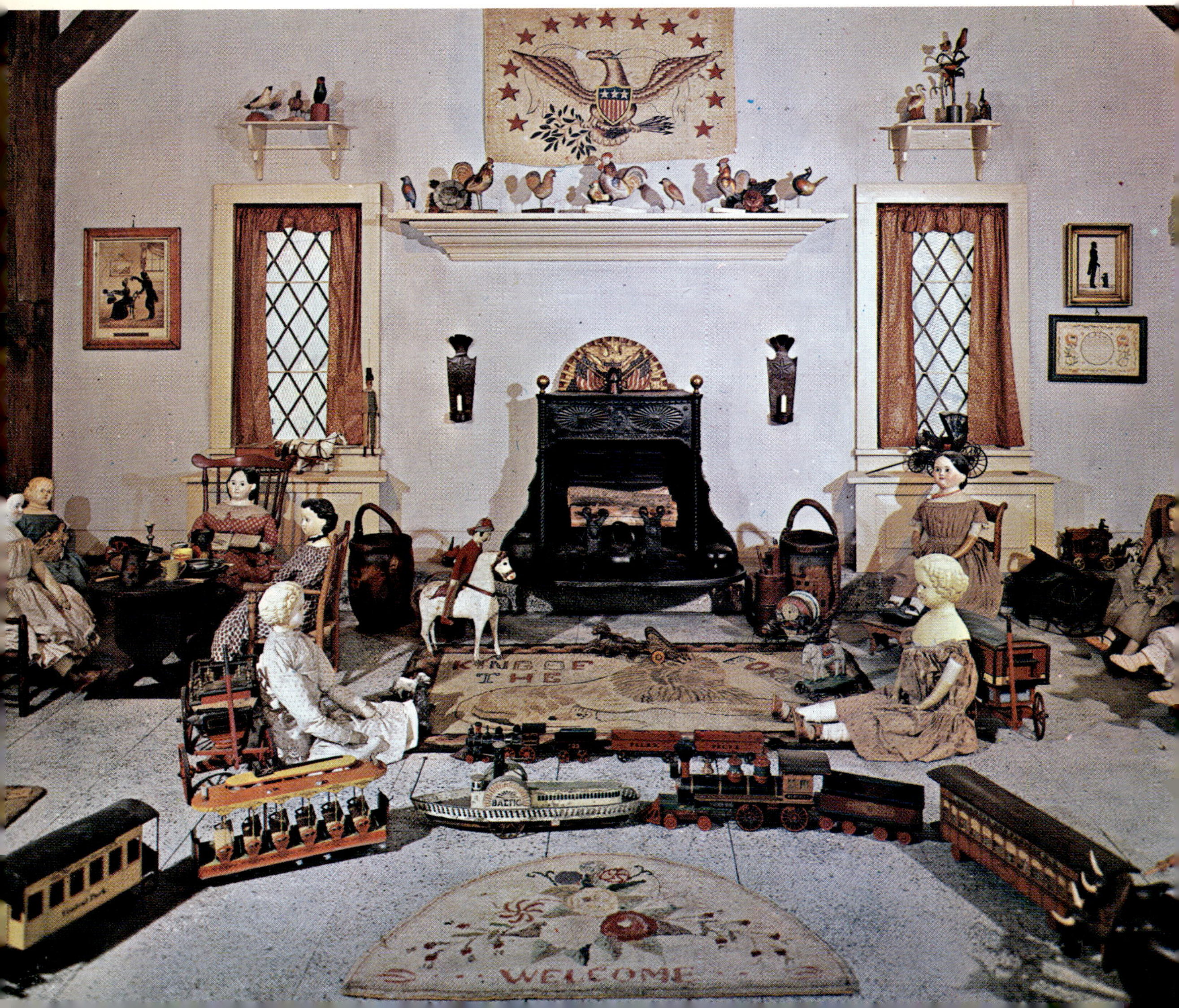

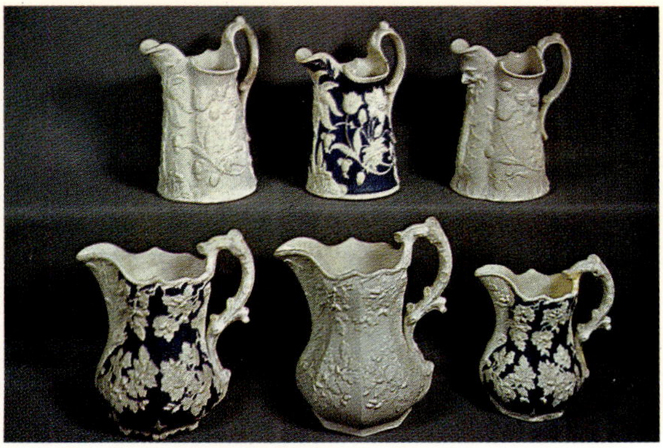

Parian and blue and white porcelain pitchers made at Bennington, Vermont. *Photo Richard Carter Barrett; Courtesy, Bennington Museum*

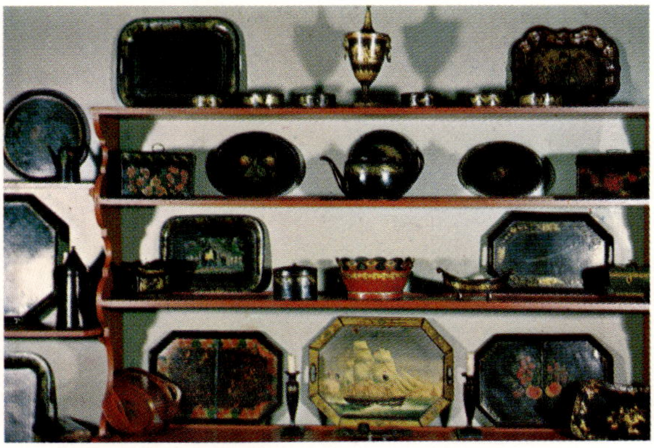

Painted tin from the Hagar Collection at the Richard Derby House, Salem, Massachusetts. *Photo Richard Merrill; Courtesy, Salem Maritime National Historic Site*

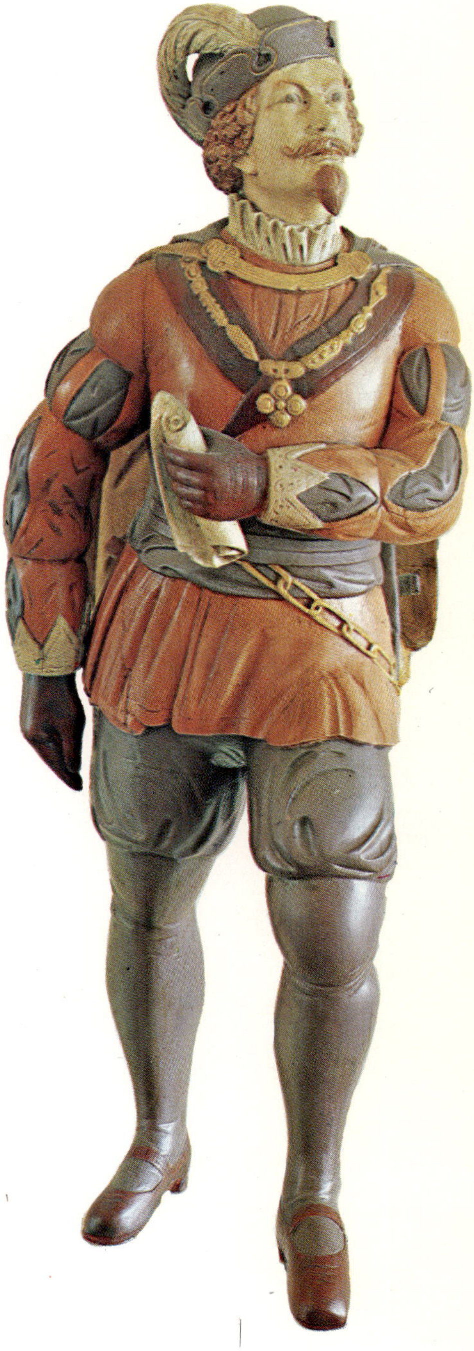

Figurehead of the ship "Grandee" displayed at the Peabody Museum, Salem. The vessel was built at Portsmouth, New Hampshire, in 1873. *Photo Eric Muller; Courtesy, Peabody Museum*

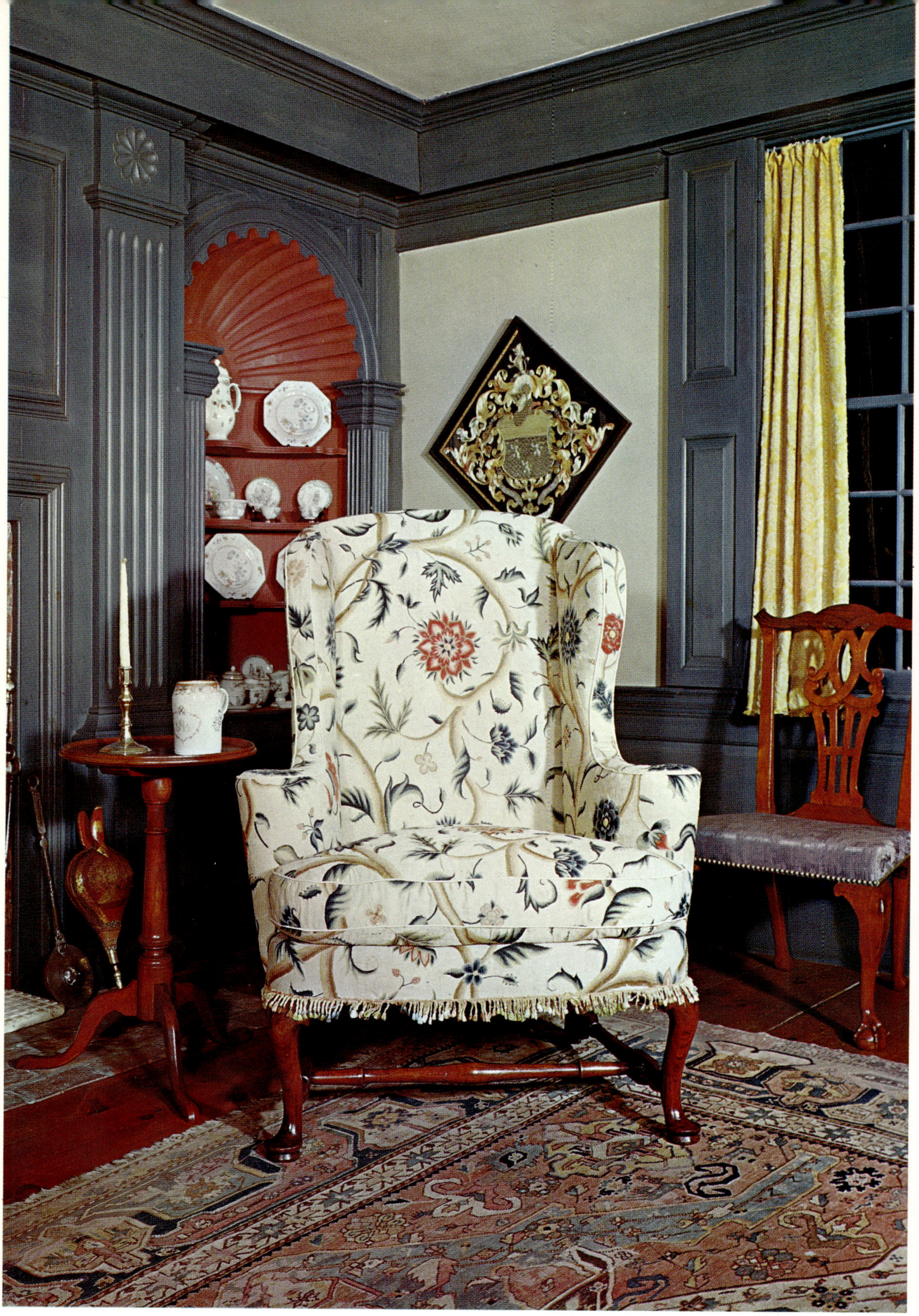

A wing chair done in crewel embroidery graces the eighteenth century parlor of the Ashley House in Deerfield, Massachusetts. The family coat of arms on the wall behind the chair and the superbly carved shell cupboard are other features of this tastefully arranged room, noted for its rich color. *Photo Samuel Chamberlain*

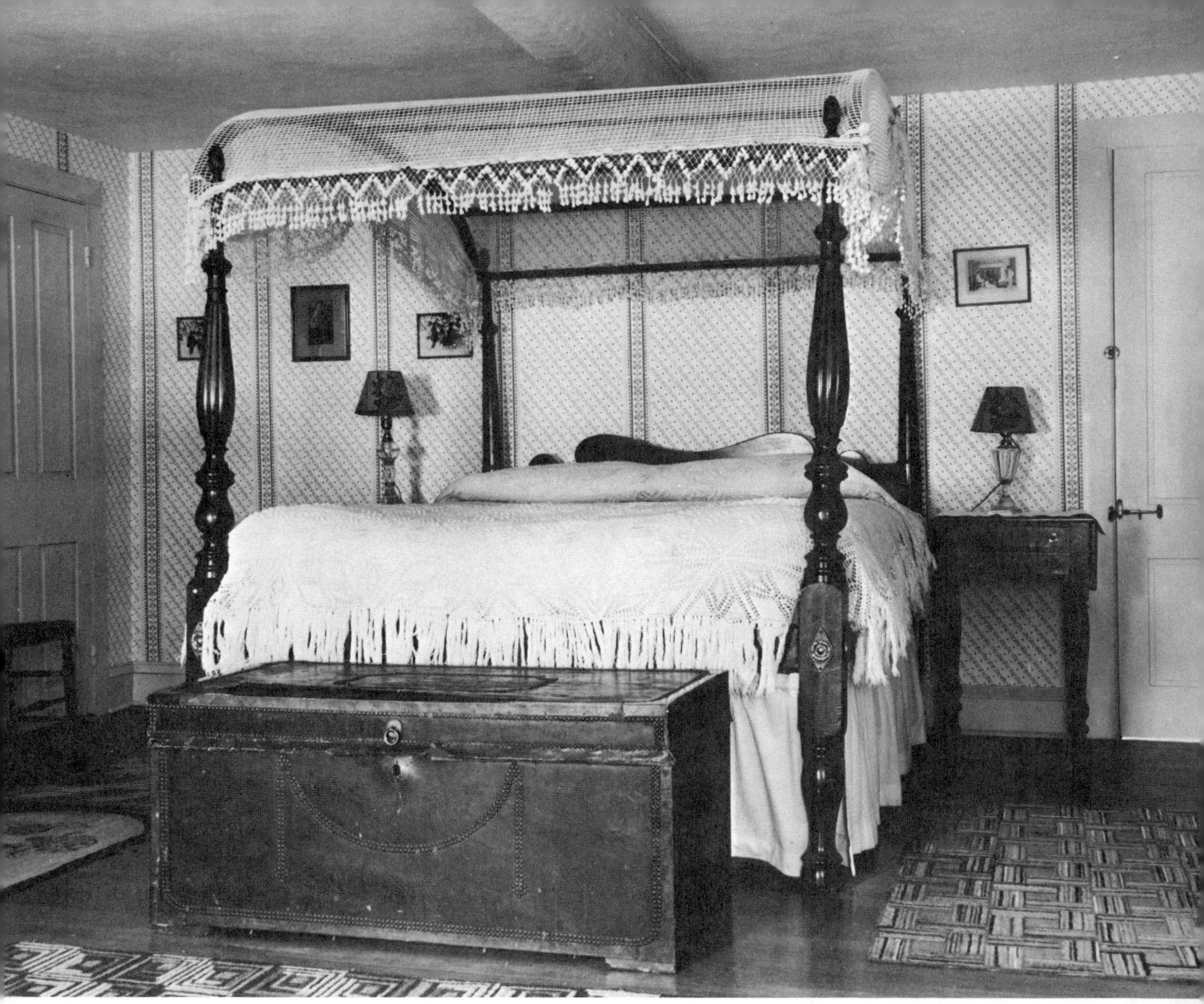

Among the truly ancient houses in Salem is that of the Pickering family, where ten generations have lived and which is still occupied by the family. In the east chamber, the bed is covered with a crocheted spread, worked on over a period of two generations. A net canopy gives the large four-poster a feeling of space in this low-ceilinged room. Two of the hooked rugs are simple, authentic, geometric patterns and the other is a floral. *Photo courtesy Samuel Chamberlain*

ment is stretched on the pillow; a pattern is then pricked in small holes on the parchment. Pins were placed over the pattern on which thread was fastened and each piece of thread was directly wound upon a small bobbin. As many as fifty or sixty bobbins were sometimes necessary to produce a single piece of lace, one inch wide. The bobbins were allowed to hang on one side of the pillow and, as the work progressed, were changed from side to side and intertwisted. As the meshes were formed, more pins were needed to secure them. The work continued in this order until sufficient yardage was acquired.

In 1822, Augustine Heard with the aid of several venturesome Ipswich citizens smuggled lacemaking machinery into town. (English law forbade the exporting of machinery of this type.) In 1824, the Boston and Ipswich Lace Company was formed; three years later, it became the New England Lace Company. In connection with the operation of the lace factory, Heard endeavored to raise silkworms in the town. He imported cocoons from China and it is said that they were brought over by a Chinese who placed them in little silk bags and carried them about his body to keep them at the necessary temperature during the long sea voyage. Mulberry trees were also cultivated to provide food for the silkworms but did not prove successful. This venture lasted but a few years and ended in 1832, because thread was scarce. All of it had been imported from England since it was of finer quality than that made in this country.

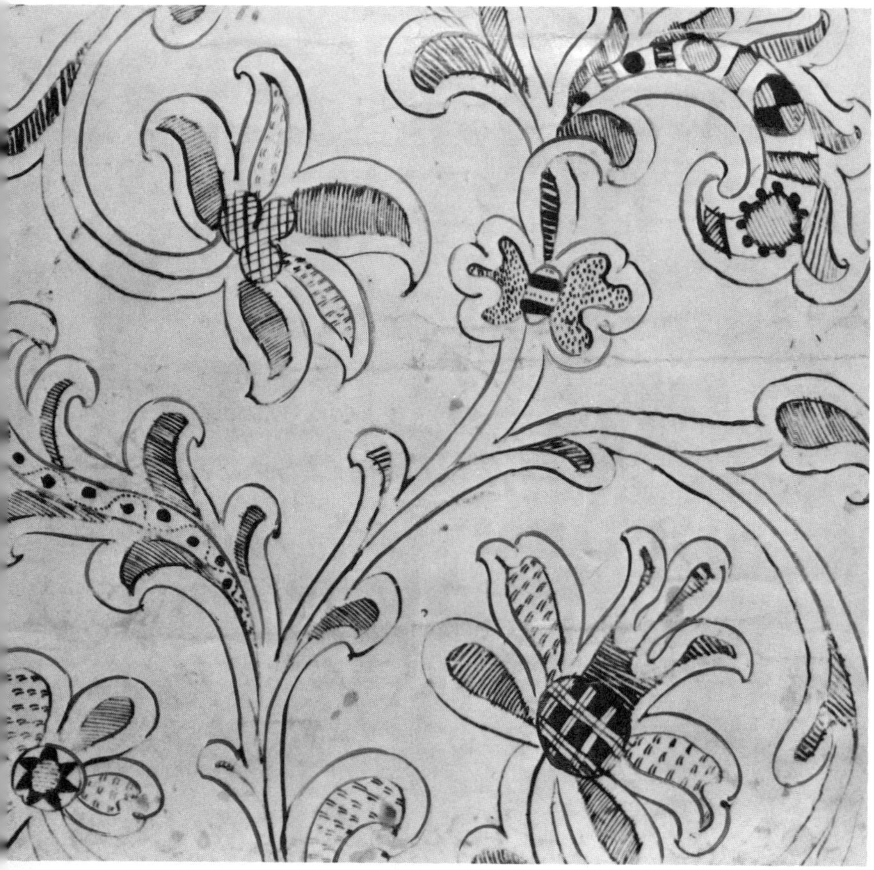

Pattern for embroidery or lace (deed on reverse). Ink on parchment. Probably made in Boston before 1719, it was intended for use in lace, or for embroidery, in white cotton or linen threads, or colored crewels or silks. *Photo courtesy Museum of Fine Arts, Boston*

Finally the lacemakers migrated to other parts of our country and those remaining in Ipswich began to manufacture stockings, so that by 1883 there were four well established hosiery mills in Ipswich.

The lace industry originated in Italy, and the Italians who migrated to these shores brought their lacemaking skills with them. The Spanish had their own distinctive lace designs and techniques—but the lace that is truly American was developed by another country—Ireland.

A strange event in the economic history of Ireland brought about the development of the lace that is truly American. Potatoes were the staple food of the British Isles; to the people of Ireland, in particular, they were the staff of life. For three months each year, when the previous year's crop had been depleted and the coming crop was not ready for harvest, the peasants survived as best they could on a scanty porridge made of ground grain. In the 1840's, disaster followed on the heels of the failure of the potato crops for two successive years. There was no money to purchase the grain for their porridge, and when during the third year the potato famine continued, as many as could manage came steerage passage to America. A few of the English gentry went as volunteers to Ireland to save the Irish peasantry in Cork. Headed by Miss Susanna Meredith, a school of crocheting was opened.

The Irish women were quick to respond and brought to the teaching a native skill. Several of Miss Meredith's friends came to assist in this fine undertaking, and soon a tremendous web of gossamer lace, roses in Irish crochet, beautifully fashioned and handsome enough to embellish any gown, came from their flying fingers. Queen Victoria herself set the fashion by wearing these laces and soon all England was clamoring for them. Many of the crocheters earned their passage to America by crocheting this lace, and thus they brought to a receptive country the art of making lace "in the air"—without the aid of bobbins, cushions, or hairpins. Quick to perceive good designs, to imitate, to improve upon, and to be creative, the Irish gave to our American neeedlework an historic first. Colonial women knew nothing of crocheting although the Indians practiced a craft similar in some respects, using a kind of fiber made from bark pulp.

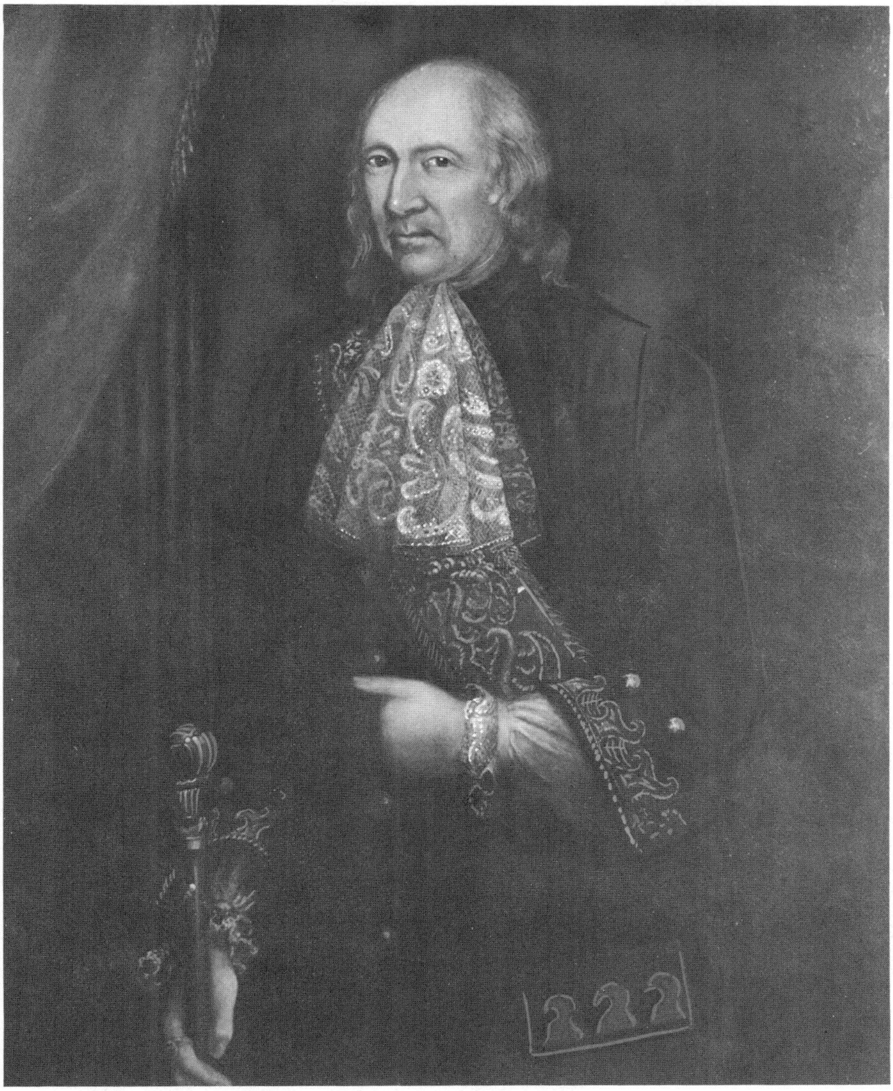

Portrait of George Curwen, 1610–1684. *Photo Eric Muller: courtesy Essex Institute*

Rose Wilder Lane tells of the day she was in the National Museum of Croatia, in Zagreb, Yugoslavia. Noticing ordinary crocheted lace displayed on velvet, locked under glass, she asked what it was. The astonished curator, rather than reply, asked her if it were not American, for she was looking at the museum's collection of the art of American lace. She was dumbfounded, and looking again at the case, she recognized the familiar popcorn pattern, the filet, the spider web, the pineapple, and the hairpin swirls. All of them treasured by a foreign land! She related that this incident occurred forty years ago and that as yet she has not seen in an American museum such a collection of American lace as she saw that day in the Balkans!

While, at the present time, lace for personal adornment is not sought after, crocheted bedspreads and beautifully crocheted tablecloths are in demand and undoubtedly will be the heirlooms of tomorrow. For years Rhode Island has been the lace "capital" of the United States. The twentieth-century industry is entirely dependent on a high tariff and the whim of women's fashions. Nylon is the most important of the raw materials used by these lace plants and their product is directly sold to the cutting trade.

Needlework Pictures

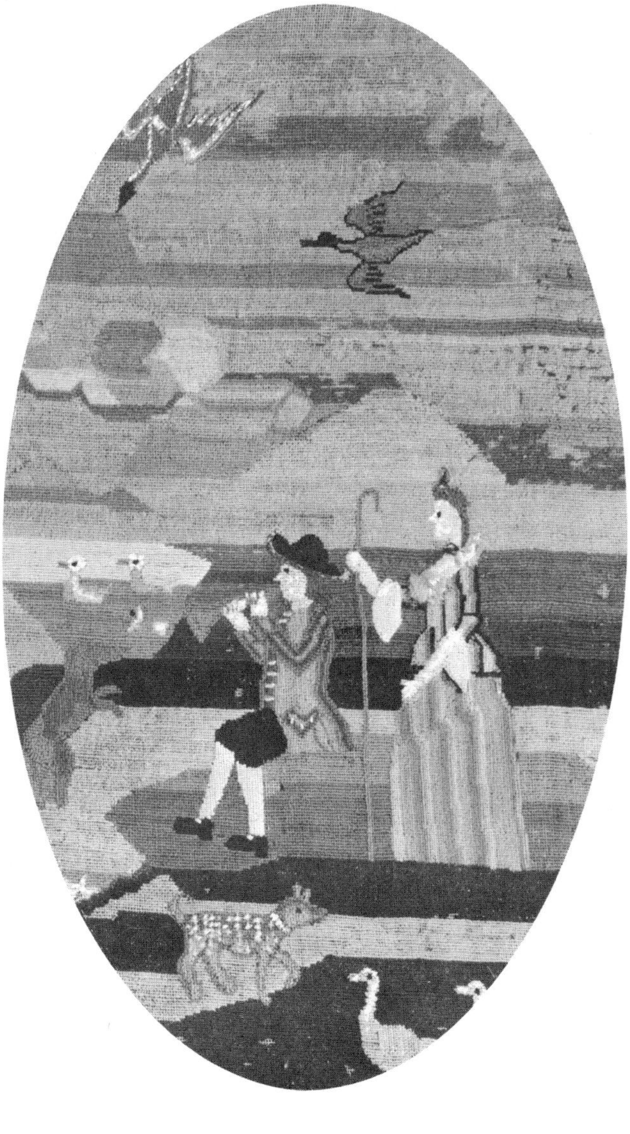

An embroidered picture of exceptional coloring, done in crewels and silks on linen, "The Piper and Shepherdess" is believed to have been made in Maine 1750-1775.
Photo courtesy Museum of Fine Arts, Boston

Martha Genung Stearns, skilled New England needlewoman and "dean" of those working in crewel embroidery in America has told the story of crewel work in *Homespun and Blue.* Masterfully written, out of a life rich in experience, it remains the most engaging exposition of this skilled craft yet to appear. She sheds bright light on the heritage of needlework that is ours to treasure and to enjoy. These are her opening lines: "Ever since woman, the mother and homemaker, began to have a history, the needle has been her intimate companion. The singing kettle and the needle and thimble are inseparable parts of our picture of a home. Needle-decoration is an art, and as the art of a people is closely bound up with its daily life, needlework has been a medium, just as the pen and paintbrush have, for recording history."

Crewel Work

Could any woman, packing a sewing kit, close her heart to all the lovely reminders of a home she might never see again? Among their most cherished memories was the affection the early colonists brought for the bright embroideries that had graced their former rooms and the techniques for making their own. Of this we can be certain, and crewel work was one of those skills. The term crewel refers to the twisted form of worsted yarn and crewel work is defined as "wool embroidery of any age worked on any ground." Among the notable examples of crewel embroidery that remain from the eighteenth and early nineteenth centuries, the work of New England women is considered the "loveliest and most appealing." Catherine Hedlund in *A Primer of New England Crewel Embrodiery* written for Sturbridge Village has evaluated our inheritance and its far-reaching significance in these words: "The many examples that remain to us in museums, in historical societies, and in the hands of private collectors reflect in the minds of their workers a love of color and design, a skill with the needle, and a sense of beauty we cannot but admire and that some few of us have been inspired to emulate. The revival of interest in crewel embroidery today is convincing evidence that the art has a charm and an appeal that have reached down across two hundred years to capture the hearts and imaginations of American women today."

By the early part of the eighteenth century, silk had superseded wool as the popular embroidery thread; thus both design and execution were finer and more appealing. Many settlers of the early colonies were from the middle and lower classes. Although some of these women had done crewel embroidery back home, practically all of them had some knowledge of it. They had been urged and warned by various colonizing companies and by letters from earlier arrivals to bring with them enough clothing and household linens to last them for some time. It must be assumed that some of these women, at least, had tucked way among their belongings, threads and patterns so that they might continue this pleasant pastime when they arrived in America. Working at it must have been primarily a question of finding the leisure. Since days were filled with the mechanics of living and evenings with poor and inadequate lighting, only gentlewomen with servants could indulge in this form of recreation. For it was definitely a pastime for the daylight hours. This may explain why almost no seventeenth-century New England crewel work survives. Lacking also were free time and creature comforts. (Some of that which has survived may well have been begun in England, for it closely resembles the embroidery of the middle-class Englishwomen of the same period.) The early American-made pieces were "blue and white," blue embroidery on a white homespun surface, the pattern copies perhaps of Canton motifs.

The Continental and English crewel work was heavy, covering the greater part of the material on which the designs were worked. The amount of labor and time involved in obtaining and preparing materials forced the New England embroiderer to open up her work, to use stitches that economized on thread. The resulting design was pleasantly simple, and perfectly suited to somewhat "stern" New England, albeit decorative and distinctively American. It had naive simplicity which was the hallmark of American embroidery from the start.

Most of the surviving New England crewel work was once part of a set of bed curtains. These hangings provided warmth and protection against chilly night drafts in unheated rooms. Since the beds of the colonists were often placed in the parlors, these hangings

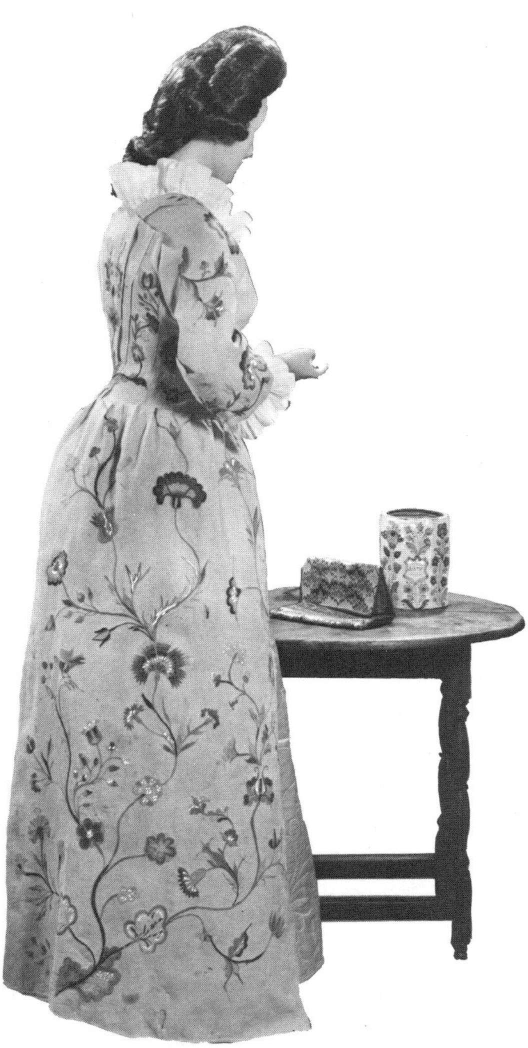

A wedding gown in crewel yarns made by Mary Myers Johnson, a Connecticut bride, in 1732. Olive green predominates, combined with shades of rose, gold, and a little blue. *Photo E. Irving Blomstrann: courtesy Wadsworth Athenaeum*

provided lovely color. This rather surprising fact is readily understandable when one realizes that the embroidery was so highly prized both here and abroad that rarely was one heir so highly favored as to receive title to an entire set of hangings in a family will.

Many other pieces of embroidery were made in New England. These included cushions, chair seats, aprons, pockets and pocketbooks, petticoats, gowns, children's dresses, waistcoats, samplers, and other pictures. While perhaps not so spectacular as were the bed hangings, they made a pleasing contribution to the surroundings and the society in which they were used.

New England embroidery has fewer stitches than the English. Outline, rope, cable, chain, coral, and couching stitches were the kinds used most frequently. Indeed, many of the best of the New England pieces surviving today were executed almost entirely in economy stitch, so named because in this stitch most of the wool appears on the surface, thereby insuring a minimum of waste. Like everything else in the colonies, thread was a precious commodity, not to be squandered where it would not show.

Beautifully colored crewels were not easy to obtain, and the embroidery fabrics varied. Much of the linen and yarn was home grown or raised, then handspun, dyed, and woven. Quantities of dry goods, including linens and twills, fine cottons and wools and linen canvas, were imported from England, and these were available to women in town shops and from peddlers' packs. A young woman who taught embroidery in Boston in 1751 advertised that she sold "canvas, crewils, floss, flowering and nuns thread, needles, pins and tapes." A shop, "At the Sign of the Spinning Wheel" sold "crewils in shades for working," in Portsmouth, New Hampshire, in 1791. When he opened his school for young ladies in New Haven in 1783, Abel Morse advertised that he offered, along with reading, writing, arithmetic, English grammar, geography, and composition, and along with the most advanced texts of the day, "the different branches of needlework." Some of these earlier embroiderers were self-taught. Chloe Hayes of Brattleboro, Vermont, was one such girl. "She had skill in needlework of all kinds and an artist's love for fancy work, copying her designs from the flowers in her garden. She loved the work so much that on Saturday afternoon as the Sabbath hours drew on she was wont to put her worsted-work in her workbasket and push it as far under the bed as she could and get it all out of her mind for Sunday."

Since crewel embroidery was dear to the hearts of pioneer women, its graceful open spaces held particular charm for, in these, the beholder could see readily the material prepared by the embroiderer's own skills. In those early years every craftswoman dyed her own yarns, spun her own linens, and even created her own designs or developed them from memory. A few had been inherited directly from English forebears and brought here by Pilgrim settlers. Later, these were modified as the result of environmental observation or individual inspira-

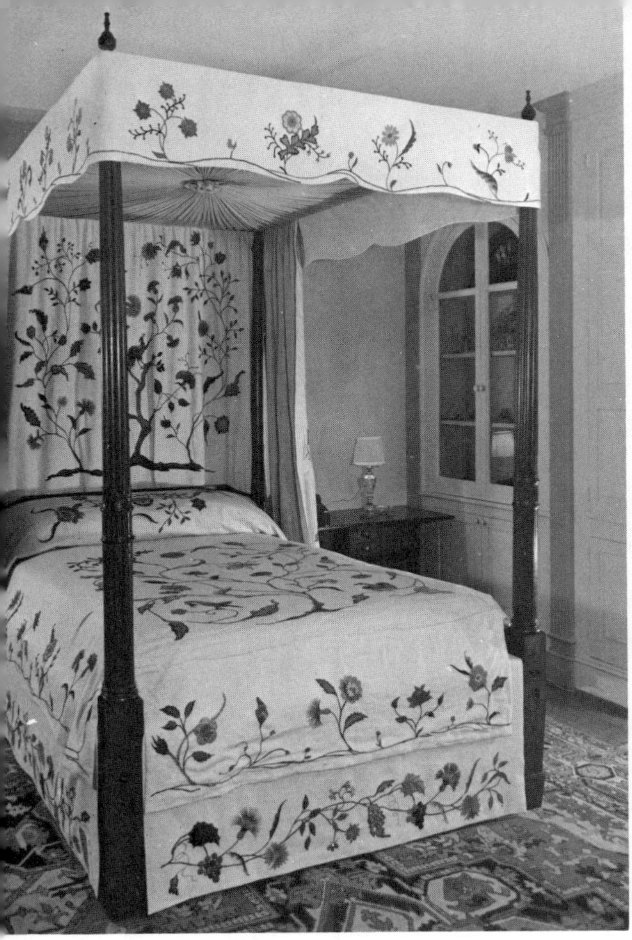

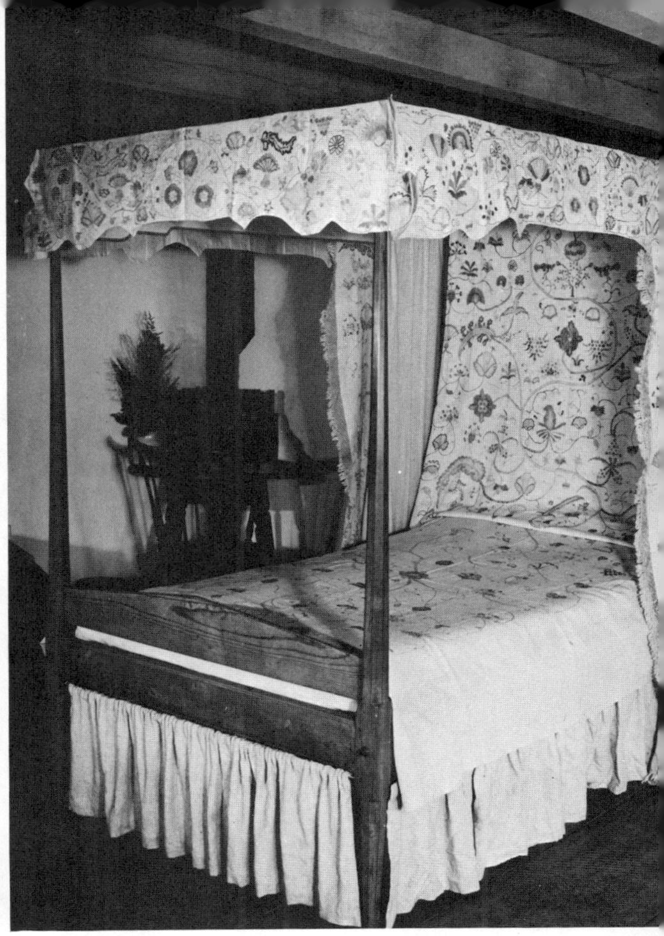

(*Left*) Crewel-embroidered bedspread and hangings designed to specifications and adapted from authentic early American embroideries. Designed in the Needlework Shop of the Women's Educational and Industrial Union, Boston, Massachusetts. The "Union," founded in 1877 as a nonprofit educational and social service organization, was instrumental in organizing and giving impetus to the arts and crafts societies in the 1920's. *Photo courtesy Women's Educational and Industrial Union, Boston*

(*Right*) Coverlet and hangings, *circa* 1773, worked by Martha Abbott Prescott of Westford, Massachusetts. Presented by Mrs. James Hammond to the Jeremiah Lee Mansion, Marblehead, Massachusetts. *Photo Alessandro Macone: courtesy the Lee Mansion*

tion. It appears that much of the needlework of this type originated in the New England colonies. A considerable number of crewel embroideries have been inherited by old families and many of these may be seen in New England homes and museums. Frequent sailings from England to the port of Boston may have encouraged the sending of patterns to friends and relatives living in New England, which would account for the fact that the majority of these embroideries seemed to have been made in this section.

In the Governor's Palace at Williamsburg, Virginia, may be seen a curtain believed to have been made in Ipswich, Massachusetts, between 1720 and 1750. In the American wing of the Metropolitan Museum of Art, the beautiful cover worked by Mary Breed of Boston in 1770 is on display. One could get lost in the beautiful embroideries and crewel work to be seen at Deerfield, Massachusetts. (The first and only dye that the colonial women had to work with was indigo, so they did the first crewel work in blue on bleached white linen. The effect was eye-pleasing and cool looking. There are many examples of this blue-and-white in Deerfield.)

A very fine dated piece of crewel work was made by Mary Bulman, in York, Maine, in an incredibly short time while she awaited the return of her husband. This unique set of embroidered bed hangings, done in 1745, may be seen in the Gaoler's bedroom in The Old Gaol Museum (1653), York, Maine. The Wadsworth Atheneum, Hartford, Connecticut, owns an embroidered wedding gown in unusual yarns, made in 1732 by the prospective bride, Mary Myers Johnson. Olive green predominates, combined with shades of rose, golds, and a little blue in this wedding gown of long ago. Even a casual

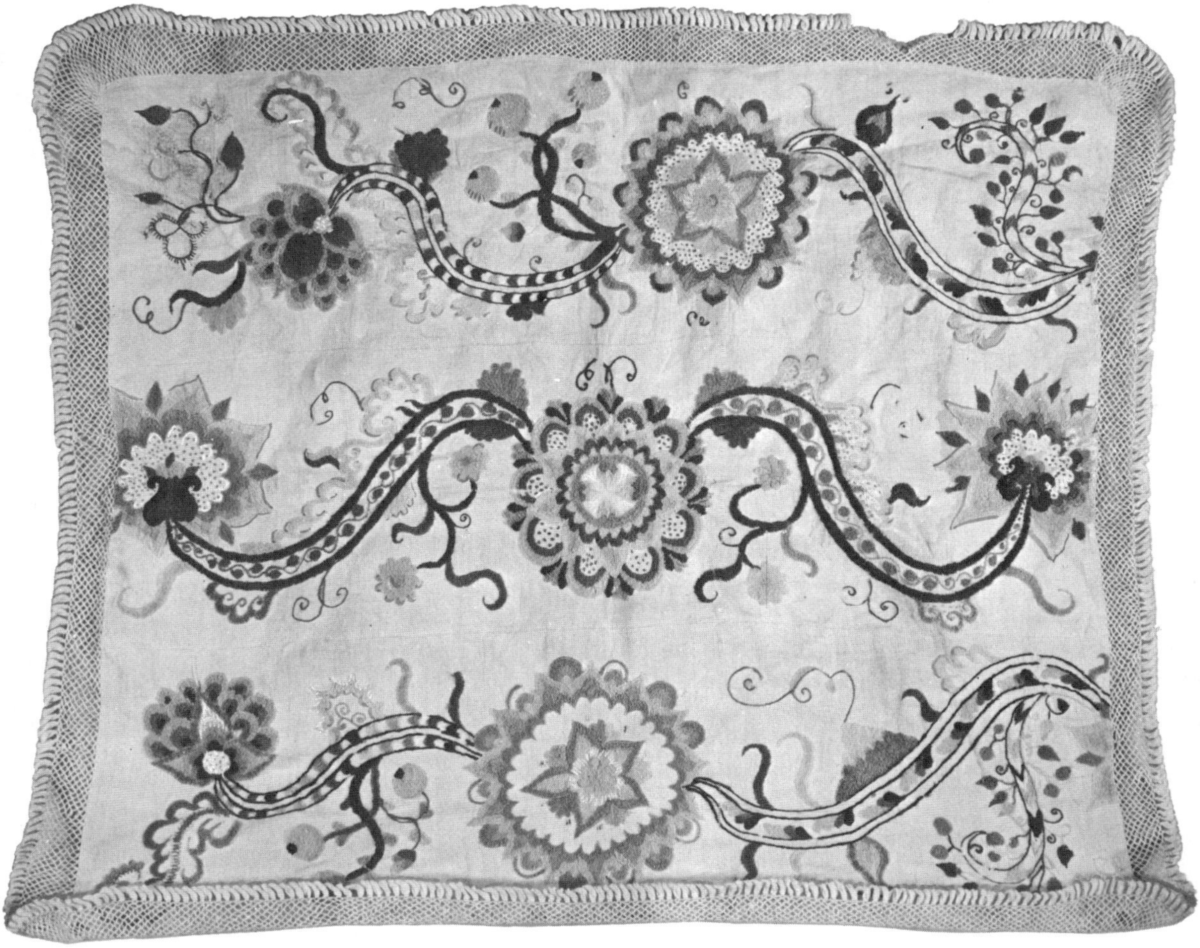

This crewel work table scarf found in Massachusetts was made of three strips of linen (22 × 26 inches overall) with a border of netted string and looped tassels. The "S"-shaped serpentine embroidered motifs accentuated with exotic stylized flowers were done in wool split-stitch. The coloring throughout is brilliant with five or six shades of green, an equal number of pinks, blues, yellows, lilacs, and other colors. *Einar Mengis: courtesy Shelburne Museum*

glance at these pieces of crewel work makes one aware that they are more beautiful than other forms of needlework for there is the loveliness of color coupled with the freedom and grace of stitches. These stitches are simple and varied, unlike the monotonous cross-stitch in samplers and those in needlepoint, both the gros and petit point stitches.

Once again, in the middle of the twentieth century, crewel work has become a household word. Paralleling the greatly increased national interest in historic restorations, there seems to be a ground swell of interest as the comfortable, easy-to-live-with designs reappear. *The New York Times* had this to say: "It is no news that this age of mass production has had its own antithesis in the 'do-it-yourself' trend. But is it not possible that some of this has sprung from a desire to keep alive, in available leisure time, the artistic craftsmanship of our own forebears? Or the desire to have finer, more individualized possessions? Or a combination of both? The revival of popular interest in fine needlepoint embroidery started some time ago. Now, the more difficult art of crewel embroidery is beginning to make a comeback."

As Mildred J. Davis of Brookline, Massachusetts, has expressed it, "Crewel embroidery is now in your hands, one hand a legatee of generations past, the other a harbinger of generations to come." It must be remembered that for women in earlier centuries a tremendous toll was taken with the many physical tasks which daily confronted them. On the other hand, their free moments were not taken up with daily newspapers, countless magazines, television and radio programs. There were not the films or the theater. Concerts were few, if any; a woman's free time was left literally to her fingers—dexterous ones at that, that long ago had ceased to play at "cat's cradle" to while the time away. Card playing was frowned upon, nor was it an obsession. Rubbing her hands with corn meal to make them less grimy she gave herself over to the crewel yarns, with which she was already intimately familiar.

It is a lucky collector who can secure a crewel-embroidered bedcover. Museums have elevated quilts to the realm of art as they are now being avidly sought.

Early crewel-traditional colors include several shades of green from gray to blue; warm chestnut brown to yellow; blues, indigos to gray; soft, dull reds—and happy disregard of nature such as a blue rabbit! Women everywhere in New England are avidly making crewelwork pieces. In so doing, they are making their homes more attractive and are carrying on the tradition of having heirloom pieces for posterity. It has been said that "Whatever we look at with delight, whatever we see that gives us pleasure, though we may think we have forgotten it the next day—will influence us all our lives."

Needlepoint

The first President of our land was beloved by all. He was a frequent visitor to New England, and the colonists had a real picture and measure of the man. What Mrs. Washington did was of equal importance, so the news of her needlework must have been the topic of conversation everywhere. Martha Washington worked ten seats for drawing-room chairs for her newly remodeled home, Mount Vernon. These, doubtless, were among the very first examples of American needlepoint. Not only the English shell-patterned canvas, but the chairs, too, were imported from England. As thoroughly American as her husband, however, Mrs. Washington did not hesitate to send to the mother land for these, nor did she have to consider the cost; few, at that time, could imitate her.

Needlepoint, which is worked with wool or silk on canvas, has been a popular domestic art for centuries. Most people, however, are familiar with variations of the half cross-stitch, which is the one most commonly used. Hope Hanley, in her book *Needlepoint,* delineates over fifty canvas stitches which may be used

Photos (below and following page) courtesy Women's Educational and Industrial Union, Boston

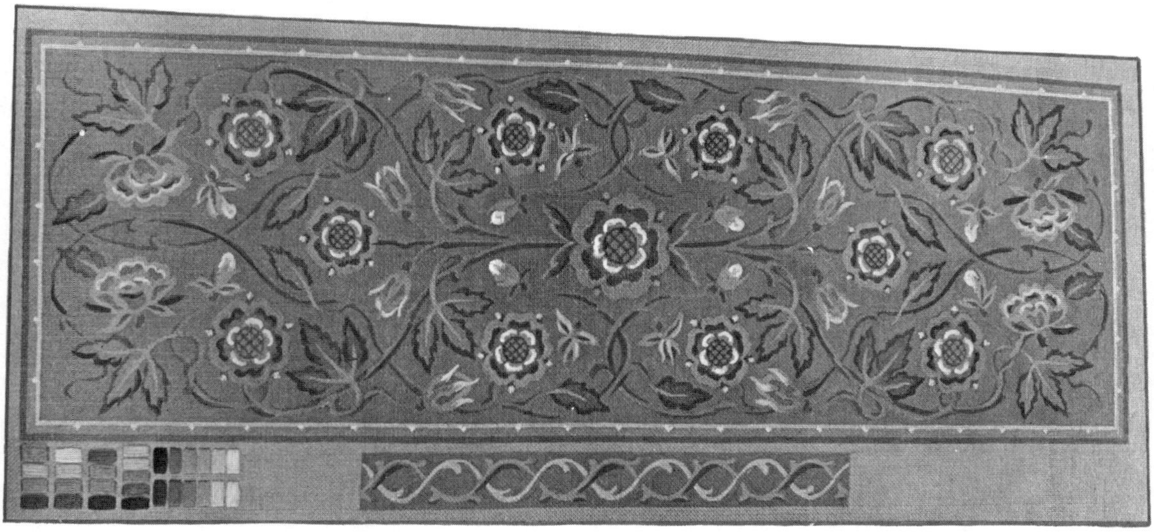

(Preceding page and above) Designs for stall cushions and kneelers worked in needlepoint were made by the Women's Educational and Industrial Union Needlework Shop for the Chapel of St. Mary in the Cathedral Church of St. Peter and St. Paul, Washington, D. C. These included the Tudor rose and the fleur-de-lis. They were worked by a group of skilled Boston needlewomen who qualified by first submitting samples of their skill, demonstrating "something of beauty for the Lord." When the handiwork was exhibited at the cathedral, it was described by a noted newspaper writer as "the gamut of human emotions told in fine needlework—the unselfconscious laughter of children, the heartbreak of bereavement—the warmth and dignity of faith."

alone, or in combination, offering infinite possibilities to the creative designer and less monotony in the actual work as well. When one stitch alone is used, the effeet of the finished piece depends on the shading and contrasting of the colors; with different stitches, the texture can be varied.

The two common stitches used in needlepoint are gros point and petit point. Petit point is a fine tent stitch. There are two basic types of needlepoint canvas: single thread and two thread or double thread. Two thread is the better known and is called penelope.

Tent stitch was the stitch taught in many of the dame schools of New England. This tent stitchery, known as tapestry or needlepoint today, was used profusely throughout the nineteenth century. During the 1700's and until about 1830, needlepoint in New England was used for embroidering portraits. George Washington was a favorite subject. Concord Historical Society at Concord, New Hampshire, has a large needlepoint picture of George Washington and also one of Benjamin Franklin. In the 1940's landscapes and Biblical scenes replaced the portraits. These were usually very large canvasses.

Then followed the "sentimental" pictures, such as "Two Little Sisters" stitched in a decorative landscape, and small wall pictures entitled "Little Birds in a Nest." Needlepoint chairs, ottomans, piano benches, stools, footrests, and other pieces of furniture, using floral designs, became fashionable.

Berlin work is a term which was applied generally to all types of needlework on canvas made during the Victorian era. The name derives from the fact that the most desirable and sought after patterns came from Berlin and were commonly referred to as the Berlin patterns. The work is characterized by the use of notably brilliant worsteds, also obtained from Germany.

Needlepoint depends not so much on the quality and refinement of line as it does upon mass effects. Differing entirely from crewel embroidery, its closely woven stitches give it a heavier and bulkier effect. Its close resemblance to tapestry when used on hangings or covers imitating that style of design, accounts for its being so-called. It is not, however, a woven technique like tapestry, but rather decoration applied to a woven surface by means of a needle, which is embroidery. Canvas foundations were originally imported from Germany and France but today they are supplied by Czechoslovakia and Austria as well.

Zealously stitching their canvasses, American women of the twentieth century deliberately take time from their many active duties to embroider. For them needlepoint is a stimulating activity which provides an easy transition from the busy, active moment to the relaxation that follows. When time lags or the brain is fogged, a bit of needlepoint eases the tension pleasantly and amusingly. In addition, it appeases the desire for beauty by releasing creative and spiritual energies which exist in everyone to some degree.

The reason for the absence of early American needlepoint is simple. The material cost too much. In New England almost any thrifty woman could hook a rug or sew a patchwork quilt from materials taken from her rag bag. She could embroider homespun linen with homespun wools, whereas needlepoint required costly imported canvas and a blunt needle useless for anything else.

On the other hand, the Republic was hardly more than fifty years old before American women began to develop needlepoint, but there was still much more interest in creating new patchwork designs for quilting and in making lace. Actually, needlepoint was not considered essential. It is not thrifty. It has no claim to utility; its value is in beauty alone.

Endless variety of wools in both color and texture are to be observed and are evident when one looks at needlepoint, and the variety in designs is equally extensive.

The needlework department at the Women's Educational and Industrial Union of Boston is widely known for its excellent instruction in the art of crewel work and needlepoint. Under the able and inspiring direction of Miss Caroline Brandley, this department has kept alive and maintained a constant high standard of fine needlework. A score of artists design and sketch original canvasses and patterns for the avid needlewoman; perfection is the aim of all. Consequently rare and beautiful pieces are wrought and a reputation for excellence of work has been heeded throughout the United States. Many notable people, concerned with the restoration of old houses, have come to Boston for help, as exemplified by the request of the National Cathedral of Washington, D.C. The Union was asked to design and make the needlepoint needed for St. Mary's Chapel, five main altar rail-kneelers, full length, and two stalls requiring a full-length cushion and kneeler, four inner altar kneelers, and three different types of designs for positions. These are magnificent specimens of the true art of needlepoint. Miss Brandley comments that while the interest in crewel work fluctuates, there has always been a constantly keen interest in needlepoint and the perfection of needle art that it exemplifies.

Excellent embroideries in needlepoint and crewel work are executed by American women today who feel the same urge which actuated women of long ago to express themselves imaginatively, and to enrich their environment with work created with their own hands.

Deacon Drowne and His Weathervanes

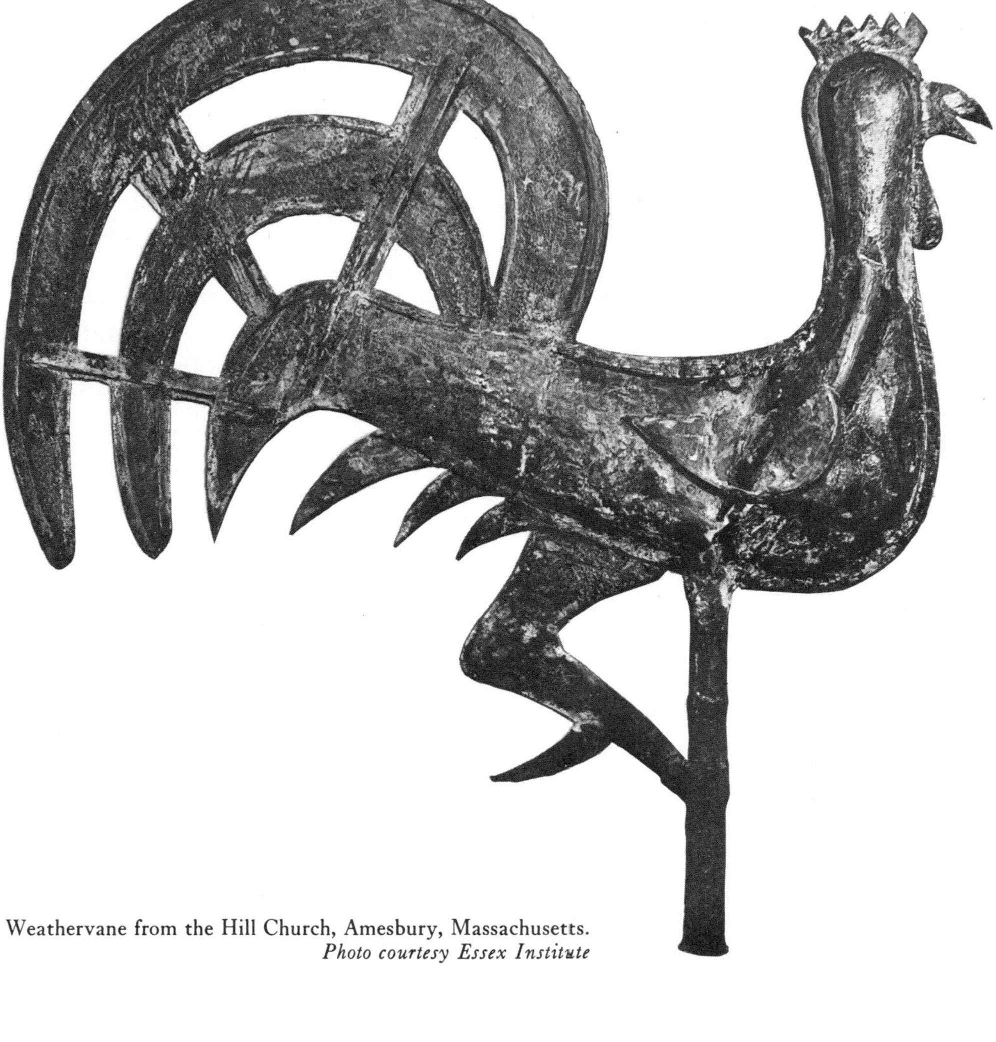

Weathervane from the Hill Church, Amesbury, Massachusetts.
Photo courtesy Essex Institute

Peter Faneuil, as a young man, was sitting one day on the grassy bank of the Charles River, looking dejectedly into the water, for he was without funds or a place to lay his head. Suddenly he was approached by a small boy who came running down a path, chasing a grasshopper. The two became friends and the small boy took the young man home for supper and a night's lodging. It is said that the boy's family also gave the young man his start in business. The boy was Shem Drowne. Years later, when Peter Faneuil became a wealthy merchant, he erected a market house and meeting hall which was called Faneuil Hall. He commissioned Shem Drowne, then a widely known coppersmith and woodcarver, to make a weathervane for the building—a giant grasshopper—as a memento of that eventful meeting. (The episode representing the first meeting of the merchant prince and the master craftsman was memorialized, two centuries later, in a painting by a Boston artist, W. M. Drowne, who based the subject of his painting on old family tradition.)

Many stories and legends have clustered around this, the most famous and one of the earliest weathervanes made in New England that still remains. The grasshopper made by Deacon Drowne was believed, at one time, to have appeared on the crest of the Faneuil family, since a similar figure was placed on the roof of the summerhouse in Peter Faneuil's garden. However, it is believed to have been adapted from a similar one erected on the Royal Exchange in London. The grasshopper was the crest of the Gresham family, and Sir Thomas Gresham was the founder of the Royal Exchange.

Shem Drowne was born in Kittery, Maine, in 1683; the family moved to Boston in 1692. He made the grasshopper for Faneuil Hall in 1742, hammering it out of copper in his shop on Ann Street. The date was verified by a paper found inside, which read in part:

> Shem Drowne Made it May 25, 1742
>
> To my brethren and Fellow Grasshopper, Fell in ye year 1753 November 18 from ye Market by a great Earthquake . . . repaired by my old Master above.
>
> Again like to have met with my Utter Ruin by Fire but hopping Timely from my Publick Scituation came off with broken bones, and much Bruised, Cured and again fixed by Old Master's son Thomas Drowne June 28th, 1780, and though I will promise to Discharge my Office, yet I shall vary as ye wind.

On the evening of March 17, 1889 (Evacuation Day in Boston), the 'bird' as it was called, was knocked from its perch by the carelessness of some men hauling in the flag, and fell to the street, losing its eyes, horns, and two feet. It was soon repaired and, feeling very proud in a new coat of gold leaf, it was given a reception in the historic hall before getting back on the perch "from which it had been much missed." In 1899 the 'bird' left the perch again, while the old wooden cupola, long considered a fire trap, was replaced by a steel one.

The grasshopper weathervanes with their green glass eyes were copied and offered for sale by L. W. Cushing and Sons in the 1840's. A favorite Boston legend held that Benjamin Franklin, once forced to prove his identity in Europe, was asked if he could describe the weathervane on Faneuil Hall. When he mentioned the grasshopper, the evidence proved sufficient to grant the favor he requested. (This old chestnut has been rolling around for a long time and has been linked with many important people.) Famed on both sides of the Atlantic was this gilded creature which looked fit enough to jump with the best of them.

Carolyn Sherwin Bailey, popular writer of children's stories, told how Shem used to mend the copper toes of the stout shoes which children of those days wore. They loved to visit his shop and watch him work. When he made the grasshopper, the news spread rapidly and everyone went to see this strange creature which filled the tiny shop with its long, slender legs stretching in every direction. To the young folk, it looked like a dragon. Among the visitors was young Sam Adams, then a student at Harvard College. Peter Faneuil saw it too, so the story goes, but soon forgot about it for he was much concerned with plans for Faneuil Hall which he had offered to the City of Boston as a gift. (At first, his offer was not well received. Among those who opposed it was Adams. It was only after Faneuil had sent young Adams a note that he succeeded in convincing him of the value and importance to the town of the proposed building. Adams suggested that he put the grasshopper on the cupola for he remembered well having seen it at Shem Drowne's shop. This

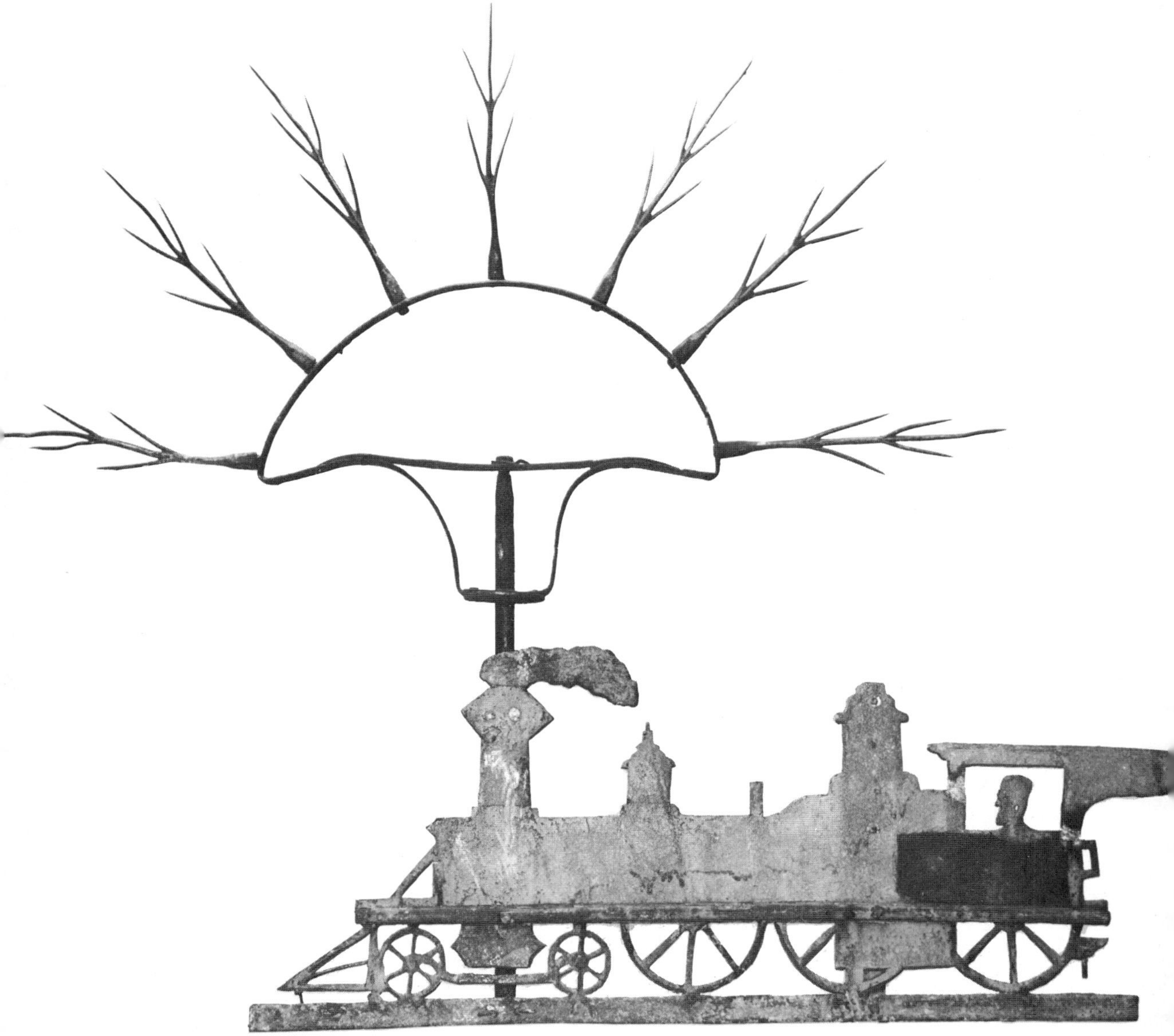

This weathervane featuring an early locomotive is distinctive for its unusual lightening rod. *Photo courtesy Shelburne Museum*

story, based on tradition, varies from the other accounts given, but it is included nonetheless as an example of the way legend and tradition usually embroider the facts.)

"Deacon" Shem Drowne is usually referred to as the first known professional weathervane maker in New England. Actually, weathervanes were only a sideline with Drowne as with other craftsmen working in metal. In addition to his trade as a coppersmith, Drowne became one of Boston's most colorful craftsmen whose life—like that of the objects he made both of metal and wood—became truly legendary as tale after tale was told at the fireside about his weathervanes and his carving. It made good talk, for what subject has more appeal in New England than *weather*. He also carved pump heads, mantle decorations, trade signs, and ship figureheads. In "Drowne's Wooden Image," Nathaniel Hawthorne described the wonderful copper Indian (four feet, six inches tall with a glass eye) which topped the old Province House, the former residence of the royal governors of the colony. "An Indian chief gilded all over, stood during the better part of a century on the cupola of the Province House, bedazzling the eyes of those who looked upward, like an angel in the sun." Tradition holds that crowds of children used to gather about the Province House at mid-day to watch for the fulfillment of the legend that the Indian would shoot his arrow at high noon.

There was trouble among the congregation at Boston's "New North" since a goodly number did not see eye to eye with the minister. Those who left the church built a new one of their own on Hanover Street which they called "New Brick"; but others referred to it as the Revenge Church, strange name indeed for a Christian edifice. "The Cockerel" which Shem Drowne hammered out of brass kettles for the steeple weighed 172 pounds and the story goes that the day it was set in place "a merry fellow" climbed the spire, straddled the cock and crowed away in a derogatory manner in the direction of "New North." Eventually, the cockerel came to a tragic end when it crashed through the roof of a nearby house and landed in the kitchen.

The weathervane was known in Greece before the Christian era. At that time, Andronicus built a Tower of Winds and topped it with a figure of a Triton made of bronze, holding a wand. Among the many innovations that William the Conqueror brought to Britain were the useful and ornamental weather vanes. That they were made in the seventeenth century in the colonies is indicated by a number of old ones still in use.

Weathervanes of every imaginable kind have been intrinsic features of the New England skyscape for generations. They stand out in people's memories as much today as in the eighteenth century. Those of later design are almost entirely the work of metal craftsmen, copper or iron, and many of them are truly distinctive. For the most part, the weathervane lost much of its charm and individuality when it began to be mass produced. Those on public buildings have always commanded more attention because of their size and often for their conspicuous or distinctive designs. Equally appealing are the stories of their makers and the lore surrounding them. A cupola on a barn was never complete without its weathercock, or a cow, horse, sheep, pig, or even a dog, all gleaming in a protective coating of 23-carat gold leaf.

Each section of New England has its characteristic types. Along the Maine coast, at Kennebunkport and inland as well, carved wood was a favored material. It was cheap and there were plenty of whittlers who enjoyed doing nautical subjects or a horse and buggy, a pair of trotting horses (inspired by Currier-and-Ives prints), arrows, and animals. The Sanford Public Library became widely known for a vane featuring a weaver at a loom. One of the noted carvers was James Lombard, born in Baldwin, in 1865. A farmer by profession, he also made furniture. He specialized in hens and roosters and a number of them have been found on barns as far away as Wells, implying that he may have been an itinerant craftsman. His figures were highly stylized, made of pine and painted in yellow ochre, a cheap substitute for gold leaf.

The rooster rates as one of the earliest designs used for weathervanes in New England and rightly so. Did he not have Biblical symbolism in his heritage, and was he not the first creature in the barn to arouse the dawning of another day? He was a favorite for many reasons, and decorative too. Intricate in design, he was usually made of copper in several parts and soldered together. For strength the legs were often of iron, cast solid. Copper lent itself to considerable detail for it could be hammered with ease. Picasso once remarked: "Cocks have always been seen, but never as well as in American weathervanes." At the time he had never been to America, but probably based his remark on pictures he had seen.

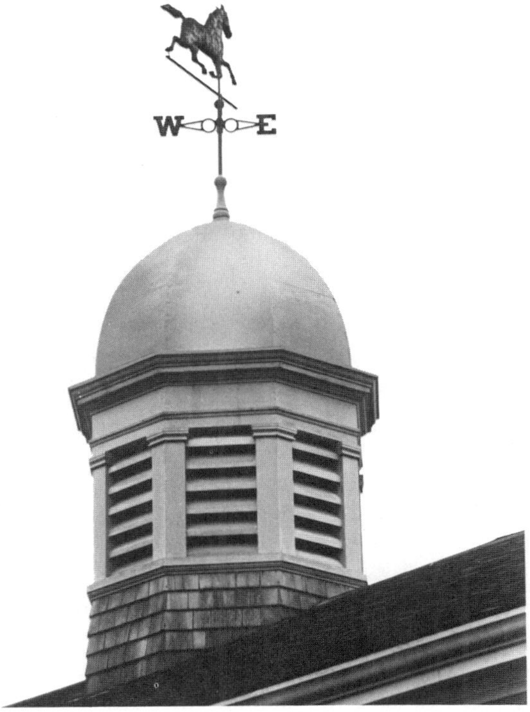

Weathervane from the cupola of the Richardson House, Newburyport, Massachusetts. *Photo courtesy Essex Institute*

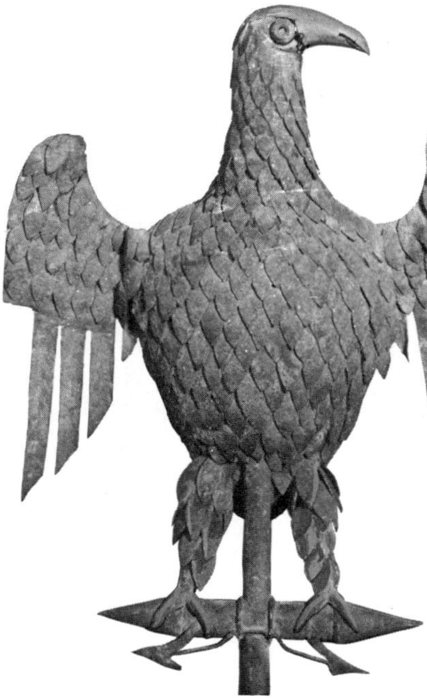

Metal eagle used for the top of a weathervane or flagpole. *Photo courtesy Shelburne Museum*

The captain of a New Bedford whaling vessel favored a sperm whale carved out of wood for his vane. Fish, spyglasses, and boats were other favorite subjects by the sea. Everyone who visits the Paul Revere House on North Square in Boston is lured to look at a fish (probably a cod) carved from hardwood and studded with copper nails. It had been formerly used at Revere's copper shop in Canton and some believe that it was actually his trade sign at the time. Lincoln J. Ceeley of Nantucket, known as a most versatile craftsman, specializing in cabinetmaking and carving, made weathervanes featuring ships and windmills and wind toys for children.

Copper takes on rich tones with age—a combination of green and soft orange, the result of weathering. A silhouette of a winged Angel Gabriel blowing his horn, or one with the archangel clothed in a flowing gown (as on the steeple of the Baptist Church at Whiting, Vermont, 1814), seemed a most appropriate symbol for a house of worship. In the 1840's these figures began to be mass produced; within a generation or two, Gabriel had lost his vigor, being reduced to a mere cupid. Such was the fate of so many examples of native craftsmanship with the coming of streamlined methods in a machine age. That ancient Christian symbol, the fish, adopted by the leaders of the Reformation as one of their insignia, has long been a favorite subject for churches and was found on many a New England steeple. A wooden angel wearing high black shoes and blowing a trumpet floated in the air on a pinnacle atop a boathouse in Nantucket.

With the passing of the horse, many an old blacksmith, reluctant to lay aside his hammer and anvil, continued his trade by making decorative and useful objects of wrought iron. Such a person was Ernest S. Rice of Camden, Maine, who became known as a true artist and not the least of his productions were weathervanes. Henry W. Merrill of East Hiram, still active at eighty-six, became known as Maine's blacksmith-botanist for his amazing knowledge of native plants. These he incorporated into his designs for andirons, signs, gateposts, and weathervanes. Wrought iron was a favorite material for weathervanes in the days when wood went out of fashion. Steam fire engines and locomotives were frequently seen and most of these were as picturesque as they were distinctive. On the steeple of the First Church in Concord, Massachusetts, the crowning ornament was a superbly made wrought-iron gilded banner dated 1673.

The subjects used for weathervanes reflect a diversity of tastes, trends, and trades. The patriotic theme was represented by Columbia, the American eagle, and Uncle Sam. The weathervane often served as a trade sign as well or marked the location of a firehouse or some other public building. A butcher, Captain David West, who owned a slaughterhouse in the New Bedford area in the nineteenth century had a curious vane in the form of a huge cleaver with the figure of a pig being driven by its owner.

Bruce Rogers of Fairfield, Connecticut, one of the nation's leading typographers and book designers, created a weathervane that delighted and amused all who saw it. It was a singing cuckoo connected to a windmill, reminiscent of the wonderful mechanical toys made in Europe in earlier centuries. He first took a cuckoo clock apart to see how it worked and how he could adapt it to the movements of the windmill he wished to use. His aim was to make a bird that would sing and raise its tail, at intervals, governed by the movement of the mill. The mechanism to make the bird "come alive" was concealed in the tower of the mill and the ingenious vane was perched on an old Ford steering wheel which served as a track on which the mill revolved. The cuckoo sang on every turn of the windmill, timed by the wind.

Needless to say, this was a vane for mild weather and was taken indoors in winter.

Iron Work

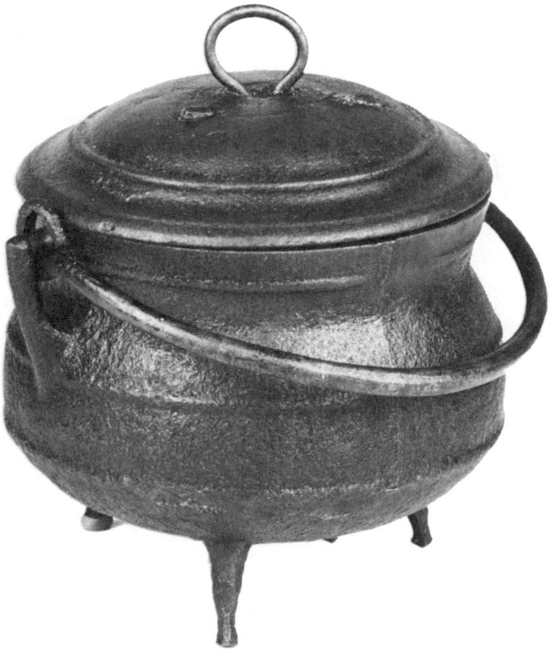

Tools made of iron which were essential in establishing settlements in the wilderness were brought from England, but these were by no means sufficient for the rapidly expanding colonies in the New World. John Winthrop, Jr. son of Massachusetts Bay Colony's first governor, launched the iron-making industry at Hammersmith on the Saugus River near Lynn. Begun in 1646, it flourished for a generation, during which time nails, pots for cooking, hinges, and various items of hardware were among the iron products produced. The ironworks, consisting of a blast furnace, forge, rolling and slitting mill, wharf, warehouse and other essential buildings, became one of the spectacles of the colonies and visitors were frèquent and numerous in the seventeenth century. However, several factors including heavy debts contributed to its closing about 1670. Today, the Saugus Ironworks Restoration at Saugus, Massachusetts, reproduced by the American Iron and Steel Institute in cooperation with the First Ironworks Association, attracts thousands of visitors annually from mid-May to mid-October. Skilled craftsmen make the exhibit a prime example of living history at the forge, in the rolling mill, the blacksmith shop, and elsewhere on the grounds. To recapture the spirit of the times, a complete series of oil paintings was produced by Charles Overly and these enhance the various exhibits in the museum, since the wilderness setting of the ironworks has long since disappeared.

Tin, Tin Peddling, and Painted Tin

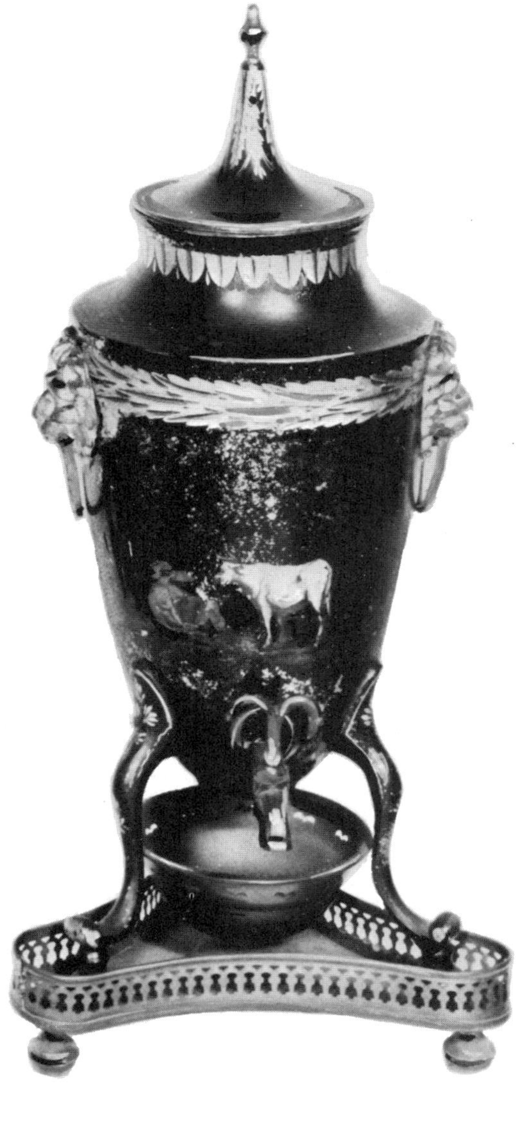

More than two hundred years ago, when Edward Pattison and his brothers, newly over from Ireland, set up a tin shop in Berlin, Connecticut, they launched one of America's most inimitable ambassadors, the Yankee Peddler. A box of tin plates, a few wooden mallets, and several pairs of strong hands coupled with an unlimited amount of Irish dexterity gave a new twist to Yankee ingenuity.

In the typical manner of newcomers, charged with earning a living, Edward and his brothers set to work at the trade they knew best, cutting, shaping, and soldering tin. First they made "a handsome line of shiny tin dinner plates, tin cups and saucers, tin teapots, lanterns, candlesticks, and candle sconces. The wares were displayed attractively on their shelves, along with a sideline of tin milk pans, pots, and pails—an irresistible exhibition for any housewife tired of swabbing the crude wooden plates and heavy bowls that were standard culinary equipment. Here at last was a lightweight, eye-catching substitute for the cumbersome old vessels. They sold almost as fast as the Pattisons could produce them. Their cellar bulged with the vegetables and potatoes taken in exchange; their pantry was a veritable storehouse of cheeses, barrels of grain, biscuits, and corned beef that represented gross income." W. Storrs Lee, commenting on the brothers in *The Yankees of Connecticut* says "Berlin was pleased with the Pattisons and proud of its new pursuit."

In the century ahead, the activities begun by these immigrant tinsmiths were to link the economic, artistic, and social life of New England with those of the rest of America in a variety of ways. From these humble beginnings came the beginning of industrial activity and the rise of the modern department store. Tin, in its various forms, served to inspire the household art of decorating by hand, utensils of everyday use and, in large measure, helped to influence the foibles and fashions of the burgeoning Republic. Tin had eye appeal especially when it was new and shiny, hence the popular name "poor man's silver."

In a day when the news of the outside world came through in a weekly newspaper, often out-dated when it reached remote communities, the Yankee tin peddler with his pack or his wagon was the principal purveyor of the latest headlines (which actually were never headlined) and the social gossip of the big towns. This he colored to suit his fancy as he higgled and haggled to sell his wares. Behind the rattling pots and pans, the shining tin lighting fixtures, the sturdy deed boxes, the salt shakers, the sugar bowls, and dozens of other useful houseold articles lies a fascinating phase of America's coming of age. The art of japanning, a form of chinoiserie, was also a by-product of the age that was to give the town housewife and her country cousin a new outlet for artistic expression, more color for the kitchen, the parlor and the front hall—not to mention that "elegant" look with the glitter of gold.

While it has often been said that Deacon Shem Drowne, the Boston metalsmith and woodcarver, worked with tin as early as 1712, the beginnings of tinsmithing on a commercial basis are more accurately traced to the Pattisons of Berlin, Connecticut. (The family name is also spelled Patterson or Paterson.) About 1738, Edward Pattison from County Tyrone, Ireland, arrived in America and settled in the town of Berlin. Shortly after his arrival, he returned to his homeland and brought back his brothers William and Noah and his sisters Anna and Jennie. He had learned the tinsmith's trade at home, but at first there was little chance to practice it in Berlin because tin was hard to come by in the colonies. In fact, it was scarce and what "tinned" pans were in use had been procured at considerable cost. Within two years of his arrival, he began to import sheet tin from England, making it into cooking utensils. At that time, tin was being made in several industrial centers in England and also in Wales where a thriving factory had been established at Pontypool.

The Pattison brothers worked at home, beating out their vessels by hand. When they had accumulated a stock, they peddled it from door to door in Berlin and the surrounding area. Soon the local demand was met, so they visited nearby towns carrying their wares in sacks on their backs, or in large baskets strapped to the sides of a horse. This new bright, shining ware was a welcome relief from the dull, drab, dented pewter and the woodenware generally in use at the time.

The tin business prospered and, with apprentices eager to learn the new trade, other

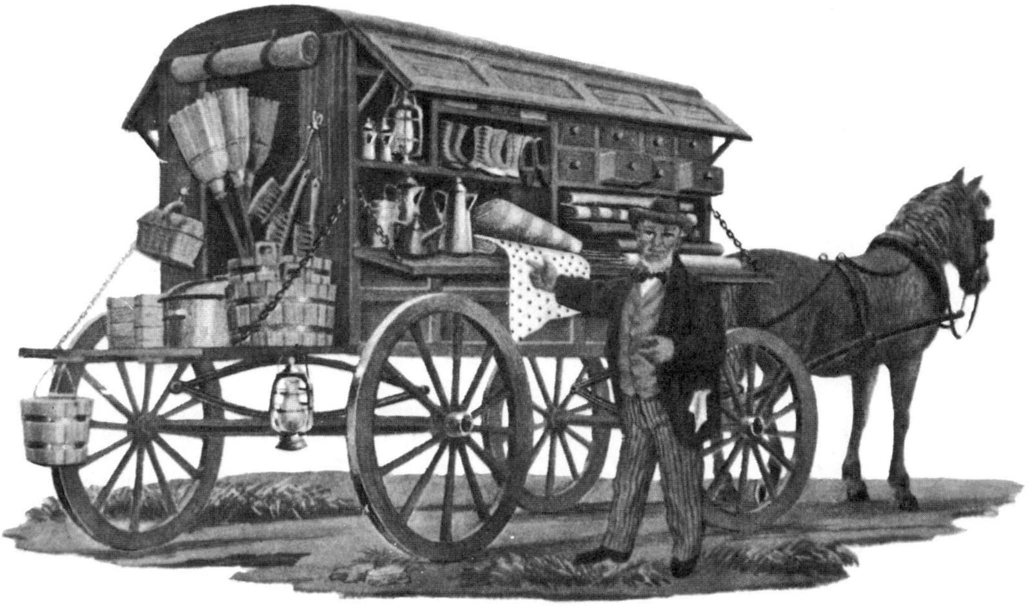

townsmen began to produce tinware as well. Soon Berlin became the center for the tin industry in New England and it continued there until 1850. There was a lull during the Revolution since sheet tin could not be obtained from Great Britain. From a modest beginning as a home industry, the work was carried on in factories which were located along streams where water power was available. Production was improved to meet the heavy demand and, by 1815, it was not unusual for the Berlin tinsmith to consume ten thousand boxes of sheet tin a year, most of which was made up into culinary utensils. Five tinsmiths could supply the demands of twenty-five peddlers. In nearby Farmington and adjoining towns other shops sprang up.

At first, tinsmithing was entirely a handcraft involving such equipment as a huge pair of shears, a soldering iron, a steel-edged anvil known as a "stock," a hammer, and a few other tools of the trade. Tinplates were the result of dipping thin sheets of charcoal-smelted iron into melted tin. Thinness was accomplished by rolling the metal. Three dippings produced single tinplate, whereas six dippings gave a much more durable product. Actually, these materials were much longer lasting than the lightweight tin produced today. Edwin Valentine Mitchell has described the simple manufacturing process in *The Romance of New England Antiques*. Of it, he wrote:

> The tinsmith, in working the sheets up into various utensils, such as pans, pails, plates, teapots, coffeepots, bake ovens, measures, and cups, made patterns for the various parts of an article and having outlined these on a sheet of tin cut them out with a mammoth pair of shears. These were then brought to the desired form by a few simple tools specially adapted to the purpose. The various parts were then soldered together with a composition of tin and lead, a small charcoal furnace being used to heat the soldering iron. But, before the tinsmith did any soldering, he turned the edges of the parts which were to be united by beating them with a mallet on a steel-edged anvil called a "stock." This was done to strengthen the seams and give the solder a chance to take hold. Iron wire was used to re-enforce the edges and handles, which required more strength than the tin alone possessed. With the growth of the industry, machines invented by Seth Peck of Hartford County and driven by water power were used to turn the edges. These machines greatly expedited the manufacture of the ware and helped to reduce the price.

Methods of distributing and selling this output also improved and increased. Since road conditions before the Revolution made wagon travel difficult or impossible except along the main highways, for some time the Pattisons and their competitors continued to carry their wares on foot or on the back of a horse. The pots and pans were stacked in large tin trunks, each weighing about fifty pounds, and a peddler could carry two of these strapped on his back. Later these trunks were carried by horses. After the Revolution modes of travel improved, turnpikes were built, and Yankee peddlers loaded down with tinware and sundry other household items took to the road in wagons. Shubael Pattison, son of Edward, made trips to Canada where he traded tinware for furs. It is said that John Jacob Astor accompanied him on some of his trips.

Timothy Dwight (1752–1817), a grandson of the Puritan divine Jonathan Edwards, and long-time president of Yale College, has left us a vivid picture of the tin peddler and his operation. His *Travels in New England and New York,* published in four volumes in 1821, is a mine of information on colonial life. Here is his account: "The manner, in which this ware is disposed of, puts to light all calculation. A young man is furnished by the proprietor with a horse, and a cart covered with a box, containing as many tin vessels, as the horse can conveniently draw. This vehicle within a few years has, indeed, been frequently exchanged for a wagon; and then the load is doubled. Thus prepared, he sets out on an expedition for the winter. A multitude of these young men direct themselves to the Southern States; and in their excursions travel wherever they can find settlements. Each of them walks, and rides alternately, through this vast distance, till he reaches Richmond, Newbern, Charleston, or Savannah; and usually carries with him to the place of his destination no small part of the gain, which he has acquired upon the road."

Continuing his account in great detail, Dwight told of the unique arrangement which the tinsmiths developed to meet the demands of the growing market. Master tinners were sent to key towns where they produced items that were popular so that the peddler was always well stocked. After completing his circuit the peddler returned to New York where he sold both his wagon and his horse. Thence by boat to New Haven, and on to Berlin or one of the nearby towns. He was home again with his pockets bulging with money and a glowing report of his travels. It was not unusual for a peddler to travel twelve hundred to fifteen hundred miles on a single trip. Some went north to Canada, others inland to Kentucky. St. Louis and New Orleans were also among the outposts where they could be met. (To the Connecticut Yankee of those days, such distant points were outposts since much of the intervening country was wilderness or only sparsely settled.)

Before long, the peddler increased his stock, adding pins and needles, scissors and cobs, buttons and thimbles, ribbons and rock candy, children's books, "cotton stuffs made in New England . . ." and other aids to housekeeping. Some loaded their large commodious wagons with dry goods, hats, and shoes along with the tinware and small articles already mentioned. These loads represented an investment by the proprietor of from one to two thousand dollars, and were intended exclusively for southern and western trade. In addition to the tin and "notions," he was bubbling over with "learning," such as it was, for many were glib of tongue, philosophy, news, shrewdness, and a wonderful stock of Yankee yarns which he spun whenever and wherever the occasion permitted itself. Not all the peddlers were ne'er-do-wells, full of guile, even though some southerners regarded these damn Yankees "in the light of a visitation" calling them "commercial Scythians" and "Tartars of the North." Bronson Alcott, father of the famed Louisa, who hailed from Wolcott, Connecticut, was both a tin peddler and a visionary as well. Upon his return from a peddling trip to Virginia, he settled down in Concord, Massachusetts, to found a school of progressive education. Henry David Thoreau, on his trip to Cape Cod, was mistaken for a peddler because he knew how to fix clocks. It was often stated by those of a practical turn of mind that between 1800 and 1835 more young men born and bred in Maine graduated from the "tin carts" than from Bowdoin College. What was more to the point, however, was the fact that there were fewer failures in life among the tin peddlers than there were among the college graduates.

In later years the tin peddler traded his wares for linen rags, referred to as "paper rags," which were sold to paper factories. In its beginning days, the famous Crane Company of Pittsfield, Massachusetts, slanted its advertising along patriotic lines with an appeal to "patriotic" housewives to save "paper" rags for the peddlers thus helping to build a new American industry. Wood ashes for the potasheries were collected in a similar way and bartered for no-

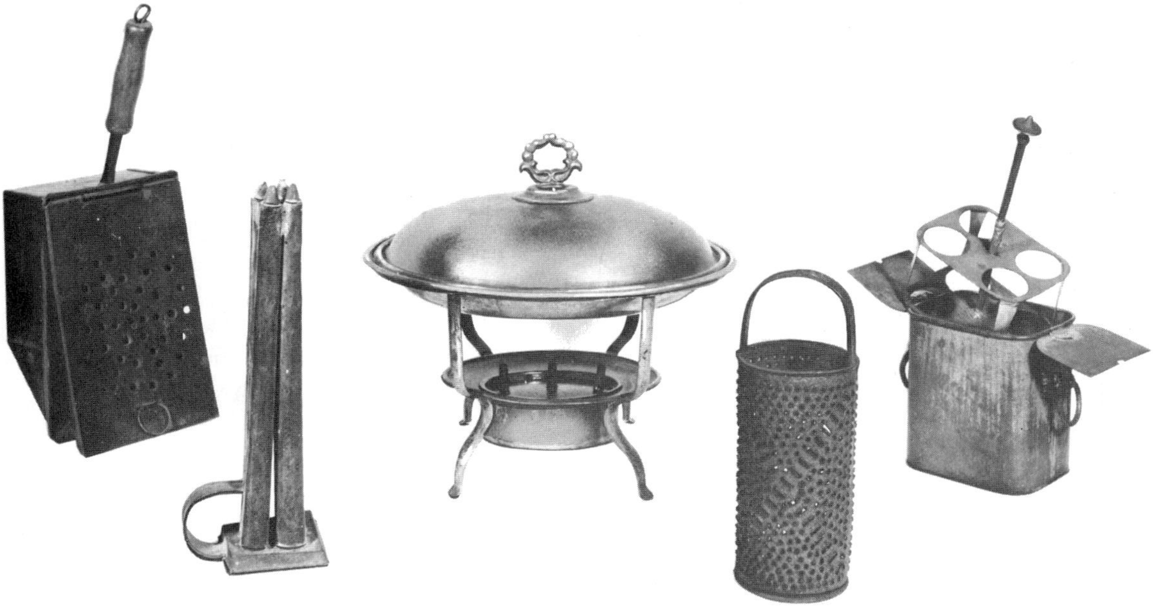

Tin was used to make many kinds of kitchen utensils. Left to right: a firepan to carry hot coals, a candlemold, a chafing dish, a grater and an egg cooker, one of the more uncommon kitchen utensils. *Photo Richard Merrill: courtesy Salem Maritime National Historic Site*

tions, ribbons, knickknacks, and cheap jewelry. The peddler was not only a traveling department store but a builder of industry as well.

Morals entered the picture in this business of peddling since, as Richardson Wright reminds us in *Hawkers and Walkers in Early America,* most of the customers of the tinware peddler lived in isolated areas and the peddler was obliged to take farm produce and articles of home manufacture in exchange for his cooking utensils. "On the face of it, this bartering and this double responsibility of the early tin peddler would seem like taking a big risk. The first tinware peddlers were not working for themselves; they were representatives of manufacturers in far-away Connecticut. Here were hundreds of young men trusted with a stock, trusted with a team, trusted with bartering, and depended upon to make honest reports and honest returns. In the light of their legendary reputation for dishonesty and slick dealing, this would seem almost like expecting the impossible of the peddlers, certainly a too artless confidence on the part of their employers, for the Connecticut Yankee has never enjoyed a reputation of having confidence in any one except himself. Doubtless there were fraudulent and absconding peddlers in these first days, but the greater part of their evil reputation lies not in their dealing with their employers but in their overreaching of uninformed customers. Later on both the tin peddler and the other sorts were 'staked' to a stock by the manufacturer or they bought it outright themselves."

Timothy Dwight, who knew his contempories intimately, feared for the evils "attendant upon the bartering of small wares" and "every other mode of traffic of the same general nature." "Many of these young men . . . start at an early period with both modesty, and principle. Their sobriety is exchanged for cunning; their honesty for imposition; and their decent behaviour for coarse impudence. . . . The only source of their pleasure, or their reputation, is gain: and that, however small, or however acquired, secures both. No course of life tends more rapidly, or more effectually to eradicate every moral feeling.

"Berlin has, I suspect, suffered not a little from this source. Were their manufactures sold, like other merchandise; the profits would undoubtedly be lessened: but the corruption of a considerable number of human beings would be prevented."

Farms and plantations were isolated. Sometimes they had to be reached by boat, but the peddler knew how to announce his arrival. He might use a horn or a conch shell to summon his customers. Often the rattling of the tin against the sides of the wagon was enough. He was always welcome for he brought news and stories and exciting new goods as well as the merchandise. Sometimes he shared a meal or a night's lodging and a welcome one too especially if he were a decent sort. Some were rogues, others tipplers, and a few of them were "downright onery" in their dealings. In any event they were sharp traders for the most part and a five hundred per cent profit was not unusual. Sometimes shoddy merchandise was offered but the stories about wooden nutmegs, sanded sugar, and clocks without works were often exaggerated.

The life of a peddler was a hard one. For nearly two centuries these stout-legged men trekked through the pathless forests of our wilderness to sell goods in the outposts of civilization. To be sure the market was a good one but the road was hard. It was at best a dog's life, knocking about afoot or on horseback, sloshing along rutty, muddy roads in winter or kicking up the dust in summer. Despite the farmer's dogs which snapped at them, the Indians who shot at them, the flies, mosquitoes, bedbugs and other pests which bit them they were a hardy lot. The more he sold the heavier his trunk became since he bartered for many of the items he offered. Honey, furs, grain, woodenware made on the farms and other items were exchanged for his tin, notions, calicoes, and a dozen other items which he carried. The peddler's life was full of adventure for it gave an opportunity to see what was on the other side of the mountain and how the pioneers were progressing. It took no experience, little cash for investment and afforded a good living, for profits were often amazing. The market was unlimited and in many cases they found new unexploited areas to set up their business. Actually, many of the leading merchants in cities far beyond New England's border began as peddlers.

Tin, plain and undecorated, is utilitarian all the way, yet there is distinct appeal to many of these pieces. Purely functional with no conscious attempt to be ornamental, even such utensils as the milk cans, the quart measures, the pudding molds, the spice boxes, and others, nonetheless convey a feeling of simplicity and beauty, of a thing well made. Even though made in quantity, these early pieces bear the mark of craftsmanship so unlike a tin can of the present day. Even the dents of age and the signs of wear on those early pieces that remain add interest. Ingenuity in producing needed items for easier housekeeping brought the "tin kitchen" or roasting oven. Cooky and gingerbread cutters, tin nursing bottles, berry and herb presses, footwarmers, and candlemolds were among the tinsmith's new products to ease the life of women in town and country.

In the early 1840's, a century after Edward Pattison had opened his tin shop in Berlin, Emma Hart Willard, noted poet, writer, and champion of higher education for women, wrote a poem entitled "Bride Stealing, A Tale of New England's Middle Age." Based on the courtship and marriage of her great-aunt Tabitha Norton who married Isaac Lee, a colonel in the Revolution, the poem recounted an unsuccessful attempt to abduct the bride on her wedding day. It was a common prank of the time for a group of lads and their girls to capture the bride after the ceremony and take her on a round of the taverns for the rest of the day, returning her home the following morning. Included in the verses were these lines recalling the success that attended Pattison's tinware when it was first made. Emma also was born in Berlin and the Pattison's tin shop was only a few houses down the road from the Hart farm.

> "Oh, what's that lordly dish so rare,
> That glitters forth in splendour's glare?
> Tell us, Miss Norton, is it silver?
> Is it from China or Brazil or . . .?"
> Thus alltogether on they ran.
> Quoth the good dame, "Tis a tin pan,
> The first made in the colony,
> The maker, Pattison's jest by,
> From Ireland in the last ship o'er.
> You all can buy. He'll soon make more!"

Those shiny tin dippers so proudly displayed by the peddlers mirrored a history that would dazzle the brightest and sharpest among them. The story of this metal can be traced back to the Gauls and the Romans; it was introduced to England at the time of the Roman occupation. The making of tin metal involved not only arduous labor on the part of the workers, but large numbers of them, and required enormous quantities of wood to make charcoal essential for steady heat. The Bohemians, who discovered deposits of tin in their own country (with the aid of a Cornish miner) as early as

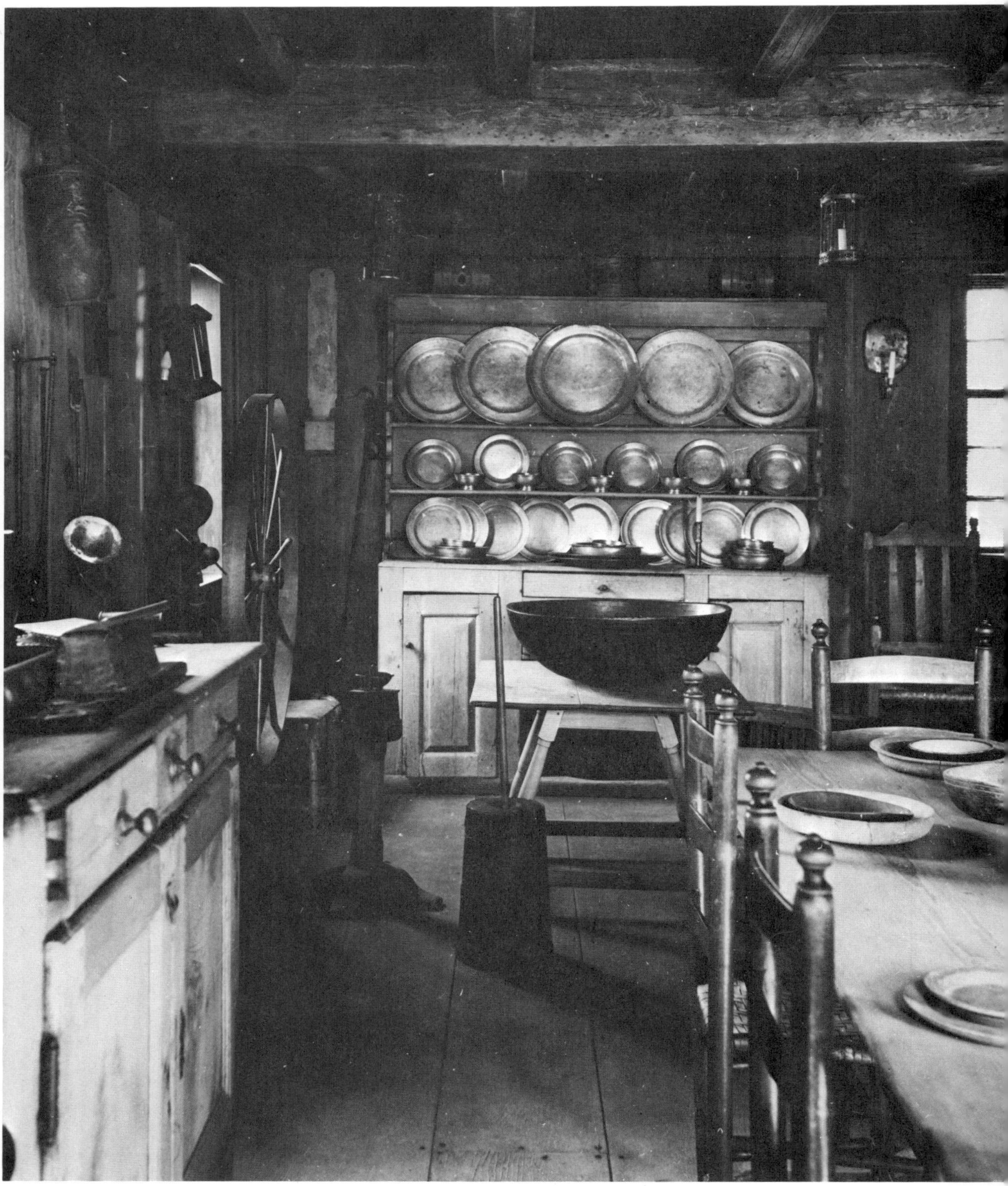

A "dress of pewter" shines in the sunlighted kitchen of the Wayside Inn in Sudbury. "Pewter bottles of Pyntes & qrts" arrived in 1629. Yet, Master Thomas Graves, "Engynere" and aid to Governor Endecott, wrote home listing "needfull things" which every Planter "doth or ought to provide" but he did not mention pewter. Not until the middle of the seventeenth century did pewter come into general household use, first as a salt—"a dish of honor." Three or four other pieces were used on more formal occasions by families of means. For, as George Francis Dow reminds us, "the wooden trencher, like the homespun coat, lingered in use for a century later." *Photo courtesy Samuel Chamberlain*

1240, found the secret to a speedier and more efficient process and this reached England in 1667. The development of plate tin or tin plate originated in the mountains of southeastern Germany sometime after 1530. Eventually, in 1620, the Duke of Saxony acquired knowledge of the process and built up a tremendous iron and tin-plating business. In Great Britain, it was at the Pontypool Mills of Major John Hanbury that tin plate was first produced on a commercial basis and there the industry was fully developed. It is believed that it is from this source rather than from other English industrial centers (where it was also produced in the first half of the eighteenth century) that the earliest tin plate used in America was obtained.

In 1749, shortly after the Pattisons launched their tin business, the English parliament passed a law prohibiting rolling and plate mills in the colonies. Tin plate was not manufactured here until after 1829, for it was then that Professor Hitchcock of Amherst College discovered tin at Goshen, Connecticut.

The tin shipped to America was not always of the best quality nor were sheets of double size (12 × 18 inches) usually sent in sufficient quantities. More than once the remark has been made that some of the shipments to America were comparable to the "end of the pot." Thus larger utensils including trays and other objects had to be pieced and soldered. Before wire was used for strengthening the turned edges of trays, they were more or less vulnerable, so that by frequent use they were easily damaged.

Pinprick or pierced tin afforded the tinker, as he was sometimes called, an opportunity to create a design with his tools, changing the appearance to give a raised perforated design which was decorative and practical as in the case of foot-warmers which held hot coals. Punched tin which gave the effect of an embossed surface was made with a blunt tool which did not make a hole but a raised or dented surface. This form of decoration is found on watertight containers of various kinds. The making of candlesticks, tin lamps, chandeliers, elaborately designed sconces and lanterns using a variety of techniques to improve the plain surface of the tin was another specialty in which design and decoration played a part. Tin had infinite uses for every conceivable kind of household utensil and for the construction trades as well, as in tin roofs. Some craftsmen used this material for weathervanes.

Britannia Ware

As the tin business in Connecticut expanded with shops opening in Meriden, Bristol, and Wallingford, a new composition metal was introduced. A Wallingford industrialist seeking to improve on tin developed a new alloy composed of tin, copper, and antimony (actually a top grade of pewter), which was called Britannia ware. At first it was cast in molds, but as the demand grew and to meet competition, it was made by spinning and stamping. Elaborate designs could be stamped easily in this soft metal to emulate the more costly silver. When the electroplating process was developed, the demand for Britannia ware ceased. It took a better polish than pewter and made the peddlers happy for they could go out on the road again with a new product and a new sales pitch.

Painted Tin

"That lordly dish so rare" was soon to look as if it had come from China for it was to lose its silver glitter and assume the rich red, orange, and yellow tones of Oriental art and later to be highlighted with gold. Young ladies in Boston and elsewhere under the instruction of John Waghorne and other teachers were captivated by a new art which had already absorbed the English and French gentry. In the years immediately following the Revolution, Paul Revere imported a sizeable collection of Roman tea trays and waiters from Bristol, England. The term Roman, used in this manner, referred to decorating in the Pompeiian style like on the walls of houses in that ancient city. Revere's shipment was to be followed by many more before the art of japanning or "flowering" was to be practiced in a popular way in New England, but the fashion for the new art had been set and it was to become more than a fad.

Essentially, japanning referred to the process of applying and kiln-drying the glossy tar-based varnish which gave tin its durable, waterproof surface. "Flowering" referred to the art of decorating the prepared surface with

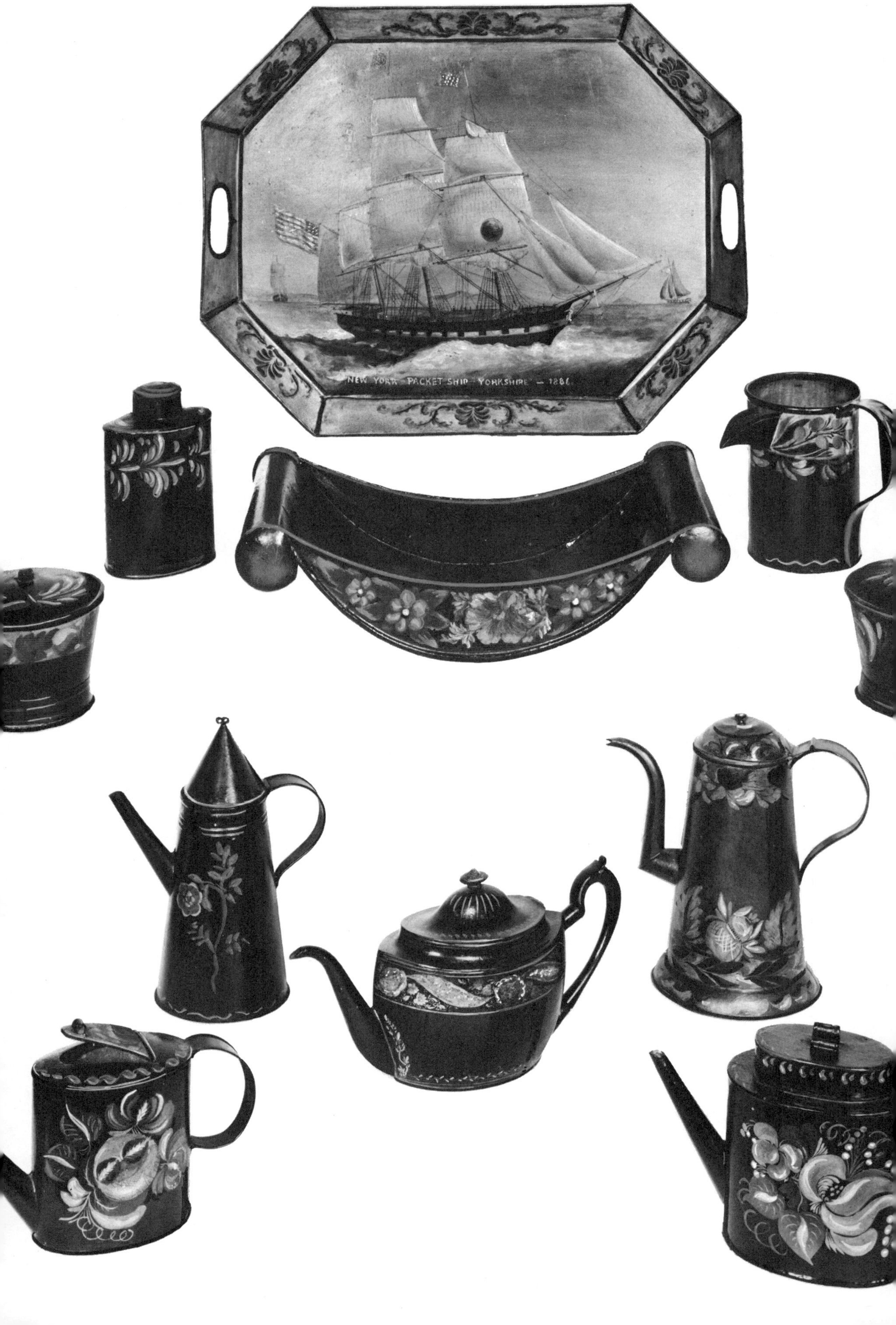
NEW YORK PACKET SHIP 'YORKSHIRE'

various kinds of motifs of which flowers were notably popular. Often these were highly stylized, but nevertheless identifiable and distinctly ornamental. They greatly enhanced the appearance of the trays, and other pieces on which they were used. Fruits, birds, Oriental scenes including landscapes, and geometric patterns were also fashionable. The French called it toleware, a name that still remains in common use to describe all kinds of painted tin.

Plain or unpainted tin is bright and shiny when new and is kept that way only by constant scouring. It rusts quickly if neglected and becomes dull and stained with use. In the eighteenth and nineteenth centuries, tin was used for so many essential items from pin boxes to bath tubs that all New England would have been hard put, so to speak, if it was not for the tinsmiths. With the introduction of japanning or "flowering" in the early 1800's the "poor man's silver" took on a new wrinkle. Painted or decorated tinware became a country folk art as women all over New England learned this new "art and mystery" which had come from Japan by way of Wales and England. Handsomely decorated trays, boxes, coffee urns, cheese coasters, and other items shipped from London began to appear in Salem, Boston, Portsmouth, New York, Philadelphia, and other seaports. The coloring was rich, the designs both floral and scenic were appealing and the gold edging (not used on country tin) added a touch of elegance to these pieces. Color such as had previously never been seen except in expensive tapestries and rugs was introduced as painting on tin. But it required skill. One did not merely trace patterns or create free style designs on black painted surfaces.

In the small community of Pontypool in Monmouthshire and somewhat later at Usk, Edward Allgood, a maker of tin plate, had been carrying on experiments to prevent the rusting of iron. He found that tin treated with a varnish made of asphaltam (a form of pitch), umber pigment, and raw linseed oil, applied in several coats, each being kiln-dried before the other was applied, produced a lusterous hard finish. This treatment resulted in a protective surface and, by adding other components, the color could be changed from black to tortoise shell or deep crimson. Applied lightly over silver foil or wire, the latter acquired the appearance of goldwork. The finished product was an excellent imitation of Japanese lacquer.

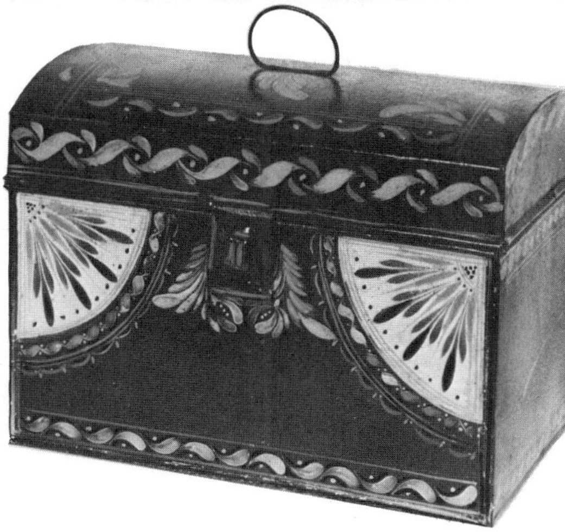

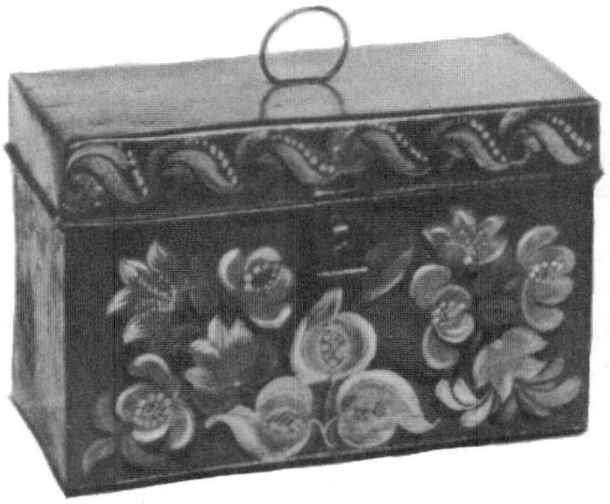

The decorated box above has been traced to Zachariah Stevens; that below shows exceptionally fine brush work. Hagar Collection. *Photo Richard Merrill: courtesy Salem Maritime National Historic Site*

(*Opposite page*) Coffin tray, at top, shows New York packet ship *Yorkshire*, 1836. Both the seascape and the decoration were done by a skilled painter. The cheese coaster is probably of English origin, but the other four pieces are typical examples of New England decorated tin. Below are a collection of tea and coffee pots showing variety in design and decoration. The pot in the center, an exceptional example of graceful form seldom found in tinware, was made in Usk; the others belong to the New England tradition of craftsmanship and decoration. Hagar Collection. *Photo Richard Merrill: courtesy Salem Maritime National Historic Site*

W. D. John in describing the wares made at Pontypool has pointed out, "They were of really excellent quality and craftsmanship, solidly made, with an exceptionally high gloss and pleasantly decorated with painted flower groups, strawberries, fruit and birds, and with quaint groups of Chinese figures carrying parasols. Enormous numbers of black and tortoiseshell round trays were made, especially at Pontypool, and these are often characterized by a pierced or turned-up rim with parallel rows of punched-out lozenge-shaped holes; some of the later large trays of oval or octagonal shapes were painted over with landscapes or historical scenes." He adds, "The japanning varnish could be applied effectively over every type of metal, including silver, Sheffield plate, brass, copper and bronze; but it is most usually found on the locally produced rolled black iron plates for the flat shapes, and on the lighter, more flexible tin plate for the moulded curved designs.

"The Monmouthshire japanned wares from their first appearance were always esteemed both for their utility and for their decorative qualities and were sold at hardware shops throughout the country and exported to the Continent and the United States. In 1764–65 Henry Johns advertised in the *Bristol Journal* that at his warehouse in St. Thomas Street he was offering Pontypool wares in the form of snuff boxes, japanned waiters, bread baskets, tea caddies, tea kettles, lamps, coffee pots, dressing boxes, weight boxes, sugar tongs, cake baskets, cheese holders, candlesticks, toastracks, pepper pots, snuffers, chestnut urns, tureens, knife boxes, Dutch ovens, etc., etc."

Sign and coach painters, and cabinet painters as well, in New England, New York, New Jersey, and Pennsylvania were beginning to decorate furniture. The vogue began before the Revolution as Nina Fletcher Little reminds us in *American Decorative Wall Paintings:* "New England was the stronghold of the japanner whose advertisements appear in the Boston papers from the early years of the eighteenth century. This branch of the decorating business was carried on by a number of men who combined with it the usual occupations of house, ship, and carriage painting. It was even considered a genteel and desirable accomplishment for young ladies of the period, as witness the following announcement made by John Waghorne in the *Boston Gazette* for May 19/26, 1740: 'Whereas John Waghorne, has lately Receiv'd a fresh parcel of materials for the new Method of Japaning, which was Invented in France, for the Amusement and Benefit of the Ladies, and is now practised by most of the Quality and Gentry in Great-Britain, with the greatest Satisfaction . . . he disigns a School at Five Pounds for each Scholar.' Many kinds of japanned furniture were made during the mid eighteenth century, including highboys, lowboys, clock cases, picture frames, mirrors, and corner cupboards." The amusement of the ladies was expressed by a young Scottish woman who wrote to her sister; "Everybody is mad about Japan work, I hope to be a dab at it by the time I see you."

In 1798, Zachariah Brackett Stevens, son of a tavernkeeper, opened a tin shop in Stevens Plains, now known as Westbrook, Maine (four miles from Portland), and continued it for more than forty years. Stevens is believed to have derived some of his inspiration from Paul Re-

Chippendale tray with elaborate decoration; Revere tray so-called because this type was imported by Paul Revere. *Photo Richard Merrill: courtesy Salem Maritime National Historic Site*

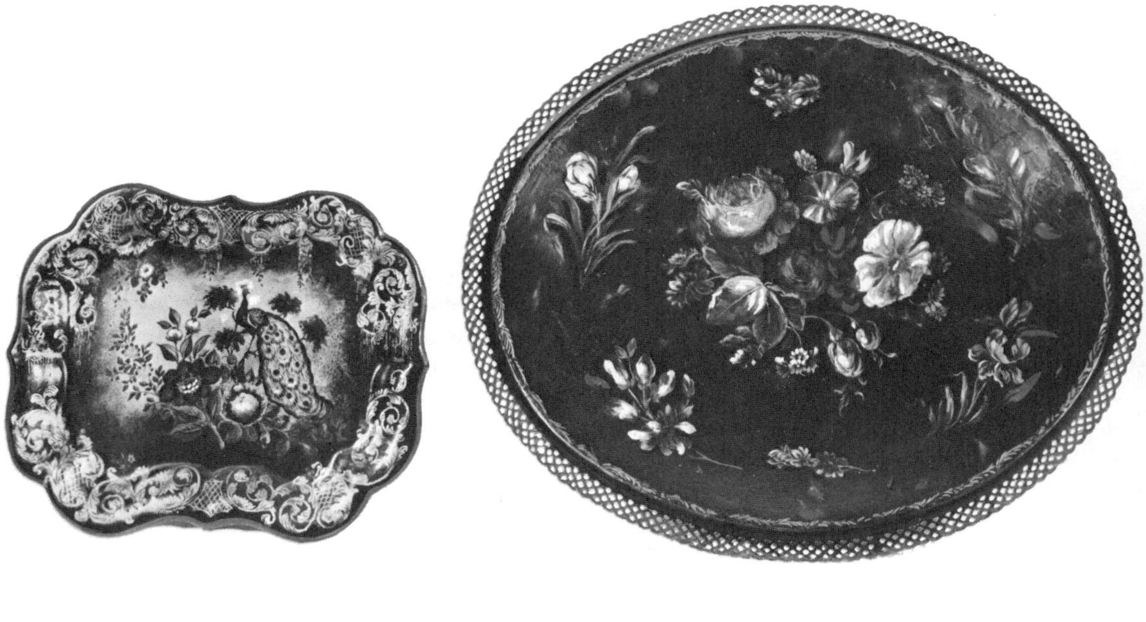

vere since family tradition holds that as a young man he lived in Cambridge for several years and knew the master craftsman. Yet another link stems from the fact that Revere's nephew, Philip Rose (who decorated tin and had a shop in Boston), visited in Stevens Plains in 1791 or shortly thereafter and made some ornamental drawings for the Brackett family. Esther Stevens Brazer maintained that Rose used a decorative device in the form of a curved line on these drawings which she had never seen anywhere except on painted trays. It was used by the decorators in Maine. Rose's sister Sarah married Thomas Briscoe, an Englishman who had learned the tin trade in the mother country; they came to Maine in 1803. "Oll Briscoe" as he was affectionately known to other peddlers and the neighbors was the first tin peddler in the area.

To meet the growing demand for decorated tin, Briscoe's wife and at least three of her five orphaned nieces, the Francis girls (whom the Briscoes adopted), became decorators. They flowered and bordered trays, tea canisters, boxes, and dozens of other items including tea-and coffeepots. Patterns were "set" for these girls to copy as they "painted for the trade." Oliver Buckley and his wife Mary Ann had come to Maine from Connecticut and he, too, not only nade tin but decorated it. Farm women also were employed to make the pieces pretty and "fancy," for such it was called. This new "art" proved to be a welcome change from needlework, and since the peddlers came frequently to pick up orders, there was always a chance to chat. Stevens Plains became a lively place and with a hundred peddlers moving in and out frequently, new trends in styles and changing tastes in decoration were noted. This community also became a center for making horncombs which were sold throughout the East. Pewter or block tin, as they called it, was another craft of the area. At this time, New England and the rest of the country as well were alive with energy for doing things. Interest in various forms of folk art was evident on every side. Women could do this kind of painting in the few leisure hours they had each day. Decorating useful objects was enjoyable and provided a new source of color for every room in the house. This was no backwoods enterprise.

It is significant that Stevens's great-great-granddaughter, Esther Stevens Brazer, published in 1940 *Early American Decoration,* which is considered the outstanding book in the field since it deals with all the early techniques relating to wall, floor, and furniture decoration as well as that of tinware. None of the Maine craftsmen signed their work so that Mrs. Brazer, in classifying the early painted tinware made in

White flowers with red details stand out in bold relief against the gold-leaf foliage of the French piece at the left. The mantel garniture in the center is of Welsh origin. Monteiths (filled with cold water to keep wine glasses cool) made of tin are rare; more often they were made of silver or porcelain. The piece shown is of English origin. Hagar collection. *Photo Richard Merrill: courtesy Salem Maritime National Historic Site*

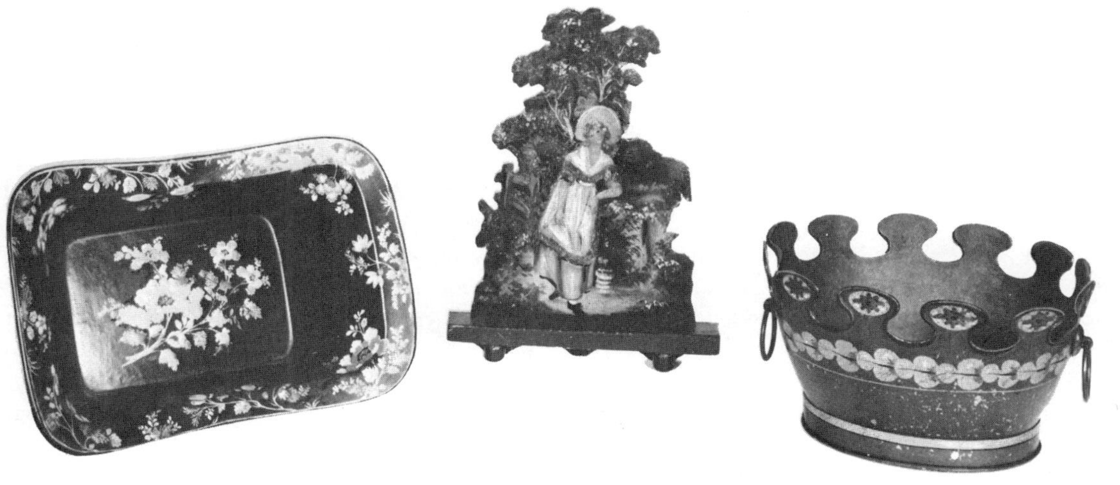

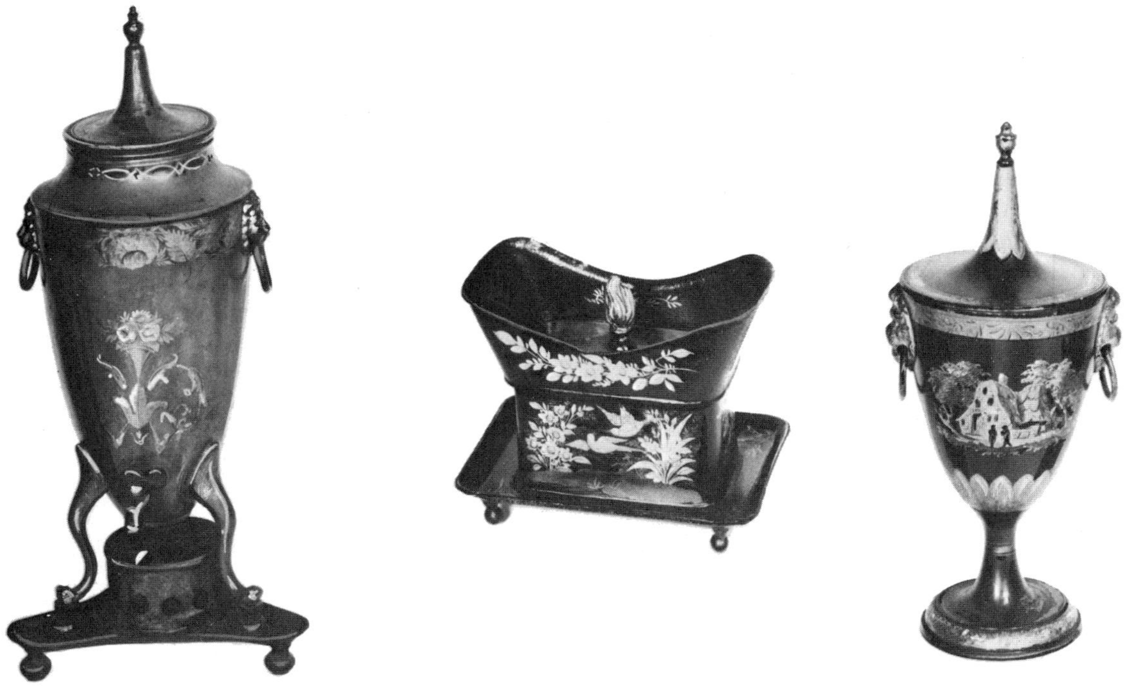

Examples of highly skilled craftsmanship in tin (*left to right*): a tea or coffee urn, an ornate box of unusual design, a chestnut urn. All are believed to be of European origin. Yet tinsmiths trained in England who migrated to America made a number of unusual items for special orders. Hagar collection. *Photo Richard Merrill: courtesy Salem Maritime National Historic Site*

Maine, evolved theories of her own for her decisions by first inspecting collections owned by the families involved with the business. She was convinced that Zachariah's work or that which he directed was done in floral designs "simply painted in the country-tinsmith manner." The elder Stevens introduced "a single and double cherry motif, in combination with flowers." Much of "Uncle Zach's" work was rendered on a cream-colored or mustard-yellow background. In 1832 he was succeeded by his sons, Samuel and Alfred, and their work is not considered the equal of the decorated ware produced under their father's production. Pieces with conventional and geometric patterns she called the "Connecticut" fashion since they were done by men who had learned their trade in Berlin and elsewhere in the Nutmeg State before coming to Stevens Plains. Among the later arrivals was Walter B. Goodrich who arrived at Stevens Plains in 1824 having spent five years of apprenticeship at Berlin. James A. Thompson, Thomas Deshon, and others were active in the enterprise.

A letter written to the Portland, Maine, *Argus* in 1888 by an old-time peddler named Will contained these reminiscences. "Paint the cart red, fill up with tinware and 'trinkets,' hitch 'Dobbin' in his place, mount the cart, boy and be off on trading ground for a few weeks! Soon the horse and man returned drawing the cart under a load of 'truck' as large as a load of hay . . . paper rags, wool, wool skins, slats (sheep skins with the wool off), hog's bristles, old copper, brass and block tin, pewter, and all sorts of peltry, etc., etc., generally worth double what they started off with."

He remarked most of the peddlers were green young men from the farms who wanted to see the world and earn enough money to buy some land. Peddlers cruised along the Maine coast in vessels known as "Old Junkmen" visiting islands to sell tin and all the other items which they carried; some of the boats used were built especially for this purpose.

In addition to japanners in Berlin and elsewhere in Connecticut, the work of Oliver Filley of Bloomfield became widely known. He later moved to New Jersey. Filley's relatives traveled far and wide making and selling their painted tin. This shop became noted for its skilled decorators. The surest way for one industry to grow in the days before railroads was to set up branches wherever there was a demand for a particular kind of goods. The names Francis, Hubbard, Mygatt, and North were on Filley's list of decorators who hailed from his native state.

Reuben Butler left Connecticut in 1799 for East Greenville, New York. His business continued to thrive until 1859. Margaret Mattison Coffin writing in *Woman's Day* has recorded some interesting notes on this family. Of Butler's tin shop and family she wrote: "The small building used as a decorating shop has been dismantled recently. A mortar still stained with vermilion paint was found along with rusted bread trays and a ledger. At least two of his daughters, Ann and Minerva, worked in the painting shop. Since six of the eleven Butler children were girls, probably others painted. Minerva, who married a peddler, John Miller, kept an autograph album. This is filled with verses ornamented with painted designs nearly duplicating those found on tinware.

"A verse suggests:

"Remember me is all I ask,
And, if remembered be a task,
Forget me."

As painted tin became increasingly popular, English tinsmiths, like the Staffordshire potters, began to use brighter colors for the wares which they shipped to America. This action was prompted by the strong competition from local craftsmen who became skilled in lacquering and improved methods of manufacture. In the middle of the nineteenth century, a group of British manufacturers, noting the change from individual to mass production, visiting here, declared: "The class of tools commonly used by tinmen are almost obsolete in New England States. In a well-furnished tinman's shop there are about twelve different kinds of machines employed."

Many of the pieces imported from Britain and those probably shipped from France were executed in a more highly stylized, academic manner than was most of the country tin decorated in America. The latter was ornamented with flowers and other set patterns, further embellished by simple or fancy borders, but it was utterly lacking in the Oriental motifs (chinoiserie) scenic effects and similar compositions which reflected the cultivated taste of an era when romanticism flourished, bespeaking the idyllic and the glorified ideal of the natural landscape. This point is made because one sees in museums and private collections such items as chestnut urns, cheese coasters, coffee urns, toast racks, tea caddies, monteiths, fancy boxes with ball-like bases, and other curious examples which by their craftsmanship and decoration are definitely earmarked as imported. That is not to say that American tinsmiths did not make similar pieces, but the distinction between the two is readily apparent.

Trays in a variety of shapes and sizes are among the most practical and widely used of all decorated tin. There were kinds for bread, biscuits, and apples and those that held cheeses were called cheese coasters. Among those used for serving were tea trays and the larger sizes referred to as waiters after the English manner. The treatment of the edges added greatly to their appearance, as lace, piecrust, and rolled edges. An octagonal form was called a "coffin" tray for in appearance it resembled the form of the coffin of an earlier day. Kidney-shaped kinds were uncommon and the oval types took their form from the trays used by typesetters in print shops. The unusually decorative round trays with lace edges of French origin were often called "Paul Revere" trays. Not all the trays or the other types of tinware had black or dark backgrounds. Other colors were used as well including white, yellow, and red. Decorating was by no means limited to freehand or traced designs. Stenciling was also used. The paint was applied with a "pouncer" (made of cotton or sheep's wool, covered with chamois or velvet) through the cutouts of the stencil.

New York state was a favorite area for selling decorated tin and so, too, was Vermont. Peddlers even carried the ware into Canada. Pennsylvania tin, easily recognized because its bright colors are Pennsylvania Dutch designs, was influenced by Connecticut japanners. Miniature pieces made for children have great charm and are widely sought by collectors.

Today, painted tin has become a favorite field for those in quest of things old and quaint. Practically every piece can serve some useful purpose in the twentieth-century household. Furthermore, many pieces have been reproduced and find a ready sale. The art of decorating trays and other items continues unabated.

Rugs and Comfort

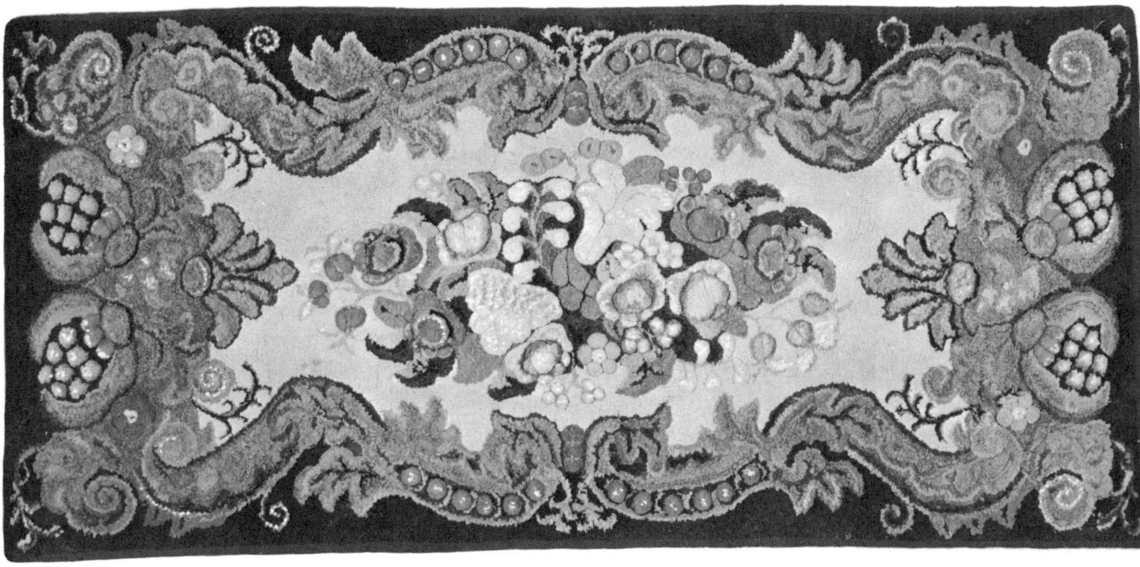

Early example of hooked rug. *Photo courtesy of Shelburne Museum*

While rugs and carpets for floor covering were not the least important articles needed for comfort in the seventeenth-century home, they were relegated to the background until material and time were available for making them. Yet, in 1634, John Winthrop, Jr., obtained from England "mingle coulrd checkered rugs, partly tawny, but the most are wholly red." Ten years later, Miles Standish inventoried the estate of Stephen Hopkins and listed both yellow and green rugs. Blue and white were other rug colors listed in Massachusetts inventories during the first forty years of the colony. Surely, there were plenty of rugs for those cold floors, but the rugs were actually bedcovers. The word *rug* is believed to be of Scandinavian origin meaning a coarse coverlet. In sixteenth-century England the term also referred to "a rough woolen material, a sort of coarse frieze" which was used for cloaks in winter. The colonists wore them, which gives new meaning to rugs being imported by the yard at an early date. The *Oxford English Dictionary* reminds us that "snug as a bug in a rug" goes back to the eighteenth century when a rug was a bedcover.

In an issue of *Antiques Magazine,* Marion D. Iverson gives us a vivid picture in *"The Bed Rug in Colonial America."* In March, 1630, while John Winthrop waited aboard the *Arbella* for favorable winds to begin his voyage to the New World, he wrote a farewell letter to his wife, who had remained at Groton in Suffolk. He assured her that their two young sons slept "as soundly in a rugge (for we use no sheets) as ever they did at Groton, and so I doe myself (I prayse God)." In September, even before he had experienced his first New England winter, Governor Winthrop wrote his son John to bring "a store of Coarse rugges, bothe to use and sell" when he came to America. When John Davis of Lynn, Massachusetts, made his will in 1661, he mentioned three "home made ruggs." The Yorkshire clothmakers who settled in Rowley in 1638 made ruggs of "cotton wool and also Sheeps Wooll." The Puritans kept warm under rugs.

The most primitive dwellings had only earthen floors which were cold and damp. But once stamped with the treading of many feet, they made a smooth hard surface on which were scattered dried leaves such as cattail rushes, bracken (the royal fern), and sweet fern. The materials were cut and dried before strewing and helped considerably to insulate against the dankness of the soil, as well as to keep down dust which "doth putyfy the ayre." They had to be replaced constantly since they were quickly ground to a fine powder under foot. When fragrant herbs were added, the effect was pleasant and the pungent leaves and stems helped to keep down "evil odours" and "humours."

Floors made of wide pine boards, with sand scattered over those on the ground level are referred to in early records. Oak, birch, and other woods were also used at a later date, but pine being plentiful, was commonplace. Undoubtedly animal skins were used in the keeping room and in the sleeping rooms on the second floor at an early date. Calf and deerskins (when they could be spared) made warm soft surfaces on which to walk, but these were subjected to hard wear and, at a later date, were replaced by hooked rugs, woven carpets, and braided rugs.

When tradesmen began to advertise in newspapers and almanacs, we find records of imported rugs which were offered at public sale from estates. Mention of rugs in wills and inventories is another source of information. George Francis Dow combed the pages of five New England newspapers dating from 1704 to 1775 and recorded his findings in *The Arts and Crafts in New England 1704–1775.* From this storehouse we learn that "a very large Turkey Carpet measuring Eleven and an half by Eighteen and an half Feet" was to be sold from the house of the late Mr. Ebenezer Holmes in King Street, Boston, on March 26, 1754. The following year three dollars reward was offered to anyone who could locate "a Turkey Carpet of various Colours. . . . fringed on each end" that was stolen out of a Boston house. In 1761 William Greenleaf imported from London and Bristol rich Persian carpets and stair carpetings. Another Boston merchant offered carpets consigned from Quebec. At this time, "matts for floors," handsome straw carpets, as well as Scotch and English carpets and rugs were listed. Frequent references are made to turkey-work during the seventeenth century. Even the most knowledgeable of modern needleworkers would not wish to make a piece of turkey-work, for its demands upon one's skill, time, and eyesight seem excessive for the result created. Turkey-work was popular in early Colonial days. Many, even in England, could not afford the Oriental rug. The idea for the style and name came to America

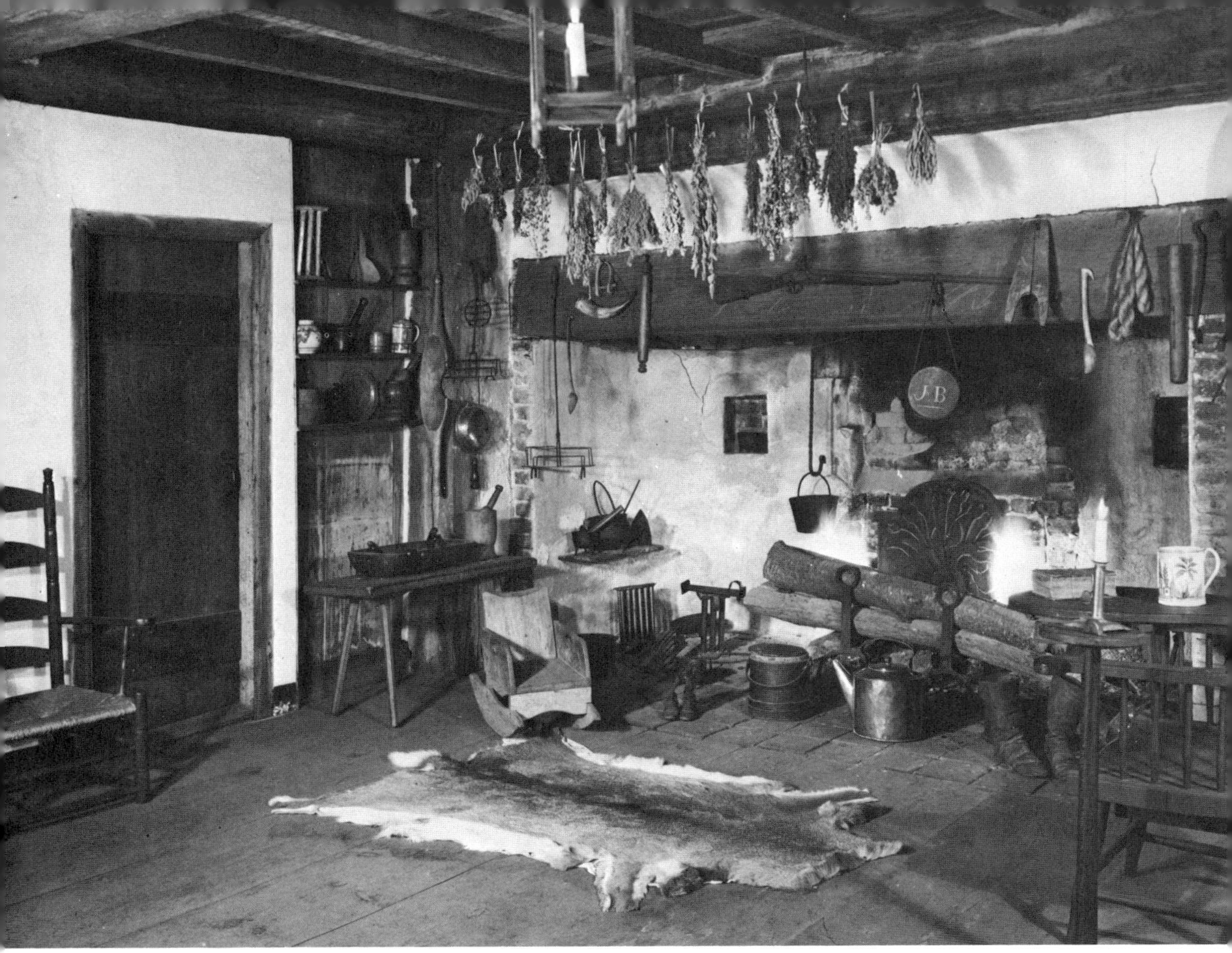

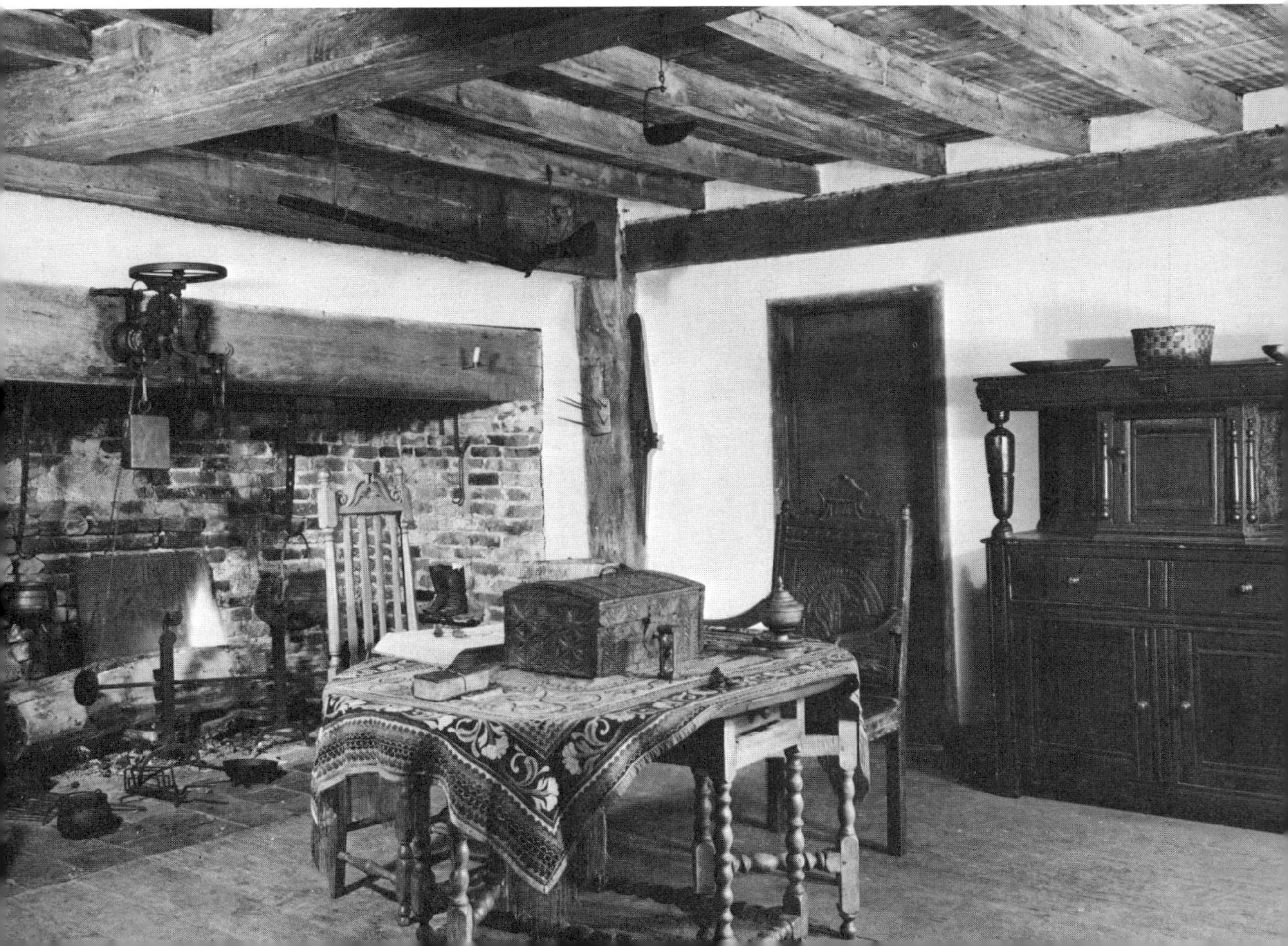

by way of England in rugs from the East that were imported to England during the seventeenth century. These Orientals were a source of inspiration for the designs used.

The colonists wishing to emulate the patterns woven in the Eastern rugs substituted a cloth foundation, upon which a needle was threaded with yarns of varying colors. Then the threads were pulled through, tied into a knot, and either cut or left uncut to achieve a pile or raised surface. Sometimes, they were able to create brocaded or damask effects by running the stitches parallel with the threads of the background material in contrast to other stitches made at right angles.

Examples of turkey-work existed in the colonies as early as 1760, according to lists of household effects dated that year. It was an effective and efficient covering and was used by many housekeepers in the earlier days of colonial decoration for chairs, tablecovers, and bedcovers. The latter sometimes were made to serve as rugs. One such example may be seen in the museum at York, Maine. This example of turkey-work was originally made for a bedspread, but in its current role it is a rug, though one must *not* walk on it. A fine example of turkey-work is to be seen at the Essex Institute in Salem, Massachusetts. This piece with its conventionalized geometric forms closely follows the design found in Oriental rugs.

In the 1750's the new country citizen began to paint his floor boards. In the March 17, 1768, *Boston News-Letter* we read: "George Killcup, jun. Informs the Gentlemen and Ladies in Town and Country That he Paints Carpets and other Articles, and Papers Rooms in the neatest manner." Another advertisement in the *Boston Gazette,* January 22, 1759: "Carpets Just imported from London, in the last ships and to be sold at Mr. Blanchard's in New Boston West End; a large assortment of fine Carpets for Rooms, very Cheap for ready Cash."

(*Top*) Deerskin rugs (also rush mats made by the Indians) were the earliest type of floor coverings used by the colonists. Kitchen of the ironmaster's house, Saugus Iron Works, Saugus, Massachusetts. *Photo Richard Merrill: courtesy Saugus Ironworks Restoration*

(*Bottom*) A Persian rug used as a cover on a gateleg table in the great room of the ironmaster's home at Saugus Iron Works Restoration, Saugus, Massachusetts. Court cupboards (similar to the one at the right) made of oak were often found in the homes of prosperous colonists in the mid-seventeenth century. *Photo Richard Merrill: courtesy Saugus Ironworks Restoration*

No mention is made at this time of hooked or braided rugs since these were made for home use and were not identified specifically in lists, although they may have been simply referred to as rugs or carpets or mats in the inventories. As Ella Shannon Bowles reminds us in *Handmade Rugs,* "The earliest history of the making of hooked rugs is wrapped in mystery . . . buried so deeply beneath unsubstantial tradition and romantic legend as almost to defy efforts to unearth reliable fragments of it."

However, by this period the women in New England and throughout the colonies had collected enough rags from their left over woolens and other materials to be making their own rugs, either by hooking or braiding them. In *A Primer of American Antiques,* Carl W. Drepperd expressed the belief that hooked rugs were brought to America in the seventeenth century by the Scandinavians—the Swedes, the Finns, the Danes, and the Norweigians—and that they were adopted almost at once by both the French and British settlers. He contended: "The hooked rug appears to have been contemporaneous with nearly all seventeenth-century furniture. Only the rugs were used as mats for tables and covers for beds, chairs, settles, etc. These rugs are quite long-lasting; in fact they might readily last a century or more as bedcovers and tablecloths. As floor rugs, however, they disintegrate faster than loomed stuffs. By 1700 almost every housewife in the northern colonies knew how to hook a rug, and did it."

Ralph W. Burnham, noted antiquarian of Ipswich, Massachusetts, used to tell the story of an old lady in his town, who related that when she was a little girl, "Mother always kept the hooked rugs bottom side upwards. When company was expected, mother would sit at the front window, watching for them, and as soon as they hove in sight, she would say 'Sally, turn the rugs, while I mind the door.' "

Stella Hay Rex, noted hooked-rug authority, claims that the hooked-rug craft flourished in the early years of the New World mostly in the New England area and the Maritime Provinces of Canada. This was partly because of the thrift of the folk of preponderantly English-Scottish ancestry, and also because the long, cold, icy winter demanded warmth for the floors. Rug-hooking, too, being a pastime of seafaring men, it was natural that it should be practiced in the seacoast settlements.

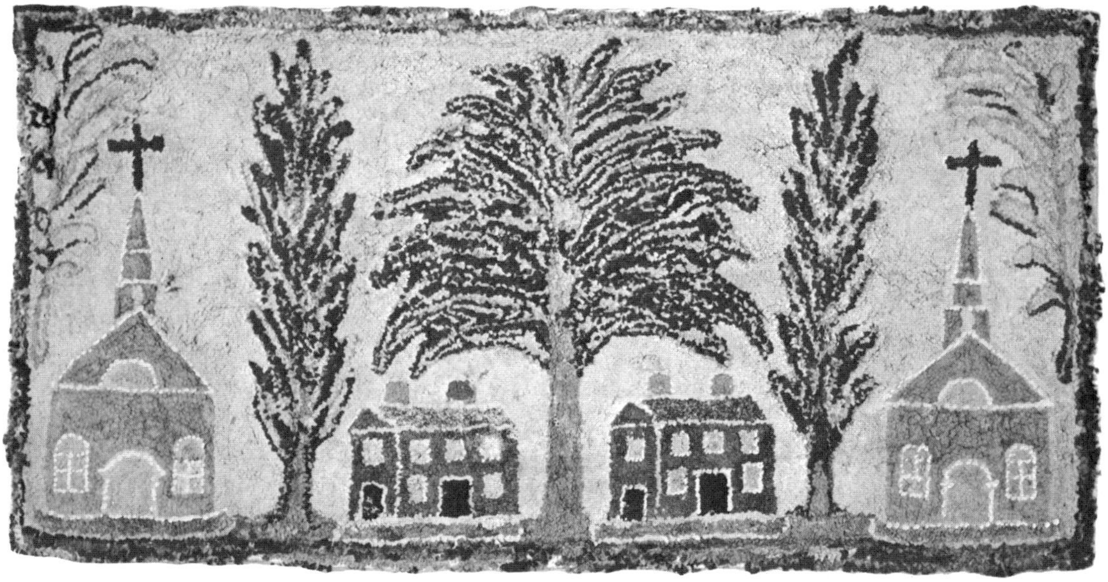

An early hooked rug on homespun foundation. The brick houses are patterned after similar designs found on eighteenth-century samplers. A sturdy pine tree forms the central motif. *Photo Frank Kelly: courtesy Currier Art Gallery*

The rug frame gave the early housewife an opportunity to relax at a productive occupation that was not a chore. From her rough hands grew a product embodying so much of native art that the examples which have survived the years are most highly treasured by private collectors and museums.

One cannot help but be impressed by the work of the early hooked-rug craftsmen. Untutored as they were, such specimens of this handiwork as are now extant show considerable natural artistic ability and vitality of individual expression. They did not go into elaborate detail and shadings; rather they favored a simplification of form that gave their primitives much vigor.

The earliest rugs had few colors; by their very restraint they have a primitive appeal lacking in the multicolored examples of a generation later. The early rughookers looked to their quilts and their embroidered pieces for the designs they chose for their hooked rugs. Canton ware, Bristol china, carvings on furniture also supplied motifs for them to copy. Except for the American eagle, it is unusual to see an old New England (or, for that matter a

A runner made in New Hampshire in the early nineteenth century by Elizabeth Spark, whose father was a noted figure in the Revolution. *Photo Frank Kelly: courtesy Currier Art Gallery*

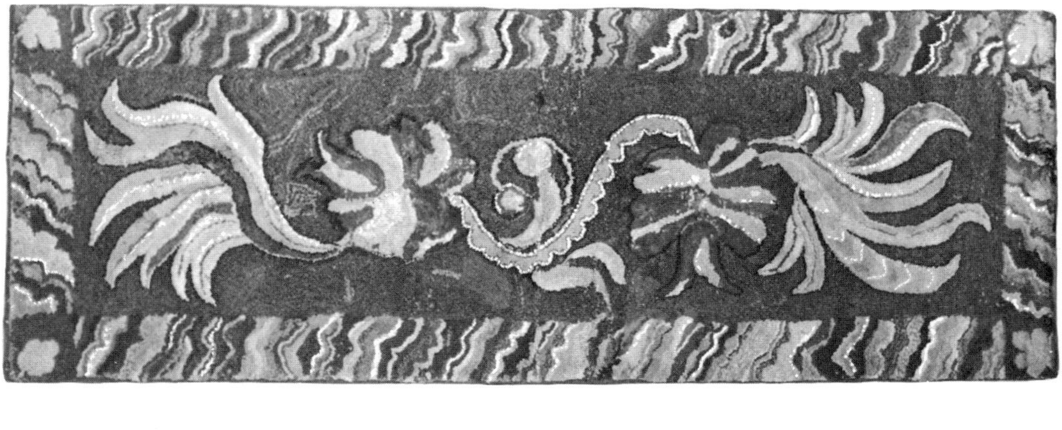

current New England) hooked rug with a bird or fowl for a subject. There are plenty of landscapes, dogs, sheep, cats, lions, seascapes, and boats. Half-rugs or door rugs were made in great quantities in the 1870's. Kate Douglas Wiggin described her feeling for one of these "Welcome Mats" in *More Chronicles of Rebecca.* "Rebecca could see the Cames' brown farm house from Mrs. Baxter's sitting-room window. The little-traveled road with strips of tufted green between the wheel tracks curled dustily up to the very doorstep, and inside the screen door of pink mosquito netting was a wonderful drawn-in rug, shaped like a half pie, with 'Welcome' in saffron letters on a green ground."

Of great historical significance to New Hampshire is a rug made in 1840 by Miss Elizabeth Stark, a descendant of General John Stark of Revolutionary fame. Hooked in the earlier part of the nineteenth century, this runner is done in homespun rags on a hand-woven linen foundation. Two large, abstract florals, resembling fuchsias, are in opposite positions on either side of the central bud. The background is a mottled blue, with white flecks. Flowers, of rich red and neutralized yellow, give life to the design. Each corner has a blue-green leaf growing from the outside to a center panel, and the background of this corner block is the same speckled mixture as the center. Leaves are done in green and blue-green, much softened by time. Unusual in the treatment of these corner leaves is an outline of complimentary red, inside a row of dull brown. The red, yellow, brown, and blue of the pattern are carried into the rug borders. Two pieces of homespun linen sewed together formed the foundation of this runner which measures 110½ inches long by 37¾ inches wide.

People have always had an interest in hooked rugs and one man who capitalized on this interest was E. S. Frost of Biddeford, Maine. He was an old tin peddler, quick to notice the hooking of rugs that occupied his buyers' time. He noted, too, that they longed to have something "new and different," so with true Yankee ingenuity he designed and sold his rug bottoms from 1868 to 1876. He made his own zinc stencils for stamping and these are still being used to make patterns for hooked rugs! His flower, scroll, and animal rugs are recognizable to anyone familiar with rug design. Collectors prefer original work in hooked rugs—but a true collectors' item is one of Frost's yet unhooked, old patterns, identifiable by the stamping ". E. Frost & Co., Biddeford, Maine."

Universally recognized as the rarest of all early handmade carpets that have survived, is the embroidered rug. The most notable example hangs in the American Wing of the Metropolitan Museum of Art in New York City. Made in 1835 in Castleton, Vermont, by Zeruah Higly Guernsey, it became known as the "Caswell Carpet." (She became Mrs. Caswell in 1846.) It was often called the "Blue Cat" rug, for Catherine Cate Coblentz made it the fascinating subject for her book *The Blue Cat of Castle Town.* Certainly this blue-colored cat had *ten* lives, for its story will live forever, caught up as it is in threads of needlecraft.

The Caswell Carpet is made of individual squares and rectangles embroidered on firm homespun with a type of chain stitch known as "double Kensington stitch." Tambour-work (that is any embroidery done stretched on

Oval hooked rug, commemorating the centennial of the United States. *Courtesy Shelburne Museum*

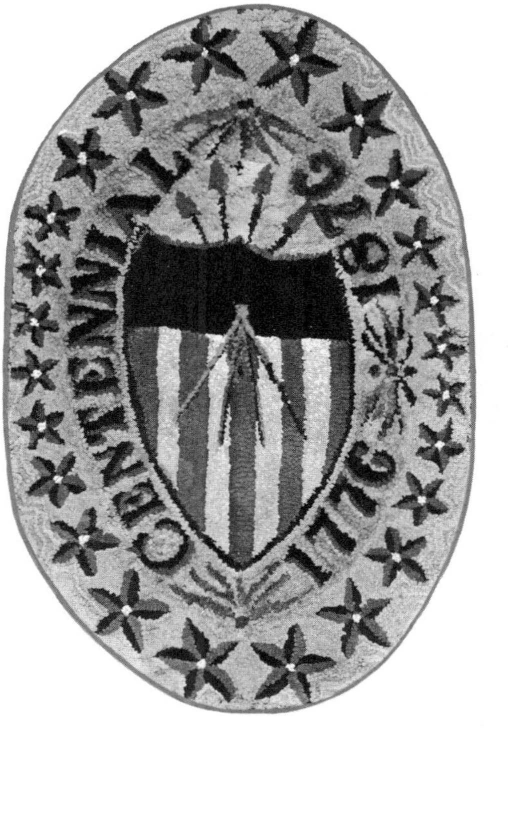

hoops like the top of a drum) was popular in those days, and it is believed that Zeruah worked the rug on a "tamber" frame, her yarn being threaded through a wooden needle made by her father. Its design includes a panel of fruit, cats, and kittens, in addition to the solitary "blue cat," shells, snow crystals, and many other motifs, but floral motifs predominate in this famed carpet.

Zeruah "started from scratch." She raised the flax and went through the tedious tasks of preparing the fibers for her hand-woven linen foundation; sheared the sheep which she had raised; washed, carded, spun, and dyed the yarn that she finally used in embroidering her many designs. The carpet itself is 12 feet wide by 13½ feet long; each square bears a different design. She made it for her father's parlor. Recently nine motifs of the Caswell Carpet were selected by a commercial rug concern. They were repeated to make a nine by twelve rug since the designs fitted well with modern interiors. That the early handmade rugs of New England and Canada have a sincerity that marks them as honest folk art has been acknowledged on many occasions.

There has always been a love of floor pattern in this country. After dirt floors were replaced by wooden planks, the latter were sanded and marked off into figures. Later on, color came into floor design through stenciling. Following this were the "floor cloths" made from sailcloth spread out like a rug. These cloths were often painted with the popular Spanish-tile design. The work was done by men engaged in the painting and paper-hanging trade, whose advertisements in the 1760's read, "Coach and Carpet Painting."

With no central heating, floors in those early days were bitter cold and while painted designs supplied pattern and color, it took carpeting to give warmth and quiet.

The term "rugg" also applied to a type of bedcover found only along the Connecticut Valley, and it is said that no more than a half-dozen are in existence today. Usually with a woolen homespun blanket as a foundation, a design was worked in yarn, sometimes a long and short stitch, often in a hooked technique. Bed "ruggs" have a shape peculiarly their own—two end corners are rounded to fit the foot of the bed, and the upper edge is straight, bearing the date and initials of the maker.

For these early rugs, original patterns were drawn on the foundation with a lump of indigo or a charcoal stick from the fire. Most of the old rugs had a looped, rather than a clipped surface. Since the early hooker was unhampered

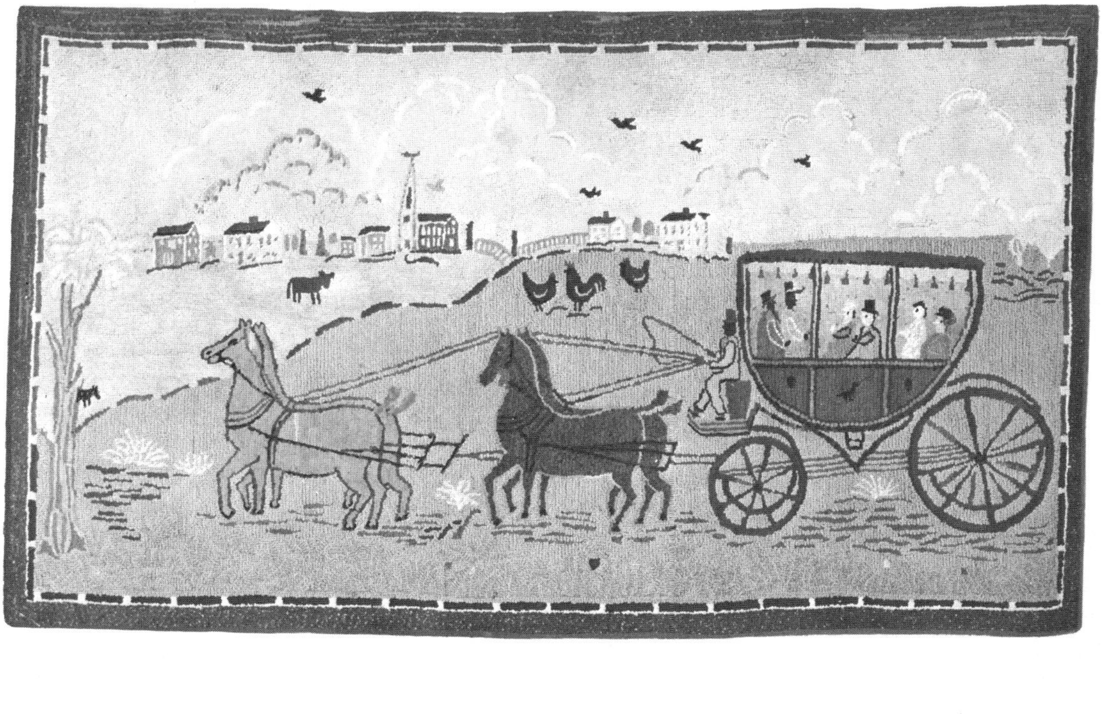

in theory, and no restriction was imposed by a prospective customer, she could give free play to her imagination. The earliest drawn-in mats were on homespun linen foundations. The finer the weave of the linen, the older the rug. Hand-made floor coverings include both knit and crocheted rugs, knitted rugs, cross-stitched rugs, woven rugs, patchwork rugs, and button rugs. Each presents its own technique to place underneath one's feet.

One of the more frequently used motifs for quilts, crewel work, and hooked rugs was the pine tree. Captain John Hull, the mint-master of the Massachusetts Bay Colony, had designed a coin on which was engraved the prevalent and beloved pine tree that the colonists saw everywhere. This shilling was to take the place of the wampum which the early settlers had adopted and adapted for their own use and which was used as exchange together with the current coinage of gold and silver money and monies from England, Portugal, and Spain. The pine-tree shilling was scarce, and one of the reasons for this was that the barter system was still prevalent, as it has continued to be. A subtle bit of evidence of what lay ahead—this shilling was one of the earliest true indications that the colonies were scheming to becoming free and independent.

Collecting as many of the old silver and gold articles as he could find, Captain Hull had his "pine-tree shillings" struck off. The account of a particular dowry of pine-tree shillings comes from the early diary of Judge Samuel Sewall, whose bride, the former Hannah Hull, was asked to step upon a weighing scale as soon as the marriage reception was over. According to Nathaniel Hawthorne's recounting of this tale ("The Pine-Tree Shillings" in his *Grandfather's Chair*) this new bride "was a fine, hearty damsel, by no means so slender as some young ladies of our own days." Step she did on the scale while her father, Captain Hull, had her weight balanced in pine-tree shillings!

(*Opposite page*) Primitive example of hooked rug, showing pastoral scene. *Courtesy Shelburne Museum*

(*Below*) The light olive green field of this yarn-sewn Bengal Tiger rug provides an effective setting for the animal done in shades of brown. Four-leaf clover designs appear in each of the four corners in pinkish tan outlined in blue and white. The Bengal Tiger is found in the warmer parts of Asia, chiefly in India and the Indian Islands. In Philadelphia about 1810 Thomas Bewick's book *The Quadrupeds,* illustrated with woodcuts, was published, and it is believed that the tiger may have been adapted from this volume. 41 × 67 inches. *Circa* 1820. *Photo Einars Mengis: courtesy Shelburne Museum*

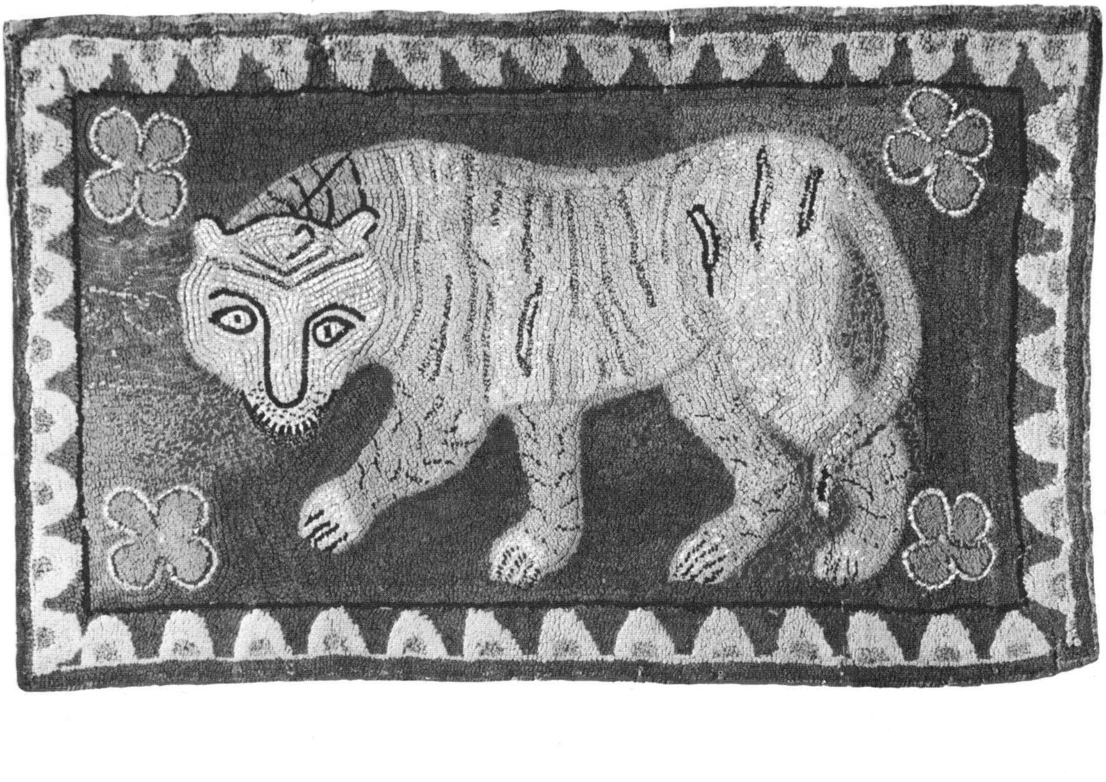

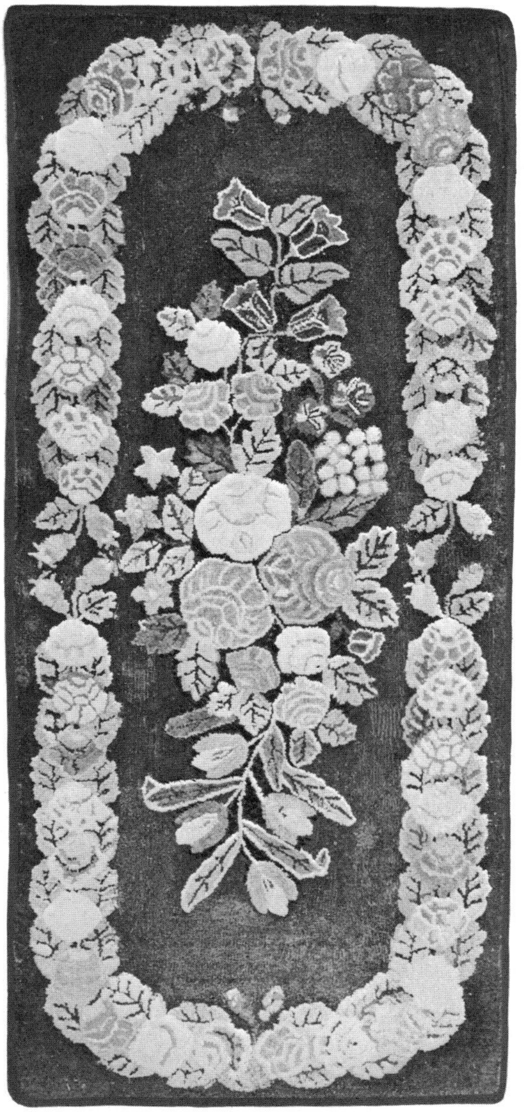

Hooked rug patterns include floral, geometric, pastoral or landscape subjects which were suggested by the immediate surroundings of home, field, and country, as in this primitive example. *Photo courtesy Shelburne Museum*

This was a dowry indeed. John Hull himself was an exponent of the versatility of this new coin. For his wedding attire, he had donned "a plum-colored coat, all the buttons of which were made of pine-tree shillings. The buttons of his waist-coat were sixpences; and the knees of his small-clothes were buttoned with silver three pences." News of this display of the pine-tree must have set the women of the colony thinking how they could incorporate this fashionable new motif into their own decoration.

Ralph W. Burnham of Ipswich, Massachusetts, wrote: "Several prominent writers upon the subject strongly contend that the deservedly popular floor coverings antedate the American Revolution. A still more venturesome writer of reputation asserts that hooked rugs were in evidence earlier than the year 1700."

Katherine Lee Bates, who wrote "America the Beautiful," tells in her *American Literature* that "a dozen factories were gathered into the farmhouse kitchen, where thin-lipped women baked and brewed, washed and ironed, canned and pickled, compounded the family physic of 'snail-water,' with ruby jellies to obliterate its taste, spun, wove, knit, quilted, made candles, soap, sausages, rug carpets, feather beds, and were by turns seamstresses, milliners, tailors, with frequent calls to dairy, poultry yard and milking stool."

In New England hooked rugs reached the height of their popularity in the Civil War period. The whaling industry, which centered in New Bedford and Nantucket, claimed nearly all the able-bodied men in the New England seaport towns, and this industry has been picturesquely commemorated in hooked rugs made by the women during the long months of their men's absence. Their destiny was often the cabin of some whaling ship. A full-rigged schooner usually formed the central part of the design, and appropriate nautical objects, such as anchors, knots, and other objects, appeared on the borders. Thoreau declared that the value of a thing is determined by the amount of life that goes into it. So home rugmaking will live on, as far as the craftswoman expresses herself in the products of the rughook, the needle, and the loom.

When sanded floors, swept with hemlock brooms into intricate patterns, gave way to those made of painted spruce and pine boards, housewives began to use up their carefully hoarded bits of cloth in another way—by braiding (or plaiting) rugs. The scraps were precious for in days when every piece of fabric was made at home from flax and wool raised on the farm, even the smallest pieces were stored away in the garret for future use. Braiding the strands for the rug is the same process as braiding one's hair, although sometimes an old rug was braided with four strands instead of three. It is possible to have braids of any desired width but rugs made of small braids are considered more valuable than those constructed in larger widths. In New Hampshire, braided rugs are called "shaded" rugs, that is they chose shades from light centres to dark borders, and only one or two colors are featured. Braids are loosely sewn together when a sufficient length has been made. Most of the braided rugs were round, but they may be oval, ovoid, or even rectangular in shape. A clover-leaf shape was used, too. These braided rugs are as popular now in homes as they were when first made.

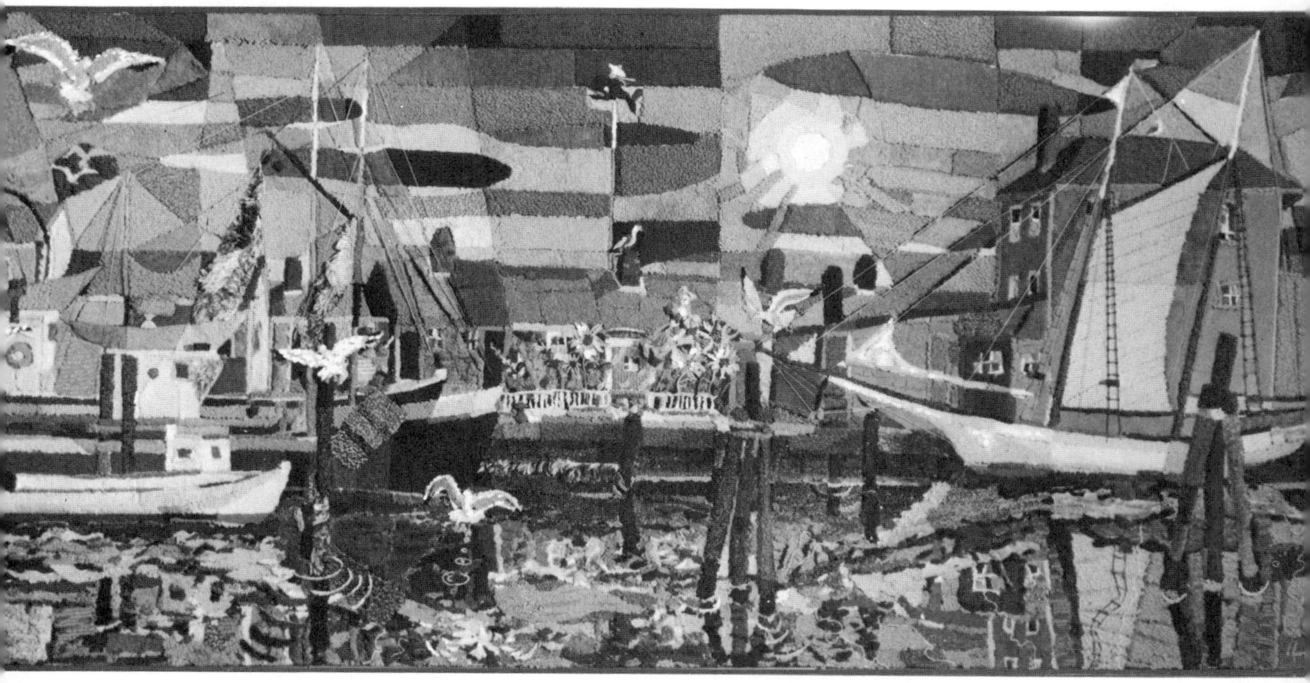

C. K. Perrin, well-known Boston and Nantucket artist, knowing that the old wharf in Nantucket, on which his beloved studio was located, was to be torn down, has perpetuated his summer place in a collage or "rugotamia" as he called it. Using scraps of carpet and rug samples, he combined the various colors and textures to create a wall hanging 10 × 5 feet. The result of Mr. Perrin's experiment reveals the possibilities of a distinctly creative medium in which the depth of piling of the rug pieces contributes greatly to the dimensional effect of the hanging.

The American Eagle

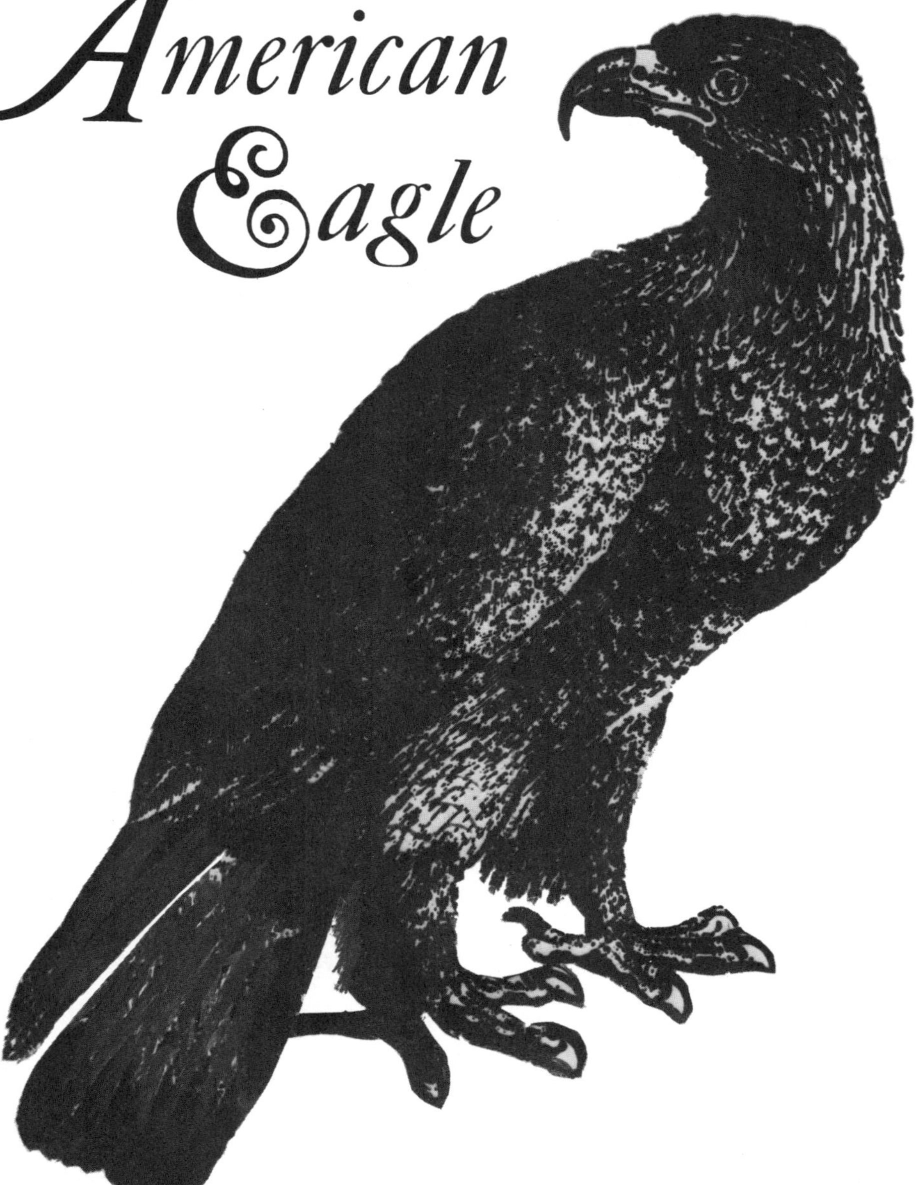

From its very first appearance as our national emblem, the eagle as a decorative motif has held precedence over all other designs, and today more than one hundred and eighty years later its popularity has not diminished. The folk art of New England and, for that matter, the creative spirit of colonial America took on a fresh outlook with the adoption of the American eagle as the national symbol of the United States. Once the eagle had been officially accepted by the Congress, every craftsman in the then sprawling Republic was eager to depict the *royal* bird in one form or another. The potter, the signmaker, the woodcarver, the glassmaker, the printer, the weaver, the buttonmaker, and all the other skilled artisans of the day wasted no time in imprinting their new symbol of freedom on everything that they made. The housewife, not to be outdone, proudly displayed the great bird on her quilts, her rugs, her embroidery, and other kinds of needlework.

The new symbol was distinctive in form—signifying virility, strength, pride, majesty. It represented, in a sense, the kind of uplift which the battle-weary colonists needed after their struggle. Had it not been the emblem of conquerors for more than three thousand years? The Romans called the eagle the Bird of Jove. Austria, Russia, and Prussia adopted it as their royal emblem. France under the Empire used it also. In heraldry it had long been considered a charge of high honor. The eagle was a proud bird which made its home in lofty places. Nor was the fiery disposition associated with this winged creature out of tune with the spirit of the times. Yet it took six years to decide that the American eagle was to become our national symbol.

At a slightly later date, in old Marblehead, Massachusetts, captains returned from the sea placed carved eagles over their doors. Today, as Hartley Alley has recorded in *A Gentleman from Indiana Looks at Marblehead,* the tradition lingers. "Eagles over doors are as thick as sea gulls overhead. Originally the carved eagle on a house was a sign that a ship's captain lived within. Skippers from distant ports were welcome to drop in for a cup of grog. While there is no lack of hospitality in Marblehead, today's sea captains might be well advised not to drop in on just any house with an eagle."

Curiously enough, somewhere between 1772 and 1779 an itinerant decorator, who remains anonymous, used his talents on the wall of a house in Washington, Connecticut, to paint an eagle with both olive branch and arrows and the motto "Federal Union." At the close of the Revolution, the adoption of the American eagle, the symbol of Liberty, was truly a godsend to the colonists of New England and the rest of rough-hewn America. As the eagle soared, so, too, the spirits of these freedom-loving people. In 1789 when George Washington made his triumphant tour of the colonies, transparent painted eagles sketched on paper were placed against the window panes of houses everywhere along his route, with lighted candles behind them. Even their oppressors in the fatherland, quick to sense the pulse of the new nation and eager to recapture the promising market, soon flooded the colonies with goods of every description marked with the new symbol of hope and freedom. Flowers, fruits, and song birds were forgotten. Eagles soared or perched on clocks, fabrics, buttons, china, glass—everywhere and anywhere that the motif could be utilized.

As Florence Peto expressed it in *American Quilts and Coverlets,* "From the Federal period to the Centennial in 1876 no craftsman felt more of a possessive attitude towards the emblem of freedom than the American quiltmaker; it was one for which she had made many sacrifices. Patched, woven or printed on cloth, the more or less easily recognized bird flew a streamer from hooked beak: *E pluribus unum.* Unabashed, always with an eye to trade, England promptly printed the symbol of America's freedom on cotton material destined for consumption in the new states. . . . During ensuing years, at any threat to the Union (there was the War of 1812, the Mexican War, and the Civil War) the quiltmakers with intense loyalty patched and stitched the patriotic motif to show where they stood." Nor were the French far behind in discovering that "Old Baldy" had eye appeal, for they, too, saw the commercial possibilities of this highly salable patriotic form of decor. Profiles of Washington and Adams, Liberty and Columbia, and fiery patriotic slogans many of which were outright anti-British in sentiment had their place as well, but the eagle predominated.

Later, when New England sea captains opened the China trade, the imperious bird in

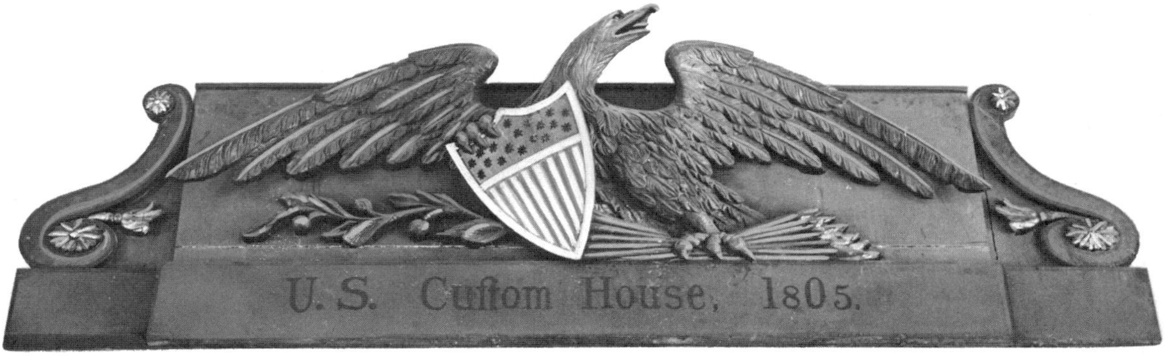
U. S. Custom House, 1805.

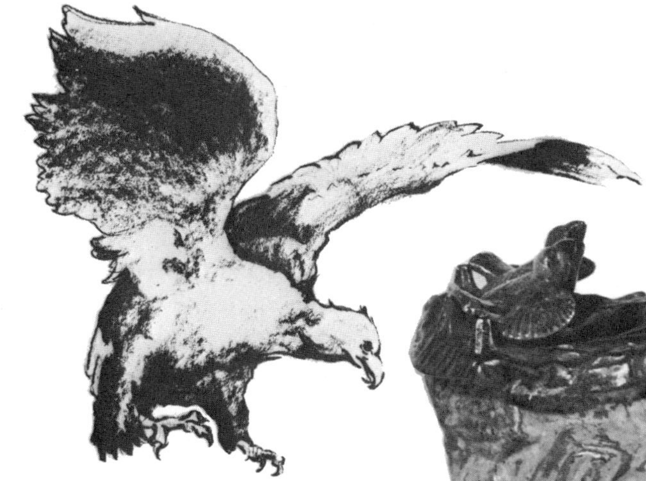

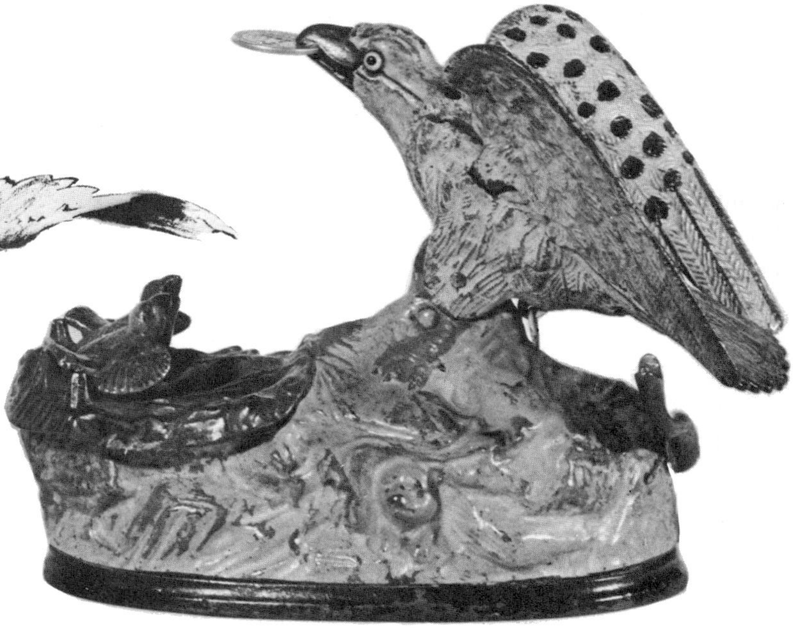

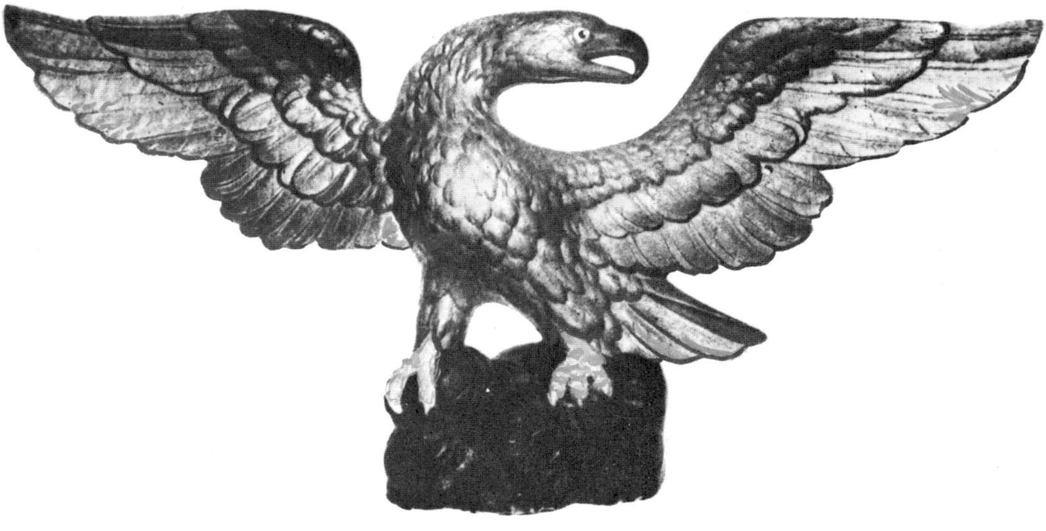

(*At left, top*) Eagle carved by McIntire for entrance to Salem Custom House in 1805. *Photo Courtesy Essex Institute*

(*Center, righthand photo*) A cast-iron penny bank. *Photo Richard Merrill: courtesy Rushford Collection*

(*Bottom*) Cast-iron eagle from an old mansion in Thomaston, Maine.

highly stylized form appeared on all types of fine china, often in gold. In many ways, the extensive and unrestrained use of the national emblem in every conceivable manner during the early days of the Republic set a precedent for the advertising techniques of later generations.

As a decorative feature, on sofas, bedposts, the backs of chairs, match boxes, in stencil designs, rugs, wallpaper, on door knockers, tavern signs, pitchers, bowls, and dozens of other household articles, the eagle appeared in some form. The ancient warrior bird soared sunward in their hearts and was everywhere present as a symbol of courage and endurance to express the independence which they cherished so dearly. This excessive use of the American emblem was obvious especially to foreign visitors, among them Captain Frederick Marryat, an English naval officer and novelist. In his *Diary in America* he wrote, "It is astonishing how little work they (the congressmen) get through in a session at Washington. This is owing to every member thinking himself obliged to make two or three speeches, not for the good of the nation, but for the benefit of his constituents. These speeches are printed and sent to them, to prove that their member makes some noise in the house. The subject upon which he speaks is of little consequence, compared to the sentiments expressed. It must be full of *eagles,* star-spangled banners, sovereign people, claptrap, flattery and humbug."

The eagle was a familiar insignia on tavern signs throughout the country, so that no traveler foreign or native was unmindful of the new-found freedom symbol. Edward Everett Hale, noted Boston preacher and writer, recalled his summer visit to northern Vermont in the 1850's. In describing the signs, he wrote: "Almost without exception their devices were of the American eagle with his wings spread, or of the American eagle holding the English lion in chains, or of the lion chained without any American eagle. These were in memory of Macomb's and McDonough's victories at Plattsburg and on the lake. They also, perhaps, referred to the fact that most of these taverns were supported by the wagons of smugglers, who, in their good, large peddlers' carts, provided themselves with English goods in Canada, which they sold on our side of the line."

On the afternoon of July 14, 1776, shortly after the Declaration of Independence had been adopted, the Congress appointed a committee composed of Benjamin Franklin, John Adams, and Thomas Jefferson to select a seal for the United States. With characteristic vigor and dispatch, they sought the advice of Pierre du Simitière, a Swiss portrait painter and naturalist who was living in Philadelphia at the time. His suggestion was a shield representing

A flagpole ornament, made of metal. *Photo courtesy Shelburne Museum*

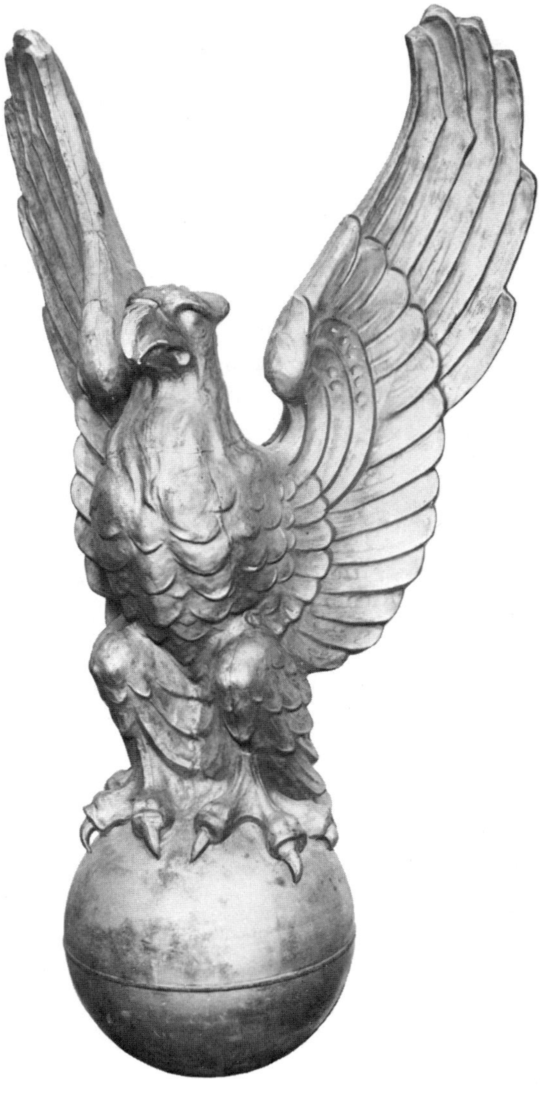

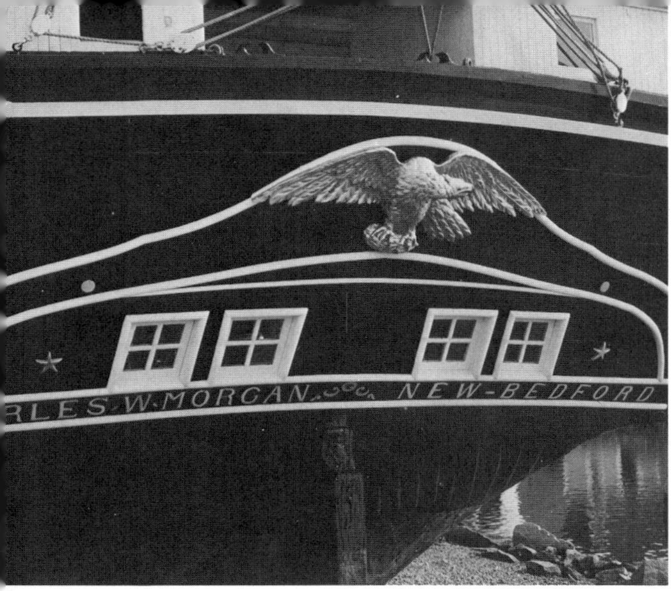

Sternboard eagle of the *Charles W. Morgan,* the last of the great whaling ships, now part of permanent marine exhibit at Mystic Seaport, Mystic, Connecticut. This vessel, built at New Bedford in 1841, made thirty-seven whaling voyages and not only sailed a greater distance than any vessel of her kind but also caught more whales. She remains today an impressive symbol of a great era in New England shipping.

the various nations whence the colonists came, flanked by the figure of a woman, Liberty, on one side and a rifleman in uniform on the other.

Franklin and Jefferson had other ideas. They favored allegorical scenes taken from the Bible. The determined Franklin advocated a sketch showing Moses lifting up his wand and dividing the waters of the Red Sea, as Pharaoh and his chariot were swallowed up. The motto was to read, "Rebellion to Tyrants Is Obedience to God." Jefferson was so greatly impressed with this motto that he placed it on the state seal of Virginia, but he had a different notion concerning a Biblical illustration. In lieu of du Simitière's design, the scholarly Jefferson favored a sketch of the children of Israel in the Wilderness, with Hengist and Horsa, the Saxon chiefs from whom so many Americans claimed descent, on the reverse.

Despite his solid Puritan background, John Adams favored classic mythology for the symbolic figures of the national emblem. He advocated the depiction of Hercules being urged by Virtue (a maiden) to ascend the mountains while the wanton figure of Sloth reclined seductively on the ground. Adams was a man of serious mien and strong determination who thought well of his own ideas, but he had to admit that his proposal was much too complicated to be effectively portrayed as a national symbol. These were stirring times and the selection of a suitable emblem for the fledgling nation was of vital importance.

Finally, the committee chose the image of Liberty supporting a shield of the states on the right and the Goddess of Justice, replacing du Simitière's rifleman, on the left. The motto, "E Pluribus Unum," taken from the *Gentleman's Magazine,* a popular London periodical of the day, seemed highly appropriate. It appears in the *Moretum,* a Latin poem attributed to Virgil. On the reverse, it was agreed that a modified version of Franklin's scene from Exodus would be suitable.

In the face of more urgent business, Congress tabled the report. A hostile army, including large numbers of Hessian soldiers, had to be dislodged from various harbors on American soil. Although Congress adopted the Stars and Stripes as the nation's flag in 1777, the selection of an emblem remained undecided. In 1780, a new committee, headed by the learned but controversial James Lovell of Massachusetts, tried its hand at the problem. The proposal that emerged portrayed a warrior holding a sword and a maiden with an olive branch; while on the reverse, there was a seated figure of Liberty holding a staff and cap. This was the first suggestion for the use of the olive branch, symbol of peace, and the first to incorporate the use of stars and stripes. However, this presentation failed to meet acceptance.

In 1782 two South Carolinians, Arthur Middleton and Edward Rutledge, and Elias Boudinot from New Jersey, were constituted as a third committee to pick a seal. They sought the aid of William Barton, a prominent citizen of Philadelphia, who was given to drawing and had a special interest in heraldry. Barton offered several sketches, among them one featuring an imperial eagle displayed on the crest, holding the flag of the United States in its left talon and a sword in its right, with a laurel wreath suspended from the point. Below was a maiden representing Virtue, holding a dove in her right hand and resting her left on a shield adorned with stars and stripes. A soldier stood to the right of the shield.

The committee accepted this design, but the members of Congress, not yet united, referred to their longtime secretary and public servant, Charles Thomson of Philadelphia. This scholarly patriot, known even in Europe for his knowledge of Greek and Latin, refined the design, stripping it of all superfluous detail, made the eagle the central figure on the seal and specified that it be an American bald eagle, rising not displayed. In the left talon he placed a cluster of thirteen arrows (one for each of the thirteen original states), emblematic of the war power; in the right, he substituted an olive branch (symbolizing peace) for Barton's sword and laurel wreath. For the crest he used the constellation of thirteen stars, and, recalling the first committee's favored motto, he depicted the eagle holding in its beak a streamer inscribed with the words "E Pluribus Unum"—One [nation] composed of many [states].

Then Barton made a final change, showing the eagle displayed rather than rising, and the much-discussed design for the national emblem was adopted on June 20, 1782. Although recuttings and minor changes have been made on several occasions since its acceptance, the basic design is unchanged. In 1884, Messrs. Tiffany of New York modified it, giving the eagle its present haircut.

Two years after its adoption, in 1784, when Benjamin Franklin was in France seeking aid for his country, a badge was being designed for the Order of the Cincinnati, a newly formed patriotic organization of American soldiers. The eagle in the design resembled a turkey rather than the proud bird. Or, so it seemed to Franklin and he wrote to his daughter, Sarah Bache:

> For my part, I wish the bald eagle had not been chosen as the representative of our country. He is a bird of bad moral character; he does not get his living honestly. You may have seen him perched on some dead tree, where, too lazy to fish for himself, he watches the labor of the fishing-hawk; and, when that diligent bird has at length taken a fish, and is bearing it to his nest for the support of his mate and young ones, the bald eagle pursues him, and takes it from him. With all this injustice he is never in good case; but like those among men who live by sharping and robbing, he is generally poor, and often very lousy. Besides, he is a rank coward; the little *king-bird,* not bigger than a sparrow, attacks him boldly and drives him out of the district.

Franklin considered the turkey "a much more respectable bird, and a true native of America." Eagles, he pointed out, are to be found in all countries, but the turkey is "peculiar to ours." Conceding that the turkey was "a little vain and silly," Franklin hailed him as "a bird of courage," who "would not hesitate to attack a grenadier of the British guards who should presume to invade his farmyard with a *red* coat on." This shrewd statesman surely knew that the Spanish raised turkeys for their holiday feasts and that they were being raised in England at the time for the same purpose.

Our National Emblem, from the collection at Mystic Seaport. *Photo Louis S. Martel: courtesy Mystic Seaport*

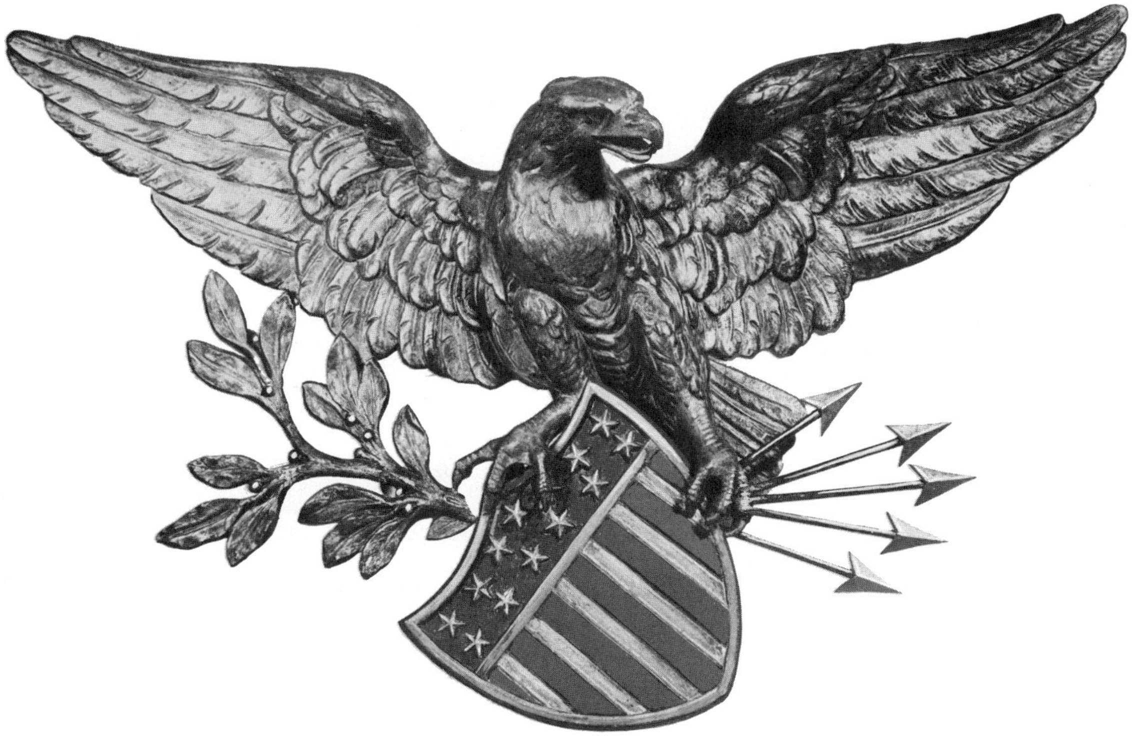

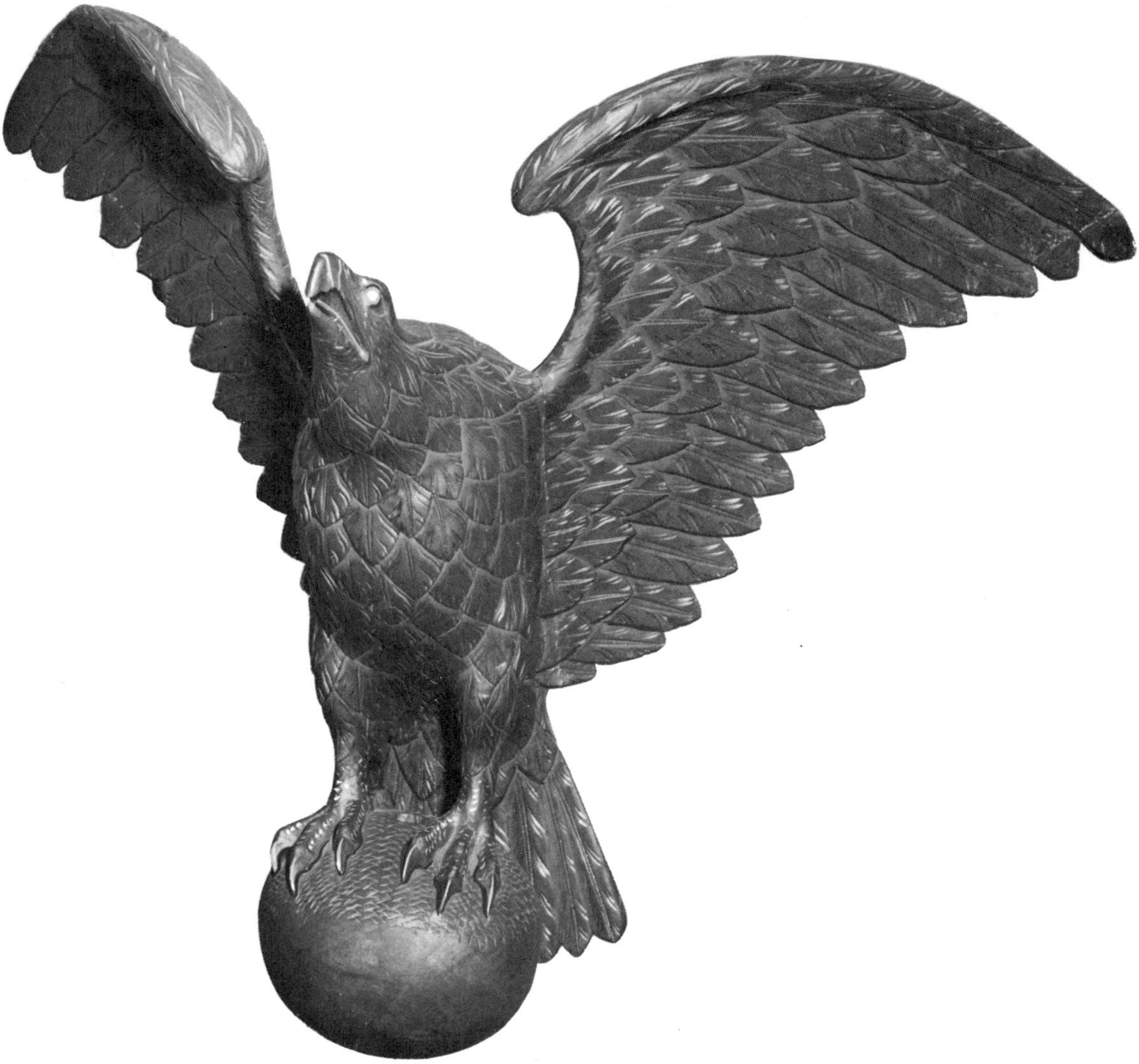

A free standing eagle carved by John Haley Bellamy. It now rests on a pedestal on the staircase landing of the spacious entrance hall in the Sir William Pepperell House, Kittery Point, Maine, where Bellamy lived during most of his life. Owned by Joseph E. P. Frost. *Photo Guy Nicholas: courtesy Joseph E. P. Frost*

He was aware that the early settlers at Plymouth had used them for their first Thanksgiving feast. Yet, this native New Englander, born in Boston (as he was wont to declare on the slightest provocation), was dead set against the eagle. A symbol may be defined as "that which suggests something else by reason of relationship, association or convention." The vain and silly turkey was hardly suited to become a traditional symbol for an aspiring new nation dedicated to liberty, justice and freedom.

Although seldom used in cemeteries, the image of an eagle appears on the gravestone of Lucinda Day who was laid away in the old burial ground at Chester, Vermont, in 1800. The appearance of the bird with wings and legs widespread suggest the design may have been adopted from a tavern sign. Replacing the shield of stars and stripes is a heart and within it is scribed an elfin face, that of Lucinda, with arched brows posing a question.

Early in the nineteenth century Putnam and Roff, a firm manufacturing paper hangings and band boxes at Hartford, Connecticut, designed a trade-mark featuring the eagle. Since no special etiquette had been devised for the national emblem, the eagle was utilized to carry the firm name on a ribbon in the bird's mouth and claws. (This was common practice with many craftsmen and tradesmen who made use of the eagle to advertise their wares.) Generous branches of olive and laurel further enhanced the design which when reproduced in four colors made a most attractive motif on a bandbox.

Free-standing eagles carved from wood or made of metal in various sizes and usually gilded have had strong eye appeal since the late eighteenth century. Their decorative uses are legion and the notable examples that have survived are greatly cherished. Samuel McIntire (1757–1811) noted architect and woodcarver of Salem, Massachusetts, made a number of them for public buildings and the cupolas of carriage houses. Several may be seen at the Essex Institute in Salem and others are in private collections. McIntire trained and inspired other craftsmen to carve eagles, among them Joseph True of Salem, who had been described as the "artistic successor of McIntire and an outstanding ship carver." True carved the imposing specimen that adorns the Salem Custom House where Nathaniel Hawthorne wrote the preface to *The Scarlet Letter* while serving as Collector. The eagle, carved from wood in 1828, covered with gold leaf, was made at a cost of fifty dollars. It is still in place gazing watchfully out on Salem Harbor. William Rush of Philadelphia, a contemporary of McIntire, also did outstanding work in modeling the symbol of freedom. In the nineteenth century, during the period following the Civil War, William Schimmel and Aaron Mounts, itinerant carvers in Pennsylvania, produced a great quantity of eagles, including some with removable wings. A sizeable number of Schimmel eagles may be seen in the great collection at the Shelburne (Vermont) Museum. One of the largest carved wooden eagles in New England is to be seen in the Stagecoach Inn at Shelburne. A superb specimen with wings fully spread and measuring nearly sixteen feet across, it is poised on a coil of rope and was formerly on display at the Portsmouth Navy Yard.

New England's most distinguished carver of eagles was John Haley Bellamy (1836–1914), often referred to as "The Woodcarver of Kittery Point, Maine." He was born there in the Sir William Pepperell mansion and resided in this historic house, which was owned by his family until shortly before he died. A woodcarving shop which he maintained for a time in nearby Portsmouth, New Hampshire, gave rise to the term Portsmouth eagle. In many respects, he was without a peer in his performance as a woodcarver. As a young man, he studied art and was apprenticed to the noted Boston woodcarver, Laban S. Beecher, prior to being employed at the Charlestown (Massachusetts) Navy Yard and later at the Portsmouth (New Hampshire) Navy Yard. He lived and worked in the heyday of the eagle in naval design and produced many notable birds including the figurehead for the U.S.S. *Lancaster* with a wingspread of eighteen feet. His work was characterized by the kind of individuality that has given rise to the term "Bellamy Eagle." As M. V. Brewington has expressed it in *Shipcarvers of North America,* "Bellamy developed marked characteristics, such as deep concave wings, the square sectional beak, and the heavily incised eye sockets."

Since many of his creations symbolized the authority of the United States government,

Eagle headpiece from the whaleship March. *Photo Louis S. Martel: courtesy Mystic Seaport*

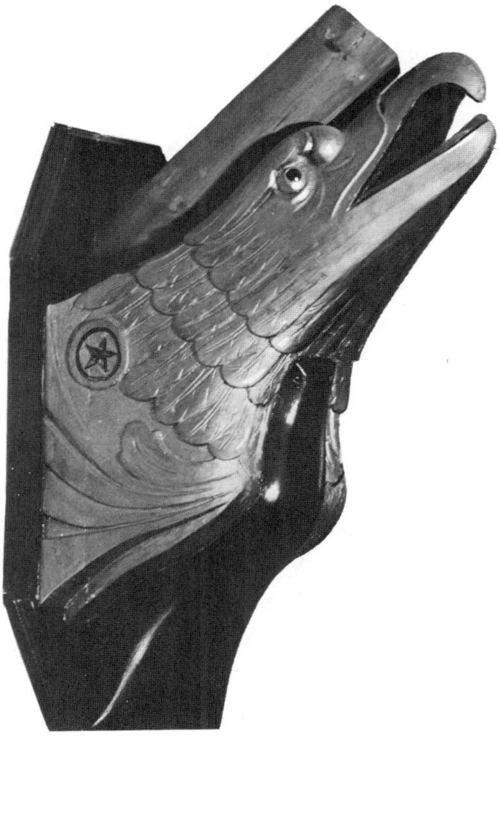

John Bellamy developed his own unique way of handling the eagle, the national coat of arms, and the American flag. Even when he carved eagles for public buildings, they were usually draped with the flag. A man of distinction in the community where he lived and worked, his countenance and bearing were said to be that of an old French chevalier. His talent was characterized by great facility and speed with tools and he turned out flocks of small spread eagles measuring two feet across which he often gave to his friends and neighbors. These were usually made of pine painted white with touches of red and blue and sometimes stars in the banners which they carried in their beaks or talons. Until recent years, practically every house in Kittery Point had at least one eagle on display. A superb example of the emblematic bird, executed in the round with its wings spread as if in flight, looks down to the front door from the landing in the front entrance hall of the Sir William Pepperell mansion. Joseph E. P. Frost who owns this eagle considers it one of the finest pieces of carving executed by Bellamy. The stuffed bird used as the model for it was only recently discarded because of its poor state of preservation.

An eagle (32 inches in height) carved by Samuel McIntire for the cupola of Lynn Academy in 1804, at a cost of $14.00. All of the free-standing eagles known to have been carved by McIntire are perched on balls with substantially heavy talons grasping the rounded surface. The wings are open as is the bird's mouth, and the general aspect is of a fierce creature of regal bearing, carved in excellent detail and striking form. *Photo Richard Merrill: courtesy Lynn Historical Society*

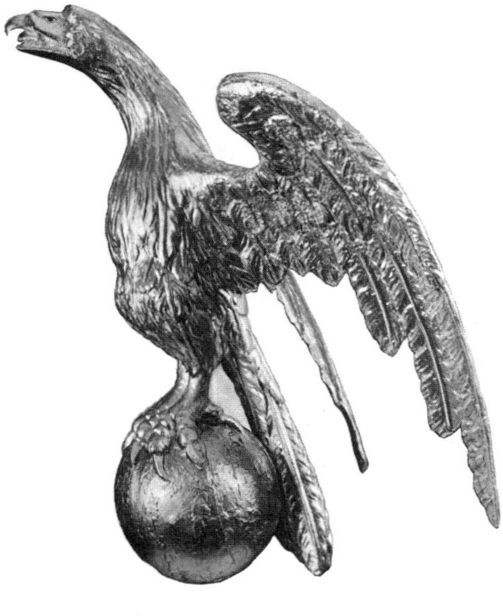

Bellamy also carved figureheads and a variety of ornamental works for naval and mercantile craft. He brought "inert wood to life with the beauty of his carving" as Frost expressed it. His technique was marked by clear sharp lines so typical of present-day carving. A variety of wooden ornaments including his own initials, an overdoor carving of roses, the head of a fox, and classic wreaths and garlands, typical of the festoons made by Samuel McIntire a century earlier, in the Frost collection show Bellamy's versatility.

Owners of whaling ships and tugboats favored eagles for figureheads. Pilot house eagles as they were called became popular for lake and river craft. During the Victorian era when cast and wrought iron were in wide use for ornamental fences and rails, the eagle was a familiar subject.

Because of his flare for poetry and for writing articles of historic and current interest, as well as his exceptional skill, "The Woodcarver of Kittery" played host to many distinguished literary and seafaring folk at his home and workshop.

During the past few decades in New England, interest in carving eagles has been revived to a marked degree. Many talented sculptors in wood, some with exceptional talent but mostly of amateur standing, have produced their own concepts of the American eagle. However, they remain anonymous for a number of reasons. A few craftsmen have become specialists, producing their work for sale. Among them is John Upton of Damariscotta, Maine. In his book, *The Art of Woodcarving,* he delineates his techniques in a highly informative manner. His work has received wide acclaim and he carries on in a lively manner the eagle-carving traditions of the state of Maine.

Now, after more than a century and a half, there are those who would scrap the American eagle as our national emblem and substitute for it the Statue of Liberty. In the *New York Times,* February 14, 1960, Professor Richard B. Morris of Columbia University wrote a lengthy plea for abolishing the eagle as our national symbol on the basis of its being un-

American. Resorting to Benjamin Franklin's claim, he declared that the big bird was "lazy, cowardly, rapacious, and hardly a fit national emblem." As a suitable symbol, he advocated the image of Liberty—based on Bartholdi's famous statue at the entrance to New York Harbor. His impassioned plea did not go unanswered.

Strangely enough, the article was inspired by the design of the new U.S. Embassy building in London's Grosvenor Square, featuring an eagle with a thirty-six-foot wingspread. Professor Morris was convinced that "this gilded bird of prey will cast a sinister shadow" on America. Most readers who replied to the plea took a firm stand in favor of the eagle as an outstanding bird and a worthy and appropriate symbol.

For centuries the Indians had revered the eagle as the tribal chieftan of all the birds. An eagle feather in his scalplock gave an Indian warrior increased courage and endurance. He feathered his arrows with those of the eagle to speed them straight and true and sang a ceremonial eagle song:

> A hat of eagle feathers
> A hat of eagle feathers
> A headdress was made for me
> That made my heart grow stronger.

The eagle was considered a sacred bird. Its feathers decorated peace pipes and with wampum were used to seal treaties. The eagle could only be hunted under special conditions; even then the custom with one tribe was to prepare a trap and strangle the bird. Sometimes the fierce fighting creatures, struggling for life, killed the hunter. Medicine men needed the feathers, claws, and whistles made of the bones for their ceremonials, hence the reason for killing eagles.

Those stirring lines from the "Invitation Song" of the Iroquois Indians have not lost their impact nor are they likely to as long as the voice of tradition is heard above the clamor of those who would rewrite history in an era when not everyone sets his sights in the right direction. Then as now, the eagle is held in high esteem:

> Screaming the night away,
> With his great wing feathers swooping the darkness up;
> I hear the Eagle-bird pulling the blanket back
> Off from the eastern sky.

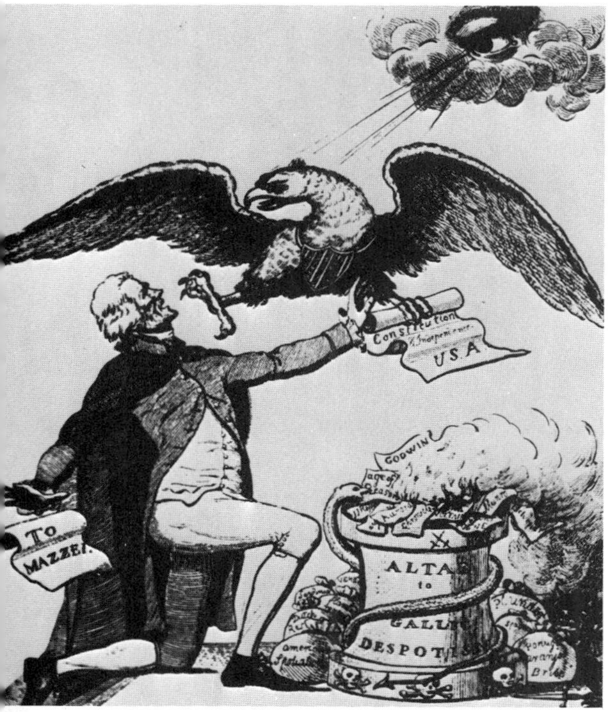

Thomas Jefferson's French sympathies were derided in a cartoon published in 1800. The Federalist is shown rescuing the U. S. Constitution before Jefferson could bury it on the Altar of Gallic Despotism. The French were believed to favor free love, and, at the time, Yale's president warned that Jeffersonianism would surely make "our wives and daughters the victims of legal prostitution."

The Itinerant Painters and Their Art

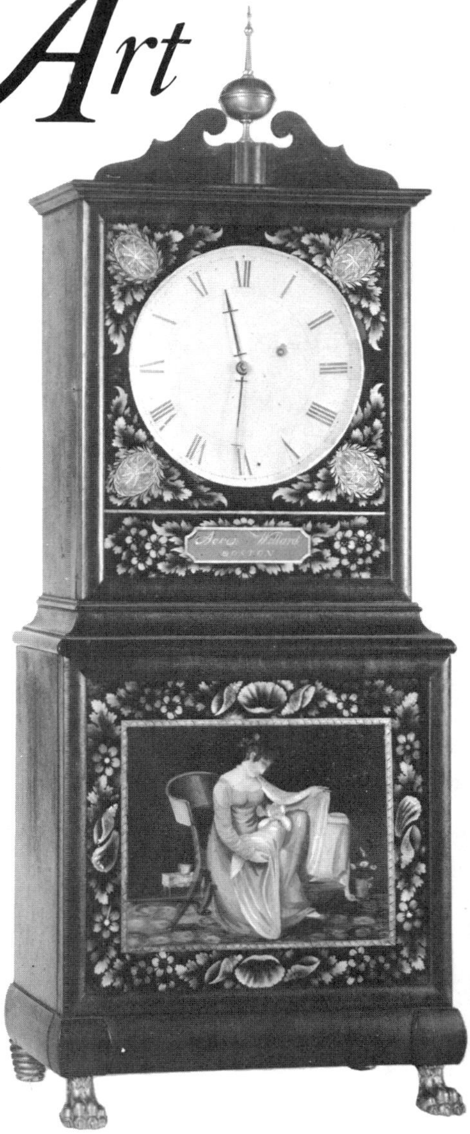

The shelf or mantel clock was an American invention designed by the Willards of Boston to serve the purpose of the tall case or so-called grandfather's clock without being as large or as expensive. Yet, it could be seen across a room. These clocks were often handsomely ornamented with brass finials and reverse painting on glass. When the decoration was done by a highly skilled craftsman, as in the case of this clock ascribed to Charles Bullard (1794-1871), the result was impressive. In decorating clocks and the tops of mirrors, craftsmen either copied contemporary European prints or local landscapes or used motifs featuring fruits, flowers, or geometirc patterns.
Photo courtesy Museum of Fine Arts, Boston

The portraits of grandfather and grandmother, cousin Martha at the age of five, Uncle Simon, just home from Zanzibar, and other faded flowers of the family tree had their day on the parlor walls and the large majority of them eventually landed in the attic, under the eaves, to gather dust. With the passage of the years, they became dry; sometimes they peeled or became water stained; more than likely, holes were punched in the canvases, accidentally in most instances. There they remained, undisturbed, until someone needed a frame for a new print or a painting. Then the canvases were either put back "up attic" or, on occasion, tossed in the rubbish heap, but usually they were saved out of respect or because mother couldn't bear to throw them away.

About forty years ago, the curious, few in number, began to collect them. Suddenly came a revival, fired with all the spirit of those old-time religious awakenings and sparked with fervor and a kind of zeal not previously known in the art world. Soon, we learned that it was perhaps easier to find out whose likeness it was that hung in Smith's Antique shop window than who the painter was. In all too many instances, he turned out to be *Anonymous,* and so, in most cases, he remains forever.

The rise of the American folk artist became a new and smart tea-table topic and marvelous were the stories about these itinerant painters that came to light. Many of them were true; some were fantastic, but, in such cases, all the facts could be verified. Others were the essence of brevity such as are found in birth records and death notices. All too frequently letters, diaries, and advertisements in newspapers of the period produced bare facts, occasionally a eulogizing paragraph or two, but a goodly number had left no mark but their unsigned paintings. Along with the biographical data came many theories explaining why and how so many of these obviously flat often notably shadowless canvases came to be painted. The oft repeated story, still generally accepted, was that the itinerant artists carried with them a stock of partially completed canvases, complete as to costume and accessories, with the heads missing. The painter would spread his collection before his patrons, bargain for a sitting, allow them to choose the finery they preferred and then paint the head of the person he "took." "Taking heads" was. an expression of the time. Like many an old tale this bit of tradition grew with repetition, often greatly embellished with each telling and was generally accepted as gospel truth.

In *The Cult of the Primitives* James T. Flexner refuted this notion clearly when he declared: "No evidence exists that this ever happened. Authentic documents are silent concerning such a practice; and half-painted headless canvases have never been found, although there remain hundreds which were abandoned when the head was completed but the body not begun. Prefabrication of background and pose and costume would have made sense for the itinerants, since it would have given them employment when the roads were blocked by winter; yet they followed immemorial European studio practice by painting heads first, even if they later put in the bodies altogether from imagination in their studios or boarding houses."

These craftsmen in "face painting" could "catch a likeness" that was often naive, frequently candid (to the point of being unflattering), and quite wooden to boot. On the other hand, many pleasing likenesses were to be found and in the most unexpected places in the back country. That they were rich in color, often eyecatching in their detail, and decidedly different from those of the known and accomplished painters of the day, no one can deny. Some are utterly charming and delightful, others amusing, and not a few are downright funny. These have been the source of many a chuckle among the families who have inherited them. It has always been the practice of one generation to poke fun at the dress, customs, and manners of their predecessors and such antics are allowable in the confines of the family circle. Far be it for two observers concerned with assembling a somewhat composite picture of the arts and crafts of New England to pose as evaluators of American primitives. Rather, the attempt is to present the record as it appears in books, magazines, and newspapers currently available. Truly, this aspect of American folk art has more champions and objective and dissenting critics than any other, and they stand in clearly defined camps.

When Clara Endicott Sears first began to collect portraits for Fruitlands Museum at Harvard, Massachusetts, she combed the countryside for pictures and accounts as well of the people represented and the men who painted

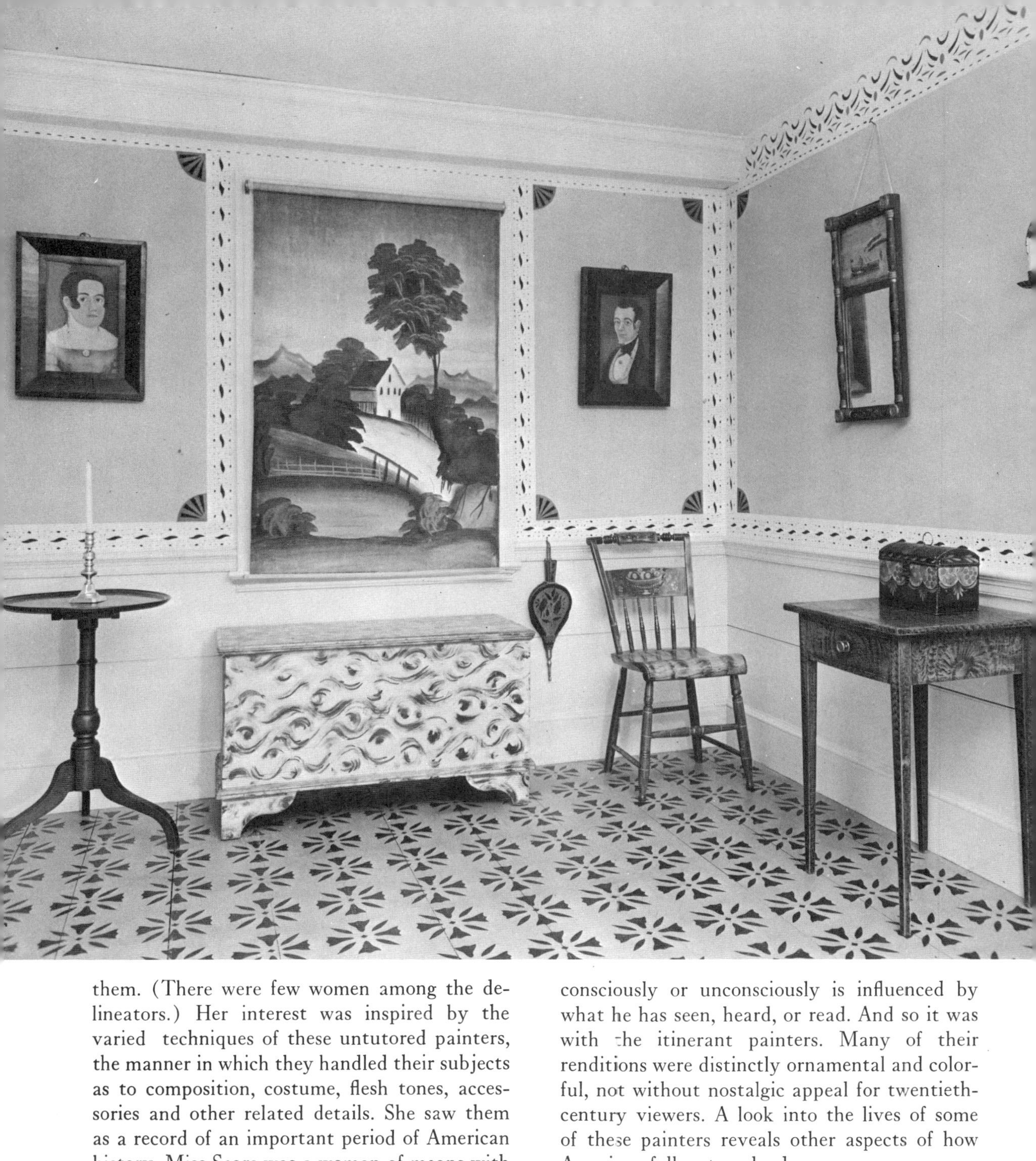

them. (There were few women among the delineators.) Her interest was inspired by the varied techniques of these untutored painters, the manner in which they handled their subjects as to composition, costume, flesh tones, accessories and other related details. She saw them as a record of an important period of American history. Miss Sears was a woman of means with a dedicated outlook and, for her, these amateurs reflected that "yeasty" period when every sort of talent "bubbled up to the surface."

Students of the period remind us that the influence of skilled academic painters of the period both here and abroad is obvious in some of the primitives. As today with the Sunday painters, the limners frequently copied objects and techniques found in the prints popular at the time. This is not to condemn copying, because imitation is not the greatest of vices by any means. Everybody, in one way or another, consciously or unconsciously is influenced by what he has seen, heard, or read. And so it was with the itinerant painters. Many of their renditions were distinctly ornamental and colorful, not without nostalgic appeal for twentieth-century viewers. A look into the lives of some of these painters reveals other aspects of how American folk art evolved.

The number of primitive or untrained painters prior to the Revolution was comparatively small compared with the outpouring that occurred from the early 1800's on, and the reason for the rise and popularity of these craftsmen is an integral part of the history of a growing nation. Richardson Wright tells us: "As soon as a people attain that point of self-consciousness where they desire to preserve their features for the delectation of their descendants, then they may be said to have passed the primitive stage." Those who could afford it and knew

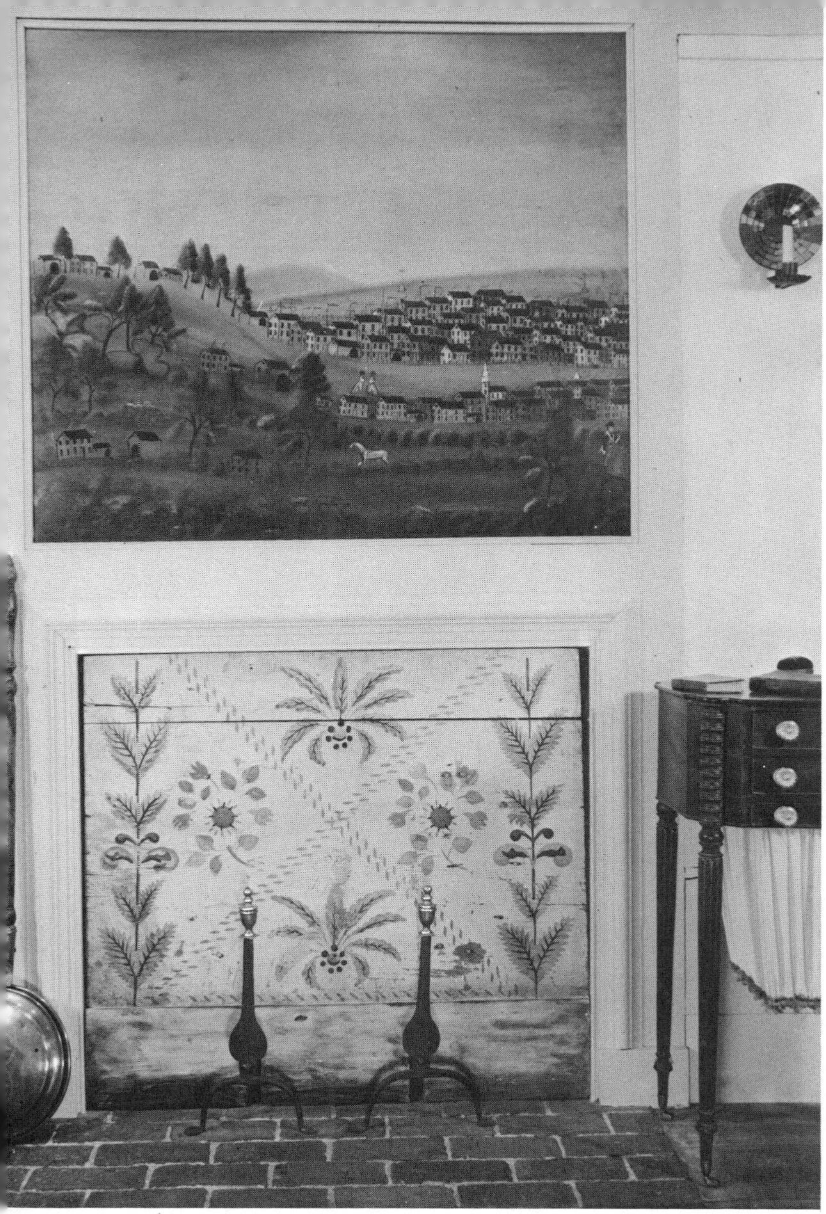

(*Far left*) Walls, floors, furniture, and even window shades in town and country houses displayed a lavish amount of color during the Federal period and in the years that followed, as shown in the Village Tavern at Old Sturbridge. Stenciled borders and quarter fans gave the effect of panel treatment on the walls. Black geometric figures accentuate the pumpkin-yellow floor. A landscape painted on the window shade recalls a fashion in home furnishings long gone. The chest, bellows, chair, mirror top, table, and tin box all have painted decorations, and the work of the limner in the portraits flanking the window shade adds the crowning touch. *Photo Courtesy Old Sturbridge Village*

A good many of the overmantel paintings and picture panels executed by the itinerant painters in the early days of the Republic have long since disappeared. Combining elements of realism from the local natural landscape with bits of fancy, these traveling painters, painter-stainers, and decorators made many a New England home bright with their creations in the "newest taste." The landscape shown above was taken from an old house in Sturbridge and is now preserved in the Perez Walker House in Old Sturbridge Village. The fireboard below is an example of stenciling in black and yellow-green on a light buff background. *Photo courtesy Old Sturbridge Village*

the importance of the professional painter had their likenesses made by British artists or the few in America who had an academic background; but the rank and file turned to the itinerant painters who came to their doors and were lured by them "to preserve their features" and those of their loved ones.

They were called limners. The term, considered archaic and seldom used today, stems from *luminare* to light up or illuminate as with the manuscript decorations in the margins of pages, typical of books handwritten or lettered in the Middle Ages. From this derivation came the term limner, a portrait painter. (Esther Forbes described one vividly in her novel *Rainbow on the Road.*) Most of them had no academic training or knowledge of the fine points and techniques of painting. To be sure, a few studied (usually for a short period) with men of recognized talent, but, for the most part, these craftsmen had graduated from their trade as sign painter, house painter, stainer, coach painter, gilder, or some allied skill and, at first, took on as a side line the craft of painting likenesses. When successful, they stayed at it.

W. Storrs Lee has related in *The Yankees of Connecticut:* "When Hartford was still little more than a village, it was supporting two portrait studios, three engravers, and six sign painters, but most of the artists shut up shop in the summer and took to the road. The road led to New Hampshire and western Massachusetts, to Vermont, the Genesee Valley, Pennsylvania, and Ohio. And occasionally they paused for a few days to sketch Mount Washington, Lake Champlain, or Niagara Falls. More often they persuaded an affluent householder that the dignity of his home called for a mural or overmantel landscape. From underneath the layers

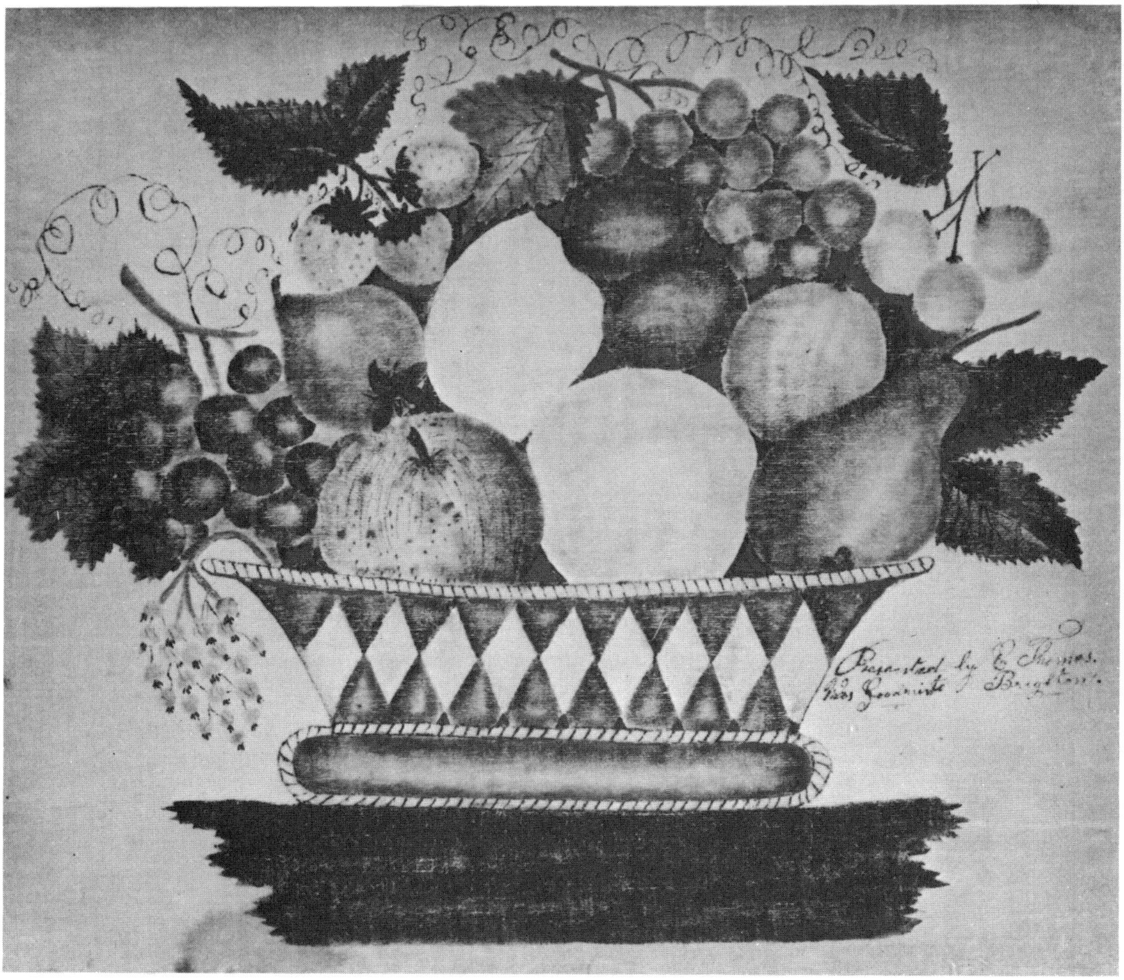

This still life of fruit in a basket is an example of stencil or theorem painting popular with young ladies in the first part of the nineteenth century. The hollow-cut paper designs made it easy to apply color, and there were instruction books published to guide beginners. *Photo courtesy Old Sturbridge Village*

of wallpaper and cheap paint, these picturesque effusions in design are still being uncovered."

These adventurous wanderers, who like the peddlers trod the rough roads of New England as long each year as weather permitted, were looked upon as belonging to the peddler class. They ranked with scissors' grinders, hairdressers, musicians, strolling players, buffoons, exhibitors of birds, puppets, and other strange phenomena. "Unprofitable laborers" described them well in the eyes of most of the country folk. Yet, more often than not, they were well and warmly received, especially in the back country, for not infrequently they had an amusing manner and could tell a story well. It was custom that they were fed and lodged. Since they often wandered in from nowhere in particular they rarely declared their intentions as to where next they might stop. Ever and always these "knights of the road" sought sitters, at any price, however modest—even bed and board would suffice in exchange for a likeness.

The standing of the painter had not risen significantly for generations as Carl Bridenbaugh has pointed out in *The Colonial Craftsman.* Of it he wrote: "Today painters would never be bracketed with artisans and craftsmen, but even during the Renaissance the great Leonardo da Vinci acknowledged in a treatise on painting that in the cultural hierarchy the artist's rank was low—inferior to that of the scientist or the mathematician or the poet—and that he was commonly regarded as a craftsman-decorator. In the English colonies the limner, or portrait painter, rated even lower in the scale than the painters of Urbino and Florence. John Singleton Copley complained bitterly of the Boston attitude toward painting in 1767: 'The people generally regard it as no more than any other useful trade, as they sometimes term it, like that of a Carpenter or shrew maker, not as one of the most noble Arts in the World.' Some master silversmiths and cabinetmakers received as much acclaim as a good painter." It has been said that paintings were commissioned in the same manner as a silver teapot, a chest of drawers, or a set of chairs. Even in England painters had no professional standing until 1760 when "The Society of Artists" was founded. They were looked upon as "upper" servants. The title of carpenter-architect associated with Samuel McIntire, Charles Bulfinch, and others typified the position of these talented men in the field of architecture.

Recognition was achieved slowly and the challenge was met by traveling about, doing as many heads as possible. Advertising was costly for the beginner whose only assets were determination, a strong pair of legs and the painting materials which he carried on his back or in a wagon. Distances between villages were great and farmhouses were scattered. In the back country, stagecoaches were infrequent. At best, the road to success had more than its share of stumbling blocks. Like the peddler's life, the traveling artist's was a highly precarious existence.

To some it was merely a means to eke out a living and to satisfy a desire for wanderlust; to others it was a desire to build a career. Men like Chester Harding in western Massachusetts and Francis Alexander in Connecticut, and James Frothingham of Charlestown, Massachusetts, achieved distinction as highly competent artists in later life. With William Matthew Prior and a host of others like him, they produced large quantities of canvases and made a comfortable living for their families. Many remained in the ranks of the lowly, dying in poverty. The environment in which they were born and in which they moved as well as any inherited talent or inclination and the pictorial prints which they saw, determined, in large measure, their destiny. A much larger group whose work survives belong forever, probably (unless art historians can uncover something about them with practically no clues to follow), to the world's anonymous craftsmen. Of these, a goodly number undoubtedly followed other trades as well.

Aside from those who did likenesses on large canvases, "ancestors" we often call them, others specialized in miniatures which included portraits in wax. For a period of several decades, silhouette cutting rose to great heights. Sign painting and coach painting were always in demand. Overmantel pictures, frescoes, and stencils for walls and woodwork, decorations for floors, and the embellishment of furniture afforded other outlets for talent—or, at least, a means of employment. They painted "in general" anything that could be improved, decorated, or made pretty with pigments. On occasion these struggling painters made "painted parsons," signposts "which, like some ministers, always point the way but seem never to follow it themselves."

Working in carriage shops, they learned to know the making of color by grinding the pigments. This experience they transferred to the painting of coaches when the railroads took

A distinctive Hitchcock chair featuring the eagle, made at the famous Connecticut chair factory. *Photo courtesy Old Sturbridge Village*

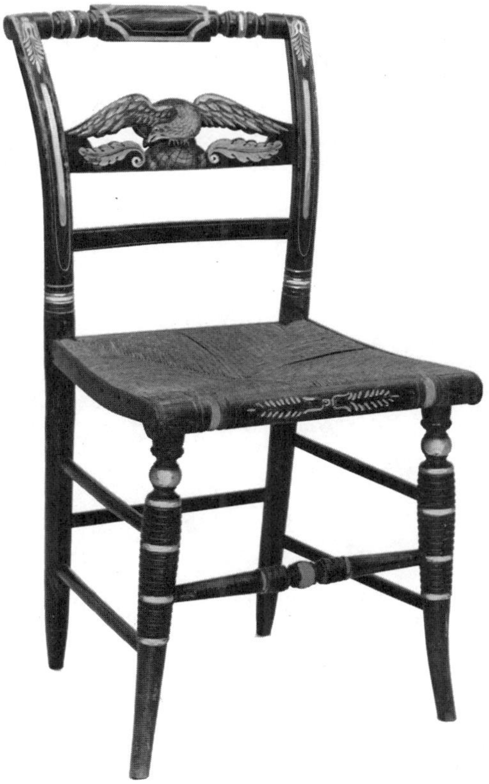

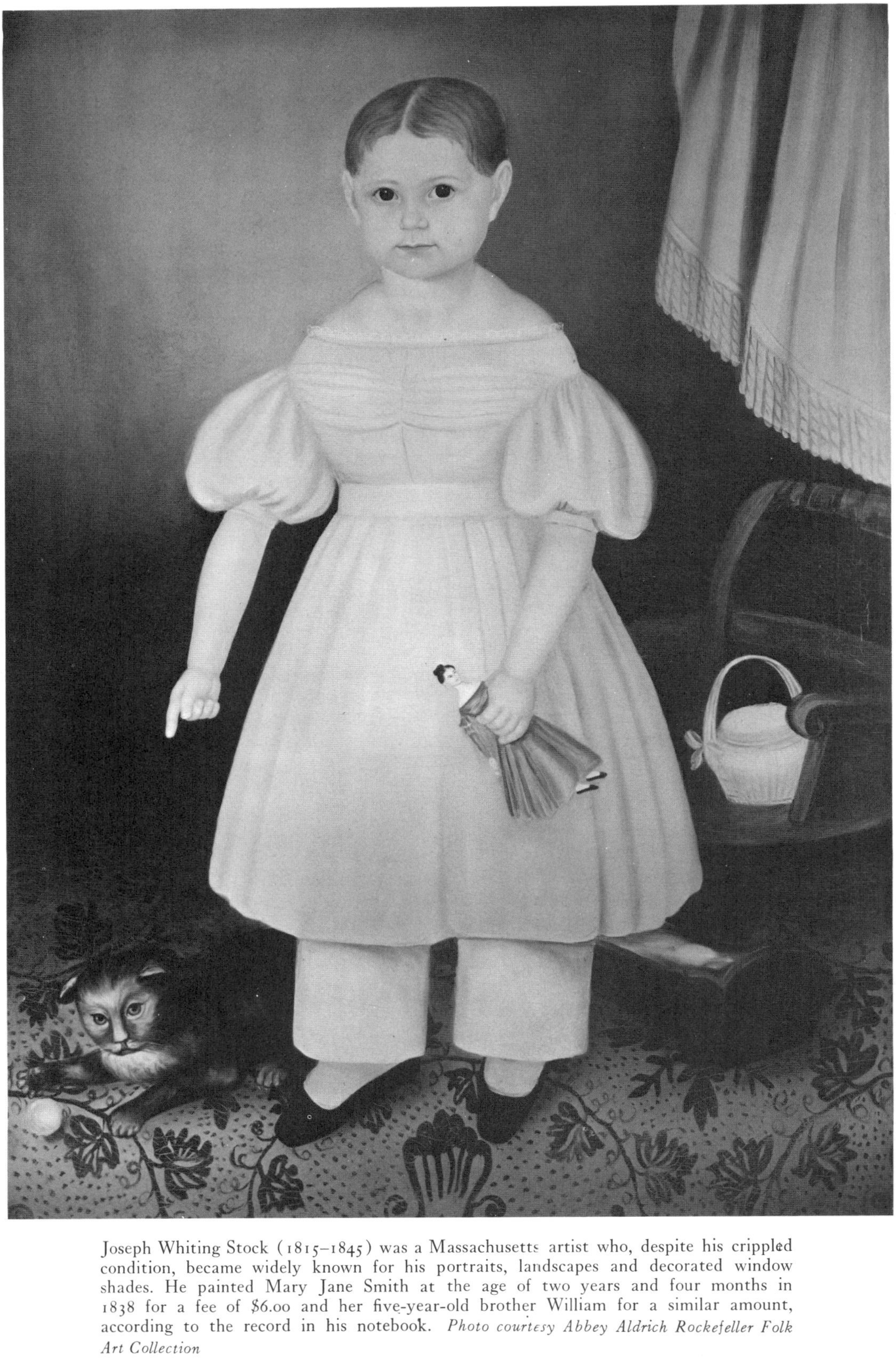

Joseph Whiting Stock (1815–1845) was a Massachusetts artist who, despite his crippled condition, became widely known for his portraits, landscapes and decorated window shades. He painted Mary Jane Smith at the age of two years and four months in 1838 for a fee of $6.00 and her five-year-old brother William for a similar amount, according to the record in his notebook. *Photo courtesy Abbey Aldrich Rockefeller Folk Art Collection*

over in the mid-nineteenth century. They "drew faces" in crayon as well as oils. Some had as many as six sitters a day. Others started a portrait and, after "catching" the likeness, took the canvases to their rooms to be finished. Isaac Sheffield of New London, Connecticut, and others like him, specialized in doing sea captains. All had red faces, all stood before a red curtain, and each held a telescope.

"An example of these lowly and obscure itinerant artists can be cited in the cultural ascendency of one Frank Alexander, a farmer's son in Windham County, Connecticut. Without the slightest knowledge of painting technique he began to paint fish, at which the family marvelled, and from fish passed on to animals, and from animals, took the dizzy flight into human portraiture. He travelled about the countryside of Connecticut painting portraits for $3. a head and board. Saving his money, the lad went to New York for instruction in art, and after his return, he staggered the neighbourhood by charging $8. a head." But, as Richardson Wright also recalled so vividly in *Hawkers and Walkers in Early America,* not all the hawkers were walkers.

"As pretty a story as you'd ever want is found in the wanderings of James Sharples the peripatetic artist. An Englishman, he was educated in France, and then came here in 1798. His mediums were crayon and pastel. Seeing that the market for his wares was scattered, he devised a special cart that would comfortably hold his wife, two boys and a girl and their clothes and food and his painting gear. It was drawn by one large sturdy horse. In this menage ambulant he travelled all over the country, going from town to town and city to city. In each city he would obtain letters of introduction to people in the next city—military, civil or literary worthies. Sharples would present the letter, beg the honour of doing a portrait for his 'collection' and, if this was granted, he would set to work. As he was a good artist, he could manage to make a faithful likeness in about two hours. Having seen himself so faithfully portrayed, the sitter, of course, was easily induced to buy the picture. The charges were $15 for a profile and $20 full face. Sharples's wanderings came to an end in 1811 when he departed this life. His portraits could scarcely be called masterpieces. Yet, several of them are to be found in the American Wing of the Metropolitan Museum of Art."

John Greenwood (1727–1792) possessed characteristics that differed greatly from some of his contemporaries in the painter's craft and from most of the limners who followed him. Like John Trumbull of Connecticut, he was well born, the son of a shipbuilder and merchant. When the family fortunes suffered, he was apprenticed to Thomas Johnston of Boston, a most versatile artisan engaged in engraving, japanning, cutting gravestones, painting houses, ships, and even fire-buckets. Johnston was a seller of maps as well and is known to have made a concert-hall organ. Training under such a person of such diversified talents could not be without its reward, but Greenwood was not disposed to accept it and set himself up as a portraitist. He had acquired more reputation than he had skill, being considered quite a genius; he was much sought after, even though very young.

The Museum of Fine Arts in Boston owns an engraving of one of Greenwood's paintings entitled Jersey Nanny. Beneath it, this verse:

> Nature her various skill displays
> In thousand shapes, a thousand ways;
> Tho' one form differs from another,
> She's still of all the common mother;
> Then, Ladies, let not pride resist her,
> But own that Nanny is your Sister.

This was a bold departure from the accepted order of things in colonial New England, but it indicates some measure of the man and smacks of Hogarthian wit. He also on a piece of bed ticking approximately 3×6 feet painted a picture of sea captains carousing at Surinam. Who knows what else he might have portrayed had he not abandoned painting as a career. Instead, he left the colonies at the age of twenty-five, and went to London where he became a successful art dealer. Like many another sea-captain's son, he became a man of the world.

Winthrop Chandler (1747–1790) hailed from Woodstock, Connecticut, and remained close to home during his comparatively short life. He is said to have been apprenticed to a house and sign painter and despite his lack of formal training showed considerable competence (that of a master, as one critic expressed it) in the portraits he painted of his friends and relatives. Two of his paintings are in the Garbisch Collection. Like many another who pursued the field, he died in poverty.

When we read that Ralph Earl (1751–1801) "may be taken as either the most notable of untrained professional or the most unskilled of the professional painters" as described by Edgar P. Richardson in *Painting in America,* it is implied that he stood out from his fellow men in a number of respects. And he did.

He was born in Worcester County and lived in New Haven after his marriage. By temperament he was decidedly unstable and was eventually "ruined by drink." One of his friends was Amos Doolittle, an engraver, who kept a shop on the site of the Yale campus. When the Governor's Guard was rushed to reinforce the struggling troops at Lexington, Doolittle and Earl joined them. Taking his position in the deep grass and behind pasture fences, he sketched the action of the battle and later rendered four paintings, each with a title, which were engraved and colored by Doolittle. Needless to say, these mezzotints had a ready sale. According to Cuthbert Lee, noted art scholar of Yale University, "They were probably the first historical pictures ever executed by an American artist." He was also one of the very earliest American landscape painters, and several of his canvases including "Falls of Niagara" remain.

Earl's earliest known portrait is one he did at the age of twenty. He had a flair for making his subjects quite human and introduced accessories revealing their interests. His talent showed itself with children, especially, and in family groups. Among those who sat for him in 1777 was Timothy Dwight of Yale and this remarkable educator and chronicler of history became one of his admirers. Never a dedicated family man, Earl left his wife and children in 1778 and departed for London. After five years, he was elected to the Royal Academy and painted, among other notables, George III. Deserting his first wife, he married a second time. His son by this marriage, Ralph E. W. Earl, studied with John Trumbull and later under the distinguished Benjamin West. Earl returned to America and pursued his profession as an itinerant, but his prime weakness overtook him and "he retired to a quiet dying-place in the silent old village of Bolten, Connecticut" and died at the age of fifty in 1801. On his death a notice appeared in the *Hartford Courant,* which shows that he was known and appreciated by his contemporaries. It called him "a portrait painter celebrated in America and respected in Europe, a pupil of Sir Joshua Reynolds and a member of the Royal Society."

Horace Bundy (1814–1883) came from Hardwick, Vermont. Apparently he stayed fairly close to home also, since his work was confined to his native state and to New Hampshire. One of his portraits now known as *Vermont Lawyer* is in the Garbisch Collection.

Among the early primitive painters was Joseph Badger born in Charlestown, Massachusetts, in 1708. A house painter and glazier by trade, he did trade signs and coats of arms as well as portraits and eventually became surprisingly accomplished. Although his early work was crude, like that of nearly all the unschooled itinerants, his later portraits earned for him a place among the early American painters who were considered creditable artists. He has been described as an intellectual painter and a possible teacher of Copley (both used squirrels in some of their portraits). Typical of many of the limners, he was plagued by debt, and expired intestate of apoplexy in 1765. He has been described as endowed wtih the creative urge to paint in an age barren of art.

A wax modeler and waxworks showman who took to the road with his show, Reuben Moulthrop (1763–1814) of East Haven traveled from his native state, Connecticut, through parts of Massachusetts and also to New York, New Jersey, and Pennsylvania. His painting shows considerable variety in style and his portraits of Job and Sally Perit in the Garbisch Collection are exceedingly interesting studies in blue tones as well as the high-styled fashion of 1790.

Ruth Henshaw Bascom (1772–1848), called the ablest of the "ladies" (and they were few in number), was a prolific pastelist whom Clara Endicott Sears "discovered" in the 1920's when she was collecting pictures for her gallery at Fruitlands in Harvard, Massachusetts. Fortunately, Mrs. Bascom kept a diary of her home life and "art doings" (covering a period of fifty-seven years) so that we have a most revealing picture of the life of a minister's wife in the early days of the new nation. Because her husband was called to various churches, she moved often and wrote that "taking profiles" was done more for her satisfaction than for the fee involved. She received "genteel finishing" at Leicester Academy in the Massachusetts town where she

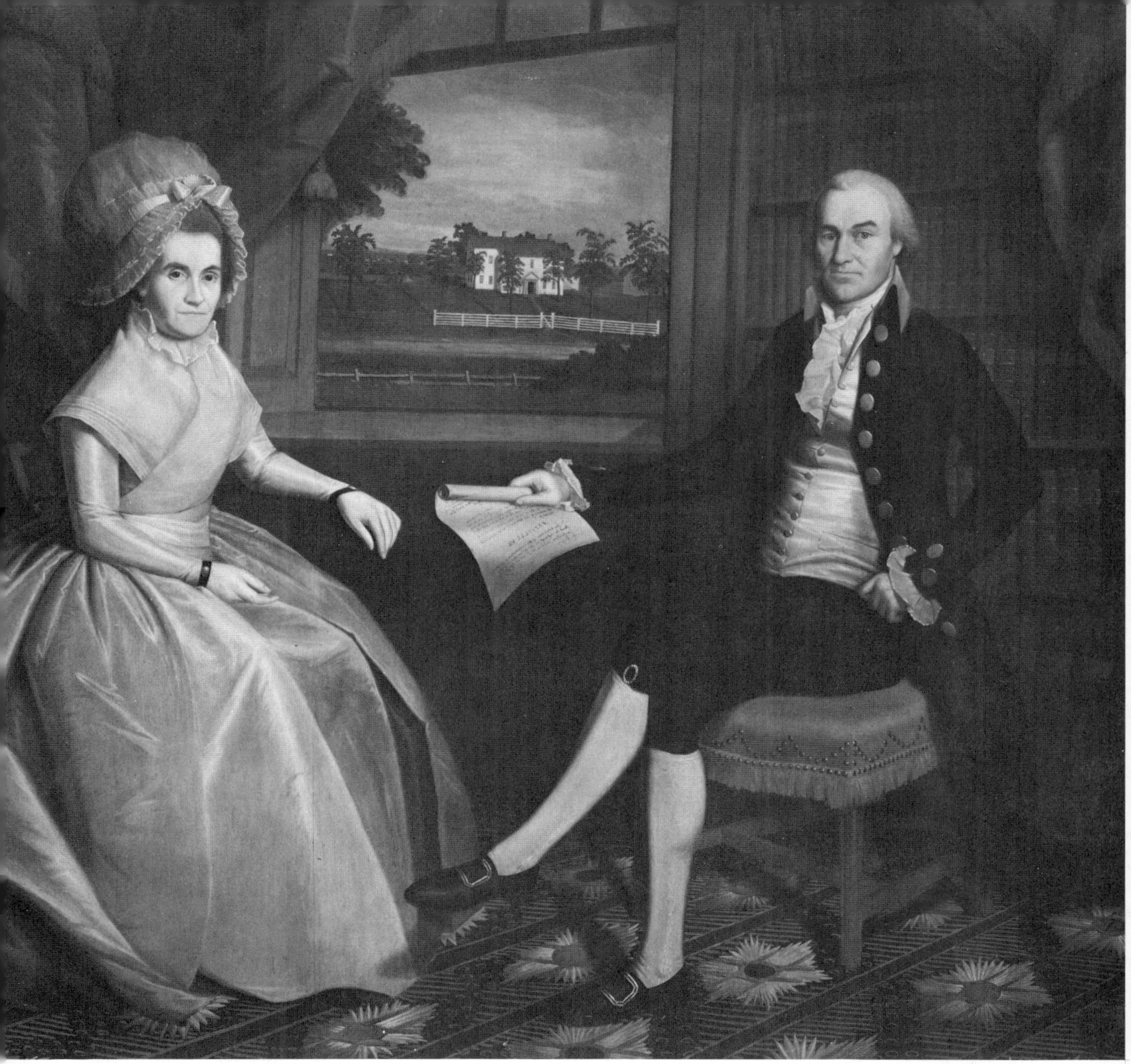

Ralph Earl was a painter of more than ordinary skill whose erratic life undoubtedly limited his achievements. This painting of Oliver Ellsworth and his wife reminds us of the statesman's position as lawyer and leader who urged the adoption of the Constitution of the United States, a copy of which he holds in his hand. Through the window is a view of the Ellsworth Homestead at Windsor, Connecticut, surrounded by thirteen elms, one for each of the thirteen original states. *Photo courtesy Wadsworth Athenaeum*

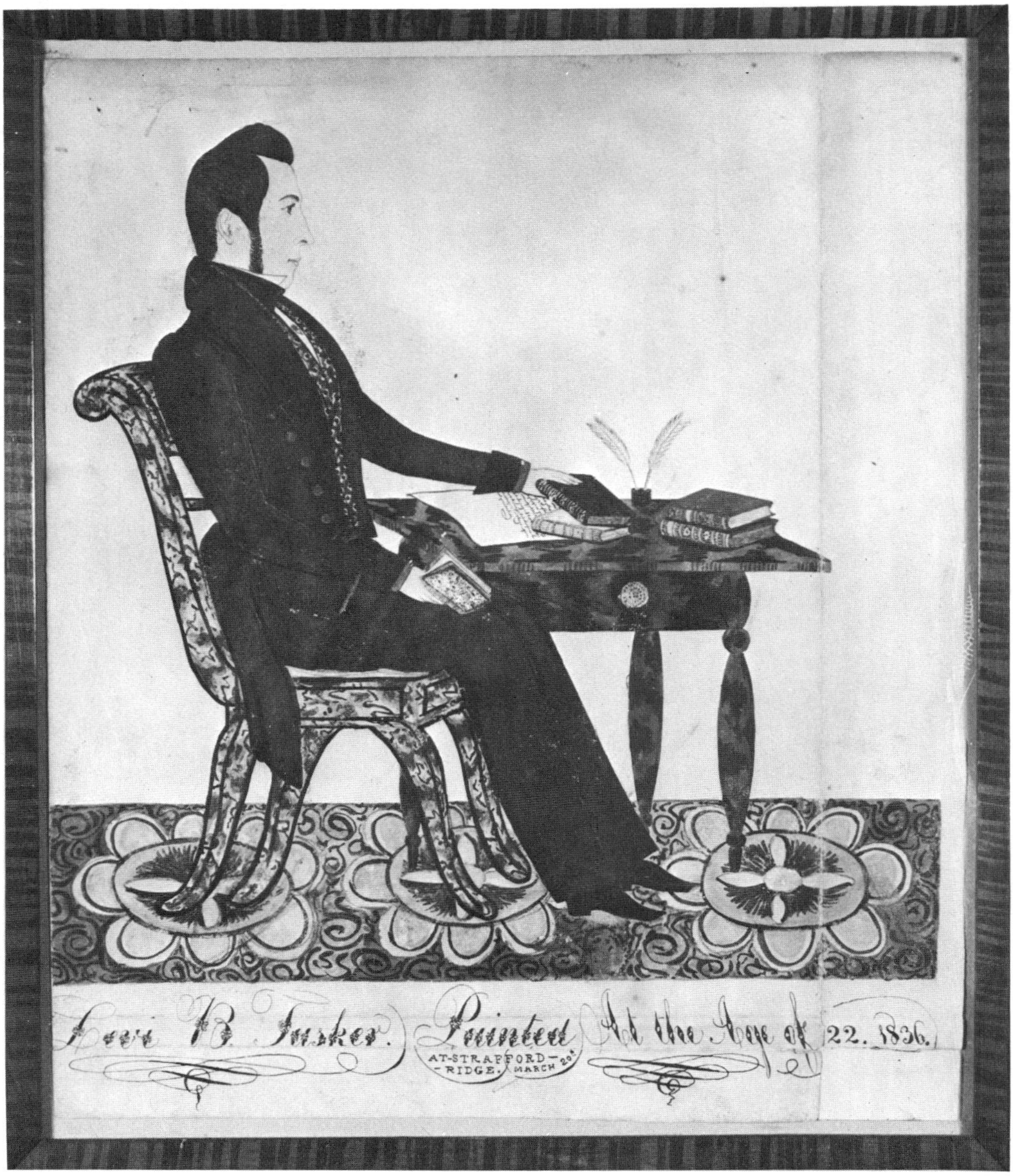

was born and as might be expected from such a background, she became an expert needlewoman. Her accomplishments with the brush were noteworthy, revealing an odd quaintness of approach, but, on the whole, she is of interest primarily as a curious kind of limner. On one occasion when her sitter wore glasses, she accentuated them by cutting spectacles out of gilt paper and pasting them on the portrait.

Anyone who has seen the portrait of Molly Whales Leonard, called the "Lady with her Pets," is not only amused, delighted, and greatly entertained but almost bound to exclaim "Who painted her?" This portrait was featured in color on the cover of *One Hundred and One Masterpieces of American Primitive Painting from the Collection of Edgar William and Bernice Chrysler Garbisch.* The artist was Rufus Hathaway (1770–1822) born at Freetown, Massachusetts. He enjoyed woodcarving,

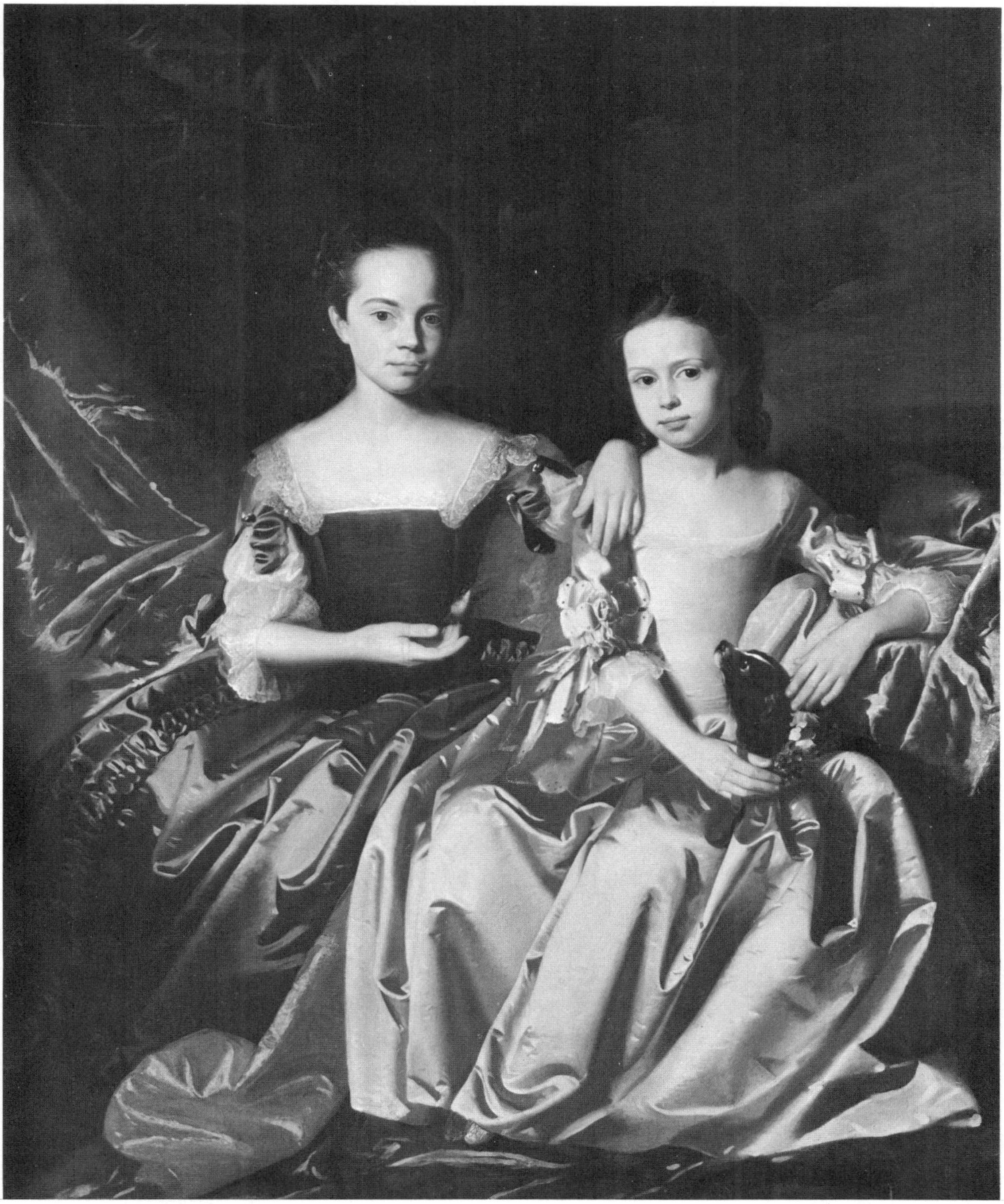

(*Opposite*) Levi B. Tasker, at the age of twenty-two, was painted in water color by Joseph H. Davis, who once signed himself as "the Left Hand Painter." Davis worked in New Hampshire and Maine during the 1830's, painting individuals and family groups. He was obviously fond of elaborate floor decorations, painted furniture, and accessories, which he recorded in meticulous detail. *Photo courtesy Old Sturbridge Village*

(*Above*) Mary and Elizabeth Royall by John Singleton Copley, 1738–1815. "This self-taught native genius, unquestionably the foremost figure of American art before the nineteenth century, in virtual isolation from the artistic currents of his day, developed his talents to surpass any of his contemporaries on this continent. Perceptive of observed nature, he portrayed prosperous merchants, then ladies and families with an uncompromising and truthful eye, but one that obviously delighted in rich fabrics and colors."—Illustrated Handbook, Museum of Fine Arts, Boston. Mary and Elizabeth were the daughters of Isaac Royall of Medford, Massachusetts. Elizabeth married William Pepperell Sparhawk of Kittery, Maine. *Photo courtesy Museum of Fine Arts, Boston*

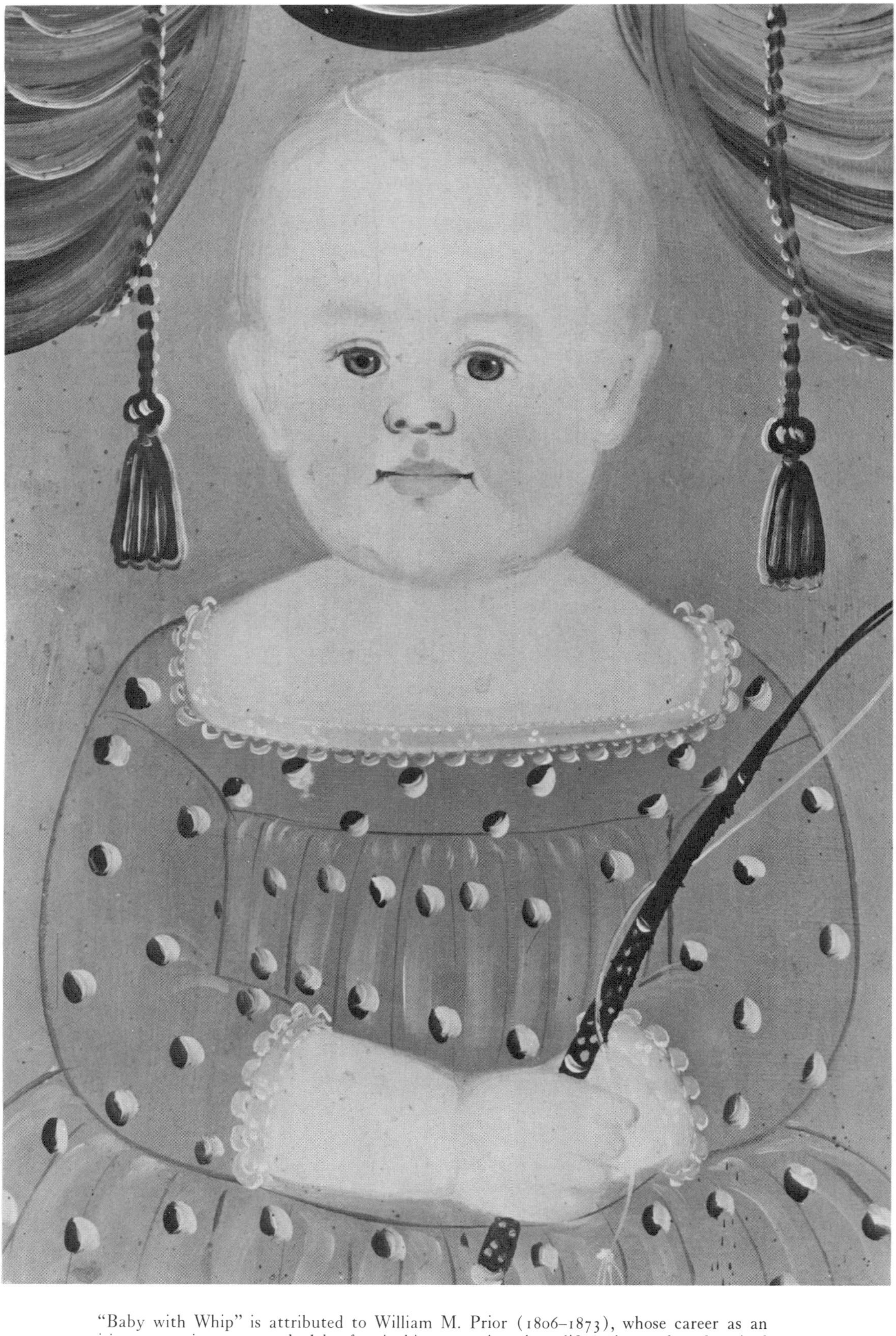

"Baby with Whip" is attributed to William M. Prior (1806–1873), whose career as an itinerant artist was matched by few in his generation. A prolific painter who advertised "flat likenesses without shade or shadow," he operated his "Painting Garret" from his East Boston home for more than a quarter of a century and became a legendary figure even during his lifetime. *Photo courtesy Abby Aldrich Rockefeller Folk Art Collection*

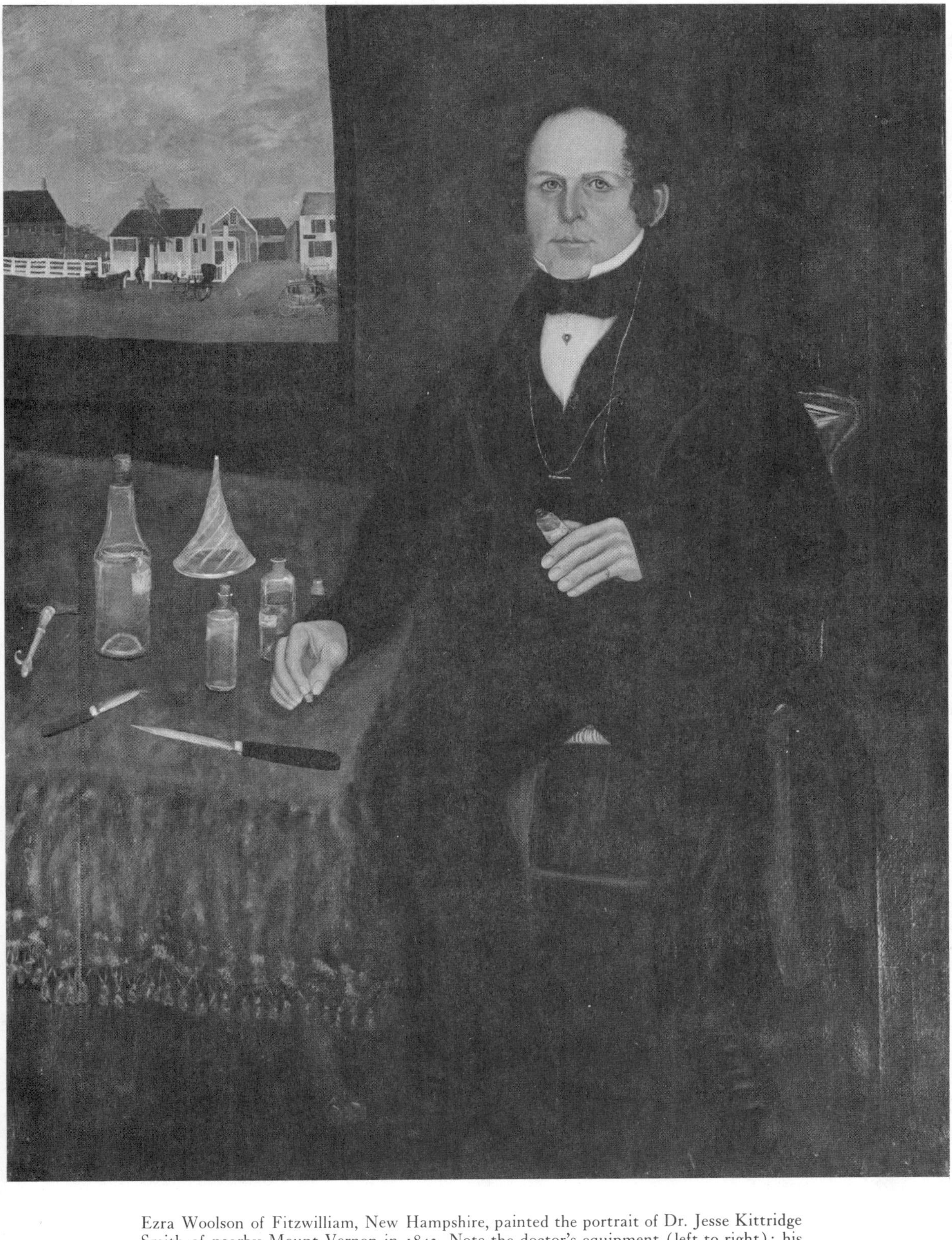

Ezra Woolson of Fitzwilliam, New Hampshire, painted the portrait of Dr. Jesse Kittridge Smith of nearby Mount Vernon in 1842. Note the doctor's equipment (left to right): his tooth extractor, vials, funnel, and scalpels. The setting was made all the more complete by the view through the window showing the doctor's house and the gig he used for traveling about. *Photo courtesy Old Sturbridge Village*

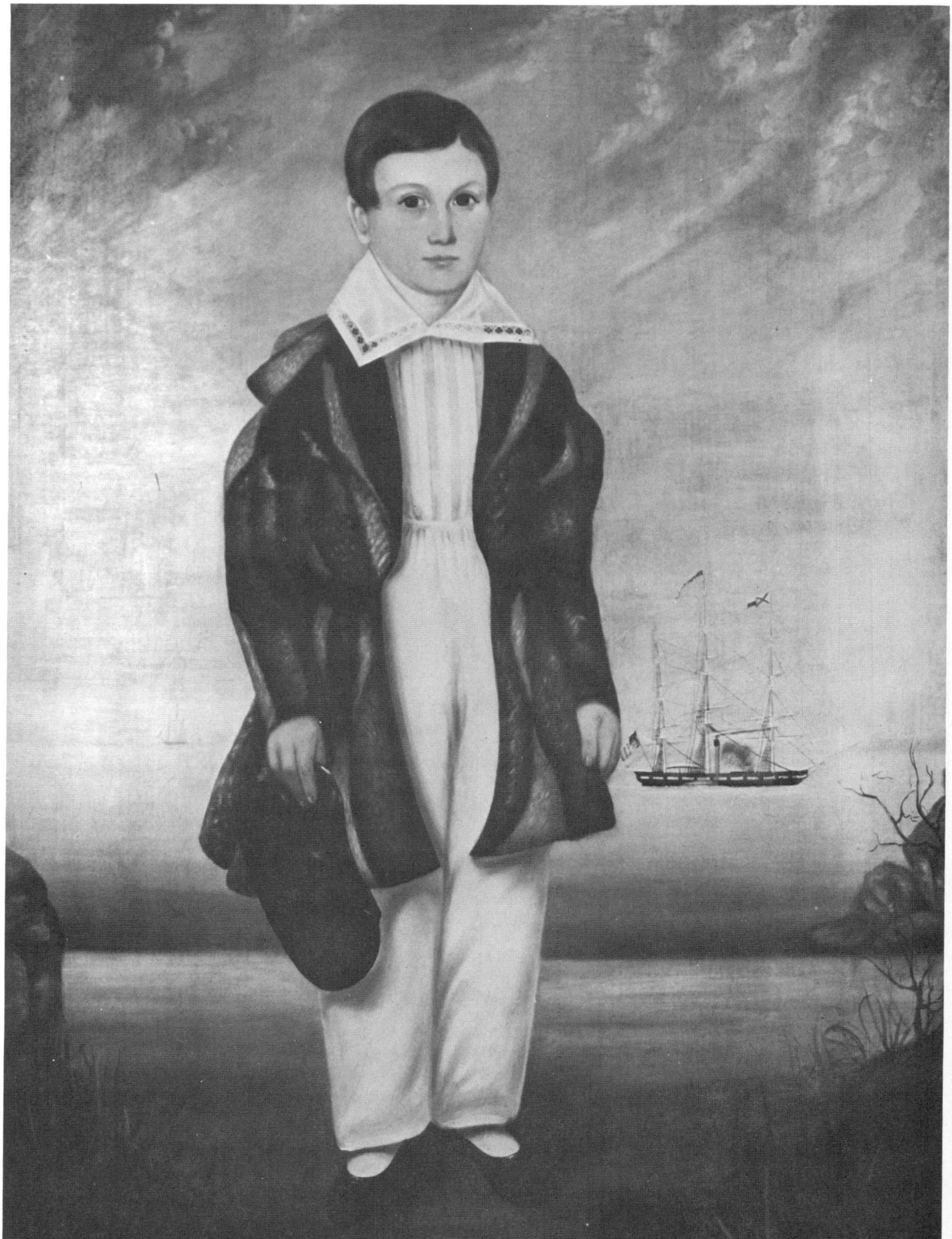

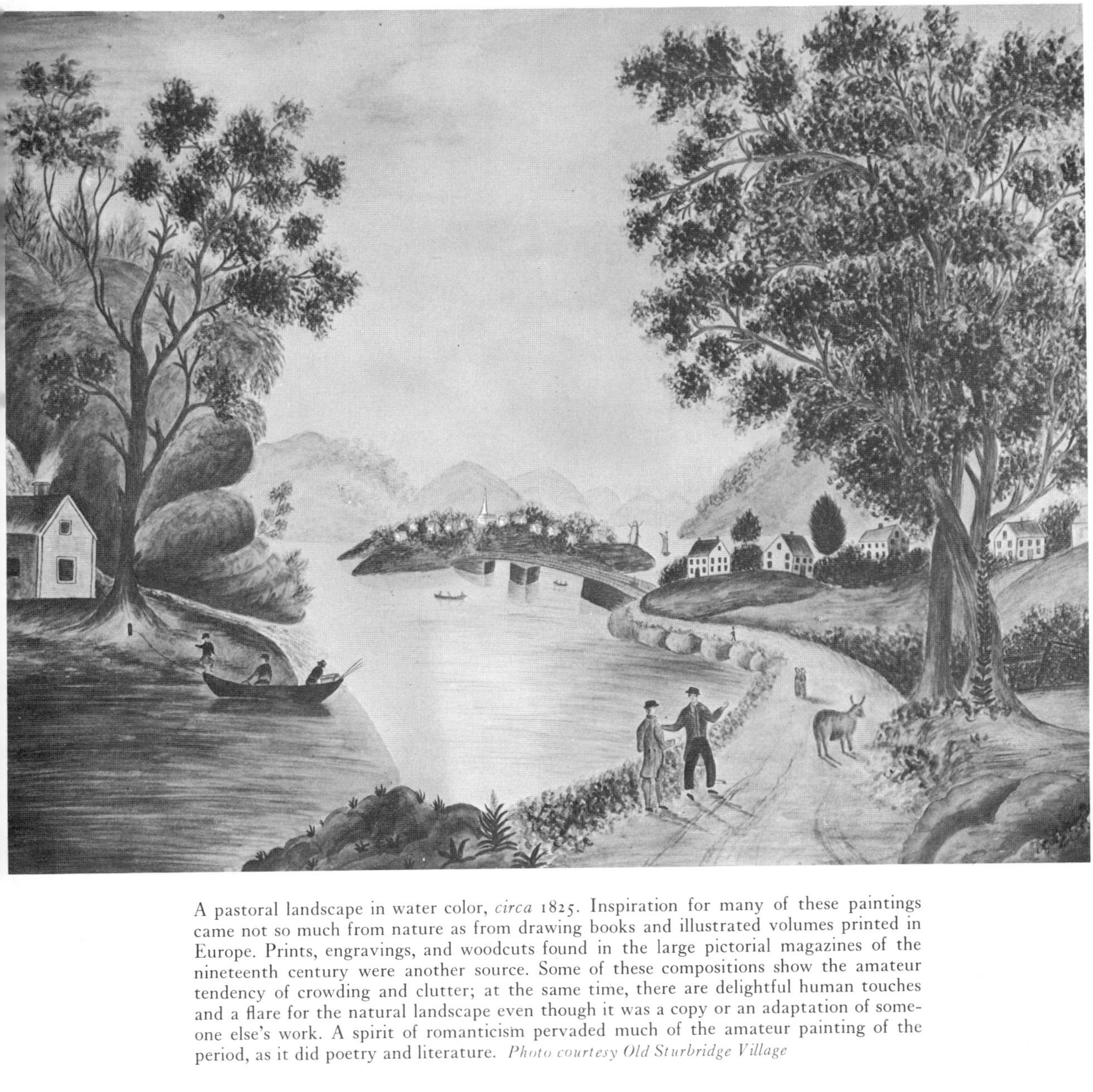

A pastoral landscape in water color, *circa* 1825. Inspiration for many of these paintings came not so much from nature as from drawing books and illustrated volumes printed in Europe. Prints, engravings, and woodcuts found in the large pictorial magazines of the nineteenth century were another source. Some of these compositions show the amateur tendency of crowding and clutter; at the same time, there are delightful human touches and a flare for the natural landscape even though it was a copy or an adaptation of someone else's work. A spirit of romanticism pervaded much of the amateur painting of the period, as it did poetry and literature. *Photo courtesy Old Sturbridge Village*

(*Opposite page*) Isaac Sheffield (1798–1845) was a Connecticut limner whose portrait of James Francis Smith painted at the age of five years and ten months is of more than passing interest. The boy is dressed in a penguin-skin coat which he wore when he landed in New London from the ship *Chelsea* on October 12, 1837, having returned from a whaling voyage to the South Sea island of Desolation. His father, Captain Franklin F. Smith, was a successful whaler who made nine voyages to the South Atlantic between 1830 and 1841 and brought back 16,000 barrels of whale oil and 1,100 of sperm oil. James also followed the sea, first becoming captain of a schooner and later a steamer.
Photo courtesy Lyman Allyn Museum

was also a joiner and even made his own picture frames for the canvases he painted. After marrying he settled in Duxbury, Massachusetts, and, having studied medicine under a Marshfield doctor, eventually became the town physician. Not many of the itinerant painters were as successful.

The story of Chester Harding (1792–1866) is surely a Horatio Alger tale in the realm of art if ever one was recorded. He did not need a biographer for *My Egotistography* published in 1866 is a record sufficiently disarming and detailed to give us a complete picture of this fabulous personality. Born in the small mountain village of Conway in western Massachusetts, he was so poor that at the age of twelve he "lived out" to a farmer in a nearby town for six dollars a month. At the age of thirty, he was still a shy young man straight from the backwoods when he wrote of the summer he spent in Pittsfield and Northampton. "I one day received an invitation to a large party . . . which I accepted; but, as the evening drew near, I began to regret that I had done so. I finally went into my room and took the matter into serious consideration. Should I go? or should I not? It was a fearful ordeal to go through. I had never been to a fashionable lady's party, and should not know how to behave. My heart grew faint at the thought of my ignorance and awkwardness. But then, I reflected, there must be a first time; . . . . So I went, and passed through the trial better than I anticipated; but I was glad when it was over."

Having painted portraits of two Boston men, he was urged to go there. Of this experience he wrote: "I did so, and for six months rode triumphantly on the top wave of fortune. I took a large room, arranged my pictures, and fixed upon one o'clock as my hour for exhibition. As soon as the clock struck, my bell would begin to ring; and people would flock in, sometimes to the number of fifty. New orders were constantly given me for pictures. I do not think any artist in this country ever enjoyed more popularity than I did; but popularity is often easily won, and as easily lost. Mr. (Gilbert) Stuart, the greatest portrait painter this country ever produced, was at that time in his manhood's strength as a painter; yet he was idle half the winter. He would ask friends, 'How rages the Harding fever?'"

After returning to America from a trip to Europe, he painted Emily Marshall, then the reigning beauty of Boston. He described the experience thus: "No artist's skill could be put to a severer test; for her beauty depended much more upon the expression of her animated face, which when lighted up in conversation, was bewitchingly lovely. I did not succeed to my own satisfaction, though others seemed well pleased." Emily so dazzled Boston in her day that it was said that laborers would forego their short lunch hour to catch a glimpse of her.

Harding could call the names of many eminent Americans and Englishmen as well whose heads he had put on canvas during the first thirty years of his career. He was widely known and loved for his buoyant personality and delightful sense of humor, which the critics claim greatly exceeded his skill as a painter. He loved to tell the story of a lady who had recently died and whose pet cat had for several days wandered dejectedly about the house in search of something which she missed. At last she entered a room where a Harding likeness of her late mistress was standing on a sofa. The creature at once gave a bound and tried to settle herself in her accustomed place on the old lady's lap.

The story of Joseph Whiting Stock (1815–1855) born at Springfield, Massachusetts, has always excited interest. Badly crippled by an accident in childhood, he was urged to pursue painting as a livelihood. Being of a methodical turn of mind, he kept a journal and, from it, we learn that he painted the Smith children of his native city, William Howard and Mary Jane, for six dollars each in 1838. He also painted landscapes, made anatomical drawings, and decorated window shades as he traveled about. Later he went into business with a daguerreotypist. From his journal we learn that he made more than nine hundred portraits in the thirteen-year period from 1832 to 1845. His first likeness was that of his sister and he delighted in painting children, often enhancing his subjects with such accessories as their favorite toys.

Not every lad who painted a neighbor's likeness on a barn door grew up to be a portrait painter, but such was the beginning of Matthew Prior's (1806–1873) career. Born in Bath, Maine, the son of a Duxbury, Massachusetts, shipbuilder, he boasted of his descent from the Pilgrims and remained a flamboyant showman throughout his life. He made every step count as he walked the dusty roads seeking buyers for his talent. Possessed of more than a little of the

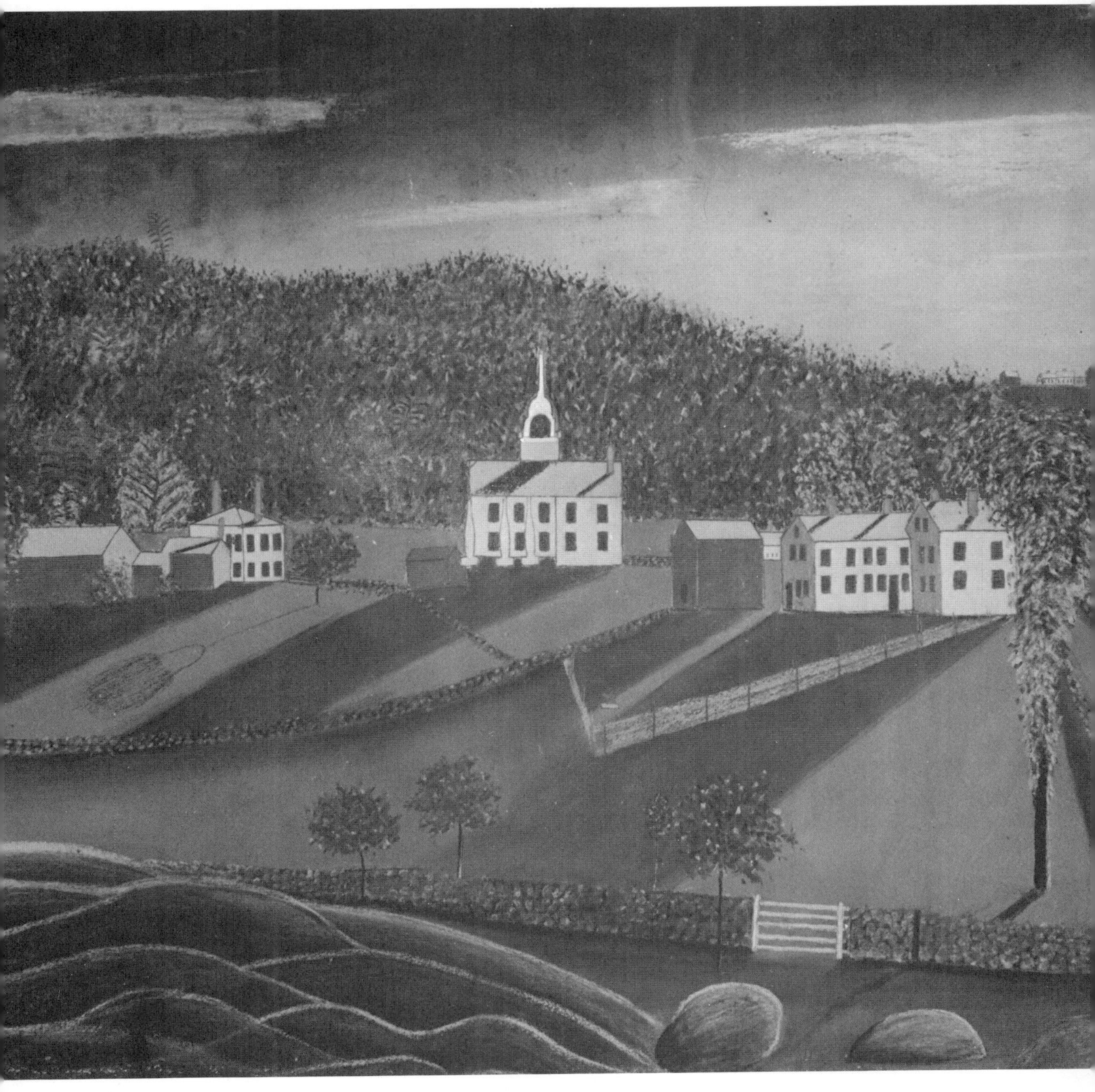

A landscape rendered in pastel on paper, believed to have been done about 1840. It may have been copied from a contemporary print as was typical with ladies of the period, who sometimes took lessons in painting or, without formal instruction, expressed their prim and genteel emotions in painting flowers or landscapes. *Photo courtesy Old Sturbridge Village*

peddler's skill at bargaining, he succeeded in getting sitters for whatever sum they could afford. He worked rapidly and turned out hundreds of likenesses over a long period of years.

Eccentric and full of notions, he built a house in East Boston which he called the "Painting Garret" and beneath the eaves he kept a hive of bees which flew daily to the flower beds in the Public Gardens. Once he had "arrived" in the profession, having painted Charles Dickens, Abraham Lincoln, Theodore Parker (of anti-slavery fame), and many other notables, he raised his prices. Not particular about using canvas, he did Andrew Jackson's portrait on bed ticking and such figures as George and Martha Washington on glass. No limner in New England or anywhere else for that matter can compare with this "character" who seems to have been the epitome of all the vagaries that one associates with people of temperament.

The fantastic pictures of biblical and mythological subjects executed by Erastus Salisbury Field (1805–1900), a New England nonagenarian, born in the hill town of Leverett, Massachusetts, have intrigued all who have seen them. He was also a painter of likenesses. He married an artist named Pheba Gilmore and they lived in Hartford, Connecticut, for a while before returning to Massachusetts where he died. Fascinated by biblical history, he painted the Garden of Eden on more than one occasion and a wonderful garden it is. Although he "looked over the shoulder" of Samuel F. B. Morse for a few months, he belongs to the American primitive school. Perhaps had he been strongly influenced by the academic point of view, he would not have expressed the fantastic imagination which his work so obviously displays. In 1876, he produced "Historical Monument of the American Republic," a marvel in size and concept of the "history of our country —on a monumental form"; it covers the period from the settling of Jamestown to the days of the whisky risings. His portraits are soft in color and his "children" are especially delightful. In the village of Sunderland (not far from his birthplace), where he spent his later years, he used his barn for a studio and the children took great delight in watching him paint.

The biographies of the limners whose records are obtainable bequeathed to us a most extraordinary collection of pictures of every sort which are as appealing and as illuminating as their canvases themselves. Many of them make fascinating reading but not all have been unearthed by any means. For those who seek a glimpse into the past, particularly into the lives of the amateur painters of the eighteenth and nineteenth centuries, there exists a fascinating and revealing field of exploration. By no means has the last word been written in this almost limitless field. As Nina Fletcher Little has expressed it in *American Folk Art from the Abby Aldrich Rockefeller Folk Art Collection:* "Fortunately, much folk art has survived. Modest in its goals, it is nevertheless proof of the reservoir of artistic strength to be found in America's early years. Popular education, modern modes of easy travel and communications provide today's artist ever new ways of expressing himself. But the folk artist has left us an intimate portrait of our social history as varied, original, and irrepressible as the democratic sources from which it came. Its freedom of expression, documentary value, and artistic charm combine to make it a significant part of our American culture—and one that is being increasingly appreciated today."

Painting on Glass

Reverse painting on glass is one aspect of the early decorator's art which, like gilding, required considerable patience and competence. Executed on the back of a glass panel in reverse, the finished effect was viewed through the glass from the front. As with other forms of artistic endeavor, both the highly skilled artisan and the amateurs attempted this form of decoration. In any event the pieces of it that remain hold a strange lure for those who enjoy working in art restoration or copying good examples for present-day use and enjoyment. The detailed portion of the design was applied first and the background last. Subjects used for the motifs varied greatly. These included flowers, fruits, shells, animals, landscapes, buildings, seascapes, figures, portraits, and geometric designs, use and adoption being governed by the surface to be covered. The decorators did work to order for their customers or for the clockmaker. A most unusual shelf clock owned by the Museum of Fine Arts, Boston, serves as an excellent example of this form of painting. Black and gold was a favorite combination, but a wide range of colors was utilized in many of the pieces.

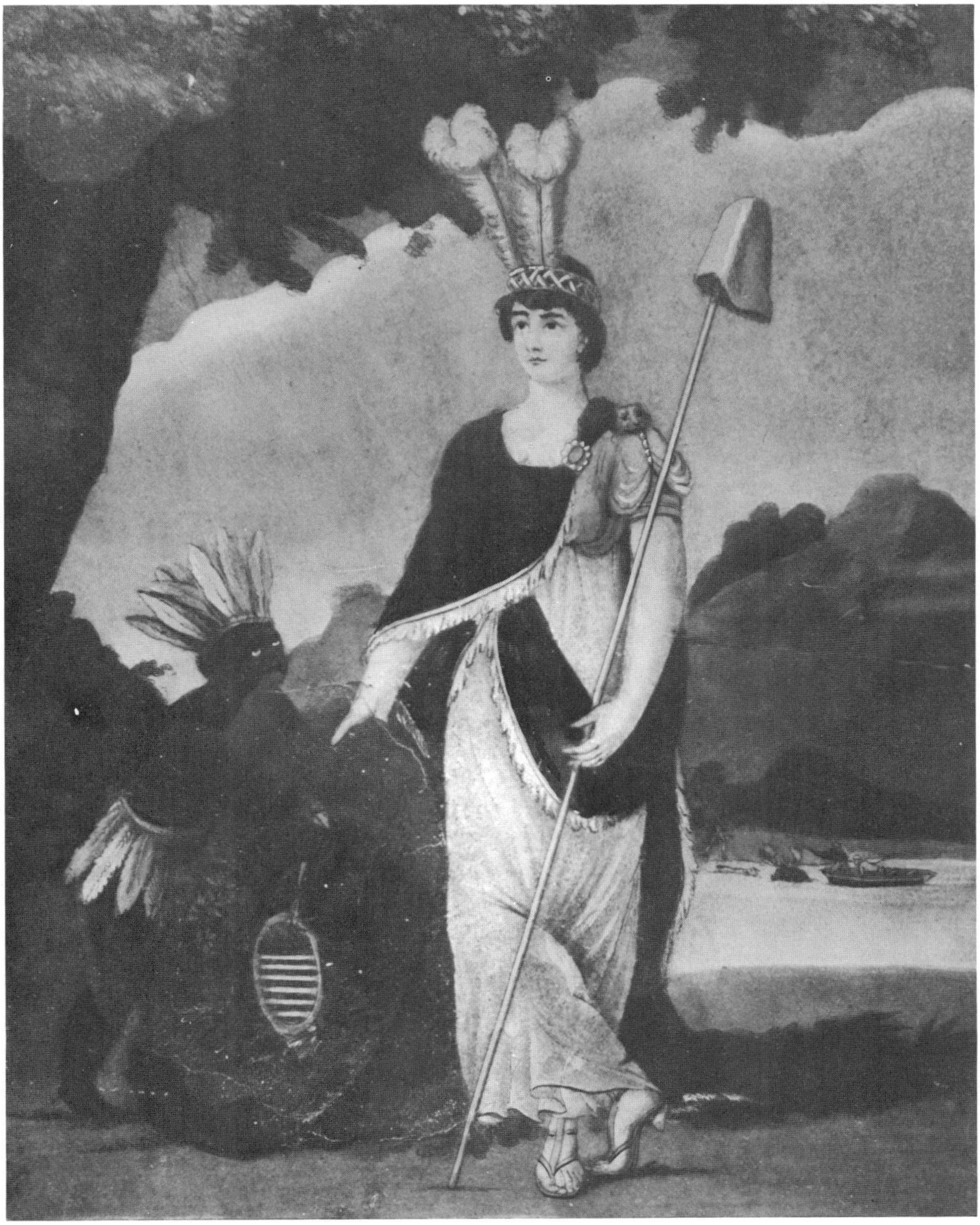

Painting on glass, which required more than ordinary skill and patience, became popular in the nineteenth century, but it was by no means a new technique, having been practiced at least two centuries earlier. Mezzotints (colored etchings) were transferred to glass by applying a sticky coating of Venice turpentine to the surface of the glass before laying the colored print on, face downward. By rubbing the back of the print with a moistened sponge, the outline was transferred to the glass. Colors were then added, in reverse order, by first moistening the glass surface with turpentine to take the highlights. Background colors were added last. The same process was used with freehand designs. *Photo courtesy Old Sturbridge Village*

Quilting—Its Place in New England History

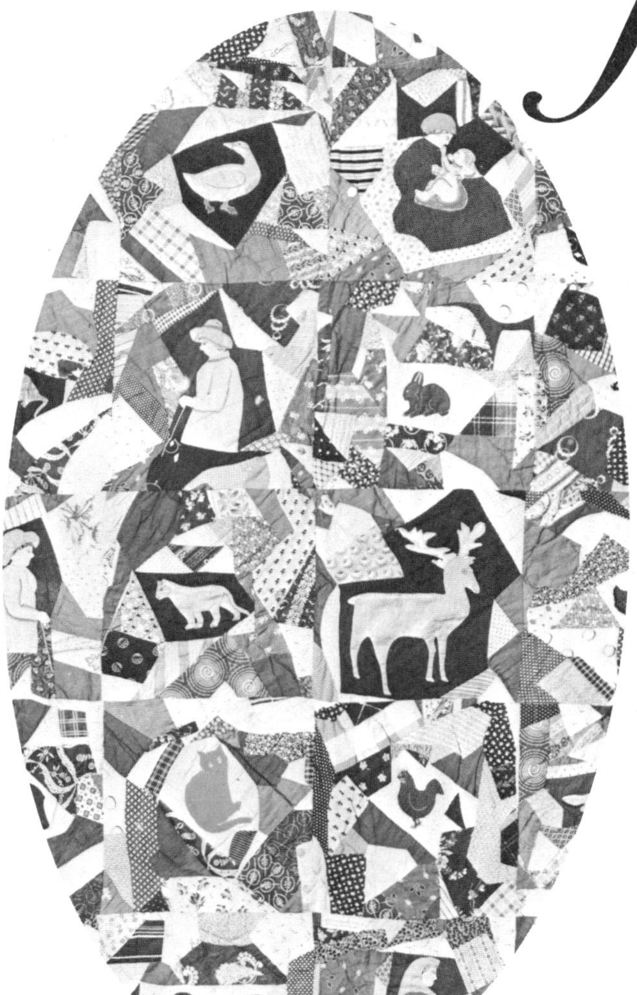

Long, long ago quilting came from the East, for the Chinese have worn quilted garments through the ages. A history of needle arts tells us that the Italians had a quilting of their own which was copied throughout the Continent; that is—quilting that held a layer of straw or tow between two pieces of covering. This would seem to be a type of mattress, and so it could be called, for it was used on the bare earthen floors or planks. Quilting to Americans means two things: a pieced quilt or patchwork bedcover; a stitching which, in design, held together a top and a bottom of an interlined coverlet.

In *Woman's Day* magazine, quilting is described in this manner: "The quality of this needle art is subtle. Perhaps the quickest way to understand it is to think of quilting as the obverse of embroidery." Embroidery dominates and decorates a fabric with stitches; quilting does not. Quilting stitches are so modestly retiring that one must look for them to see them. Only their effects strike the eye, and these effects are lights and shadows—the same technique used by competent artists in landscapes, portraits, and still life. Thus one may *quilt* a quilt. When the quilt is an appliqué type, the method of quilting the quilt is usually employed. After making a "Friendship Knot" or a "Tulip" quilt, one would not wish to obliterate the pattern of the design that was sewed together; rather, one would quilt around these designs, using such stitches as the "Princess Feather," the "Spiderweb," the "Running Vine," the "Serpentine" to name but a few of the many quilting stitches. For the most part, quilting patterns are simple, and they must be for they quilt only the background, thus producing light and shadow effects.

Nathaniel Hawthorne once noted that "women are never more at home with their own hearts than while they are sewing." Quilting is simple, straight sewing, employing, as it does, cloth, needle, thread, scissors, and exactness in imagination. The Puritan homemaker had little time and few materials with which to make quilts; the cutting and piecing of quilts require time and there must be adequate light for the task. If the cover is not to be quilted, some method must be employed to hold together the top and bottom layer and the padding in between. This method is called tacking.

At first the colonial wife resorted to woven coverlets; when materials were more accessible she made her quilts. The extra padding which the quilt provided was actually a kind of insurance for the family who slept in cold, drafty bedrooms. The little children who slept in trundle beds built close to the floor were open-sesame to chills, tuberculosis, pneumonia, and the other respiratory diseases that follow in the wake of bitter cold rooms, swept by the icy, deathlike fingers of winter winds and blizzards. The only warmth that could be provided for the beds in those earliest days came from heated stones and bricks wrapped and placed in the beds. Then followed the warming pan filled with hot coals.

Although the fire in the fireplace roared, heat could only radiate a limited distance, and those beyond were chilled to the bone. One can easily conjure up a mental picture of those earliest structures put up by the first settlers. Some were sod-roofed dugouts, made of logs, cut into the side of a hill; where there was no hill, no protection from the wind was possible. The English wigwams, so-called, made of bark were makeshift at best, and the thatch-roofed wooden houses were easy prey to both fire and wind. Even a casual look at the restorations at Plimoth Plantation on Cape Cod and Pioneer Village in Salem are proof of their primitiveness. The first completely wooden houses with shingled roofs and board siding were no great improvement either. They were, all of them, through those early years cold, windswept, and barren. Since the women found that there was a dearth of material to make quilts, they began to save every scrap of left-over, worn-out clothing and this economy gave birth to the rag bag.

The fashioning of quilts was practiced in Europe as early as the eleventh century, so that when the English, Dutch, French and other immigrants settled here, they brought with them their own patterns and methods of making quilts. Prior to 1750, practically all the quilts made in this country were pieced quilts.

We must not overlook the fact that American coverlets and quilts, like all other early crafts, were made under great handicaps and under the most unbelievable hardships, all of which are described elsewhere in these pages. As with so many commonplace and essential articles, letters and diaries reveal little about the patchwork or pieced quilt prior to 1750. But, in the hundred years between 1750 and 1850, an uncounted number of quilts were pieced and patched. Many of these remain and may be seen in museums and private collections. Others are described in numerous books on quilting.

In the *The Romance of the Patchwork Quilt in America,* by Carrie A. Hall and Rose G. Kretsinger, we read: "The slow changing of our social patterns has been recorded in many ways, but no one product has so closely reflected the folkways of some portions of American life as has the patchwork quilt. Although quilt making is one of the world's oldest arts, the pieced quilt is our own American production. The patchwork quilt, as such, has come to be a distinctly American art form, indigenous to our native soil and well embedded in the background of our national consciousness. It has played a part in the history of our nation, and many aspects of early American history are reflected in its development."

Quietly, but nonetheless poignantly, and in a symbolic way, the homecraft art of quilting has left its mark on the record of American life. This form of stitchery depicts the growth and development of every-day activity from earliest colonial times to the present in a kind of panorama. First, it reveals the vital, necessary integral part of homemaking that made survival possible.

Once this was achieved, from it there emerged a true desire to capture a new kind of beauty in the home. At this stage, quilting reached its fullest height. Today we can look back on a revival that occurred earlier in this century and notice that the daily papers and current periodicals all have quilt designs and directions for making them in the columns featuring home decoration.

The pieced quilt is simple to make. Using up left-overs as it does, the appliquéd type is apt to be a more artistic expression of the quilters' craft, in that it is created "out of whole cloth." The *quilted* quilt, on the other hand, is a coverlet of plain material sewed together into designs using both quilt patterns and quilt stitch.

When quilts were in their heyday, there were numerous ways of classifying them. For example there were "Friendship Quilts" for which the maker begged from each of her friends, enough material for an individual block. While every block was uniform in size, each might

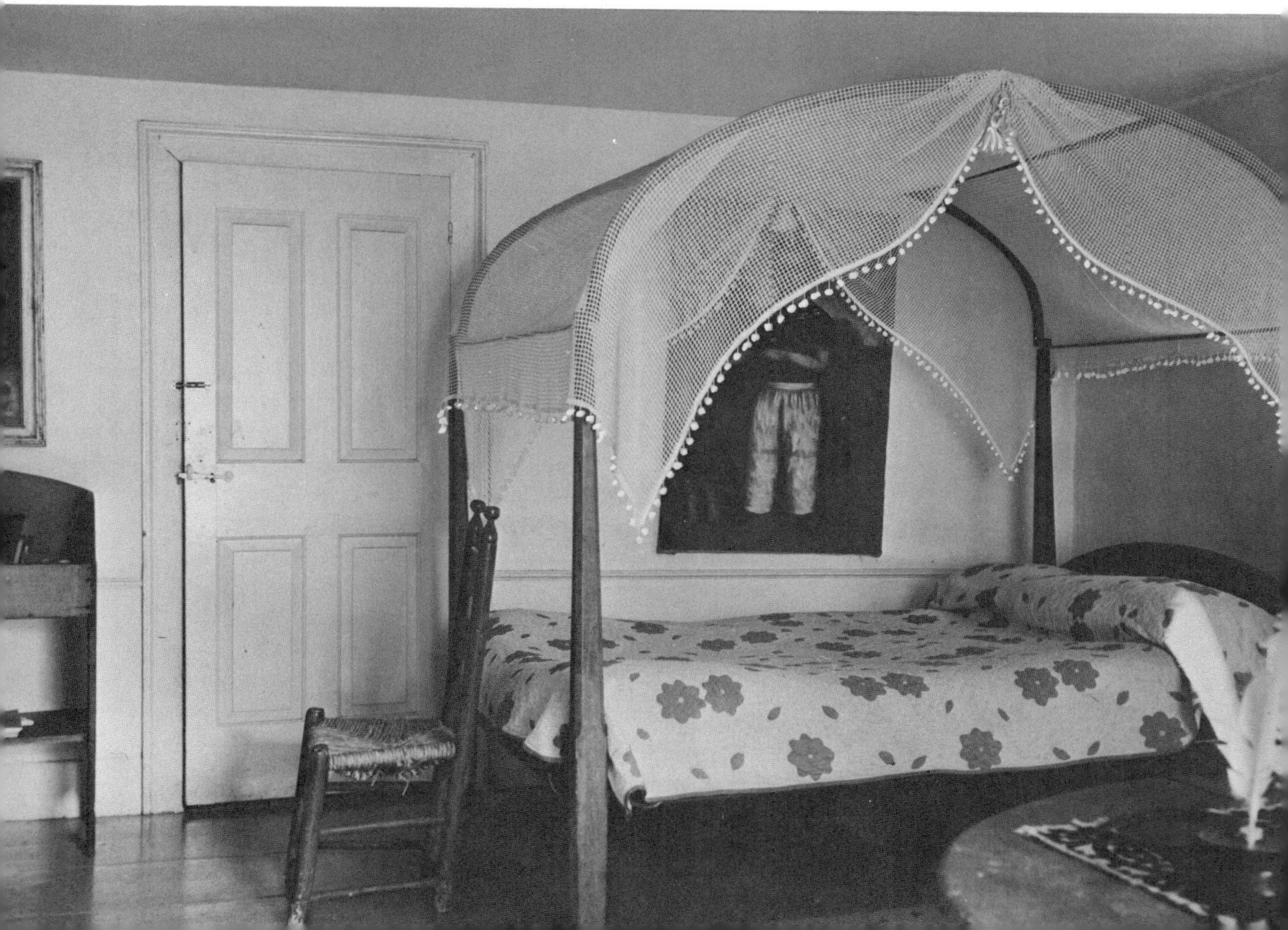

have a different pattern. The one who asked for these contributions was she who put it together. A "Friendship Medley" quilt was one where each block was made by a friend who brought it finished. There were even "Friendship Medley Surprise Parties" for this type of quilt and we read that they "were a sprightly and genteel mode of entertainment some years before the Revolution."

Then, too, there were "Freedom Quilts." These were made to commemorate a young man's twenty-first birthday, and one of these was often a gift of the recipient's feminine friends. Scraps of their prettiest frocks were brought by the girls to his home; there they spent an afternoon piecing them together. This chatter-filled afternoon was followed by a supper provided by his mother; the result of their cooperative labor was laid away until the young man married.

Album quilts included many types. Sometimes a needlewoman made an entire quilt and, when the quilt was completed asked her friends to come to her home and autograph a block. Sometimes the donors of an album quilt met to present the blocks at one time having stitched and autographed them beforehand. As was the way with women, they lingered to admire the other blocks, and to suggest an appealing arrangement.

A goodly number of the oldest quilts that remain in museums are unusually large in size. (The Shelburne Museum at Shelburne, Vermont, contains an extensive and impressive col-

(*Left*) A plain fish-net canopy covers the bonnet-top frame of this simple field bed with its gracefully tapered posts. The appliquéd bedcover and the hooked rug together with the portraits lend warm touches of color to this seventeenth-century room in Rockport. *Photo courtesy Samuel Chamberlain*

(*Below*) Governor Gore's mansion (1804) in Waltham, Massachusetts, is one of the notable historic landmarks of New England. The handsomely proportioned bed, in a second floor chamber, with its reeded posts is tastefully fitted with a net tester and white quilted quilt. The antimacassar on the chair had a purpose—to protect the upholstery from the macassar oil which the men used in their hair. *Photo courtesy Samuel Chamberlain*

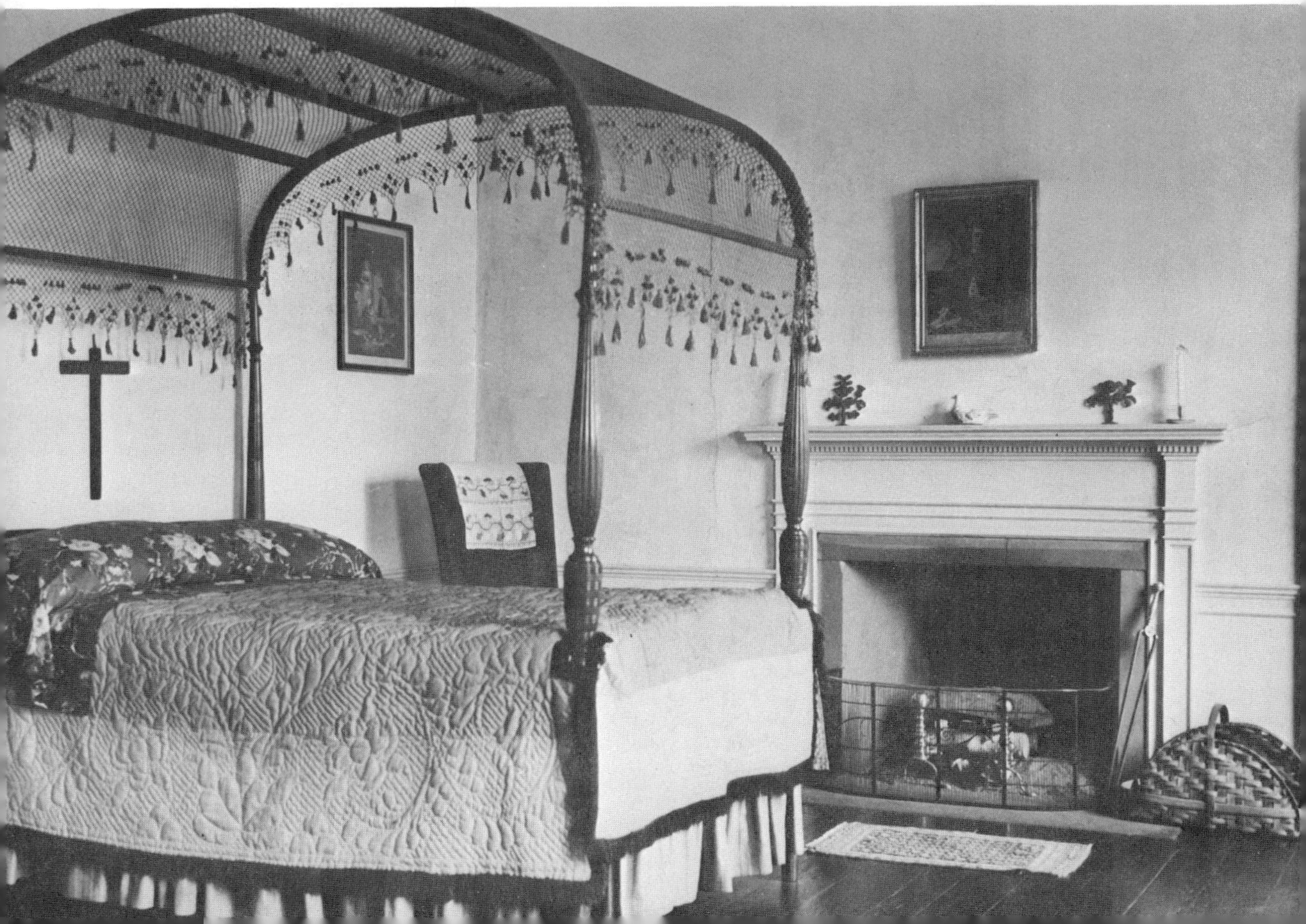

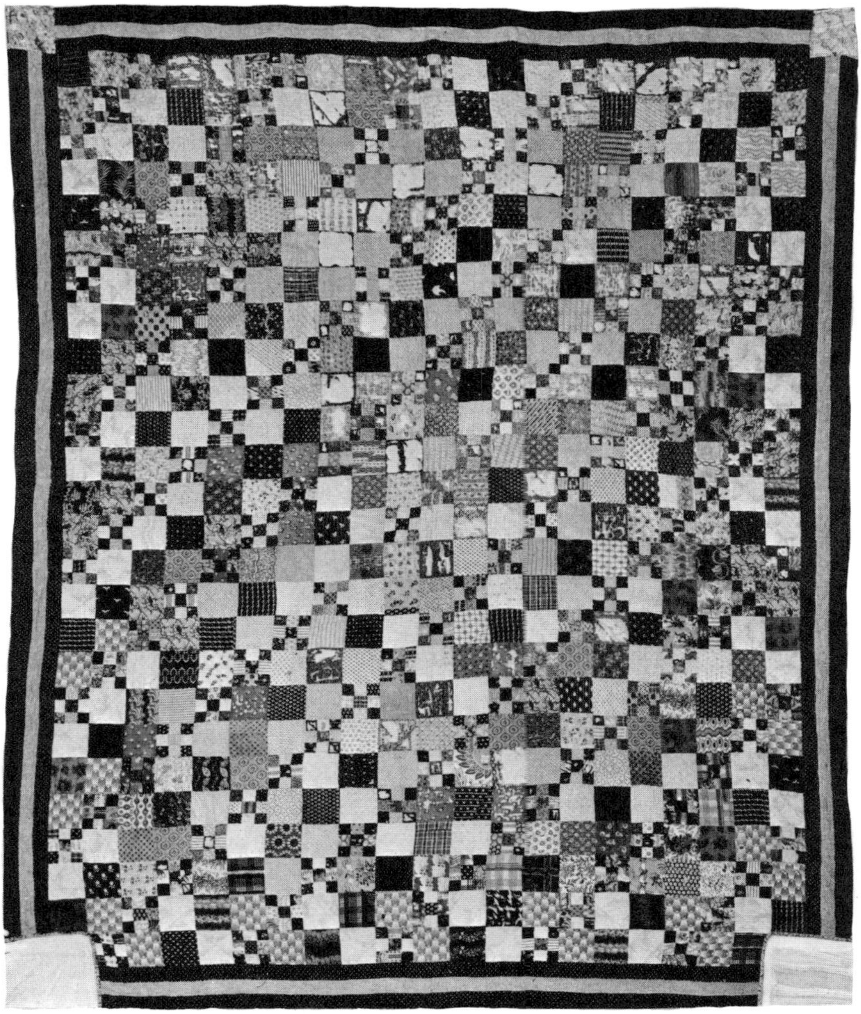

This Nine Patch Chain quilt (1825–1850), found at the old Brock Farm, South Newbury, Vermont, was probably made by Harriet E. Brock. The stitches seaming the blocks together are meticulous and tiny and every remnant of material in the scrap bag—no matter how small—has been utilized. Each of the miniature blocks making up the nine patches is less than one inch square. Even in the larger 3×3 inch blocks, the material, although of the same print, has been pieced (in some cases) to get a block of this size. Two dark blue strips on either side of a pink-patterned cotton band form the border. The backing is of homespun linen which has been turned in and the two edges sewed together with over-and-over stitches. A thin cotton fill has been used, quilted with a simple diagonal pattern. 69×81 inches. Second quarter nineteenth century. *Photo courtesy Shelburne Museum*

lection of great historic value; all are superbly displayed.) Florence Peto, a widely known authority on quilts, has an ingenious and simple explanation for these large quilts. She points out that in the Paul Revere House in Boston there was but one sleeping room for Revere, his wife, and their twelve children. The youngest child probably slept with his parents while the others were tucked into the trundle bed and on pallets, laid on the floor. In the morning each pallet and its bedding, together with that of the trundle, was placed on the parents' bed, making a mound so high that a large quilt was necessary to cover it.

In *Old Patchwork Quilts and the Women Who Made Them,* Ruth E. Finley, another authority, reminds us of the facts: "It is in the nature of a folk craft that its products reflect the personal whimsy of the individual worker. There is a living reason for all that human fingers create. Sometimes it is a mere matter of convenience, as in the curves of a candlestick, graceful beyond words yet accurately fitting the hand. Today we admire the beauty of a wing chair, little thinking that its enclosed back was originally designed to cut off the drafts of the illy heated houses of our ancestors. Such creations do more than serve the purpose for which they were intended; they remain as aids to understanding of the long since past."

The quilters of long ago used the materials and colors close at hand. Sometimes, it is a shock to see purple and shocking pink in the same square, and we are apt to think of our forebears as lacking in color sense. It is curious to note that the truly old quilt patterns, particularly those of geometrical design, fit admirably with the angles and the straight lines of the severely designed modern or contemporary house—the Frank Lloyd Wright type of architecture. Indeed, it may be observed that some of the so-called "new" fabric designs are so nearly duplicates of the antique quilt patterns as to appear to be direct copies!

Although quilting, like patchwork, was first used for utilitarian purposes by those of little means, it eventually became an art in which the well-to-do excelled as well and were proud of their accomplishments. The average eighteenth-century home was small, but families were large. The furniture of the period was made mostly by journeymen cabinetmakers, who made beds according to their customers' dictates. A charge of twopence per inch of bed was the going fee, so that some fourpost beds were only four feet wide! It was easy to judge a man's wealth by looking at the width of his beds. As stated previously, the bed usually accommodated mother, father, and the youngest child. Sometimes children slept on feather beds arranged on settles, and the servants, if any, had to be satisfied with a straw pallet on the floor. As neatness was the order of the day, all these makeshifts had to be "stashed" away, either on top of the bed or under. Probably this accounts for the origin of the valance. (The function of the outsize quilt has already been accounted for.)

Quilting was a generation-to-generation affair. A woman pursued the inclination of her fingers and fancy, and designed a quilt which pleased her as much as the purpose which it served. She taught her daughter to quilt, and a lazy girl it was, who, when she was asked in marriage, did not have at least fourteen quilts which she had made herself in "family" patterns and her own as well!

The existence of pre-Revolutionary and Revolutionary quilts is explained by the fact that certain quilts were "best" quilts. These counterpanes were placed on the bed only when the minister came to call, and were immediately removed when he left. Then, an "everyday" one went back in its place. Why? Remember that *the* bed was most generally in the parlor! This "best" quilt was always fashioned from the *best* of the homespuns, or whatever material was used.

The scrap bag was a treasured one and any snippets or samples that could be spared were put into this bag; one such hung on almost every doornob. How different today; with a wealth of material, color, and designs, we do not have to *save* for the quilt. There is even a Cloth-of-the-World Club, which monthly brings to your very door swatches of different, tantalizing materials from everywhere.

A bedspread, little known because of its rarity, is the wool-on-wool coverlet. These are among the most interesting and least known of all early New England bedcovers. One, a bisected specimen (1774), has been preserved in Chelsea, Vermont, only because it was used formerly as a padding for a carpet. When the carpet wore out and had to be replaced, the coverlet was found underneath. Made on a woolen foundation, wool was either hooked in or coarse needlework was employed to produce this distinctly different coverlet. They had their origin in the Connecticut colony. Another rarity is described by George Francis Dow in *Everyday Life in the Massachusetts Bay Colony:* "In the days immediately following the settlement many a New England bed was covered with a rug. When William Clarke of Salem, Massachusetts, died in 1647, in the parlor of his house was a bed with a green rug covering which was valued by the appraisers at fourteen shillings."

Quilting was also done on frames. After the pieces had been sewn together, the quilt top, filler, and bottom were stretched up by two horizontal bars, about two feet long and two vertical bars about four feet long. The bars were approximately two inches wide and thick, held together at the corners with clamps.

The "Crazy Quilt" is the quilt put together without "rime or reason." Various pieces are sewed together in matching-sized squares. In the 1870's the Crazy Quilt was being made of odds and ends of ribbons, satins, velvets, and silks, all featherstitched together. At the height of the Victorian era, the Crazy-Quilt designers embroidered scenes, or whatever they chose, to make a quilt that was decidedly more than elaborate, to say the least.

At this same period another trend occurred in spreadmaking: a white, tufted type. One Olive Dennett, who lived near Newburyport, Massachusetts, made such a spread which shows candlewicking, the loops of which had been sheared.

Quilts have always held a strange fascination for men. They have been designed and collected by men and some have even made them. In a book, printed privately, a Maryland physician, Dr. William Rush Dunton, proved to be one such enthusiast. He urged that all "nervous ladies" take up the fascinating art of quilting to relieve their tension and be caught up in the great satisfaction of creating something lovely, working in color!

In *Occupational Therapy and Rehabilitation,* Thelma Brackett tells the interesting story of a quilt made by an ancestor of Dr. Grace Helen Kent, in 1840:

"The Rev. Mr. Kent and his wife had among others, two small children; a delicate boy of three and a baby girl of one year, whose care absorbed practically all of the time of Mrs. Kent. One day, the baby girl, being ailing, a physician was called, who found the boy also ill. So much so that he died that night, his sister dying the next morning. Naturally the mother was greatly distressed and was without occupation as the household duties had been performed by an adopted daughter and several older children. In order to relieve her depression her husband suggested she make a quilt, which she had planned to do some time before. He drew for her the central design of a sixteen-pointed star, which he copied from that which was on his watchcase. The central design that she made come alive in her quilt was a border of a somewhat unusual garland of laurel, morning-glory leaves and smilax. The remainder of the quilt was a running feather, rather large leaves and a background of diagonal lines in quilting. She completed it and went on to do more."

Occupational therapists recognize the benefit and lasting effect derived by those emotionally disturbed when they can be induced to work with gay-colored patches, creating pleasing designs. Women everywhere have turned to work, often needlework, for solace for their grief and for the relief of monotony and boredom. This applies to men as well and one quilt made by a wounded Union soldier toward the close of the Civil War proves the point.

The names of the quilts vary in different localities, just as the names of some flowers do. Whenever an historical event was a popular one, so was the contemporary quilt: Washington's Inauguration; the adopting of the eagle as a national symbol resulted in eagles flying on many a bedspread; "Mohawk Trail"; "Nelson's Victory"; and "Star Spangled Banner" to mention only a few. The category of names is long and interesting: Alphabet, Baskets, Birds, Bushes and Shrubs, Flowers, Fruits, Games and Puzzles, Geometric, Insects, Leaves, Nature-Animals, Plants, Politics and Place Names, Proper Names, Religion, Seeds, Shells and Fish (the Clam Shell originated in New England), Social, Stars, Stones, Sun, the Elements, Trees, Vines, Wreaths, and good old Miscellaneous!

One modern quilter, harassed because she could not quilt all the patterns that she wished to, hit upon a startlingly original idea. In a series of twelve units arranged around a central panel, gray-gowned ladies spread their quilts for display. Each quilt was a replica in miniature of a fullsized bedspread, each complete with its own different pattern and border! The border of this unusual quilt has small squares of those designs not incorporated in the main theme.

At quilting bees, after the supper dishes

had been cleared away, it was the custom to put a cat in the middle of the quilt. The young man or woman over whose head it jumped was thereby expected to be the next person to marry.

The quilting bee was highly important in the life of a prospective bride, from the functional as well as the social point of view. Harriet Beecher Stowe's classic, *The Minister's Wooing,* contains a detailed account recording the English customs and manners of that period when such an affair was of utmost significance. Even the question of whether the Oak Leaf was to be preferred over the common Shell pattern was discussed. From the sought-after invitation to the day-long gathering, to which guests brought

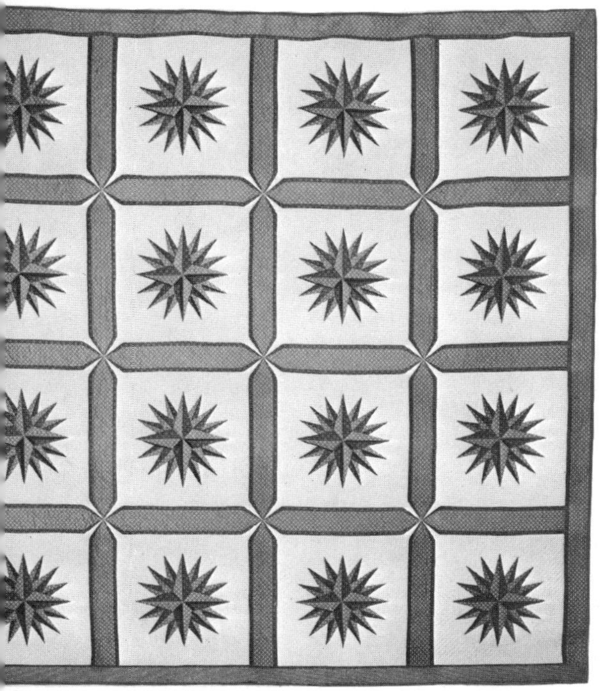

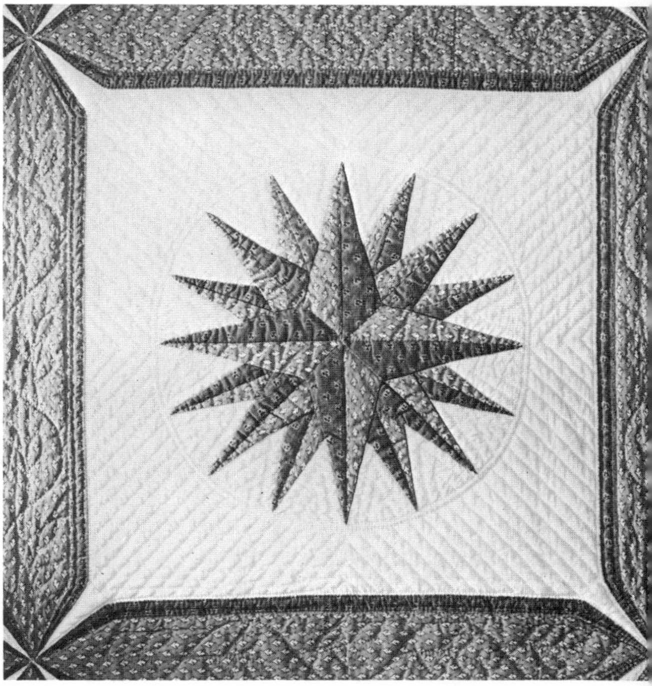

This Mariner's Compass quilt from Vermont is made of flag colors in a clean-cut nautical design of bright red, white, and blue calicoes. The compass is pieced of red (painted with tiny yellow figures) and blue (printed with white). All sixteen motifs are set together with pointed strips of blue marked off with thin red borders at the edges. The quilting pattern follows the compass points and each block is finished off with a series of diagonal quilting lines extending to the four corners. Serpentine waves are quilted on the blue set.

Mary Canfield Benedict, who married Fayette Shephard Baker of Arlington in 1852, made the quilt prior to her marriage. Her family conducted a sheep shearing and carding industry on the Battenkill River, and she was descended from Remember Baker, an early settler in Arlington, first cousin to Ethan Allen of the Green Mountain Boys.

Although Mary had probably never studied geometry, she had to divide a square horizontally and again vertically to construct her compass. Then she drew a tiny circle at the intersection of the marks and joined the points of the square to the circle where it touched the dividing lines. The four points of the star that resulted from this artful manipulation were then slit in half lengthwise, and seamed together again with corresponding halves of the sharply contrasting color; thus, the clean-cut nautical-center star motif evolved. Adding the twelve other points required additional calculation, but the consequences of Mary's effort remain as something to marvel at. 90×94 inches. *Photo courtesy of Shelburne Museum*

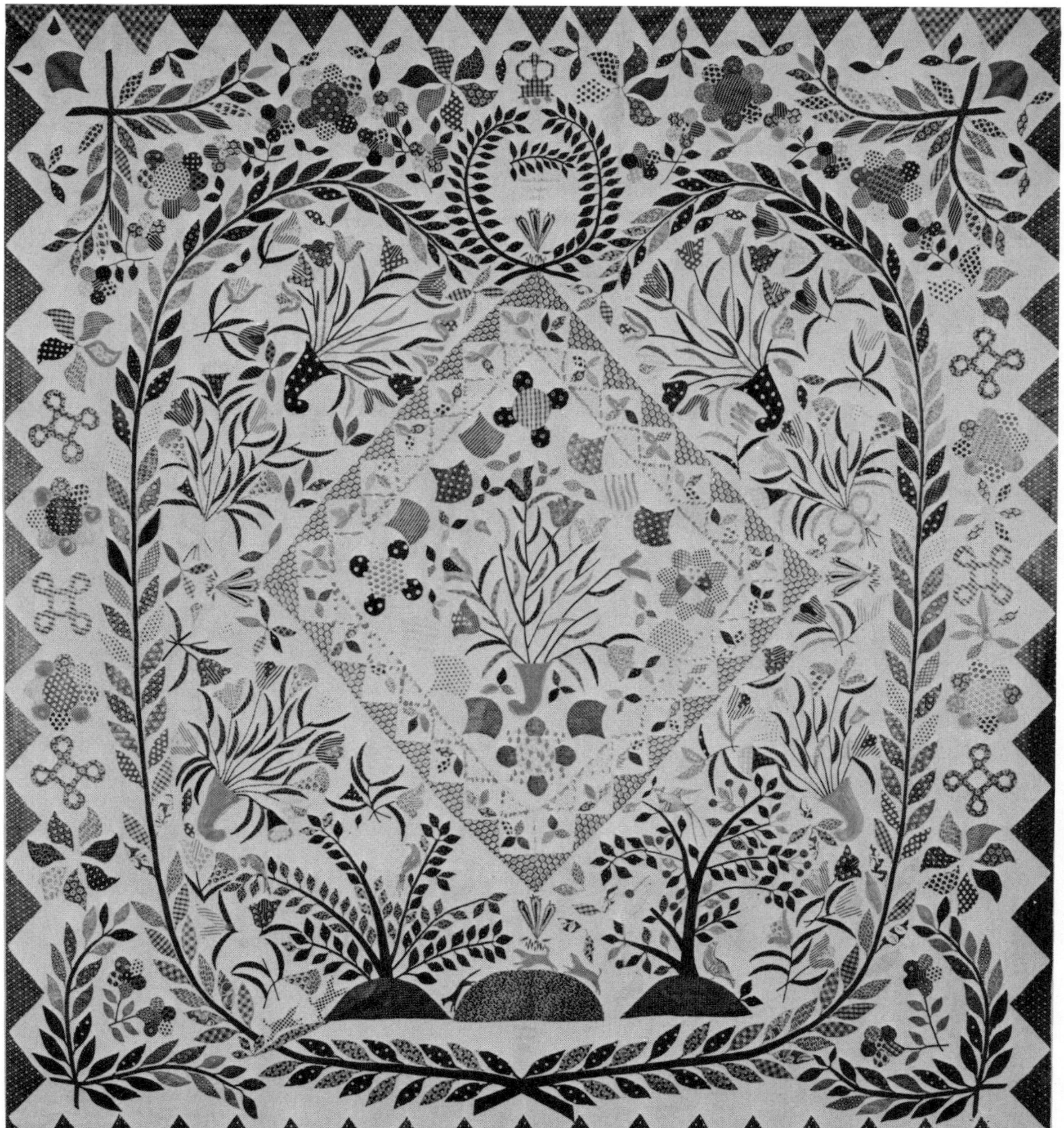

Ann Robinson of Connecticut started this spread on October 1, 1813, for she cross-stitched this information into her counterpane for posterity (See enlarged detail at right). She also appliquéd a matching bolster cover measuring 37 × 20 inches in a similar design of calico patches.

This spread shows a saw-tooth border of blue and white triangles and laurel branches of vari-colored calicoes. Cornucopias spill out a profusion of tulips and other flowers, and additional floral bouquets fill the intermediate spaces. Two trees rise out of calico hummocks at the bottom of the spread and a sleek cat bounds over another small mound with two dogs in hot pursuit. Others bay at birds (carefully cut from printed chintzes) preening themselves in the tree branches.

Ann used hexagons of parti-colored calicoes, poinsettia blooms, laurel branches, and a four-looped curvilinear interlacement motif in the spaces between the outside border and the laurel-enclosed center portion of her spread. The gingham crown at the top with its three circles of calico probably represents the Triune Deity (Father, Son and Holy Ghost) who reigns over all. 95 × 100 inches.

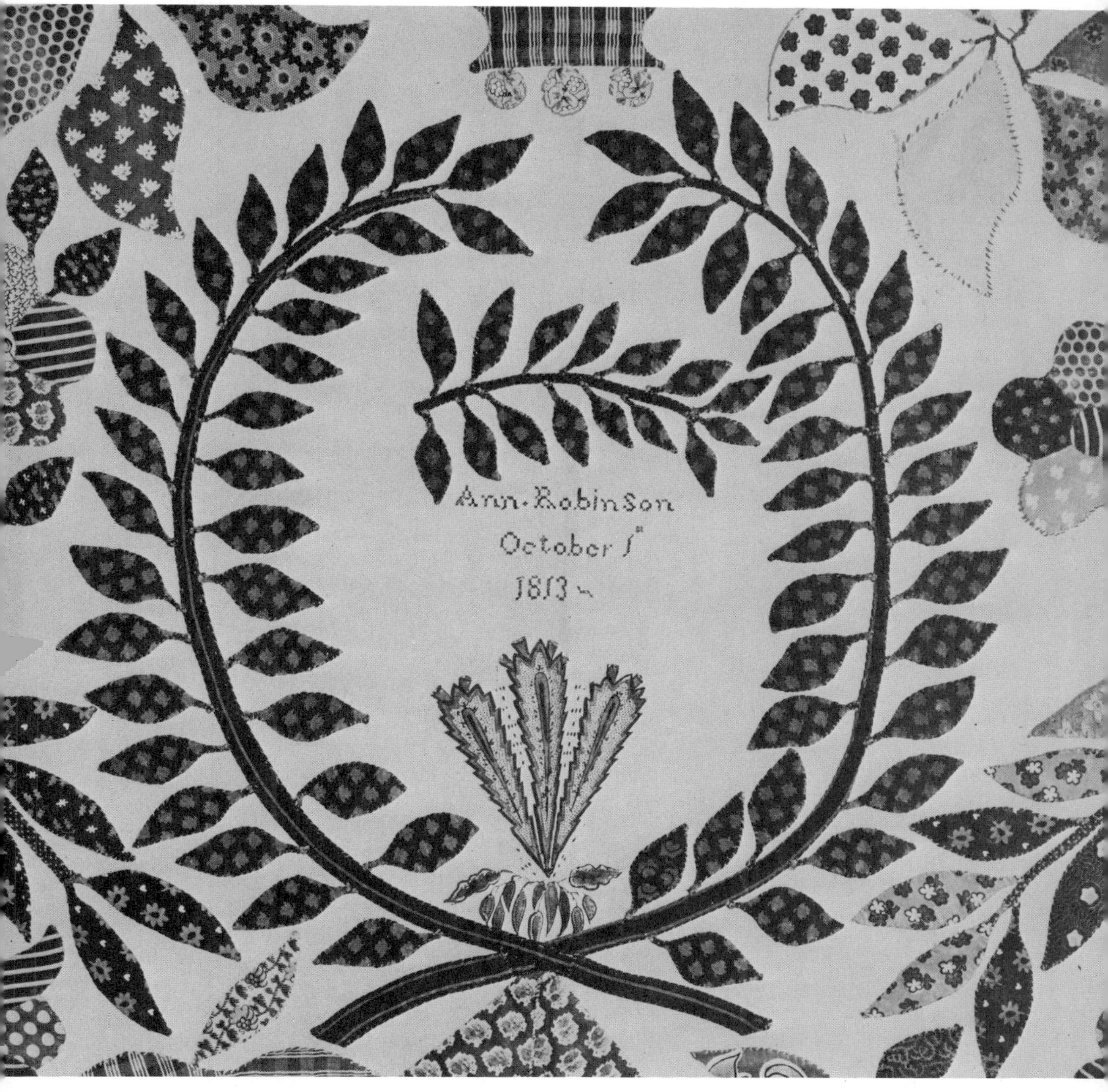
Ann·Robinson
October 1st
1813

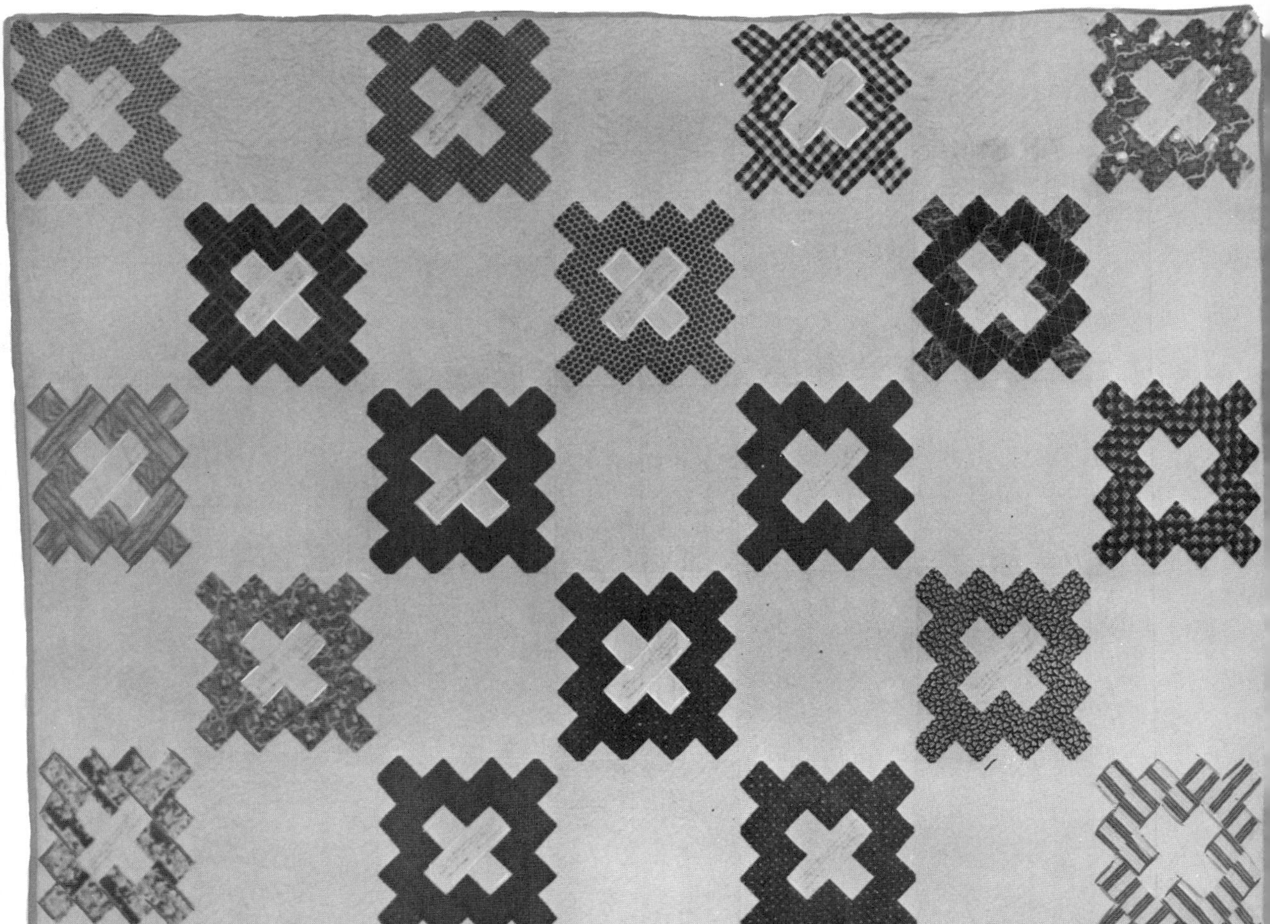

Simple straight-forward rectangles and squares of vari-colored calico put together with white rectangular strips form the pattern of this signature Bible quilt. Each of the crosses has been signed by a donor, who has also written her favorite verse. (See enlarged detail above right.) Intermediate white blocks, quilted in a feather wreath with diagonal bars, form the center, and the pieced squares are quilted in parallel oblique lines. The quilt is backed with white handwoven linen, bound around with a strip of the same. This souvenir Bible verse quilt was made in 1848 at Proctorsville, Vermont, for Lois Willard Stevens as a parting gift from friends in her town and neighboring Vermont communities. *Photo courtesy of Shelburne Museum.*

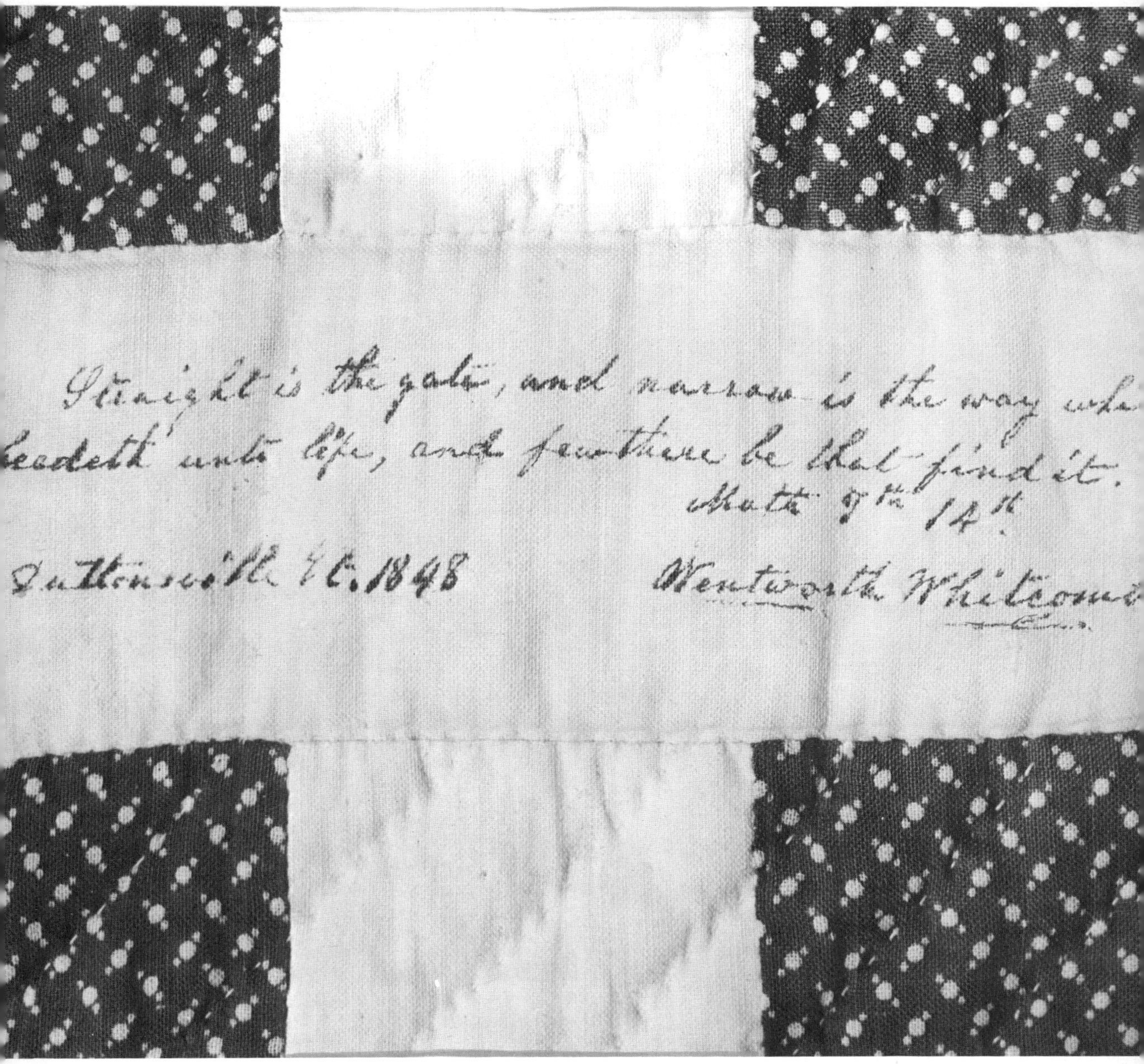
Straight is the gate, and narrow is the way wh
leadeth unto life, and few there be that find it.
Matth 7th 14th.
Duttonsville Vt. 1848
Wentworth Whitcomb

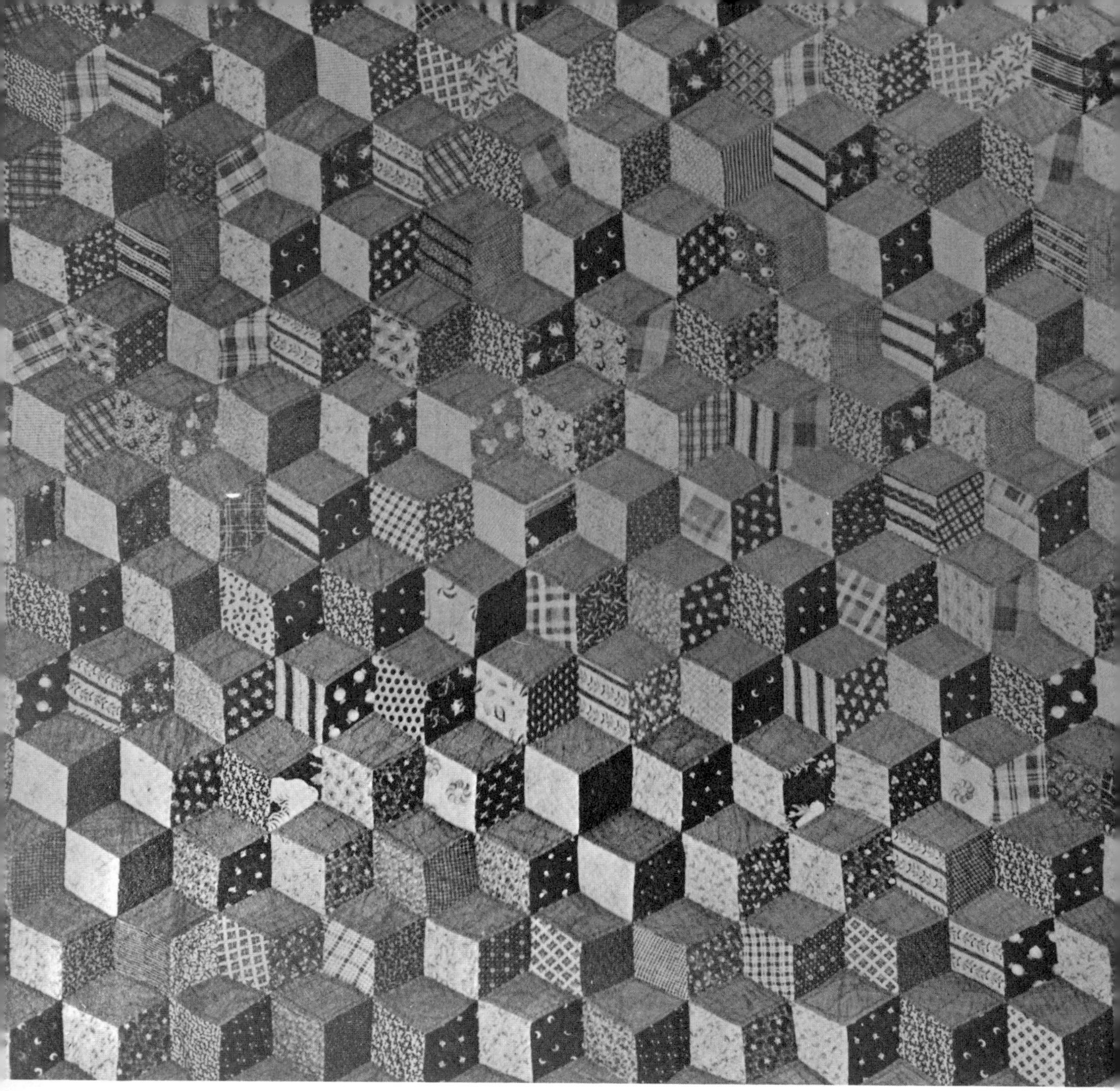

This popular design, an optical illusion in pattern, known by many names—Stair Steps, Diamonds, and Box Patchwork—was made by Sarah Weir Ely in the mid-nineteenth century. A variety of printed cottons cut in diamond form were stitched together with similar shapes of Turkey red to give the effect of depth, as well as height and breadth, to the boxes. The brilliant red color, practically fast to washing, known as Turkey red was brought to England from the East in the eighteenth century. Papillion, a Frenchman, is credited with founding the first Turkey-red dye works in Glasgow. The coloring matter, formerly obtained from alizarin, was produced from madder; today the color is synthesized from coal tar. 70 × 83 inches. *Photo courtesy of Shelburne Museum*

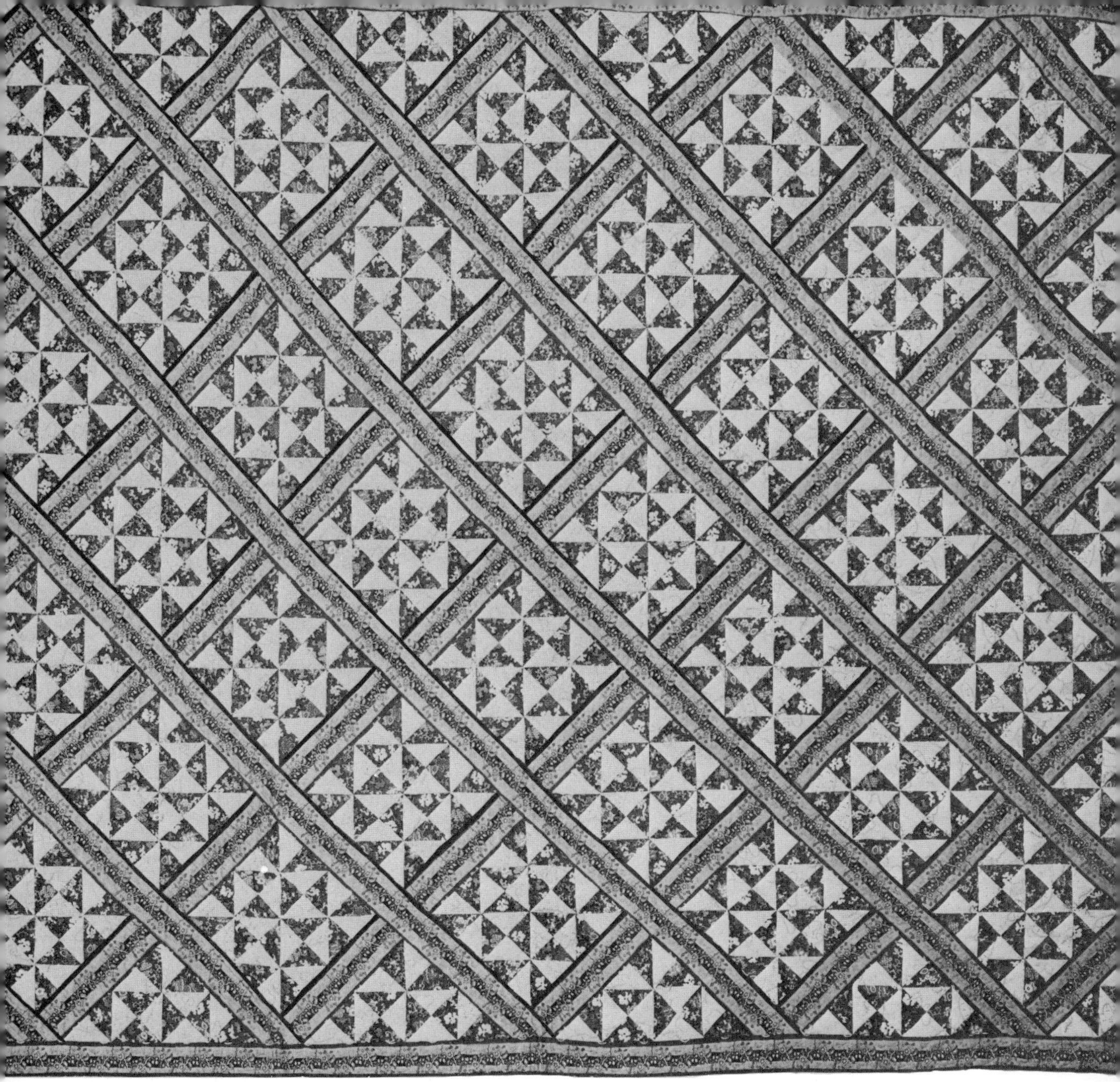

Triangular patterns were comparatively easy to fashion and, with a simple rearrangement of the diagonally halved squares, offered almost endless variety. In this Windmill or Broken Dishes quilt, all the calico patches were taken from the same print. A glazed cotton strip printed in a floral pattern sets the pieced blocks together. The border repeats the pattern of the chintz set and is twined over the backing and hemmed down. Backing is in a geometrical design in calico of beige and brown in a striped pattern.

For the proposed pieced-work quilt top, sufficient material of matching design or planned contrast had to be available. The quilt-maker cut each piece individually and pieced them together in a predetermined precise pattern. Such a bed covering was not an "economy" quilt, but by using simple geometrical forms such as the triangle, there was no waste of the expensive glazed cotton. 82 × 98 inches. Second quarter nineteenth century. *Photo courtesy Shelburne Museum*

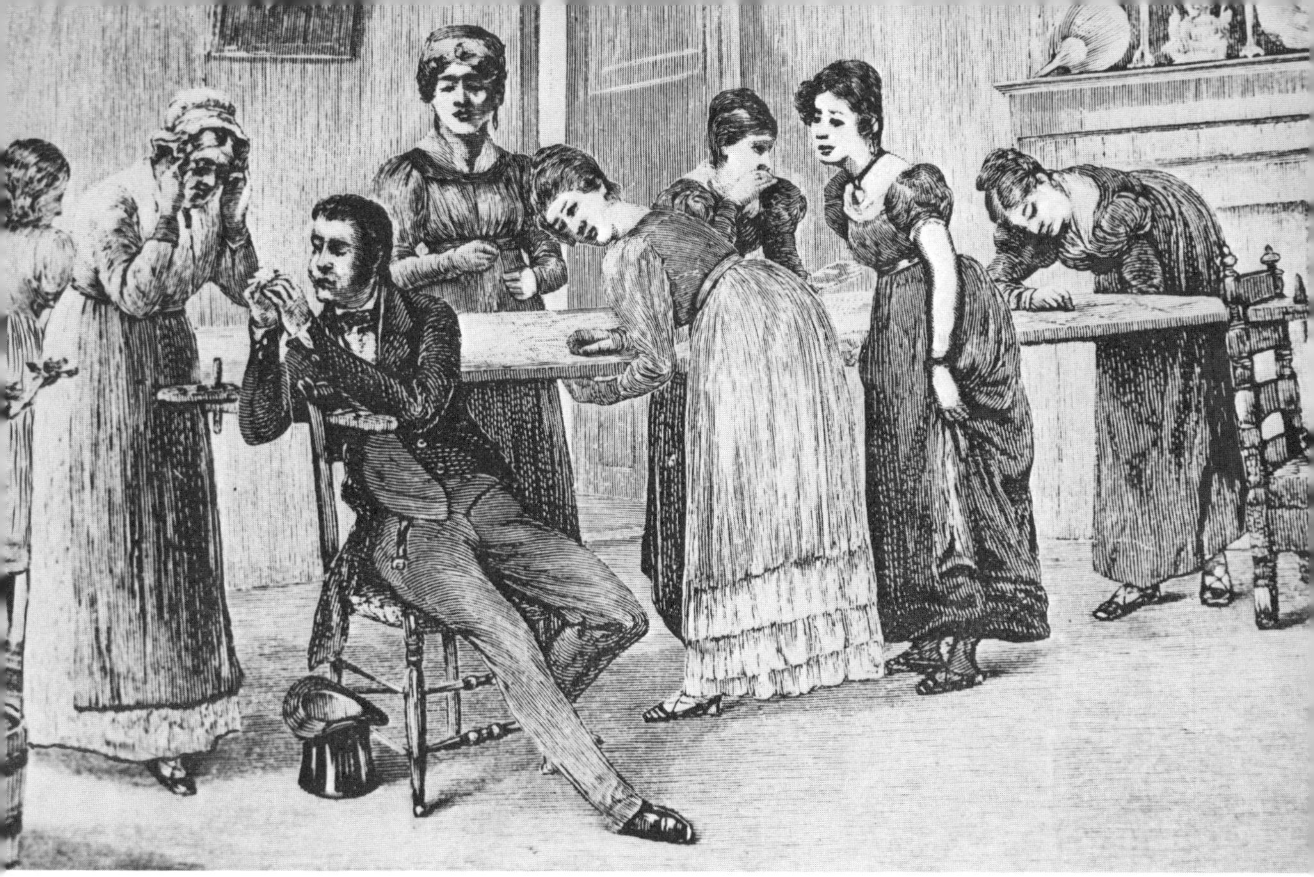

"The needle's eye that doth supply
The thread that runs so true,
It hath caught many a fair young heart,
And now it hath caught you."

gifts as well as their sewing skills and chatter, to the evening when the gentlemen were invited to a great supper, and through the last "Goodnight," the quilting bee was indeed the high point in the life of every betrothed young lady.

That old and young alike enjoyed quilting parties is best illustrated by the tale told about Amanda Brown, a little girl of long ago, in Vermont. A secret, known only to herself, of her plan to get everyone to come to her home for a quilting party, was executed and brought to fruition by this determined little girl. Distances meant nothing to this Vermont child, so she started out early one morning to bid the neighbors to come to her mother's home for a quilting bee.

Pleased with the reception of her invitation, the guests began to arrive before she had scarcely returned home. Somewhat startled at first, Mrs. Brown seemed nonplused, but she hurriedly went to the attic for her rag bag. Fortunately it was always full. As quickly as these pieces were distributed she engaged her unexpected guests in setting up the quilting frames. As busy fingers cut and basted, stitched and tacked, she hastily prepared food for the men who would be sure to come for their share of the evening meal and the singing afterwards. When quiet came to the home again, that day had unexpected profit for Mrs. Brown—a new and always useful quilt!

To quench their thirst in the daylong quiltings, before, during, and after the troublous days of the Revolution, the women drank many a cup of "Liberty" tea—that concoction that was of American make. English tea was not in favor. Many a tale was told at these gatherings including one of the old Bell Tavern in Danvers, Massachusetts. Like most inns of the period, it was a place for the exchange of village gossip and the discussion of the events of the world beyond the town. Among the popular topics was the unpopular Stamp Act. Tea was proscribed and the sale of it forbidden under penalty of a ride on a rail and the brand of being classed as a Tory. However, Isaac Wilson, a tea dealer, convicted of violating the law, obtained a reprieve by furnishing the villagers with a bucket of punch. His neighbors saw to it that he received his share, while he repeated three times as he drank:

I, Isaac Wilson, a tory I be;
I, Isaac Wilson, I sell tea.

Tea was a luxury, and although our male ancestors were willing to deny themselves, they found difficulty in preventing the women from doing the same. In spite of the vigilance of the men, the fair sex found ways and means of sipping in secret.

It was well known at the Bell Tavern taproom what was going on. There was there a certain enormous coffee pot, which was a "few sizes smaller than a common lighthouse." The huge container was known to migrate from place to place where the ladies were meeting. One evening a large party of dames gathered at the house of one of their number. The master of the house was known to stay at the tavern until the last of his companions had gone. So in his absence the ladies were enjoying their tea, secure in the knowledge that they were safe from prying eyes. Tea having been brought in, it was put into the big pot and left to simmer on the hearth. Then it was poured out, with many a sly joke at the expense of unsuspecting men in general. And for Isaac Wilson, the "Tory who sold tea," a very special compliment.

And now it was time for the master of the house to return. The tea grounds must be buried of course, and coffee put into the pot. So the big lid was removed and the pot tipped up; and to the accompaniment of shrieks from twenty tea-filled ladies, along with the leaves out came the body of a big toad, speckled and bloated, sprawling on the hearth. Forgotten were the many tributes to the brew; there remained only disgusted exclamations. It is said, and without doubt truly so, that the consumption of tea among the fair sex dropped off noticeably for a while.

This story is perpetuated by the ceramic mugs being handcrafted today in Vermont. The unsuspecting woman who has finished her delightful brew may be as aghast as our ladies in the tale of old, at finding, embedded in the bottom of the mug, a perfectly proportioned green ceramic frog!

Wamsutta is now manufacturing a sheet which is a printed replica of the old quilts grandmother used to make. The design, printed in lovely colors, is called "The Aster Quilt" or "Friendship Ring" as identified in Ruby Short McKim's *One Hundred and One Patchwork Patterns.*

This elaborate version of the old-time Crazy Quilt, a detail of which is shown, was made by a member of the Haskins family of Granville, Vermont. It is composed of forty-two pieced blocks; the figures probably represent members of the family. Third quarter nineteenth century. *Photo courtesy Shelburne Museum*

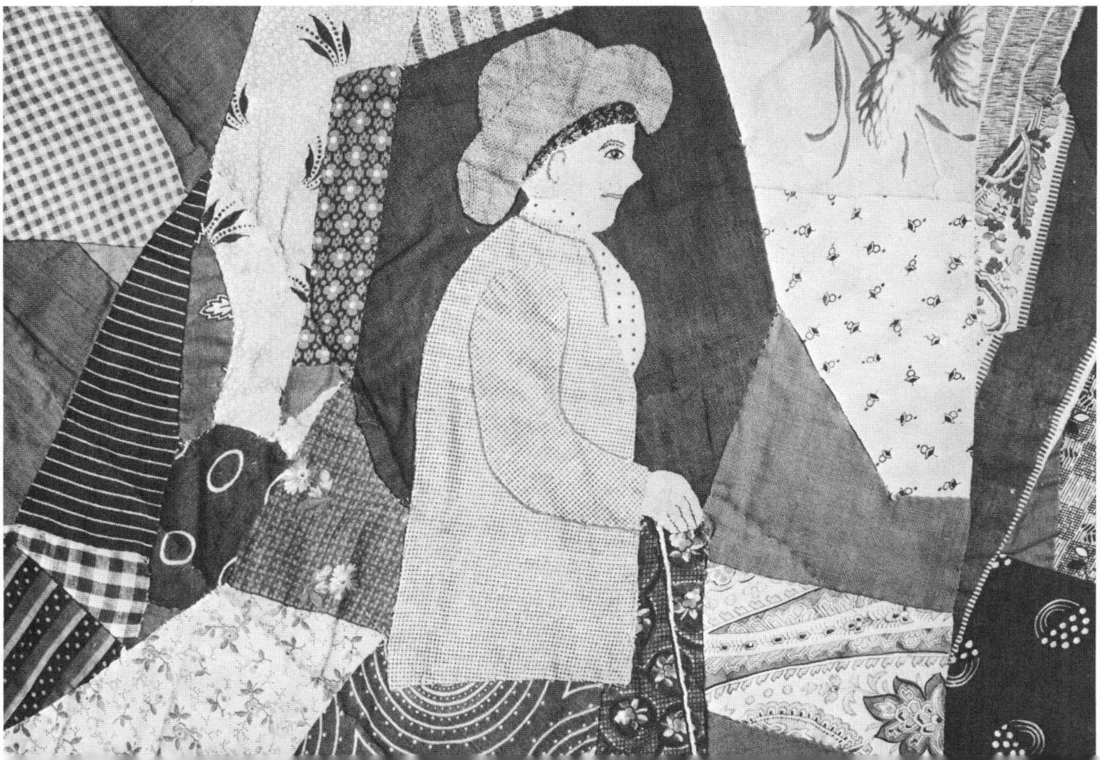

Miss Christine Batchelder of Wyoma, a section of Lynn, Massachusetts, used silk yarn and fabrics of various textures for her "Crazy Quilt." She divided the coverlet into twelve rectangles and, using her home and surroundings as her motif, created a series of landscapes and seascapes. Each was given a portrait-like character by working some of the porches and garden urns "in relief . . . . This feature, recalling certain English embroideries of the Tudor and Stuart periods, taken together with the quilt's relation to a New England tradition for silk-embroidered seascapes . . . . places our newly acquired quilt well into the great traditions of domestic needleworker's art." (*Bulletin,* Museum of Fine Arts, Boston.)

Photo courtesy Museum of Fine Arts, Boston

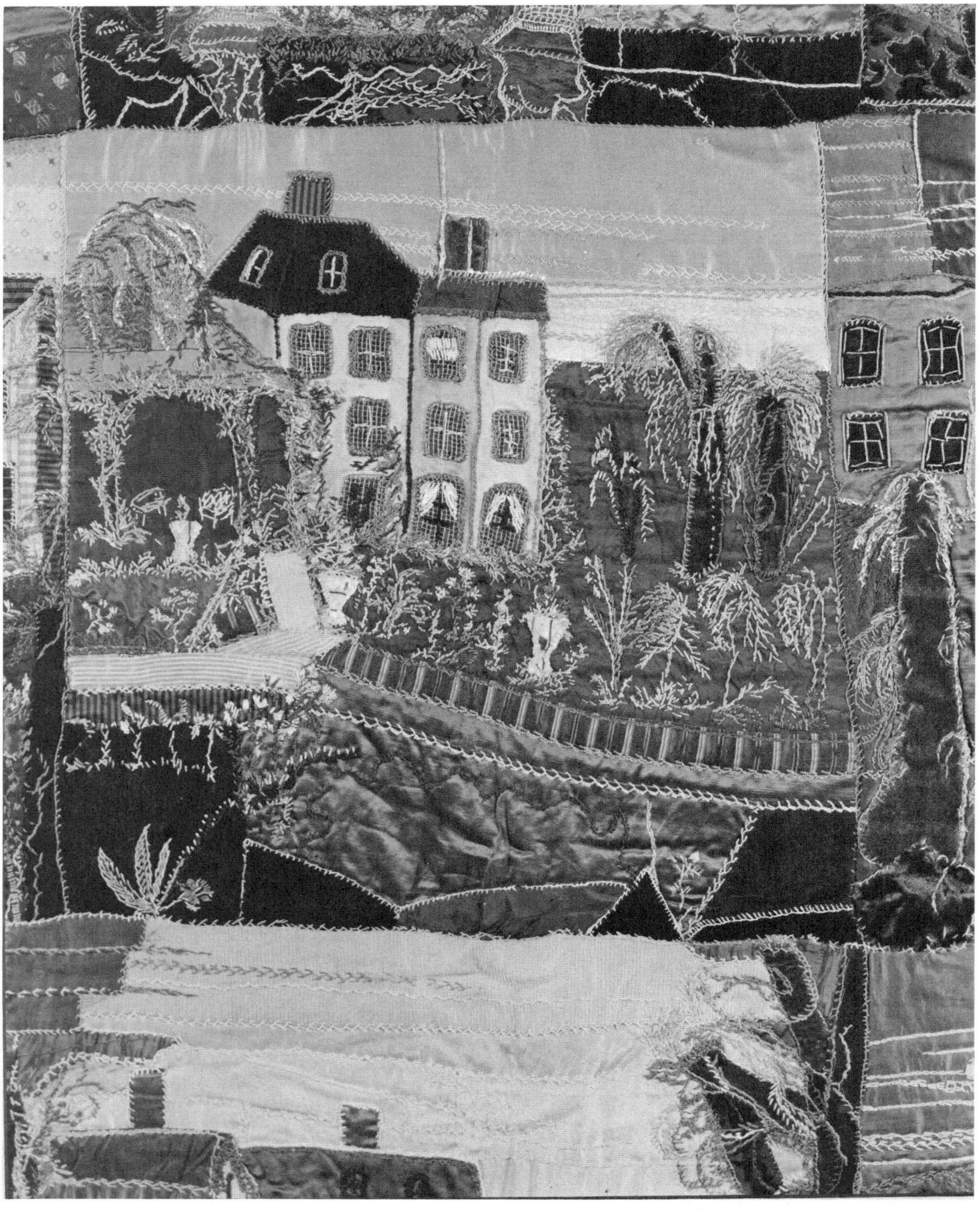

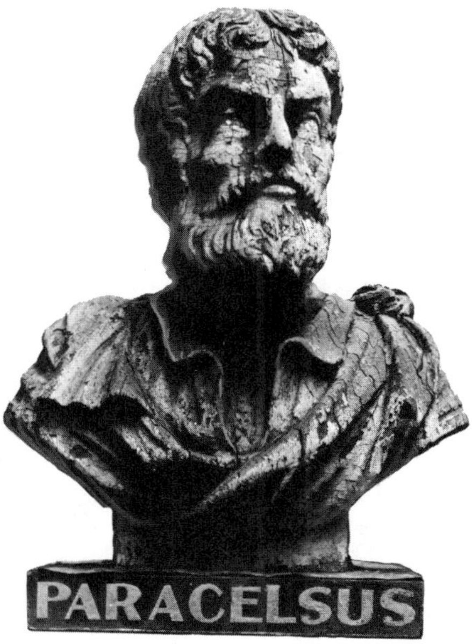

The bust of a Swiss-German physician of the sixteenth century who assumed the name of Paracelsus was sometimes used as an apothecary symbol.
Photo courtesy Essex Institute

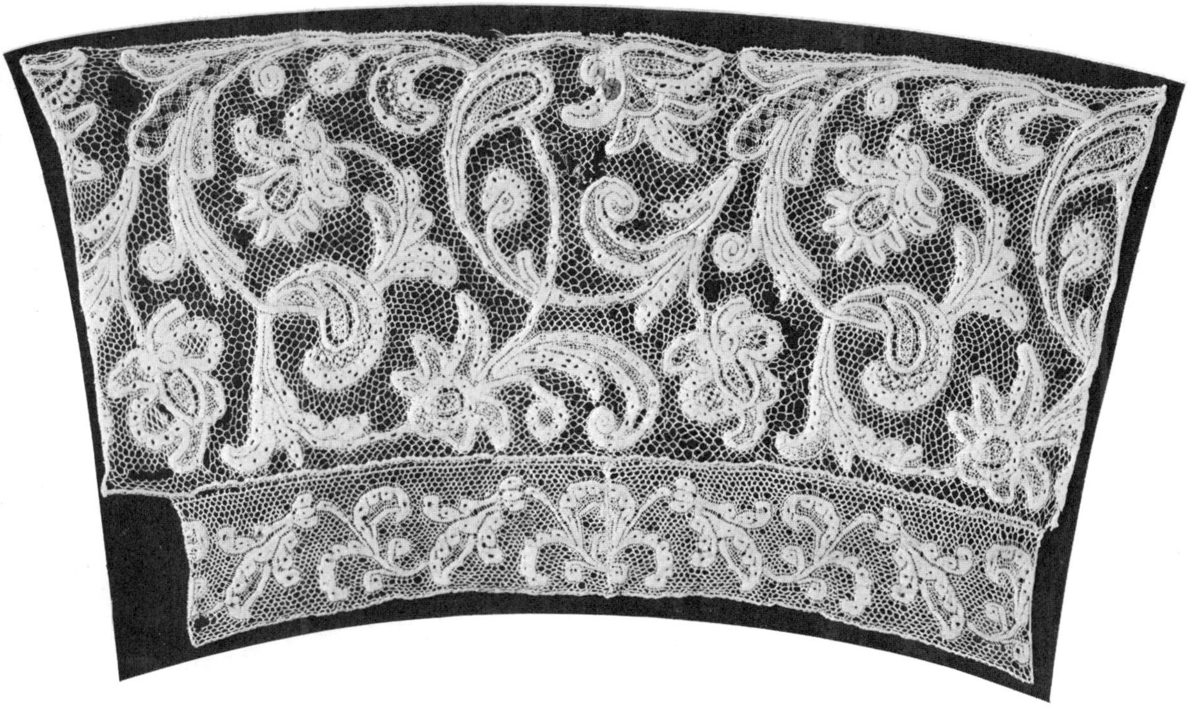

Lace band worn by George Curwen. William Bentley, reporting on a visit to Ipswich made in 1819, wrote in his diary: "We . . . saw a woman making lace, the same as that in the Curwen band in 1653."

Tavern Signs, Trade Signs, and Cigar-Store Indians

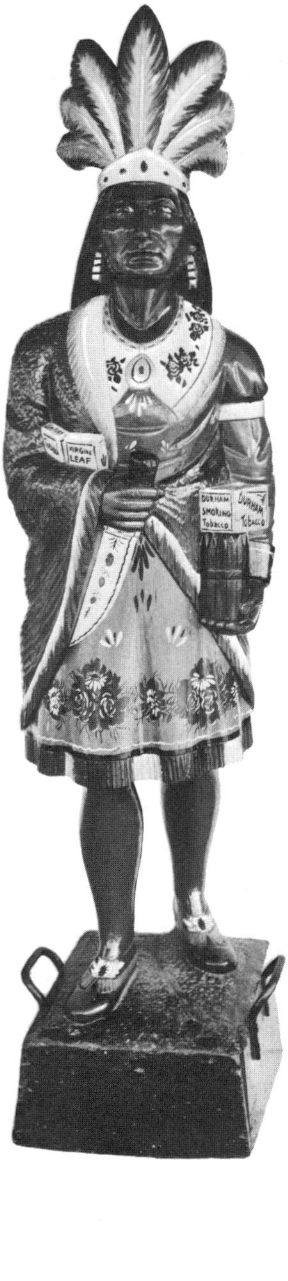

Elaborate dress was characteristic of Indians carved in the heyday of the cigar-store symbol, and brand names of tobacco were conspicuous as with this figure at the entrance to the Country Store at Mystic Seaport. *Photo courtesy Mystic Seaport*

Every tavern and trade sign in New England might well serve as a jacket for a book and what a library this collection would make, stacked by size, on a dozen sturdy shelves, each portraying some phase of the life and manners, the foibles and fashions, the spirit, the genius and the ingenuity of young America!

Tavern signs told their story by means of a distinctive design and often a rhyme and usually carried the proprietor's name as well.

> Gentlemen you are welcome;
> Sit down at your ease.
> Pay what you call for;
> And drink what you please.

Even when the rhyms did not appear on the sign everyone around knew the descriptive couplet or verse that described the place and, with the help of a few drams, could add a few additional lines of his own. When freshly painted, they shone in the sunlight and served as a warm welcome to the weary traveler. Just as the innkeeper was the town or village greeter, so the sign was his business or trade card. These old "beacon lights" were landmarks for wayfarer and coachdriver alike. Directions were given with reference to their location.

The inn itself was a hospice for the dispensing of food, drink, and shelter. What is more important, next to the meetinghouse, it was usually the most important building in the community. No wonder the landlords were proud of their signs. They conveyed a message unmatched by the most profound sermon. In the seventeenth century an inn or a tavern was sometimes spoken of as an ordinary, a term referring to the room or building where food was served. The word tavern by its very derivation implies a place where wine and liquor were served. Invariably the inn or tavern was in close proximity to the meetinghouse or within viewing distance of it.

The trademark of the innkeeper was an emblem of innumerable services and activities from the seventeenth through the nineteenth centuries. The village inn was also the daily meeting place of the community. Many were large enough for sizeable social gatherings and civic meetings. Not a few served as temporary art galleries for limners, silhouette cutters, sign painters, and other types of craftsmen, even traveling entertainers. The inn was used by peddlers to display their wares.

The story of tavern signs and trade signs is more than the way in which they were made and what they said or implied. The real story concerns the person or persons whom they represented. How these people lived and worked, what they believed, what they accomplished and contributed, can best be told by recalling the words of writers at the turn of the present century since many of the old signs were still in place at the time. Furthermore many of them were so aptly described that it would be presumptuous to attempt to improve on these word pictures. Also, it should be stated that not a few of the reminiscences gathered sixty years ago came directly from leading citizens who possessed clear memories and vast knowledge. Plagiarism is neither implied nor intended, but only by borrowing liberally from volumes long out of print is it possible to present this phase of folk art in its true light.

Abraham Stafford who opened a new tavern in Salem some years before the Revolution was exceedingly proud of his "elegant sign of King George the third" and he so advertised, but it came down in a hurry once the war began in earnest. The same fate attended "The King's Arms" and "The King's Head" in nearby Boston, but in Newburyport the portrait of General Wolfe hung in front of the Wolfe Tavern until the 1950's. Despite controversies, criticism, and frequent denouncements by the local newspaper, it swung in the breeze in defiance of the best-ordered opinion in that old Republican town until the tavern was finally closed. So precious did the old sign board become, that it was stored in winter, according to the late Allan Forbes of the State Street Trust Company. A sign that carried the likeness of the Duke of Cumberland still exists, clearly pierced with a hole made by an unknown patriot's musket, proving the point that symbols of royalty in any form were distasteful to the colonists, especially a tavern sign which implied hospitality, good cheer, and freedom from the cares of the world.

Names like the Red Lion, the Blue Lion, the Green Dragon and others, often used for taverns, had their origin in the crests of noble families. In the Middle Ages when inns were few in number, it was not uncommon in England and elsewhere on the continent for the homes of noblemen to be used as hostelries while they

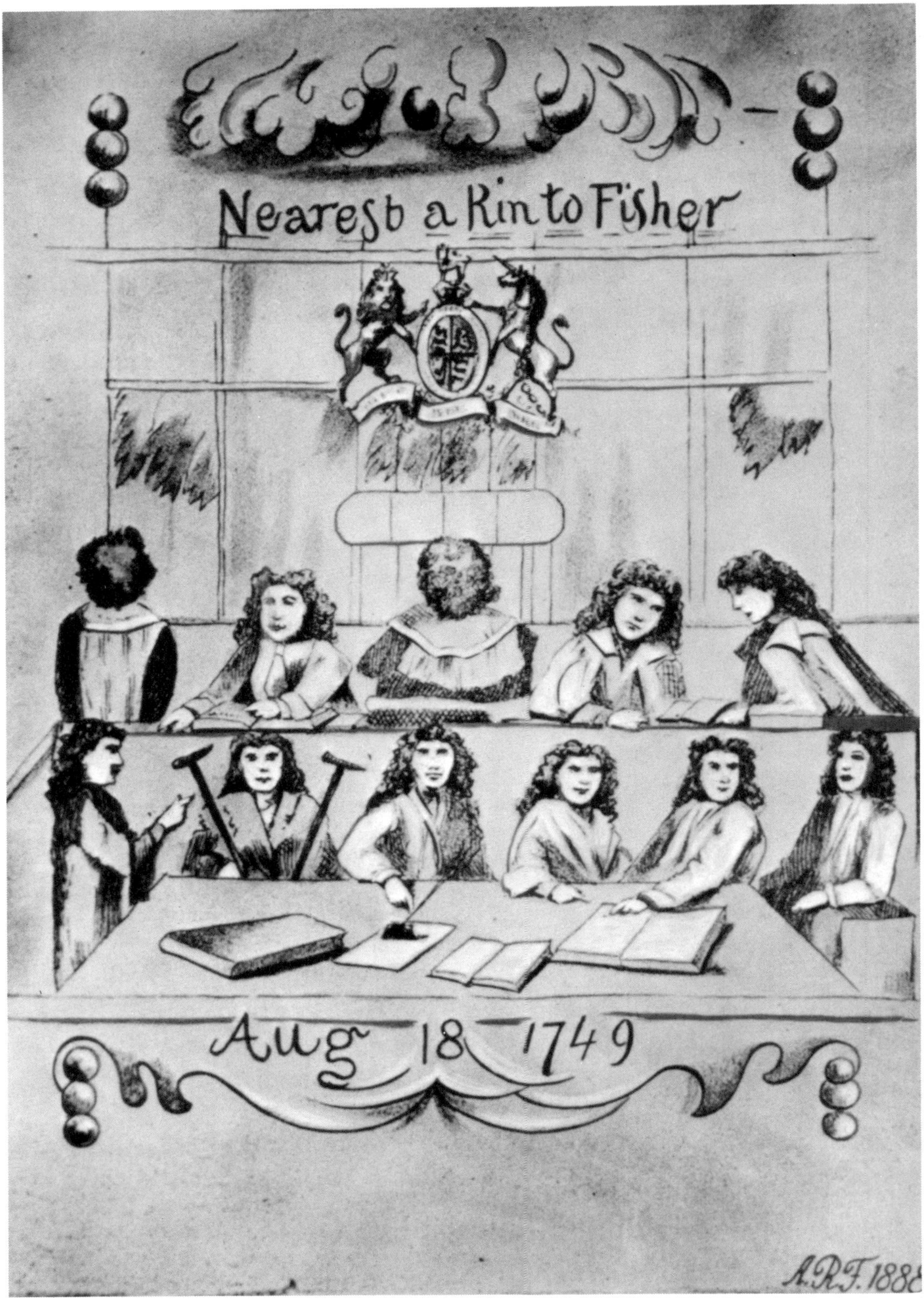

Sketch of the Fisher-Ames-Woodward Tavern sign desiged for Nathaniel Ames of Dedham, Massachusetts, to lampoon the General Court of Massachusetts. The sign cost £40 old tenor and swung from its brackets for only a week. At the time, William Hogarth used a similar approach for several English taverns, but his caricatures were vastly more satirical in their biting wit.

were absent. Most appropriately, these houses were marked with the family coat of arms and travelers unfamiliar with heraldic language used to identify an establishment by some conspicuous device on the shield such as the red lion and the like. As Larwood and Hotten remind us in *The History of Signboards* these insignia "became a very popular intimation that there was

> Good entertainment for all that passes,—
> Horses, mares, men and asses!

Perhaps the most unique tavern sign in all New England was the one that swung from a famous old hostelry in Dedham for a period of less than a week.

Dedham had been an important stagecoach center on the road to Connecticut and New York, via Hartford since the days of the first four-wheeled vehicle. In 1832, some sixteen hundred stages came to and departed from Boston every week and a goodly number stopped in Dedham each day so that the pert remark "taverns were as thick as fiddlers in hell" in Dedham had its point. With so many taverns, it is not surprising that many a memorable toast was offered by traveler and townsman as well. One to the female sex ran "the best and handsomest piece of domestic furniture is a virtuous and admirable woman."

Oliver Wendell Holmes, impressed by the importance of Boston as a travel center, was impelled to write "Boston has opened and kept open more turnpikes that lead straight to free thought and free speech and free deeds than any other city of live or dead men."

The hostelry around which the story revolves was the Fisher-Ames-Woodward Tavern which was operated continuously from 1658 until after the Revolution. Its first owner, Lieutenant Joshua Fisher, surveyor, apothecary, innholder, and "officer of ye trayne band" was succeeded by his son of the same name who held the title of captain. In the early 1730's one of his daughters married Dr. Nathaniel Ames, the compiler of the famous *Ames' Almanack*. With the aid of his astronomer father, he had published the first issue in 1726 when he was but seventeen years old.

After the death of his wife and an infant child, Ames entered into a famous lawsuit with the Fisher family to obtain the inn and the land on which it stood. The turningpoint of the suit hung upon the settlement of the term "next of kin." According to ancient common law and English law, real property was never inherited by a father or mother from a child; in absence of husband, wife, or lineal descendant, it passed on to the "next of kin," which might be even a

Temperance signs like this one from a tavern in Colchester, Connecticut, indicate the willingness of tavern keepers in the early nineteenth century to cooperate with the temperance movement. Beer and wine were advocated in place of hard liquor. *Photo courtesy Connecticut Historical Society*

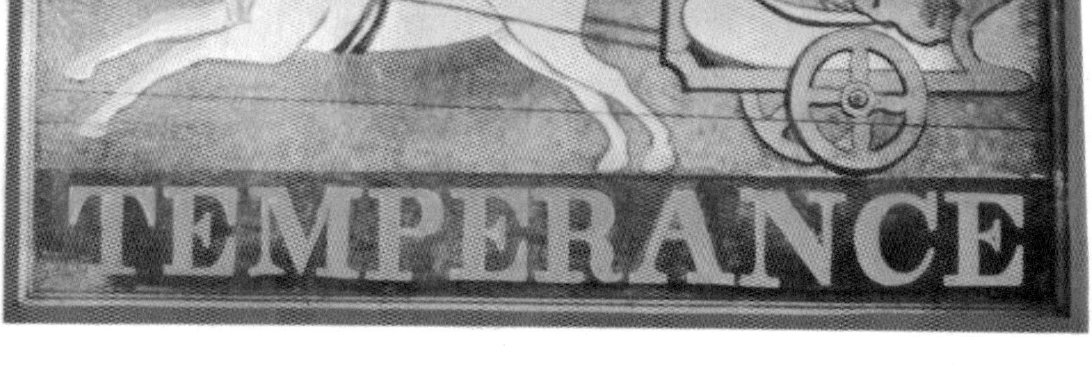

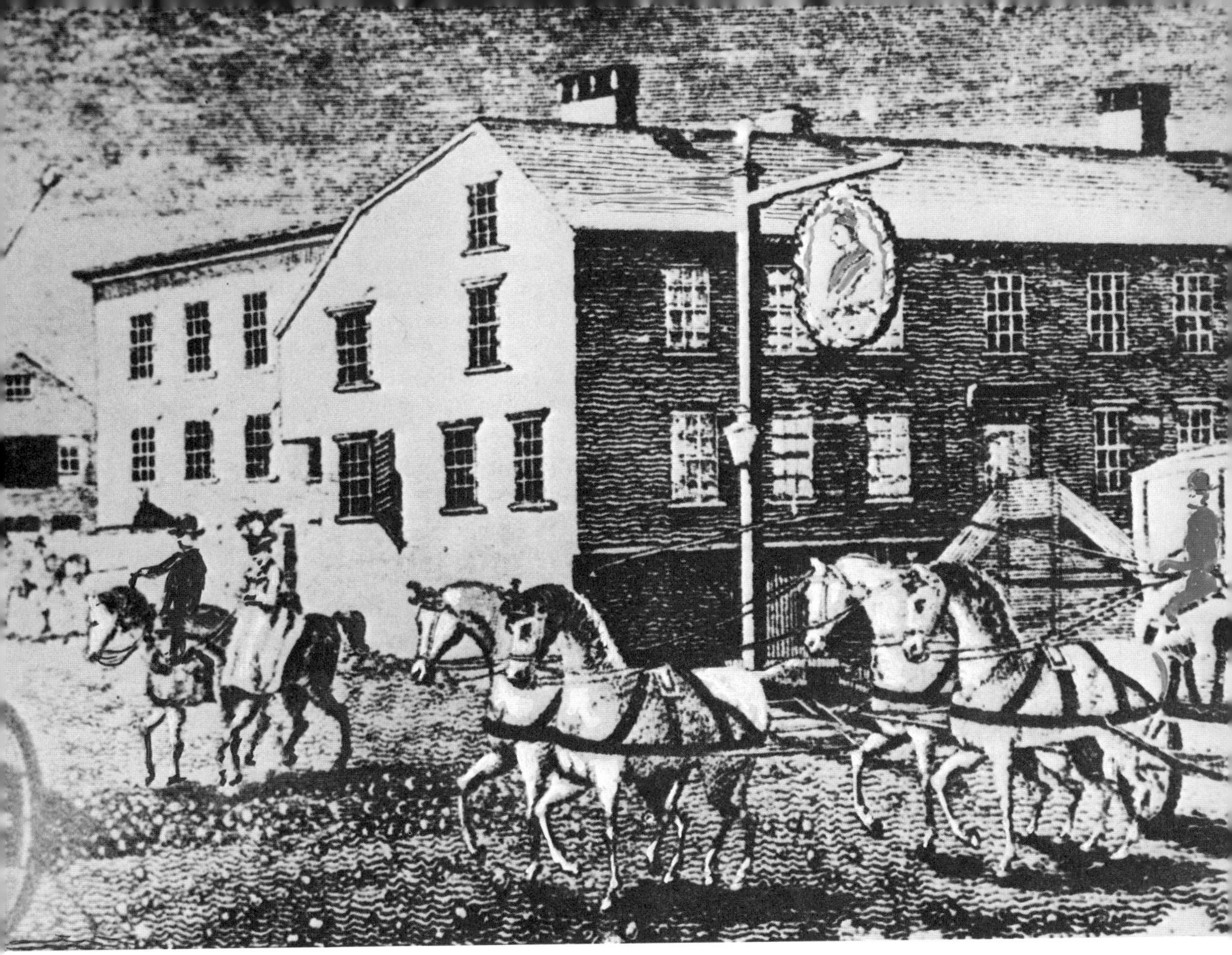

distant cousin. However, the Province Laws substituted the so-called "civilian" method of counting kinship, by which the father could inherit. Although twice defeated in the courts in 1748, Dr. Ames boldly pushed his case before the "Superior Court of Judicature, etc., of the Province of Massachusetts Bay." He prepared the case and argument, unaided, and he triumphed. As a result, he gained possession of the property and the inn became Ames Tavern.

Brilliant but erratic, as Alice Morse Earle reminds us in *State Coach and Tavern Days,* he was nervous in temperament, excited by his victory, indignant at the injustice and loss to which he had been subjected. Loudly intolerant of the law's delay, and especially of the failure of Chief Justice Dudley and his associate Lynde to unite with the three other judges, Saltonstall, Sewall, and Cushing, in the verdict, he had in anger and derision painted for him and his tavern a new and famous sign, and he hung it in front of the tavern in caricature of the court.

The sign is gone long ago, but in that entertaining book, *The Almanacks of Nathaniel Ames 1726–1775,* the editor, Sam Briggs, gives an illustration of the painting from a drawing found among Dr. Ames's papers after his death. On the original sketch these words are written:—

'Sir:—I wish could have some talk on y[e] above subject, being the bearer waits for an answer shal only observe M[r] Greenwood thinks y[t] can not be done under £40 Old Tenor.'

This was a good price to pay to lampoon the court, for the sign represented the whole court sitting in state in big wigs with an open book before them entitled *Province Laws.* The dissenting judges, Dudley and Lynde, were painted with backs turned to the book. The court, hearing of the offending sign board, sent the sheriff from Boston to bring it before them. Dr. Ames was in Boston at the time, heard of the order, rode with speed to Dedham in advance of the sheriff, removed the sign, and it is said had allowance of time sufficient to put up a board for the reception of the officer with this legend, 'A wicked and adulterous generation seeketh after a sign, but there shall no sign be given it.'"

The old roadhouse, after this episode in

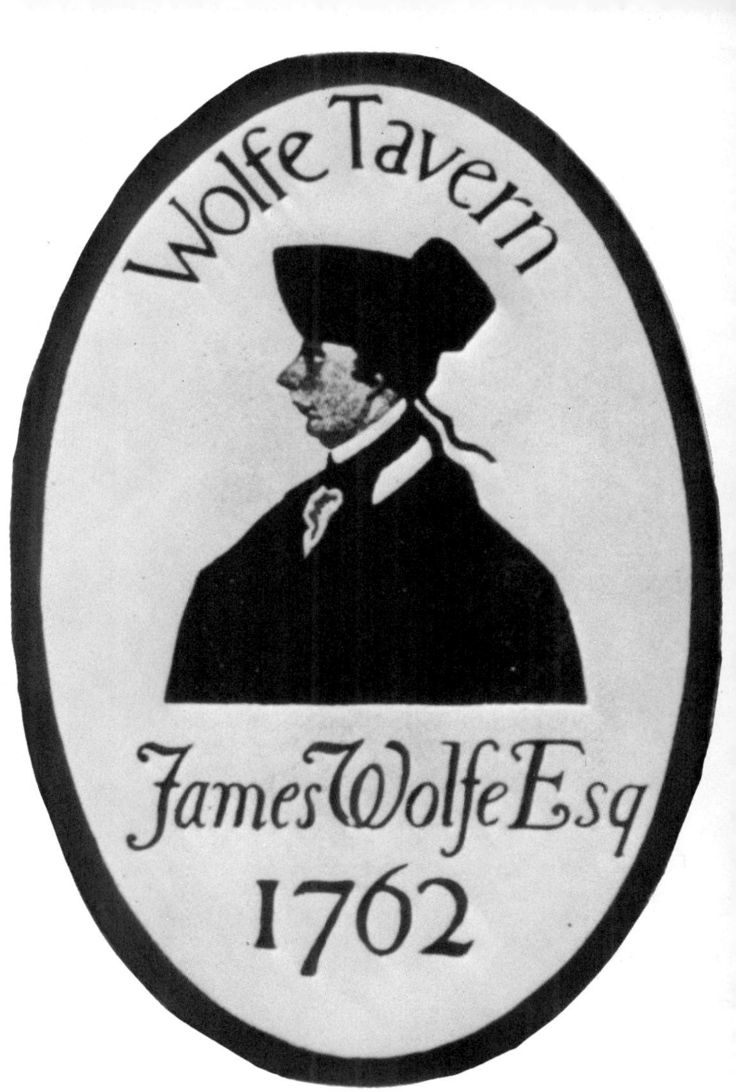

(*Far left*) Wolfe Tavern, Newburyport, Massachusetts, from an old print. Established in 1762, this widely known hostelry was operated continuously for nearly three hundred years.

(*Left*) An early sign that hung outside the Wolfe Tavern at Newburyport, Massachusetts, commemorating General James Wolfe, a British general killed in 1759 on the Plains of Abraham, Quebec. William Davenport, who served with him, hung the sign in 1762 when he opened a tavern in his home.

its history, became more famous than ever before; and *The Almanack* was a convenient method of its advertisement, as it was of its distance from other taverns. In the issue of 1751 is this notice:

ADVERTISEMENT

These are to signify to all Persons that travel the great Post-Road South West from Boston That I keep a house of Public Entertainment Eleven Miles from Boston at the sign of the Sun. If they want Refreshment and see a Cause to be my Guests, they shall be well entertained at a reasonable rate.

N. Ames

Ames operated the tavern until 1766 followed by Richard Woodward. It ceased to be a landmark in 1817. Sam Briggs, who later edited Dr. Ames's almanacs, wrote, "If there ever was anything in *Ames' Almanack* which more than another caused my heart to go out to that enterprising New England Astronomer-Physician, it was the knowledge of the fact that he was an innkeeper, who fully appreciated the importance of his calling, and hesitated not to own the "sorry trade," yet withal, to caution the guest against the serpent that lurked within the bowl."

Some of the signs within a tavern were even more significant than the symbol of hospitality swinging near the front door. Usually in some conspicuous place in the taproom, where all could read them with ease, were lettered, boldly and in good typographic style, lines such as these:

Greadly Bob, he does live here,
And sells a pot of good strong beer;
His liquor's good, his measure's just,
But Bob's so poor he cannot trust.

Smiles were bound to broaden the faces of those who read:

Within this hive we're all alive,
With whiskey sweet as honey;
If you are dry, step in and try,
But don't forget the money.

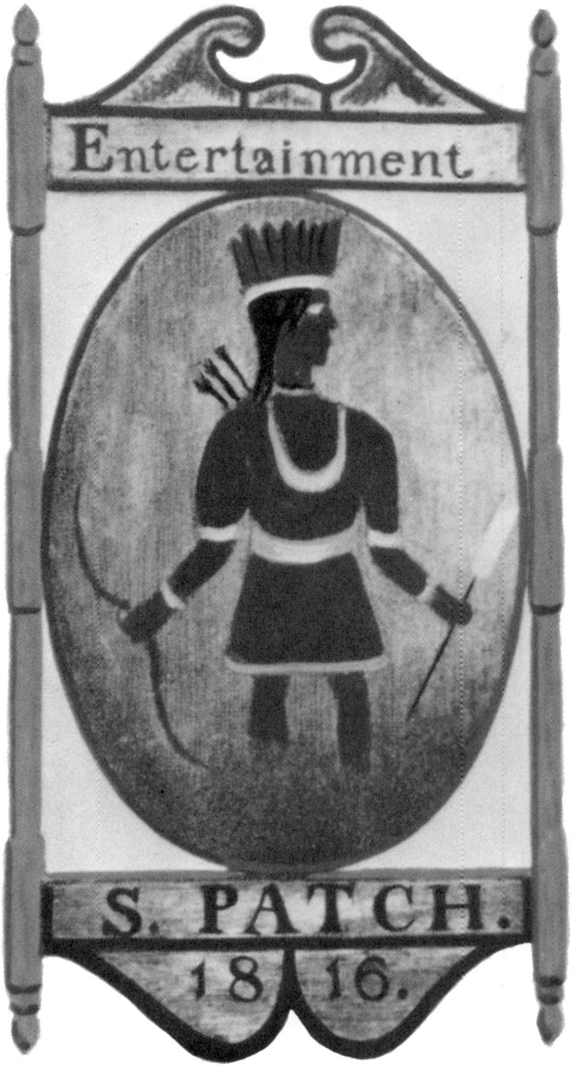

Tavern sign from the Patch Tavern, Concord, Massachusetts. *Photo from a private collection.*

(*Center*) Although proverbs were never as common on American tavern signs as they were in England, what more effective way for the tavern-keeper to declare "no credit given" than to make use of an adage that was familiar? *Photo courtesy Connecticut Historical Society*

(*Right*) Oliver and Mary Pomeroy kept a tavern known as the Yellow House in Rocky Hill, near Middletown, Connecticut. The Duke of Cumberland on his spirited horse corroborates the pre-Revolutionary date since all trace of association with the mother country, even where popular British figures were concerned, disappeared from tavern signs after the Revolution. *Photo courtesy Connecticut Historical Society*

Another form used was a board fashioned into the shape of a tombstone, set in one corner of the room, whereon was inscribed:

> This monument is erected to the memory of Mr. Trust, who was some time since most shamefully and cruelly murdered by a villian called Credit, who is prowling about, both in town and country, seeking whom he may devour.

Neither this one or any of the other quotations needs amplification:

> The rule of this house, and it can't be unjust,
> Is to pay on delivery, and not to give trust;
> I've trusted many to my sorrow,
> Pay to-day, I'll trust tomorrow.

A short phrase on a small box gave new meaning to a simple English word and every traveler knows it well. One of the important accessories of the "great room" of a tavern was a small box nailed to the wall. At the top was a small opening into which coins were dropped, and on the face of this box, printed in letters easily read, were the words "To Insure Promptness." It was expected that guests would drop into this receptacle such amounts as they deemed proper in return for services rendered. From time to time, the money collected in this way was taken out and divided among the servants of the house. Frequently, it became necessary for some employee of the tavern to remind a thoughtless guest of the location of the box. In doing so he would point with his finger in its direction and speak the first letters of the words, T.I.P. Gradually it came to be known as the "Tip" box, and later as a tip. Although the box has long since disappeared, the practice is firmly entrenched. No words need to be spoken, only

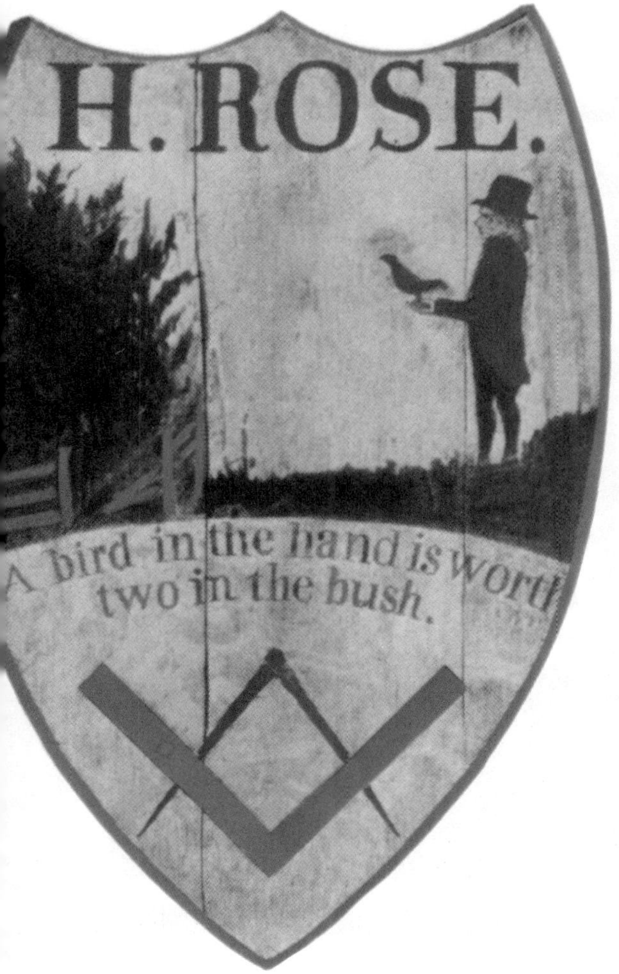

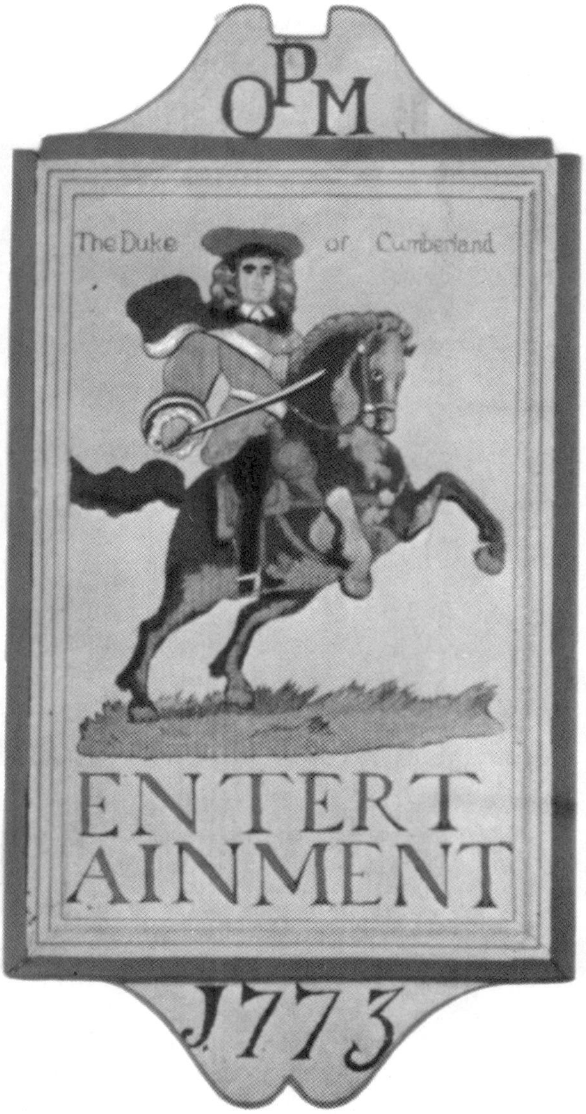

an inquiring look which when translated means, "Have you forgotten me?"

Benjamin Franklin, who was a constant traveler on the turnpikes and highways of colonial America, claimed that in his younger days the first step he took, "for his tranquillity and to obtain immediate attention at the inn" was to anticipate all unwelcome inquiry by telling the innkeeper: "My name is Benjamin Franklin. I was born in Boston. I am a printer by profession, and am traveling to Philadelphia. I shall have to return at such a time, and I have no news. Now, what can you give me for dinner?" No further questions were asked.

In 1710 in Massachusetts, an act of the General Court granted to the sheriff or deputy of the county the power and authority, when a taverner had his license revoked for any irregularity, "to cause his sign to be taken down."

Occasionally tavern keepers received payment for hospitality and refreshment in curious forms. Not a few of them dispensed a good deal of charity. When they fed those who were incarcerated in local jails, they were allowed a mere pittance by the community or the county for furnishing a prisoners' meals. Obviously, the Widow Carey treated four British navy men well since they showed their appreciation in a handsome manner, as recounted by E. O. Christensen in *Early American Wood Carving*. "In 1776 four British prisoners of war found themselves together in one jail in Windham, Connecticut. They were fed by the inkeeper, Widow Cary, whom they presented upon their release with a carved figure of Bacchus. One of them, John Russell, was a ship's carpenter. With his three cell mates he carved the plump infant Bacchus seated astride a keg and holding before him a basket filled with fruit. The back of his head is overlaid with grapes and leaves; the fig-

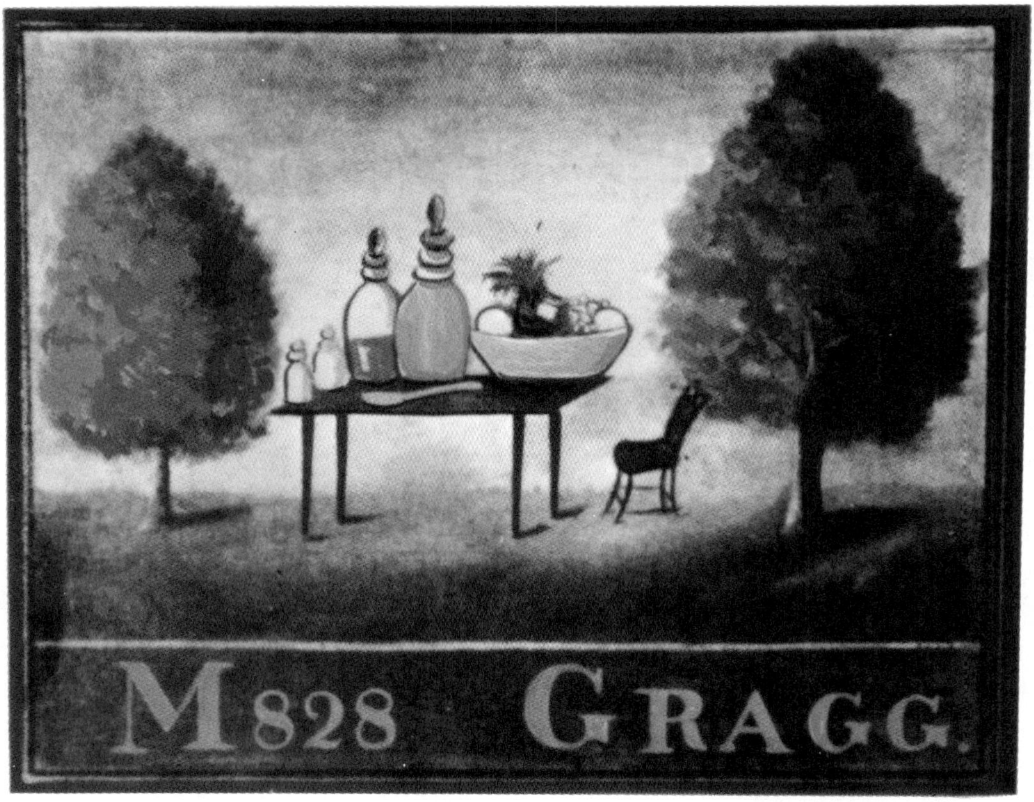

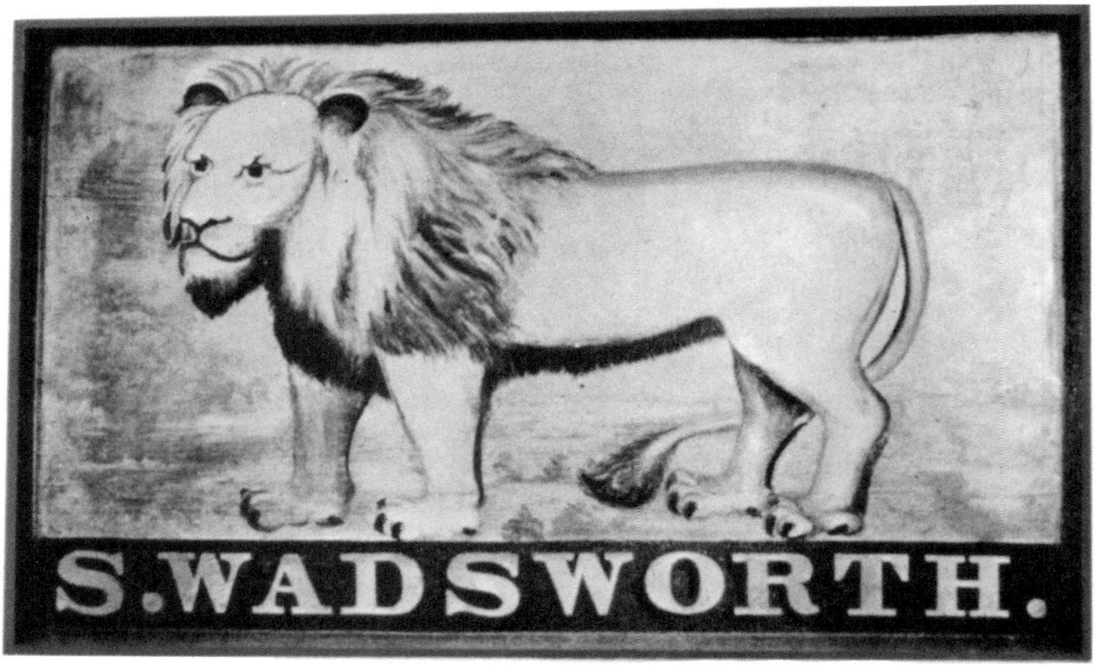

(*Top*) Moses Gragg's tavern at Milton, Massachusetts, later known as the Blue Hill Hotel, was a "famed resort for fancy dinners and high living." Before he kept a tavern, Gragg was a hostler. The reverse of the sign showed a sketch of the Blue Hill observatory. *Photo courtesy Dedham Hsitorical Society*

(*Bottom*) One side of the Wandsworth Tavern sign, Hartford, Connecticut; the reverse was a distinctive drawing of an eagle. The sign was painted in 1844. *Photo courtesy Connecticut Historical Society* ure is painted flesh color; the barrel is red with black hoops and the date, 1776, is carved across the front of the keg. The figure is about twenty-six inches high; the keg twenty-one inches long. Here we have a sample of eighteenth century English folk carving executed with gusto and good humor. According to tradition, the prisoners were only allowed the use of a pocket knife. The Windham Bacchus, a landmark, is now kept at the library." There are undoubtedly other mementos extant revealing the skill of British soldiers and sailors and the Hessians as well who were quartered at Newport in Revolutionary times. One account tells of toys which English seamen carved for Salem children while their vessel was held captive in the harbor of that old seaport town.

When toasts were offered in taverns, which was early and often in the course of a day, the American eagle was seldom omitted. Hawthorne reminds us of this custom in his story "The Bald Eagle," published in 1833. In the opening paragraph he paints this colorful word picture of the omnipresent freedom symbol:

> In one of the little villages sprinkled along the delicious valley of the Connecticut, there stood, not many years ago, a little tavern called the Bald Eagle. It was an old-fashioned building with a small antique portico in front, where of a lazy summer afternoon, the wise men of the village assembled to read newspapers, talk politics, and drink beer. Before the door stood a tall yellow signpost, from which hung a white sign emblazoned with a fierce bald-headed eagle, holding an olive branch in one hand and a flash of forked lightening in the other. Underneath was written in large block letters, "The Bald Eagle: Good Entertainment for Man and Beast: by Jonathan Dewlap, Esq."

The most notable Bell Tavern in all New England (and there were many which incorporated the name Bell) was located in South Danvers, Massachusetts, but all that remains of it is recorded in history and tradition. The sign of the house was a wooden bell in silhouette on which the host informed the public of his desire to serve them.

> Francis Symonds Makes and Sells
> The best of Chocolate also Shells.
> I'll toll you in if you have need,
> And feed you well and bid you speed.

Before the separation from the mother country, the colonists sought this place for shelter and refreshment, and the jolly taverner, Francis Symonds, was ever eager to fulfil the promise of his signboard, which also included "Entertainment for man and beast." Nor to the wayfarer alone was its promise extended. It was the resort for the villagers to learn the news of passing events and every traveler was expected to furnish his quota. It was the village exchange, where prices and every-day gossip were discussed, and the public affairs of the colonies and the mother country settled. Here too, on Sundays, the more remote villagers dismounted from their beasts at the old horse-block, and walked to the meetinghouse, again to return after the two-hour sermon and partake in a snug corner of a dinner from their well-filled saddlebags. As Fitch Poole recalled in 1840:

"The loyal neighbors here collected, to mourn the demise of good Queen Anne and rejoice in the accession of the first George. His departure and the rise of his son, George II, were here commemorated over the same bowl of punch. George III, was also welcomed with a zeal that was only equalled by that with which they drank to the confusion of his ministers. The odious Stamp Act and all Parliament taxes on the colonies were patriotically denounced. Tea was proscribed and its sale forbidden, under penalty of a ride on a rail and the brand of toryism. One conviction only took place, and the unlucky wight obtained a reprieve from his sentence."

It was at the Bell Tavern that Elizabeth Whitman lived and from which she was buried in 1788. Here, too, it was that the episode occurred regarding the toad in the coffee pot that made the tea taste so good. This yarn was spun at many a quilting bee for generations after it happened.

Trade Signs

The trade signs of artisans and craftsmen frequently were more elaborate than those of the tavern keeper. Often they were fancy in design and rich in color, even carved or decorated with gilded borders, or gilt was used for highlights. All the village would flock to see a sign, newly hung from brackets of forged iron. It functioned to sell goods, to advertise services,

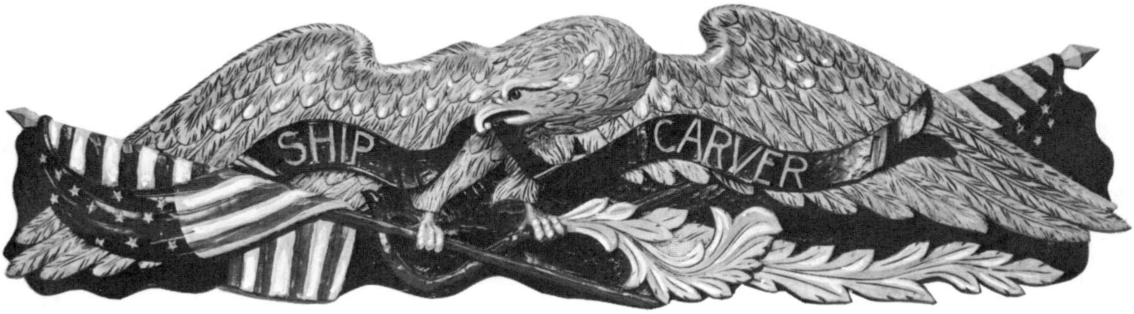

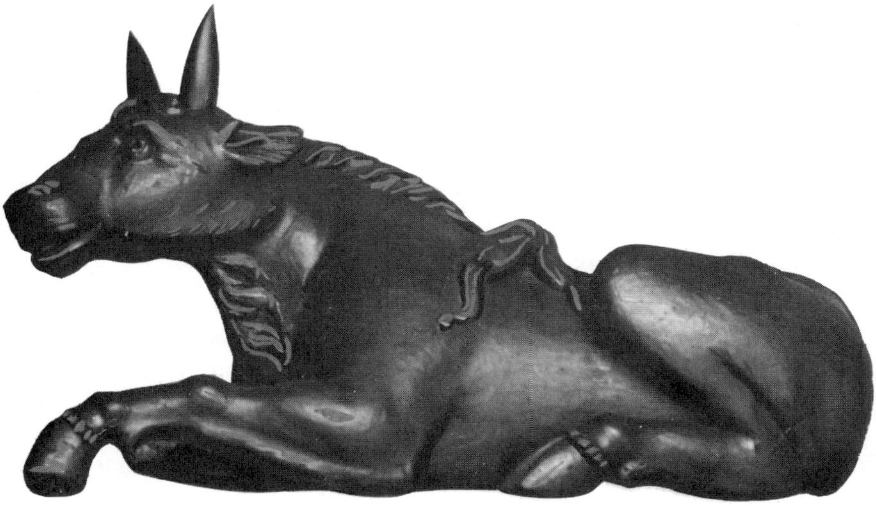

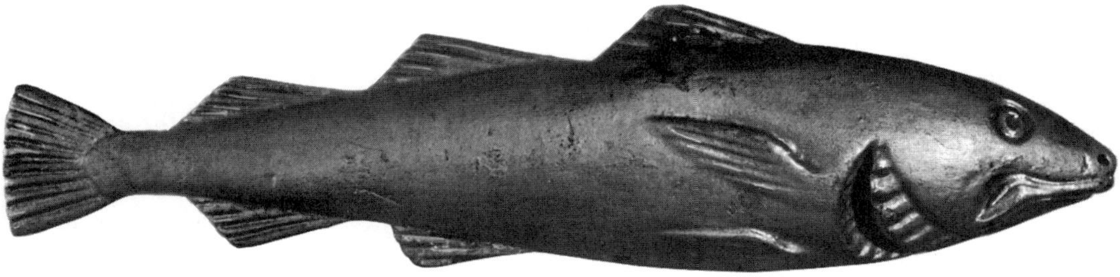

(*Top*) The sign on the carver's shop at Mystic Seaport is the work of Richard Orr whose woodcarving techniques delighted visitors for several years. Other examples of his work exhibited there attest to his high skill as a twentieth-century craftsman. *Photo Louis S. Martel: courtesy Mystic Seaport*

(*Center*) A tanner's trademark. *Photo courtesy Essex Institute*

(*Bottom*) Fish mongers in Europe and America often sought woodcarvers to make their trade signs. *Photo courtesy Essex Institute* and, in a sense, it was a status symbol which revealed the position, wealth, and standing of the tradesman or artisan in the community. Many of them were costly to produce, but in the case of a particular craftsman they served to reflect something of his personality. With many tradesmen, signs had been traditional emblems of a particular trade for centuries. Old prints and present-day photographs of cities and towns in the Old World attest to this fact to a marked degree and add not a little to the charm and atmosphere of European shops. In short, these pictorial images served not only to fix locations in the minds of the villagers and townspeople, but also to identify the craftsmen.

The origin of signboards can be traced with certainty to ancient Pompeii and Herculaneum. A few were painted on walls, but most of them were made of stone or terra cotta. A goat served to mark the site of a dairy, while a mule driving a mill indicated the location of a baker. Even the schoolmaster had his emblem—a boy receiving a good thrashing with a birch rod. Taverns were known by a figure of Bacchus pressing a bunch of grapes. Cupid carrying a pair of ladies' shoes, one on his head and one in his hand, was a shoemaker's trademark. A street in Rome carried these words *"Vicus Ursi Pileati,"* the street of the Bear with the Hat on.

Also from Roman times came the characteristic sign of the bush for a tavern. It was used much later in England and from it came the proverb "Good wine needs no Bush." When traced to England, the insignia used for trade signs reveal a similar practice—a knife for the cutler, a stocking for a hosier, a hand for the glover, a pair of scissors for the tailor. Signs served to mark every conceivable kind of business enterprise involving goods and services and not a few reflected a sense of humor, lusty or restrained according to the inclination of the owner.

In England, in the century preceding the settlement of Plymouth, Salem, Boston, and other seaport towns, "reading was a scarce acquirement" and it was useless to letter the owner's name on a sign. Symbols took their place. From *The History of Signboards* by Jacob Larwood and John Camden Hotten we get a bird's eye view of the language of signs. "Those who could advertized their name by a rebus; thus, a hare and a bottle stood for Harebottle, and two cocks stood for Cox . . . new subjects were continually required. The animal kingdom was ransacked, from the mighty elephant to the humble bee, from the eagle to the sparrow; the vegetable kingdom, from the palm-tree and the cedar to the marigold and the daisy; everything on earth and in the firmament above it was put on contribution. Portraits of the great men of all ages, and views of towns, both painted with a great deal more of fancy than of truth; articles of dress, implements of trades, domestic utensils, things visible and invisible . . . everything was attempted in order to attract attention and to obtain publicity." This was the background of the sign painter's trade and it was from this reservoir of tradition that he garnered his ideas for the signs that swung in front of the shops and taverns from the Canadian border to Long Island Sound.

A century and a half ago a street in a New England town or village spotted with shop and tavern signs was as colorful as any outdoor art gallery. There was considerable variety and originality in the display. Some were painted or carved by itinerant craftsmen, who because of the impecunious position in which they frequently found themselves worked off their debt for bed and board by painting a sign. More than one limner eked out his existence in this way when he was getting his start in life.

In 1770, Paul Revere, that supreme craftsman of many skills, designed, carved, and painted the sign for the Red Lion Inn in Boston which was kept by his friend Edward Proctor. However, most of the sign painters were self-taught and possessed little knowledge of academic techniques. Yet, they usually acquitted themselves admirably. Sometimes highly imaginative, their designs, especially the landscapes, may have been lacking in perspective, and the portraits of Washington, Adams, Hancock, and other public figures were a bit flat, but in total effect, these examples of the colonial sign painters' art were colorful, often striking in appearance, and frequently marked with true originality.

The lettering was usually distinctive, sometimes amusing in the way the lines were handled, but always readable. Wood was the material most commonly used and the construction showed the hand of the skilled artisan whose knowledge of architectural detail was reflected in the moldings, carvings (when used), and general embellishment. While rectangular

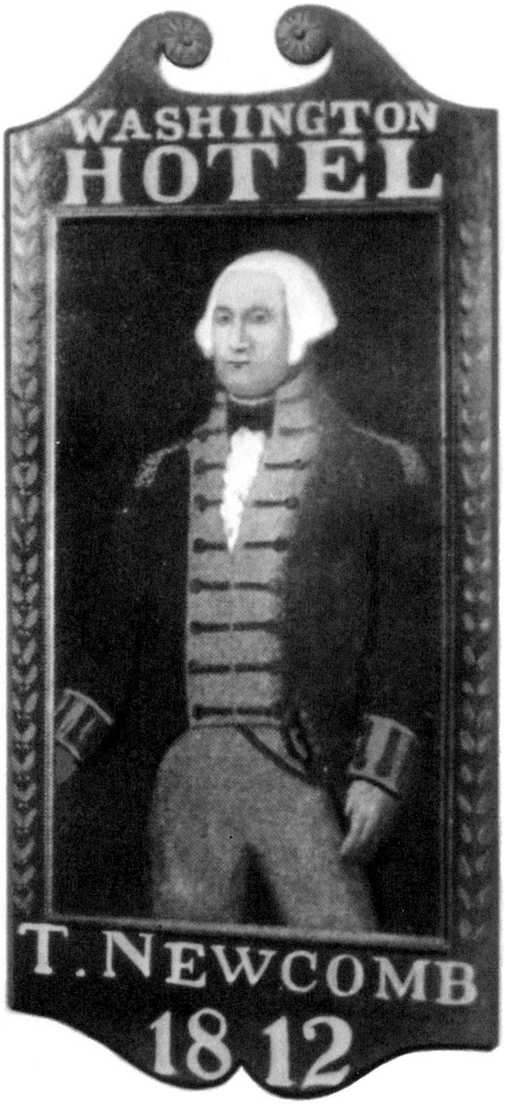

Washington was honored by having many hotels and taverns named for him and it might be added that his distinguished portrait added an air of prestige to the establishment so named. *Photo courtesy Essex Institute*

and square shapes predominated, there were shields, ovals, bells, and other types of cutouts. As we look at them today, in museums, they stand as pleasing, highly personalized ornaments of a heritage that discerning folk have come to reverence. Even before the present vogue for folk art, students of history and lore, both amateur and professional, considered these tokens of the earlier centuries important footnotes to history.

Signs in some towns became numerous enough to give the streets a somewhat cluttered appearance. Craftsmen and shopkeepers, motivated by the desire to attract attention and get as much publicity as possible, caused these emblems to literally "grow" larger and larger. Rivalry among tradesmen, competing for business, also spurred them on to demand bigger and better signs. They became more costly, too, as gold leaf and fancy designs, dictated by a desire for quaintness, became the desiderata. Elaborately carved figures became popular with some craftsmen and shopkeepers. These required considerable skill to make and, besides requiring frequent coats of paint and repairs, they had to be fastened securely on brackets or pedestals to avoid weather damage or theft. In the 1850's a cigar-store Indian might cost as much as $125.00, a tidy amount in those days of the five-cent cigar. Nor was the size the only problem. On wintry nights, they creaked and squeaked as they swayed back and forth in the wind, but as John Gay reminds us in his "Trivia," they sometimes served as a weather warning to the wayfarer:

> But when the swinging signs, your ears offend
> With creaking noise, the rainy floods impend.

Present-day complaints about billboards bring to mind the fact that similar objections were frequently made to tavern and trade signs a hundred years ago, but especially to the latter. Not only were these "beacons" growing larger with the years but they were often suspended between tall poles for better display. In some instances signs were so greatly enlarged that they came toppling down in high winds and stormy weather. Or, the sheer weight of a sign on a poorly placed pole eventually caused it to fall; in some instances, even the guests were not safe. Signs were sometimes lighted at night by placing lanterns of pierced tin (made in Connecticut) at strategic places on the framework.

It would take a heap of digging into old records to obtain the name of the unfortunate man who passed John Duggan's tavern on Corn Court in Boston on a windy day and was killed when the sign blew down on him. Duggan was very proud of the sign that hung outside his hostelry since it featured a portrait of his good friend John Hancock; the place was known as the Hancock Tavern. He had the sign painted (believed to have been adapted from a Copley portrait) when Hancock was governor and when the great patriot died he draped it in black crepe.

Moreau de St. Méry who paid a visit to America after the Revolution kept a journal which Kenneth Roberts translated and called *American Journey* (1793–96). In it St. Méry wrote: "There are artisans who make a specialty of painting remarkably beautiful signboards with backgrounds of different colors, speckled with gold and silver." Of the spelling he observed: "In America children might take spelling lessons from the signboards."

Cigar-Store Indians

To many of the present senior generation, the image of the American Indian was personified in those colorful "segar"-store effigies that decorated the counters of the local tobacconist's shop or stood outside, sometimes near the curbstone. Many a preoccupied soul hurrying home at dusk or later came to grief as he walked straight into one of those imposing carved figures—standing immutable outside a shop door or near the curb. Often with a menacing look on his face, he stood complacently gazing at some distant object and holding a bunch of cigars or tobacco leaves in his hand or wielding a wooden tomahawk.

Carved figures in infinite variety had special appeal as trade signs. They ranged in size from the miniature to the heroic, including boots for the shoemaker, navigators for the nautical shops, ladies of fashion for milliners' establishments, Indians for tobacco shops, and a host of others. They have been called the "homely antecedents for the advertising art of our day," the nostalgic symbol of business in the "good old days," and "vital documents of the American past." Today they are avidly sought by collectors and many are in museums. The cigar-store Indians sold at the Parke-Bernet Galleries during the past three years fetched prices ranging from $725 to $2050.

Best remembered of all because they were in common use and nearly always executed with skill, those brightly colored eye-catchers, the cigar-store Indians, have special appeal to our nostalgic sense. The genealogy of this "true American" is strongly entwined with his first appearance in the mother country in the seventeenth century. When the gallant Sir Walter Raleigh returned from his first trip to the New Land, he told Elizabeth I of the strange people and customs he had observed. She listened intently as he recounted the story of the "Indian weed" (tobacco), and the practice of smoking the peace pipe. Soon after John Rolfe shipped the "weed" to England. From what they gathered, English woodcarvers created a strange character—a Negro wearing a feathered head-

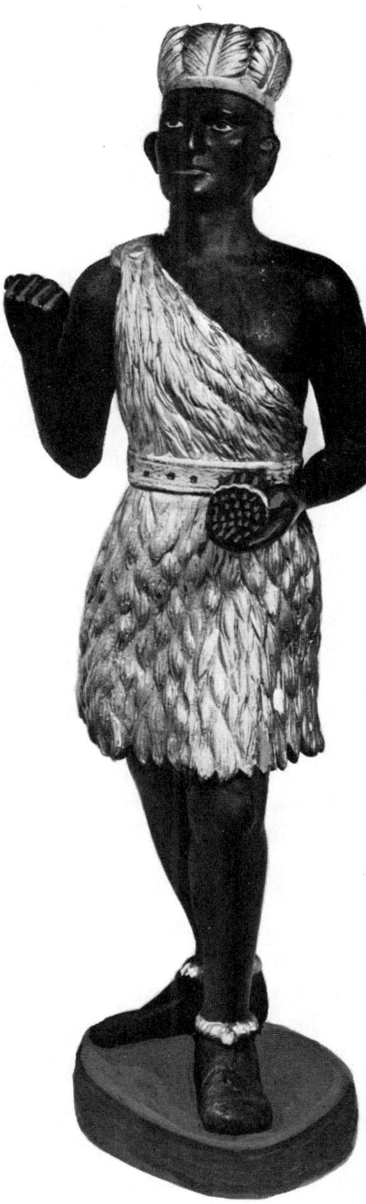

Cigar-Store Indian carved in Massachusetts and used by an Essex County shopkeeper. *Photo courtesy Essex Institute*

dress and a kilt of tobacco leaves, referred to as a Virginian. (These figures were used in England and Holland in the 1600's.) Needless to say, the English became confused with the reports which they had received over the years. On the one hand, the Indian who first raised and smoked tobacco had copper-colored skin, while the colored man who later raised the crop for the Virginian planters actually gave them the inspiration for their portrayal.

In New England and elsewhere in America, the cigar-store Indian became a common trade sign in the generation prior to the Civil War and lasted until the closing days of the nineteenth century. A sizeable number held their proud places until the early years of this century and prompted people like Kate Sanborn to write *Hunting Indians in a Taxi-cab* in 1911. E. O. Christensen reports that as late as 1937 there were about six-hundred wooden Indians in active service. Few remain today. We meet them mostly in museums, in private collections of folk art, or rarely on the auction block.

Most of the carvers remain anonymous, but some of the early sculptors were undoubtedly carvers of ship figureheads. A. W. Pendergast and W. Porter Ware in their book *Cigar Store Figures* mention five woodcarvers who made Indians in New York City in the 1850's. At least one of them worked in Boston carving figureheads. It is fairly certain that at least some of the figures used in shops along the Maine coast and elsewhere in New England were made by local craftsmen whose know-how with the hammer and chisel had been used previously. The day of figureheads and elaborate shipcarving was over. Many of the early figures show distinct individuality in treatment. Some one has said that they were more lifelike than those made after the Civil War. This quality of vitality was derived from the skill, the feeling, and the kind of dedication that one senses as he looks at some of the great ship figureheads of the late eighteenth century and early nineteenth century. Naturally, when they were mass produced, they took on a more static wooden look. Yet the appeal of color was there.

The figures varied in size from those used on store counters, two feet or more in height, to life-size or nearly so that posed on pedestals (sometimes with wheels attached) outside the door. When leading cities passed ordinances relating to public safety, the figures had to be taken in at night.

William Demuth with a shop at 403 Broadway in New York City began to advertise metal show figures in the early 1870's. These were heavy and less likely to be stolen and they were much more weatherproof than their wooden brothers and sisters. On the whole, they were more realistic and notable for their detail. Pewter, iron, bronze, lead, and even papier-mâché were the materials used. Demuth's advertisement speaks for itself.

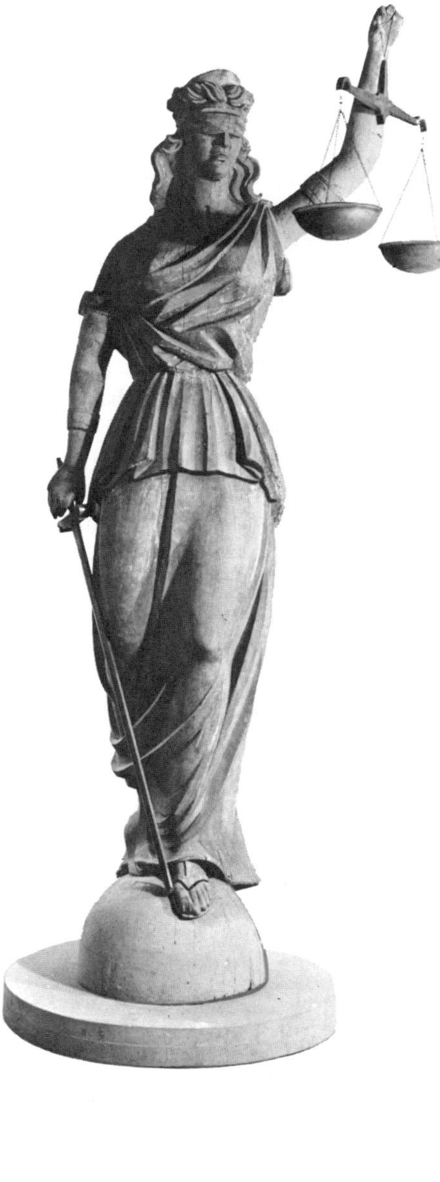

The figure of Justice sometimes appeared on courthouses in the nineteenth century. This carving found in Barnstable on Cape Cod was made of pine, measuring ten feet in height. *Photo courtesy Shelburne Museum*

WOODEN SHOW FIGURES

which we are constantly manufacturing for all classes of business, such as SEGAR STORES, WINE & LIQUORS, DRUGGISTS, YANKEE NOTIONS, UMBRELLAS, CLOTHING, TEA STORES, THEATRES, GARDENS, BANKS, INSURANCE COMPANIES, &c.

Before we commenced Manufacturing Show Figures, their use was almost entirely confined to Tobacconists, who displayed before their Stores a figure of what by a great stretch of imagination might have been recognised as an Indian—the workmanship of which, to say the least, was not very artistic.

Since then we claim not only to have Manufactured Figures which are both carved and painted in a manner which cannot be excelled, but also to have introduced a number of entirely new and original designs for same, to which we are constantly making additions to suit many other classes of trade (as stated above) besides the Tobacco.

But although our Figures invariably gave full satisfaction, still we wished to make a greater improvement in the line, and by the use of some more durable substance than wood, thus prevent cracking, which will sometimes occur in Wooden Figures, especially when exposed to the climate of our Southern States.

For this purpose, after incurring a heavy outlay for Designs, Moulds &c. we commenced the Manufacture of our New

METAL SHOW FIGURES

(being the first parties in the country to introduce same), which have now been before the public for over two years, during which time we have sent large numbers to all sections of the country without ever having received the slightest word of complaint in regard to them.

We claim for these Figures the following qualities: that they are durable, and as light as wooden figures; are designed and executed in a highly artistic manner; and can be furnished at comparatively low prices.

We are constantly receiving orders for Statues and Emblematic Signs, and can furnish same, of any required design, to order, with promptness.

WILLIAM DEMUTH & CO.,
403 Broadway, New York

Popular figures of the day also helped the tobacconist to sell his cigars. Immortalized in wood and dressed in easily identified costumes, every imaginable personality from Punch to Uncle Sam and Yankee Doodle did yeoman service in all kinds of weather. Titled Britishers, rugged frontiersmen, actors, singers, preachers, and even ladies of fashion held down their accustomed places with dignity and confidence. Many stayed on even after the curtain of the Gilded Age had dropped for the last time.

Small carved figures like this one were often placed on the counters in tobacco shops. *Photo courtesy Essex Institute*

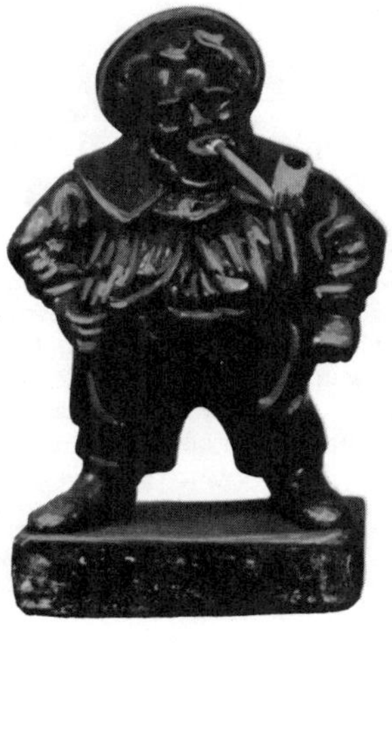

New England Silversmiths

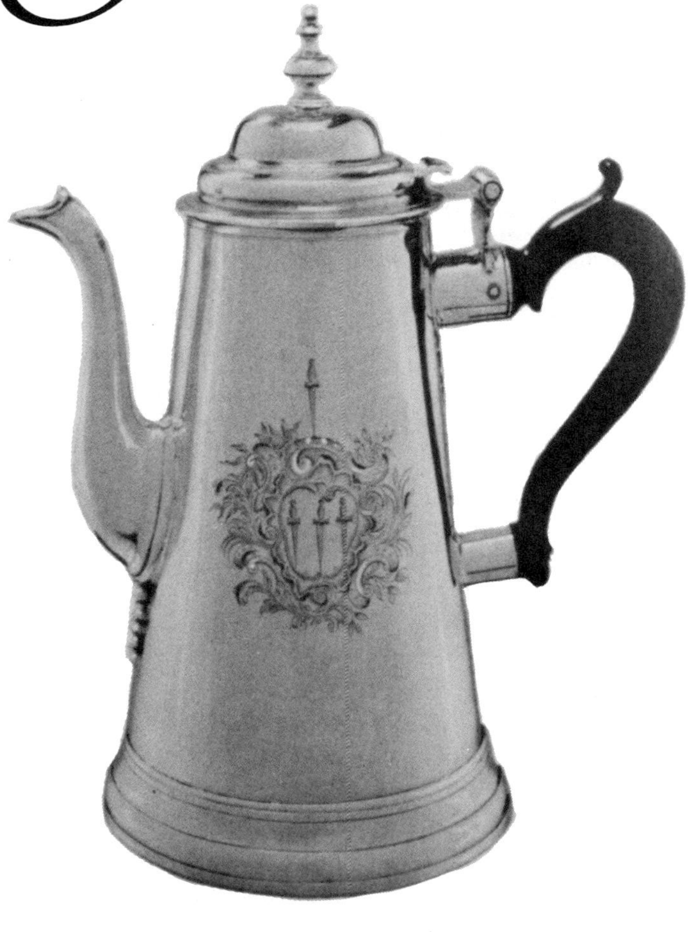

Among New England silversmiths, the name of Jacob Hurd is no less distinguished than the handiwork which he wrought. This coffeepot is 10¼ inches high, engraved with the Clarke coat of arms, and is considered notable for its proportion and craftsmanship. *Photo courtesy Henry Francis du Pont Winterthur Museum*

One of the young men graduated from Harvard College in 1662 was Benjamin Tompson who became master of the grammar school in nearby Charlestown. He had probably been told the story of the setback in business a generation earlier which prompted him to write a poem entitled "New England Crisis" in 1676.

John Hull, Boston's "godly goldsmith" and its first, was a young man at the time and "the chinking bitts of eight" to which Tompson referred in the poem brought good business to Hull. He melted them down to make plate or silver as it was commonly referred to, for silverware was in great demand by churches and wealthy citizens for their homes. As Samuel Eliot Morison recalled in *Builders of the Bay Colony:* "The vessels that he made expressly for the communion service of a church were in the traditional form of the chalice and paten. A few such, like the cup of which Governor Winthrop presented to the First Church of Boston, had been brought over from England. Presumably John used those as models, but attempted little in the way of ornamentation. His work is distinguished for dignity and beauty of proportion, rather than for richness of detail.

"In addition to the orders for churches, the burghers of Boston, waxing rich, ordered silver cans, salts, tankards, beakers, tumblers, bowls, candlesticks, caudle cups, platters, porringers, and wine tasters, for their family use. Many of the drinking vessels and round plates in course of time found their way by will or gift into the possession of the churches, and so were saved for us. For in the eighteenth and nineteenth centuries there was a deplorable practice of melting down ancient pieces of family plate to have them reworked in the latest style."

Prior to the establishment of our banking system, silverware was considered the safest and soundest kind of investment. From the West Indies and other trade routes, Spanish and Dutch coin flooded the seaports of New England. As the motto on the city seal of Salem, Massachusetts, expressed it, the sea captains sailed "to the farthest ports of the rich East," and returned with cargoes, treasures for their families, and Spanish silver dollars. The surest way to protect money was to take it to a local silversmith to be transformed into tankards and teapots, candlesticks and caudle cups, platters and porringers and countless other articles of use and beauty.

In converting silver coin, the silversmith first melted it in a crucible and cast the silver in solid pieces by pouring it into iron molds. After forging the plates on an anvil, he reduced them to an even thickness by passing them through steel rollers several times. Since pure silver (1000 parts fine) is too soft for common use, coin silver (900 parts fine) was preferred for plate or tableware. The present-day sterling standard, fixed by federal law, 92.5 parts pure silver, has copper added to provide greater solidity plus wearability.

Four ways of working the metal are: hammering, stamping, casting, and spinning. The method used was determined by the type of article to be made. Thus, it was the silversmith's decision to choose the right technique to achieve both durability and beauty. This craft demanded not only consummate skill but artistic talent as well.

The making of the teapot, described by E. V. Mitchell in *The Romance of the New England Antiques,* required the rolling and forging of fifteen separate pieces. "The knob, the spout, and handle were either cast or the two parts composing them were cut from the plate and shaped by stamping them with steel dies. The various parts were then soldered together with an alloy composed of about three parts of silver and one of brass and copper. But before the spout and handle were added, the body was polished on a lathe, first with a file, then with a scraper, and afterward with pumice stone. It was next removed from the lathe and held against a rapidly revolving brush charged with fine brick dust and sweet oil. Then, after the handle and spout had been soldered in place, the teapot was annealed and placed in pickle, that is, in a weak solution of oil of vitriol. On removal it was scoured with sand and water and finally burnished with a steel instrument." Decoration by means of chasing or engraving gave the maker a further challenge.

In addition to their own trades, silversmiths, who, of necessity, had to be versatile, functioned as clockmakers, bell founders, cabinetmakers, blacksmiths, and decorators of painted tin. Sometimes they were referred to as whitesmiths" because they worked in a light metal whereas the blacksmiths used iron which was dark or black. Whereas the silversmith could

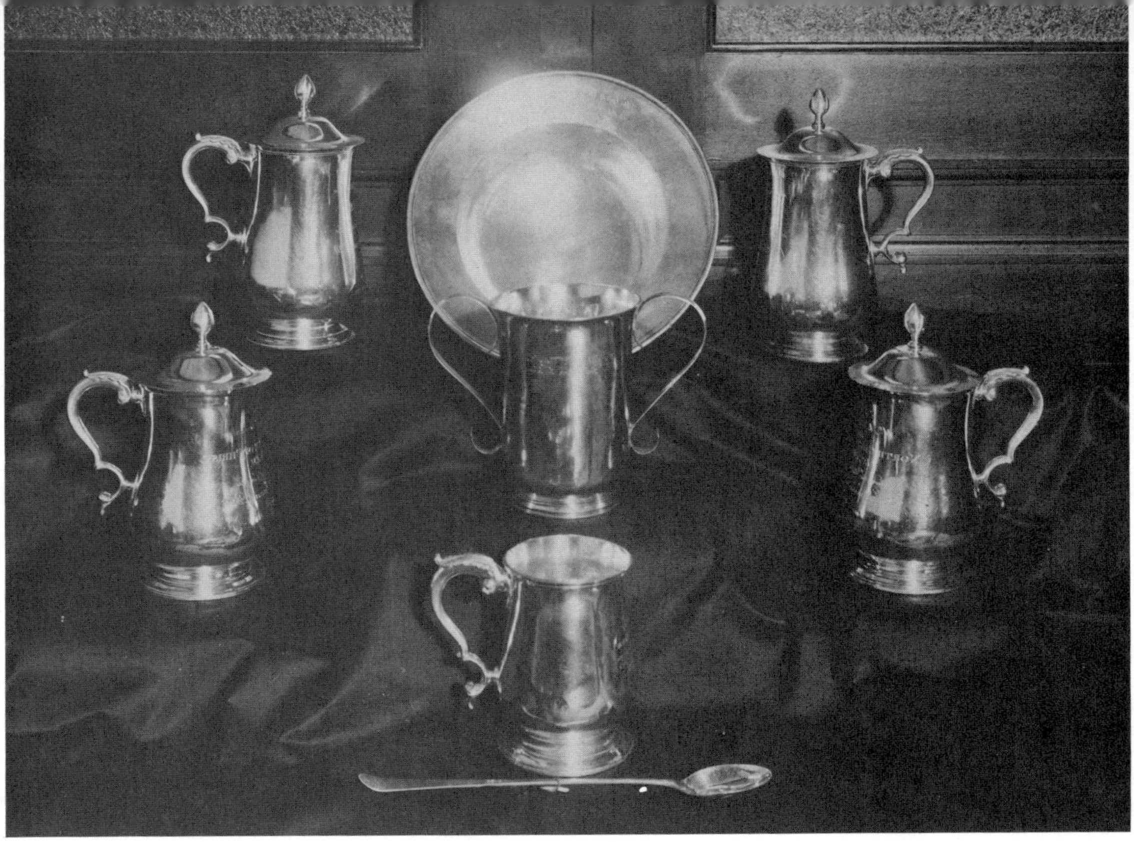

A number of New England churches own notable collections of early American silver, some of which were commissioned for use in Communion service. Other pieces bequeathed by leading citizens were sometimes melted down and the metal used to make additional pieces for church use. However, a goodly number of these heirlooms have been preserved in their original state. The pieces shown above represent a small part of the collection of the First Church, Salem, Massachusetts. *Photo courtesy Essex Institute*

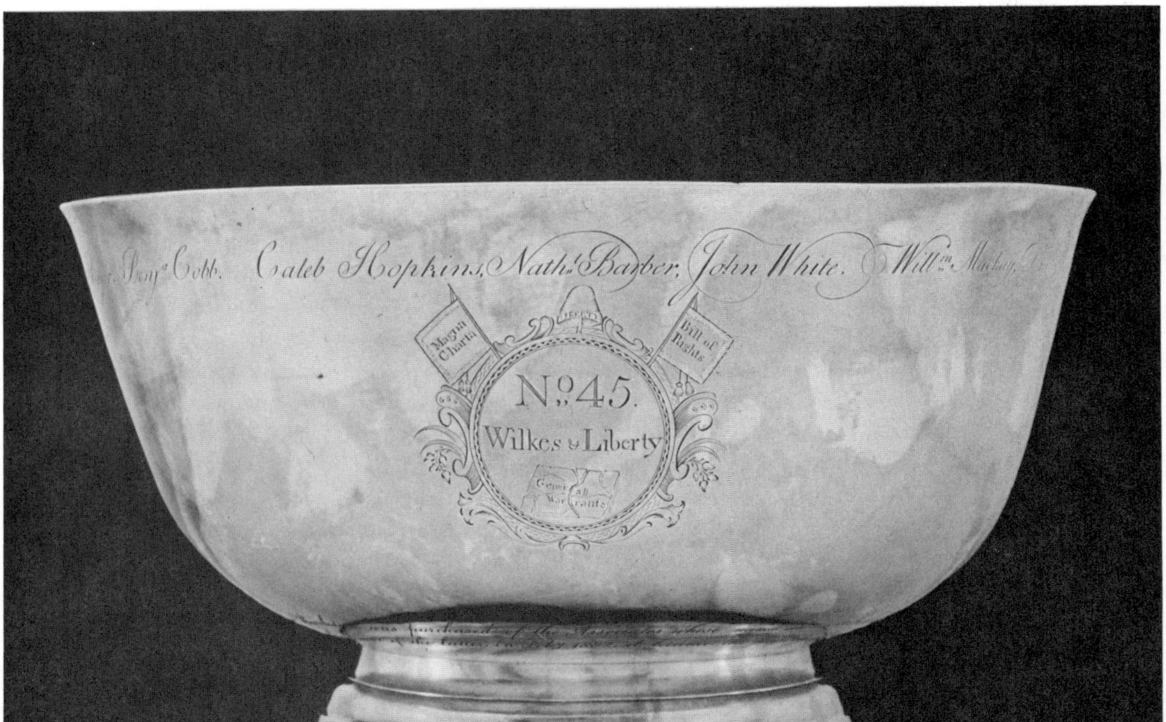

wield an anvil and knew the handling of metals, he was well equipped for the task of blacksmith and bellfounder as well. The large, powerful hands of Paul Revere, portrayed by John Singleton Copley, immediately capture the attention of anyone who looks at this famed portrait. In Middletown, Connecticut, there was a woman silversmith named Minerva Dexter, but this was no craft or art for women.

Every housewife longed to own a sizeable collection of silver spoons in various sizes and she prized them highly. The story told by Benjamin Franklin, the most notable of all early American raconteurs, could probably be matched by many a rising young colonialist of the time, but few could tell it in so inimitable a manner. Here is the story: "We have an English proverb that says, *He that would thrive, must ask his wife*. It was lucky for me that I had one as much disposed to industry and frugality as myself. She assisted me cheerfully in my business, folding and stitching pamphlets, tending shop, purchasing old linen rags for the papermakers, etc., etc. We kept no idle servants, our table was plain and simple, our furniture of the cheapest. For instance my breakfast was for a long time bread and milk (no tea), and I ate it out of a twopenny earthen porringer, with a pewter spoon. But mark how luxury will enter families, and make progress, in spite of principle: being call'd one morning to breakfast, I found it in a China bowl, with a spoon of silver! They had been bought for me without my knowledge by my wife, and had cost her the enormous sum of three-and-twenty shillings, for which she had no other excuse or apology to make, but that she thought *her* husband deserv'd a silver spoon and China bowl as well as any of his neighbors. This was the first appearance of plate and China in our house, which afterward, in a course of years, as our wealth increas'd, augmented gradually to several hundred pounds in value."

When the British occupied Boston in 1775, food became scarce during the summer and General Gage decided to evacuate large numbers of residents. He posted a notice to receive the names of those who wished to leave, stating that no silverware was to be removed and that no more than five pounds in cash might be taken by each person. More than two thousand people agreed to leave; many, though eager to leave, feared to because they knew well the plundering habits of soldiers. The women who did leave quilted silver spoons into their garments, and coin as well. During the "trouble" a sizeable quantity of American silver was taken to England by families of Tory sympathy.

In the spring of 1791, Mrs. Anstice Updike Lee of Rhode Island made a trip to Hartford by horseback, accompanied by her brother and put up at Bull's Tavern, where she was delighted by the fresh Connecticut River salmon. She was asked to tea at the home of Colonel George Wyllys along with President Stiles of Yale College and gave the following description of the silver she saw. "The room where we sat was spacious, and there was a greater display of silverware than I had ever seen before. There was a large mahogany table in the parlor, and under it stood a finely-wrought silver chafing-dish, and a silver kettle on it; there was also a large silver tea urn. On the table stood a large

(*Opposite*) Sons of Liberty Bowl fashioned by Paul Revere. In the *Boston Gazette*, August, 1768, the following announcement appeared: "We hear that the Week before last was finished by Order and for the Use of the Gentlemen belonging to the Insurance Office kept by Mr. Nathaniel Barber, at the North-End, an elegant Silver BOWL, weighing forty-five ounces, and holding forty-five Jills. On one side is engraved within a handsome Border—To the Memory of the Glorious Ninety-two Members of the Honourable House of the REPRESENTATIVES of the MASSACHUSETTS-BAY, who undaunted by the insolent Menaces of Villains of Power, and out of a strict Regard to Conscience, and the LIBERTIES of their Constituents, on the 30th of June 1867, VOTED NOT TO RESCIND. Over which is the Cap of Liberty in an Oaken Crown. In the other side, in a Circle adorned with Flowers, etc., is No. 45. WILKES AND LIBERTY, under which is General Warrants torn to Pieces. On the Top of the Cup of Liberty, and out of each Side, is a Standard, on one is MAGNA CARTA, the other BILL OF RIGHTS.—On Monday Evening last, the Gentlemen belonging to the Office made a Genteel Entertainment, and invited a Number of Gentlemen of Distinction in the Town, when 45 Loyal Toasts were drank, and the whole concluded with a new song, the Chorus of which is, In Freedom we're born, and in Freedom we'll live, etc." *Photo courtesy Museum of Fine Arts, Boston*

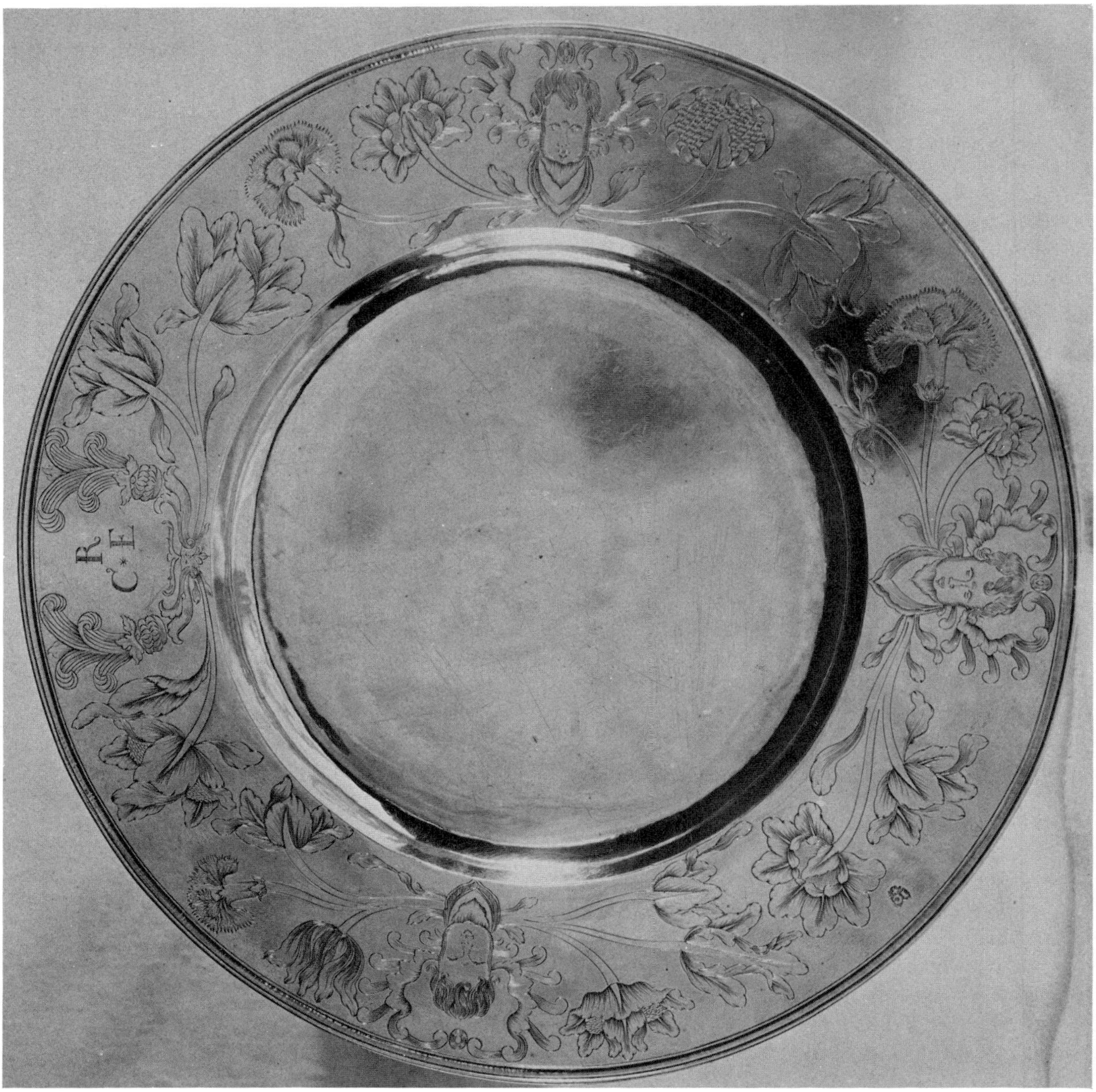

A broad-rimmed silver plate, richly engraved with cherubs' heads, tulips, and carnations, made by John Coney (1655–1722), is among the rare examples of early American engraved silver. Owned by the Musuem of Fine Arts, Boston. *Photo courtesy Museum of Fine Arts, Boston*

silver waiter and a large silver teapot, silver sugardish, and silver cream pot. This was surrounded by a richly ornamented set of China service; in unison with that were elegant chairs, carpets, and mirrors. It was impressive evidence of an ancient family of wealth."

While the making of such objects as tankards, mugs, flagons, caudle cups, porringers, and beakers occupied the silversmiths of the seventeenth century, those who followed produced a wide variety of useful articles. These included snuffboxes and patch boxes, candlesticks and candlesnuffers, shoe buckles, saltcellars and pepper shakers, cruets and trays, sugar tongs and nutmeg graters, saucepans and sauce boats, cream pitchers and basins, hatbands and thimbles, inkstands and sword hilts. For the ladies they also made buttons, beads, rings, hair combs, and even gold toothpicks. Making jewelry was a prime occupation of the silversmith, and the favored metal was gold. With the exception of mourning rings, spoons, and gold beads (all standard items), most of the articles in the silversmith's shops were made to order. A piece

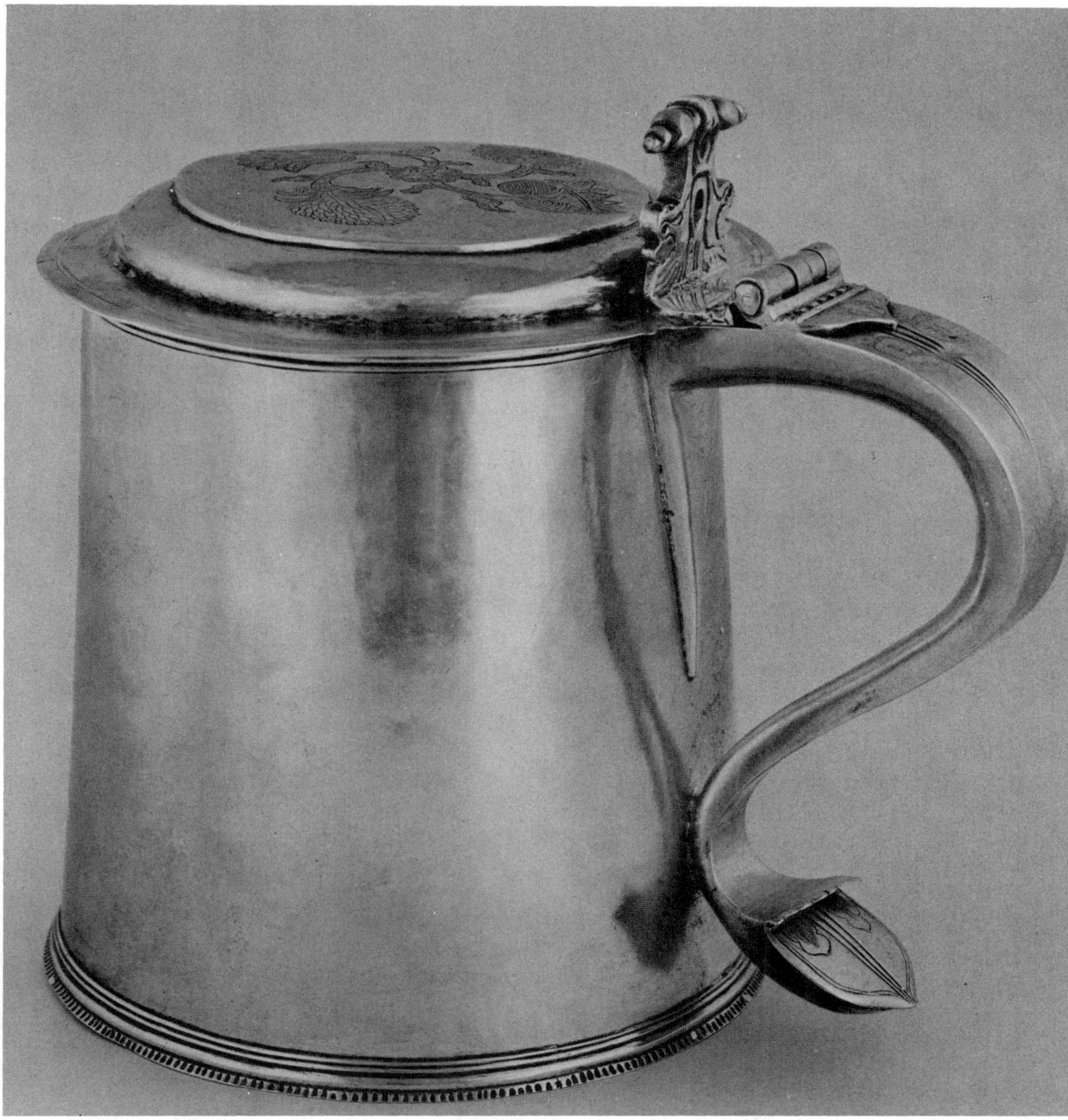

Robert Sanderson (1608–1693), partner of John Hull, the mintmaster of Massachusetts, was commissioned to make this large cider tankard for Isaac and Mary Vergoose. Eventually, Isaac's second wife Elizabeth inherited the tankard. Often referred to as "the original baby sitter," she used to sing rhymes to Boston babies and her son-in-law, Thomas Fleet, published these as *Mother Goose's Melodies. Photo courtesy Museum of Fine Arts, Boston*

of silver represented an investment of money and labor which most of the craftsmen could not spare.

In the prosperous towns, like Salem, Newburyport, and Boston, Massachusetts; Newport and Providence, Rhode Island; Hartford and Norwich, Connecticut, the business of the silversmith flourished, whereas, in the smaller towns, the making of spoons, mourning rings, and jewelry occupied the craftsmen, with occasionally a commission for a piece of plate. Yet, many of the small-town whitesmiths were men of considerable ability as their work so clearly reveals. It was only natural for wealthy citizens to turn to a craftsman who had a reputation. Then, as now, performance was the best kind of advertising, and the lure of the large-town, often fashionable-to-patronize silversmith was ever present. Nor, has it changed—that maxim of the prophet without honor. . . . Thus, the country silversmith assumed the role of Jack-of-all-trades. The glamorous life associated with a

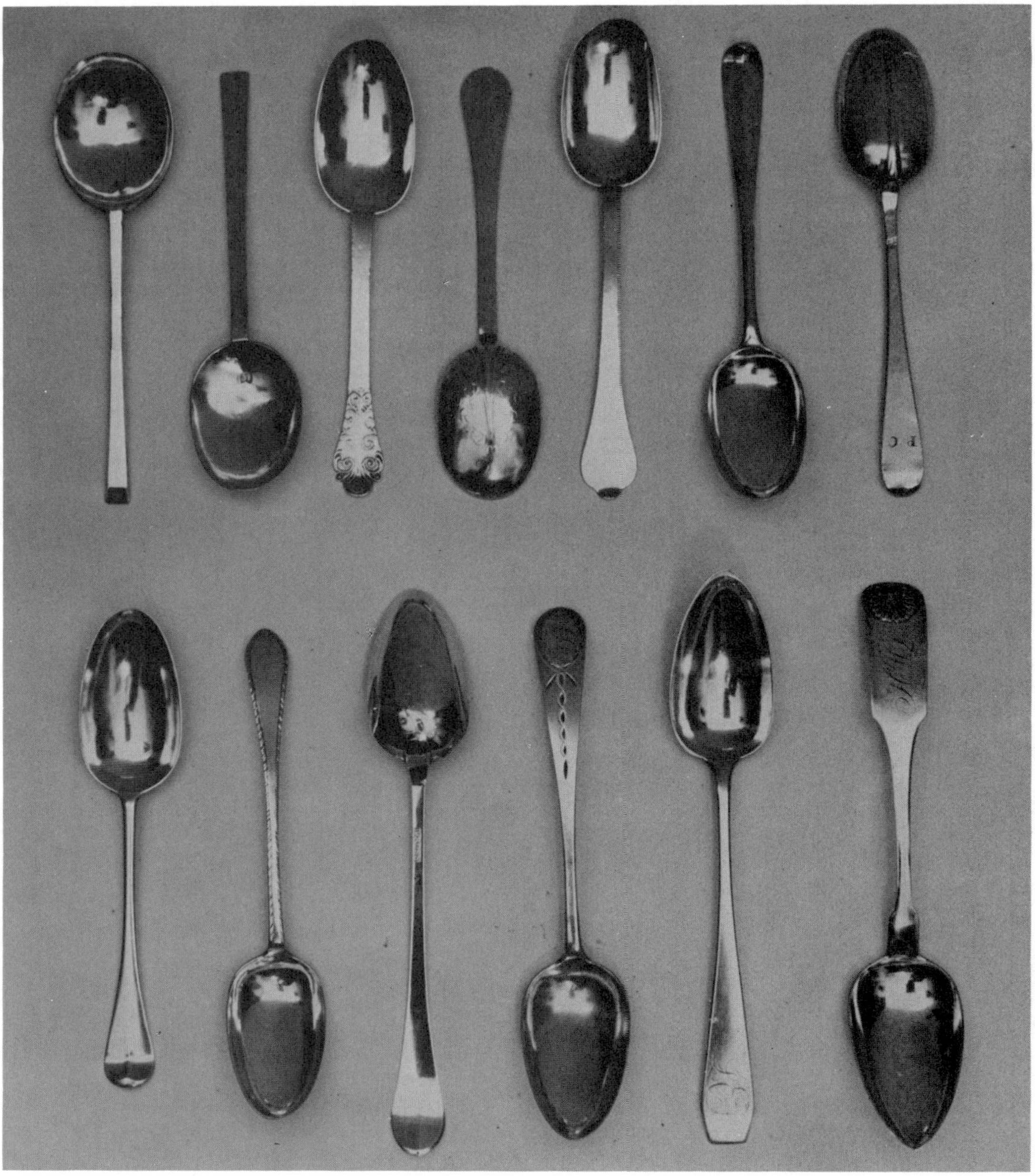

In 1746, when Joshua Hempstead of New London, Connecticut, loaned his grandson some money, he recorded that he lent him "so much Silver Money as his silver spoon weighs and took ye spoon for security." The development of the silver spoon from 1650 to 1850 is of interest to all who enjoy using and collecting old silver. Top row, left to right: (1) slip-end c.1650; (2) puritan c.1660; (3 & 4) trifid c.1690; (5) wavy-end c.1700; (6 & 7) mid-rib c.1715. Bottom row, left to right: (1) modified mid-rib c.1750; (2) feather-edge c.1770; (3 & 4) bright-cut c.1785; (5) coffin-end c.1800; (6) fiddle-shell c.1830–50. *Photo courtesy Yale University Art Gallery*

master craftsman like Paul Revere hardly could be matched by a silversmith in a small town. Joseph Carpenter, Jr. (1747–1804), lived in Norwich, Connecticut, and carried on his business in a little shop which is still preserved by the "Society of Founders." The account book which he kept also remains and from it we can glean an idea of what he made, what he spent, and how he prospered. He also did engraving and, for twelve years, was a clockmaker as well. From his earnings he was able to build a substantial house.

It is not surprising that every type of drinking vessel was in constant demand—mugs, tankards, cans, caudle cups, punch bowls. Drinking was a well-established custom of long standing, firmly intrenched in the colonial way of life. It was one way to keep the stomach warm and the spirit lively in those cold unheated houses and taverns. It was an outlet for the stern sense of duty, responsibility, and Puritan theocracy of the day. All too often, as is the way with men everywhere and in every age, the amount of spirits consumed often overpowered the spirit, and this led finally to the temperance movement of the early nineteenth century. The result was that many pieces, displaying the finest kind of craftsmanship, were melted down or remodeled.

John Mansfield (1604–1674), New England's first silversmith, arrived in Boston in 1634. While no example of his work is known, it is believed that he may have taught the art to John Hull. (See Chapter 19.) Then followed Robert Sanderson (1608–1693) who joined John Hull in partnership in 1652, the year that Hull became mint-master of Massachusetts and began to coin the pine-tree shillings and six pences. The minting of these coins, the first to be made in America, was continued for thirty years. Jeremiah Dummer (1648–1718) learned his trade with the famous Hull; so, too, Timothy Dwight (1654–1691). It was Dummer's brother-in-law, John Coney (1655–1722), who claimed as one of his apprentices the father of Paul Revere. Silversmiths in large numbers were at work throughout New England in the eighteenth century.

For one-hundred and twenty-five years, the Moulton family of Newburyport, Massachusetts, through six generations, handed down their silver business from father to son. William Moulton (1664–1732), who founded the business in 1690, was both a black- and whitesmith. In all, there were three Williams and three Josephs in direct line of descent who plied the silversmith's craft. Following the Moultons, two apprentices of the last Joseph carried it on. One of these men was Anthony Towle, and the Towle Silversmiths of Newburyport are still operating,

An impressive punch bowl made by Jeremiah Dummer in 1692. Wines of quality and variety, as well as rum, brandy, and other ingredients were mixed, according to the receipt favored by the host, for the pleasure of his guests. Punch was popular in the colonies and, then as now, overindulgence was not uncommon. *Photo courtesy of the Mabel Brady Garvan Collection, Yale University Art Gallery*

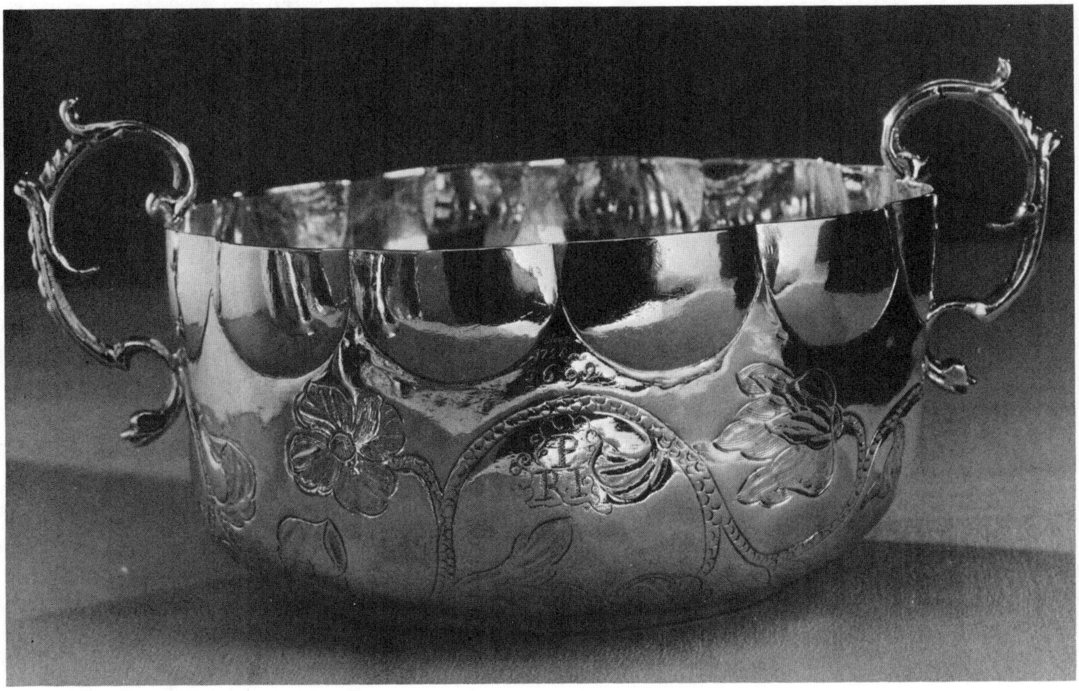

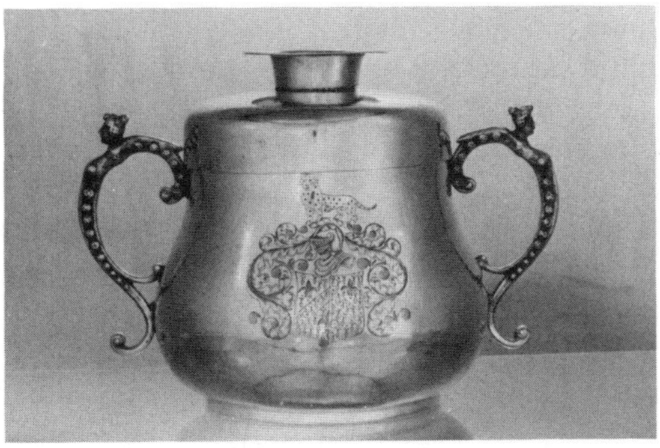

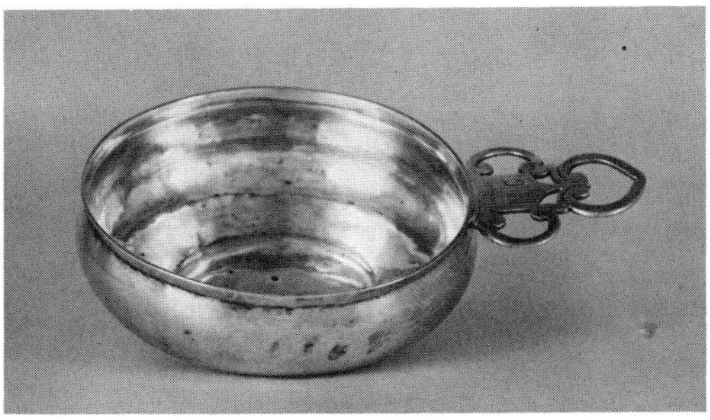

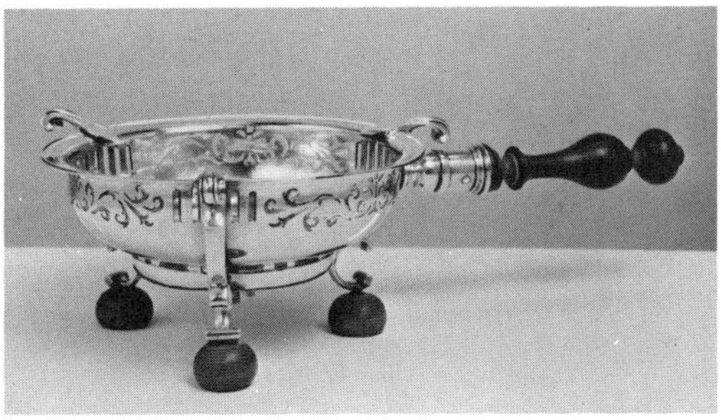

(*Top*) A covered caudle cup made by John Coney of Boston in 1679, inscribed with the Addington coat of arms. Caudle, a warm drink made of thin gruel mixed with wine or ale to which spices and sugar were added, was served on all festive occasions ranging from baptisms to funerals. *Photo courtesy of the Mabel Brady Garvan Collection, Yale University Art Gallery*

(*Center*) Porringers like this one made by Jeremiah Dummer (1645–1781) were originally used for porridge and broth and later as sugar bowls. These shallow circular silver bowls with their single intricately designed handles are prime examples of utility of purpose combined with beauty of design. *Photo courtesy Museum of Fine Arts, Boston*

(*Bottom*) John Potwine (1698–1792), son of a Huguenot physician, was born in Boston but moved to Hartford, Connecticut, in 1739. The superbly fashioned chafing dish which he made is one of a pair. Later in life Potwine operated a general store. *Photo courtesy Henry Francis du Pont Winterthur Museum*

carrying on the traditions of distinguished craftsmanship in silver for 276 years.

The famous punch bowl made by Paul Revere is the most highly prized piece of colonial silverware in America. It was acquired by the Boston Museum of Fine Arts for fifty-six thousand dollars which was raised by public subscription. At the time, it was said that the Liberty Bowl would have been worth every penny of the price paid even if it were a battered relic. Actually, this superb example of the silversmith's art was in pristine condition and it was rumored that one of the wealthiest men in America had offered nearly twice the amount paid if only he could possess it. No other piece of silverware is so closely linked with American history and its story merits repetition. Although Revere kept a ledger from 1761 to 1797, the bowl is not mentioned.

When the Townshend Acts were passed, placing a small duty on tea, paper, printer's colors, and glass, the colonists were annoyed but hoped to handle the matter by boycott. The mother country was obviously determined to regulate trade and they would have no part of it. More taxes were bound to follow. The Massachusetts General Court had expressed its views to the colonies, and George III demanded that they "recind" them. Seventeen members complied, but ninety-two flatly refused. To celebrate the event, fifteen Sons of Liberty commissioned Paul Revere to make a generous punch bowl that would hold a gallon. How many, many times it had to be refilled to quench the thirsty throats of the objectors, Esther Forbes has not declared. But, in that most readable of biographies, *Paul Revere and the World He Lived In,* she has given us a spirited description of the bowl. The strong, easy lines and the exquisite finish are all Revere's but the innumerable thoughts engraved all over it suggests those fifteen bright Whiggish minds, all cooking up something together and, like the traditional too-many cooks, spoiling the broth. Although Revere may have been pleased politically by these noble thoughts, it must have been hard for him as a craftsman so to mar the surface of his bowl. Everything is on it: wreaths, Liberty caps, No. 45 (referring to a pamphlet by the English John Wilkes), and 'Wilkes for Liberty.' Two standards bearing the words 'Magna Charta' and 'Bill of Rights.' One bright idea follows another, a torn document for 'general warrants,' and a long effusion to the 'glorious 92.' The names of the donors. Revere's own name appears simply on the bottom."

Revere showed his talent as a silversmith to the fullest even before he was thirty and, in his pursuit of perfection in design, it has been said that he never sacrificed purity for the sake of embellishment. Even when fashioning pieces in the rococo manner, the high style following that of the Queen Anne period, the great silversmith showed his grasp of his art in the restraint which he used. Some of his finest work left Boston with some of its best citizens, the Tory families who sought refuge in the mother country, but various pieces have returned home, to round out the distinguished collection of Revere silver housed in Boston's Museum of Fine Arts. His church silver is as highly praised today as when it was made.

At the turn of the present century, collectors directed their attention to old American silver. Prior to that time, it was believed that much of the heirloom silver to be found in New England was English, whereas it was part of the proud heritage of an earlier America. Theodore W. Wolsey focused attention on American silversmiths in an article which appeared in *Harper's Magazine* in 1896. Then followed the great exhibition staged by the Boston Museum of Fine Arts in 1906; this astonished all who saw it and the search was on.

E. V. Mitchell, in *The Romance of New England Antiques,* writes: "One reason, perhaps, why people had been misled into thinking that there were scarcely any silversmiths in this country was because the craftsmen of the period followed more or less closely the changing fashions in English design. Yet they were not slavish copyists, but adapted the designs to American taste, which demanded simple lines and good proportions. Fortunately, these silversmiths were fancy free and did not try to follow the elaborate and flamboyant ornamentation that was characteristic of some of the silver made abroad in the eighteenth century. Another factor which may have thrown people off the track was the high quality of the workmanship. Apparently people could not believe that such excellent work could be that of provincial silversmiths."

The hallmark of the maker is the key for identifying old silver. In England, for generations, the Goldsmith's Company required that a mark be placed on articles made of gold and silver to designate the standard of purity of the metal used by the craftsmen. However, this practice was not in use in the colonies. Instead, colonial craftsman used either their names or their initials and, with this distinguishing mark, they sometimes combined some insignia which they had chosen as a trademark. A typical example was John Coney of Boston who used a rabbit; cony or coney is an Old English word meaning rabbit. Jeremiah Dummer marked his work with the initials I. D. with a fleur-de-lis in heart. Jacob Hurd's stamp was his name in a small rectangle. The word *coin* appears on some of the early pieces, but the term *sterling* was not used as a hallmark until 1865. The present federal law requires the use of this mark and indicates that the metal meets the required standard for "solid silver."

From the very beginning, New England led the country in the production of silverware and still holds that lead in Rhode Island, Connecticut, and Massachusetts.

Styles in silver changed with the prevailing taste in England, and because of the constant importation of fine silver by wealthy merchants, long before the Revolution, New England silversmiths were able to keep abreast of the newest fashion. Consequently, as Martha Gandy Fales has stated in *American Silver in the Henry Francis Dupont Winterthur Museum,* "The development of American silver more closely parallels the stylistic development of the major artistic movements than does any other art practiced in early America. Because of its early and continued patronage and the esteem in which silver was held, it was one of the first arts to flourish in America and therefore merits particular study." Moreau de St. Méry, who visited in America shortly after the Revolution, was impressed not only with the signboards of our craftsmen but also with "all the silver . . . displayed on the sideboard in the dining room."

Shades of Our Ancestors

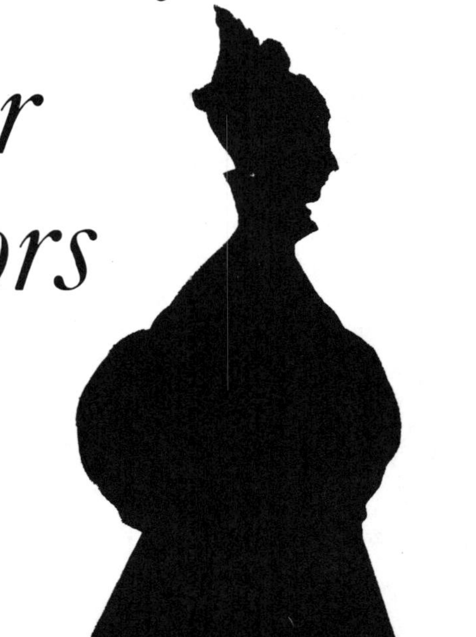

Undoubtedly, it was George Washington who, not only "first in peace, first in war . . ." but also the most silhouetted of his countrymen, made the silhouette or profile (as it was often called at the time) popular in America. Our first president had a distinguished countenance and his profile was unforgettable. It was the ambition of every profilist in America to have him as a subject, and at least six widely known silhouettists succeeded. Even his beloved Nelly Custis tried her hand at his likeness and many amateurs followed suit. While on a trip to London, Benjamin Franklin wrote to his wife: "I send you the little shade that was copied from the great one. If it will be acceptable to my good Friend, Mr. Robert, pray give it to him."

Patience Wright, a vivid Quaker lady who lived in Philadelphia, not only modeled wax figures for a living, but on the side cut profiles of all who would sit for her and did animals and flowers as well. As Alice Van Leer Carrick tells us, she was an "odd old woman" noted for her "energetic mildness." Abigail Adams paid her a visit in 1784 and while this prim and proper New Englander was "immensely impressed by her genius," she was most critical of her appearance for as she wrote: "Her person and countenance resemble an old maiden lady in your neighborhood, Nelly Penniman, except that one is neat, the other the queen of sluts, and her tongue runs like Unity Bedlam's." (However much they tried to conceal it, most New Englanders did not take kindly to the Quakers, and Mrs. John Adams was no exception.) Continuing, Mrs. Carrick remarked: "Still after such disparaging words it is only fair to add that, left a widow, Patience Wright supported her family by her wax modeling, first in America, later in London, where she became the rage and was able to give her son Joseph, the artist, a chance to study in Paris and to work under Benjamin West and John Hoppner."

It has been said that like the Roman Empire, the art of silhouette cutting had its rise and its fall. Franklin used the term "shade" in his letter to his wife and this together with "profile" were the names in common use when the art was first practiced on both sides of the Atlantic. Actually, *profile* is the term preferred for it preceded *silhouette* and is all inclusive; it referred to the various types of shadow pictures both cut and painted. Shadowgraph, another name used, derived from those cut by John Casper Laveter's wonderful hollow-cutting apparatus, developed in the eighteenth century.

In 1757, a most extraordinary Frenchman, Étienne de Silhouette, was made controller general of his country at a time when government costs were reaching staggering proportions. He immediately instituted so many widespread and far-reaching procedures of economy that, in France, anything cheap was referred to as a silhouette. The controller general died ten years later, but this bit of jargon, which persisted for generations, was the name to be linked with the shadow portrait which became popular in England somewhat later. In 1826, Augustin Edouart, left France and took up residence in England and advertised himself as "Silhouettist," thus starting the vogue for the term in common use today. As if this mode of expression did not have enough names to describe a simple profile, there were those who advertised their ability in "Skiagraphy"; others called themselves "Scissor-graphists" and the inimitable "Master" Hubard announced himself as "Papyrotamist." The simplest type of profile was snipped from black paper and mounted on white card. Other techniques included outlining on silk, glass, ivory, or metal, and filling in with black, or occasionally with color.

It was the American itinerant silhouette artists who introduced the style of cutting the portrait out of the centre of the card itself and pasting black paper or cloth behind it. Amateurs, including children, used the easy method of fastening a piece of paper to a wall behind the sitter whose profile was simply traced, later to be blocked or colored according to choice. The "sheet method" using specially made screen and a lighted candle, as described in the following paragraph, was one type of "machine." Moses Chapman, who wandered around Essex County in Massachusetts in the early part of the nineteenth century, had his own contraption which he carried about with him. Prior to the introduction of the daguerreotype in 1839, and the photograph somewhat later, the silhouette was the cheapest and easiest method of obtaining a likeness. Many of the cutters were itinerants and a few were even youthful prodigies. Exhibitions of silhouettes by the itinerants were popular and frequent.

John Casper Laveter's description of his hollow-cutting process appeared in his *Essays on Physiognomy* in England in 1797. With typi-

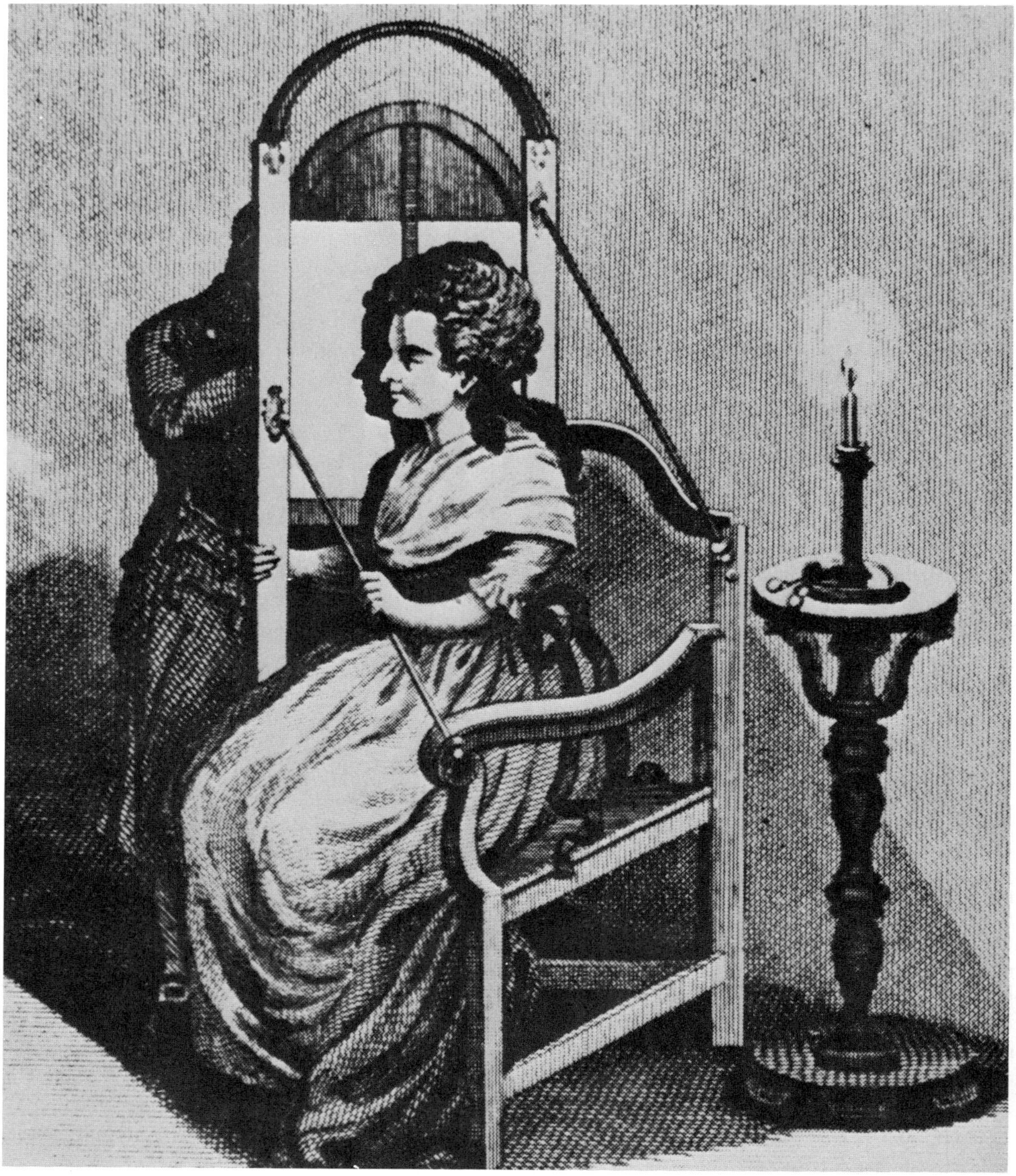

A silhouette machine.

cal French sense of detail he stated: "The shade should be taken on post paper, or rather on thin oiled paper, well dried. Let the head and back be supported by a chair, and the shade fall on the oil paper behind a clear, flat, polished glass. Let the drawer sit behind the glass, holding the frame with his left hand, and, having a sharp black-lead pencil, draw with the right. The glass, in a detached sliding frame, may be raised or lowered, according to the height of the person. The bottom of the glass frame, being thin, will be best of iron, and should be raised so as to rest steadily upon the shoulder. In the centre, upon the glass, should be a small piece of wood, or iron, to which fasten a small round cushion, supported by a short pin, scarcely half an inch long, which may be raised or lowered, and against which a person may lean. By the aid of a magnifying lens or solar microscope, the outlines may be much more accurately determined or drawn." And he added: "Coughing, sneezing or laughing are to be avoided as such movements put the shadow out of place." For those who were gifted with the scissors, these "sundry wonderful machines" were hardly necessary.

The Pantograph (also called "Stork's Beak" or "Monkey") was used to reduce the size of the silhouette thus made. With this instrument, silhouettes could be made in brooch and locket size. On occasion, these tiny paper portraits were mounted on glass and inserted in the tops of snuffboxes.

Commenting on the endless variations in the making of silhouettes, Ethel Stanwood Bolton noted: "Some artists, not content with plain black paint, have used a combination of pine soot and beer, which gives a very intense blackness. There appears to have been a time when beer was the do-all and cure-all, for at about this same period is found the receipt for cleaning pewter by boiling it in beer and hay. Be that as it may, these silhouettists covered glass with the mixture of pine soot and beer, and then removed the portrait and left the background. The glass was then backed with gold leaf, silver leaf, or tinsel, so that the result was a gold or silver portrait in a black ground or the reverse. Sometimes delicate lines are left to traverse the more brilliant background."

"Papyro-Plastico" was the high-flown name for the art of modeling in paper. In a pamphlet published before 1825 we read that "by sticking three or four sheets of paper together, and by working at the back with a polishing steel, one can actually make a profile portrait in slight relief out of a silhouette cut from white paper." It adds that this process gives "it the appearance of a marble tablet or a plaster cast done by a sculptor. Thus can one attain great ends from base beginnings."

The peripatetic antics of William King, temperamental profilist of Salem, Massachusetts, are the makings of a good novel, and thanks to that indefatigable diarist the Reverend William Bentley we know a great deal about him. King was also a cabinetmaker, and a scamp to boot, once compared to the migrant tumbleweed, but for all his shortcomings, he was not without talent. He belonged to the singing company at Bentley's East Church and was often invited to spend "a pious evening of song and prayer" at the minister's rooms (Bentley

Deputy Sheriff Daniel Dutch. *Courtesy Essex Institute*

was a bachelor) in Crowninshield's boardinghouse. Sometime in the 1780's he went to the West Indies, but returned to Salem where he married. When his wife was expecting a second child, without any warning, he wrote a letter of his intentions to abscond and without any good reason. He departed with a neighbor's

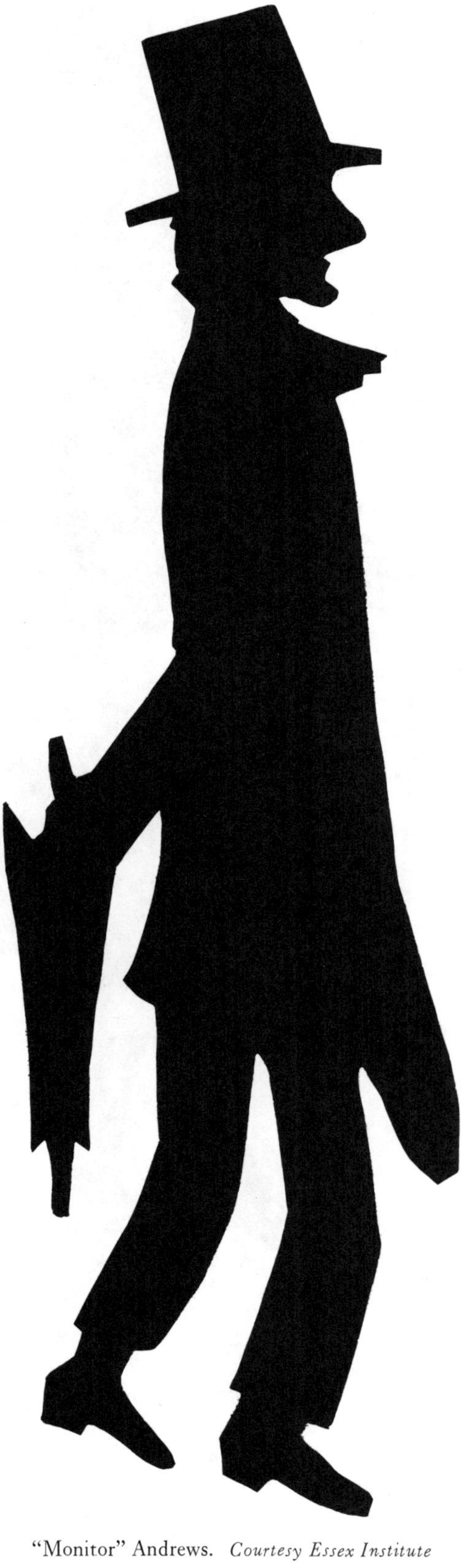

"Monitor" Andrews. *Courtesy Essex Institute*

horse and sulkey and reached East Haven, Connecticut, before he was apprehended. For this performance he paid £16 damage. Two years later, he turned to the ivory trade and offered at his cabinet shop "genteel canes and Riding-Sticks, Fifes, Dice and Dice Boxes, Back Gammon Boards and Men, . . . a good price given for ivory and Sea Cow teeth." When King's son died at "Martinico" the death notice in Bentley's diary read, "The father a wanderer. An ingenious mechanic, but full of projects, and what he gains from one, he loses in another." In an advertisement in the *Salem Gazette,* July 27, 1804, King told of his talents in this manner:

WILLIAM KING

Respectfully informs the Ladies and Gentlemen of Salem and its vicinity that he takes

Profile Likenesses

of any size with the patent Delineating Pencil, which for accuracy excells any machine before invented for reducing or increasing the object. He flatters himself, from the exactness of his profiles and the moderateness of the price (only twenty-five cents for two likenesses of one person) he shall give a pleasing satisfaction to those who favor him with a call, at the next house from Captain Joseph White's in St. Peter's Street—where may be had Oval, Round and Square Frames—Gilt and Black—Also, Turn'd work in Ivory, Wood and Iron—and Canes manufactured.

N.B. He has for sale a handsome Mahogany Turning Lathe, suitable for a gentleman's amusement, or a Jeweller.

He continued to be a wanderer, going first to Boston then to Hanover and Portsmouth, New Hampshire, and from there to Portland, Maine. In a two-year period, he claimed in his advertisements that he had made twenty thousand profiles; "one in six minutes" was his claim. Alice Van Leer Carrick once described him as one of her "favorite hollow cutters."

For the most part, the profile cutters were either unusual characters or somewhat eccentric, or they were showmen with a flair for the theatrical. In 1806, Martin Griffing, originally a steeplejack, fell from the steeple of the

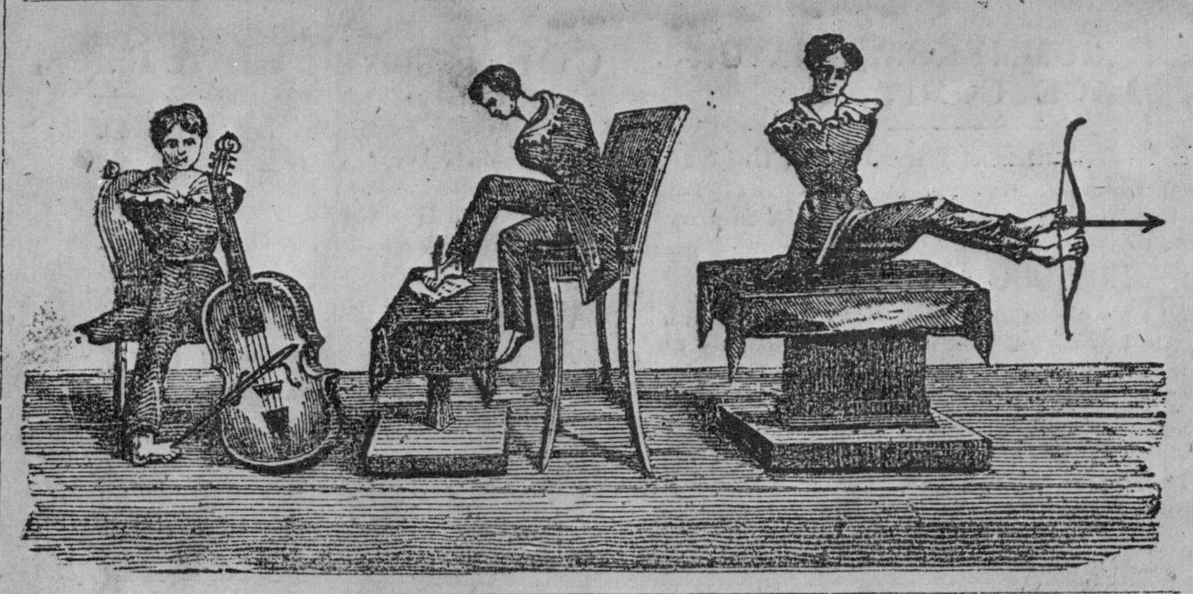

EXTRAORDINARY

EXHIBITION

OF THE WORKS OF

NATURE AND ART!

MASTER SANDERS K. G. NELLIS,

BORN WITHOUT ARMS.

CELEBRATED throughout the principal places in the United States for his wonderful performances, will gratify the Ladies and Gentlemen of Salem, with an exhibition of the same at WASHINGTON HALL. THIS, TO-MORROW, AND MONDAY EVENINGS

This unfortunate Youth, although deprived of those Limbs so essential to the usefulness and beauty of the Human Form Divine, will nevertheless execute many difficult feats altogether unattainable by many of the finished race of mankind

ORDER OF PERFORMANCES.

1st. With Scissors in Toes, MASTER NELLIS will cut Valentines and Watch Papers very ingeniously, and will also cut the Likeness of persons very correctly.

2d. He will make a Paper Fly Box and fold a Letter in the True Love style.

3d. With Pen in Toes he will write a very fair hand, and execute several Drawings of Animals, Birds, Fish, &c.

4th. He will open and wind up a Watch, also take out and put in the Crystal, open Penknives, screw up his Inkstand, and lock his desk

5th With Bow and Arrow he will shoot a Quarter of a Dollar at the distance of eight or ten yards. This performance invariably astonishes the beholders by the almost unerring aim with which the Archer uses his Bow and Arrow.

6th. On the Violoncello he will perform accompaniments truly astonishing.

After which, MASTER NELLIS will sing a number of Sentimental and Patriotic SONGS, and Dance a FAVORITE HORNPIPE.

The whole to conclude with a number of highly interesting COMIC SONGS, by the celebrated MR. FOSTER.

☞ The Exhibition will be accompanied with good Music. Doors open at 6½ o'clock, performance to commence precisely at 7.——Admittance 25 cents.—Children half price.

☞ Tickets for sale at the Lafayette Coffee House, the Mansion House, and at the Bookstores of Henry Whipple, and W. & S. B. Ives, and at the door of the Exhibition.

Salem, Jan 29, 183C.

FLOUR, COFFEE, &c.

300 BARRELS Richmond Flour...

Salem Classical School.

From a Salem newspaper, January 29, 1836. *Photo courtesy Essex Institute*

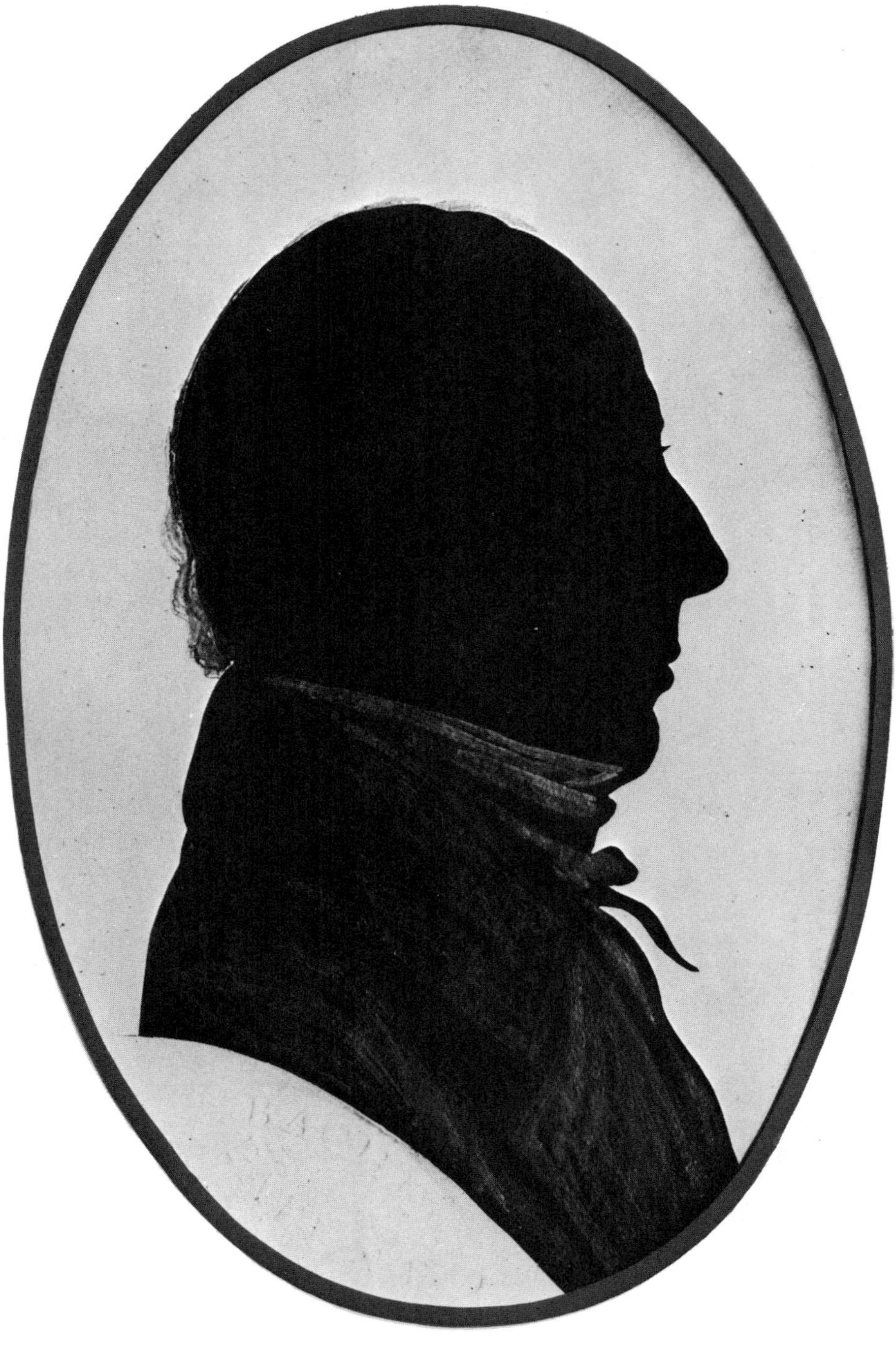

Captain John Barr. *Courtesy Essex Institute*

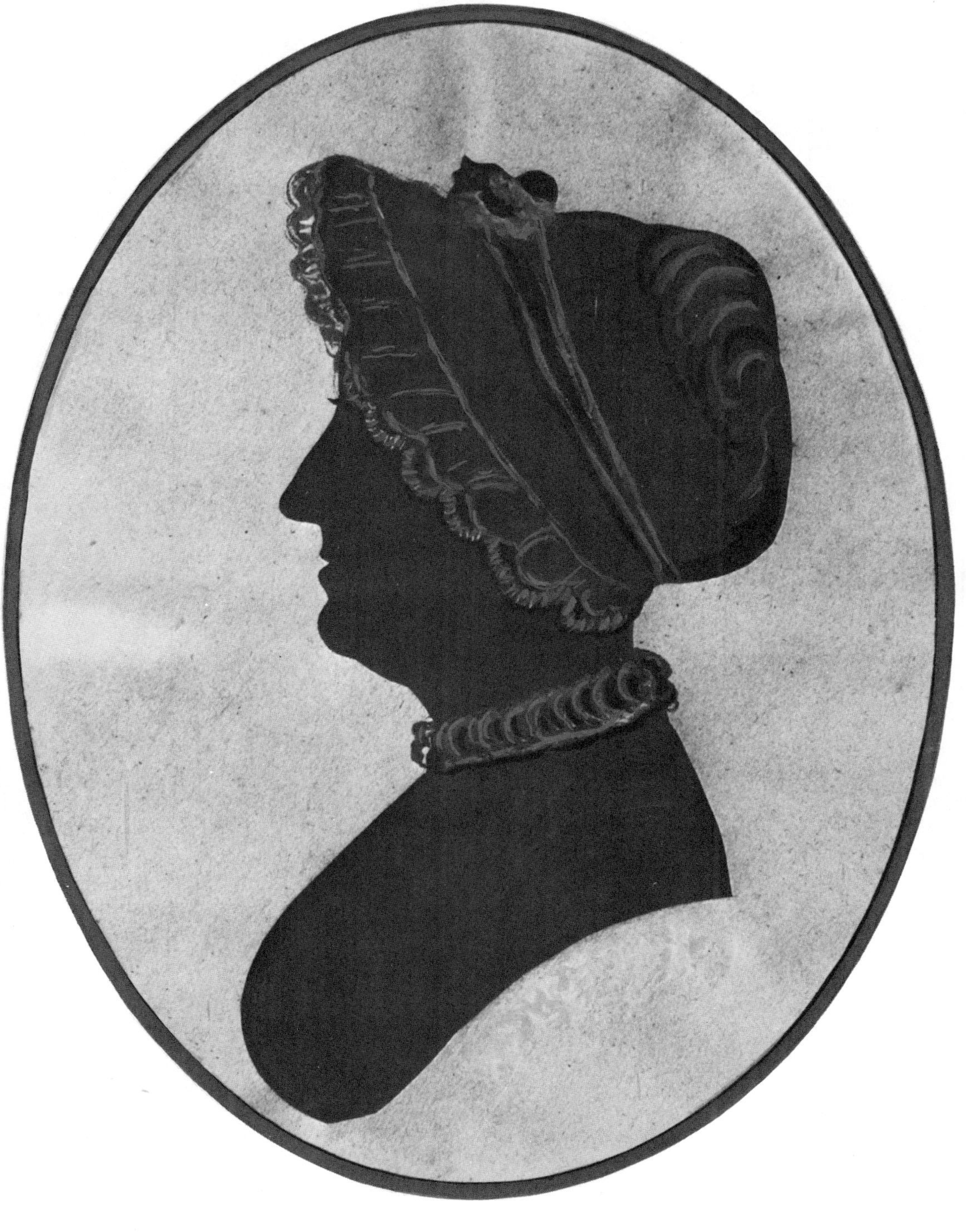

Mrs. Elizabeth (Ropes) Hodges. *Courtesy Essex Institute*

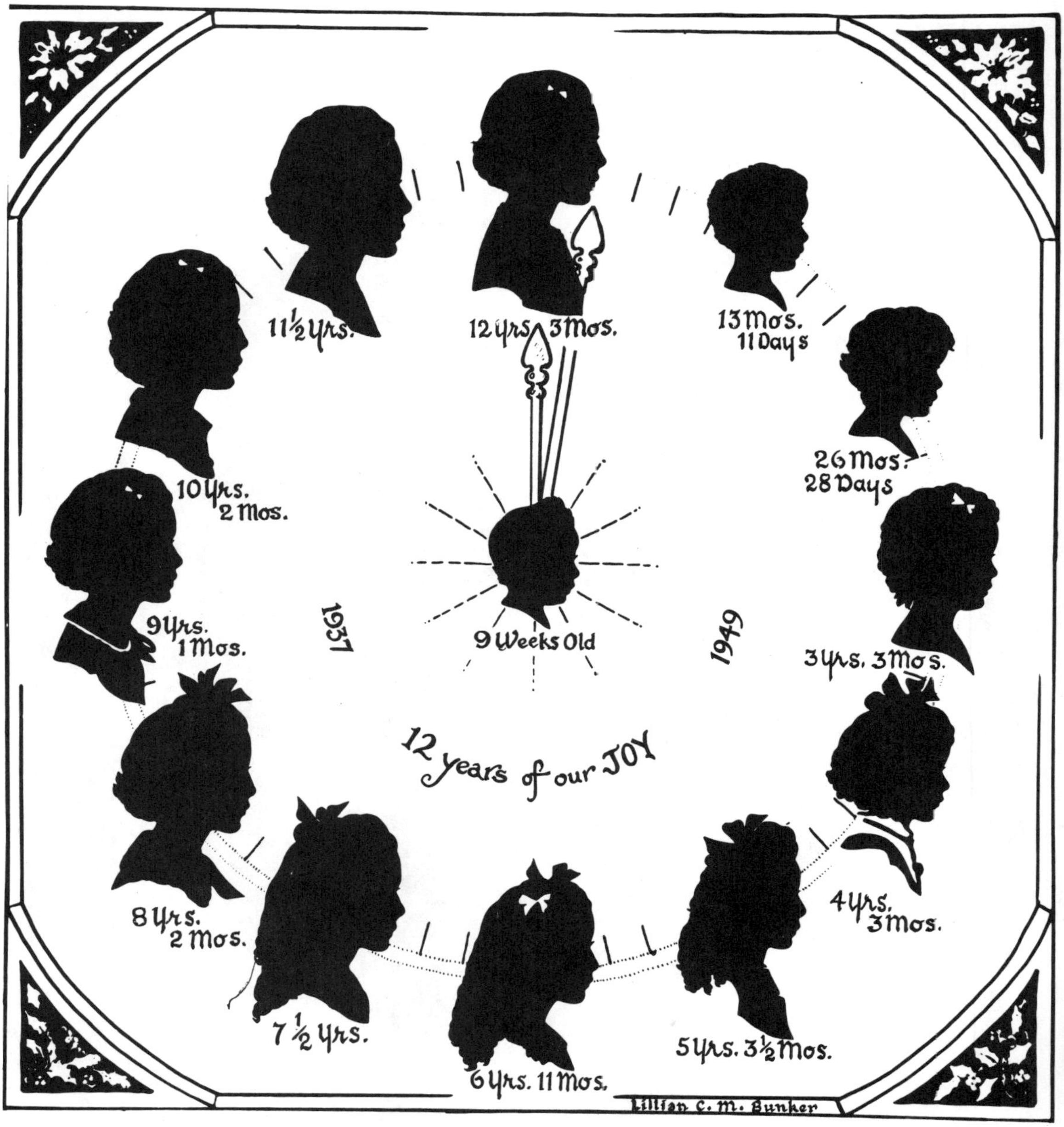

Silhouettes tell a story. *Photo courtesy Lillian G. Clarke*

Congregational Church in Richmond, Massachusetts, while he was painting it. He was only twenty-two at the time. When picked up, he was at first thought dead for he had broken his back. When he recovered, he took up profile cutting and traveled about in the Berkshires, even going into New York State and Vermont. However, travel in a horse and wagon was difficult for this man with a crippled body, so he gave up his "itinerating" and returned to his hometown where he became a shoemaker and lived until he was well past seventy. People took pity on him and he made a good deal of money in a short time, fifteen hundred dollars the first year, so he claimed. Some of his silhouettes were colored.

Master Hankes was considered the *ingénue* among silhouette artists. Not only did he make money cutting silhouettes, he gave exhibitions of his skill and charged twenty-five cents admission. His collection of "works" was called a Papyrotamia. In a few seconds, he could snip out of a black paper an exact likeness of any person he saw. He traveled about New England in great style and in 1828 he was advertising in the following manner:

Novel and Interesting Exhibition
Concert Hall
For a short time
The Papyrotamia
Accompanied by the talented young artist
Master Hankes
the immediate and only successor to the
celebrated
Master Hubard

The Papyrotamia is a numerous collection of Cuttings in Paper executed in a style which has astonished the first Artists in Europe, and attracted admiring crowds in Great Britain and America. It consists of Sporting, Military and Architectural Subjects, Flowers, Trees, Portraits of distinguished individuals in Europe and America.

Admission 25 cents

For which each visitor is entitled to see the Gallery of Cuttings, and to obtain a Correct Likeness in Bust, cut in a few seconds without drawing or machine. By sight alone! and simply with a common pair of scissors by Master Hankes a youth who possesses the rare talent of delineating every object in Nature or Art, in the same extraordinary manner. Full length Portraits 1, 25. Likenesses elegantly finished in bronze by Mr. Reynolds 50 cents extra and upwards, Likenesses in colors.

Open daily at the Concert Hall, from 10 to 1—from 3 to 6—and from 8 till ½ past 9. Catalogues furnished. The room is brilliantly illuminated every evening.

Once, Oliver Wendell Holmes, after one of his almost daily visits to the Boston Athenaeum, wrote a bit of verse to a charming unknown lady whose portrait he had seen on exhibition there.

Pray did you ever hear, my love,
  Of boys that go about
Who, for a very trifling sum,
  Will snip one's portrait out?
I'm not averse to red and white,
  But all things have their place;
I think a profile cut in black
  Would suit your style of face!

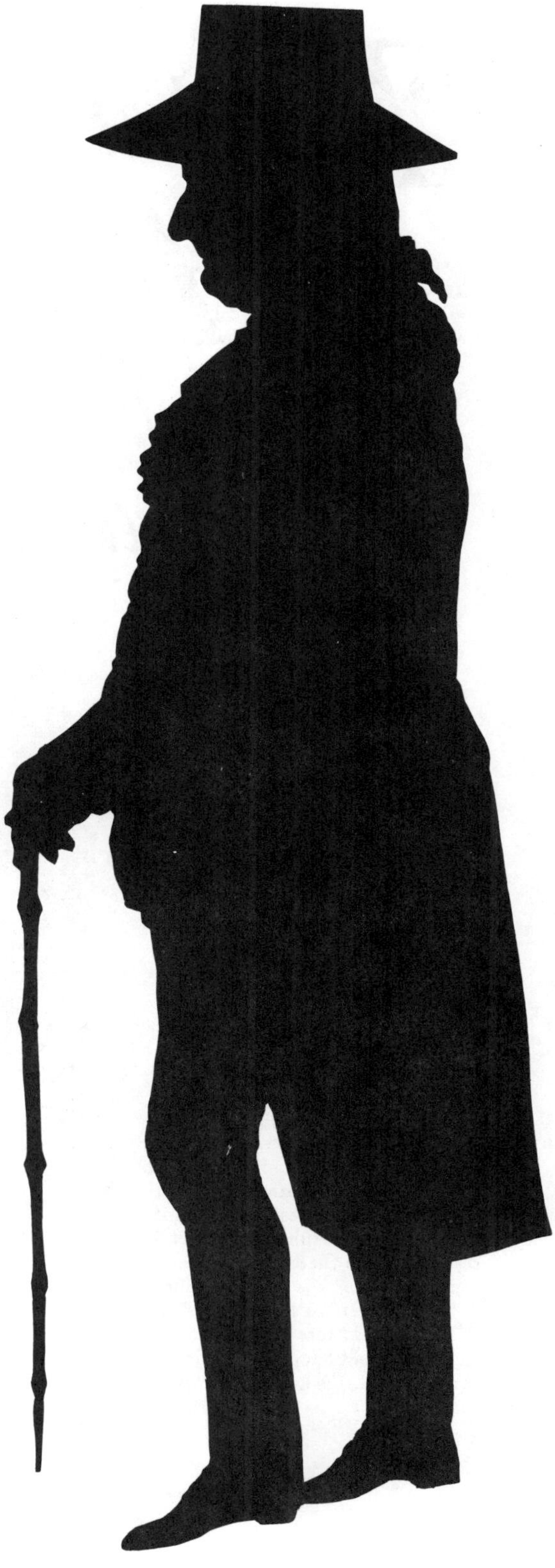

Dr. Edward Augustus Holyoke. *Courtesy Essex Institute*

Basketry—Heritage from the Indians

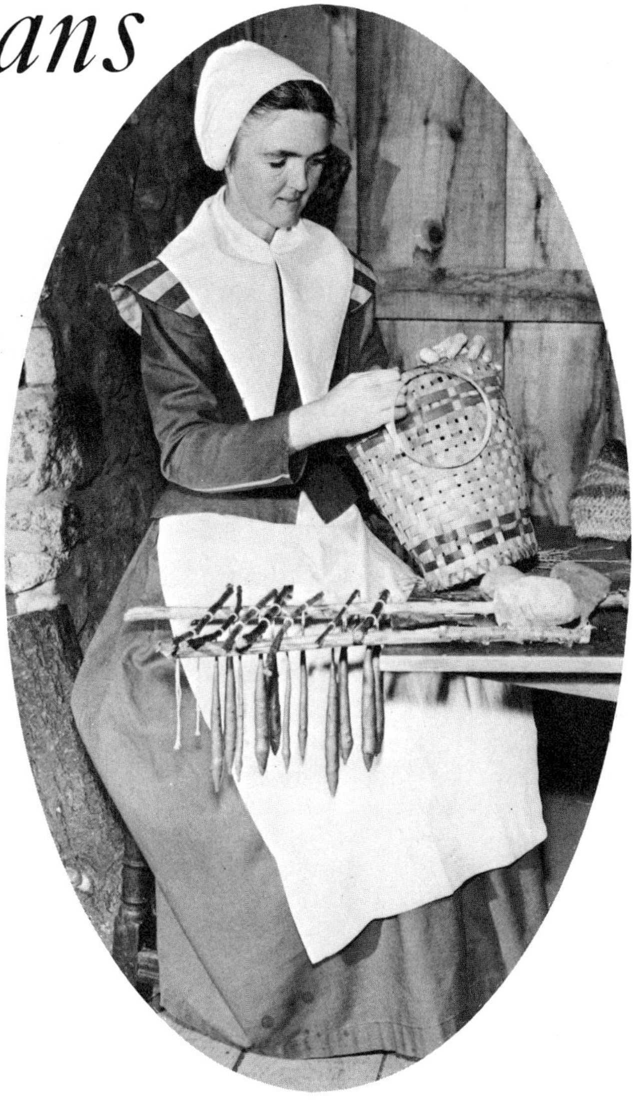

Household crafts as presented at the Brewster House and elsewhere in the restoration at Plimoth Plantation reveal the ingenuity and resourcefulness of the early settlers. While the bayberry candles were hardening, the housewife made baskets as shown here. This so-called "tote bag" was one of many types adapted from Indian crafts. *Photo courtesy Plimoth Plantation*

Did I hear you say you collected baskets? Well I've got some. They're either up attic or out in the back shed." This kind of talk is seldom heard now, but there was a time when every New England house had an extensive array of baskets. And they were kept either in the places mentioned or in the summer kitchen or the back kitchen or in the cellar or the hall closet or somewhere about the house, serving a useful purpose. New Englanders have always been "saving" people who seldom throw out anything that might one day be useful.

Most people who had them had had them for so long they could not remember who made them or how they got them. They were much like the itinerant painters of an earlier day; nobody seemed to know where they came from. (And the painters seldom let it be known where they were going.)

Baskets in this part of the country antedate the earliest settlers since the art of making them was perfected by the various Indian tribes, many generations before the white man came to this rockbound coast. There are baskets to meet every conceivable New England need and there were and always will be ingenious ways to use them. They vary in shape, size, and the kind of material used, ranging from small trinket cases to clothes baskets. Many are intricate in their patterns and rich in color. Some are for treasure or picnics or pies; others serve to hold potatoes, apples, pears, onions, or what have you. Still others were for the family wash or for clothespins, market baskets, flower baskets, even a basket to fetch home a pot of baked beans from the bakeshop on Saturday night. This in brief is the tradition of baskets in New England. Even the most commonplace among them has a bit of distinction and beauty in its appearance. The early settlers at Plymouth more than welcomed some of the first Indian baskets which they found since these containers held precious corn which saved them from starvation.

A glance backward into history reveals that baskets preceded pottery by centuries. Unlike pottery, which breaks with hard use or cracks with the passage of time (age cracks, they're called), baskets are more perishable and more easily destroyed. But the materials of which they are made have always been plentiful and they are not difficult to make once the skill has been attained. In bygone days basketmaking was a spare-time occupation in the country and there was always a market for them. So many people of all ages engaged in basketmaking that little is known about individual craftsmen.

The scholars tell us some of the earliest forms of pottery were molded in or around baskets in the time before clay was hardened by sun or fire. Among the Egyptians, the preserving effect of the dry climate and the sand has resulted in the discovery of predynastic types used for storing grain that date back four thousand years.

The ash-splint basket, made from the black or hoop ash, probably the oldest type still being made, was turned out at an early date by both the early settlers and the Indians. This ash differs from all other trees in that the branches and twigs of each year's growth can be peeled off and separated by a pounding process. Thus, a natural splint is obtainable to make sturdy baskets for hard usage. On the other hand, delicately made types, of almost paper thinness, can be produced when the splints are divided several times. Furthermore, these are flexible and can be bent, twisted, or curled without breaking. For centuries splint baskets have been an industry among the Penobscot Indians of Old Town and the Passamaquoddy tribe in eastern Maine.

The Abbe Museum in Acadia National Park near Bar Harbor, Maine, owns a notable collection of baskets made by the various Indian tribes of New England. The women at Old Town are noted for two types of baskets, the curlicue or porcupine and a tiny horsehair basket. The first is made by curling paper-thin ash splints as the weaving of the filler progresses. Known also as a birthday basket, it is used for a variety of purposes, but shouldn't be confused with the true porcupine-quill baskets. In contrast, the horsehair basket is a miniature, the largest of which is no bigger than a thimble. The Indians at Old Town have long depended for their livelihood on the sale of baskets in the summertime.

Native sweetgrass found in the swamps particularly in the Penobscot area is one of the most satisfactory of all basket materials. The stems are tough and pliant which makes it possible to produce very fine weaving and braiding, and the various shades of green of the fragrant grass hold their color well, even when dried. These baskets have long been favorites with the

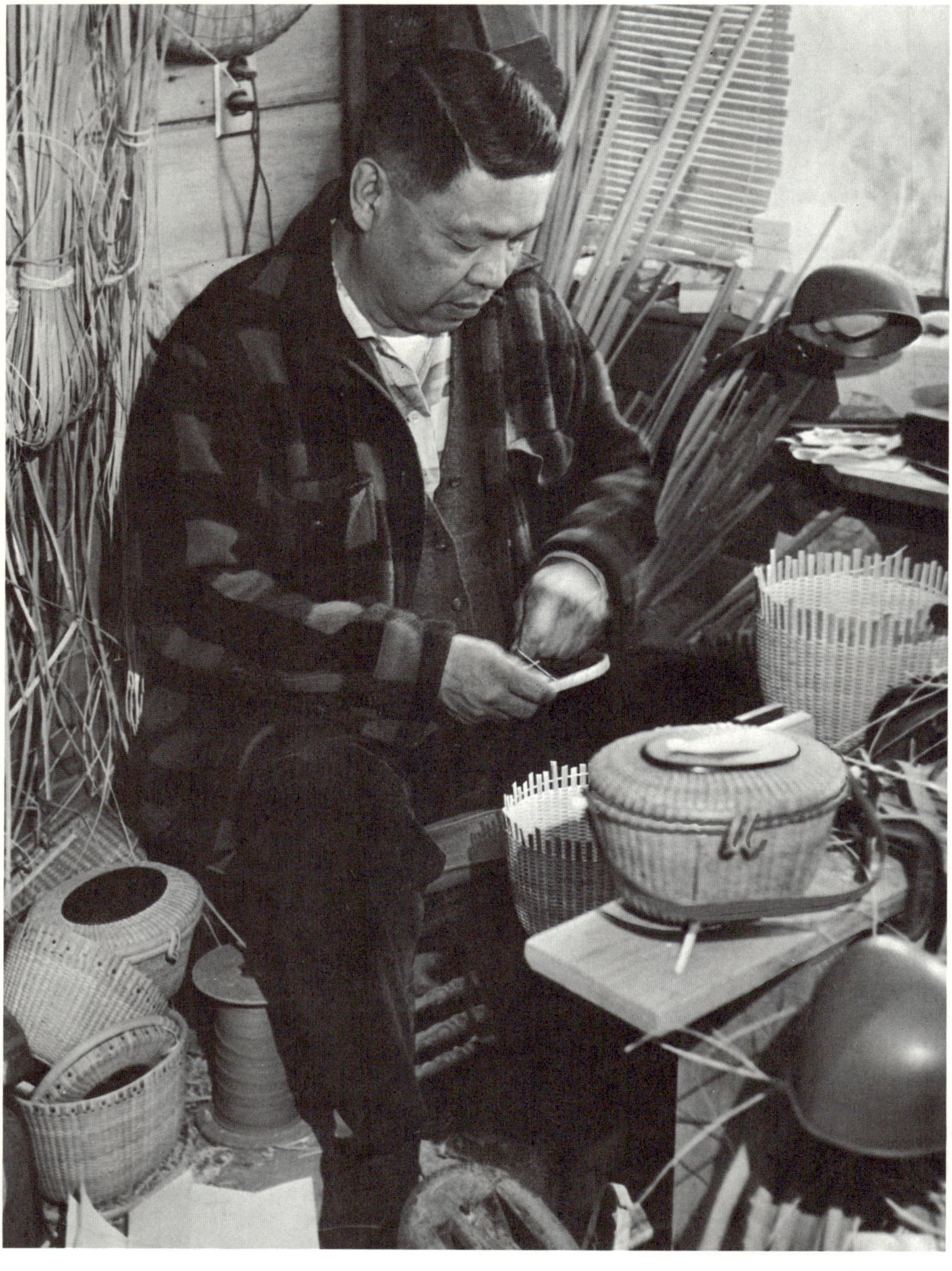

José Reyes, the accomplished basketmaker of Nantucket whose craftsmanship has earned for him an international reputation. *Photo courtesy Nantucket Chamber of Commerce*

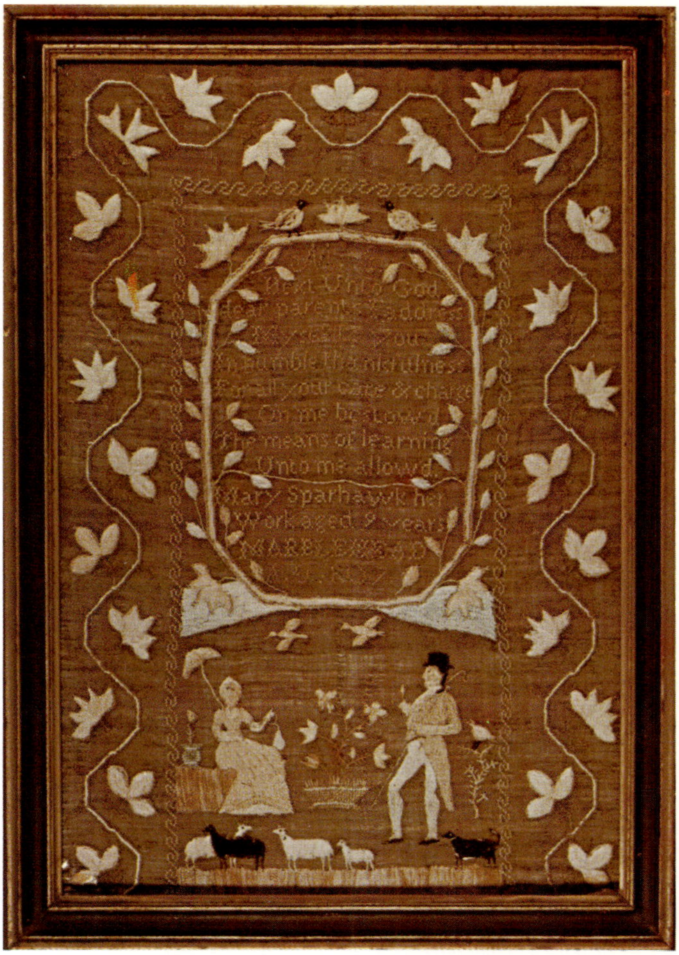

In 1807, at the age of nine, Mary Sparhawk of Marblehead, Massachusetts worked this elaborately designed sampler measuring 14½ by 16 inches. *Photo Richard Merrill: Courtesy, Mrs. Norris Bull.*

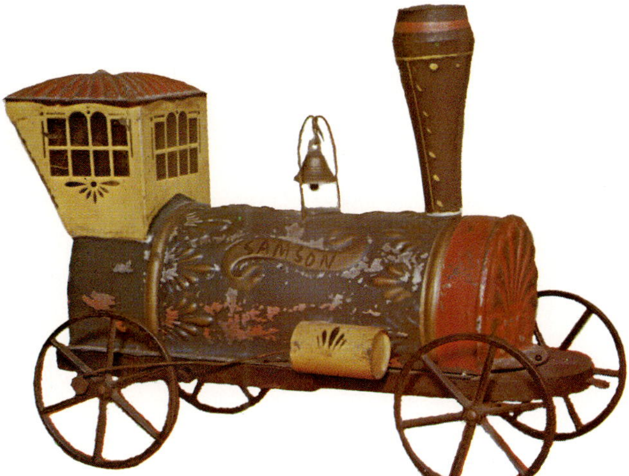

This soldered-tin toy steam engine "Sampson" was made about 1860 by Hull and Stafford Co., Clinton, Connecticut. *Photo Richard Merrill: Courtesy, The Merrill Collection.*

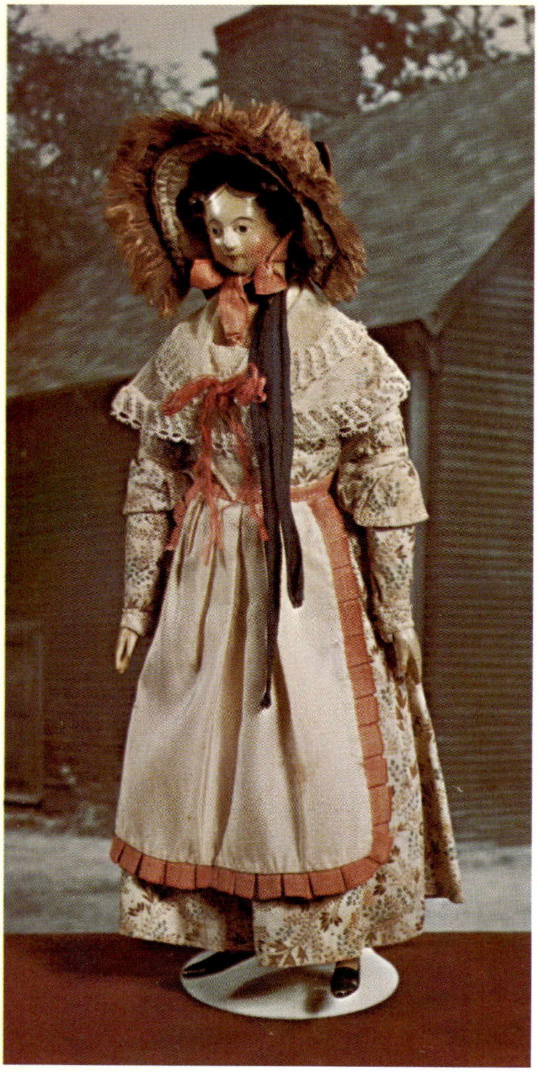

(*Left*) Polly Upham, Melrose, Massachusetts, owned this papier-maché doll in 1830. The costume is original and the bonnet worn over an exaggerated hairdo is considered unusual by collectors. The Upham family homestead in the background was built in 1703. *Photo Richard Merrill: Courtesy, Collection of Madeline O. Merrill.*

(*Below*) (L.) Crazy quilt made from bits and pieces of old nineteenth century silks and satins by Emelyn S. Sawyer in 1900. (R.) Patchwork quilt made about 1860 by Mary Hartwell Wright Hayward. *Photo Richard Merrill: Courtesy, Mrs. P. H. Lord.*

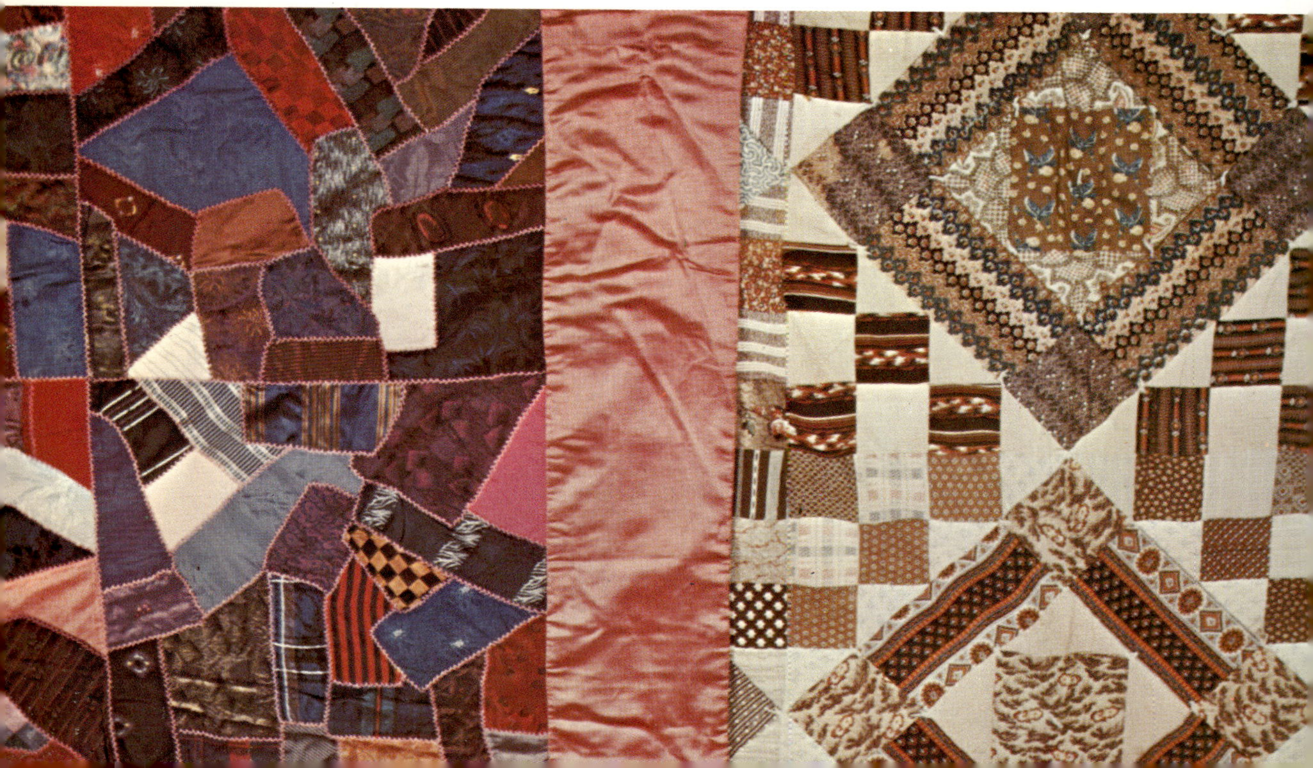

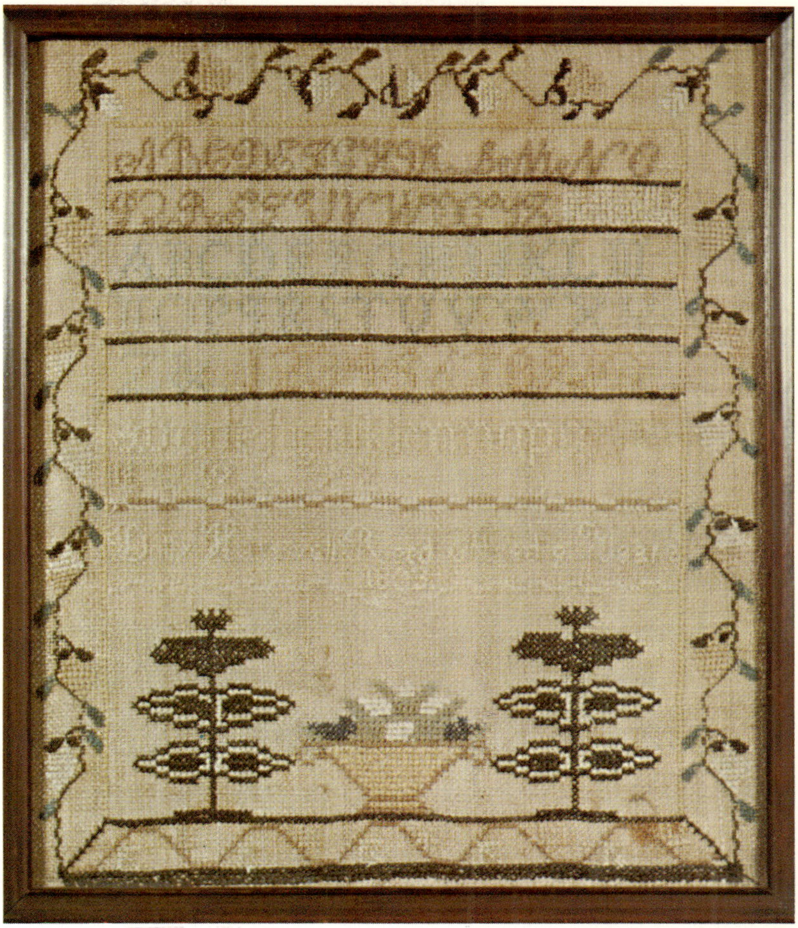

Dolly Hartwell Reed of Lexington, Massachusetts adapted the tree motif for her sampler from the Pine Tree Shilling. She completed the task at the age of nine in 1803. *Photo Richard Merrill: Courtesy, Mrs. P. H. Lord.*

Examples of wood carving made between 1860 and 1875 include: (l. to r.) a meadowlark, by an anonymous carver; model for a circus horse, carved by Joseph Brown, Salem, Massachusetts, who built a merry-go-round at Salem Willows in 1875; a miniature rooster, probably a toy, modelled by a New Hampshire craftsman about 1860. *Photo Richard Merrill: Courtesy, Edward Banks Rushford Collection.*

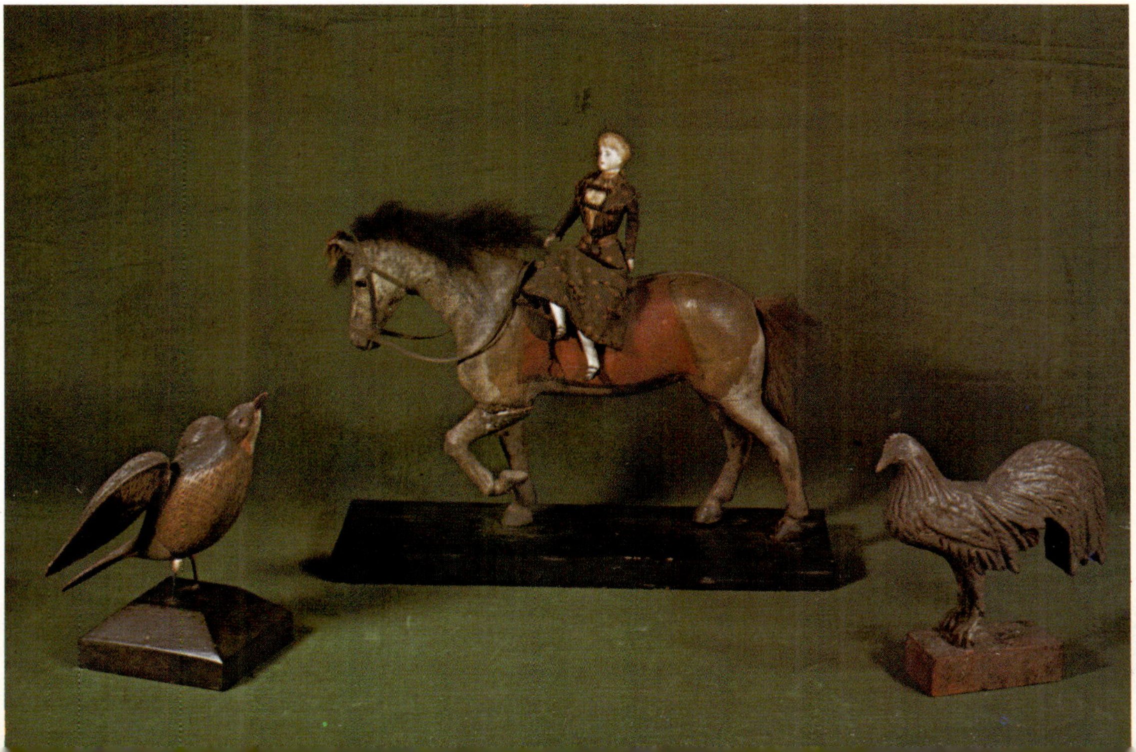

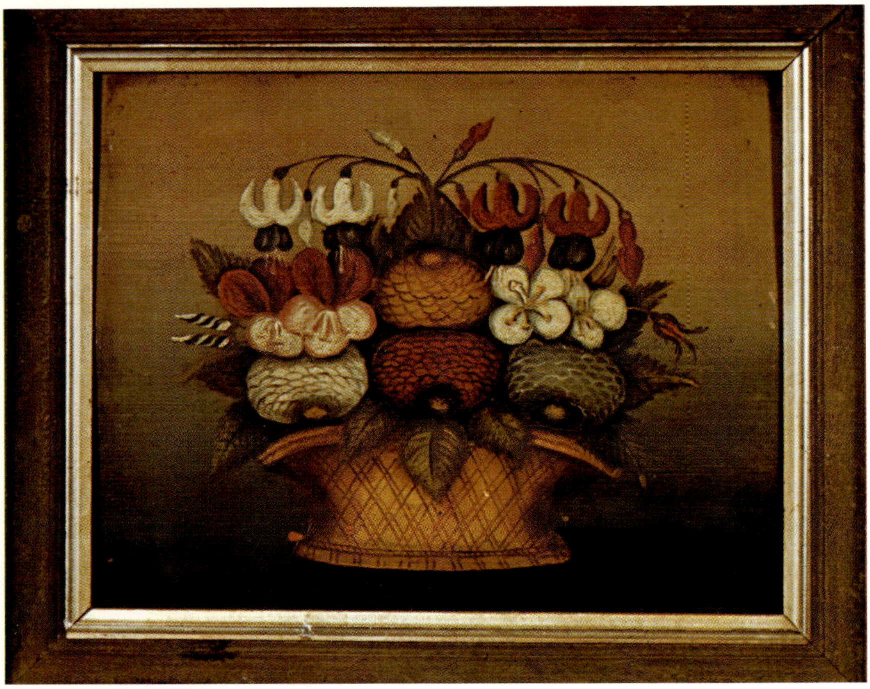

Oil painting on a board, c. 1830. *Photo Richard Merrill: Courtesy, Edward Banks Rushford Collection.*

(*Opposite page*) A unique nineteenth-century double desk made of pine, 84½ x 48 x 16⅝ inches, stained rose-brown, at the Shaker Community, Hancock, Massachusetts. Contemporary in feeling, it is impressive for it height and pleasing proportions. *Photo Richard Merrill: Courtesy, Hancock Shaker Village, Hancock, Massachusetts.*

(*Below*) Victorian afghan made about 1850 by Mary Hartwell Wright Hayward who used the afghan crochet stitch to create her elaborate floral design. *Photo Richard Merrill: Courtesy, Mrs. P. H. Lord.*

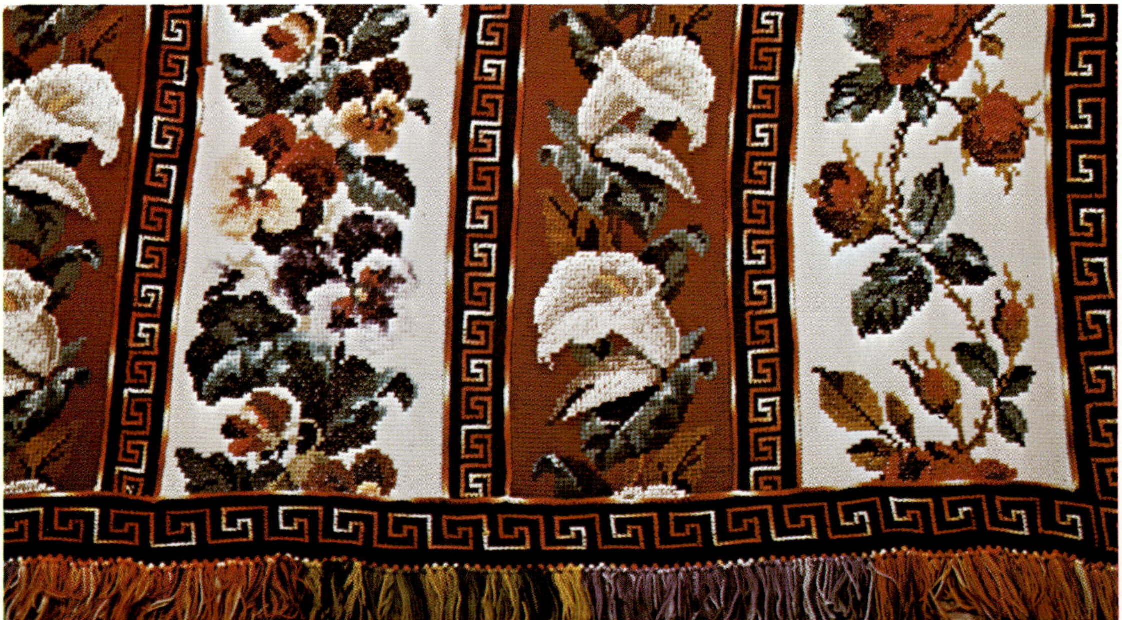

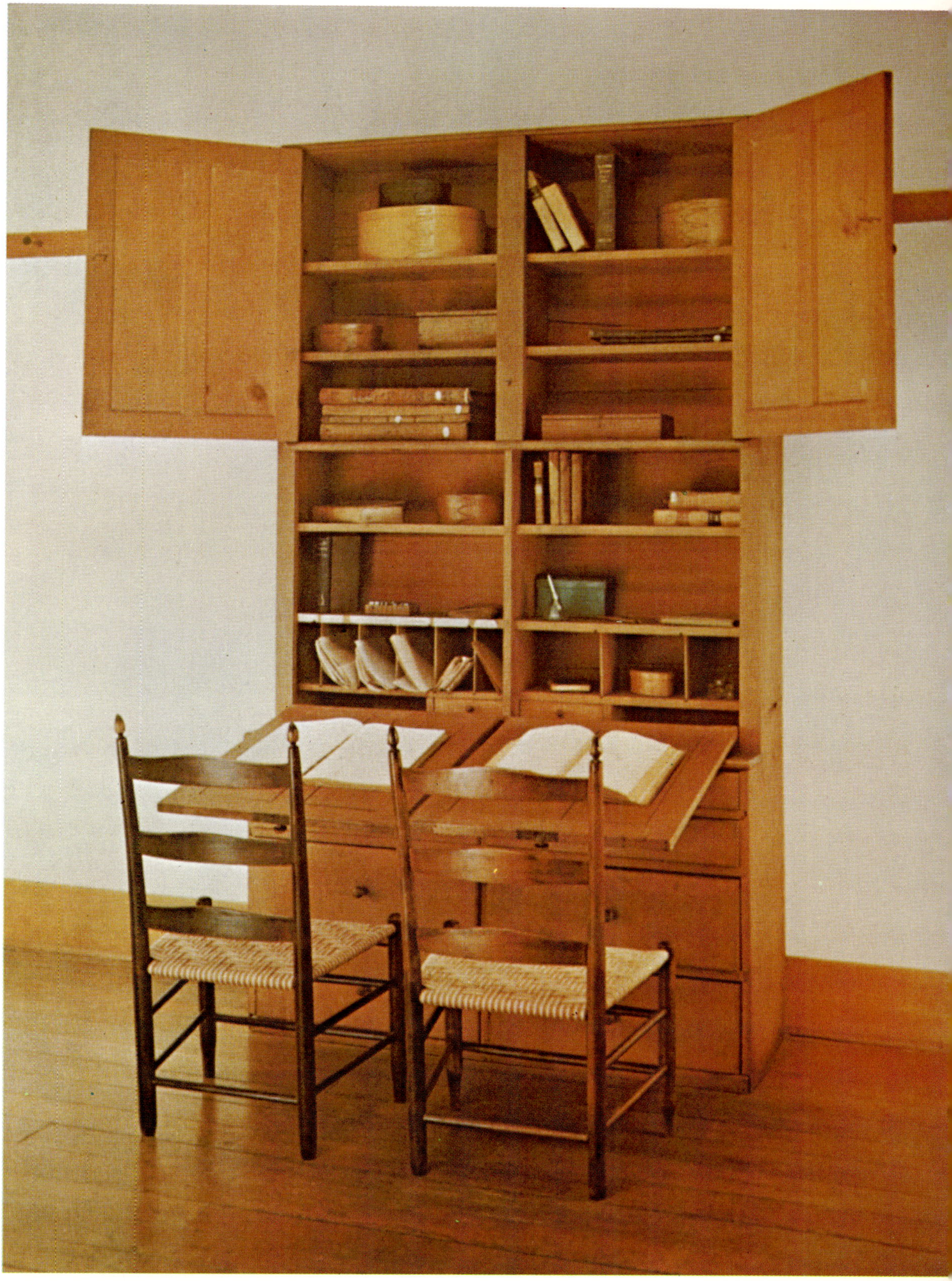

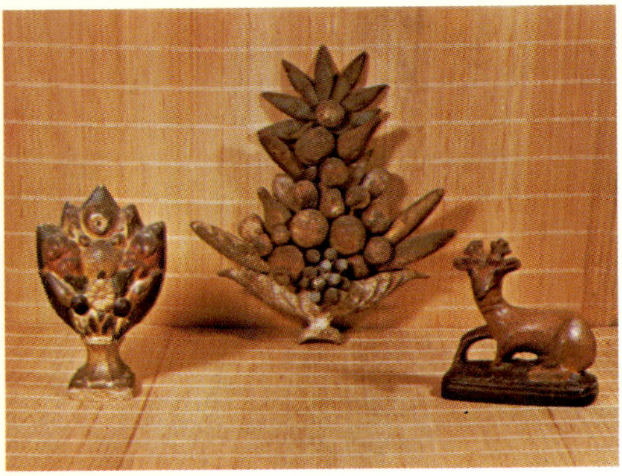

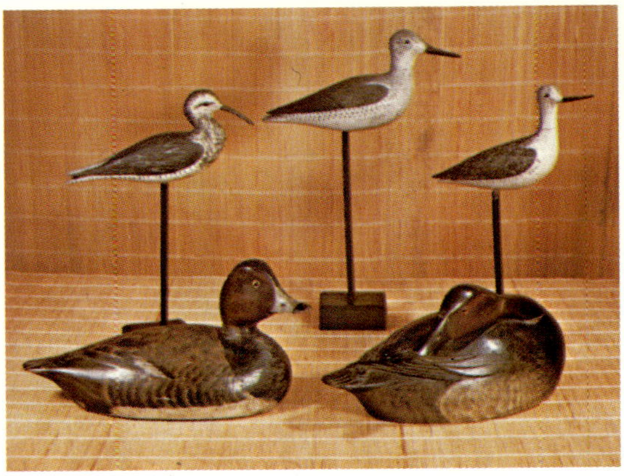

(*Above*) Decorative objects, fashionable in the early nineteenth century include: (l. to r.) basket of fruit in chalkware c. 1830-1840; carved wooden fruit in basket, c. 1820; deer in chalkware, c. 1830-1840. *Photo Richard Merrill: Courtesy, Edward Banks Rushford Collection.*

(*Above right*) Wildfowl decoys, first carved by the American Indians, are highly collectible objects of New England folk art. Top row (l. to r.) a curlew by George Boyd, New Hampshire; sandpipers by an unknown New England carver; redhead ducks by Elmer Crowell, Harwichport, Mass. *Photo Richard Merrill: Courtesy, Edward Banks Rushford Collection.*

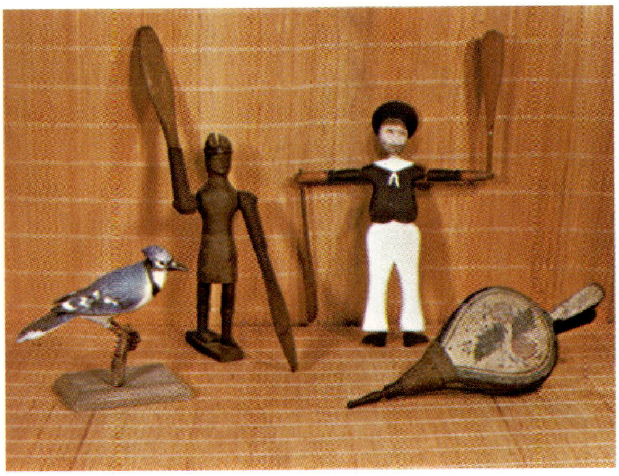

(*Right*) Carved and painted wooden objects displaying various skills include: (l. to r.) a blue jay carved from a pine block by Richard Merrill; a nineteenth-century whirligig in the form of an Indian; another featuring a sailor from Marblehead, Mass.; a pair of bellows, with stencil decoration, c. 1820. *Photo Richard Merrill: Courtesy, Edward Banks Rushford Collection, Richard Merrill and Mrs. Norris Bull.*

Late seventeenth-century needlepoint of Huguenot origin used to cover a settee brought to Salem, Massachusetts about 1685. *Photo Richard Merrill: Courtesy, The Essex Institute.*

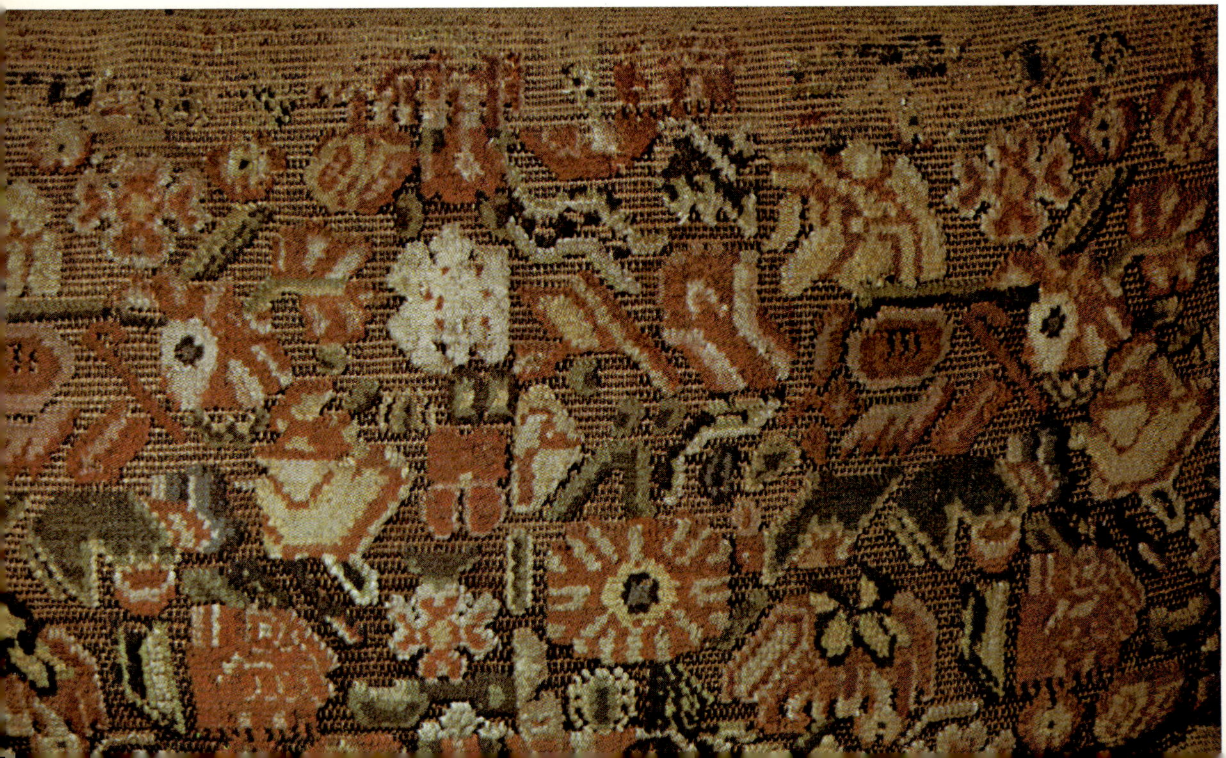

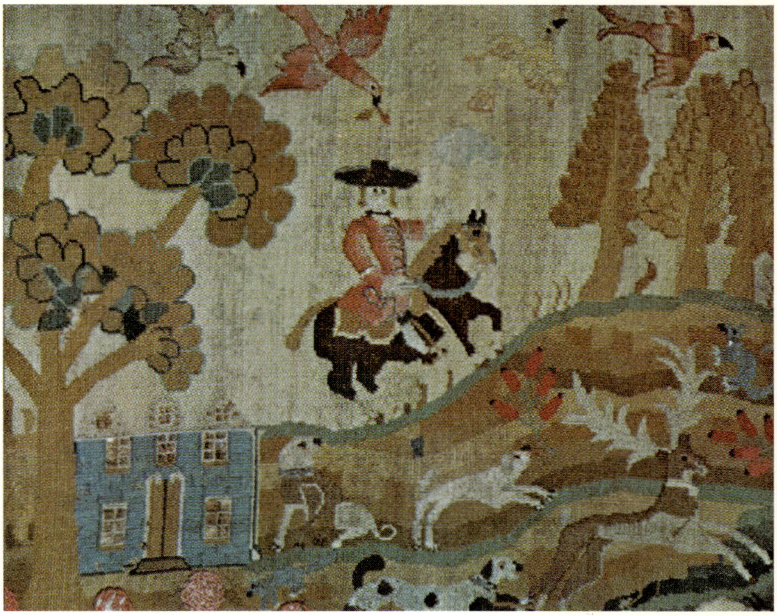

A pettipoint picture, in a Hogarth frame, made c. 1770-1780, hangs in the Richard Derby House, Salem, Massachusetts. *Photo Richard Merrill: Courtesy, Salem Maritime National Historic Site.*

Pottery wooden ware and pewter in the kitchen of the Crowninshield-Bentley House, Salem, Massachusetts. *Photo Richard Merrill: Courtesy, The Essex Institute.*

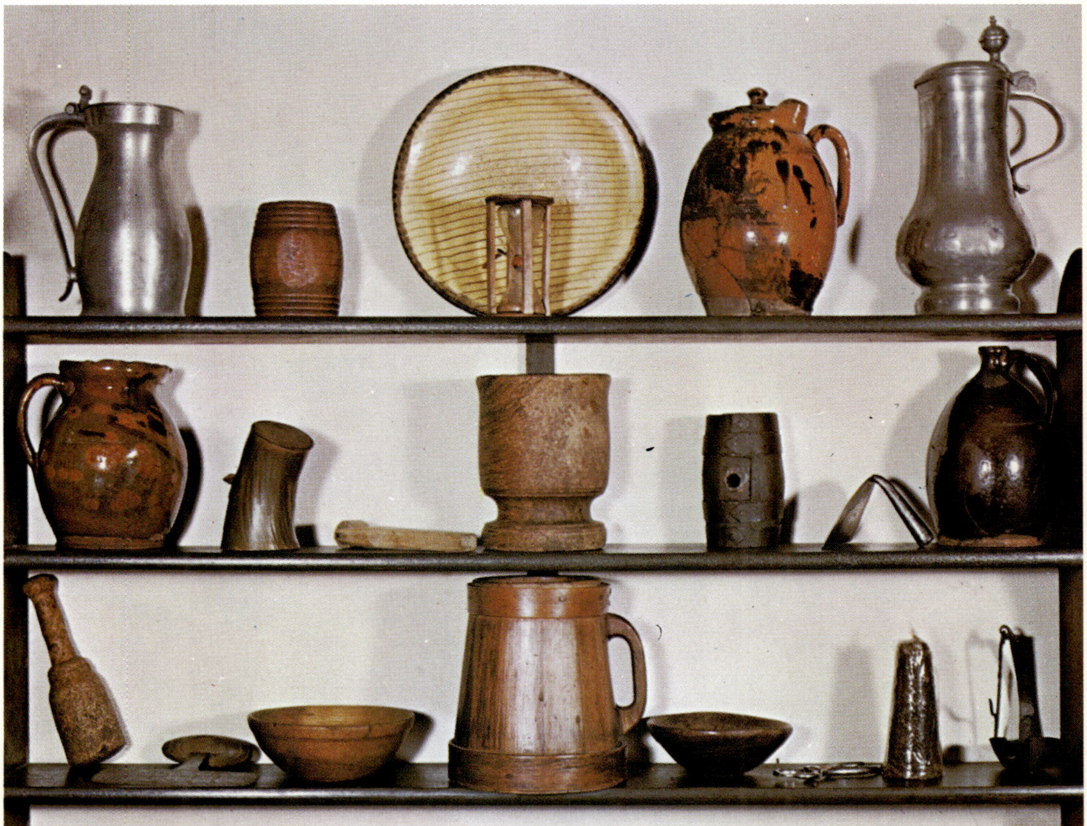

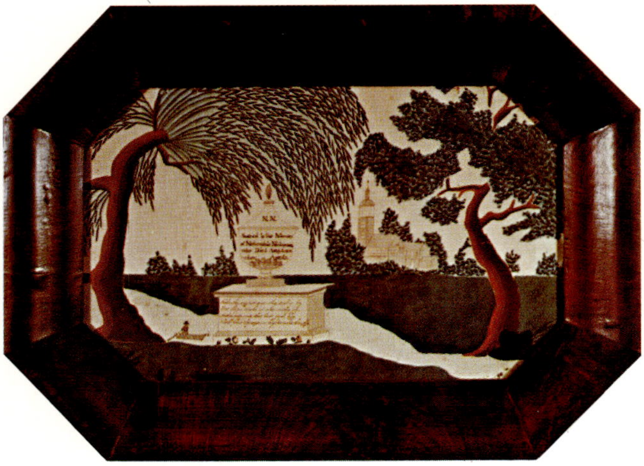

Memorial picture rendered in watercolor records the death of a boy named Nehemiah Nickerson who passed away on August 6, 1812 at the age of seven. *Photo Richard Merrill: Courtesy, Edward Banks Rushford Collection.*

An inspirational drawing of the *Tree of Life*, 1854, by Hannah Cohoon, a Shaker artist who produced an exceptional collection of watercolor drawings, all of which she signed. The work, dated "City of Peace Monday July 3rd 1854," refers to the Shaker Community at Hancock, Massachusetts where she lived as a sister. *Photo Richard Merrill: Courtesy, Hancock Shaker Village.*

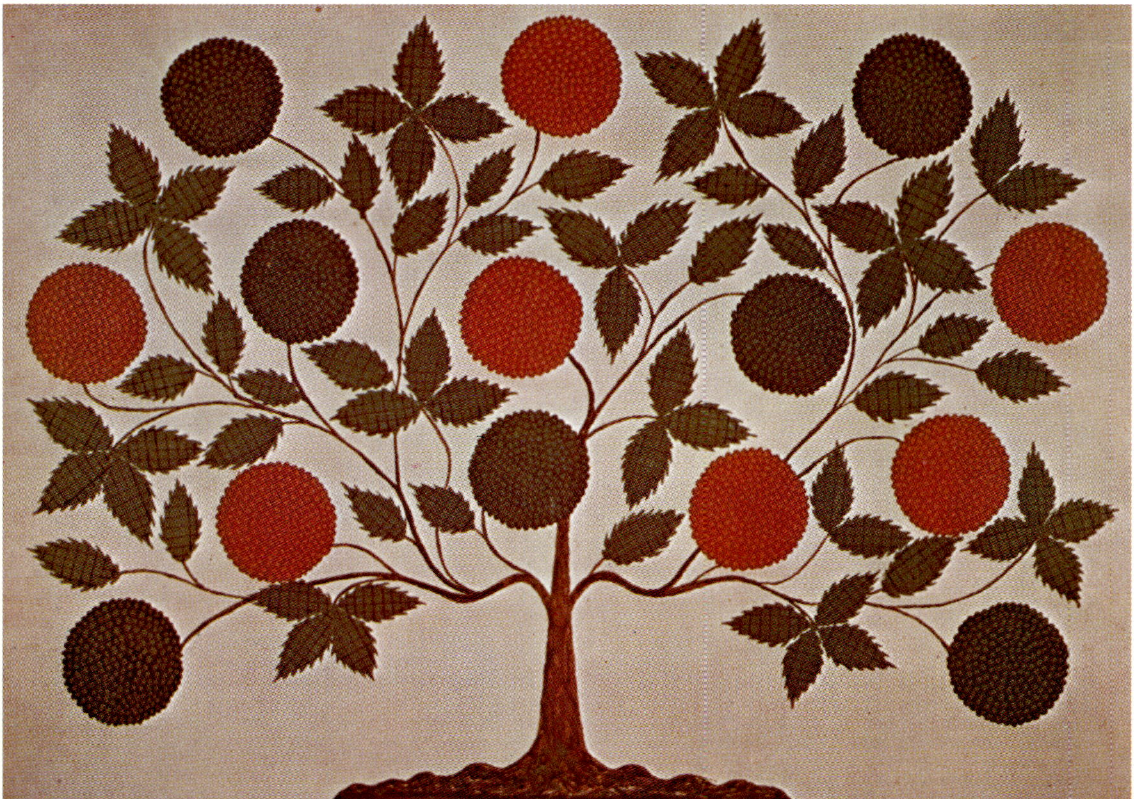

Indian women. For centuries, the Indians have utilized all types of baskets for a variety of household purposes in storing and carrying food. Watertight kinds served for cooking; heated rocks were dropped into a basket of water to make it boil. Sap from the maple was gathered in birch-bark baskets. When color was used for the designs, it was obtained by steeping the roots and bark of native trees and shrubs.

Baskets made from willow twigs are also of ancient origin; handsome in appearance, they have a multitude of uses. In the absence of other materials, pine roots and branches have served to make this type of container. The Scandinavians brought to these shores wider use of birch bark for basketmaking.

Among the Shakers, the fine splints obtainable from the native poplar or basswood were popular. With the exception of selected kinds of Indian baskets, those made by the Shakers at their colonies in Maine, New Hampshire, Massachusetts, and New York stand at the top of the list for craftsmanship. They also used wheat and rye straw, weaving and plaiting these materials to produce baskets of exceptionally delicate woven texture. In *Handicrafts of New England,* Allen H. Eaton has described their technique. "Using a fine strong white thread as warp, they weave a woody filler on a special loom designed for that purpose. The splints are very carefully laid in, and when once woven into a web, a kind of grass cloth is produced, which can be used to cover a box or basket frame."

One of the best-known examples of present-day New England craftsmanship, in any field, and surely one of the most highly prized by all who are fortunate enough to own one is the Nantucket lightship basket. It outclasses all the baskets produced in the last century for durability and beauty. It is so named because it was made for many years in the South Shoal lightship established in 1853 at the island of Nantucket. Although Indian sources have been suggested, it is believed to be of Quaker origin since that sect had a large following on Nantucket in the early nineteenth century when whaling was an important industry there. A similar basket has been made in Europe by a colony of Quakers for many years and it is believed that the origin of the Nantucket basket came with the exchange of ideas on religious philosophy. Charles G. Coffin of Nantucket wrote a detailed account of the technique used in making these baskets, from which these comments have been gathered. "Each whale ship carried a cooper. To this day the vertical splints of the basket are called 'staves,' the circular top binding finish 'hoops,' the boards 'bottoms,' . . . Nests of baskets were much prized; such baskets were of round or oval shape, usually 8 in number, with the smallest one pint size, the largest 12 quarts. . . . These baskets were very strong and durable. . . . They were used for everything from gathering potatoes, fire wood, and carrying fish to holding knitting. . . . Some have lasted in good condition well onto one hundred years."

In bygone days, Sherwin Boyer devoted part of his time to basketmaking. Mitchell Ray and Ferdinand Sylvaro gave practically their full time to it. Ray, known as "Mitchey," for many years had his shop in a long, low building (open to every passer-by) at the end of Starbuck Court. Both his grandfather, Captain Charles B. Ray, and his father had been skilled in the same craft. Mitchey used a crude little shaving horse or bench which once belonged to his grandfather and nearly the same tools, namely, a drawing knife and a jackknife. In November, 1886, Captain Ray declared that he had just completed his two-hundredth rattan lightship basket, one hundred and forty of which he had sold.

For the past thirty years, José Reyes, a native of the Philippines, has been the leader in the craft. It was he who conceived the idea of putting a cover on the basket, to make it a suitable and highly practical (and prized) handbag for ladies. Known as friendship baskets, these are decorated with carved ivory figures of whales, porpoises, gulls and various kinds of fish. In recent years, these baskets have become so popular and so highly regarded that a woman carrying one, almost anywhere in the world, is sure to be asked "When were you last in Nantucket?" A rhyme used as a trademark (attributed to Mitchey Ray) for the basket reads:

I was made on Nantucket
I'm strong and I'm stout.
Don't lose me or burn me,
And I'll never wear out.

Several women in Nantucket specialize in ivory carving and scrimshaw. Miss Aletha Macy described as a "topnotch carver" is not only a highly talented woman, but also a direct descendant of Thomas Macy, the island's first

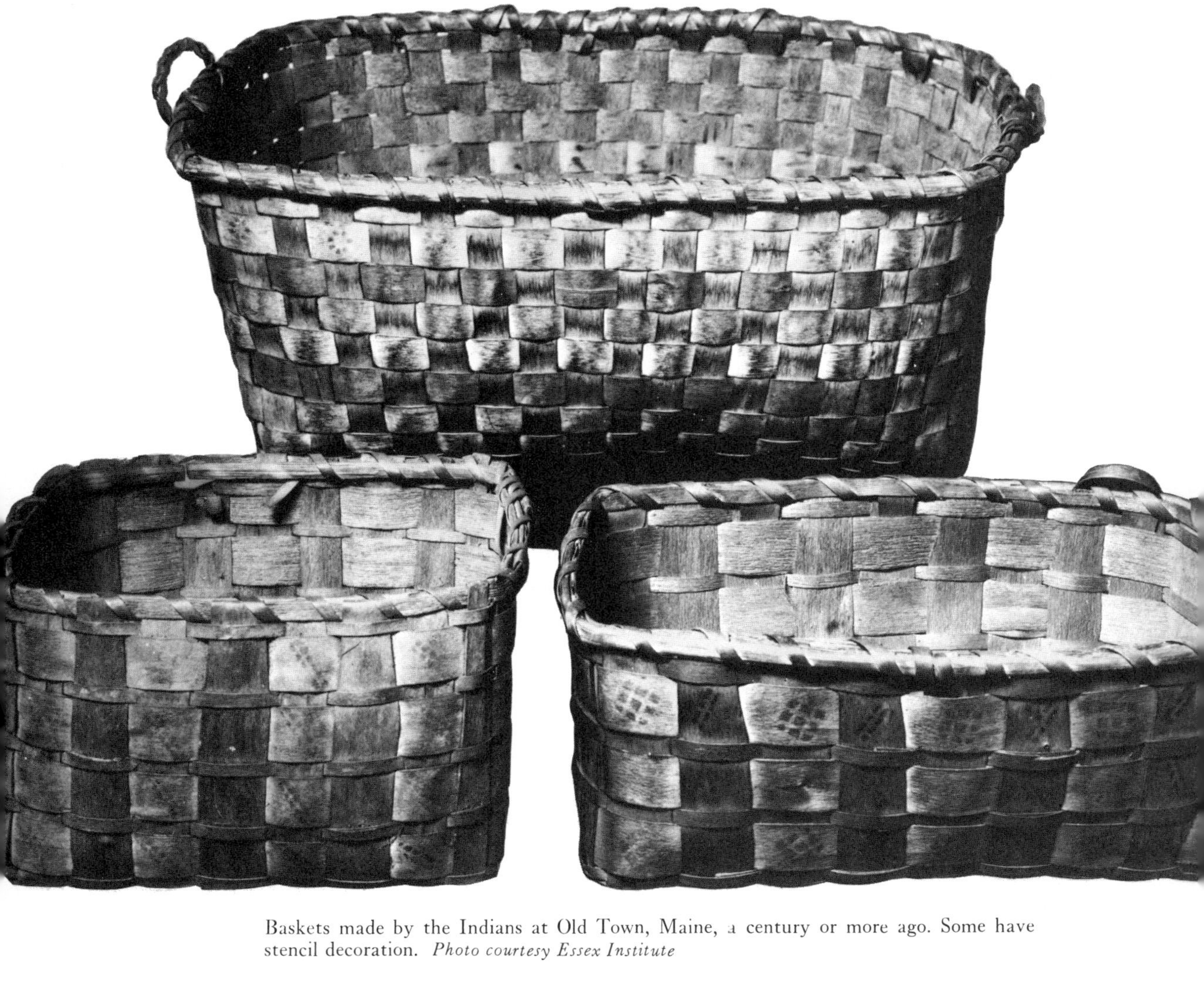

Baskets made by the Indians at Old Town, Maine, a century or more ago. Some have stencil decoration. *Photo courtesy Essex Institute*

settler. She obtains her whalebone from Norway and her ivory from Africa, carrying on the importing tradition of the whalers of the nineteenth century who brought treasures home from everywhere. Her panels, featuring scale models of whales, have been widely sought by museums and private collectors. Jewelry featuring these nautical subjects has been another outgrowth of her carving skill which was derived from a long apprenticeship with Lincoln Ceeley, a well-known cabinetmaker of "the faraway island," as Nantucket is often called.

Other crafts for which the island has become widely known include needlework in all its variations (especially crewel work) and the hand-looming of materials for draperies, upholstery, rugs, blankets, and coverlets. Excellent tweeds, *couturier* fabrics in silk, and specially woven and designed materials for embroiderers, are typical of the work launched by the Nantucket Historical Trust since 1961. Knitted and crocheted bedspreads also deserve mention. Summer courses in these skills taught by distinguished craftswomen under the direction of the Nantucket Needlewomen have made this comparatively new enterprise outstanding in the arts and crafts movement which is making itself felt all over New England. In many ways the work of the Nantucket Needlewomen reminds one of the revival started at Deerfield before the turn of the century.

The Glassmaking Art

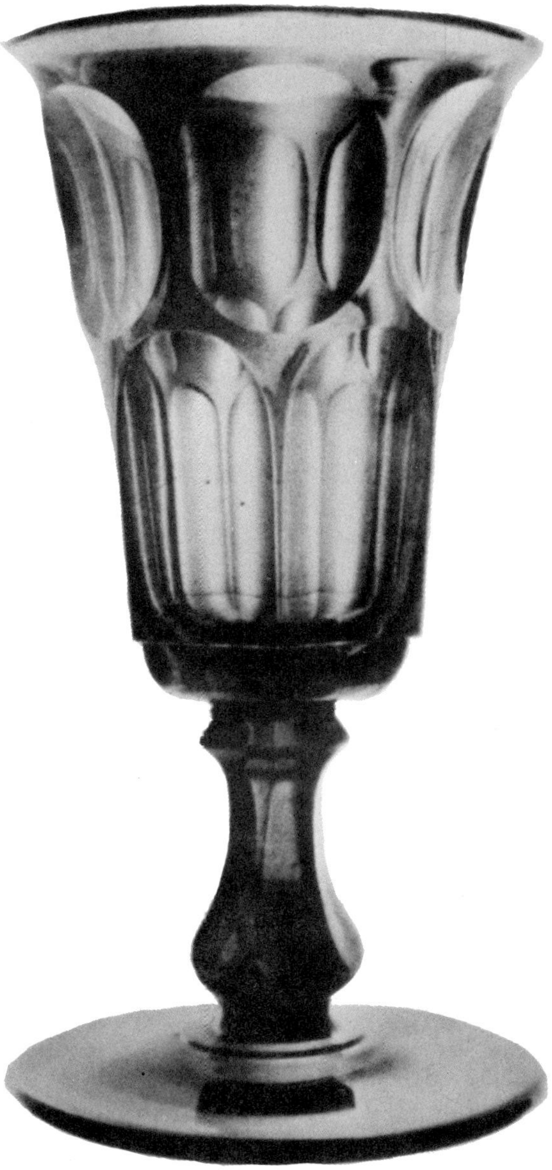

Extremely rare amethyst Ashburton celery vase. Believed to be the only one in existence today.
Photo Haydn Mason: courtesy Sandwich Historical Society

In the dim, distant past, a ship laden with natron (sodium carbonate) owned by Phoenician traders, was moored at the mouth of the river Belus in Syria (Palestine), near Mount Carmel. While the crew were preparing their food on the shore, they placed their pots and pans on blocks of this material. It is said that the heat from the fire melted the sodium compound and formed a flux, reducing the sand to glass.

This in a nutshell is the first written account of the discovery of glass given us by Pliny, nearly two thousand years ago. Undoubtedly, there is more to this story since scientists tell us that chemicals in the riverbed may have contributed to the composition and that the natron referred to may have been of a different makeup than the substance bearing that name today. However, Egyptian tombs dating back to 1500 B.C. contain drawings of glass blowers. Silica (derived from sand), alkali, and a base such as lime or lead oxide are the simple ingredients needed for making glass and color is obtained by the use of metallic oxides.

It is the esthetic aspect of glass with which we are concerned primarily. While New England can lay no claim to "Baron" Stiegel of Pennsylvania or to the Wistars and Stangers of New Jersey (famed for their eighteenth-century glass), it produced in the short span of fifty years in the nineteenth century some of the loveliest and most varied kinds of glass made in modern times. The story of glass and the "mysteries" surrounding its origin and making have always been clothed in romance and a certain amount of fantasy, even wonder. In all of these respects, the story of Deming Jarves and the Sandwich Glass Works is one of the sagas of American enterprise. It embodied many aspects of idealism, including distinguished leadership, top quality production, pleasant relations with craftsmen and supporting labor as well, sound business methods, a spirit of progress, and a high degree of skill.

For more than one hundred years, failure pursued every attempt to establish a glass house in New England. In fact, the same ominous cloud seemed to hover over glassmaking in other parts of colonial America as well. Even when manufacturing was successful and pieces of quality and distinction were produced, the ventures were short-lived. In nearly every instance, the men behind such enterprises, such as Baron Stiegel at Manheim, Pennsylvania, were not to prosper. That the attempts failed in early colonial times stemmed not so much from lack of know-how in craftsmanship, as perhaps from that vital requirement—sound business acumen. Glass blowing was not only an ancient, highly technical skill, known to comparatively few, but also one that required amazing dexterity and almost superhuman endurance in the presence of intense heat. From earliest times, glass had been valued highly and was greatly sought after because of its intrinsic beauty and fragile quality. It was a distinct luxury in the seventeenth century—rare and costly and found only in homes of the wealthy and affluent. In those days, drinking vessels were made of leather, wood, pottery, or metal such as pewter; to be served a drink in a glass was most unusual. Unlike pottery which was comparatively easy to make, glassmaking was an involved and elaborate skill requiring considerable equipment, construction, time, and a sizeable outlay of capital.

Except for windows, glass was not a prime necessity for survival in the early days. Yet, the high price demanded by English exporters plus the need for bottles and other items prompted the ambitious colonists to establish many kinds of industry at an early date. The Puritans looked forward to every kind of trading venture and glass was one of the commodities they considered. At any rate, a glass house was built in Salem in 1641 under the direction of Obadiah Holmes and Lawrence Southwick who sought the help of Ananias and John Conklin, skilled glassmakers. Capital was needed and this was advanced by the governing authorities. Many problems beset these pioneers and while a few bottles were blown, production was spasmodic. Attempts were made in 1645 and again in 1661—but the early records reveal little of the venture. However, the site of the first glasshouse was carefully recorded and, more than two hundred and fifty years later, excavations were made revealing a variety of glass samples.

In 1748, Joseph Crellins, a German, chose a site for a glasshouse in the towns of Lee and Williamstown in the Berkshire hills. Wood for the fires was plentiful and the local sand proved suitable for glassmaking. (It was later used at Sandwich.) However, the German glassworkers whom Crellins had hoped to employ did not arrive within the time specified by the colonial government and the project failed. Crellins then

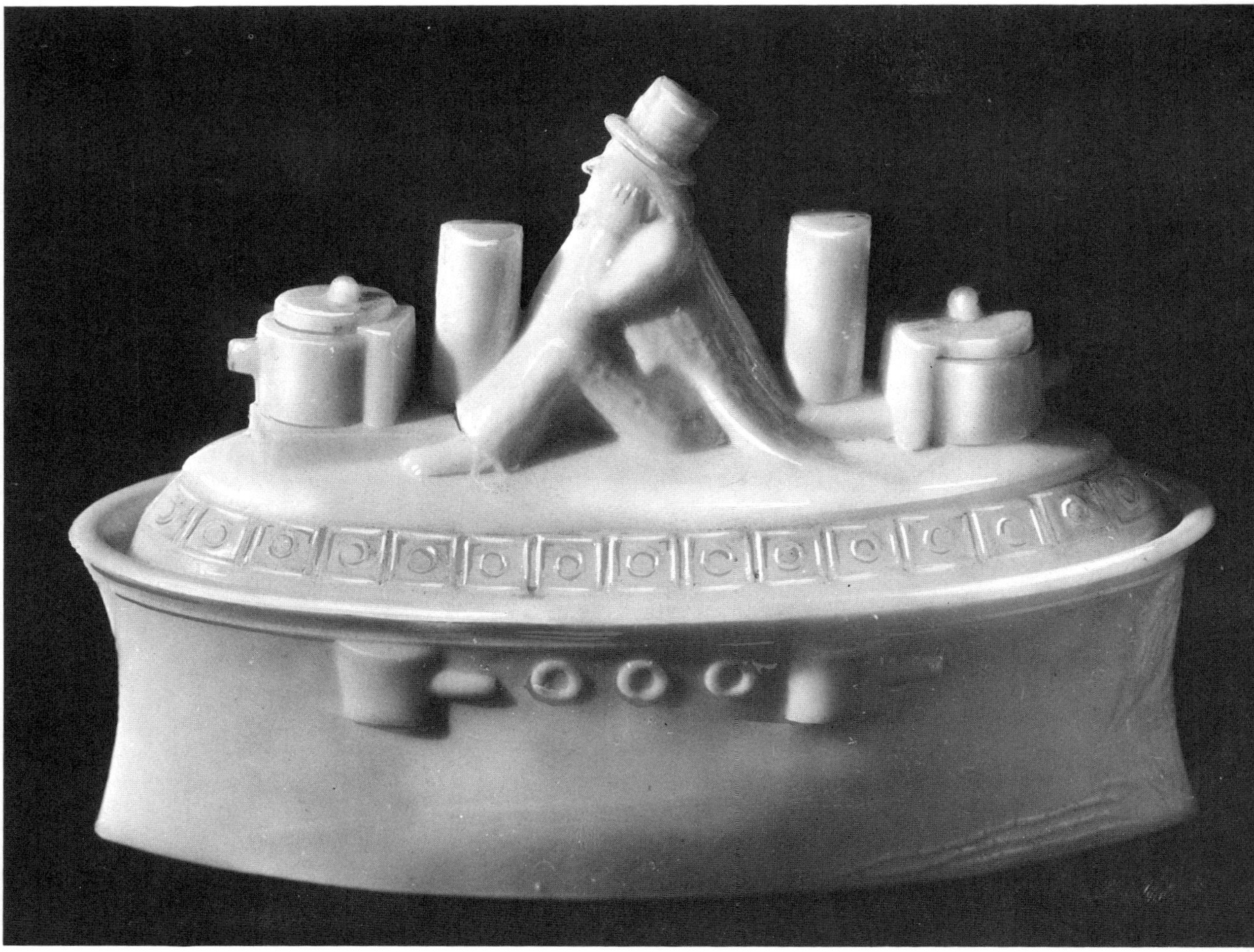

Sandwich glass mustard pot. *Photo courtesy Essex Institute*

secured the interest of several prominent men in Boston and hoped to establish the glass industry in nearby Quincy. Although elaborate plans were made, buildings were designed and even a village for the glassworkers was proposed, this, too, failed to materialize. In a later attempt Joseph Palmer and Richard Cranch advanced a scheme including a diversity of industries along with a glassworks, which included a pottery, a salt works, a chocolate mill, and a spermaceti plant, but it was all to no avail. They could not sell their bottles after they were blown and, shortly thereafter, a fire destroyed the property.

At Templeton, New Hampshire, Robert Hewes, a young Bostonian, started a glasshouse. He employed Hessian deserters from the British Army for workers, but the factory had hardly begun operating when it burned. Hewes rebuilt immediately, but the second furnace made of stones, hauled by oxen from Massachusetts, was affected by a hard frost, and, at the first firing, it came tumbling down. That was the end of the Templeton experiment. Hewes, determined to make glass, organized the Essex Glass Works at Boston in 1789 (later known as the Boston Crown Glass Company) and made crown or window glass noted for its quality. "Boston Crown," as it was called, was in great demand throughout the country. The War of 1812 put an end to the business and the Great Gale of September 15, 1815, destroyed the works. Robert Hewes was a "natural bone setter," who not only treated fractures, but marketed "Hewes' Liniment" in bottles made in his own factory. He was also a fencing master and the author of several military books.

In 1783 when an amicable treaty was signed between the United States and Great Britain, William and Elisha Pitkin along with Samuel Bishop, obtained a twenty-five year monopoly for the manufacture of glass from the state of Connecticut. The Pitkin Glass Works at Manchester became Connecticut's first glasshouse, and the monopoly was a form of patronage because Captain Richard Pitkin, father of William and Elisha, had made gunpowder for the patriot army during the Revolution. Since the new government was without funds, the permit for the glass monopoly was granted instead. Manchester's one natural advantage for glassmaking was an abundance of wood for fuel, but the local sand being unsuitable, it was imported from New Jersey together with gaffers or foremen, glassblowers, and other skilled workers. The sand was transported up the Connecticut River to Hartford by barge and on to Manchester in ox carts. Hartford, the trade center of the Connecticut Valley, carried on a brisk business in horses and mules with the West Indies for which molasses, sugar, rum, salt, and cider were exchanged. The Pitkins made huge long-necked bottles or carboys covered with plaited wicker to hold the distilled cider (applejack or cider brandy) which, when returned, held rum and molasses.

The Pitkin glasshouse was essentially a bottle works. At the time, all bottles were handblown, a fascinating process to watch. The glassmaker, grasping a lump of semi-molten glass on the end of an iron tube, blew hard until he succeeded in shaping the type of bottle needed. To be a glassmaker, a man had to possess powerful lungs. E. V. Mitchell relates that European glassblowers used to eat quantities of snails to strengthen their lungs. During the winter, when the Connecticut River was frozen, the Pitkins used sleighs to transport their wares to market. Children, who rode the sleighs when the return trip was made, visited the glassworks and received miniature bottles as souvenirs.

The Pitkins became noted for the design and color of their bottles and flasks which were considered among the best made in the country. E. V. Mitchell has pointed out that the so-called "Pitkin type" of swirl flask and the "Sunburst" pattern which originated in the Manchester glasshouse were later produced at Keene, New Hampshire, "but the Keene Swirl flask differs in that the swirl is to the right, whereas that of the Pitkins is to the left. The bodies of these flasks were double-dipped and were thicker than the necks, which were dipped only once. Writers on glassware believe the Pitkins were the first to use this German method of producing flasks." After more than forty years of production, the business terminated in 1830, due to competition and a lack of fuel.

Thomas Stebbins, who in 1820, took over the Coventry Glass Works which was founded in 1812, was a skilled glassmaker and a true artist as well. He was among the first to decorate whisky flasks with the portraits of famous men. His "Lafayette" and "De Witt Clinton" bottles are believed to have been made to commemorate the visit of Lafayette to America in 1825 and the opening of the Erie Canal that same year. Work ceased in 1847 when the supply of wood ran out.

Glass was made in Keene, New Hampshire, in two factories after the War of 1812 where both window glass and bottles were the chief products. After rather uncertain beginnings they prospered, the former one was under the management of Justus Perry, the other was directed by Aaron Appleton and John Elliott. The Keene bottles, flasks, and decanters were, like the Connecticut bottles, made in different shades of green, amber, black with some bluish ones. "Success to the Railroad," was blown to commemorate the building of the Boston and Lowell Railroad. There were two other glasshouses at Stoddard, one built in 1844, the other in 1850, which produced colored glass. However, the introduction of clear glass for liquor bottles dealt a serious blow to the industry. The Chelmsford Glass Works (1802) near Lowell, Massachusetts, moved to Suncook, New Hampshire, because conditions for glassmaking were considered better there.

Practically all the New England states had glassworks but little glass seems to have been made in Rhode Island or Maine. The 1840 census listed a dozen glasshouses in the region. Two of them, the New England Glass Company at Cambridge and the Boston and Sandwich Glass Company on Cape Cod, ranked among the largest glass manufactories in the country. Glassworks were opened at Salisbury and East Middlebury, Vermont, during the War of 1812, when the supply of European glass was cut off, and flourished for a short time, but closed soon after the war. In 1827, the Champlain Glass Works was established at Burlington producing window glass and bottles. The Champlain glassblowers also produced some of the finest "offhand" examples made in America. The fuel shortage closed this business too.

Wood was deemed the most suitable fuel for glassmaking, but it took immense quantities of good burning quality to keep even the smallest glasshouse in operation. Even after the industry converted to coal, New England glassmakers could not compete with the Midwestern manufacturers, who were using oil and natural gas. It was for this reason that the New England Glass Company at Cambridge, Massachusetts, moved to Toledo, Ohio, in 1888, and became the Libbey Glass Company.

The year 1817 marked the beginning of a fabulous career in glassmaking. Deming Jarves, who was to become the most accomplished of all Yankee glassmakers, and several associates bought the Boston Porcelain and Glass Company at East Cambridge. By a special act of incorporation, the new company was authorized by the commonwealth to make all kinds of flint and crown or window glass in Boston and Cambridge.

Flint glass, made with lead, and used for all types of table and ornamental ware derived its name from the fact that when first developed in England, bits of ground-up flint were mixed with the other ingredients. In bygone days, the making of glass was a closely guarded secret. (This same condition existed with many skills where formulas were involved and was a particular characteristic of some types of crafsmen. Even today there are some who keep their methods and procedures of operation inviolate.) It was well known to glassmakers that the use of lead in the manufacture of glass had given England the prime advantage in the world market in the seventeenth century. As a result of its use, clearer and more brilliant glass could be obtained, and English ware was shipped even to the established glass centers of Europe. The method of obtaining red lead or litharge was closely guarded. American glass manufacturers were dependent entirely on this material and had to import it from England. During and after the War of 1812, red lead was not available.

To Deming Jarves, a man of great talent and ingenuity, this was a prime challenge. In 1818, he set up an experimental lead furnace at Cambridge and discovered the "secret" of its production in his first attempt. From Cooper's *Emporium of Arts and Sciences* he secured a sketchy plan and with his own resourcefulness and the aid of a London trained engineer, he achieved his goal. In his *Reminiscences of Glassmaking* Jarves wrote: "For over 30 years, they (his company) monopolized the business in all its branches from the highest quality of pure Galena and painter's red lead to common pig lead."

He was only twenty-eight when he made this significant discovery. At the age of thirty-four, the measure of the man expanded when, after visiting the Pittsburgh firm of Bakewell and Page (then considered the most progressive

The apothecary shop in the John Ward House, Salem, Massachusetts, contains a varied collection of glass bottles and jars. *Photo courtesy Essex Institute*

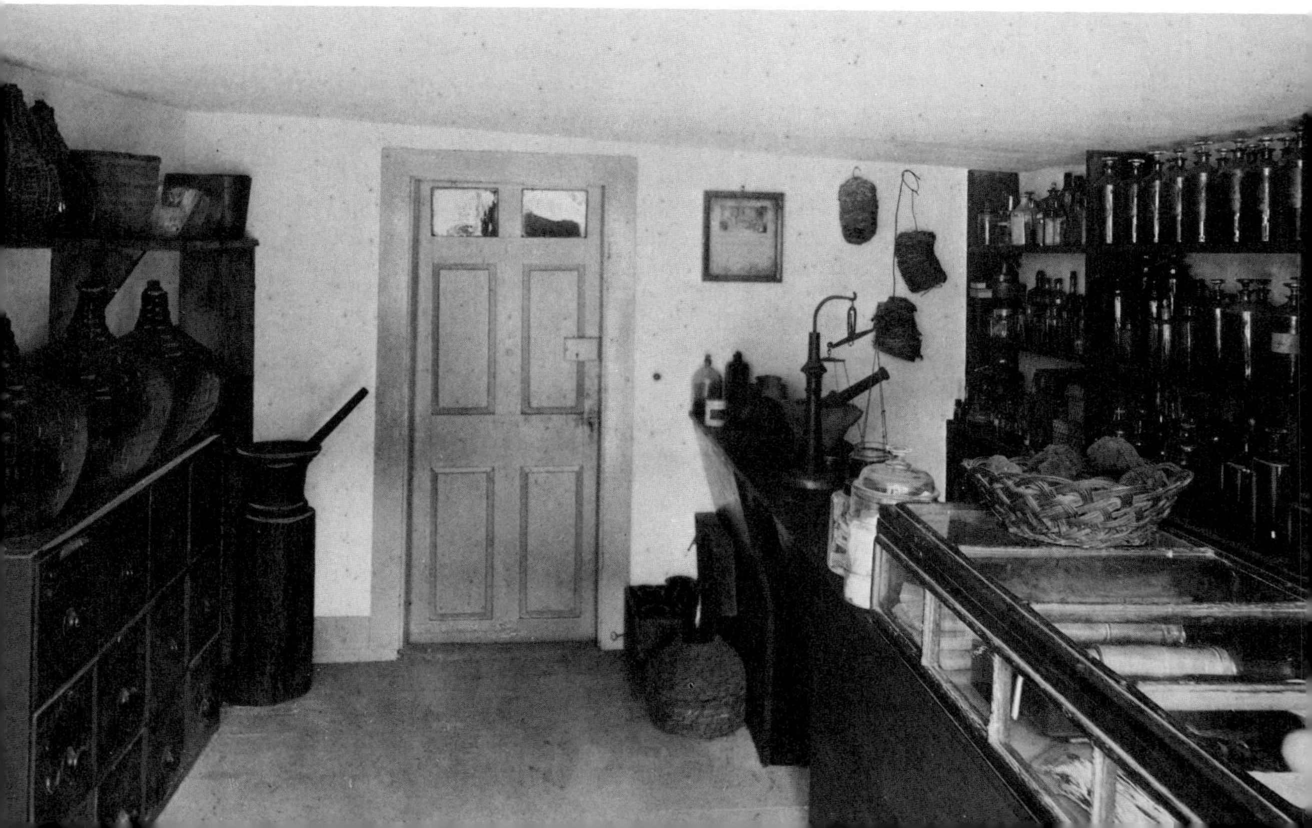

in America), he decided to sever connections with the Cambridge firm so that he might experiment with new methods and techniques in glass making in his own way. He then formed the Boston and Sandwich Glass Company, which made American glass history. Jarves chose Sandwich on Cape Cod as the site for his glassworks primarily for its fuel supply. The silica in the Cape sand was not suitable and sand had to be shipped (as ballast) all the way from Demerara in British Guiana; later it came from New Jersey and eventually from the sand beds of western Massachusetts. A man of vision and enterprise, Jarves obtained rights to more than twenty thousand acres of woodland and the farmers were paid fifty cents a cord to cut it. The logs which were small were cut to fit the furnaces and kiln-dried before burning. Later, when the glassworks was converted to coal, Jarves built a wharf on Buzzards Bay and hauled his fuel across the neck of the Cape. Since there were no railroads in 1825, transportation was entirely by boat. The factory, located on a tidal creek, was easily accessible for the delivery of sand and the shipping of glassware. When rails were run to Sandwich, and rates became high, a steamer named the *Acorn* was built which covered the fifty-mile run between Sandwich and Boston in a few hours. Glass House Village, as it came to be known—homes for the workers and the glasshouses—was erected in record time, and on July 4, 1825, three months after ground was broken, the first glass was blown at Sandwich.

Every conceivable object that could be made of glass was produced at Sandwich. A vast assortment of tableware, in various colors, brought a new kind of appeal to dinner tables all over the land. Today, collectors search avidly for the punch bowls and decanters, the tumblers and salts, the candlesticks and lamps, even the miniature glass hats in various colors and toy dishes, not to mention a wide array of ornaments made at this fabulous glasshouse. One branch of the business specialized in glassware for chemists and apothecaries.

But despite his lofty aims, Jarves was to be best remembered for his pressed glass, the invention of which revolutionized the glass industry in America and caused it to expand greatly. Prior to this time, all glass had been blown by the same methods used for centuries. With the new process, molten glass was pressed into molds instead of being blown into them. This new technique was speedier and cheaper and naturally dealt a severe blow to the glassmaking centers of Europe. They simply could not compete with this new, mass-produced American glass.

Although Jarves claimed credit for the invention, it was disputed by two workers at the Cambridge firm. The controversy finally reached the courts when he tried to patent a press which he had improved, and the Cambridge workers won the case. As with many developments of this sort, both firms were conducting experiments simultaneously, and both achieved the desired results at about the same time. Beautiful and appealing as was his glass, there was something absorbing about this man Jarves which has captured the imagination of all who have studied his career. Few businessmen in New England had his wisdom and approach in obtaining loyalty from his workmen. He showed them every consideration and even discussed his dreams with the men in the town of Sandwich before he opened his glassworks. In seeking new ideas, he not only brought skilled craftsmen from England, Ireland, Belgium, and France, but he and his associates traveled about learning how others in the business conducted their glasshouses. Mabel M. Swan wrote of him: "His lifelong ambition seems to have been to perfect a glass which would be equal to that of Venice. Despite all his efforts, he failed in this respect and his reputation rests to-day on what he considered 'the potboiler stuff'—pressed glass." *The Dictionary of American Biography* had identified Deming Jarves as chemist, inventor, organizer; Mrs. Swan preferred the title his own father gave him in his will, "gentleman."

What Carl Drepperd has written in *The ABC's of Old Glass* expresses the sentiment of all who enjoy collecting and living with it. "Glass, when first made, was undoubtedly considered out of this world. A mystery made concrete, tangible, and useful. Glass has enchanted billions of people, and has had the attention of scientists, philosophers, scholars, students, and just folks, since it was first discovered and made. Glassmaking began with enchantment and has continued its mysterious charm down through the years. There is pleasure, delectation, and satisfaction in collecting it. No matter how much factual data there are about it and its making, it forever holds more connotations of the unreal and imaginary than of tangibility and consolidation."

Hat and Bandboxes

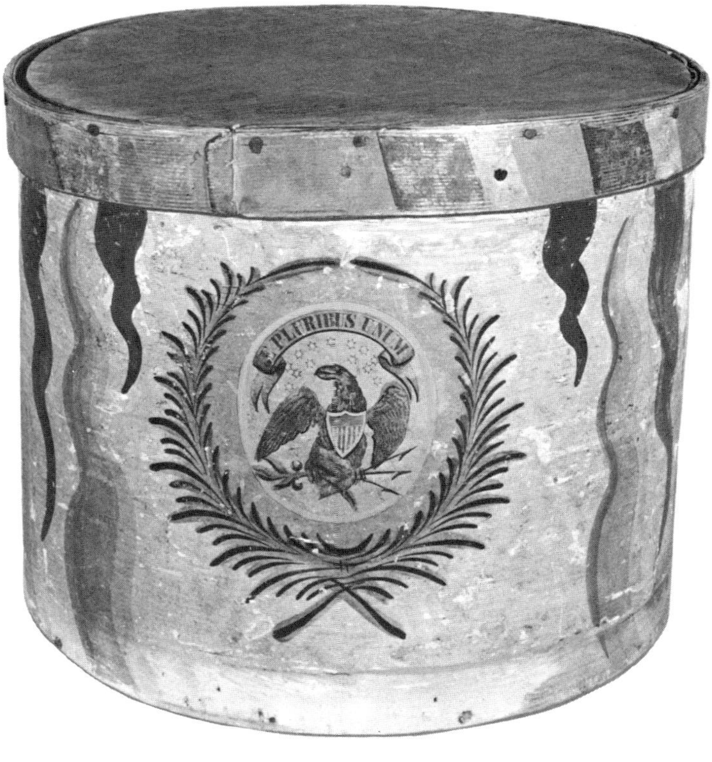

This wooden box, with cover and bottom of pine covered with gesso, is painted white and decorated with streamers or pennants of blue, green, yellow, and orange. An open wreath frames the lithographed eagle, which is tinted in color, and the banner above its head carries the motto *E. Pluribus Unum. Photo Einars Mengis: courtesy Shelburne Museum*

Hats. Daniel Jones, at the Hat & Helmet, South-End, Boston, makes and sells Beaver, Beaveret, and Castor-Hats, and has also a good Assortment of English Castor and Beaveret Hats, English and Felt ditto, Hat Linings and Trimmings of all sorts: Red Wool, Coney Wool, Camel's Hair; Logwood by the 100 wt. by Wholesale or Retail, cheap for Cash or Treasurer's Notes."

The gentleman who pursued this advertisement after reading it in his copy of the *Boston Gazette,* December 10, 1759, knew that he would either have to purchase another hatbox or bandbox to store it in. Hat- and bandboxes were not merely trappings for frivolous women. Men used them extensively, too. They were made in shapes and manners so contrived that they could only accommodate men's headgear, and they served for ye gentleman as a place to store not only fishing flies and other gadgets but whatever pleased his fancy. And these masculine hat- and bandboxes occupied their rightful places in the hall closet or wherever the storage place for this clothing was.

In *The Customs of New England,* Joseph B. Felt records: "The Massachusetts Bay Company sent over in its stock, in 1629, a hundred black hats made of wool and lined in the brim with leather and at the same time came one hundred Monmouth caps, so-called from the place where they were manufactured, and valued at two shillings each." In 1675 a Bostonian wrote to a friend in London that the local market for sugar-loaf or high-crowned hats was dull.

The Monmouth, or military cocked hat for men, began to come into fashion about 1670, with an average width of brim of six inches. Their "inconvenient width" would mean that another type hatbox would have to be designed, for the men not only had their hats, they kept them from generation to generation. The bandbox was also used for the gentleman to carry around his large, stiff, starched ruff.

Even three days is not a long enough time to visit in the fascinating Shelburne Museum at Shelburne, Vermont. There visitors may be absorbed in looking at the fine, complete collection of many an item of antiquity, and thanks to the avid searching of the donors, Mr. and Mrs. J. Watson Webb, it contains an unusually outstanding collection of hat- and bandboxes. Not only does one see all shapes and sizes, but all kinds of papers. A rich pictorial history of papers greets one, and the linings are equally of historic interest, for each is lined with an old, old newspaper, many of them perfectly decipherable. The Bandbox Room at the museum is also known as the "Hat and Fragrance Unit," for surrounding the two hundred bandboxes (the result of forty years of collecting) are fine examples of embroidery, feminine bibelots, and accessories. The names of the designs on these bandboxes read like a decorator's motif-list, and if you wished to look at only these, they would please you.

The collector of bandboxes is ecstatic when she finds a bandbox made by Hannah Davis. This spinster was to become the one most famed of all bandbox makers, and whose work has become the most searched for. This Jaffrey, New Hampshire, woman possessed qualities so inspiring and a personality so vibrant and endearing that she has been the subject of many a feminine "character" paper. Born a descendant of self-reliant, sturdy pioneer stock, Hannah first saw light of day in 1784. Her grandfather, John Eaton, had moved from Bedford, Massachusetts, to Jaffrey in 1774 one year after Jaffrey became a town. He was a millwright by trade, but his skills encompassed many other fields. Although his spelling was poor, his old account book attests the evidence of some of the work he tackled as a matter of course. He made flax and wool wheels, "dugg graves," made carts, "tuggs," "Corfens," and sleds among other things. His interest and skill in working with wood he bequeathed to succeeding generations.

Hannah's own father, Peter Davis, was a maker of wooden clocks. He died when she was a young woman and her mother died when Hannah was thirty-four. Thus, she became a spinster who had to make her own livelihood. Nor for naught was Hannah a "dyed in the wool Yankee." She remembered her menfolks' skill with wood, and looking carefully over the field, she decided to make wooden hat boxes. Miss Davis's methods of work were truly simple. She would hunt through the woods until she located the perfect tree for her use—a fine, big spruce tree. Then she would bargain with the owner of the tree-land, and when she had paid for the tree, she hired a man to cut it and haul it to her home. This log was to be cut into lengths which

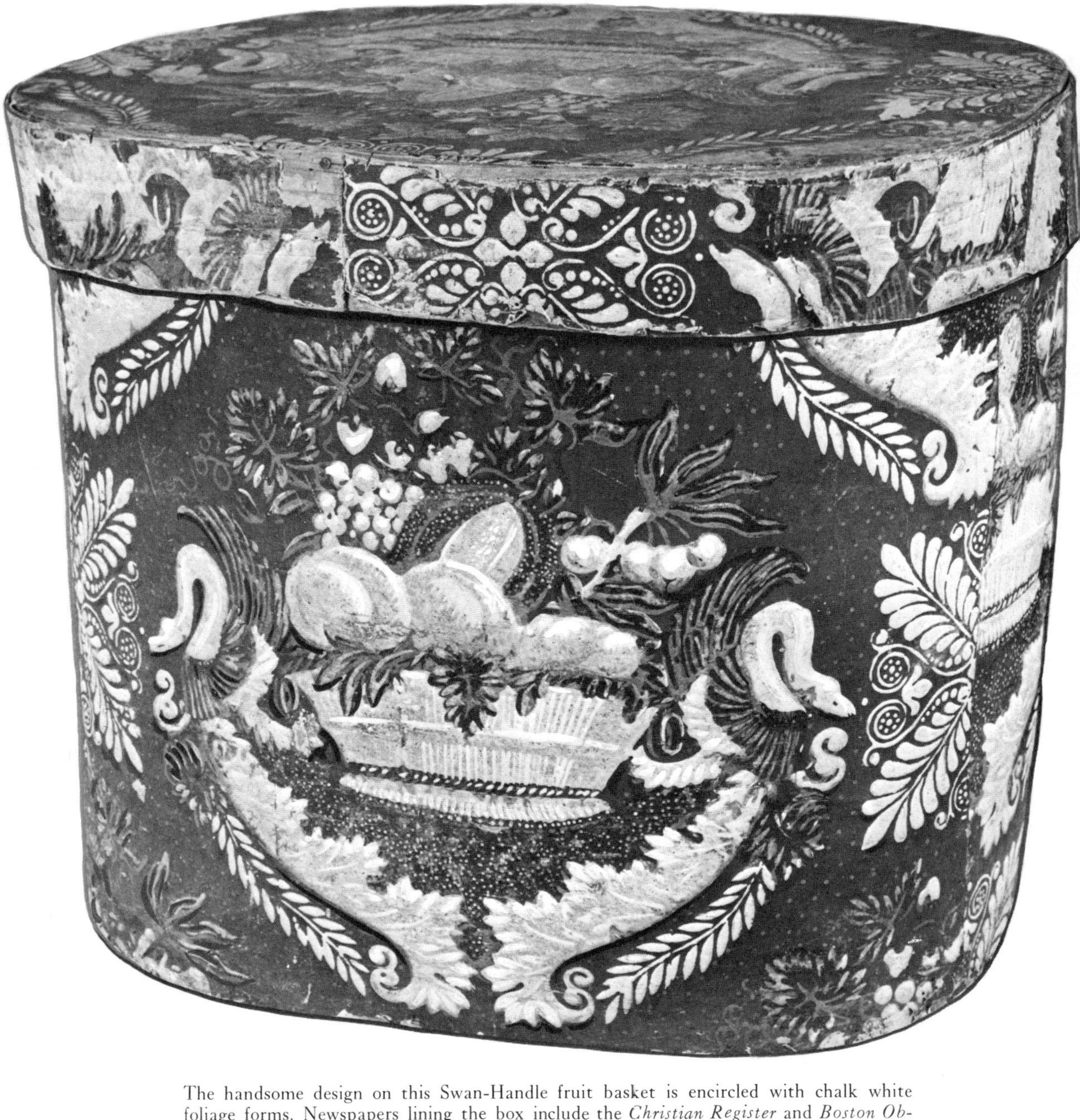

The handsome design on this Swan-Handle fruit basket is encircled with chalk white foliage forms. Newspapers lining the box include the *Christian Register* and *Boston Observer,* August 13, 1836; also Rhode Island news items of 1840. The cover is inlined with the *Christian Register* for August 13 1831. The colors are yellow, pale green varnish, and white on an unusual brown background. *Photo Einars Mengis: courtesy Shelburne Museum*

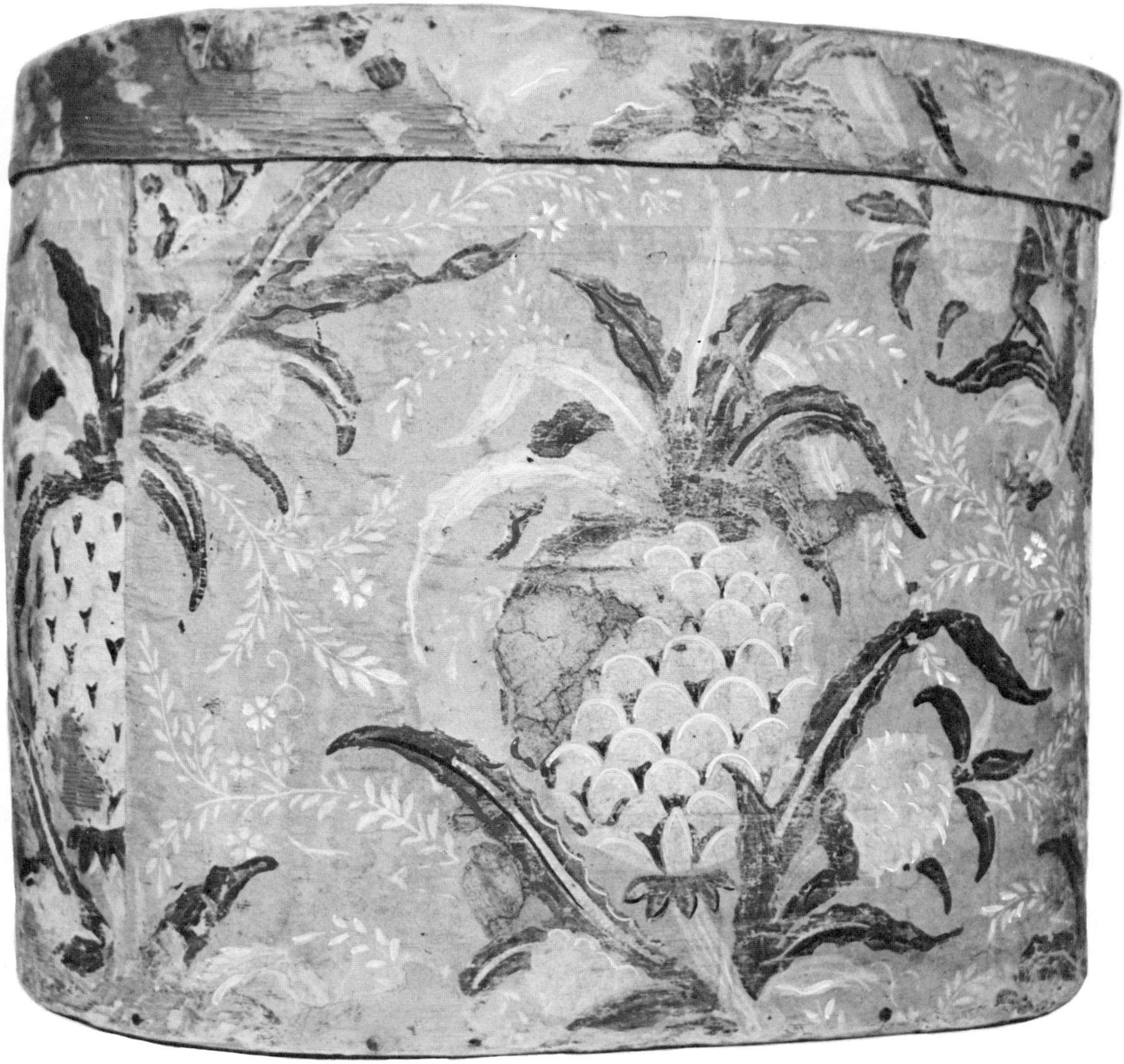

One of the most charming of the wallpapers used by Hannah Davis on her boxes is the pineapple design. It has been reproduced by Jones and Erwin of New York City and entitled: "Portsmouth Pineapple—a documented design with a handsome representation of the exotic fruit which became a symbol of hospitality in the 18th century." *Photo Einars Mengis: courtesy Shelburne Musuem*

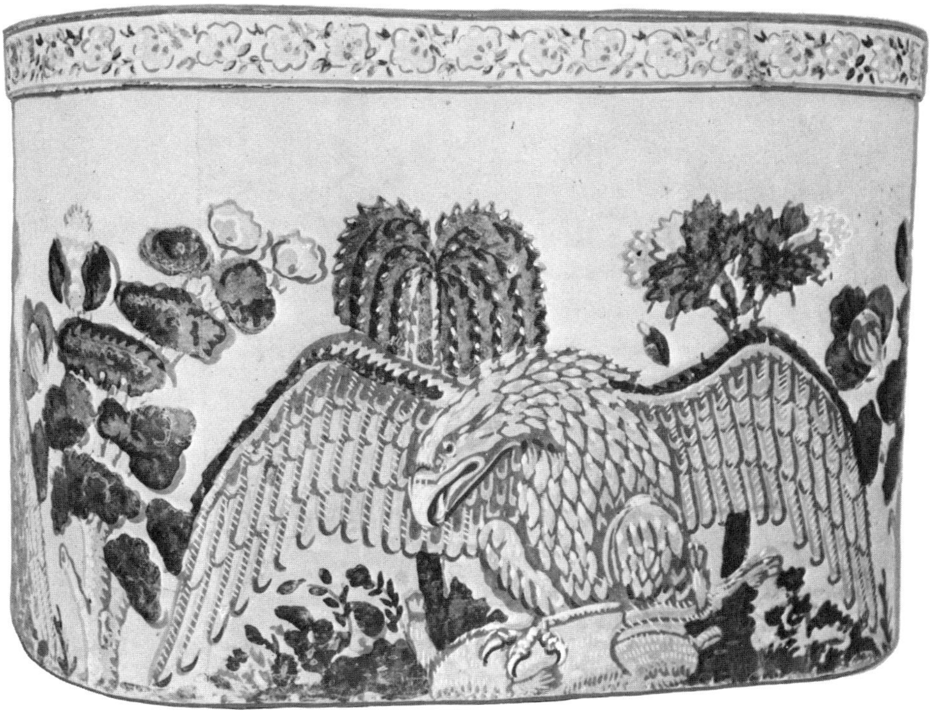

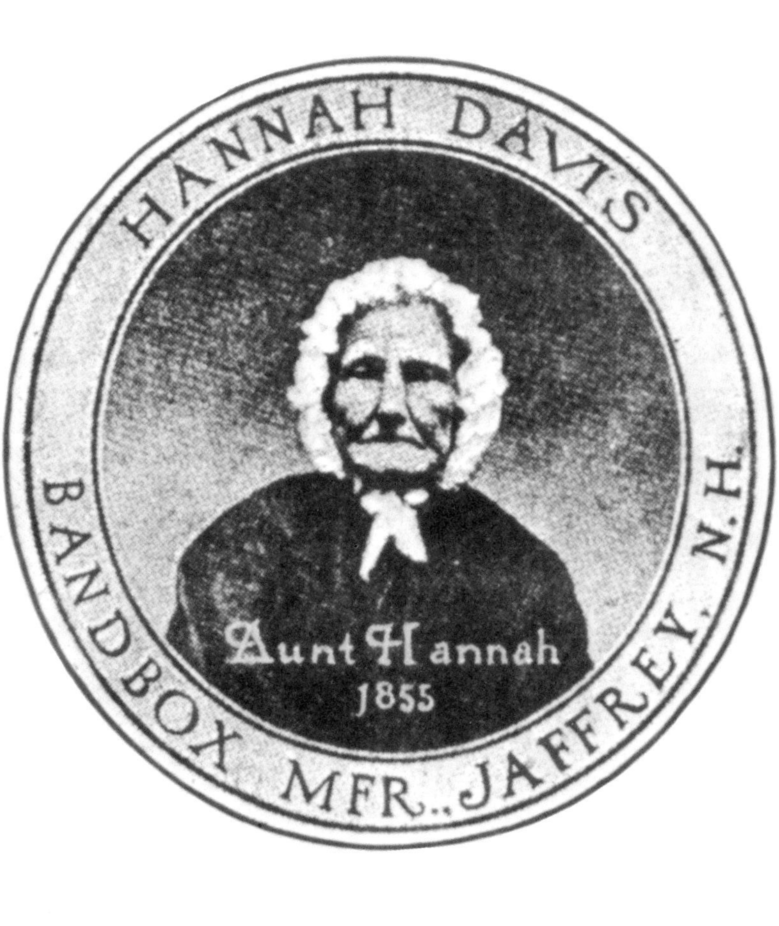
HANNAH DAVIS
BANDBOX MFR., JAFFREY, N.H.
Aunt Hannah
1855

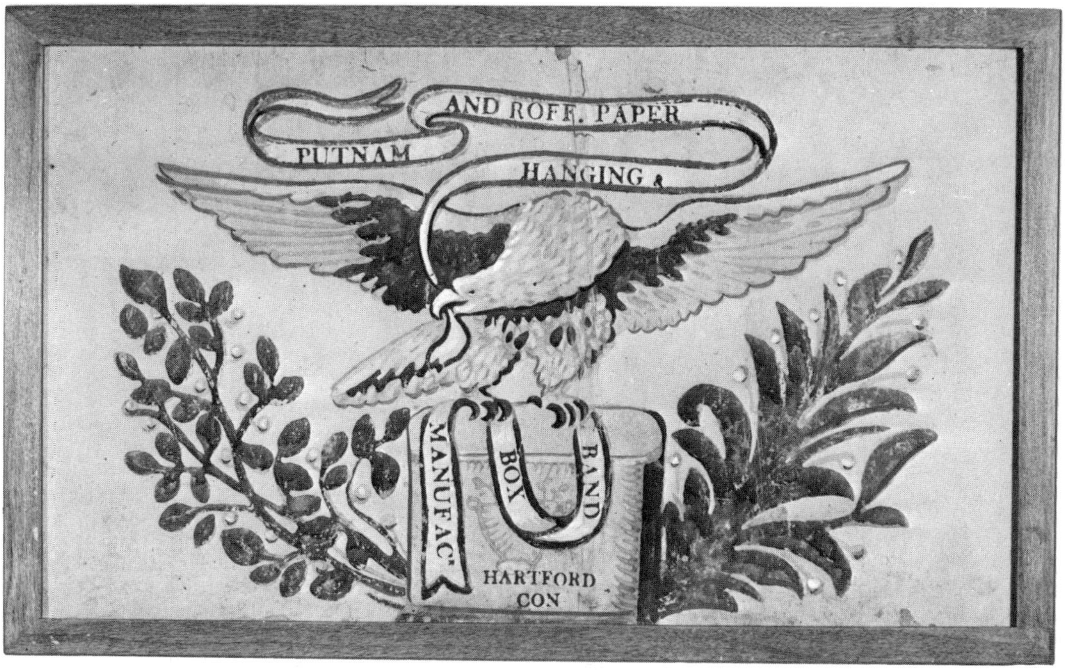

(*Above*) Threaded through his beak and looped through the talons of this spread eagle are ribbons advertising *Putnam and Roff Paper Hangings and Band Box Manufacturer.* The olive branch and laurel spray balance the motif on either side of the trunk which is stamped with the Hartford, Connecticut, address of this early nineteenth century wallpaper manufacturer. The fragment is printed in black, brown, white, and green varnish on pale blue background. *Circa 1823.*

(*Opposite, above*) The eagle made a notably ornamental wallpaper design and Aunt Hannah used it frequently on her boxes. (*Below*) Hannah Davis marked her products with this trademark. *Photos Einars Mengis: courtesy Shelburne Museum*

were stood up on end on a wooden platform. This inventive woman designed a machine to be run by man foot-power, using a sharp blade which cut off vertically thin slices from the log, about an eighth of an inch thick. These she used for the sides of the bandboxes. For the bottoms and covers her choice was pine; these were cut a little thicker.

All of her boxes were lined with newspapers. Hannah, herself, did not hoard these newssheets; rather, she bartered with her neighbors for theirs, and in return they were allowed to choose, for their own, any one of the many boxes she had made. The outsides of the boxes were covered with hand-blocked wallpaper, in a rich array of colors with ever so many blue backgrounds.

At first Hannah was successful in selling her boxes to the local merchants (fifty cents for the big ones, while the small ones brought only twelve cents). Her largest group of buyers were the young factory women of the day. The only deterrent to her business was the fact that she did not own a horse. Once again she was resourceful. She hired a "gentlebeast" from a nearby neighbor. In the winter she drove a sleigh and in summer used a large wagon with a white prairie schooner canopy top.

When her factory-girl customers went home they would carry with them into the stagecoach one of Aunt Hannah's bandboxes.

In her late life, Hannah broke her hip. She had endeared herself to everyone in Jaffrey, and each tried to outdo the other in caring for her. She died in 1863, and thirty years later, still remembered by the daughters of "her girls," a church window was installed, "In memory of Aunt Hannah Davis."

Jewelry and Its Importance in the New Land

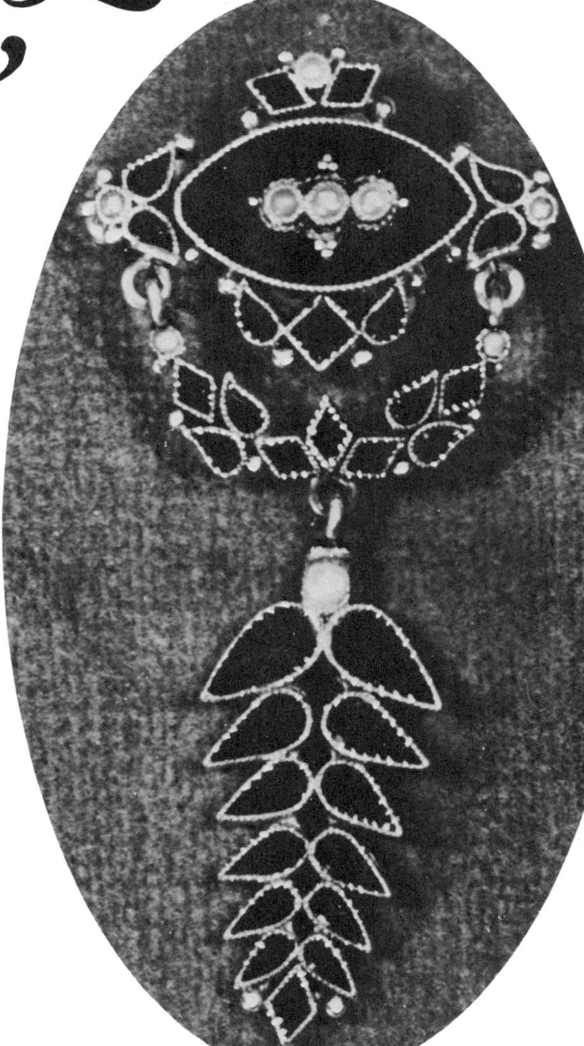

A chased gold and black enamel brooch, *circa* 1820. Among their heirlooms, many New England families proudly display elongated, oval brooches with a bar bisecting the oval as shown in this brooch. The bar gives the effect of a tongueless buckle. *Photo Richard Merrill: courtesy E. S. Sawyer Collection*

From the dawn of history man has had an avid interest in jewels and jewelry, not only with which to adorn himself but to possess. He has chased gold to the ends of the earth and to many a rainbow's curve. Some of the first explorers who came to our shores were lured here only by the thought of gold. Surprised they must have been to find a country lacking in that precious metal, but one which, nonetheless, had produced a native civilization of its own.

The making of jewelry is one of the oldest trades—arts—of which the American historian can find record. While the manufacture of such articles of adornment occupied a position of minor importance until several years after the arrival of the colonists, jewelry was made by the native Indians many years before the first European traveler set foot upon American soil. The Indians made bracelets, necklaces, and earrings; some had even found pearls to use for adornment. All these manifestations bespeak the Indian's vanity and love of personal embellishment, a trait that took precedence even over clothing. Wampum was the Indian's most prized possession. Wampum worn as ornament became the Indian's badge of wealth and position, his record book and tribal history, his ceremonial gavel, and his communications system; and, through the favor of the Great Spirit, its possession was believed to be his passport to the Happy Hunting Ground. Of the beads made by the Indians, wampum, the cylindrical shell bead, is the best known. As stated, it was used for a number of purposes, and its use as money was adopted by the white man for his monetary system. This step was accomplished quickly for the colonists brought little money with them.

Wampum was of two colors: white, "wompi," and dark purple, "sacki." White wampum was the most plentiful and its value was about one-half that of the purple. The white was made from the central part of the coiled shell of the whelk or periwinkle, while the purple came from the shell of the quahog. The pieces were formed into tiny cylinders one-eighth inch in diameter, and one quarter inch long. Because of their small size and the brittleness of the shell, the labor of making them with what tools the Indian had was difficult and tedious. They were polished by being rubbed smooth on a stone and then bored by means of a flint awl. There is plenty of evidence that they used this method before the introduction of steel tools. The little beads thus made were strung on thongs of deerskin and worn as a necklace; sometimes, strings of wampum hung from the waist. Wampum was also sewed on belts or clothing, arranged in patterns or designs. King Philip of the Wampanoag tribe (Cape Cod) treasured his deerskin wampum belt which was nine inches wide; designed in black and white wampum were figures, flowers, birds, and animals. A string of wampum may be seen at the Old Mill in Brewster, Massachusetts. When the colonist used wampum as money, it took three black beads or six white beads to equal one English penny. In 1677 Governor Winslow sent royalties of wampum of the Wampanoag federation to King Charles II of England. (The beadwork which is so prominent in the decoration of Indian costume owes its origin to the introduction of small Italian glass beads, brought by the white traders.)

Wampum jewelry still has its place in adornment in Massachusetts for, on Cape Cod, a retired couple make beautiful pieces. Its modern version has its own fascinating story. Several years ago a retired Boston mechanical engineer, Edwin L. Dayton, went to Cape Cod and, wishing to fill his days with creativity, searched the beach at South Yarmouth for treasures and found some interesting pebbles. He polished these stones to a remarkable luster, but still he was not satisfied. One day when he was beachcombing, an impulse to pick up a quahog shell led him to the hand-crafted jewelry business that is his today.

Quahogs, members of the Venus clam family, are the chief commercial clams of the eastern United States. Taking a quahog back to his workshop, Dayton cut it open and discovered that the rich purple color on the exterior of the shell actually penetrated into the shell itself. After grinding and polishing a piece of the shell, he found himself holding a beautiful bit of pearl. It was a native fisherman who identified Dayton's "discovery" as wampum. Research followed proving that what he had made was "sacki"—the old dark wampum. Pursuing his venture farther, he learned that he had to cut the quahog shell out-of-doors for it gave off a chalky dust and a peculiarly offensive odor. With the cutting accomplished, the pieces are put into a "tumbler" for an initial whirl to smooth off their rough edges. The first tumbling finished, the quahog pieces are fastened to "dop

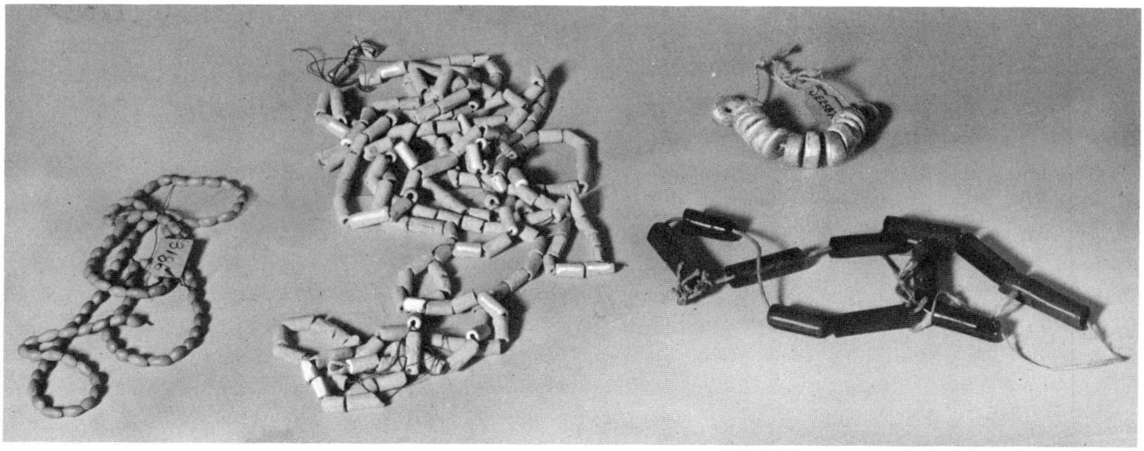

Prior to the arrival of the colonists, the Indians used disc-shaped wampum (upper right) but the Dutch introduced the tubular forms shown in the other three strings above. Trade beads were even larger and more showy in appearance. *Photo Richard Merrill: courtesy Peabody Museum*

sticks" and then ground into the desired shape. The play of color dictates the shape of the piece. It is cut and highly polished, bringing out the intrinsic beauty of each piece which ranges in color from pale violet to deep purple. Then the pieces are set in silver. Each finished piece is as attractive and as appealing as its counterpart in mother-of-pearl or abalone shell. What is more, it makes history live again—for the creator and for the wearer!

As we have said, almost everyone thinks of the Puritans as being garbed in sombre, sad-colored garments and living a life devoid of color, warmth, fragrance, and adornment. But sad color was not dismal and dull save in the name itself. It was a brown tone and brown is warm; being a primitive color, it is, above all, cheerful. The Puritan dressed in honest russet kersey, a pleasant shade, and his garment often was gay, with the bright stamell-red of his waistcoats and its grain-red lining. He was enlivened, too, with a scarlet-hooded cloak. Prim and precise as the Puritans were supposed to have been, it is a mistake to imagine that they were too primitive in their opinions to appreciate the advantage of a little jewelry as adornment of their persons. The English settlers brought such ornaments with them to the new world and one's personal attire was not complete without the buckles, brooches and rings in vogue at that time in the Old World. As a natural result of this demand, one of the first industries to be established in the colonies was the goldsmith's shop.

While the jewelry of the mid-seventeenth century was somber, the business it entailed was a very flourishing one, for mourning rings were a standard part of all funerals. At first, mourning rings were made of plain gold, usually enameled in black or black and white, but gradually they came to be more and more decorated. The decoration usually took the form of a death's head or a coffin with a full-length skeleton lying in it or a winged skull. Sometimes these rings held a framed lock of hair of the deceased. Also, the ring could be shaped as a serpent with his tail in his mouth. Many bore a posy. It was so customary a practice to give these rings that the goldsmiths kept a supply of mourning rings on hand constantly. There are even accounts of ministers and prominent citizens having tankards filled with these rings, secured at funerals, which they bequeathed to their heirs.

When Andrew Pepperell (son of Sir William) died, March 1, 1751, at Kittery Point, Maine, his father announced the death to his friend Mr. Kilby of London by sending him a mourning ring. In replying Mr. Kilby accepted "that melancholy token of y'r regard to Mrs. K. and myself at the expense of four guineas in the whole. But, as is not unusual here on such occasions, Mrs. K. has, at her own expense, added some sparks of diamonds to some other mournful ornaments to the ring, which she intends to wear."

During the Revolution, the jeweler's trade received little encouragement; yet, the custom of distributing mourning rings survived even that upheaval. At the death of Washington, the country was literally flooded with a deluge of lockets, rings and brooches, each bearing a lugubrious little painting of Grief symbolized by a dejected damsel mourning over his tomb.

The real heyday of the mourning piece was reached in the nineteenth century. Emulating the English style, one could display sentimental melancholy for its own sake by wearing a piece of mourning jewelry, for this insignia stood as the hallmark of gentility and refinement. The lockets portrayed standardized allegory: a weeping female drooping, all disconsolate over a large tomb; or, amid a number of funeral urns, a weeping willow was part of this scene, emphasizing the downward sweep of all-consuming sorrow. These scenes in miniature, set in gold, jet, or seed pearls were worn in rings and brooches to grace the person of the bereaved.

At this time too, came the hair-jewelry —rings, lockets, brooches, bracelets, watch-chains, scarfpins. Any form of jewelry was likely to include human hair and it was ingeniously introduced, one way or another, into its design. Sometimes the hair was that of a living person, but more often that of some dear departed. The most obvious and simple method of using the hair for decoration was by mounting it under crystal, to be used as a ring, brooch, or locket. Even bracelets and watch-chains were made of hair, intricately braided in many strands. Sometimes, the braid was caught at intervals by ornate medallions of wrought gold.

In the English-speaking towns in the seventeenth century, no man's attire was considered complete without buckles and buttons of silver. Except for a few pieces which the Pilgrims and Puritans brought with them, there was little or no jewelry made here at first. However, in 1636 one Captain Cromwell, "a jolly, generous vagabond" after ten years of "free-booting" on the high seas, came to Boston. Of him, Governor Bradford wrote: "He spent liberally and gave freely; he scattered a great deale of money and more since, I feare than money. He had great store of plate and jewels, and he gave Governor Winthrop a fair sedan chair worth £50." A privateersman, he returned again and again to Boston until, one

Beaded bags were often made with intricate designs, scenic, floral and geometric, and brought a good price. *Photo courtesy Essex Institute*

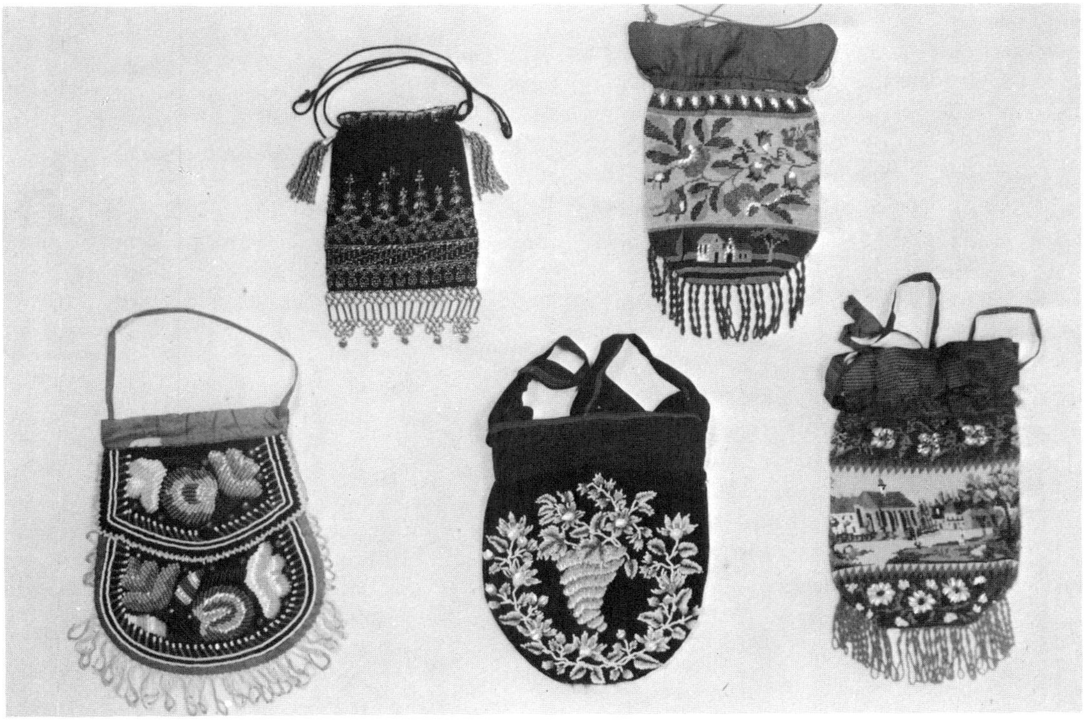

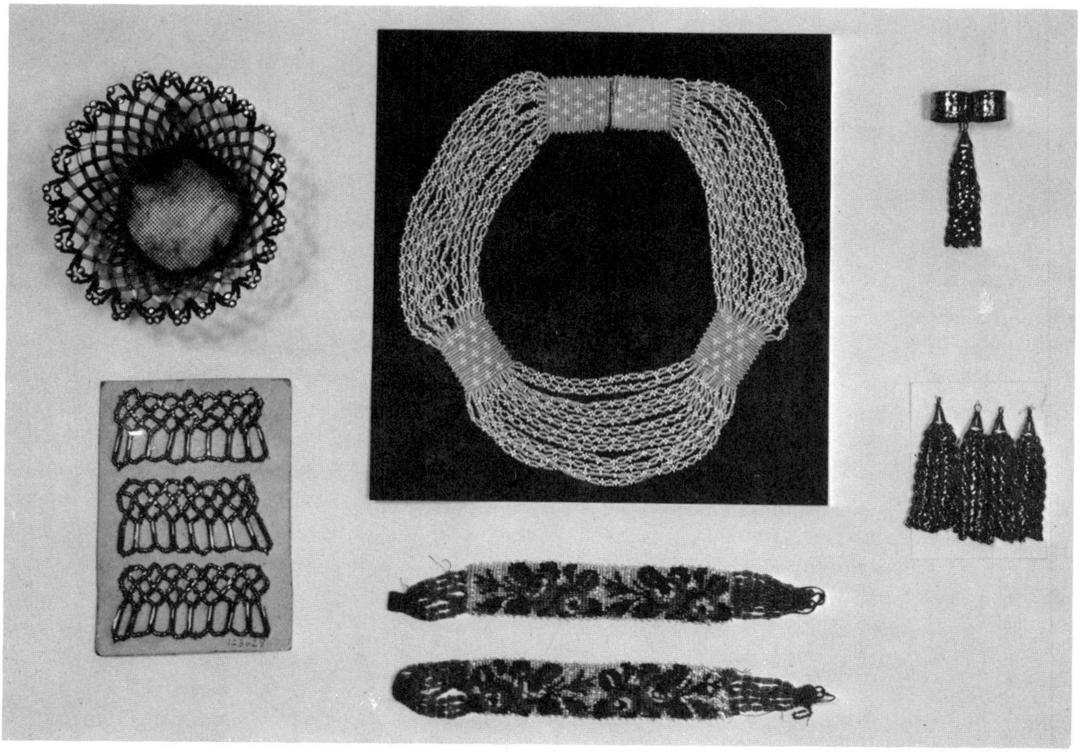

Beadwork required good eyesight and was painstaking as well. *Photo courtesy Essex Institute*

time in the "somer, having gott a fall from his horse in which fall he fell on his rapier hilts, and so bruised his body as he shortly after dyed."

The early goldsmiths and silversmiths were versatile craftsmen. They incorporated the skills of the jeweler, the watchmaker, the silversmith, and even the coppersmith all in one. The craftsmen of these early days could chisel out a ring, repair their own handiwork thoroughly(and in a completely satisfying manner) and were equally competent in each of those jobs. It was impossible to draw a sharp line of distinction between the jeweler, the goldsmith, the silversmith, or the watchmaker, the clockmaker or the maker of fine mathematical instruments. Necessity demanded that these craftsmen branch out into the various stages of precision work and divide their time and skill among these kindred crafts in order to earn a living.

An amazing advertisement, confirming the versatility of the jeweler, appeared in the October 22, 1767, issue of the *Boston News-Letter:*

> *Daniel Boyer*—Imported from London, to be sold by Daniel Boyer, Jeweler, at his shop opposite the Governor's in Boston. Stone Shoe, Knee & Neck Buckles, Stone Broaches, Pair Cluster Earings with three Drops, Steel top Thimbles, best Brilliant & Cypher Ear-ring & Button Stones, Brilliant and Cypher Ring Stones, Garnets, Armethistes and Topazes, Ring & Buckle Sparke, Diamond Sparks, Locket Stones & Cyphers, Ruby, white & amethiste foyle Coral Beeds, Corals for Thistles, best Shoe and Knee chapes, rough and smooth Files binding wire, Brass ditto, Brass Stamps, friezing Punches and Gravers, blow Pipe, Brass Borax Boxes, money Scales and Weights, Buckle & Ring Bruskes, Polishing Ditto, Small Shears & Plyers, Screw Dividers, fine Drawing Irons, Large Ditto, Hand Vices, small & Large Ditto, Anvils, Spoon Teasts, planishing Ditto, Thimble stamps, Ingots and Skillets, Forging and Drawing Tongs, upright Drills with Bitts, Turkey Oyl Syones, Borax & Salt Betre, Large Pumice Stone, Rotton Stone, Crucibles and black Pots, moulding Sand &.
>
> At said shop may also be had most sorts cf Jewellerie and Goldsmiths Work, cheap for Cash.

It was not a strange sight for the Pilgrim or the Puritan to see a male with earrings on. Many Indians wore earrings. James I of

England wore them, and they continued to be the fashion for both sexes under Charles I. Adam Winthrop, the grandfather of Massachusetts' first governor John, wore earrings. In 1800 American men who followed the sea often had their ears pierced and wore earrings. The miniature portrait of Captain George Taylor, a Salem shipowner and a man of wealth, shows him wearing earrings. Women not only wore earrings, but they also wore earstrings and ribbons drawn through the ears—for all ears were pierced. Small girls also wore earjewels. Many primitive portraits show them. These little girls also wore small lockets on chains, tiny rings, and sometimes gold beads. Even today, earrings have continued in fashion, in one form or another.

The early watches were large globose-shaped affairs and there were not many around. These clumsy watches had a detached outer case. Few among the first colonists owned either watches or clocks. We have the contemporary evidence in the case of Roger Williams. In 1672, when he rowed thirty miles down the bay and disputed with the Foxians at Newport, it was agreed that each party should be heard in turn for a quarter of an hour. But no clock was available in Newport, Rhode Island, and among the whole population that flocked to the debate, there was not a single watch. Williams wrote, "unless we had Clocks & Watches & Quarter Glasses (as in some Ships) it was impossible to be exactly punctual, so they guessed at the time."

A collection of silver buckles. *Photo courtesy Essex Institute*

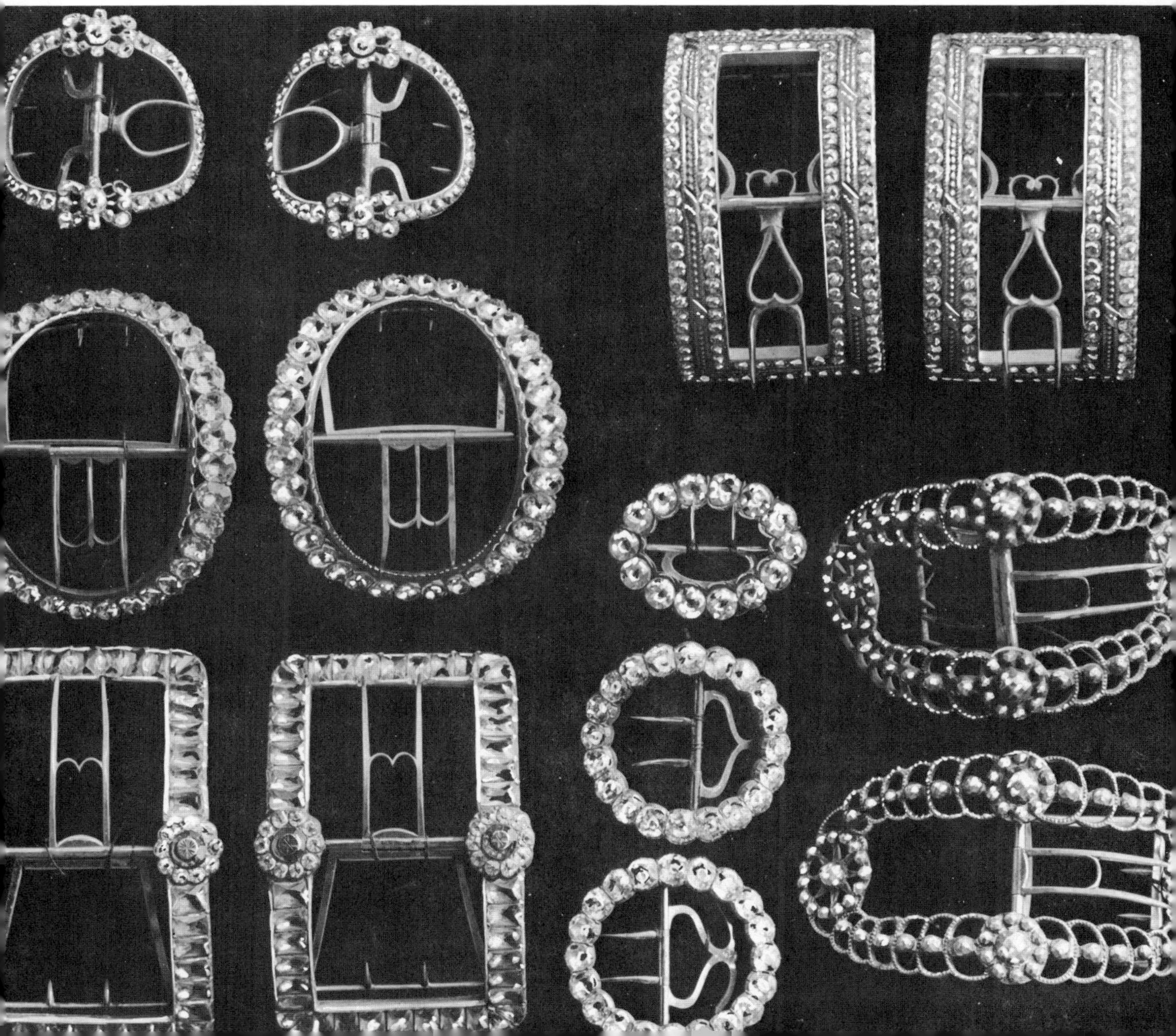

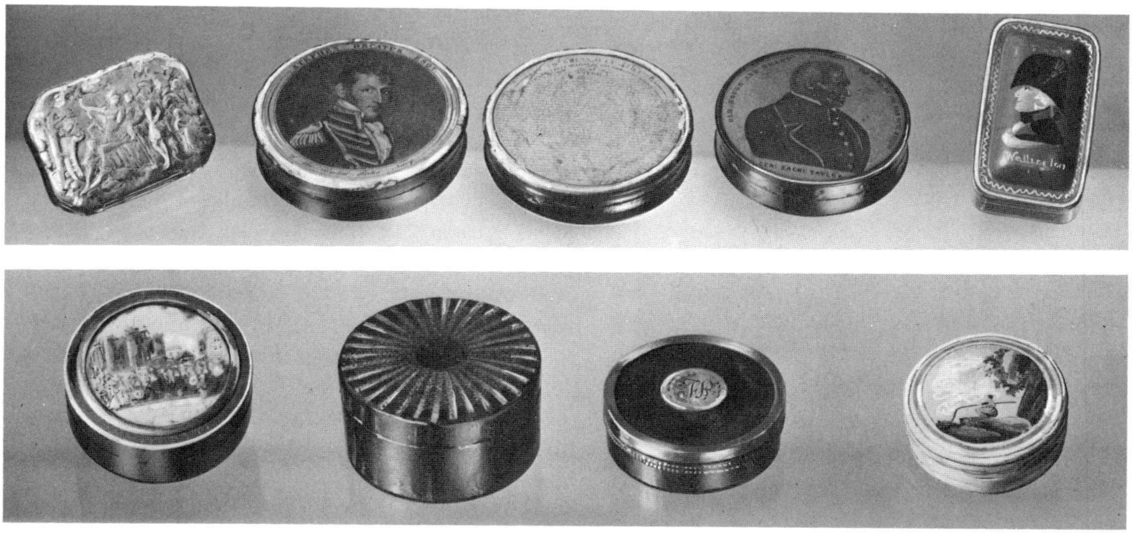

Snuffboxes were often elaborately ornamented and featured portraits or landscapes in miniature. *Photo courtesy Essex Institute*

As the watches did not fit snugly in their cases, watch-papers were made for insertion to keep them from rattling. Some of these papers were fine examples of papyrotamia—the art of cutting paper in ornamental designs. This art was taught girls in the dame schools, and while it is fascinating and amazing that such intricate cuttings could be managed with scissors, in this day and age, it seems a strange waste of teaching time. However many pieces of papyrotamia were made for watch-papers to serve as cushions, also to prevent jarring and wear; sometimes a case would hold several. Some were cut in various open-work designs using gilt and silver paper; others were embroidered in hair, and painted in water colors. Thomas Jefferson, writing as a young man, bitterly deplored his inadvertent tearing of his watch-papers, "my cursed fingers gave them such a rent as I fear I shall never get over. I would have cried bitterly, but that I thought it beneath the dignity of a man."

The use of snuff was common among the early colonial settlers, and there was great rivalry among the early silversmiths and goldsmiths in the production of beautiful snuffboxes. Alexander Hamilton, while defending the liberty of the press in New York in 1734, had the citizenship of the city bestowed upon him by the presentation of a snuffbox in which was enclosed the parchment conferring the honor. Later, others were presented to Lafayette and Washington. Snuff is actually powdered tobacco, and to take it was one of the imperative elegances of the times. The social ritual of offering a pinch of snuff to a friend, delicately snuffing a pinch for one's self, then delicately flipping one's fingers with a flourish to scatter the brown dust was an art to practice before performing in a parlor. Snuffboxes were small, dainty affairs, but rich in decoration; every conceivable motif possible was bestowed upon the snuffbox. The true gallant always carried more than one in his coattail pockets!

One of the prettiest trinkets of the colonial times, almost a companion piece to the snuffbox, was the dainty nutmeg holder made of wrought silver or Battersea enamel, just large enough for a single nutmeg. The inside of the cover was pierced or corrugated to form a grate. With a nutmeg in a pocketholder, the "exquisite" traveler, man or woman, could be sure of a dainty-spiced wine flavored to taste. Wine was everywhere to be found, but nutmeg was a luxury so one had to have one's own!

And the recipe?

Mulled Wine

A quart of boiling hot madeira, half a pint of boiling water, six eggs beaten to a froth, all sweetened and spiced with a nutmeg.

Madam Sarah Knight, the Boston resident who rode alone and on horseback to New York in the autumn and winter of 1704, made other claims to fame. She will never be forgotten in the annals of the women of her day. She taught school in Boston when it was rare for a woman to even have an education. Two of her pupils were Benjamin Franklin and Samuel Mather. She also wrote poetry and, to assure herself of a reading public, she etched her verse with her diamond on several panes of glass in the Mansion House. She sold the estate to Peter Papillion; he and the successive owners kept Sarah's diamond etched verse intact; the house and these panes were finally demolished by fire in 1775, when Charlestown was burned by the British on June seventeenth. Eventually Sarah moved to Connecticut where she died. To her only child, Elizabeth, she bequeathed a sizeable amount of silverware, jewelry, and other property. From Elizabeth's inventory we find listed:

> A negro woman, Rose; man, Popey; Indian man, named John Nothing.
> Silver plate, amounting to £234.
> A damask table-cloth, 80s.
> Four gold rings; one silver ring; one stoned ring.
> A pair of stoned earrings; a stone drop for neck.
> A red stone for a locket; two pairs gold buttons.
> A diamond ring with five diamonds (prized at £30)

The two Hawthornes, Nathaniel and his wife, Sophia, etched their names on window panes with their diamond rings—Sophia's name and date may be seen in the Old Manse in Concord, Massachusetts, and Nathaniel diamond-pointed his in a window of his birthplace in Salem, Massachusetts.

In Europe, the rose-cut diamond in 1700 influenced a great change in jewelry. However, it was to be a long time before the colonials had any diamonds with which to dazzle their friends.

Although gold and silver were expensive, both were used and articles in both metals were custom made. The September 21/28, 1732 issue of the *Boston News-Letter* contained the advertisement of one of Boston's famous craftsmen, Jacob Hurd: "Jacob Hurd, at the southside of the Town House, Boston advertised a reward of forty shillings for the return of a string of gold beads of small size with a heart stone locket." These gold beads were high fashion in this period and the making of them was a slow process.

In her scholarly article "Daniel Rogers, Ipswich Goldsmith" (in *Essex Institute Historical Collections*), Martha Gandy Fales has delineated the work of Daniel Rogers. "By far the largest accounts were with William Homes (1742–1825) of Boston who paid Rogers cash and gold for literally dozens of strings of beads in the years from 1796–1800. No doubt the busy Boston goldsmiths were delighted to have the strings supplied by Daniel Rogers, since these

Bar pin ("safety clasp" visible top left) with dove ornamented with "sparks of diamonds" and a "spark of diamond" eye, *circa* 1830. Chased gold and black enamel brooch with popular "bar," *circa* 1810. *Photo Richard Merrill: courtesy E. S. Sawyer Collection*

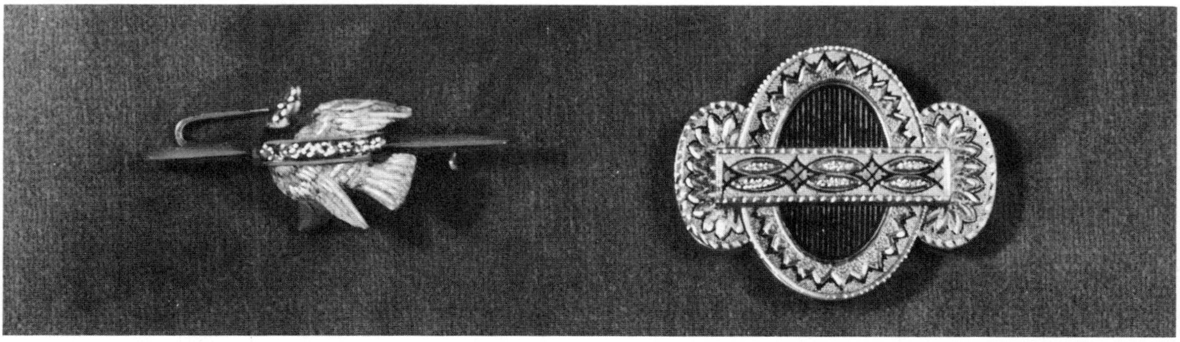

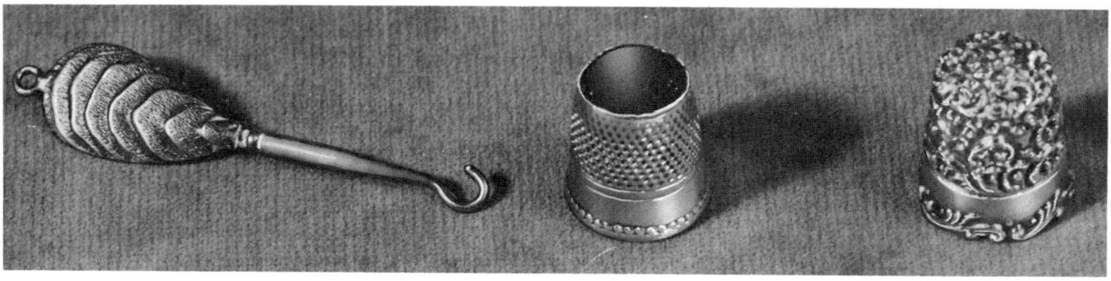

Silver glove hook, *circa* 1820; topless silver thimble, and rococo silver thimble, *circa* 1800.
Photo Richard Merrill: courtesy E. S. Sawyer Collection

little gold beads required a great deal of labor in their manufacture. A contemporary description of how they were made in two half-globes put together like two halves of a grapefruit can be found in the memorandum book of Daniel Burnap of Connecticut who described the whole process about 1779 as follows:

A RECIPE FOR MAKING GOLD BEADS.

> First, after your gold is plated down, boil it out in alum & water & then scouer it with sand. (Rule for plating: allow 9 pennyweight of gold to be made about 3 feet in length which will cut out 58 beads of a common size, which ought to be 11 inches & an half long when finished). Then cut it out & punch out the centers, and then half hollow them, and then anneal them and hollow them up, & then rub them down, and then cramp them, and then charge them, & then solder them, & then boil them out, & then file them up, & then polish them, & then anneal them, & then color them, & then boil them out in clean water, & then burnish them, and then open the holes to a suitable bigness & they are completed, which ought to weigh, when done, about 4 pennyweight 8 grains, which comes to 30 shillings (at 7s pr Dwt & 3d pr grain) and 20s for making comes to 50 shillings for a necklace.

Small wonder that Robert Evans, David Tyler, Isaac Townsend, Joseph Loring, and Samuel Minott, all Boston goldsmiths, Samuel Davis of Plymouth and Boston, and William Moulton of Newburyport, all found it feasible to have Daniel Rogers make gold beads for them.

By the middle of the 1700's all girls had an interest in jewelry and there is a sprightly description left by Anna Green Winslow, who wrote as a little girl of twelve in the year 1771. "I was dress'd in my yellow coat black bib and apron, black feathers on my head, my paste comb, all my paste, garnet, and jet pins, together with my silver plume—my locket, rings, black coller round my neck, black mitts, 2 or 3 yards of blue rubbin striped tucker & ruffels & my silk shoes compleated my dress." (She attended the Old South Church of Boston, Massachusetts.)

Commenting on woman's dress and accessories in *5000 Years of Gems and Jewelry,* Frances Rogers and Alice Beard report, "The Greek influence which during the early eighteen hundreds so greatly shaped the styles of women's clothes in Europe, crossed the sea and reached America. Our stylish great-great grandmothers —then girls of the period—outdid the Greeks. They dipped their muslin dresses in water and wrung them out before putting them on so that the dampened material would cling in classic folds. And for ornament, of course the classic cameo and intaglio were the appropriate jewels.

By 1830, fashion had flown to the opposite extreme. Full skirts and puffed sleeves made a new silhouette, but still the ladies wore their cameos."

George A. Frankovich in his monograph *The Jewelry Industry* claims that it was a chance discovery in England that shaped the future of costume jewelry in America. In his pamphlet, he wrote: "It was in 1742 that a Thomas Bolsover who had a little silversmithing shop in Syracuse Hill in Sheffield township of Yorkshire, England, had an accident that had a profound effect on modern-day jewelry. As he was working on a crack in a sterling silver knife, finding his bench vise insufficiently tight, he wedged in a copper coin next to the silver blade. While applying heat to the knife, he suddenly heard the voice of the town crier shouting the day's news. During the time his attention was diverted from his work, the silver blade fused to the copper coin. Naturally the knife was ruined, but with the loss of the knife, a great discovery was made. Being a man of imagination, Bolsover examined the silver knife with the copper coin permanently fused to it and began to experiment. When he put the knife through his hand rolls, he found that the silver and copper elongated as a single piece of metal. He had found the original process of mechanical plating."

Down through the centuries Bolsover's discovery became known as the "Old Sheffield" process. Its modern jewelry application is in the making of gold-filled and rolled gold-plate jewelry. A precious metal bonded to a base metal gives the appearance of karat gold, with many of the wearing qualities of karat gold, but at a price much closer to that of a product made entirely of base metal. Shortly after this, one John Butler in Boston announced in the *Boston News-Letter,* November 30, 1758, "Goldsmith, at the corner of Clark's ship yard, Boston, Advertised the loss by robbery of stone rings, grape gold rings, Heart and Hand rings, stone Buttons, Stone Ear-Rings set in Gold, silver buckles, neck clasps, etc.—"

Red coral classic cameo delicately carved and set elaborately in gold. Brooch and earring set, *circa* 1840. *Photo Richard Merrill: courtesy E. S. Sawyer Collection*

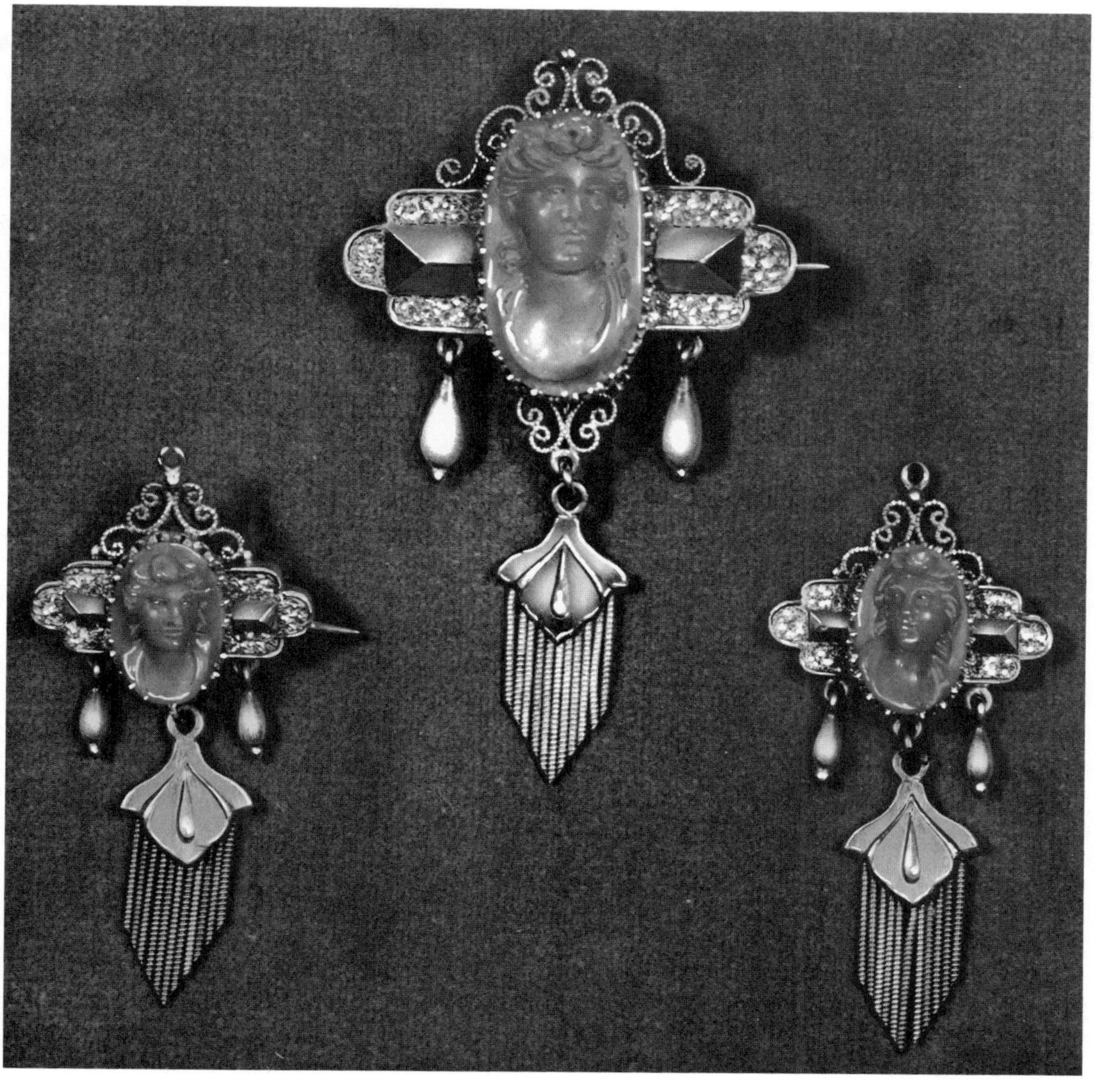

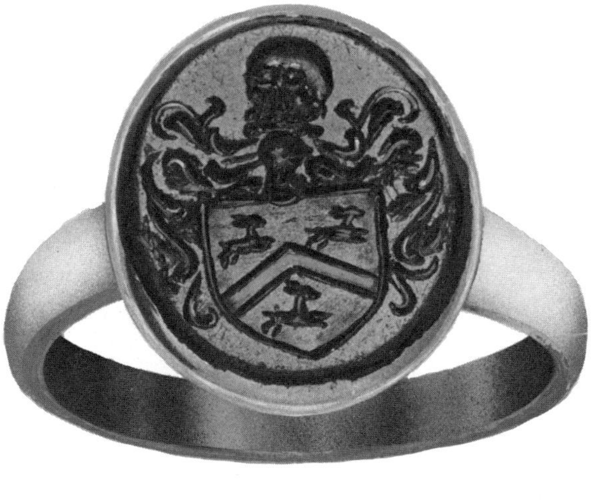

Gold ring with carnelian setting worn by Governor John Leverett (1616–1679), displaying the family coat of arms. *Photo courtesy Essex Institute*

In the 1740's one may find lists of orders for gold lockets, silver buckles for shoes and gold ones. At that time three dozen gold-wrought vest buttons cost one customer over one hundred dollars!

In *The Colonial Craftsman,* Carl Bridenbaugh declared that the work of the village artisan could not be compared with the silver or jewelry produced in the cities, either in design or craftsmanship. A clear picture of the kind of commissions which the craftsmen of colonial days undertook may be had from the account of the pieces stolen from John Jenning's shop at Norwalk, Connecticut, in 1763: "A silver cream pot, 6 large spoons, 2 or 3 dozen Tea Spoons, a great many pair of Stone Buttons, Gold Studs, Jewels and other Silver Buttons, several Pair of Silver Buckles, some with Fluke and Tongs, and some without, and sundry other Articles, to the Value of £ 100."

Shortly before the Revolution this advertisement appeared in a Boston paper (it would be difficult for a modern jeweler to match it): "Imported in the *Neptune* (Cap. Binney) and to be sold by Daniel Parker, Goldsmith. At his shop near the Golden Ball, Boston. An Assortment of Articles of the Goldsmith's and Jeweller's Way, viz. Brilliant and cypher'd Button and Earing Stones of all Sorts, Locket Stones, cypher'd Ring Stones, Garnetts, Amethysts, Topaz and Sapphire Ring Stones, neat Stone Rings sett in Gold, some with Diamond Sparks, Stone Buttons in Silver, by the card, black ditto in Silver, best Sword Blades, Shoe and Knee Chapes of all sizes."

Of all New England, Rhode Island was to lead in jewelry making from the beginning and through the present day. Several silversmiths settled in Rhode Island in the latter part of the seventeenth century, chiefly because of the increasing wealth in the colony. In those early, early days before banks were established and safe-deposit boxes were available, prosperous merchants would convert their silver coins to tankards, beakers, and other articles of silver, which were easy to identify and claim if stolen. Therefore, silversmiths were to be found in or near practically every center where wealth abounded. Providence and Newport, Rhode Island, were two such centers.

Arnold Collins of Newport, the colony's first silversmith, plied his trade in the latter part of the seventeenth century and is remembered today as the engraver of the 1690 seal for the colony. During the eighteenth century, Newport was to become familiar with several other silversmiths—Isaac Anthony, John Coddington, Benjamin Brenton, Daniel Russell, Jonathan Olis, and Samuel Vernon. The last, noted for his outstanding workmanship, was the most important of them all. Another should be mentioned who proved to be a rascal, but a beloved one. At Little Rest (now Kingston), Rhode Island, the most capable silversmith was one Samuel Casey who enjoyed considerable success for an extended period of time; but he fell upon hard times and became a counterfeiter. Alas for Samuel, he was caught, jailed, and condemned to be hanged. Luckily for him, since he had proved himself a good silversmith

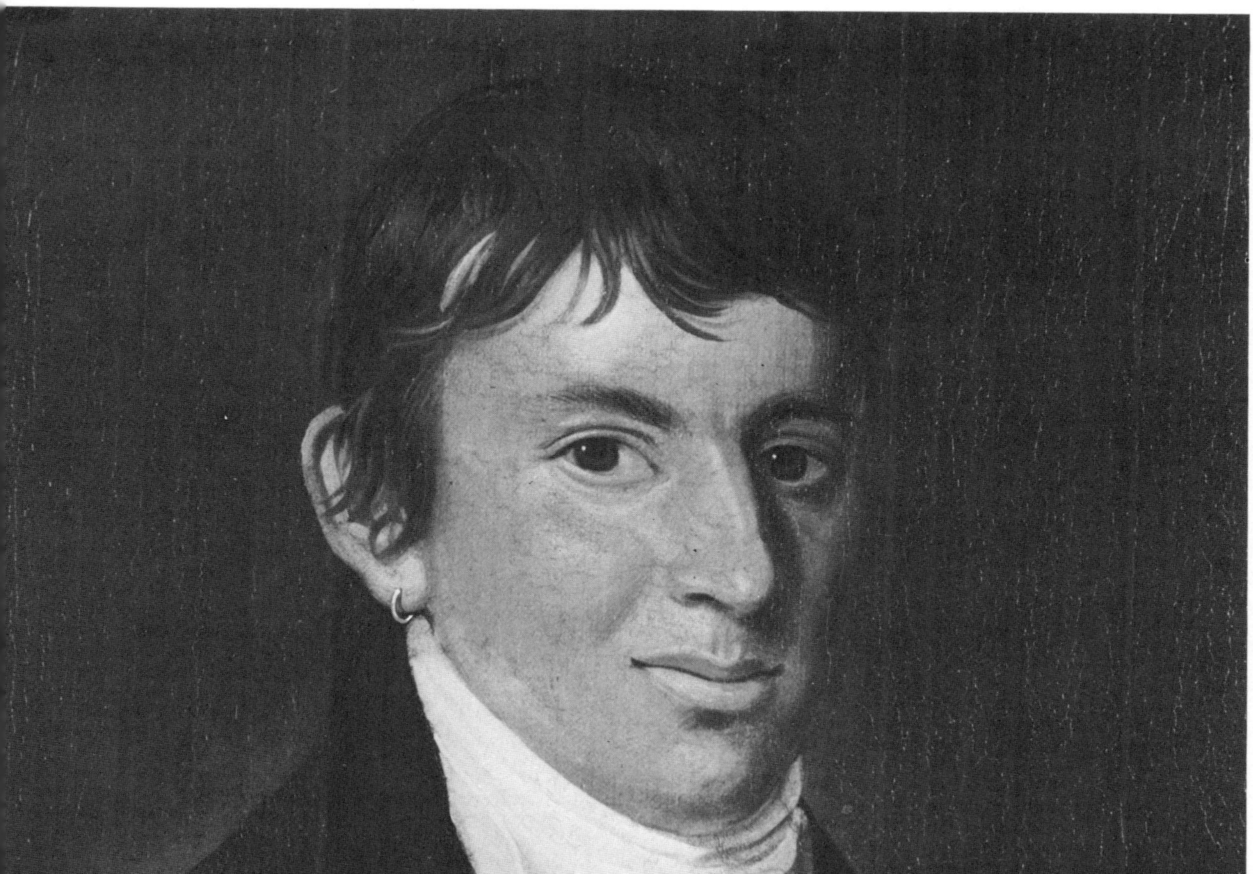

In the sixteenth century earrings were often worn by men not considered dandies. Adam Winthrop, grandfather of Governor John Winthrop, and William Shakespeare, as well as many titled Englishmen, had their ears pierced. Men who followed the sea made it common practice in the belief that pierced ears prevented and cured sore eyes. Among American sailors, in bygone days, the inference was that those who had pierced ears had seen the world and been around the Horn. The style was followed by sea captains as well. A miniature of Salem's Captain George Taylor showed him with a precious stone in his earring, while Captain William Orne (1752–1815) preferred a simple gold ring. *Photo Richard Merrill: courtesy Peabody Museum*

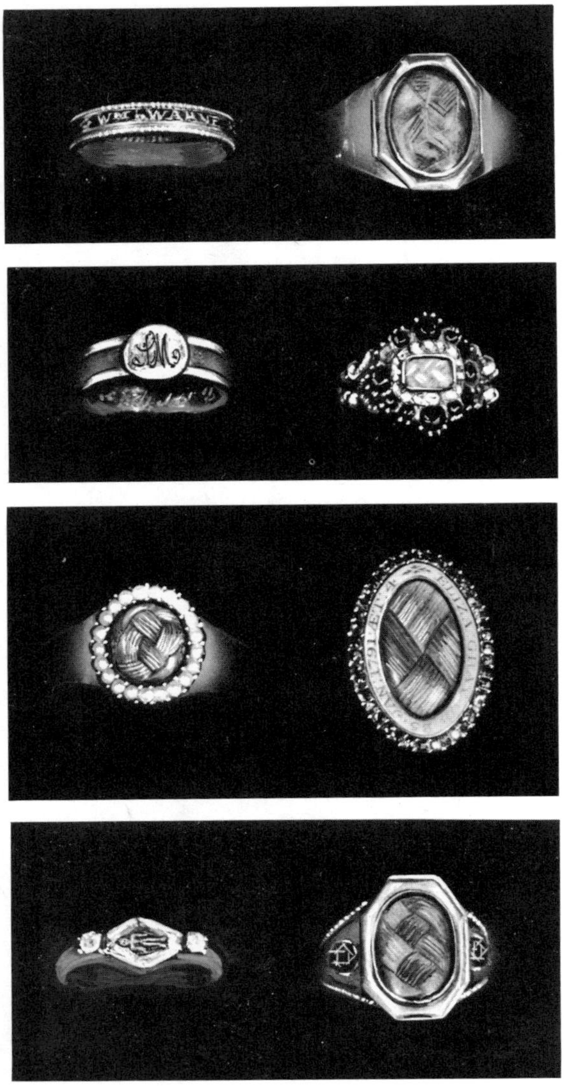

Mourning rings were often elaborately designed and set with precious stones. *Photo courtesy Essex Institute*

and a popular person as well, some of his friends not only helped him to escape from the prison itself, but provided him with a horse. The last anyone saw of him was his coat-tails as he rode away to the west, leaving neither trail nor clue behind him—only his silver remained!

There was little demand for ornamental jewelry in the colonial period; being made of solid gold or silver, it was too costly for the average colonist. After the Revolution, however, the demand increased and a number of Providence craftsmen, mainly watch- and clockmakers, made jewelry. They also produced rings, shoe buckles, and knee buckles.

Seril Dodge (1786), who attained a position of prominence, kept a shop on North Main Street, Providence, where he specialized in the production of shoe buckles. Nehemiah Dodge, his brother, opened a shop on North Main Street also; his location was near Roger Williams' spring. To Nehemiah, a goldsmith, silversmith, and watch repairer, belongs the title of founder of the costume-jewelry industry in America. Until the end of the eighteenth century all gold ornamental jewelry had been made from gold 18 karat fine. Nehemiah conceived the idea of increasing his business by using a less expensive kind of metal. He is reported to have perfected a system of washing baser metals (the prototype of the electro-gilding process) which reduced the price of jewelry to popular level. This process assured Rhode Island the lead in the production of costume jewelry and so it has remained through the years.

This "new" process also enabled the Rhode Islanders to find a fresh market in England. They shipped lockets, pencils, and pencil cases hitherto unknown in England (heretofore all American jewelry was frowned upon); thus, the colonies and the mother country exchanged ideas again, since the 1742 discovery of Thomas Bolsover had been adopted quickly here. The new trade established by Dodge prospered and by 1805 there were four firms in Providence with thirty employees. Jabez Gorham, one of Nehemiah Dodge's apprentices, became a journeyman silversmith and made silver spoons that he sold from house to house. It was he who was to establish Gorham's, the most famous of the Rhode Island silverware manufacturers. Gorham's shop was on Steeple Street in Providence where he advertised as a manufacturing jeweler. However, after 1831 he discontinued the production of jewelry and concentrated on the manufacture of silver spoons.

Attleboro, Massachusetts, is also an important jewelry-producing center. The industry traces its origin to Revolutionary days, when a soldier of Lafayette's army, now called simply "The Frenchman," opened a silver-buckle business in the area. Certain old families have preserved among their ancient treasures unusually long oval brooches with a bar extending across from end to end—the longest way to the brooch. Sometimes these were made with topaz or moonstone, garnet, marcasite, heliotropium, or paste jewels. The bar gave the effect of a tongueless buckle, or perhaps it was like a long, narrow buckle to which a brooch pin had been affixed to keep it firmly in place.

Bracelets were deemed very elegant, especially when set with miniatures or locks of hair. Of them, the poet Robert Herrick wrote:

> I saw about her spotless wrist
> Of black silk a curious twist
> Which circumvolving gently there
> Enthralled her arm as prisoner.

In the Victorian period red coral, delicately carved and mounted in gold, was extremely popular, as was purple amethyst set with pearls; amber and carnelian were wont to add their charm of color to a woman's appearance.

Mineral adornment has been a feminine passion since a day in 1444 when King Charles VII of France placed a diamond necklace around the attractive throat of Agnès Sorel. One of the "gem capitals" of the United States is Washington, D.C.; certainly, every woman is interested in the jewels which the First Lady chooses to wear. Of the thirty-six Presidents only four of the first ladies were New England born—Mrs. John Adams, Mrs. Franklin Pierce, the second Mrs. Theodore Roosevelt, and Mrs. Calvin Coolidge. Abigail Smith Adams, the wife of the second President was born in Weymouth, Massachusetts. In 1786, it was the fashion to wear cheap, imitation jewels with a gauze headdress. Mrs. Adams wore one of these, a very pretty thing, and these headdresses were worn by people of "great dignity." At the time, paste jewelry was worn by all the ladies in Washington. Paste buckles were set with imitation crystals as well as the highly polished forms of iron pyrite—"marcasite"; moss agate was also used.

Ishbel Ross in her biography of Grace Coolidge tells us that Grace Anna Goodhue Coolidge, born in Burlington, Vermont, wife of the thirtieth President, insisted that Howard Chandler Christy, while he did her portrait, should paint on to her red dress the Pi Beta Phi pin which she wore with pride. When this portrait was unveiled in the White House in April, 1924, "Mrs. Coolidge wore for this function a soft gray georgette crepe trimmed with crystal. She wore a jeweled eagle on her shoulder, a chain with a crystal pendant, a gold bracelet, and the diamond-studded arrow she had received the day before from a group of personal Pi Phi friends to take the place of the simple pin with opals that she had worn since her college days. . . . In 1927 Mrs. Coolidge gave her original pin to be attached to her gown in the Smithsonian Institution."

Interest in jewelry has not decreased and today hand-crafted jewelry in homes and small shops vies in popularity with the machine-made and with the exquisite, beautifully cut stones that come from professional jewelers. All the familiar metals are used—pewter, silver, gold, copper, aluminum, and others. Miniature, painted pintrays may command your attention, as may a pin, a carved wooden duck, a bit of beautifully molded ceramic piece in pin, earring, or pendant form. Jewelry is made from bits of beachglass, twisted wires, all kinds of material. One bit of jewelry, linked with the past, is that fashioned from Sandwich glass.

The Sandwich glass jewelry from Bourne, Massachusetts, is made of pieces of Sandwich glass which have been unearthed from the dump heap where Deming Jarves's glassworks once stood. It is significant that the singing colors of Sandwich have never been successfully reproduced. Every piece used in this new jewelry ranges from seventy-six to one hundred and thirty years old. The fragments, the result of factory breakage, reveal lovely colors—emerald green, sapphire blue, milk, canary, molasses amber, and vasa murrhina—to mention only a few. In many respects, Deming Jarves and his method of operation were in advance of his generation for he employed all who came to him, regardless of race, color, creed, sex, age, or physical disability. As a result of this policy, he obtained the aid of many men of high skill, and some of the glass produced at Sandwich has not yet been equaled for quality and beauty.

Today, there is keen interest in polished, native stones set and fashioned into pins, rings, earrings, and bracelets. Actually, New England is rich in tourmalines, garnets, quartz, some amethysts, and other semi-precious stones. Stan-

Chased gold and black enamel cuff links, *circa* 1820.
Photo Richard Merrill: courtesy E. S. Sawyer Collection

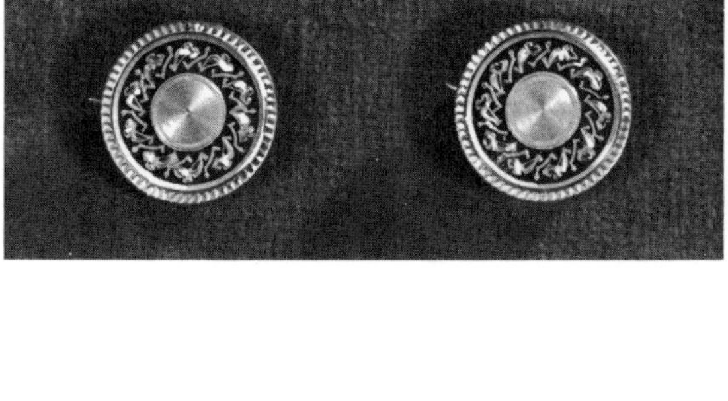

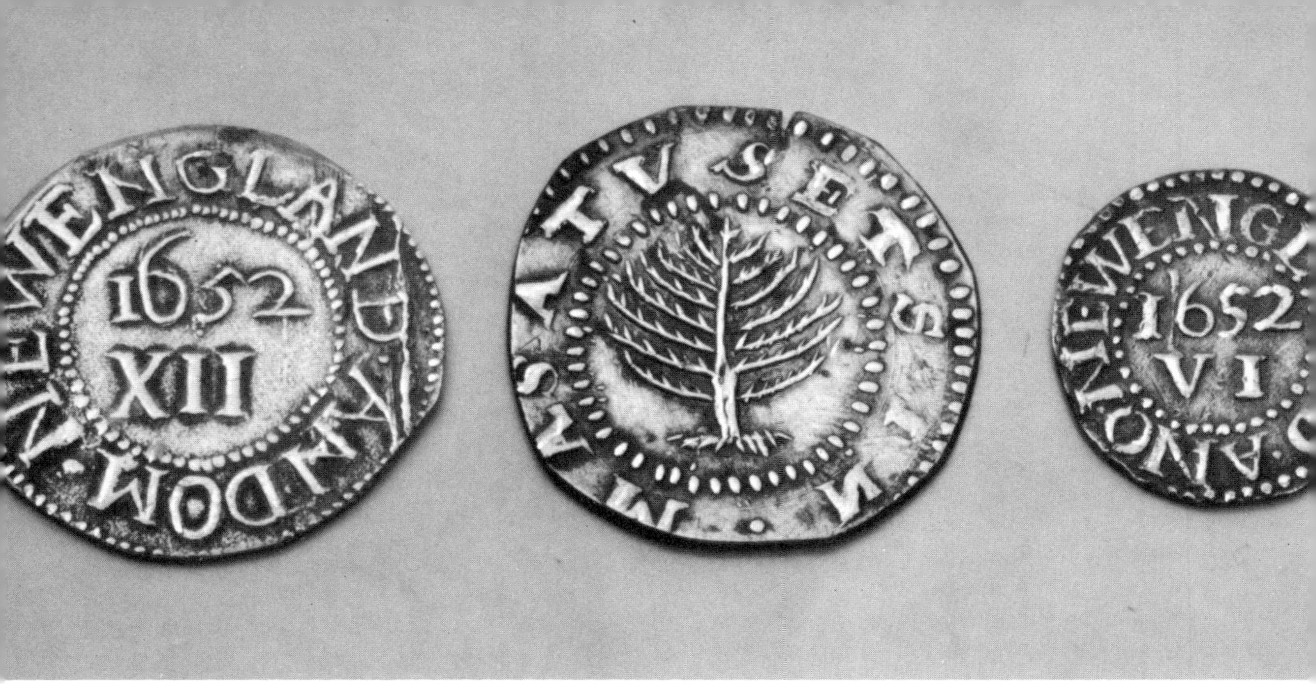

Oak-tree shilling, pine-tree shilling, and six pence minted by John Hull and Robert Sanderson. Hull, who was appointed first mint-master of Massachusetts Bay Colony in 1652, was paid for his services in the coin which he minted and gave his daughter a dowry in shillings equivalent to her weight. *Photo courtesy Henry Francis du Pont Winterthur Museum*

ley Perham's Lapidary in West Paris, Maine, specializes in native stone jewelry as does the Jewel Mill on U.S. Route 1, Rowley, Massachusetts. This mill, in its dramatic setting, is America's oldest operating waterpower mill. An unspoiled bit of early seventeenth-century engineering, it was anciently known as Rowley Mills, and is remarkable because the original dam, canal, and wasteway remain almost as they were when first laid out in 1640 for Thomas Nelson by Richard Holmes, an English millwright.

Over the years, the mill has been adapted to meet the changing needs of the times. John Preston set up the first falling stocks in America in 1643, for finishing woolen cloth. Later, Nathaniel Dummer pioneered in the milling of whole grain health flours and in packaging methods in the nineteenth century; today, the Parker family is one of the few to have perfected the modern art of gem tumbling. The great waterwheel is still used every day to grind and polish not only indigenous stones but gems from all over the world, and the steady splash of water in this unique setting is an example of New England at its best.

Not jewelry but accessories were the bead bags in the nineteenth century. An elaborate and much admired form of knitting was the making of bead bags and purses. In 1800, the accepted price for knitting one was five dollars. Considerable variety in design was shown in these bags. Some bore landscapes and figures; others were mourning designs. Exceptionally beautiful bags were knitted to match wedding gowns. Frequently, knitted purses were a gift to be given a husband or fiancé. In all these knitted bags, the beads had to be strung by a rule in advance; for an elaborate pattern of many colors, it may be seen readily that the misplacement of a single bead in the process of stringing would mar the entire design. Accordingly, they were never cheap. In one New England town, Matilda Emerson reigned as queen of bagmakers; her patterns were beyond compare: one of a Dutch scene with a windmill was the envy of all who beheld it. With Ann Green, she was a rival for the affection of the minister. Upon request from the parson's sister, Martha gave her the rules for making the wonderful bead bag. The parson's sister, determined that her brother should marry Ann, became so agitated as she knitted, that she mixed the directions up and declared to her brother that Matilda had mixed the instructions purposely. However, his busybody sister need not have stooped to this kind of deceit; her brother married neither Ann nor Matilda!

Another accessory that awaited milady was the comb. The comb-making industry in this country had its beginning in 1759, when Enoch Noyes of Newbury, Massachusetts, at the age of sixteen, began to make combs by hand from the horns of cattle. From this humble beginning, grew a sizeable industry which remained in the Noyes family for one hundred and sixty-two years. Before horns were obtainable from packing houses the early comb-maker toured the countryside in his own horse and buggy gathering up horns; steer horns were those most in demand since they made superior combs because of their size. Before the introduction of steam power, a man could make four to five dozen combs an hour. For generations, the city of Leominster, Massachusetts, has been the center of comb-making in this country. Andrew Lord of Saybrook, Connecticut, first made ivory combs in 1789. Using a handsaw, he cut out the plates and teeth of the combs, and followed with a delicate tool to shape and point the teeth—a slow and tedious process.

Fans were a necessary part of the woman's costume in the late 1800's and early 1900's. Their designs were many and beautiful and there was a real technique to using the fan properly. Edward Soper Hunt of Weymouth, Massachusetts, is credited with starting the first fan factory in America in 1867.

Art in the Graveyard

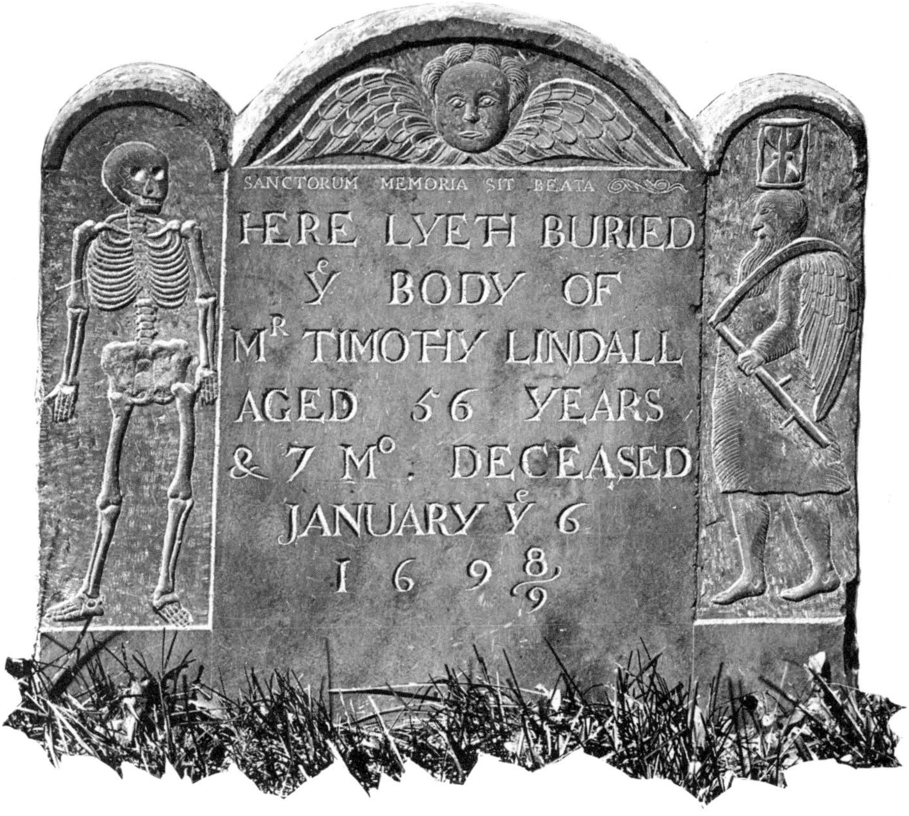

Father Time, showing the earmarks of hoary age and depicted with his symbols, the scythe and the hourglass, was obviously bent on his mission, for the lifeline of Timothy Lindall was cut on January 6, 1699. The other grim symbol, the skeleton, leaves no doubt in the mind of the passer-by of the surety of death. *Photo courtesy Essex Institute*

The hallmark of simple beauty and a quality described as "seemly" characterized not only the houses and the furniture of the Puritans but also their pewter, pottery, and what silver and brass they had. But little of their philosophy is revealed in these and other manifestations of artistic expression that remain or in the painting of the period. Rather, it is in the carvings on the gravestones, often distinctive in their simplicity and design, that we find "the most characteristic expression of the Puritan as artist. What the totem pole was to the Alaskan Indians the gravestone was to the first six generations of New Englanders." (When Harriette M. Forbes made this statement in 1927, comparatively little attention had been given to the gravestone art of New England.) Using symbolism and simple imagery, familiar at the time to both the learned and the unlettered, skilled stonecutters chiseled out varied ornamental patterns. Graphically, in one form or another, these pictorial messages conveyed the thought:

> As I am now so you shall be,
> Prepare for Death and follow me.

To those who have seldom, if ever, visited an old burying ground it may come as something of a revelation that many of these early stones are remarkable for their originality of design. Ancient patterns, mostly symbolic, which today may seem like strange flights of the imagination were typical of a truly distinctive art form practiced by local stonecutters throughout the colonies during the seventeenth and first half of the eighteenth centuries. Stonecutters were men with strong hands and each blow of the hammer against the chisel was made with sureness and deftness in delineating a skull and crossbones or Father Time; a cherub or a bunch of grapes; or even Adam and Eve standing unabashed in their nakedness. Even a casual glance reveals that many of the stones, patiently cut by hand, were executed with the broad and obvious strokes of a knowing craftsman. Some of the sculpturing reveals exceptional talent in delineation with unusually delicate tracery.

Despite neglect and the erosion of time, the gravestones "stand shoulder to shoulder, in hundreds of New England graveyards, the one unchanging record of the Puritan's reverence for death, and appropriately enough, the most lavish and original of all their artistic endeavors. The colonists used their finest skill and raised their most enduring and characteristic works of art in *memento mori*." (Mrs. Forbes who also wrote these words was one of the most dedicated researchers of Puritan lore in America. Her fascinating book was the result of several years devoted to visiting the ancient graveyards of New England. With equal zest she found time to aid her daughter, Esther Forbes, in researching her memorable novels on New England, and continued to be active into her nineties. Her distinguished work was both an art and a craft in the best sense of the terms.)

Hardly a town exists in all New England where ancient cemeteries have not only been neglected but almost forgotten completely. Down through the years there have been a few devotees of graveyard lore, who pursued their esoteric hobby with marked enthusiasm and sometimes urged better care for old graveyards —pleas which are for the most part ignored. In many instances, writers of fiction, intrigued by the age-worn inscriptions on gravestones, sometimes cryptic, often humorous and frequently poetic, have found in them inspiration for their plots. For the most part, the epitaph hunters have been concerned primarily with the idiosyncrasies of the inscriptions as to spelling, sentiment, and obvious errors and inconsistencies. But on the whole, the graveyards and their stones have gone unnoticed. Meanwhile, the passage of time has caused many of the old gravemarkers to sink and sag and nature has encrusted a goodly number with lichens, blurring both the inscriptions and the designs. Wind, weather, and vandalism have left their mark as well. Yet such stark reminders as:

> Keep death and judgment always in your eye,
> None's fit to live but who is fit to die

are still decipherable on some of the old markers.

This and other evocative epitaphs which have a familiar ring bring into sharp focus the strange exaltation of spirit with which early New Englanders greeted death. It was one of the great realities of life to them and a distinct diversion at a time when the monotonous routine of everyday living was often apparent. The grave was as familiar as the cradle, a natural wholesome reality. They looked forward with wondrous calmness to the certainty of heaven

The old burying ground at Bennington, Vermont, is noted for its gravestones showing varied examples of the stonecutter's art. *Photo courtesy Samuel Chamberlain*

and the glory and triumph that would be theirs when united with their loved ones.

No man of his time expressed the Puritan obsession with death more vividly than Thomas Smith.

> Why why should I the World be minding
> Therein a World of Evils Finding.
> Then Farewell World: Farewell thy Jarres
> thy Joies thy Toies thy Wiles thy Warrs
> Truth Sounds Retreat: I am not sorye.
> The Eternall Drawes to him my heart
> By Faith (which can thy Force Subvert)
> To Crowne me (after Grace) with Glory.
> T. S.

Strangely enough these lines were inscribed on a piece of parchment on which rested a skull, held firmly in Smith's right hand. He was a portrait painter and a sea captain as well who came to Boston about 1650. Obviously, he felt it his duty to express his philosophy in a literal manner in the self portrait which he left to posterity. Harvard College paid him four guineas for a portrait in 1680, but no evidence of it remains.

The designs and the sentiments cut on the early New England gravestones remain as mute testimony of the Puritan that "Death was the event, the condition, which brought him near to God and that unknown world, that 'life elysian' of which he constantly spoke, dreamed and thought; and he rejoiced mightily in the close approach, in that sense of touch with the spiritual world. With unaffected cheerfulness he yielded himself to his own fate, with unforced resignation he bore the loss of dearly loved ones, and with eagerness and almost affection he regarded all the gloomy attributes and surroundings of death." Alice Morse Earle, who wrote these words in 1893, knew well the convictions of her Puritan ancestors. Boston's distinguished Judge Sewall of witchcraft fame often visited his family tomb, and looked on the heart-rending sight of the coffins therein, declaring that it was an "awful yet pleasing Treat." Another Bostonian, Joseph Eliot, expressed the strange feeling "that the two days wherein he buried his wife and son were the best he ever had in the world."

A funeral big or little was an event and a spectacle not to be missed. Many came who did not even know the deceased. As Harriette Merrifield Forbes reminds us in *Gravestones of Early New England,* "There were no circuses to come to town. There was no Christmas, no May Day, no Fourth of July. A good funeral was appreciated by everyone, especially if the wealth and importance of the deceased justified not only black housings and black stockings upon the horses, but death's heads upon their foreheads and glittering armorial escutcheons upon their flanks." Funerals were costly and the tendency was to be lavish in obtaining all the proper trappings including mourning rings and embroidered gloves.

In 1690, Lady Andros, the wife of the royal governor, was buried with true splendor when she died in Boston. There were six "mourning-women" who sat in front of the pulpit, and the hearse was drawn by six black horses which wore escutcheons on their sides and death's heads on their foreheads. In addition, scutcheons (decorated shields) were placed around the room where she was laid out and hatchments were hung in front of the mansion. At the turn of the present century four of these old hatchments were known to be in existence in leading cities from Boston to Charleston, South Carolina. Similar mementos of Sir William Pepperell have been preserved to this day in the Congregational Church at Kittery Point, Maine. When Waitstill Winthrop died in 1717 the trappings for the horses alone cost twenty-two pounds—a sizeable amount for the times—and the entire burial cost amounted to approximately one-fifth of his estate. Sometimes the symbols of mourning, especially the crests bearing coats of arms, were saved as mementos and used to decorate the home of the deceased or the local church pulpit. Like the mourning gloves and rings and the verses or mourning broadsides often printed after the funeral, they served to recall the beloved departed ones.

Gloves and sometimes scarves were given to the minister and the doctor, as well as friends and servants. At the funeral of Governor Belcher's wife in Boston in 1736, more than a thousand pairs were given away. At the funeral of Andrew Faneuil, wealthy Boston merchant, the number was three thousand pairs. This family name has a royal ring in Massachusetts since Andrew left his fortune to his nephew Peter who in turn gave Boston the funds to build Faneuil Hall which James Otis, in 1763, called the Cradle of Liberty. By 1769, mourning gloves, black, white, or purple, were being made in the colonies of American materials and it was suggested that they be stamped with the Liberty

Tree or a similar device. Mourning rings made of gold and marked with the name or initials of the deceased together with his date of death and his age were also distributed to the minister and close relatives. When Dr. Samuel Buxton, a Salem minister, died in 1758, he bequeathed his heirs "a great tankard of mourning rings." It is not surprising that the General Court of Massachusetts passed an act limiting the amount spent on funerals in 1741. Again in 1788, a more rigid act was passed which practically banned all that had been "splendid in ashes, and pompous in the grave" as Sir Thomas Browne expressed it.

Dr. William Bentley, long-time minister of the East Church in Salem, Massachusetts, and noted scholar, kept a remarkable diary from 1784 until 1819 when he died. He recorded attendance at more than a hundred funerals and he was exceedingly careful to note details. Dean A. Fales, Jr., editor of the *Essex Institute Historical Collections,* described Bentley as the prize observer and recorder of funeral customs in this area in the late eighteenth and early nineteenth centuries. His observations on the woods for coffins are interesting, since other woods, in addition to the native white pine of country areas, were used in Salem.

The earliest coffin observed by Bentley was that of Sarah Crowninshield who had died in 1779. Her coffin was made of pine, locust, and mahogany and was 'all sound' even after an interment of twenty-eight years. The coffin of Richard Derby, the father of Elias Hasket Derby, was made of oak and locust in 1783. Bentley mentions that the locust grew in front

Old cemetery at Lenox, in the Berkshire Hills. *Photo courtesy Samuel Chamberlain*

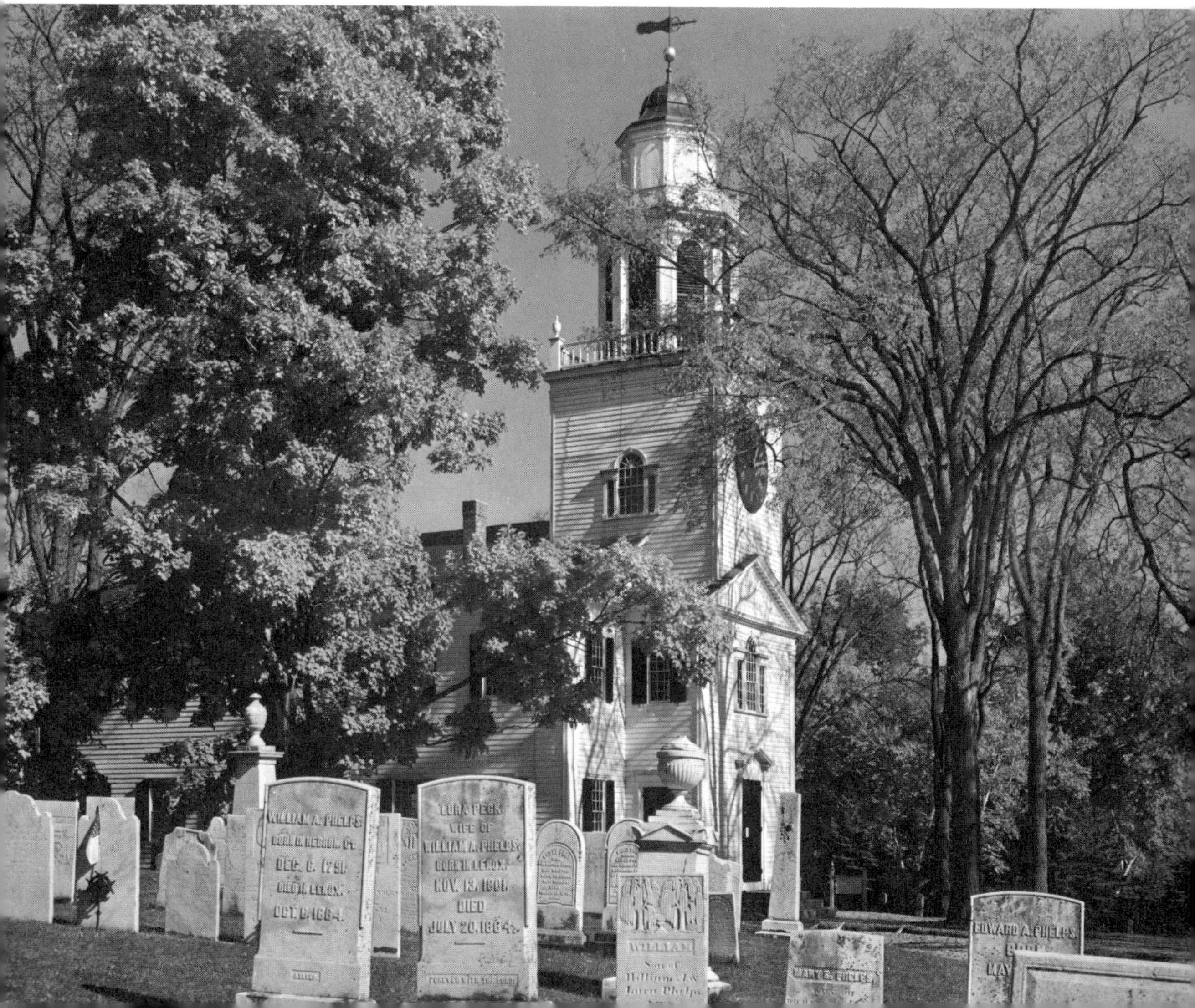

of the door of the elder Derby who had it cut down for his own coffin. Reverend James Diman's coffin, made by Mr. Ward in 1788, was mahogany, as was that of Thomas Briggs who died in 1803.

Two exceptional coffins attracted Dr. Bentley's attention. The first was at a Quaker funeral in 1798. Bentley remarked that "A White naked Coffin was among the singularities of the occasion." This refers to a plain, undraped coffin. The most amazing one, however, was that in which Dr. William Stearns was finally laid to rest in 1819:

> The superstitious fears which had accompanied a tale of a man buried alive induced Dr. Stearns to request he might not be buried immediately & the body has been kept for interment the unknown time of four days. To complete the folly of these fears against the common sense of his neighbors the children have not sealed the tomb, but ordered guards until the seventh day is over. I saw the sexton with his lanthorn, rum jug & blanket going to the place of his guard. A thing I never knew or heard of in New England before. The coffin was in the form of my first days. Not with a lid but a place cut over the face, with a shutter. The use of glass over it I do not recollect, tho not now uncommon. The Dr. has been under his screws these five days. He has a wonderful family.

Funeral customs held a strange lure for Hawthorne and as a young man he was forever roaming in old graveyards and pondering the obsession with death which his own Puritan ancestors lived by. Not the least of his observa-

Fishtown Chapel and Cemetery, Mystic, Connecticut. *Photo courtesy Mystic Seaport*

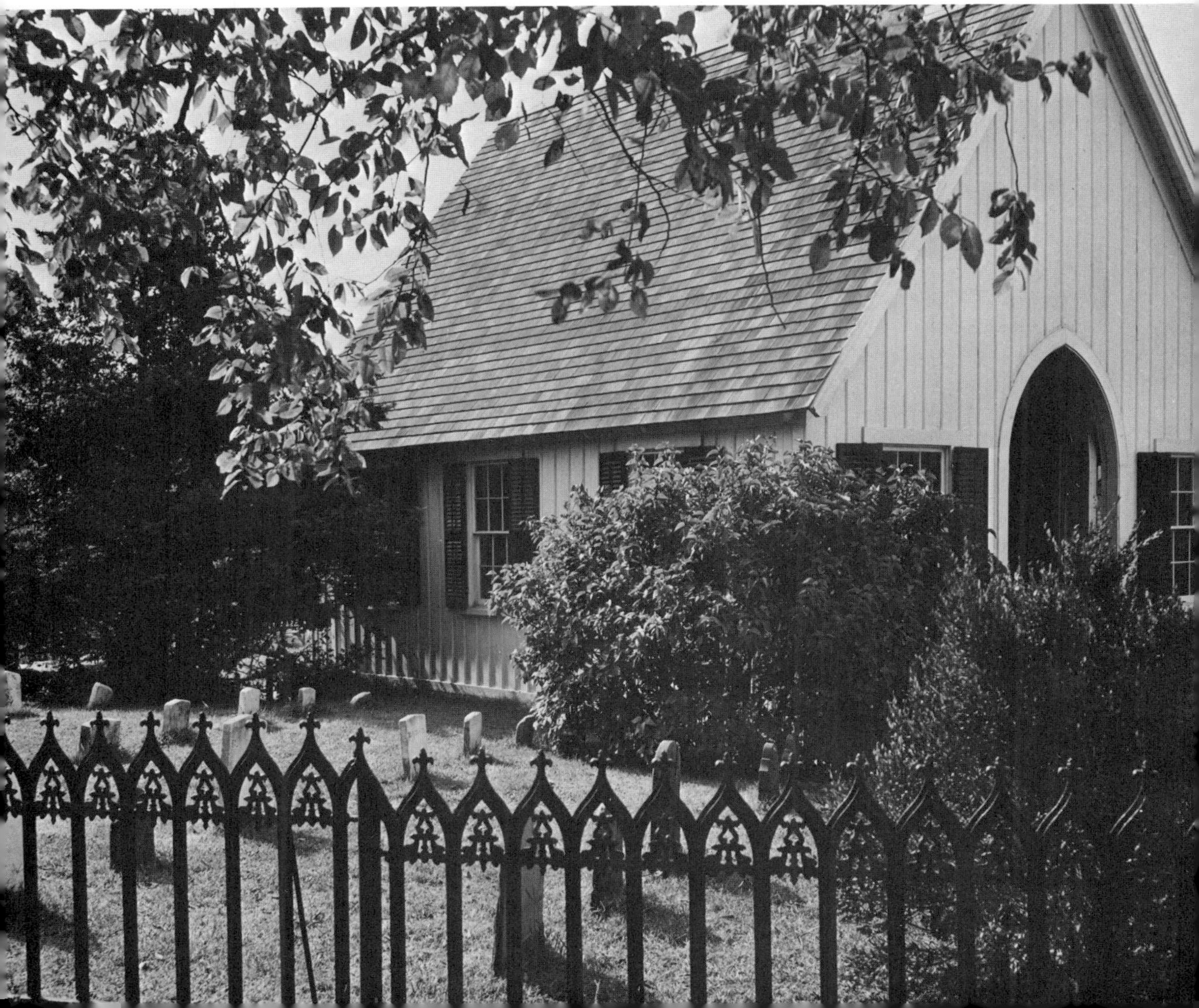

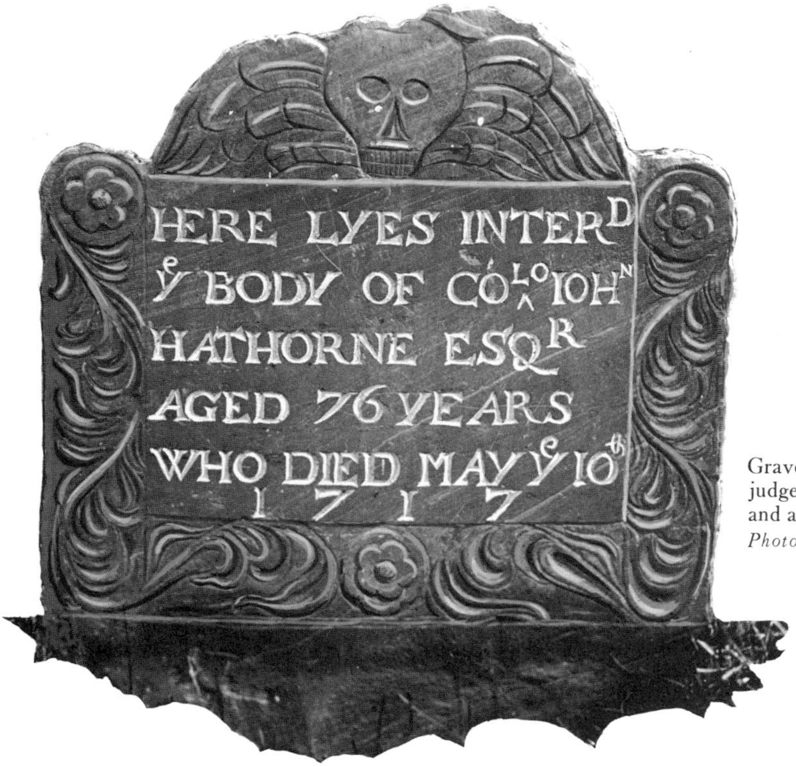

Gravestone of Colonel John Hathorne, judge at the witchcraft trials in 1692 and ancestor of Nathaniel Hawthorne.
Photo courtesy Essex Institute

tions was the following on the use of strong drink at funerals.

> They were the only class of scenes, so far as my investigation has taught me, in which our ancestors were wont to steep their tough old hearts in wine and strong drink and indulge in an outbreak of grisly jollity. Look back through all the social customs of New England in the first century of her existence and read all her traits of character, and find one occasion other than a funeral feast where jollity was sanctioned by universal practice. . . . Well, old friends! Pass on with your burden of mortality and lay it in the tomb with jolly hearts. People should be permitted to enjoy themselves in their own fashion; every man to his taste—but New England must have been a dismal abode for the man of pleasure when the only boon-companion was Death.

This was a philosophic approach indeed to a custom which often caused great concern to families in time of bereavement for practically every account book and probate record of the first century and a half in colonial times showed sizeable expenses for wine and hard liquor.

In his Diary, Dr. Bentley described a funeral among the Presbyterians in Windam, New Hampshire: "A prayer was made at the house, after which a dram of New England Rum was regularly distributed to each person of every age & of each sex, then another prayer & dram & then the funeral procession." He also referred to a funeral in the Church of England in Salem, where the singers, a Marblehead group he called "Bacchanalians," were "entertained with punch in the organ loft, which gave the true air to their music."

The "monumental sculpture" which

marked the graves of many of the "defunct worthies" of Edgartown on Martha's Vineyard greatly impressed Nathaniel Hawthorne and he wrote of it in "Chippings with a Chisel." It was his feeling that the "lugubrious emblems of mortality" cut into the old stones were "beyond colonial skill" and were probably carved in London and sent across the ocean. However, this popularly held notion seems to be without foundation since there was an abundant supply available locally and mention of stonecutters appears very early in colonial records. Kinds included flinty slate, sandstone, clay stones, greenstones or beach boulders, and others. Quarried marble appeared in the late eighteenth century. Some of the early stones were of poor quality and occasionally they were used more than once, since evidence of erasure, turning, and relettering have also been noted. Sir William Pepperell of Kittery Point, Maine, ordered from England in 1737 "a handsome marble tombstone with proper marble pillars or supporters to set it on" for his father's grave. It was engraved with the "three pineapples proper" of the family coat of arms, but this was not common practice.

That the making of gravestones was more than a matter of passing concern to the

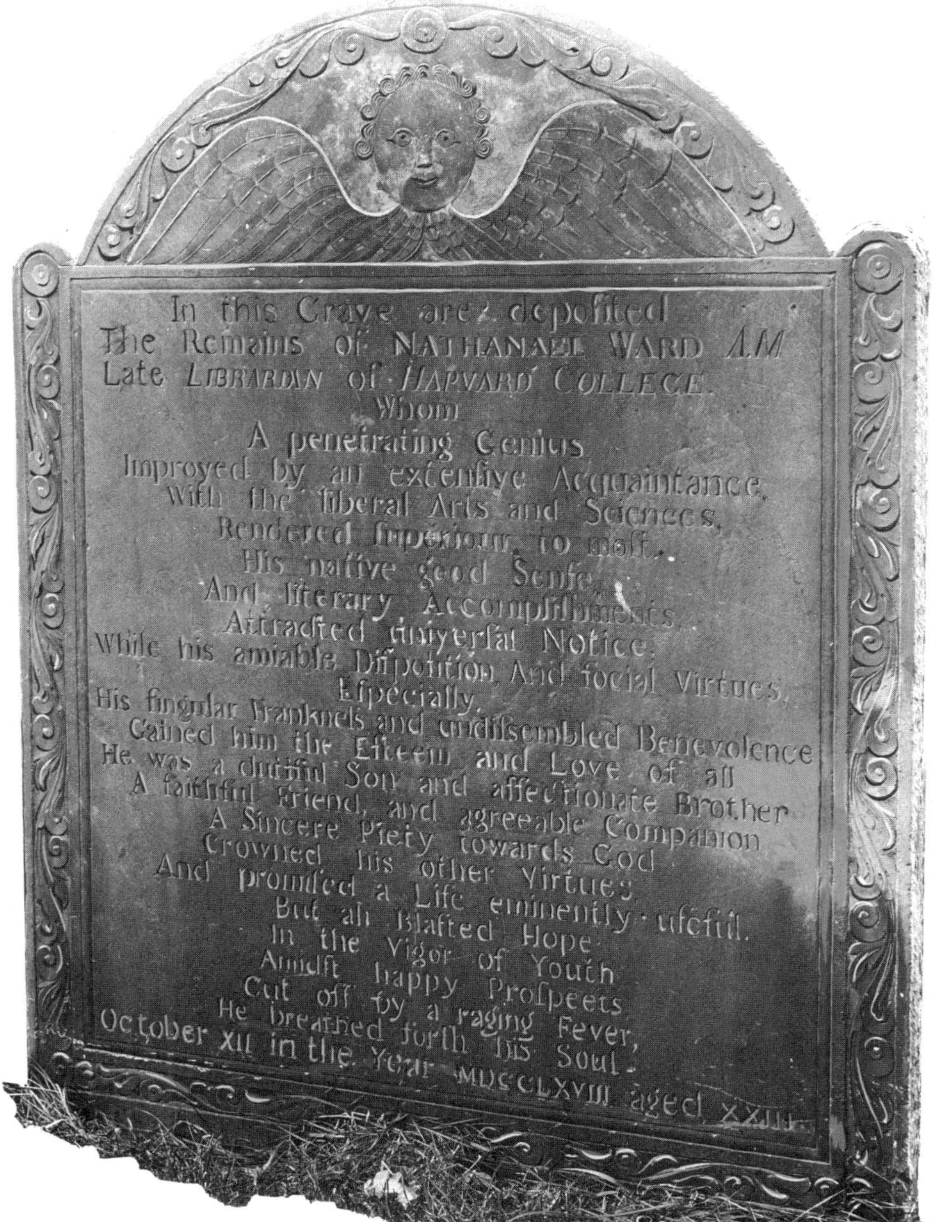

colonists is indicated by the comment of Cotton Mather referring to the epitaph of the Reverend Urian Oakes (1693): "And know, reader, that though the stones in this wilderness are already grown so witty as to speak, they never yet that I could hear of, grew so wicked as to lye." He could express this thought with conviction for it was the minister and the stonecutter working together who inspired and often wrote the epitaphs.

Stonecutters or artisans with skill in stonework were numerous in the colonies and often plied other trades as well. Some were mariners while others practiced bricklaying, masonry, cordwaining (which included making and mending shoes, saddles, leather chair seats, powder pouches, wallets, and the like), and the craft of the brazier. Often, they were farmers.

Their styles in designing like those of handwriting could be identified by the shapes of objects, the way in which the wings were drawn or hourglasses were sketched as well as the type of lettering used. Designs came from their own imaginations and the memory of stones which they had seen or worked on in the British Isles. Then too, inspiration could be had from the carved furniture of the period, the tooled leather, and the coats of arms which came from the Old World. Printers decorations were another source. In any event, the handling of the designs was usually original and seldom did a man copy the work of another.

It was common practice to visit the village graveyard and the men of the family often tarried there sometimes before church, especially if the "bury-place" was near the meeting-house as was often the case. The thought that "for aught he knew he might be next" was a form of Puritan meditation. To the educated minds of the day the passages and characters of the Bible were as familiar as those of mythology and "the two walked together in most friendly fashion." No need to be able to read to comprehend the meaning of the death's head, the coffin, the spade and the pickax, or the more consoling figure of the cherubins and the Resurrection scenes. All had hidden meanings but these symbols were very real to the Puritans. Odell Shepherd, noted Yale scholar and essayist, held the theory that the progression of the death symbols from the skull and crossbones to the winged cherubins reflected a spiritual development.

Eye appeal and a sense of fitness as well as an endeavor to interpret the epitaph and teach a lesson, albeit give a warning to those still living, were the challenges which the stonecutter met.

"Time flies and death approaches and each day brings us one step nearer the grave" was often quoted to remind all of the flight of time and the certainty of death. The occupation of the deceased, the Christian manner in which he lived, and the resurrection of his body, as well as the things that most surely would occupy him in the "elysian world" were all represented on the gravestone.

Symbols of fleeting time included the hourglass, or Father Time, an old man with flowing beard holding a scythe in one hand and an hourglass in the other. Sometimes the design included a candlestick resting on the world (the lamp of life) which the hand of death nearby was about to snuff out. Lightstands or candlestands as they were usually referred to, small tables with candlestick, candle, and snuffer resting on them, may be seen in cemeteries in and around Providence and elsewhere. The scythe used alone symbolized the passage of time.

Even the early New England tradition of the marriage trees was embodied by a Connecticut sculptor. It was an Old World custom for the bride and groom entering a new house to plant a tree on each side of the door. Many beliefs were held regarding the way the trees flourished. John and Elizabeth Norton, of Durham, planted two trees. Elizabeth died in 1751. John, left alone had the two trees carved upon her stone—hers already cut down, and his threatened by an ax which was held by the hand of death, dangling from the clouds.

The death's head was the most recurrent symbol in general use. These were anything but cheerful; usually they had not only that haunting look of horror but also wings like a griffin. Occasionally an entire skeleton was etched in the stone, holding the venomous darts of death in his hand, a reminder of tragedies caused by Indian attacks. Coffins too were depicted, usually closed, but occasionally open, showing the occupants. Nor were drawings and verses from the *New England Primer* forgotten even unto death.

Scribing a coat of arms, that most important symbol to those who were entitled to use it and often greatly desired and sought after by those who were not, provided a lucrative business for the artisans. Military trappings were also in vogue to indicate one's station in life.

Life's little ironies and inconsistencies often crept in as in the observation made by Mrs. Forbes: "On the stone of Sarah Cole, Warren, Rhode Island, 1770, there is a trim, self-satisfied young gentleman in dress uniform and wig, who without doubt was Sarah's husband, Lieutenant Isaac, who survived her. It would be quite in keeping with the self-effacement of the loving wives of that day had she chosen to have her memorial thus adorned. But, when we chance upon the stone of Deacon Josiah Cushing, Rehoboth, Massachusetts, 1787, and see represented thereupon the face of a cheerful lady smugly wearing her gold beads and locket, we decide that honors were even, at least on gravestones, in the 18th century."

The appearance of a ship on a tombstone often depicted honorable service in the navy or the resting place of a sea captain or mariner. A minister was recognized by his gown and collar bands or sometimes by the bands alone. Mrs. Tripp, of Newport, had lost her arm and the severed limb was engraved with her epitaph. Decorative borders made with the humble scallop shell were emblematic of our earthly pilgrimage. "Used by the Pilgrims for cup, spoon and dish; later it symbolized for them their crusade and was even adopted on their coat-of-armor, as an honorable and dignified device." And as Mrs. Forbes has so aptly expressed it, "It was especially appropriate for 'the honoured, ancient Thomas Faunce' as Sewall calls him, whose earthly pilgrimage covered nearly a century and who in his early days had known the real first Pilgrims of Plymouth."

Symbols of Christian life included the grapevine, emblematic of Christ, since the Church was the vineyard and its members the vines. The soul partaking of celestial food found expression in a vine with a bird perched on it, sometimes a dove which has long been the Chistian symbol of constancy and devotion. A squirrel cracking a nut meant religious meditation. There was a squirrel etched on what remains of the marker of Benjamin Hills who was laid away in the Old Granary Burying Ground in Boston in 1683 but there was no evidence of nuts. However, squirrels romped there then as now, providing no end of amusement to passers-by.

In no other city in New England can it be said, as of Boston, that it grew up around its cemeteries. Five still remain in the teeming downtown area. Among them is Old Granary on Tremont Street, laid out three centuries ago, which contains more than sixteen hundred graves. Here lie Judge Samuel Sewall, Paul Revere, the parents of Benjamin Franklin, John Hancock, three signers of the Declaration of Independence, and a host of other illustrious figures of colonial times.

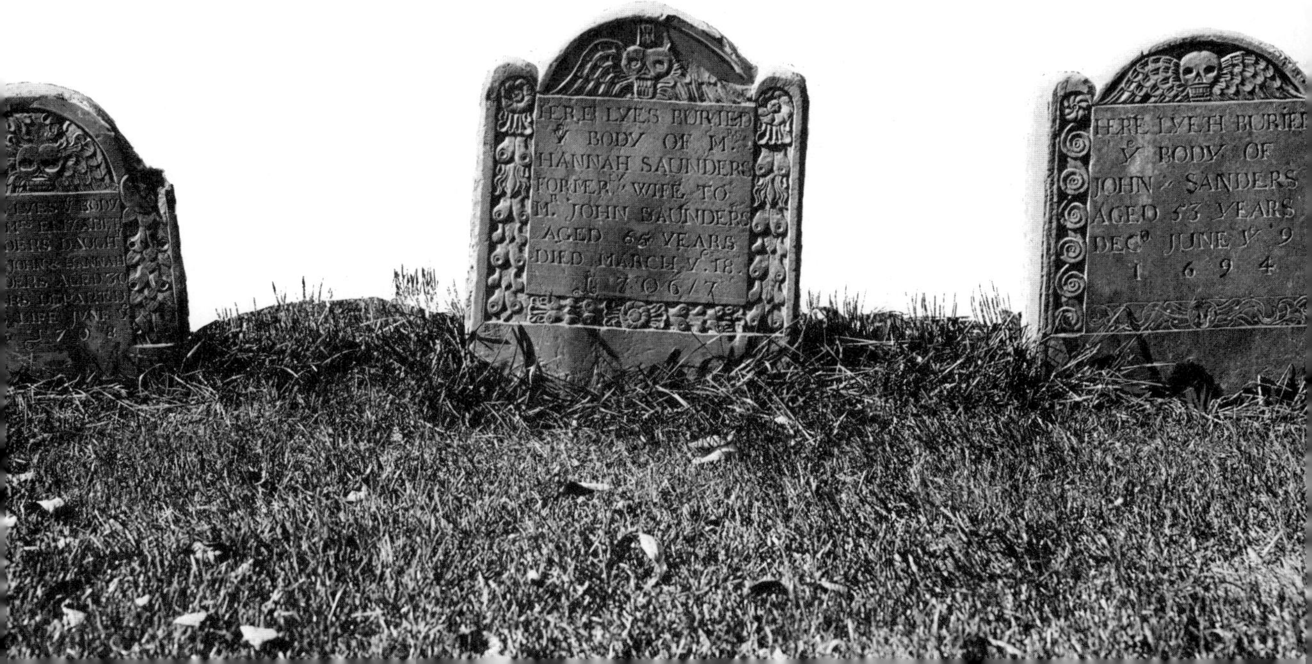

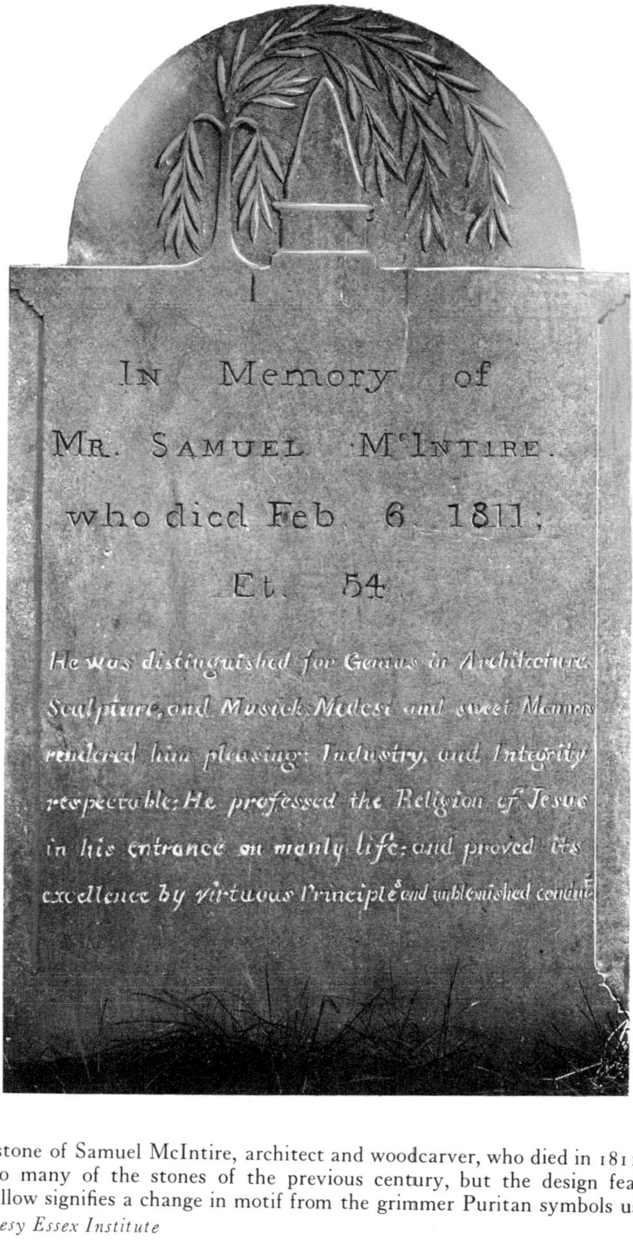

The gravestone of Samuel McIntire, architect and woodcarver, who died in 1811, is similar in shape to many of the stones of the previous century, but the design featuring the weeping willow signifies a change in motif from the grimmer Puritan symbols used earlier.
Photo courtesy Essex Institute

Mythology entered into the design of Benjamin Hills' stone as well. It belongs to a fascinating group which Mrs. Forbes called "The Urn and Mermaids." The figure of a mermaid on a Puritan gravestone is somewhat startling until one traces the symbolism in search of a spiritual meaning. As Christ was God and man, and the ancient symbol of this dual nature was the mermaid, part fish and part human, we see in this figure evidence of the fusing of Christian symbolism with that of ancient mythology. Harking back to pagan times, we find that both the mermaid and the siren were represented in the same manner. The sirens, the messengers of Proserpina, carried departed souls to Hades. Thus they were portrayed with wings, holding an urn, filled with ashes, from which the soul was separated. This was symbolic of the end of earth by Christian life, rather than of death or the resurrection. It signified man's final journey on this earth.

Pomegranates, figs, the pillars of Solomon's temple carved with pomegranates, trumpets, and the rising sun conveyed the feeling of the resurrection of the body and the activities of the soul, released from human bondage. An angel with bobbed hair trumped "Arise Ye Dead" on the stone of Thomas Nichols of Wakefield, Massachusetts, 1765. Trumpets were fairly common. Even the peacock, an ancient symbol of the incorruptibility of the flesh and the glories of heaven, appears on the stone of John Cleverly, a Quincy, Massachusetts, blacksmith, who died about 1703. The world, the sun, the moon, and the stars were used in various ways.

Henry Christian Geyer carved a most unusual stone for Susanna Jayne, wife of a Marblehead schoolmaster. The hourglass denoting the passing of time and the crossbones signifying mortality appear at the top, while the serpent with his tail in his mouth appears below. "Death with his dart is crowned with laurel, denoting victory, and he holds in his two hands the earth and the sun, the new heaven and the new earth. Under his feet are two bats signifying the evil of the world which by Death has been conquered, and in the upper corners are the winged cherubs which redeem the rather gruesome effect of the whole and indicate to us that Death as a conqueror changes us to more. happy and more innocent beings." As Mrs. Forbes points out so vividly in this description and in those that follow, the gravestones of the Puritans reveal a high degree of artistic skill and craftsmanship.

Possibly most frequently employed of all symbols of the resurrection is that of the redeemed spirit emerging from the tomb or floating through space, making heavenly music on some appropriate instrument. There is a stone in Plymouth, that of Mrs. Betsey Shaw, 1795, where there is represented the brick tomb under a tree, as there are many tombs under trees on Burial Hill. The urn at the side reminds us that the tomb had been occupied, but above it is the redeemed spirit of Betsey just unfolding her wings for its heavenly flight.

Sometimes, as on the stone of Martha Green, Harvard, 1770, we see the reëmbodied person just stepping out of her tomb, in this case with her baby in her arms. This was a favorite design of William Park, and this stone, in spite of the unfortunate condition of the noses of both the mother and the child, is interesting for its very early delineation of a willow tree which, if carved a hundred years later, we should consider an example of Japanese influence.

The stone erected to the memory of Colonel Jonas Clark, Chelmsford, 1770, has upon it a portrait of the Colonel as he looked when upon earth—a rather typical New England face, shrewd but kindly. Above this are two representations of the arisen Colonel, both resembling the portrait, but scantily clothed in garments he never knew, with wings on his shoulders, a book of heavenly tunes in one embodiment, and a wind instrument held to his lips in the other.

On other stones are represented various denizens of the heavenly world—the future companions or attendants of the departed soul. Nathaniel Phelps has depicted such spirits on the stone of Mrs. Sarah Porter of Hadley, each upholding by one hand her heavenly crown and bearing in the other the legend 'Gloria in excelsis Deo.'

Perhaps the most daring portrayal of the visions of the heavenly life is on the stone of Charles Bardin, Newport, 1773. Here we see the Lord Almightly above the clouds with his arms stretched out to receive the incoming soul—a way perhaps chosen by the sculptor to say, 'Blessed are the pure in heart, for they shall see God.'

In early colonial times, Vermont was a long way from Boston, Hartford, New Haven, and other large communities. The settlers who forged the way into the wilderness toward Canada had few resources and had to depend on their own ingenuity and imagination. Thus the work of the stonecutters of Vermont was distinctly original. The death's heads and angels which they carved on gray slate had almost human characteristics. However, in the southwestern part of the state where marble was plentiful, these tireless workers who were notably skilled became artists in their own right. Ann Parker and Avon Neal have told the story of the Vermont stonecutters in a recent issue of *Vermont Life*. Their approach to this neglected art form of early New England has been through an extraordinary collection of rubbings of gravestones which they have made. In describing the white marble stones, they wrote: "In form and content they were probably as baroque as anything ever to appear in this whole phase of early New England gravestone carving. Angels developed fancy wings and faces tended toward the round. The elaborate, free-flowing shapes of the crowns were filled in with lush fruits and flowers symbolizing the Kingdom of Heaven. The carving was intricate, perfectly designed, and struck with a sure hand."

Among the burying grounds where many of these old stones can still be seen is the one adjoining Rockingham Meetinghouse "which stands in stately splendor on the crest of a knoll overlooking a broad expanse of hillside farms and forest. In the autumn this imposing structure is serene and white in a sea of flaming colors. Soft breezes play over its rooftop and in late afternoon the sun's last rays strike irregular window panes to reflect a glory of their own. In the shadows behind the meetinghouse neat rows of slate and marble slabs march shoulder to shoulder down a gentle slope of hill. At this hour the fading light works a subtle magic. Carved images seem to peer from every stone. Crude and curious lettering deepens until whole epitaphs become softly visible. One recalls local legends in half-forgotten names, and traces genealogical data until entire family histories fit together."

Many of these stones were cut by the Wright family, father and sons, who worked together from the closing years of the eighteenth century well into the 1800's. They signed some of their stones and occasionally cut the price inconspicuously beneath the verses. Using the best of hard slate, these craftsmen produced finely cut images, so delicate that often they are not easily seen except when the light is right. These two researchers in gravestone art were strongly attracted to the tiny stone cut for the Bellows children in which "two lamb-like faces are depicted attired in lacy nightcaps and staring solemnly from twin mounds of checkered quilts as though they'd just slipped into bed."

The tree-of-life design utilized to encompass a mother and her brood of fourteen, a three-toed angel in a shepherd's robe, grapes and twining vines, and rosettes as well as fruits and flowers were used by the various craftsmen in stone. The name of Zerrubabel Collins, a native of Connecticut, is linked with the making of many of the stones in Shaftsbury. The intricacy of many of the designs and the delicate line-work testify to extraordinary skill and even the faintest line obliterated by time and age with dirt and grime reveals itself when rubbings are made.

Countless monuments to the departed have been the subjects of novels, but perhaps no other epitaph cut on a gravestone in all New England evoked more discussion in 1788 when it was erected and for more than a hundred years afterward than that of Elizabeth Whitman. Today all that remains of the historic red sandstone gravemarker that stood in the Main Street Burial Ground on the edge of South Danvers (now Peabody), Massachusetts, is a small fragment and the record of the epitaph.

"And the tears of strangers watered her grave." This pathetic sentiment, carved on the weather-beaten remnant of a century-old, red sandstone gravemarker in the old burying ground, all that remained of a much longer epitaph, was one of the few clues to a great tragedy of love, the life of Elizabeth Whitman. In 1899, claims were made that Hawthorne, who was born and lived in nearby Salem, drew the inspiration of his famous romance, *The Scarlet Letter,* from her tragic story.

Both Elizabeth Whitman and Hester Prynne, heroine of *The Scarlet Letter,* were beautiful women of extraordinary strength of character. Like Elizabeth Whitman, according to tradition, Hester Prynne sinned. Elizabeth Whitman, with her child, swiftly passed from the anguish of the harsh world, while Hester Prynne endured a living death. Both suffered the deepest pain of human hearts, unsoothed by tender care, or the consolation of dear ones, and both, with true devotion to their false lovers, kept their secrets. Elizabeth confided her mystery to the silence of that greater mystery, the grave.

Now, with the passing of more than a century the mystery of Elizabeth Whitman remains unsolved. Hawthorne ravelled the tangled skein of Hester Prynne's life, but the stern Puritans of Salem ever maintained the purity of the life of the Reverend Arthur Dimmesdale, according to the closing chapter of *The Scarlet Letter.* Thus, in New England tradition, the mystery of Hester Prynne was as impenetrable as that of Elizabeth Whitman.

That Elizabeth Whitman was born, and that she died, appear to be the sole points agreed upon by those who have attempted to describe her life during the past one hundred and fifty years in fact and fiction. The influences upon her life, her character, her loves, and her acts have been disputed by biographers. Yet, above the snarling controversies rises clear and free the fact that Elizabeth Whitman loved, whether in purity or in guilt is unknown, but with a faith so great, even as she passed into the valley of the shadow, that, for years afterward, courting couples of Peabody and nearby Salem made pilgrimages to her grave and stood there vowing to love as truly as she did who lay beneath.

The unfortunate woman was born in Hartford, Connecticut, in 1752, the eldest daughter of the Reverend Elnathan Whitman, a graduate of Yale College and minister of the Second Congregational Church in that city. She grew to be a woman of uncommon beauty, both in person and mind, and had a deep interest in poetry, as her writings show. Her heritage was closely linked with the leading families of Connecticut and Massachusetts including the Wadsworths, the Trumbulls, the Pierreponts, and Jonathan Edwards.

She was first courted by the Reverend Joseph Howe, a young man of talent and piety who was driven from his pulpit in the New South Church, Boston, by the outbreak of the Revolution. He found shelter in the home of the Reverend Mr. Whitman, and fell in love with the beautiful Elizabeth. Her parents approved and, like a dutiful daughter, Elizabeth obeyed their wishes, and accepted his love. But the young man became seriously ill and Elizabeth cared for him until he died. Actually, she did not love him with her heart, and her grief was short-lived. Howe lacked spirit. (Curiously enough, Joseph Howe lies in an unmarked grave in Connecticut while Elizabeth's grave, less than twenty miles from Boston's New South Church, became widely known all over New England and even beyond its borders.)

Shortly afterwards, Elizabeth went to visit the family of the president of Yale College, a friend of her father. While there a number of gallants sought her hand, chief among whom was the Reverend Joseph Buckminster, a tutor at the college. Elizabeth soon learned that he was given to fits of depression, but she consented to marry him to please her family. Her marriage had been especially urged because the Revolution was seriously affecting the economy, and her father's salary as a minister was suffering. However, her friends protested this match, and while she was discussing it with her cousin, Judge Pierrepont Edwards (a married man), in the arbor of her garden, Buckminster surprised her. In mad jealousy he broke the engagement, and departed to settle as pastor of a church in Portsmouth, New Hampshire.

Despite this cruel blow, Elizabeth continued to be brave and cheerful, passing the bloom of her youth in pleasant, social, and often helpful charitable activities with her friends. But the record of her maturer years is a sealed book, which several have vainly tried to transcribe. *The Coquette,* a novel which was published in thirty editions, from its appearance first in 1797 until 1866, claimed to relate the true story of Elizabeth Whitman's life. She was renamed Eliza Wharton by the novelist, Mrs. Hannah Foster, who stated that she was a cousin of the unfortunate woman, and that she came into possession of her papers. The author held up Eliza as a wanton and a coquette, but Mrs. Caroline H. Dall, âuthor of *Romance of the Association* published in 1875, who also claimed to possess papers of the unfortunate woman, declared her faithful and strong and true loving. Mrs. Dall furthermore avered that Eliza's relations with Judge Edwards were most proper and that actually she had been secretly married. She stated that Eliza, in her dying days, displayed no sense of guilt, but showed perfect trust in God's love, and insisted that her wedding ring be buried with her.

Her death saddened and discouraged her family, which had been unfortunate in money matters, and none had the courage to deny Mrs. Foster's cruel allegations, hence the marriage was never verified. However, it is significant that these statements were made by Mrs. Dall nearly a century after Elizabeth's death and twenty-five years after *The Scarlet Letter* appeared.

The historic account as recorded by Danvers historians and pieced together by Charles K. Bolton in 1912, reveals how Elizabeth reached South Danvers.

On a bright June day a woman who registered as Mrs. Walker arrived at the old Bell Tavern. She told the taverner that she would await her husband, who was coming in a few days. She wore a wedding ring and during her stay both received and posted letters to her husband, she claimed. She was gentle and graceful in all that she did, and, as she passed along the street, an old chronicler wrote "Old and young turned to look after the beautiful, strange lady." She used to sit at the south window of her chamber, apparently watching for somebody, and she wiled away the hours playing her guitar, or plying her needle, and she is said to have possessed that marvelous skill in sewing which Hawthorne attributed to Hester. She won the sympathy of the neighbors who frequented the tavern daily.

One day, Elizabeth wrote with chalk the letters "E.W." before the door, but some children at play rubbed them out. At dusk, a soldierly looking man rode by, studied the door, failed to note the erased chalk marks, and passed on. Elizabeth exclaimed, "I am undone." Soon after, she gave birth to a dead child, and within two weeks she sank to her grave of a broken heart and the news of the death of the mysterious guest at the Bell Tavern spread quickly. She was laid to rest with great tenderness by strangers in the little burying ground, on the town boundary at the Salem line. In great numbers, the townspeople who had marveled at her beauty, mourned her sad fate by accompanying the body to the grave.

Shortly after her death, an unknown person erected over her grave a sandstone tablet, bearing the following inscription:

> This humble stone, in memory of Elizabeth Wharton, is inscribed by her weeping friends, to whom she endeared herself by her uncommon tenderness and affection. Endowed with superior genius and accomplishments, she was still more endeared by her humility and benevolence. Let candor throw a veil over her frailities, for great was her charity to others. She sustained the last painful scene far from every friend, and exhibited an example of calm resignation. Her departure was on the 25th of July, A.D., 1788 in the 37th year of her age, and the tears of strangers watered her grave.

For many years afterward the tears of strangers continued to water her grave, and occasionally, so tradition says, an old man wept upon it. Visitors chipped off and took away little bits of the headstone in remembrance of her whose love was strong even in death, and in apparent desertion. More than a hundred years later, in 1899, barely six inches of the weatherbeaten stone, bearing the last few words of the inscription as quoted at the beginning, stood in the tall grass of the cemetery.

An examination of her papers threw no light on the mystery although it revealed her beautiful and strong character. One letter in particular, said to be in cipher, was published in the *Massachusetts Sentinel,* September 20, 1788:

"Must I die alone? Shall I never see you more? I know that you will come, but you will come too late. This is, I fear, my last ability. Tears fall so, I know not how to write. Why did you leave me in so much distress? But I will not reproach you. May God forgive in both what was amiss. When I go from hence I will leave you some way to find me. If I die, will you come and drop a tear on my grave?"

A fragment from her poems, written in her chamber in the Bell Tavern, also showed more character than a few words could describe. In her earlier life, she had been an intimate friend of Joel Barlow, noted Connecticut poet of the time.

> O! Thou for whose dear sake I bear,
> A doom so dreadful, so severe,
> Many happy fates thy footsteps guide,
> And o'er thy peaceful home preside.

In the long, tiresome days of the year 1849 Hawthorne paced the floor of the Salem Custom House, where he was Collector, struggling to master the inspiration for a great romance. The daily life of his colleagues had furnished him the introductory chapter, which brought down upon his head a storm of abuse from the retired shipmasters whom he pictured. At this time the tradition of Elizabeth Whitman was still burning in the public mind, and her name had not been cleared of the taint of sin.

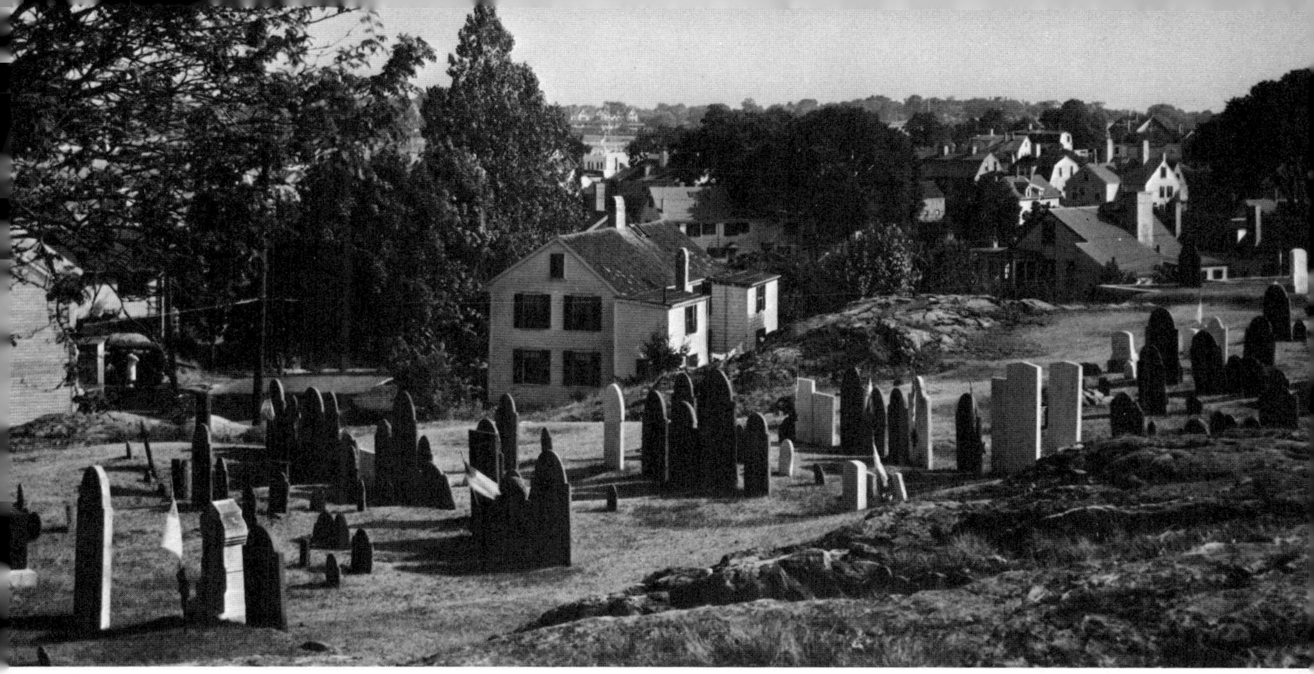

Six hundred Revolutionary soldiers lie at rest in the rocky ground on Old Burial Hill in Marblehead, Massachusetts. *Photo courtesy Samuel Chamberlain*

This was a Salem as much as a Danvers tradition, for South Danvers (renamed Peabody in 1868) adjoined Salem. Surely, Hawthorne knew this story and all its details. Throughout the nineteenth century, it was discussed at every fireside and in taverns as well, and copies of *The Coquette* were as commonplace as the Bible on the parlor table. That the great romancer seized upon the beautiful and unfortunate life, and drew it and enlarged upon it with all the strength of his mind, seems not unlikely.

He knew, as did every Salemite, of the old punishment for adultery, the wearing of the letter "A" upon the breast, for it had been several times inflicted, according to the colonial records. Indeed, he mentions the punishment in his story of "Endicott and the Red Cross." The romance, the emotions, the conflict of sentiments and facts to be found in the life of Elizabeth Whitman may have formed the basis of the romance. In the midst of writing *The Scarlet Letter* he confessed that he did not know how to end his story. Hawthorne's best works are based on traditions of his native city.

There seems to be no other character in New England tradition or history so much like Hester Prynne as was Elizabeth Whitman. If Hawthorne drew his character from tradition, consciously or unconsciously, then Hester Prynne could be no other than the unfortunate Elizabeth.

Gravestones have given way to endless lore regarding customs and traditions as they relate to families interred there and the stones that make them so intriguing. In most burial grounds, the arrangement of the stones was often haphazard, but sometimes there was a distinct pattern and a reason for it. A prominent family of long standing in the Berkshire Hills carried out many old practices when members of the family were buried and these are still followed. Horse-drawn vehicles covered with pine boughs are still used to carry the coffin to the cemetery. The graves in the lot are so arranged that all direct descendents are buried clockwise in a circle with their feet facing the grave of the patriarch of the family so that when the appointed day comes all will rise together, facing their original ancestor and ascend to meet their Maker. Tradition dies hard in New England.

Today, the harshness and starkness associated with death are not evident in the old burying grounds of old New England. It has been said that the Puritans lived so intimately and amicably in the presence of the Black Angel, that they gave "the Devil his due" as the old expression goes. Thus, like St. Francis, they could look upon him as "my brother—the death of the body."

What remains of the sagging gravestones in old New England burying grounds is often surrounded by fields of daisies and clover which lend color and life to these hallowed spots of eternal repose. Since the certainty and the glory which the future held was foretold in these *memento mori,* how else can one say Amen?

Amusements for the Children

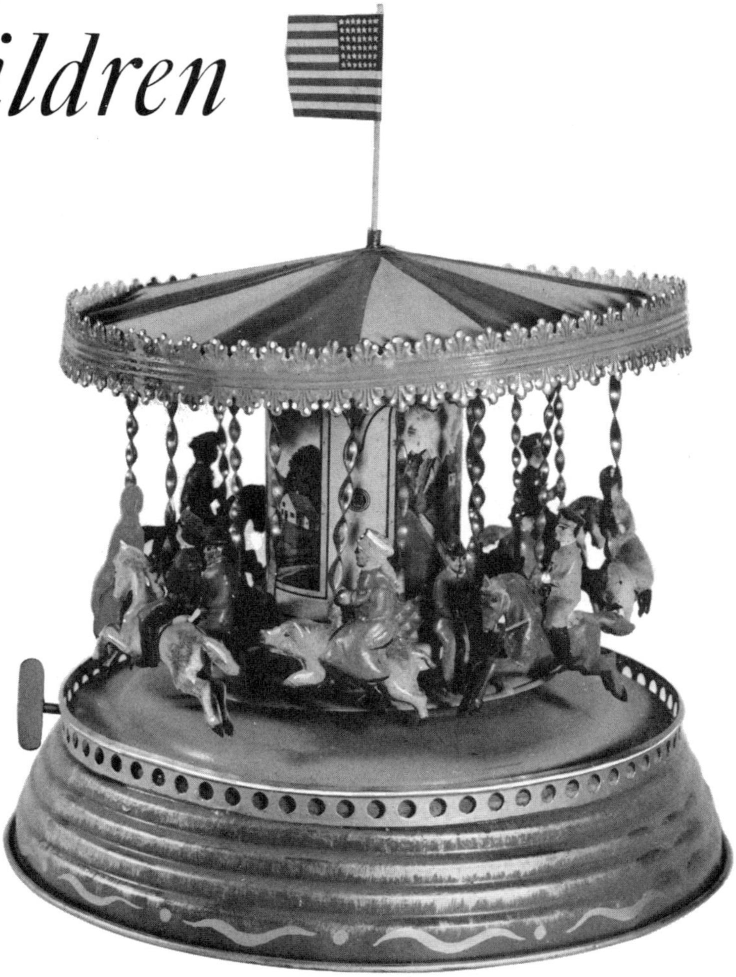

A carrousel, possibly of European origin, which inspired the making of innumerable mechanical toys in the United States from 1880 to 1920. This toy brings to mind the carrousels or "flying horses" and the spirited music of the steam pianos which were so vital a part of summer picnics at amusement parks from the Gay Nineties on. *Photo courtesy Richard Merrill*

Toys tell the story of civilization in miniature, since practically every major scientific discovery, every important historic event, and every whim of fancy in the world of fashion is chronicled in the realm of toys. Craftsmen on every level have always delighted in making toy models of the objects of their own skill for children. Usually these were executed to scale and often reveal an amazing perfection of detail. Even the crudest of wooden toys reveal the characteristic marks of the maker. The same is true of early pottery, glass, and tinware. Many items of so-called children's furniture and doll furniture were actually peddler's or drummer's samples carried about on the salesman's back or in his wagon to obtain orders for cabinetmakers and joiners. Chairs, tables, chests, even miniature highboys and settees were among the pieces made and used in this manner.

Many treasures from the shops of the tinsmiths remain to delight present-day collectors. All of these miniatures tell a vivid story of the development of folk art and the achievements of the various crafts in New England. In an era when space in most homes is at a premium, collecting of miniatures has special appeal. Then, too, many of these items are more than merely decorative.

A toy paved the way to friendship with the Indians on this continent nearly four hundred years ago. Several elaborately dressed dolls were among the first gifts distributed to the Indians by the English colonists who arrived at Roanoke Island, off the coast of North Carolina, in 1585. An expedition sent by that intrepid adventurer, Sir Walter Raleigh, was led by Sir Richard Grenville for the purpose of claiming some of the New World for England. It had been nearly a hundred years since Columbus's visit, and both Spain and France were already laying their claims to the untamed wilderness. Thomas Hariot, the chronicler of the expedition, recorded, "Wee offered them our wares, as glasses, knives, babies, and other trifles, which wee thought they delighted in. Soe they stood still, and percevinge our Good will and courtesie came fawning uppon us, and bade us welcome."

The gift of a toy was bound to create a common bond of friendship, especially a doll, for no other toy says so much by its appearance. When offered as a gift, it conveys a feeling warmer than words, particularly when language is a barrier. What matter the strange and fancy costume—it was a doll. All the Indian tribes of North America were familiar with dolls since they made them for their children. Like the early types found elsewhere in the world, they were made of whatever materials could be obtained easily. Wood, leather, and corn husks were typical, and beads, in bright colors, feathers, and various homemade trinkets were used to make them pretty.

The corn-husk doll is often referred to as having originated with the North American Indian, but it was also a favorite toy in various parts of Europe in the fifteenth century and much earlier. Actually, it is a remnant of the ancient harvest festivals held throughout the Old World. When the harvest was brought into the barns, the last sheaves gathered were fashioned into a variety of curious objects called corn dollies. The custom is still observed in Devonshire, Cornwall, and elsewhere in rural England. Both the husks and the cobs from the Indian corn, planted by the early settlers, furnished the materials to make dolls. With a little ingenuity and paint, considerable variety can be achieved in costumes. Farm women in the southern mountains continue to make corn-husk dolls which are sold at modest prices in arts-and-crafts shops. Many of them to be seen in New England museums and in private collections have remained in good condition for a century or more.

In the time of Queen Elizabeth I, dolls were called Flanders' babies, or Bartholomew babies, since many of them were made in Holland and shipped to England, where they were sold at fairs, especially the Bartholomew Fair. These "babies" were usually made of wood and, even in the time of Good Queen Bess, had movable arms and legs. Dress was typical of women's costumes of the period, elaborate in its tailoring, complete with ruff and fancy hat, cap or bonnet. A drawing of an Indian squaw and her child, made at the time of the Roanoke Island expedition by John White, shows an Indian squaw carrying a water jug made of a gourd, while her child hugs a smartly dressed Elizabethan doll, which is all the more conspicuous because both mother and child are clad in scanty garments. The attempt to establish an English community failed, but the records and drawings tell us the Indians enjoyed many kinds of sports, including their own kind of ball game.

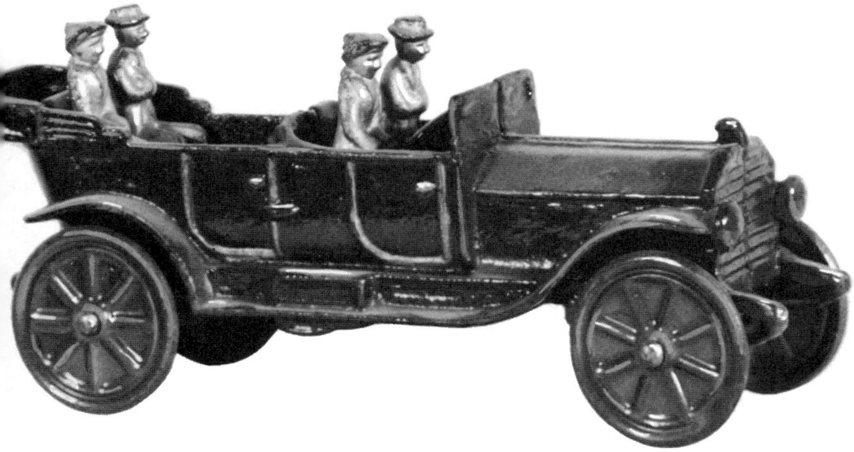

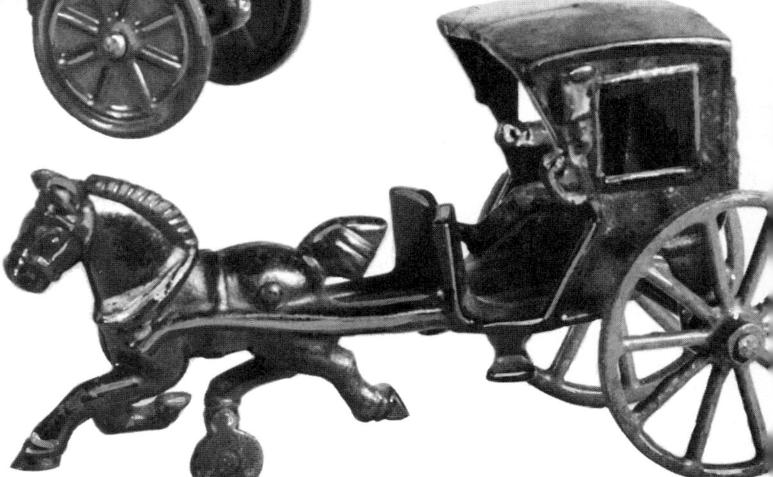

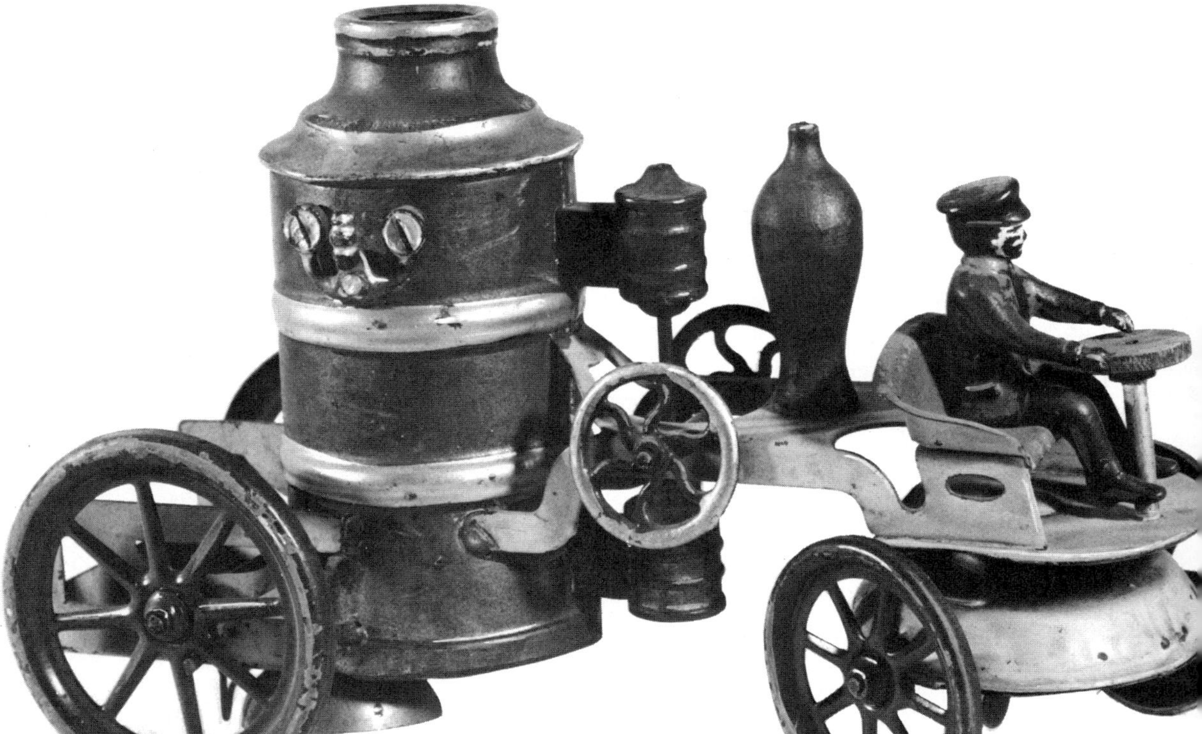

The children who came to Plymouth and the Puritans who arrived at Salem were not without their favorite dolls and other trinkets of childhood. Despite the hardships endured and the severity of the regulations which were strictly enforced to prevent indolence, some toys were provided, mostly of homemade origin. The daybook of George Corwin of Salem reveals that a farmer came to his shop in 1651 and bought "sugar for the goodwife, and for the children a doll (probably made of wood or rags) and a bird whistle." The letters and journals of the period were so much concerned with the more pressing needs of life in the wilderness, that it is easy to understand why such items as toys might have escaped mention.

Simple toys and dolls were favorites with the Indian children. Both parents and children used bits of wood and bones to carve toy animals. Nuts, shells, yarn, hollow-stemmed twigs, acorns, gourds, cones from various evergreens, and bits of leather were the beginnings for trinkets of all kinds, whistles, dolls, balls, and other toys. The pits or seeds of fruits, colored black on one side and white on the other, served as dice. Ideas for adapting these toys to their own uses were soon picked up by the children of the colonies and their parents.

Dolls made from dried apples with the most extraordinary faces imaginable belong to the craft tradition of early New England and this skill is still practiced. The art can be traced back five hundred years or more to the Iroquois Indians who lived in the eastern part of the United States and Canada. Apple carving is patterned after the faces made for the Iroquois spirit doll "Loose Feet." As apples become wizened in drying, the effect of wrinkled age that results gives to these faces that expression of wisdom, contentment, and happiness acquired only with age. Sandy and Paul Banse of Craftsbury, Vermont, have become specialists in this ancient craft, dressing their dolls in the costumes of Vermonters of the early 1800's.

Cat's cradle, that fascinating game played with string or yarn, which has been a favorite of primitive tribes in various parts of the world, was a common leisure-time activity of the women and children of all the Indian tribes. It was well known to the English settlers. Many kinds of string figures, in a wide variety of patterns, are possible, once the art has been mastered. When toys were lacking or some new form of amusement was sought, here was a game which two could enjoy to their heart's content. Scientists have observed this game being played by primitive people all over the world. Many detailed accounts have been written, including a four-hundred-page volume entitled *String Figures* by Caroline F. Jayne.

For an intimate picture of the homemade toys used by children, we may well consider those which are still being made by the crafters of the Southern Highlands. A piece of wood, a jackknife and a little skill were all that was required. Naturally, few or practically none of the early examples remain, for they were meant to be used, enjoyed, and discarded. Popguns made from twigs of the elderberry bush, whistles from chestnut wood, windmills, water wheels, and various kinds of traps for catching animals were typical of jackknife production. Doll's furniture from birch bark and wicker cradles and "chaises," or carriages, similar to those used for babies, delighted the girls. Some of these are sold in the country stores at Sturbridge Village, the Shelburne Museum, Mystic Seaport, and other restorations.

The "play pretties" of the Southern Highlands, which include the mountain areas of Maryland, the Virginias, the Carolinas, Georgia, Kentucky, Tennessee, and Alabama, include a variety of handmade toys whose origin can be traced back several hundred years, to England and other parts of Europe. They were known by curious names such as the gee-haw whimmy-diddle. The mechanics of this toy are simple, but why it works as it does has been a puzzler,

(*Above*) An endless variety of children's toys made from cast iron were produced in Connecticut in the era between the Civil War and World War I. They are believed to have been made either by Jerome B. Secor Co., of Bridgeport, Connecticut, or by J. & E. Stevens Co., Cromwell, Connecticut. *Photo Richard Merrill: collection of Richard Merrill*

(*Left*) A representation of a horse-drawn steam pumper of 1900 which was "motorized" about 1915 with the use of a Christy front-wheel-drive engine. Manufactured by the Wilkins-Kingsbury Mfg., Keene, New Hampshire. *Photo courtesy Richard Merrill* even to scientists. By rubbing two sticks together, the propeller on the end of one will turn, but its direction can be controlled. Another is the fly killer, made of mountain elder with a piece of split hickory used for a spring. This toy hurls a wooden peg powerfully and accurately for about twenty yards.

The howler, a type of bull roarer, is a gadget the boys, down through the centuries, have found made people sit up and take notice. Made from a long, narrow piece of thin wood with string or rope attached to one end, it makes a roaring sound when hurled about in the air. This ancient noisemaker is known to both primitive and civilized people around the world. It was used for religious purposes in ancient Greek ceremonies, to round up the cattle at milking time in Europe, as a rain charm in South Africa, and as a noisy symbol in the snake dances of the Indian tribes of Arizona. Other names for this noisemaker are hummer, buzz, bummer or buzzer, swish, thunder-spell, and thunderbolt. Sometimes the bull roarer is notched with tooth-like edges and may have a small hole in the end opposite to the point, where the string is attached.

Another favorite among the southern mountaineers is the flipper-dinger, made of river cane, rhododendron stalk, pith from a corncob, and a piece of wire. Air blown through the horizontal cane forces the light pith ball off its launching pad toward the ring at the end of the twisted wire. A good flipper-dinger operator can catch the pith ball on the wire ring. The resemblance between the rattle trap—another noisemaking toy—and many of similar design which are especially popular at Halloween is easily apparent.

Toy weapons were also fashioned with the jackknife. Clubs, slingshots, air guns, as well as bows and arrows, were the common kinds made. As early as 1645 the Court of Massachusetts ordered that all boys from ten to sixteen should be taught how to use the bow and arrow.

The mere mention of a jackknife brings to mind the fact that the term means a boy's knife. It was the aim of every growing boy to own a knife with a sharp blade of the best steel, for with it he could make all kinds of gadgets,

This Connecticut-made toy engine (1860–1880) of soldered tin and wood is a fairly accurate model of the type of railroad engine used in Civil War days. *Photo courtesy Richard Merrill*

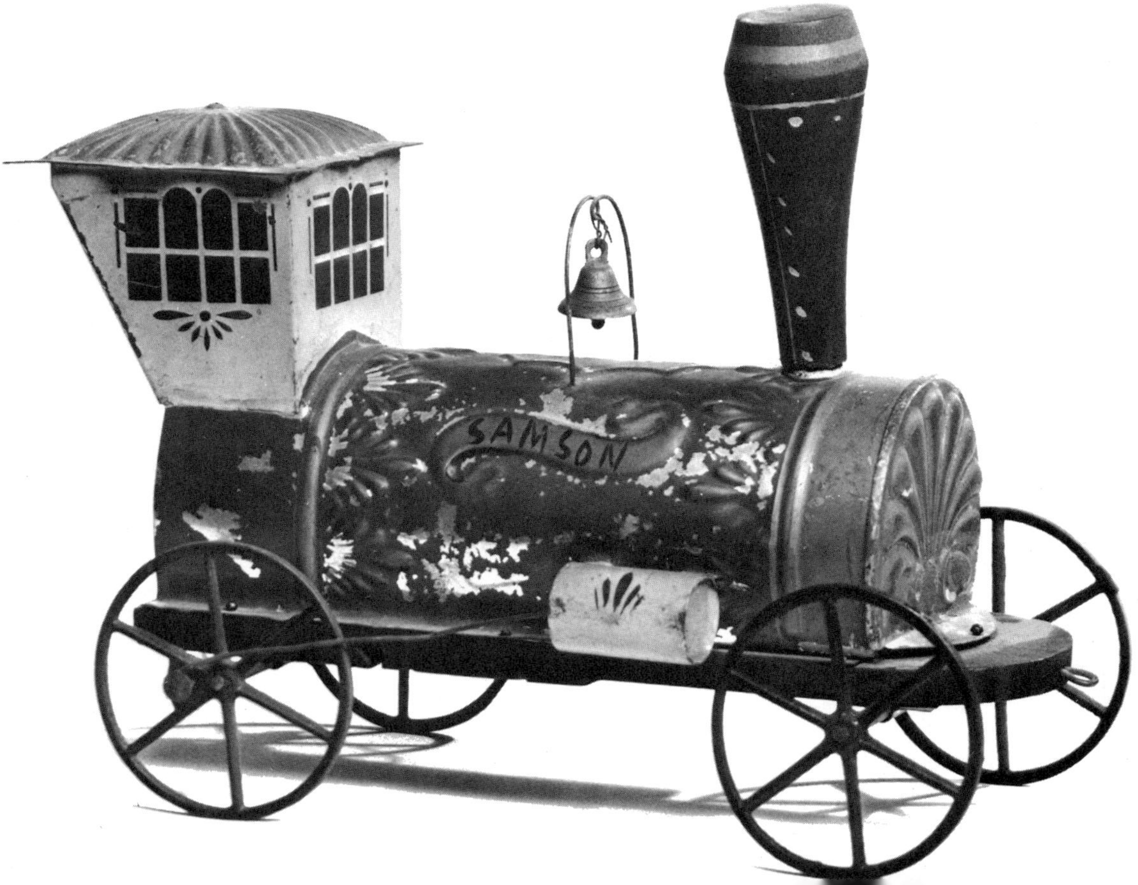

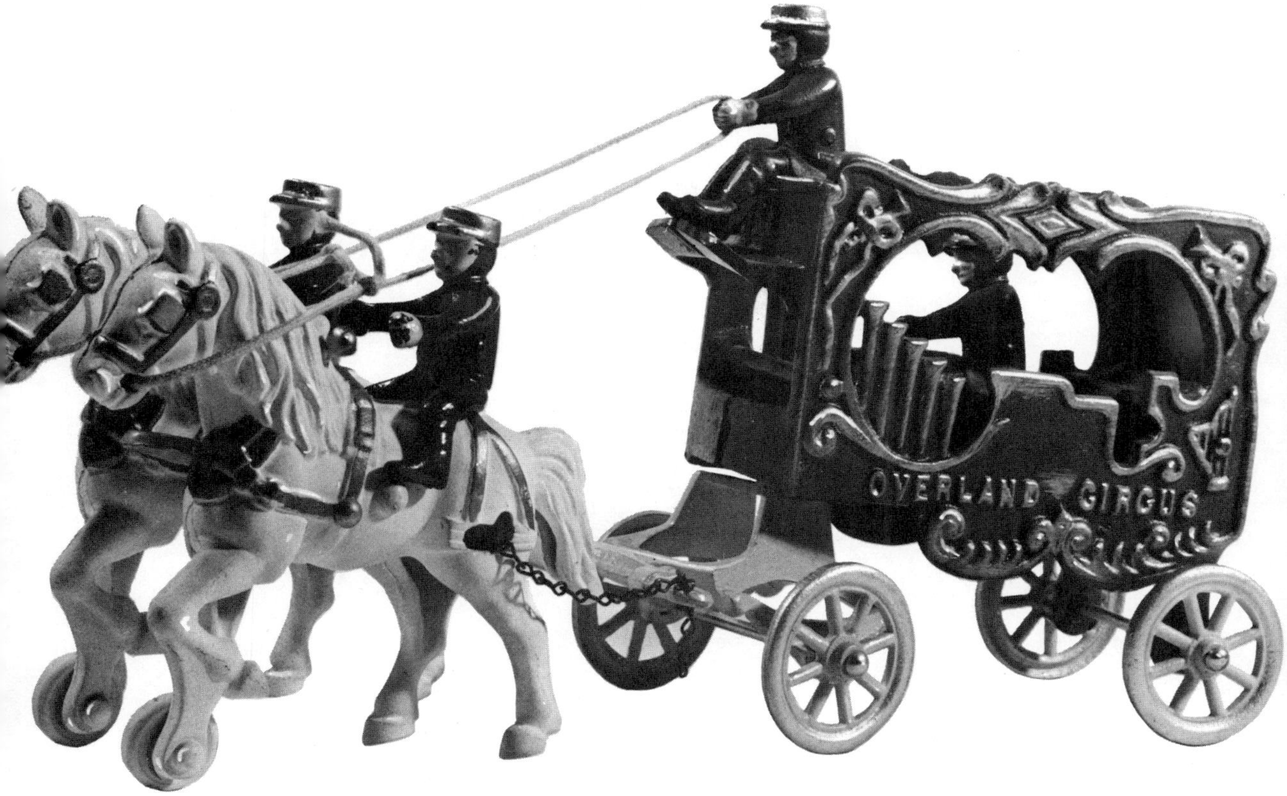

The famous Overland Circus consisting of a bandwagon, other wagons filled with various animals, and a calliope, was a prime favorite among New England children circa 1880–1925. *Photo courtesy Richard Merrill*

as well as necessary implements for household use. Perhaps not a toy, but it was the implement with which he made many of his own toys and those for younger brothers and sisters. The best ones were Barlow knives, made in England.

There was little in the way of waste material around any farm that did not produce the makings for toys. Corncobs, like corn husks, were stuff for a doll and, fastened together, they could be shaped into a fort or a cabin, while the kernels could be used in games. Even the feet of turkeys and chickens held a fascination for children when there was little else to amuse them. Colorful rocks and shells could be had for the collecting. An amusing doll could be made from the wishbone of a turkey or chicken, or, when dried, it served as a bit of amusement to see who could get the larger piece when it was pulled apart.

Dandelions and buttercups, daisies and milkweed, hollyhocks and roses, and many another flower have been transformed into the most fanciful of toys whenever children have been so minded. The flower lore of childhood is a traditional form of play, so old and so deeply entwined in the folklife of many races that origins are not easy to trace. Nor are they important. The joy they provide is brief at best, but this does not concern children.

The flowers, the fluffy seeds, and the curly stems of the dandelion are the makings of toys galore. The golden blossoms, like those of the buttercup, tell of a child's liking for butter when held under the chin. "What time is it?" or "Does my mother want me?" can always be determined easily by blowing the right way on a head of dandelion fluff. Best of all, the stems make wonderful curls or chains of beads, good enough for any little woodland queen. Another kind of chain, made with daisies, is as old as the hills, and so too is the practice of picking petals off the daisies.

Milkweed pods made tiny cradles and many other fanciful toys, while the silk within them could be used to make the softest pillows imaginable for a doll. Acorns or chestnuts, hollowed out, were transformed into pipes when attached to a hollow stem cut from a nearby shrub. Filled with the dried leaves of sweet fern, there was no need for tobacco to enjoy a smoke.

Toys that packed a wallop as noisemakers included trombones made from the

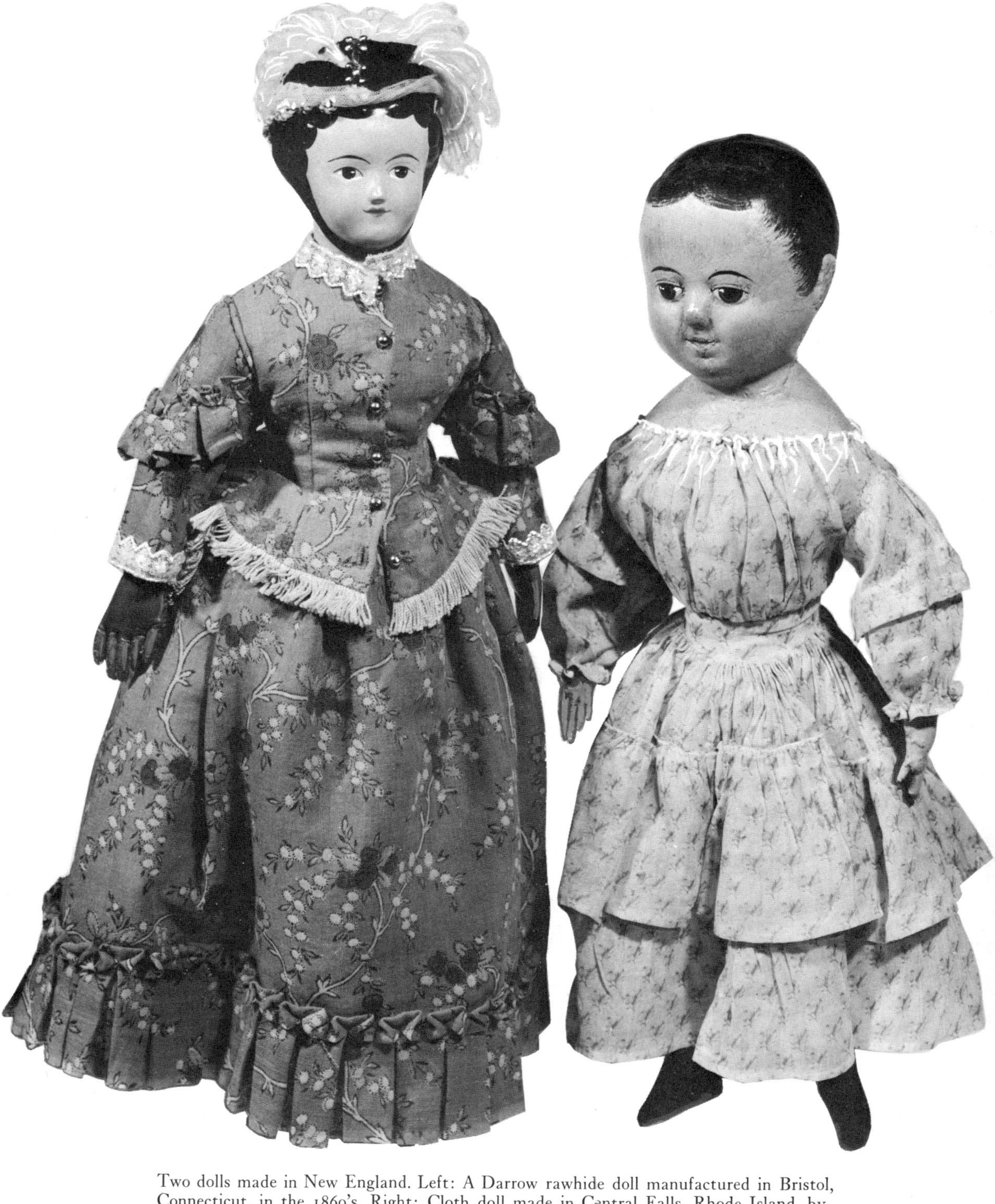

Two dolls made in New England. Left: A Darrow rawhide doll manufactured in Bristol, Connecticut, in the 1860's. Right: Cloth doll made in Central Falls, Rhode Island, by Izannah F. Walker, patented June 28, 1873. *Photo Richard Merrill: collection of Madeline Merrill*

spiny leafstocks of pumpkins and squashes. A whistle that could wake the dead was one made from a willow branch. Blades of broad-leaved grass, placed between the thumbs, need only the lusty breath of a pair of powerful young lungs to produce the loudest of noises. These and dozens of other toys could be made at the drop of a hat from wayside weeds.

Garden flowers, too, offered many possibilities, ranging from hollyhock dolls to dollhouse toys. Pioneers' children, in nearly every part of the world, have always made the most of whatever was near at hand and easy to obtain in order to fashion toys to their liking.

Skating and sledding in winter, and marbles and jackstones in spring, together with various kinds of ball games, hunting, boating, swimming, and fishing, required little in the way of elaborate toys and provided welcome outlets for youthful energy in colonial days.

In marked contrast to the messages of good will expressed in the gift of dolls at Roanoke Island, was the grim evidence which dolls presented at the witch trials of Massachusetts Bay at Salem Village in the 1690's. The former minister, the Reverend George Burroughs, was accused of having brought poppets to witch meetings. Two innocent women, Bridget Bishop and Goody Glover, were accused of possessing poppets made of "rags and hog bristles stuffed with goat's hair and other such ingredients." For these and other changes, they were hanged. These, according to testimony, were used in various ways to bring harm to others. Such was the part that dolls played in those dark days when dolls were referred to as images, poppets, puppets, and babies, as was commonplace in the seventeenth century.

Among the numerous items listed in "Rates of Imports and Exports," established by the parliament in 1660, were "babies or poppets for children" and "babies' heads of earth." By the end of the century, we read that John Higginson, of Massachusetts, wrote to his brother in England that toys imported in small quantities would sell.

At the opening of the eighteenth century, four or five generations of Americans had planted their roots deeply in the soil of the New World. Despite the fact that large quantities of household goods were imported from England, and settlers from various parts of Europe were introducing their own goods and customs, many kinds of local industry were being developed. The village potter was likely to turn out a few dishes for his own children and those of the neighbors. Older brothers whittled a variety of wooden toys for their small sisters and brothers, including animals, carts, miniature wheelbarrows, doll furniture, whistles, and other favorites. Girls made doll's clothes. Itinerant limners, waiting for a canvas to dry, would daub paint on a "penny wooden," the everyday type of doll which children found amusing. These were often carved of pine or maple, sometimes with pegged joints which allowed the arms and legs to move. Although they were stiff and clumsy and truly wooden in appearance, little girls loved them and dressed them elaborately with scraps of homespun calico and even finer materials when available. Penny woodens continued to be popular until 1850 even after dolls of more

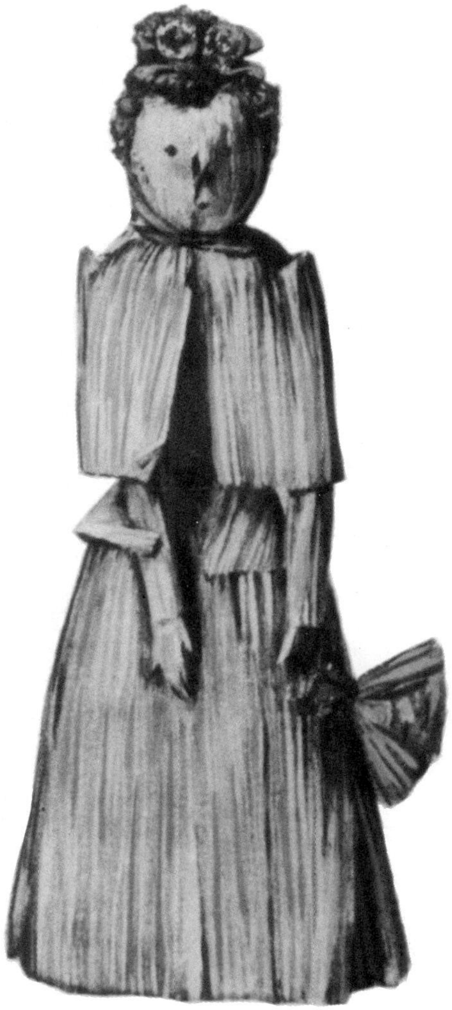

Corn-husk dolls were made to amuse children on both sides of the Atlantic long before the early settlers came to New England. They are typical examples of the century-old tradition of primitive toymaking practiced in many parts of the world, and they are still made in rural areas along the Atlantic seaboard and inland as well. *Photo courtesy Essex Institute*

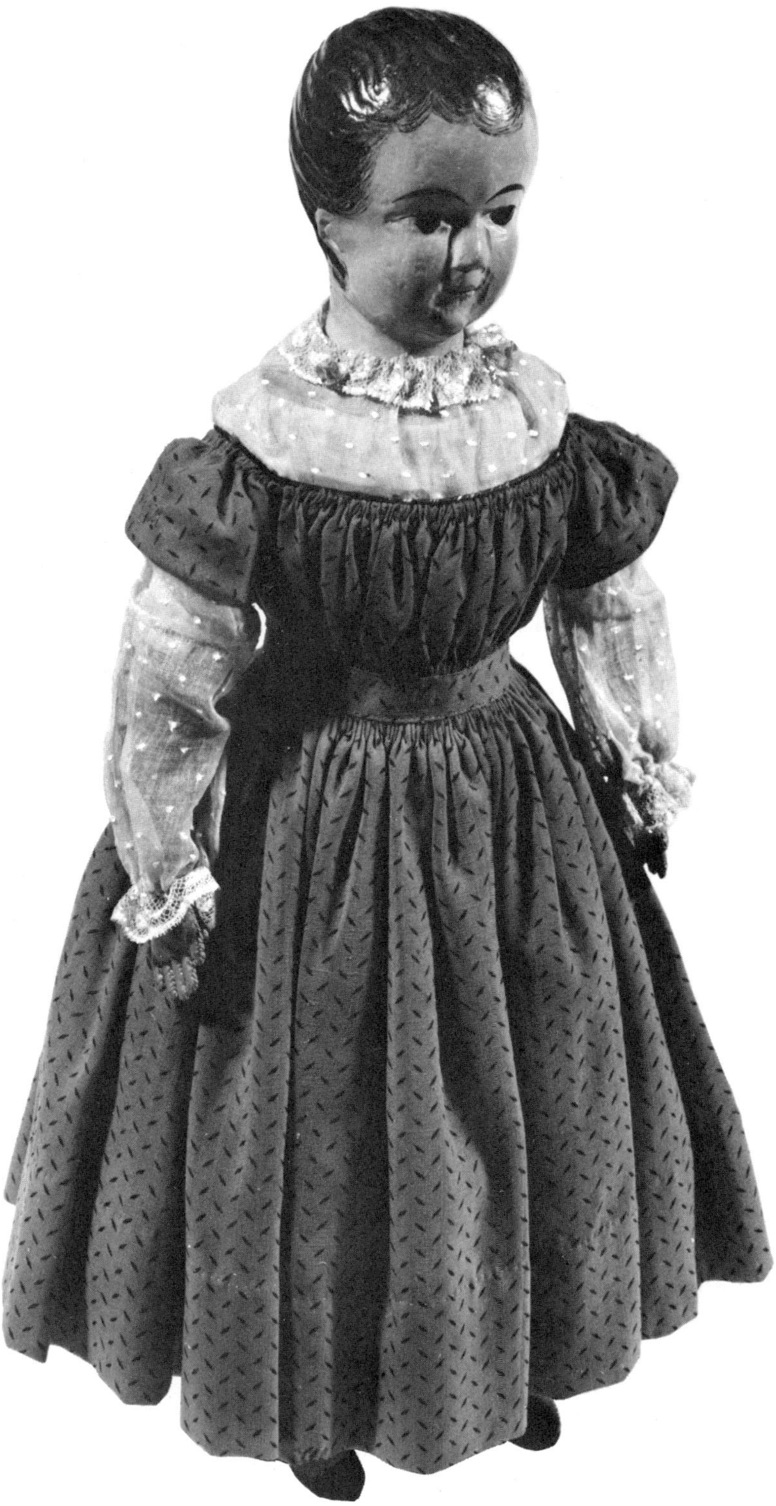

A nineteenth-century doll with hand-carved solid wooden head, hollowed shoulders, and cloth body. One of three known to have come from the Bath, Maine, area, 23 inches in height. *Photo Richard Merrill: collection of Madeline Merrill*

lifelike appearance were being sold. The wood-turner made kitchen-ware in miniature. Yet, the arrival of every returning ship was awaited with keen excitement by families whose fathers and sons were aboard. And all the neighbors were curious, too, to learn of the new and strange cargoes which the vessels carried.

It was music to children's ears to read in a Boston newspaper in 1712 that a privateersman had brought boxes of toys into Boston harbor. Every child in town who could earn a penny or two or had been given one as a reward for good behavior would make his way to whatever shop was offering the new treasures. Thus, the arrival of cargo at every seaport town in the colonies was bound to produce something new and amusing, particularly if toys were included. Both the captain and the crew, usually, had young ones awaiting their return, and they seldom disappointed the children. Then, as now, homemade toys were good enough to play with when there was nothing else at hand, but the lure of something new, strange, or curious was and always has been a mark of every growing child.

Benjamin Franklin was seven years old in 1713. He lived in Boston, one of seventeen children, and his father was often hard put to it to support his big family; but somehow Ben, the youngest, managed to get a few pennies. How the money was spent is told by Franklin. "My friends, on a holiday, filled my pockets with coppers. I went directly to a shop where they sold toys for children; and, being charmed with the sound of a whistle that I met, by the way, in the hands of another boy, I voluntarily offered and gave all my money for one. I then came home and went whistling all over the house, much pleased with my whistle, but disturbing all the family. My brothers and sisters and cousins, understanding the bargain I had made, told me I had given four times as much as it was worth, and laughed at me so much for my folly that I cried with vexation, and the reflection gave me more chagrin than the whistle gave me pleasure.

"This, however, was afterwards of use to me, the impression continuing on my mind; so that often when I was tempted to buy some unnecessary things, I said to myself, do not give too much for the whistle, and I saved money.

"As I grew up, came into the world, and observed the actions of men, I though I met many who gave too much for the whistle."

This bit of reminiscence was written by Franklin on November 10, 1779, and was printed on his own press at Passy, a suburb of Paris. It was part of one of his lighthearted essays, which he referred to as bagatelles. This one was written to his friend Madame Brillon, a beautiful and brilliant figure of the French court, where Franklin, as "envoy extraordinary and minister plenipotentiary from the United States," had won the hearts of all France by his simple and gracious manner. Franklin's bagatelles were games of delight, literary toys, as it were, written for the pleasure and edification of his friends with a certain lightness of tone. Recently, they were reprinted in *Franklin's Wit and Folly,* by Richard E. Amacher.

Little that was lighthearted in the way of merriment or entertainment was to be found in the early children's books published in colonial days. Even the crudest of homemade toys or the smallest trinket offered more in the way of amusement. However, as the eighteenth century drew to a close, a change of attitude was apparent in all forms of social life, and the inherited spirit of fun, so characteristic of everyday England prior to Puritan times, began to show itself in many ways. Then, too, the impact of life in other countries was being felt as settlers of various nationalities appeared in larger numbers.

The sea captains from coastal towns stretching from Eastport to Block Island, who sailed to faraway ports, came back bearing strange tales and equally strange souvenirs to provide new excitement for their families. The change of attitude was gradual, but it is revealed even in the titles of the children's books turned out by local printers. Mostly young men in their twenties, these mariners were actually roving ambassadors eager to learn of the ways and thoughts of other races and nationalities. That many of them were collectors at heart is evidenced by the rare and unusual items seen in our museums today. Naturally, many of the toys which they brought home were soon broken, but a few remain. Today, even the early children's books are rare collector's items.

In *A Family Well Ordered,* Cotton Mather, the eminent seventeenth-century Puritan divine, reminded undutiful children of "the Blackness of darkness forever that was to be their reward." It was not life, but the gloomy shadows of death, that permeated most of the early books for children which, all too often,

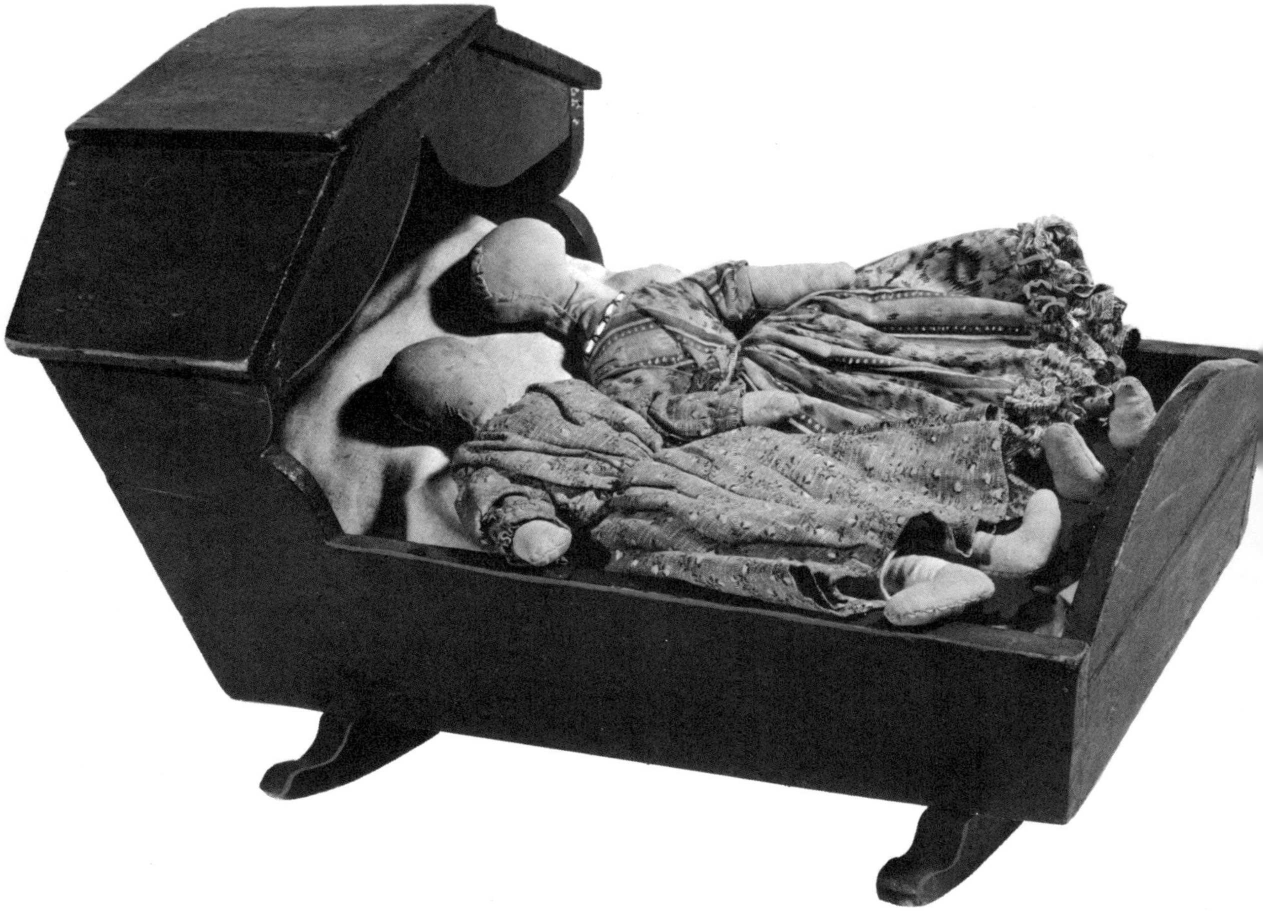

Two homemade rag dolls in a wooden cradle. The inscription on bottom reads: "Made by D. S. Edgerly for his daughter Augusta H. in the year of our Lord 1852." From Northwood, New Hampshire. *Photo Richard Merrill: family dolls from collection of Madeline Merrill*

were concerned with accounts of the passing of "pious and lovely" children. Or, when children quarreled over a rag doll or some other toy, dutiful mothers were likely to quote:

Birds on their little nests agree;
And 'tis a shameful sight,
When children of one family
Fall out, and chide, and fight.

Let dogs delight to bark and bite,
For God hath made them so;
Let bears and lions growl and fight,
For 'tis their nature to.

However, in marked contrast were these touching lines from Dr. Watts's *Cradle Hymn,* sung as an evening lullaby to comfort babies and small children as they were put to bed:

Hush, my dear, lie still and slumber,
Holy angels guard thy bed,
Heavenly blessings without number
Gently falling on thy head.

This verse was undoubtedly familiar to every New England child, for it was printed in the *New England Primer,* the most important book in the eighteenth-century nursery. Thousands of copies were printed between 1680 and 1830.

In April, 1726, William Price was advertising "children's toys sold at reasonable prices" in the *Boston Gazette,* and a quarter of a century later "London babies, English and Dutch toys, by wholesale and retail." A gold whistle, with bells and coral, was offered at public auction in Boston in 1762. Whistles made of gold or silver with a bell and coral attached were never common, and now are choice collector's items. Sometimes, ivory was used instead of coral. These handsomely wrought toys, sold by silversmiths, served as teething rings, but not every child's parents in colonial times could afford such imported luxuries. Those hammered out by colonial silversmiths were made on order and like children's mugs and plates were marked with the initials of the recipient. Alphabet blocks were known at the time, and as with all the new fashions and trends in England, news of them soon reached the colonies. They were offered for sale in New York in 1767—and may have been available here at an even earlier date.

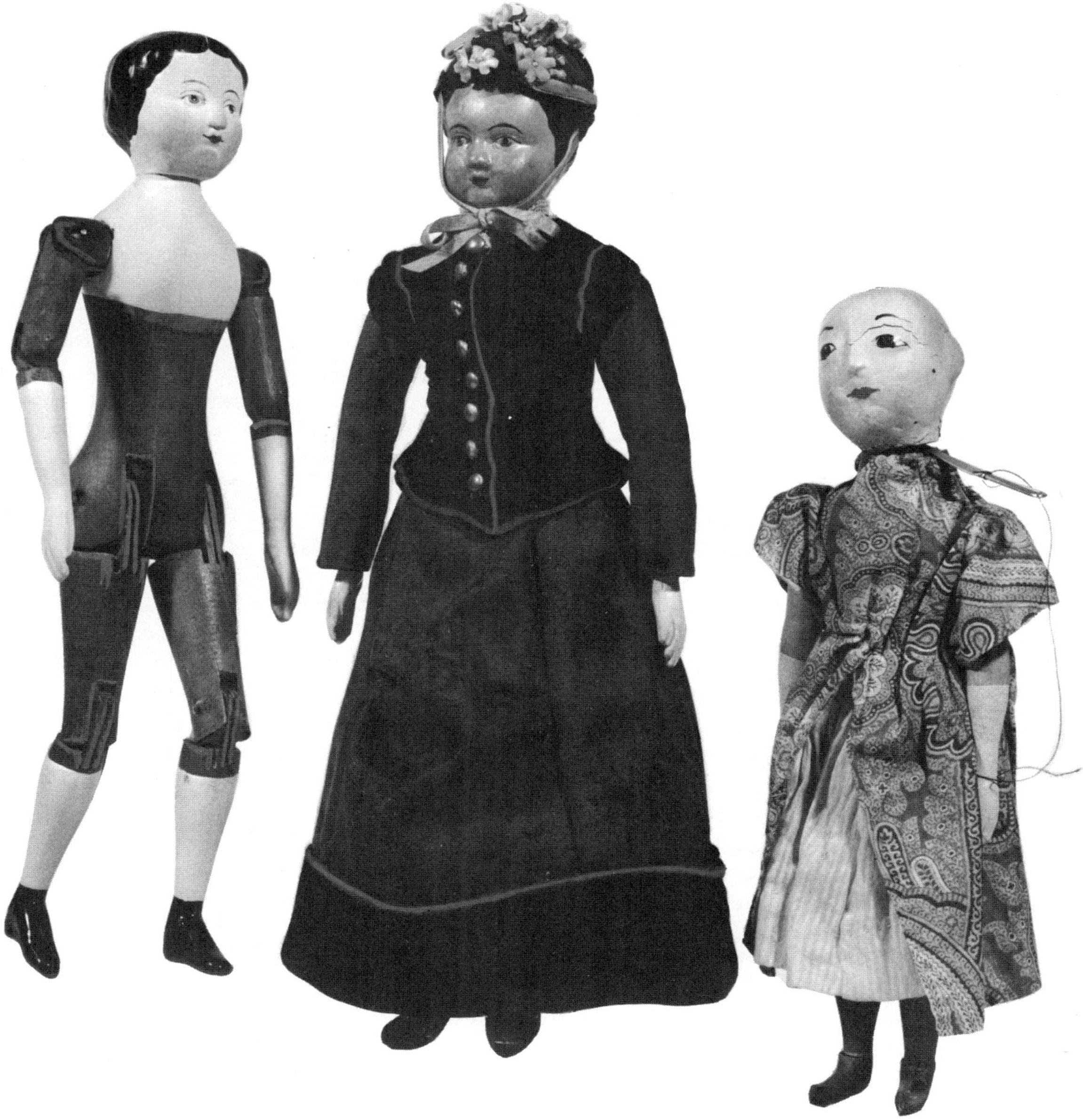

Dolls made in Springfield, Vermont. Left and center are identical Joel-Ellis Wooden dolls of 1873, with heads and bodies of hardwood; hands and feet are cast pewter. Doll at left shows the Joel-Ellis method of joining the arms and legs. Right: Mason and Taylor "Witch or Wizard Doll," 1880. Made for export to the Orient, it features a unique toggle arrangement connecting the head to body so a knife may be passed through the neck without disconnecting the head from the shoulders. *Photo Richard Merrill: collection of Madeline Merrill*

"Several compleat tea table sets of children's cream-colored toys" were offered at the "Three Sugar-Loaves" in Cornhill, Boston, on November 28, 1771.

No doubt those intinerant painters known as limners, who went about selling their talents by "taking" a likeness, painting a landscape or a still life, were instrumental in attracting children to the art of painting. Colored pencils were offered, along with battledores and shuttlecocks, in 1740. Musical instruments, so popular in Pennsylvania, were to be found in various parts of the colonies; for the small children there were whistles, Jew's harps, drums, and flutes, long before the drum and the flute figured so dramatically in the "Spirit of '76," enacted at old Marblehead.

In the days following the Revolution, children in the "New Republic" were playing with toys of all kinds, including "Lilliputian dolls," tin drums, Jew's harps, rattles, rocking horses, alphabet blocks, carts, chairs, and other toys. Practically all of these were made by local craftsmen. Wigs for dolls were offered for sale in shops, as well as "naked" dolls, for it was the custom for children to make their own doll's wardrobes. Then, too, dressed dolls were more expensive.

Toys go hand in hand with good things to eat, and, for centuries, cookies, cakes, and candy in the form of toys have delighted grown-ups and children alike. Edible dolls are as old as the toy doll. In German culture, dolls or figures made from dough were called "picture bread." During the Middle Ages, dolls of bread cut in the forms of saints were made for the children on the feast days of favorite saints.

In *Dolls and Puppets,* Max von Boehn observed, "The gingerbread doll had a tenacious life, perhaps because it appealed to the stomach and not to the spirit. The shapes which it assumed remained the same for centuries." So popular was gingerbread in England that there were fairs where only gingerbread and toys were sold. Each year in Birmingham, two gingerbread fairs were held until well into the nineteenth century, and, as Mrs. E. Nevill Jackson reminds us in *Toys of Other Days,* the warrant for holding the fairs was given back in the thirteenth century. Long lines of market stalls, filled with gingerbread in every imaginable shape and form, were interspersed with booths filled with toys. Gingerbread men were called "husbands" at the English fairs, and were often referred to as "Jim Crows" in nineteenth-century America. Nathaniel Hawthorne mentions them as favorites in Hepzibah Pyncheon's cent shop in his *The House of the Seven Gables,* along with elephants made of gingerbread. In Europe, it used to be a custom of shopkeepers to give gingerbread men, various kinds of cookies and candies, often with the shop name stamped on them, to children, either to pacify them when they came to the shop with their mothers, or as a friendly gesture, or as good-will advertising. This old-time custom found its way to America at an early date.

Of all the toys of yesteryear, none met with warmer approval from both young folk and parents than the Noah's arks. Charles Dickens wrote about them on many occasions, and no author of his day knew better the deep-seated sentiments of his readers. He was lionized on his first visit to Boston in 1842 and young and old all over New England literally devoured his books and many knew his stories by heart. Dickens retained vivid memories of his childhood, and his own children enjoyed many of the wonderful toys of which he had been deprived. In that beloved story, *The Christmas Tree,* he wrote, "Oh, the wonderful Noah's ark. It was not found seaworthy when put in a washing-tub, and the animals were crammed in at the roof, and needed to have their legs well shaken down before they could be got in, even there—and then, ten to one but they began to tumble out at the door, which was but imperfectly fastened with a wire latch—but what was *that* against it! Consider the noble fly, a size or two smaller than the elephant: the ladybird, the butterfly—all triumphs of art! Consider the goose, whose feet were so small, and whose balance was so indifferent, that he usually tumbled forward, and knocked down all the animal creation. Consider Noah and his family, like idiotic tobacco-stoppers; and how the leopard stuck to warm little fingers; and how the tails of the larger animals used gradually to resolve themselves into frayed bits of string!"

Noah's ark was familiarly known as the "Sunday toy," a curious way, indeed, to speak of any plaything by present-day standards. Yet, from the close of the Revolution until late in the nineteenth century, the Sabbath was observed with the greatest dignity and austerity in New England, and toys were put away on that day. However, the one toy, or rather the one collection of toys, which was allowed was

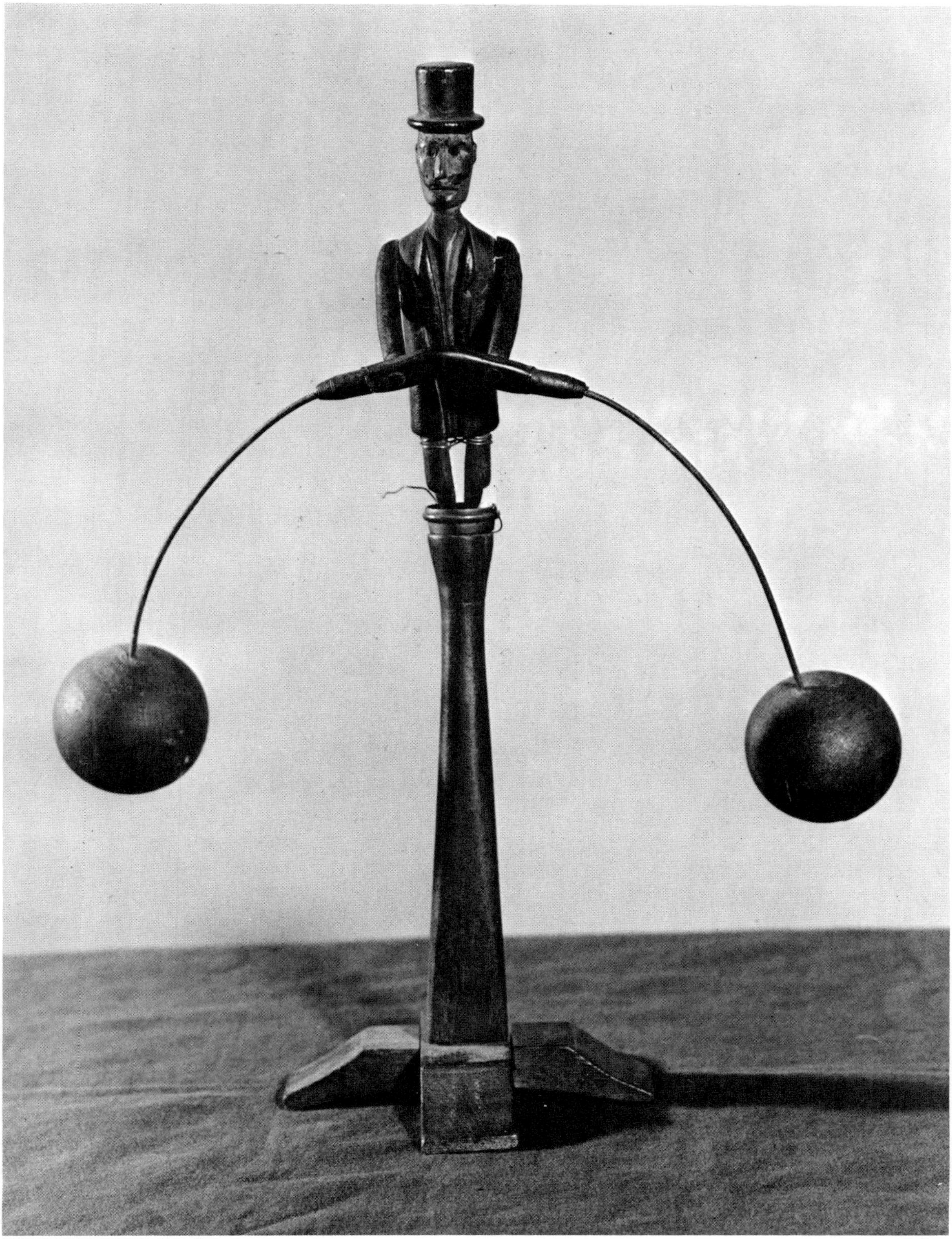

Balance toys of this type copied from Old World models, imported or brought home by sea captains, are found from time to time under the eaves in New England attics.
Photo courtesy Abby Aldrich Rockefeller Folk Art Collection

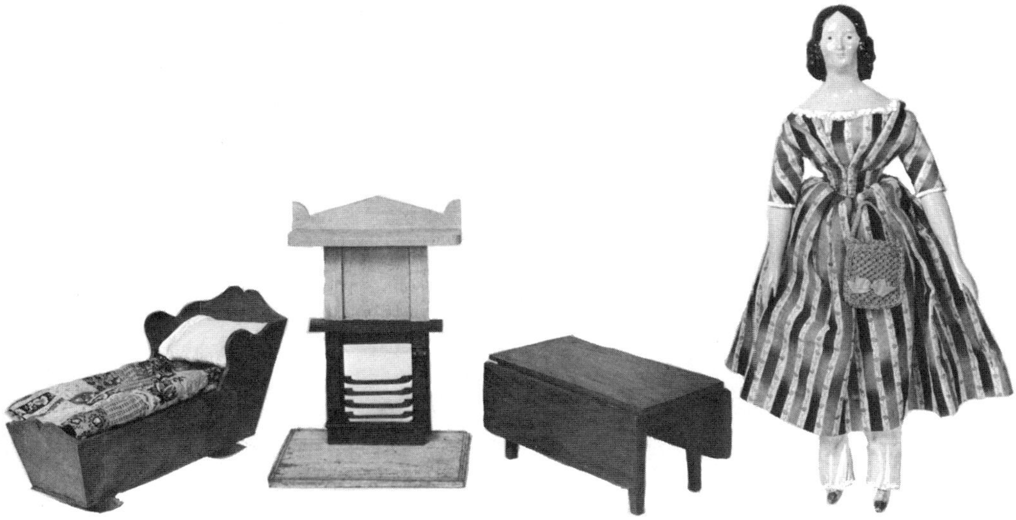

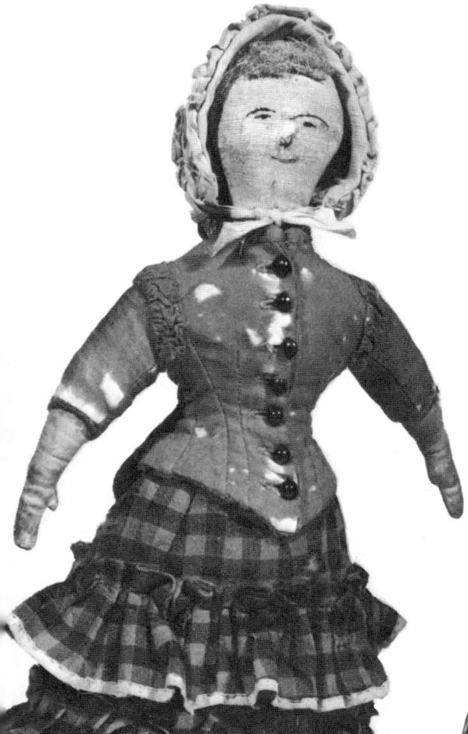

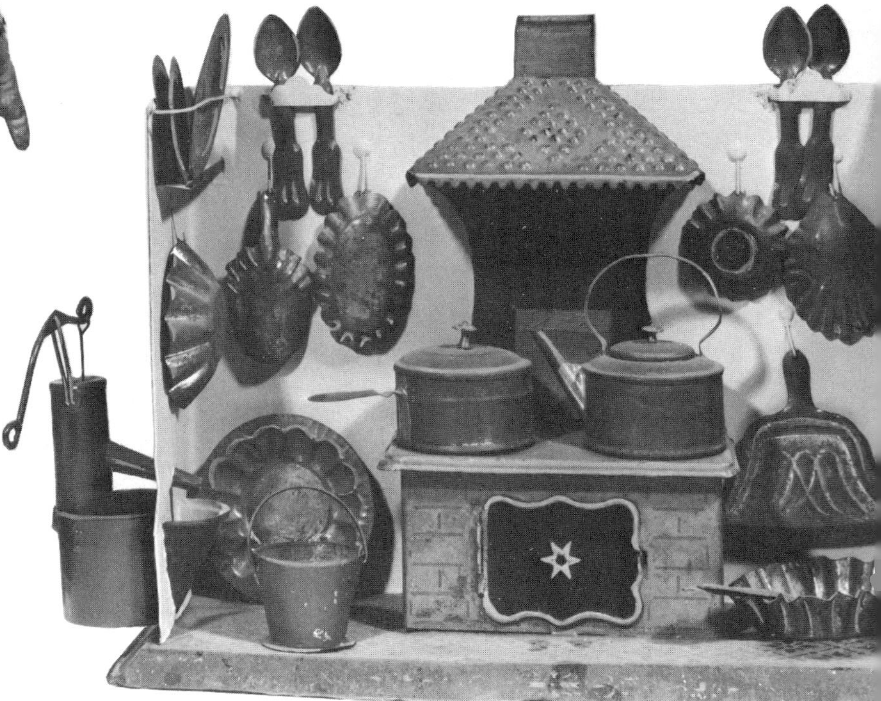

(*Opposite page top*) Doll furniture and a doll dating from the mid-nineteenth century. *Photo courtesy Essex Institute*

(*Opposite page bottom*) An early cloth doll from Bath, Maine, with painted complexion, stitched features, and hair of tow. *Photo Richard Merrill: collection of Madeline Merrill*

(*Below*) A toy whale whose carver is unknown. *Courtesy Abby Aldrich Rockefeller Folk Art Collection*

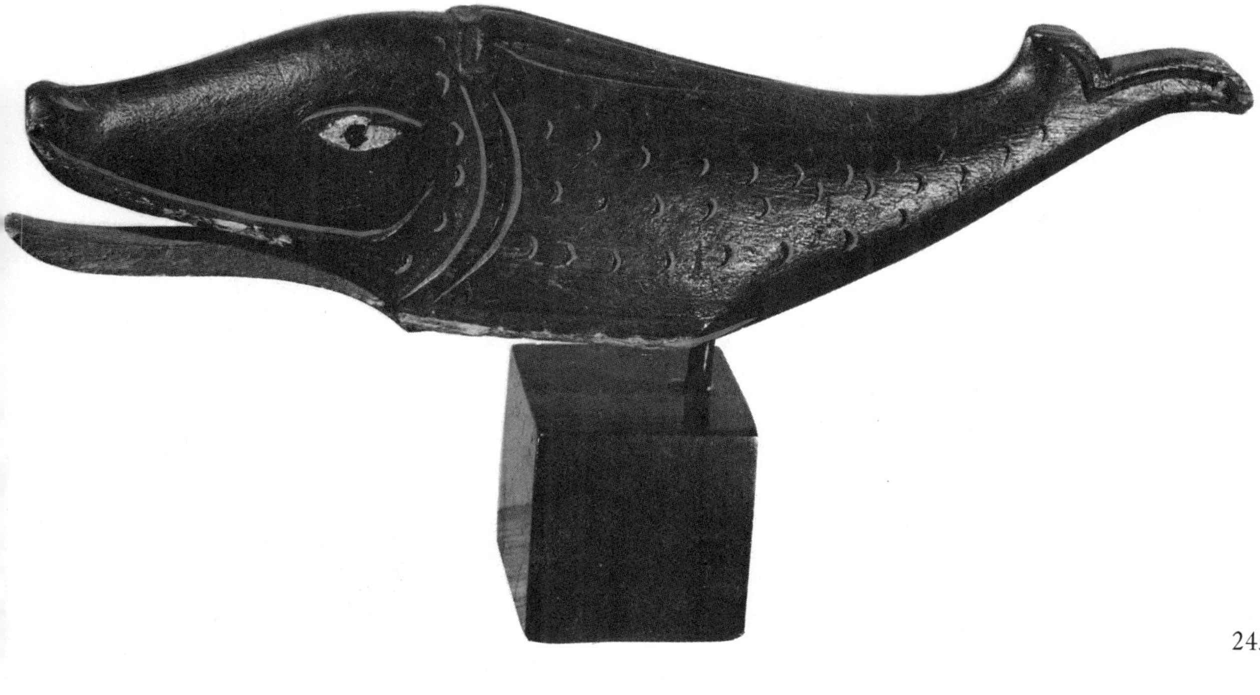

Noah's ark. It had the same important family status in England at the time.

Often, the arks were made more like canalboats than the skillfully designed vessel which, in our imagination, we attribute to Noah. As carved in wood, Mr. and Mrs. Noah were usually depicted bent with age, wearing either long, dark robes or the fashion of the period in which they were carved. Their sons, Shem, Ham, and Japheth, were sometimes dressed in animal skins, while their wives were clothed in garments of a much later period, often in vivid color. They were often so similar in appearance that it was difficult to distinguish the three brothers, and many a childish battle ensued over who was who. But it was the animals that held greatest appeal for the children, however crude they were in appearance. Although they were usually painted in bright colors, some interesting examples survive in natural wood finish. The birds, cats, dogs, pigs, goats, sheep, cows, and other familiar animals were easy enough to recognize, but with the strange animals, such was not always the case. Monkeys, lions, camels, and elephants were easy enough to identify and the comment can be left at that, for the young folk who played with them knew them in another way, and that was what mattered.

Just as the woodcarvers in many German villages used their skill to carve animals during the long winter months, so many a whittler in New England did his bit in making a menagerie of his own concept for the delight of his children.

When paper toys became popular advertising novelties in the Gay Nineties, the Willimantic Thread Company of Connecticut offered Noah's arks with a sizeable collection of animals. These paper cut-outs were reproduced in bright colors, with easels attached for display. A verse on the back of each animal read:

> Noah launched his ark on the raging main,
> And saved these animals out of the rain,
> We send them, with kindest regards to you,
> And what they say of *Star thread* is true.

Sunday dolls were sometimes permitted, especially in families whose theology was on the liberal side. The "Sunday" doll was a very special person, who appeared once a week and, always dressed in her very best, was carefully put away at the proper time. As the observance of Sunday was gradually expanded to include genteel forms of recreation, tea parties for dolls made it possible for the neighbors' children to bring their dolls to call. But the idea of any rough play was greatly frowned upon, and such gatherings were supervised carefully to maintain an air of proper decorum.

At an early date, blue laws were enacted in Connecticut, forbidding its residents to play any instrument of music except the drum, the trumpet, and the Jew's harp. Of the drum and the trumpet, little needs to be said, but the Jew's harp is hardly known today. This amusing toy, long a favorite at various fairs in England and on the Continent, was sold in many of the New England cent-shops in colonial days. It has been suggested that it had an Old Testament flavor, which appealed to the rigorous worthies who founded and governed their colony on Old Testament theology. At any rate, the Jew's harp was acceptable. Its popular name is derived from the fact that it was one of many items sold by Jewish peddlers and one of the few cheap musical instruments, at that.

The two-wheeled bell toys at least are the earliest type of pull-toy made in Connecticut, dating from about 1860, and are believed to have been made by the Ives-Blakesley Toy Co. of Bridgeport. The three four-wheeled toys on the right were made by Hull and Stafford, Clinton, Connecticut, about 1860. The figures are painted; the horse car is stenciled.
Photo Richard Merrill: collection of Richard Merrill

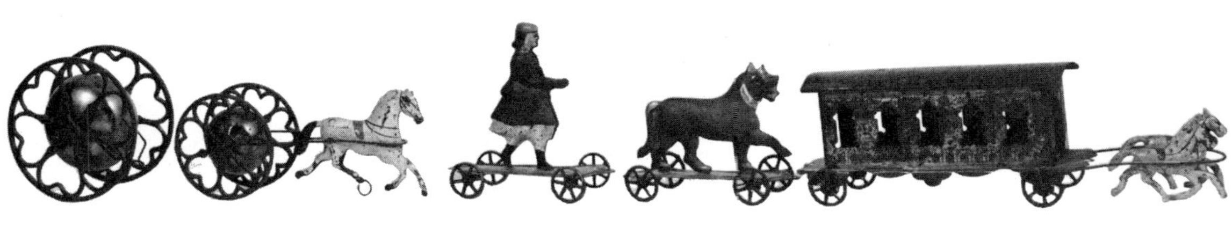

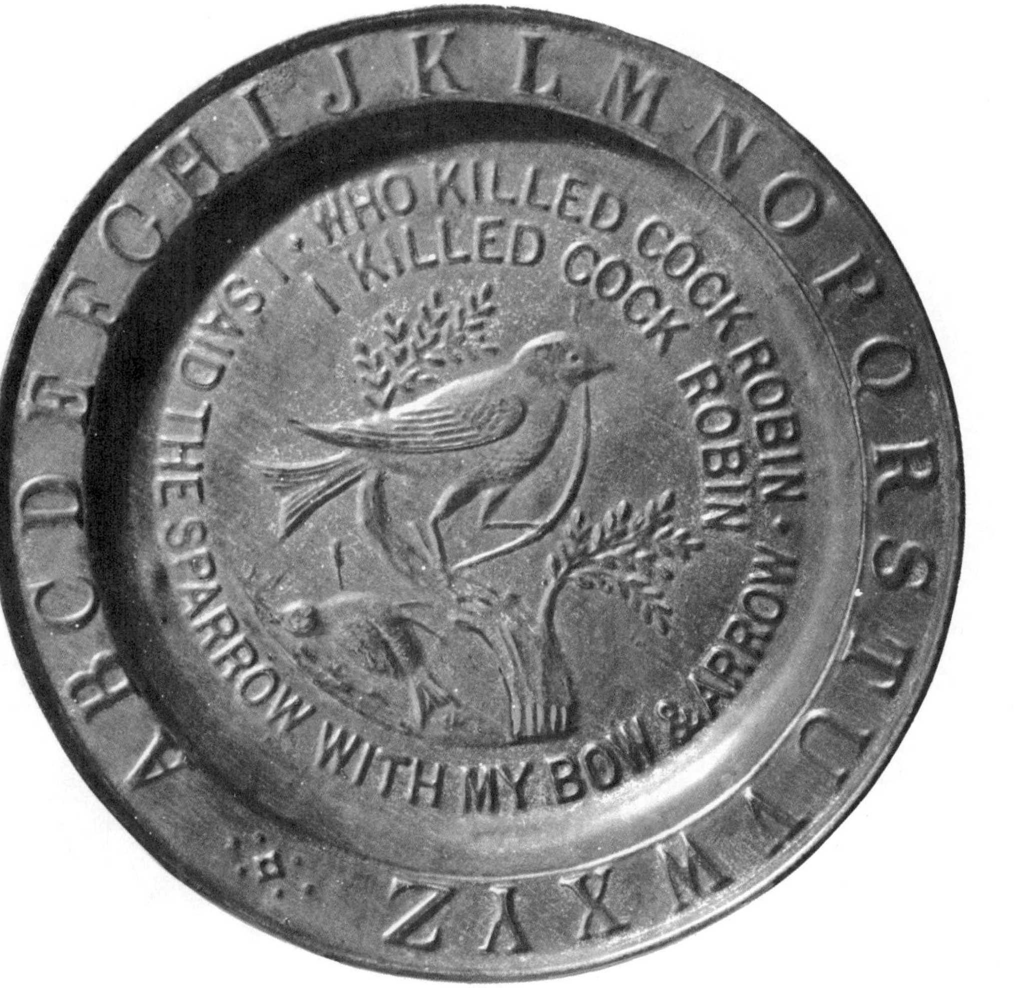

Tin plate with designs and rhymes is reminiscent of nineteenth-century nursery days. *Photo Richard Merrill: courtesy Rushford Collection*

Of all the truly musical toys of childhood popular for more than a century, none was more greatly enjoyed by all ages than the hand organ or "monkey" organ. The organ grinder with his monkey was a blend of musician and clown, often a craftsman of sorts and sometimes possessed of many skills. He was something of a philosopher too, as he moved down the street playing old-time tunes.

If the crowd did not gather soon enough, he was always quick to change his tune. If his music seemed a bit dull at times, his friendly monkey, usually with a long rope or chain attached to his waist, made up for it with his antics. Here, indeed, was a glimpse of nostalgia and charm from street scenes of the Old World, and fair days, too. In the heyday of these performers, most of the hand-organ men came from Italy. Until a few decades ago, all types and kinds of hand organs and hurdy-gurdys were to be seen on the streets of busy towns and cities, but like so many of the earmarks of gracious living in the nineteenth century, they have disappeared. The organ grinder used to be as punctual as the first crocus in spring. He made the summer days pleasant and gay for young and old, for he was always on hand for parades and fairs, and whenever the circus came to town. As Autumn came, he was still a familiar figure as we traveled to and from school. Only winter sent him into hibernation, since cold weather was not to the liking of the monkey. Actually, monkeys are known to be extremely sensitive to cold, and the commonest cause of death

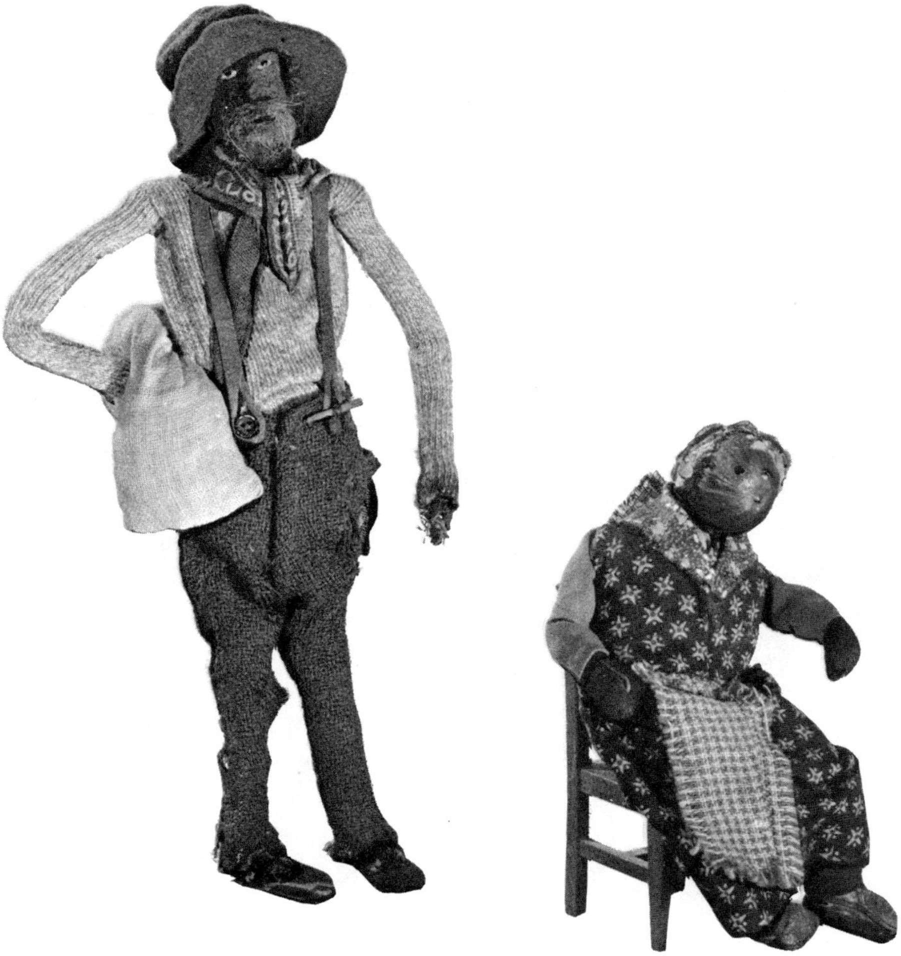

Necessity was often the mother of invention and, in every age since the beginning of time, children and their parents have created toys from commonplace materials to "make do." Today these primitive dolls made of nuts, twigs, and bits of cloth hold a curious kind of charm and appeal among people of sophisticated taste. *Courtesy Abby Aldrich Rockefeller Folk Art Collection*

among them is one due to exposure. It took considerable time to train a monkey, and since he was so important to the success of the operation, owners took the best of care of the "little fellow." Actually, during the winter months organ grinders, like peddlers, plied their trade south, and some even traveled to the orange groves of California.

When Nathaniel Hawthorne wrote *The House of the Seven Gables* in 1851, organ grinders were something of a novelty in the seaport towns of New England. The organ which Hawthorne described was a sort of combination peep show and music box. It contained a panel encased in glass, in which a series of little paper figures moved as the Italian boy, with the broad-brimmed hat, turned the crank. "The cobbler wrought upon a shoe; the blacksmith hammered his iron; the soldier waved his glittering blade; the lady raised a tiny breeze with her fan; the jolly toper swigged lustily at his bottle; a scholar opened his book with eager thirst for knowledge, and turned his head to and fro along the page; the milkmaid energetically drained her cow; and a miser counted gold into his strongbox,—all at the same turning of a crank. Yes; and, moved by the selfsame impulse, a lover saluted his mistress on her lips!"

After the Civil War, when tin and iron came into common use for the making of toys, every youngster could follow the development of the rapidly expanding railroad system in miniature, as well as all the latest models of vehicles that were being made in both America and Europe. These metals provided an amazing variety of toys from the cheap tin watches sold in "five-and-ten's" to the most elaborate mechanical figures, such as the dancing Negro, a girl playing a piano, a musical elephant accompanied by a monkey, a fox chasing a duck, and many more. Mechanical banks became all the rage, and so did every imaginable kind of novelty in the world of toys. Since they were being mass produced, prices were moderate. The introduction of electric trains eventually led to the popular fad for miniature railroads to amuse Dad as well as the boys. The story of miniature trains and railroads, *Riding the Tinplate Rails,* has been written in vivid detail by Louis H. Hertz, and the enthusiasm for this hobby has all the overtones of the "tin" soldier mania of an earlier age.

Model automobiles, kiddie cars, bicycles and tricycles, roller skates, and all the rest of the fun on wheels made growing up something of a problem for those who wanted to linger longer in that glorious age from eight to twelve. There was no end to the American toys that were being made, and in such infinite variety.

What started the wild enthusiasm for penny banks, also referred to as toy or mechanical banks, in the 1870's? Was it a campaign to teach young America to save? Had the staggering costs of the Civil War, so wasteful of human life, energy, and worldly goods, given some New England Yankee manufacturer an idea of using his materials and his labor for a by-product during his dull season? Or did someone suddenly remember the old maxim, "A penny saved is a penny earned"? In 1857, the minting of large copper cent pieces had ceased, and with the introduction of smaller coins to represent the lowest unit of American exchange, tin banks were produced in quantity. These were followed by a flood of cast iron banks as well as others made of glass, china, and pottery.

In 1870, the J. and E. Stevens Company, manufacturers of hardware, tools, and toys in Cromwell, Connecticut, began to make iron banks with movable parts which handled a penny in a variety of amusing ways and eventually pulled it away from its owner for safekeeping. Three years later, this same company had twenty-one different patterns which ranged in price from $2.50 to $3.00 each. Before the bank-making craze ended, more than two hundred different kinds were made. The simple mechanical contrivances did not possess the refined detail or the expert workmanship of the automatons made in France and Germany at an earlier date, but the automatic action that occurred when a penny was inserted came as a surprise and the question soon arose, "Whose bank is it, mine or Dad's?" Sometimes, buttons from Mother's sewing box were substituted for coins, just to see the bank work. Surely in the desire to demonstrate the newest and latest model, many a penny was inadvertently saved that might otherwise have gone into the coffers of the local candy shop.

Manufacturers' catalogs show us easy-to-identify pictures of these banks made from hand-carved wood blocks. The treasured relics in museums and private collections are much more real. But until these old-time mechanical toys are seen in action, they have little appeal. Insert a cent or two in the slot and watch what happens. They still have appeal to collectors who seek them out avidly, and an increasing number of types that are being reproduced now have a ready sale in gift shops and department stores.

In an old issue of *Antiques,* Willard Emerson Keyes wrote nostalgically of the days when penny banks "reposed on the mantel—the carved, white marble mantel of mid-Victorian years—the mantel which never knew the glow of a cheerful blaze upon the hearth be-

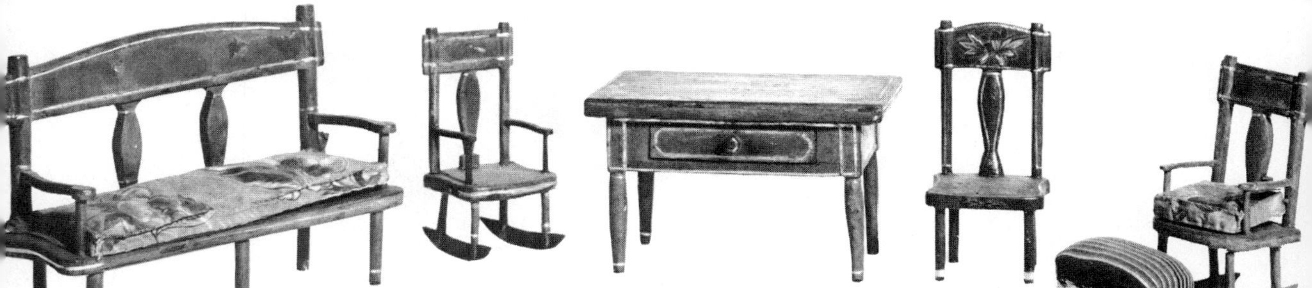

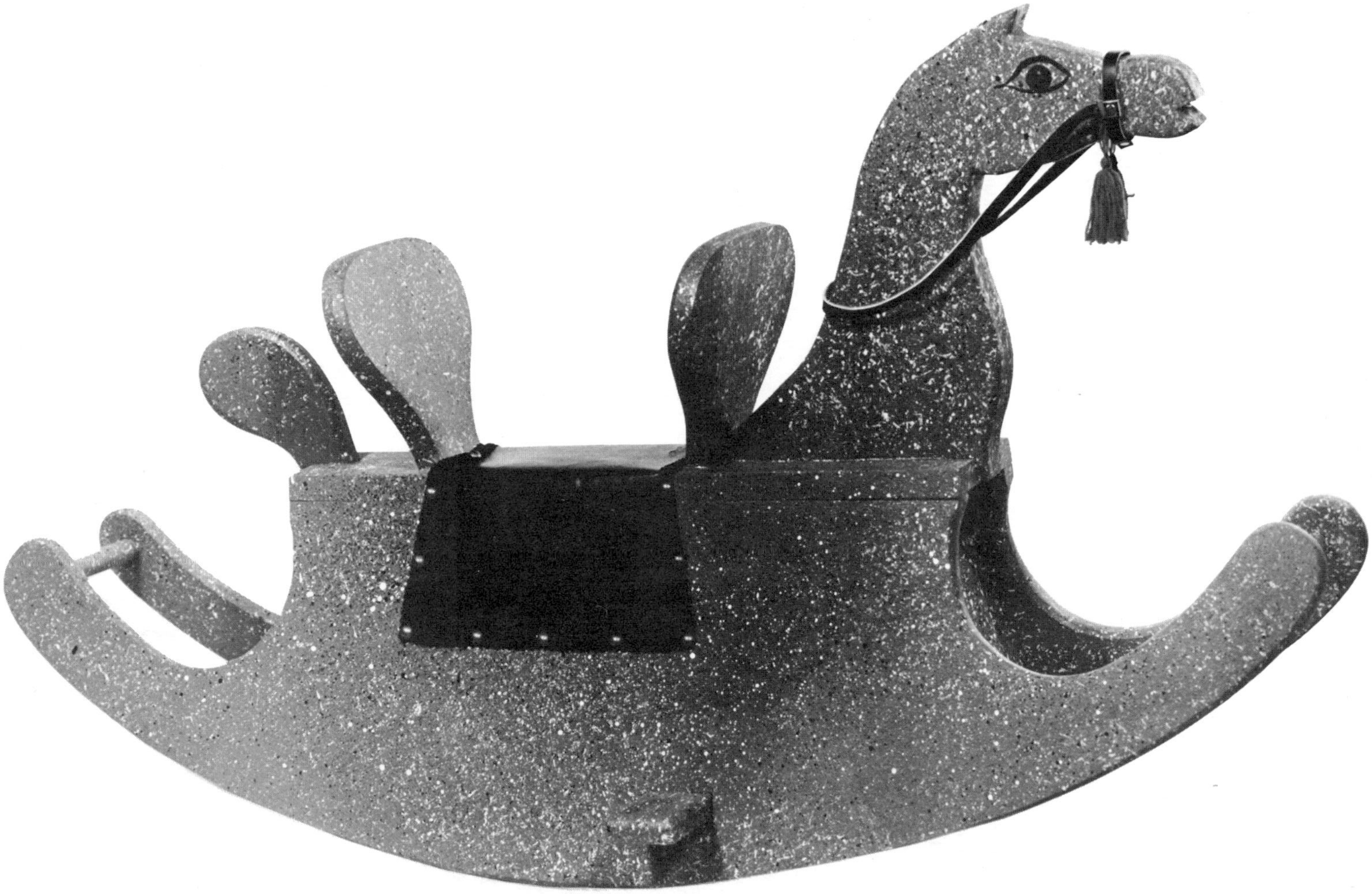

A rocking horse made at East Thetford, Vermont, designed after a late eighteenth-century model. *Photo courtesy Ruth Prevost*

neath. Perhaps it rested on the whatnot in the corner, facing those delirious forms in sable haircloth and tortured black walnut which seemed to the eyes of their generation to establish a standard of beauty in household furniture that should endure to be the envy and despair of all posterity to come; but it was there—childhood's penny bank."

Because mechanical banks have a strange fascination for those who collect them, and usually the hobby is pursued avidly by private collectors and savings banks, many of the scarce items have brought exceedingly high prices, ranging from twenty to twelve hundred dollars. This was the price range for banks in the collection of Walter P. Chrysler, which was sold in the 1950's.

Mechanical banks commemorate a number of public figures of the day in such a way that these people will never be forgotten as long as any of the cast-iron banks are preserved. The bank known as "Tammany" is the figure of a little fat man which represents Boss Tweed in his palmy days. When a coin is placed in his right hand, it drops into his pocket and he nods his head as a thank you. "Teddy and the Bear" represents Theodore Roosevelt, who, while on a hunting expedition in Mississippi, refused to shoot a bear cub. He shoots into the tree trunk and the bear pops out from the top of the stump. "Uncle Tom" of Harriet Beecher Stowe fame receives the coin on his tongue, while "Uncle Sam" accepts money that is dropped into his carpet bag and, dressed in full regalia, he leans on his umbrella.

"Always Did 'Spise A Mule," also called "The Kicking Mule," portrays a colored man sitting on a bench in front of a mule. As the spring is released, the mule turns completely around, kicking the man over the bench backwards—and the coin falls into a receptacle under the bench. Other banks feature acrobats, bears, dogs, boys stealing watermelons, buffaloes, a cat chasing a mouse, clowns, elephants, monkeys, owls, and rabbits. "Santa Claus at the Chimney," "Old Woman in a Shoe," "Humpty Dumpty," "Punch and Judy," "Help the Blindman," and on and on it goes, to nearly two hundred fifty named banks which are illustrated and described in *A Handbook of Old Mechanical Penny Banks,* by John D. Meyer.

Farm set, with animals, outbuildings, and human figures; Late nineteenth century. *Courtesy Abby Aldrich Rockefeller Folk Art Collection*

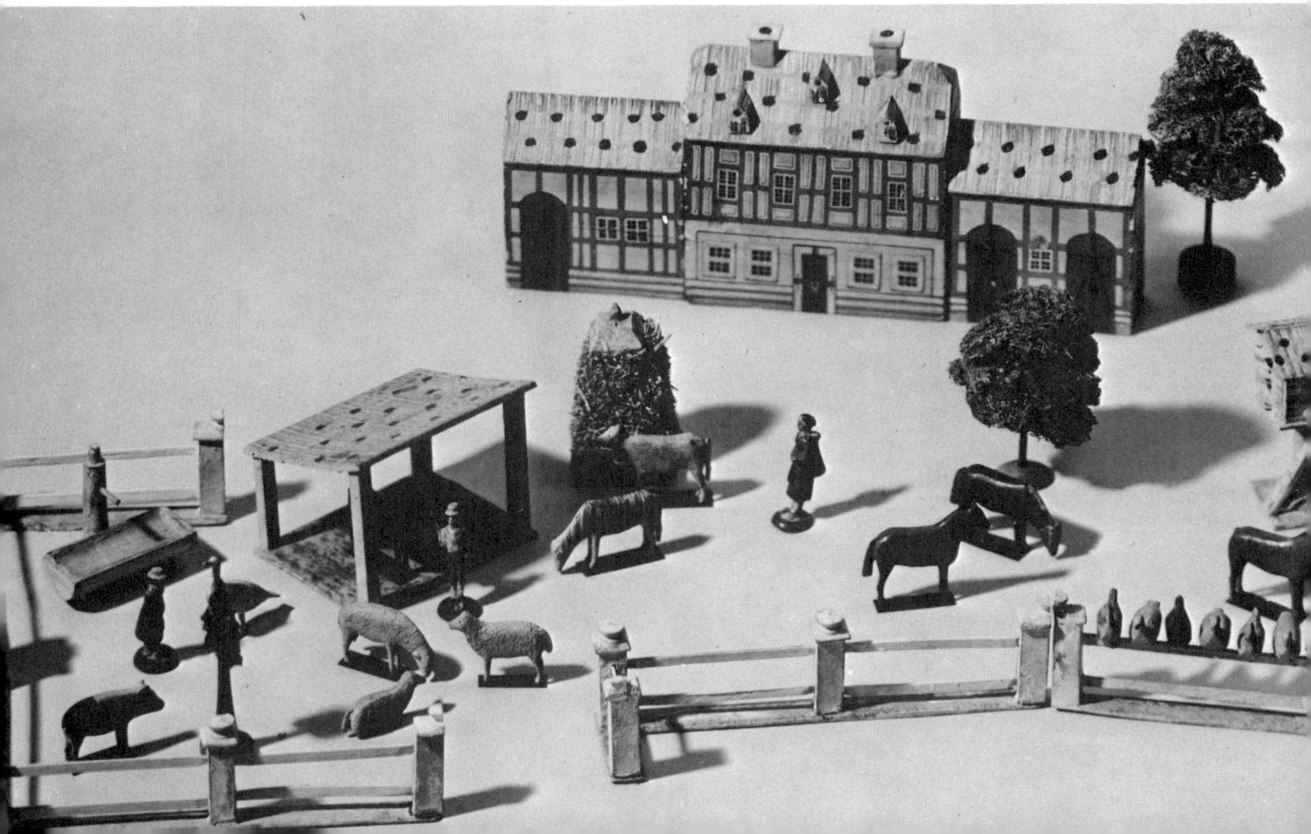

Scrimshaw: The Whaler's Art

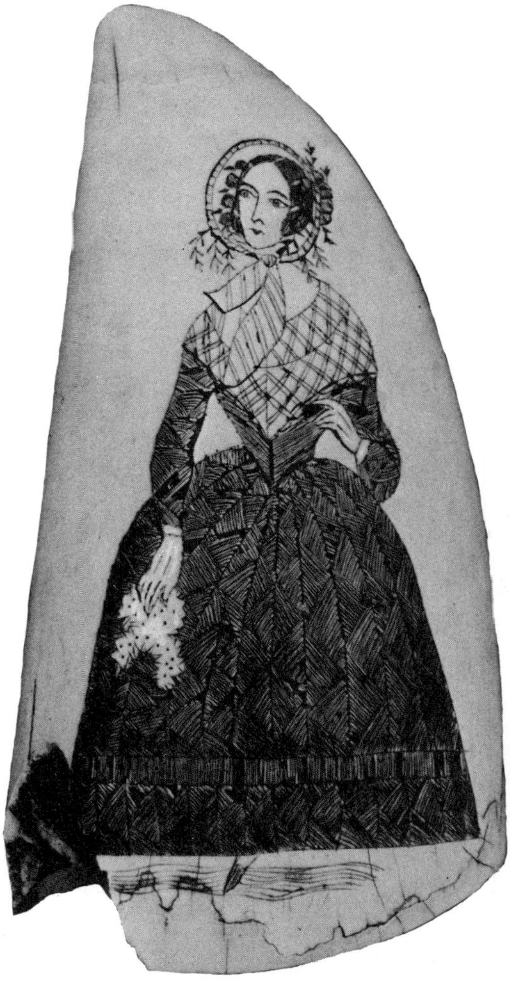

Scrimshaw, the art of carving useful, pictorial, and ornamental objects from the teeth and jaw bone of the sperm whale is often referred to as an indigenous form of American folk art, perfected by whalemen and sailors in the nineteenth century. Actually, this seaman's art can be traced back to earlier centuries in various parts of the world. French, English, and Scandinavian sailors as well as natives of Africa, Hawaii, and the Pacific Islands practiced it, using elephant and walrus tusks centuries before the teeth of the sperm whale came into use. However, American whalemen and the crews who manned the ships developed scrimshaw to a degree where it became a versatile and absorbing form of folk art.

The origin of the term scrimshaw and the variety of ways in which it was spelled by unlettered sailors adds a colorful note to its etymology. From ship logs and letters, we find references such as scrimshoning, scrimshorn, scrimpshong, skimshontering, and others. The art itself is generally referred to now as scrimshaw whereas the term scrimshander may refer to the maker or to the object itself. For those who would pursue the term in all its minutiae, see *Scrimshaw and Scrimshanders* by E. Normann Flayderman published by the author in 1972 in New Milford, Connecticut.

The fascination of this art lies not only in the techniques involved, but in the endless variety of useful and decorative objects produced. Ingenuity and skill, linked with imagination, patience, and a keen memory for detail which many of the objects reveal, are convincing evidence that this painstaking pictorial art was more than a mere pastime. The whalemen pursued it in their effort to while away the long, lonely hours at sea which otherwise would have resulted in utter boredom and eventual insanity. Whaling was a strenuous life, involving constant danger, illness, and monotony endured under cramped, primitive conditions where food often became scarce and off-duty hours were seemingly endless on voyages of two to three years duration.

In 1836 Captain William Reynard recorded in his log of the New Bedford whaler *Abigail:* "An idle head is the workshop of the devil. Employed scrimshon." An observant Frenchman named de Crevecoeur who visited Nantucket and Martha's Vineyard in the 1770's corroborates this fact in his *Letters from an American Farmer:* "Idleness is the most heinous sin that can be committed in Nantucket: . . . Even if they go to the coffee-house of the town, either to transact business or to converse with friends, they always have a piece of cedar in their hands, and while they are talking, they will, as it were instinctively, employ themselves in converting it to something useful. . . . I have never seen more ingenuity in the use of the knife; thus the most idle moments of their lives become usefully employed." Little wonder that the whalers took to scrimshaw with enthusiasm and produced such outstanding examples of folk art. Nantucket was the leading whaling port in the heyday of the trade. Martha's Vineyard, New Bedford, and Salem in Massachusetts, and Stonington, Connecticut, and other seaport towns furnished their share of captains and crews for the trade as well. All were deeply ingrained with the same puritan ethic.

While the essential materials used were the teeth of the sperm whale (the only whale which develops teeth), the great jaw bone, baleen (the black fibrous whalebone obtained from the mouths of toothless whales), narwhal ivory, and walrus tusks were also utilized. For inlay and embellishments, a variety of tropical woods including mahogany, teak, sandalwood, camphor, gum, rosewood, ebony, and native kinds such as pine and cedar, mother-of-pearl, silver, tortoise shell, abalone shell, bones of birds and animals, and other oddments provided material to further enhance the beauty and interest of the objects produced. The skin of the shark supplied ready sand paper for finishing the ivory.

Memories of home life and good eating prompted the making of elaborate jagging wheels for crimping pie crust. Rolling pins of tropical wood bore sperm ivory handles. Apple corers, pastry tubes, cookie cutters, and other useful kitchen tools were typical examples of the whaleman's art. He made whalebone handles for knives, forks, and spoons and sometimes a handsome ivory inlaid box to contain them. The uses to which his carving skill could be put seemed limitless. He would fashion needlecases, delicate in the beauty of their inlay, bird cages, card cases, parasol and buggy-whip handles, and ornately cut walking sticks. Practical objects like clothespins, coatracks, door knobs, footscrapers, and bootjacks were made with the same skill and pride as cuff links and buttons, clock cases and watch holders, candlesticks and

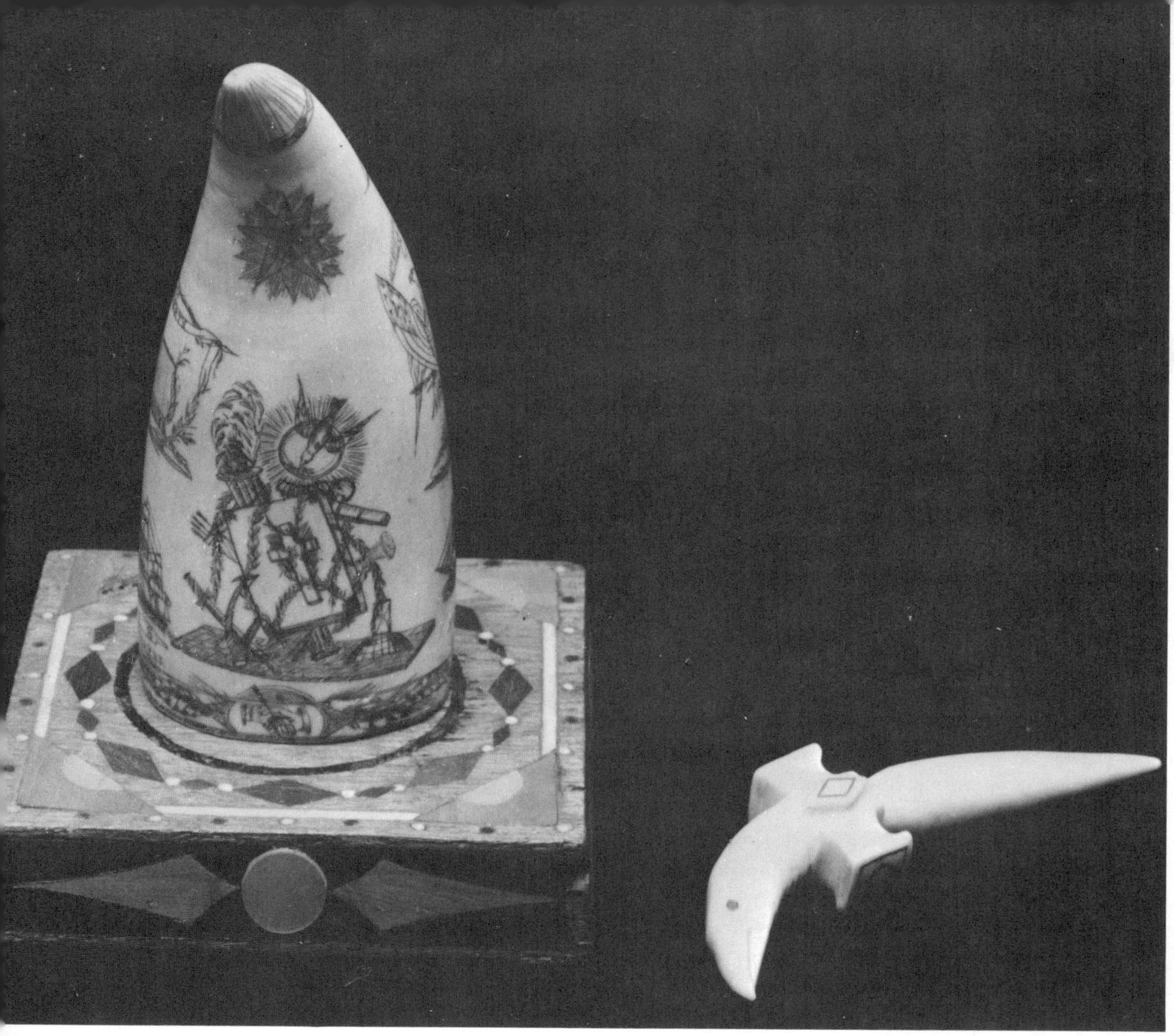

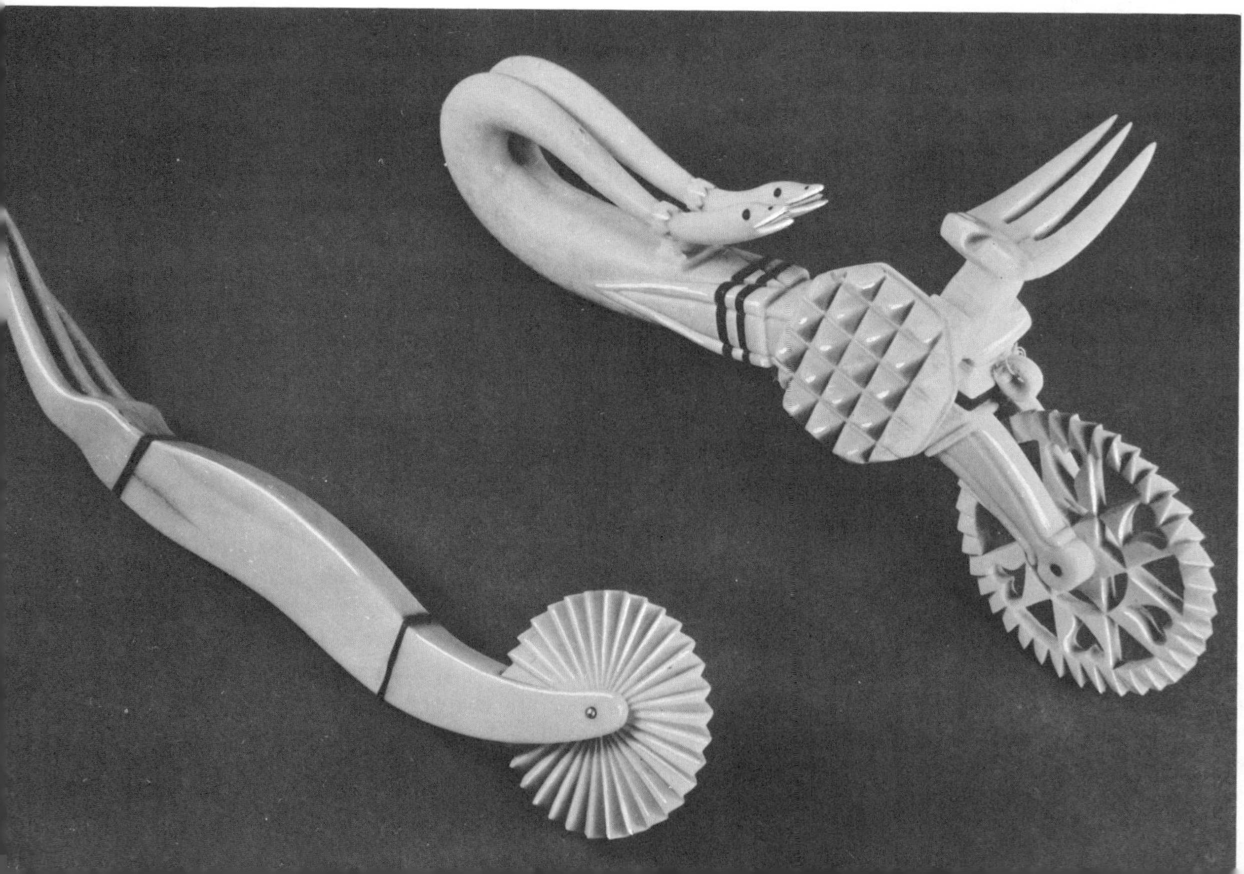

vases, baskets and boxes of varying sizes and shapes. Nor were the children forgotten. Toys of every description and dainty dollhouse furniture, sturdy enough to withstand careless handling, were obviously cherished. More than a century later, they remain the most collectible objects of the great whaling era.

For his own amusement, the sailor made snuff boxes, checkers, checkerboards, and chessmen as well as inkstands, portable writing desks, ditty boxes, rulers, letter openers, and numerous other useful items ranging from shoehorns to watch chains.

Aside from the trophy-like whale's teeth which seamen turned out in great numbers during the prime years of the whaling trade, one of the commonest and most popular of all scrimshaw articles was the whalebone busk, a bodice stay used in corsets worn by ladies in the nineteenth century. It varied in length from eight to twelve inches, measured approximately 1½ inches in width and ⅛ inch or slightly more in thickness and was usually rounded on both ends. This very personal item, carved by a sailor for his wife or sweetheart, was fashioned from either panbone, baleen, or wood and was elaborately decorated, often with romantic and sentimental motifs in picture and verse. Some depicted the adventures and hazards involved in whaling; others were adorned with compasses, rope borders, anchors, fish whales, or a bit of tropical landscape. Sometimes the designs were of hearts, flowers, birds, patriotic themes, or geometric designs. Occasionally, a portrait of the carver appeared. When a sentimental verse appeared on the reverse side of the busk, it came straight from the heart and conveyed more in feeling and thought than any letter possibly could.

While most jagging wheels or pie crimpers were elaborately designed and displayed the consummate skill of the maker, the swift or wool winder proved to be the most difficult and intricately designed of all scrimshaw pieces. The swift was designed as an expanding reel, operating like an umbrella, with a thumb screw to hold it open. A typical swift contained more than a hundred separately made pieces of polished ivory which were assembled with metal rivets (copper, brass, or silver). The silver usually came from coins. Some of the swifts were placed on stands; others were designed with a type of clamp for attaching to a table or sewing box. The most elaborate were those mounted on handsomely made inlaid boxes, complete with drawers to hold knitting needles, needle holders, thimbles, and other sewing equipment, most of it made of ivory or whalebone. Although the majority of the twenty thousand or more whalemen who plied their trade are believed to have turned their hands to scrimshaw, comparatively few attempted to make a swift. Not only was it a time-consuming, painstaking task, but it required more space to assemble than most of the small crowded whaling ships could provide. Thus, the scrimshaw wool winders that remain are among the rarest of collector's items today.

The accomplished etcher and carver attempted precious bits of jewelry for his wife or mother, his sweetheart or the girl he hoped to court when he reached home port. These included earrings and buttons, brooches and breast pins and hat pins (which could also be used as bodkins to pierce cloth), bracelets and sometimes puzzle boxes with swivel covers of intricate design and locking devices. Stars, hearts, and flowers were typical of the romantic emblems used in the designs.

For the most part, the basic tools of the whalemen were his jackknife, ground to a fine point, and those indispensible needles used by sailors. On occasion the ship's cooper could be pressed into service to make needed items. In *Moby Dick*, Herman Melville refers to "little boxes of dentistical-looking implements, specially intended for the scrimshandering business. But, in general they toil with their jackknives alone; and with that omnipotent tool of the sailor, they will turn out anything you please, in the way of a mariner's fancy." Gimlets, awls, and files were often needed.

(*Left*) Whale's tooth engraved on board the ship *Carolina Augusta*, by J. B. W. Walton, 1848, for Captain Creamer, Salem, Massachusetts. The tooth is mounted on an inlaid stand. Engraving is of remarkably fine quality. The significance of the emblems was recorded in a poem which the engraver presented to Captain Creamer. (*Right*) An eagle's head carved as a finial for a bodkin. *Photo, M. W. Sexton; courtesy, Peabody Museum, Salem, Massachusetts*

Examples of the jagging wheel or pie crimper, each with a fork attached. These indispensable kitchen implements were the joy of every housewife and the whalemen who made them were always proud to display them. *Photo, Louis S. Martel; courtesy, Mystic Seaport, Mystic, Connecticut*

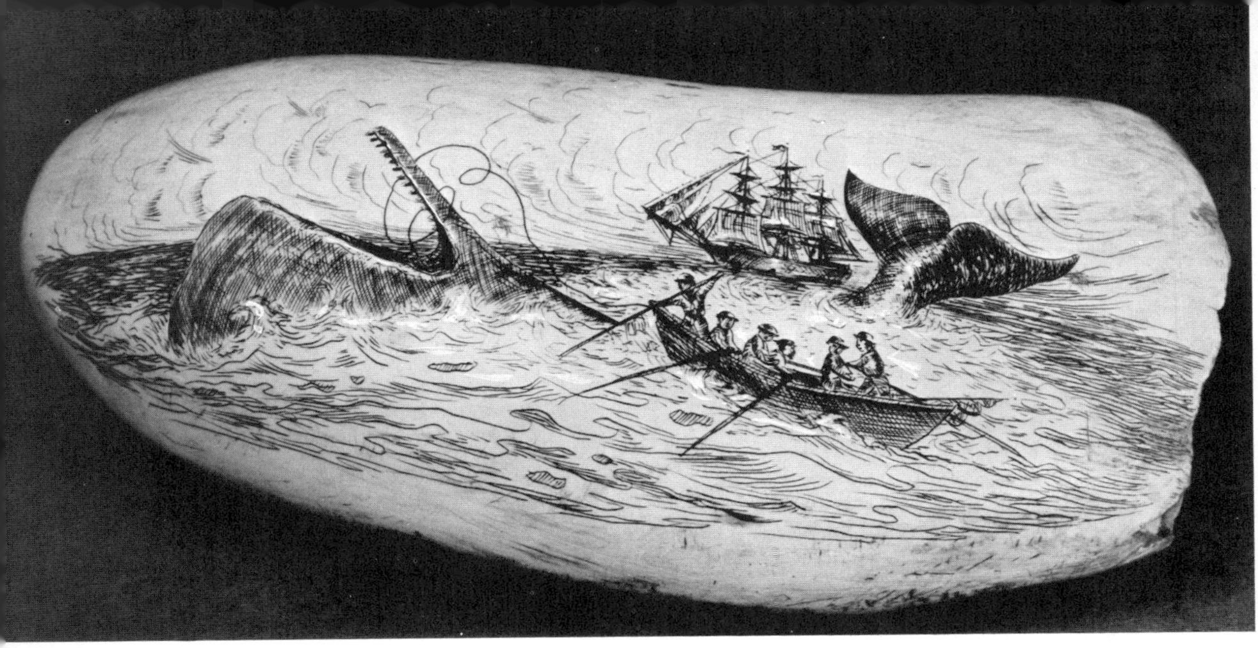

A longboat approaching a captured whale with the whaleship in the background. Action scenes of whaling were favorite subjects for etching on whale's teeth. *Photo, Louis S. Martel; courtesy, Mystic Seaport, Mystic, Connecticut*

Examples of engraved whale's teeth featuring various motifs, all executed in minute detail. *Photo, L. S. Martel; courtesy, Mystic Seaport, Mystic, Connecticut*

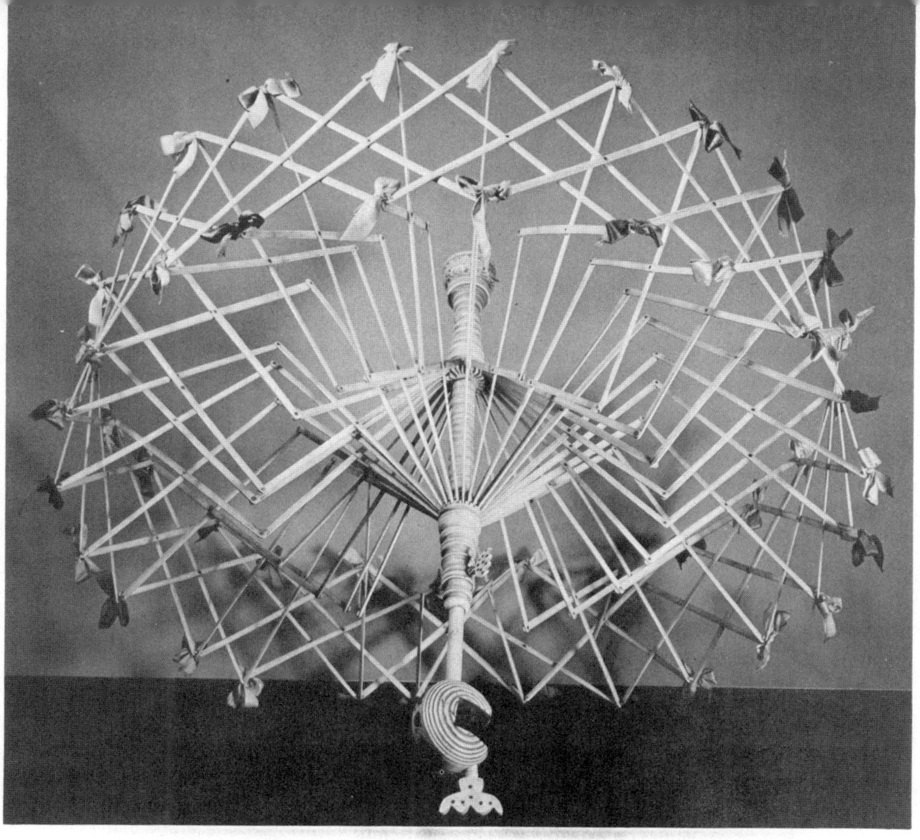

A swift or wool winder required more than ordinary patience and skill to make and to assemble. Metal rivets and bits of ribbon were used to hold the separately made pieces of polished ivory together. The clamp was attached to a table or sewing box to provide the housewife with a marvelous contraption for winding yarn. *Photo, Louis S. Martel; courtesy, Mystic Seaport, Mystic, Connecticut*

The teeth and whalebone had to be carefully scraped with a broad-bladed knife before it was cut. Brine or hot soapy water served to soften the surface. Ashes, pumice, and whiting were needed to make the ivory smooth. Sharkskin served as sandpaper.

Designs taken from books, newspapers, and magazines or recalled from memory were outlined or traced on the surface. Then came the task of engraving which required patience, skill, and a sure hand, especially when designs were intricate and sharp detail was desired. Once the design was completed, it was inked or painted, depending on the material available. These included India ink, paint, lampblack, soot, or even tobacco juice, and sometimes colored inks were used.

The subject matter that appealed to the scrimshaw carver was obviously determined by his personal interests and background, his political leanings, or whatever he happened to see pictured in the reading material to be found on board the whaler. Naturally, female figures appear frequently in scrimshaw designs, especially in those etched on the teeth. Patriotic personages like Liberty and Justice contrast vividly with replicas of Lady Godiva on horseback, Fanny Campbell, widely known female pirate captain, and Alwilda, a sword-wielding female whose exploits were described in *The Pirate's Own Book* published in Portland and Philadelphia in 1837. This book was a prime favorite of sailors. Fashion plates for *Godey's Ladies Book* and other fashion publications were obviously the inspiration of the well-dressed girls and women whose gowns were usually portrayed in minute detail.

The American eagle, the flag, whaling ships, and other kinds of sailing vessels, port scenes, and innumerable renditions of scenes featuring the capture of a whale were popular subjects of depiction. Occasionally, religious art appeared. Lincoln and Grant and other political figures, scenes from the War of 1812, as well as factories, an occasional embassy, a log cabin scene, and memorials to departed friends added to the variety of pictorial interest. Patriotic slogans, bits of verse, an occasional American Indian, Bunker Hill Monument, and Independence Hall reveal the widespread interest of scrimshaw themes as history, folklore, and romance were etched in ivory by American whalemen in the nineteenth century.

Bibliography

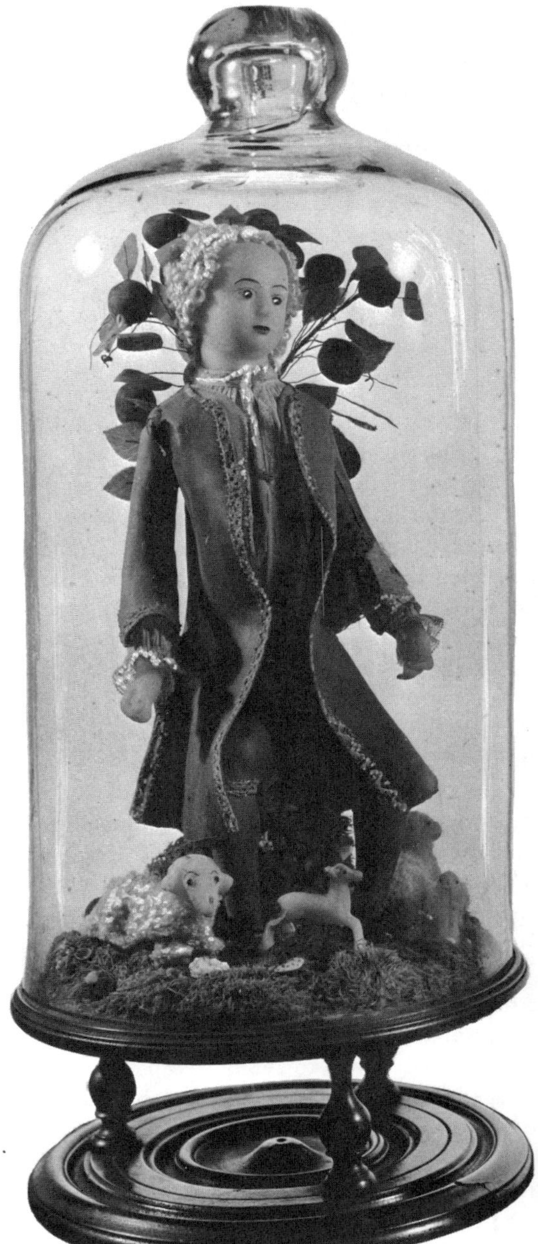

General

Adams, Alexander B., Editor. *Thoreau's Guide to Cape Cod.* New York: Devin-Adair, 1962.

Adams, James Truslow. *The Epic of America.* Boston: Little, Brown, 1932.

Adams, James Truslow. *The Founding of New England.* Boston: Atlantic Monthly Press, 1921.

Bailey, Carolyn Sherwin. *Boys and Girls of Colonial Days.* Chicago: A. Flanagan Co., 1920.

Belknap, Henry W. *Artists and Craftsmen of Essex County, Massachusetts.* Salem, Mass.: Essex Institute, 1927.

Bliss, William Root. *Colonial Times on Buzzard's Bay.* Boston: Houghton, Mifflin, 1889.

Botkin, B. A., Editor. *A Treasury of New England Folklore: Stories, Ballads and Traditions of the Yankee People.* New York: Crown, 1947.

Bradford, William. *History of Plymouth Plantation.* In, *Original Narratives of Early American History.* New York: Scribner's, 1908.

Bridenbaugh, Carl. *The Colonial Craftsman.* New York: New York University Press, 1950.

Buxton, Henry. *Assignment Down East.* Brattleboro, Vt.: Stephen Day, 1938.

Chamberlain, Narcissa. *Old Rooms for New Living.* New York: Hastings House, 1953.

Chamberlain, Samuel. *Beyond New England Thresholds.* New York: Hastings House, 1937.

Note: All of the following titles were published by Hastings House, New York. These volumes are especially noteworthy for their exceptional photographs showing exteriors and interiors of New England houses covering a period of three centuries.

———. *Cape Cod in the Sun.* 1937.

———. *Ever New England.* 1944.

———. *Fair Is Our Land.* 1952.

———. *Gloucester and Cape Ann.* 1938.

———. *Historic Boston.* 1938.

———. *Historic Cambridge.* 1938.

———. *Historic Salem.* 1938.

———. *Lexington and Concord.* 1939.

———. *Longfellow's Wayside Inn.* 1938.

———. *Martha's Vineyard.* 1941.

———. *Nantucket.* 1939.

———. *New England Image.* 1962.

———. *Old Marblehead.* 1940.

———. *Open House in New England.* 1948.

———. *Portsmouth, New Hampshire.* 1940.

———. *Salem Interiors.* 1950.

———. *A Small House in the Sun.* 1936.

Chamberlain, Samuel and Flynt, Henry N. *Historic Deerfield.* New York: Hastings House, 1965.

Chamberlain, Samuel and Hollister, Paul. *Beauport at Gloucester.* New York: Hastings House, 1951.

Christensen, Erwin O. *American Crafts and Folk Arts.* Washington, D. C.: R. B. Luce, 1964.

Christensen, Erwin O. *The Index of American Design.* New York: Macmillan, 1959.

Clarke, Mary Stetson. *Petticoat Rebel.* New York: Viking Press, 1964.

Coatsworth, Elizabeth. *Maine Ways.* New York: Macmillan, 1947.

Crawford, Mary C. *The Romance of Old New England Rooftrees.* Boston: Page, 1902.

Cutler, Carl C. *Mystic: The Story of a Small New England Seaport.* Mystic, Conn.: Marine Historical Association, 1945.

Dodge, Lawrence G. and Alice Cole. *New Puritan Paths from Candle to Countdown.* Newburyport, Mass.: Newburyport Press, 1964.

Dodge, Lawrence G. and Alice Cole. *Puritan Paths from Naumkeag to Piscataqua.* Newburyport, Mass.: Newburyport Press, 1963.

Dorian, Edith and Wilson, W. N. *Animals That Made United States History.* New York: McGraw-Hill, 1964.

Dow, George Francis. *The Arts and Crafts in New England, 1704–1775.* Topsfield, Mass.: Wayside Press, 1927.

Dow, George Francis. *Domestic Life in New England in the Seventeenth Century.* Topsfield, Mass.: Privately printed, 1925.

Dow, George Francis. *Everyday Life in the Massachusetts Bay Colony.* Boston: The Society for the Preservation of New England Antiquities, 1935.

Dow, George Francis. *Two Centuries of Travel in Essex County, Massachusetts.* Topsfield: Topsfield Historical Society, 1921.

Drepperd, Carl W. *Early American Prints.* New York: Century, 1930.

Drepperd, Carl W. *A Primer of American Antiques.* New York: Doubleday, 1945.

Dwight, Timothy. *Travels in New England and New York.* 4 vols. New Haven: Timothy Dwight, 1821.

Dyer, Walter A. *Early American Craftsmen.* New York: Century, 1915.

Earle, Alice Morse. *Child Life in Colonial Days.* New York: Macmillan, 1899.

Earle, Alice Morse. *Colonial Dames and Goodwives.* Boston: Houghton, Mifflin, 1895.

Earle, Alice Morse. *Customs and Fashions in Old New England.* New York: Scribner's, 1893.

Earle, Alice Morse. *Home Life in Colonial Days.* New York: Grosset, 1898.

Earle, Alice Morse. *Margaret Winthrop (Women of Colonial and Revolutionary Times).* New York: Scribner's, 1895.

Earle, Alice Morse. *Stage-coach and Tavern Days.* New York: Macmillan, 1900.

Earle, Alice Morse. *Two Centuries of Costume in America.* New York: Macmillan, 1903.

Eaton, Allen H. *Handicrafts of New England.* New York: Harper, 1949.

Federal Writers' Project. *American Guide Series. The Berkshire Hills.* Funk & Wagnalls, 1939.
Federal Writers' Project. *American Guide Series. Maine. New Hampshire. Rhode Island. Vermont. Massachusetts. Connecticut.* Boston: Houghton, Mifflin, 1937, 1938.
Felt, Joseph B. *The Customs of New England.* Boston: T. R. Marvin, 1853.
Forbes, Harriette Merrifield. *Gravestones of Early New England.* Boston: Houghton, Mifflin, 1927.
Franklin, Benjamin. *Autobiography.* New York: Modern Library, 1932.
Franklin, Benjamin. *The Ingenious Dr. Franklin. Selected Scientific Letters of Benjamin Franklin.* Edited by Nathan G. Goodman. Philadelphia: Univ. of Pa. Press, 1931.
Franklin, Benjamin. *The Writings of Benjamin Franklin.* Edited by Albert Henry Smythe. New York: Macmillan, 1905–1907.
Gleeson, Paul F. *Rhode Island: The Development of a Democracy.* Providence: Rhode Island State Board of Education, 1957.
Greene, Welcome Arnold. *The Providence Plantations for Two Hundred and Fifty Years.* Providence: Reid, 1886.
Hartley, E. N. *Ironworks on the Saugus.* Norman: Univ. of Oklahoma Press, 1957.
Hawthorne, Nathaniel. *The Complete Writings of Nathaniel Hawthorne, Old Manse Edition,* 22 vols. Boston: Houghton, Mifflin, 1900.
Heath, Dwight B. Editor. *A Journal of the Pilgrims at Plymouth: Mourt's Relation.* New York: Corinth Books, 1963.
Hill, Ralph Nading and Carlisle, Lilian Baker. *The Story of the Shelburne Museum.* Shelburne, Vt.: The Shelburne Museum, 1960.
Hoag, Edwin. *American Houses: Colonial, Classic and Contemporary.* Philadelphia: Lippincott, 1964.
Holliday, Carl. *The Wit and Humor of Colonial Days (1607–1800).* Philadelphia: Lippincott, 1912.
Holloway, Edward S. *The Practical Book of American Furniture and Decoration.* Philadelphia: Lippincott, 1937.
Humphrey, Zephine. *A Book of New England.* Howell, Soskin, 1947.
James, Sydney V., Jr., Editor. *Three Visitors to Early Plymouth by John Pory, Emmanuel Althem and Isaack De Rasieres.* Plymouth, Mass.: Plimoth Plantation, 1963.
Johnson, Captain Edward. *Wonder-Working Providence of Scion's Savior in New England.* New York: Scribner's, 1910.
Kelly, J. Frederick. *Connecticut's Old Houses: a Handbook and Guide.* Stonington, Conn.: Pequot Press, 1963.
Kerfoot, J. B. *American Pewter.* Boston: Houghton, Mifflin, 1924.
Lambert, M. and Marx, Enid. *English Popular Art.* London: Batsford, 1951.
Larcom, Lucy. *A New England Girlhood.* Boston: Houghton, Mifflin, 1889.
Larkin, Oliver W. *Art and Life in America.* New York: Rinehart, 1949.
Lathrop, Elise, *Historic Homes of Early America.* New York: Tudor, 1927.
Lee, W. Storrs. *The Yankees of Connecticut.* New York: Holt, 1957.
Lichten, Frances. *Decorative Art of Victoria's Era.* New York: Scribner's, 1950.
Little, Nina Fletcher. *The Abby Aldrich Rockefeller Folk Art Collection.* Boston: Little, Brown, 1957.
Lockwood, Luke Vincent. *Colonial Furniture in America.* New York: Scribner's, 1926.
Lockwood, Sarah M. *Decoration, Past, Present and Future.* New York: Doubleday, 1934.
McClelland, Nancy. *Furnishing the Colonial and Federal House.* Philadelphia: Lippincott, 1947.
Manley, Seon and Lewis, Gogo, Editors. *Teen-age Treasury of the Arts.* New York: Funk & Wagnalls, 1964.
Mann, Helen R. *Gallant Warrior.* Grand Rapids, Mich.: Wm. B. Eerdsmans, 1954.
Mann, Helen R. *Plenty, Priscilla.* Grand Rapids, Mich.: Wm. B. Eerdsmans, 1956.
Morison, Samuel Eliot. *Builders of the Bay Colony.* Boston: Houghton, Mifflin, 1930.
Morison, Samuel Eliot. *Maritime History of Massachusetts.* 1783–1860. Boston: Houghton, Mifflin, 1921.
Morison, Samuel Eliot. *The Puritan Pronaos.* New York: New York Univ., 1936.
Morton, Thomas. *The New English Canaan.* Force's Tracts, II. Washington: 1836.
Mussey, Barrow, Editor. *Yankee Life by Those Who Lived It.* New York: Knopf, 1947.
Nutting, Wallace. *The Clock Book.* Framingham, Mass.: Old America Co., 1924.
Phillips, James D. *Pepper and Pirates.* Boston: Houghton, Mifflin, 1949.
Phillips, James D. *Salem in the Seventeenth Century.* Boston: Houghton, Mifflin, 1933.
Phillips, James D. *Salem in the Eighteenth Century.* Boston: Houghton, Mifflin, 1937.
Phillips, James D. *Salem and the Indies.* Boston: Houghton, Mifflin, 1947.
Pound, Arthur. *Native Stock.* New York: Macmillan, 1931.
Rich, Louise Dickenson. *State o'Maine.* New York: Harper and Row, 1964.
Robotti, Frances Diane. *Chronicles of Old Salem.* Salem: Newcomb & Gauss, 1948.
Ross, Marjorie Drake. *The Book of Boston: The Colonial Period.* New York: Hastings House, 1960.
Ross, Marjorie Drake. *The Book of Boston: The Federal Period.* New York: Hastings House, 1961.

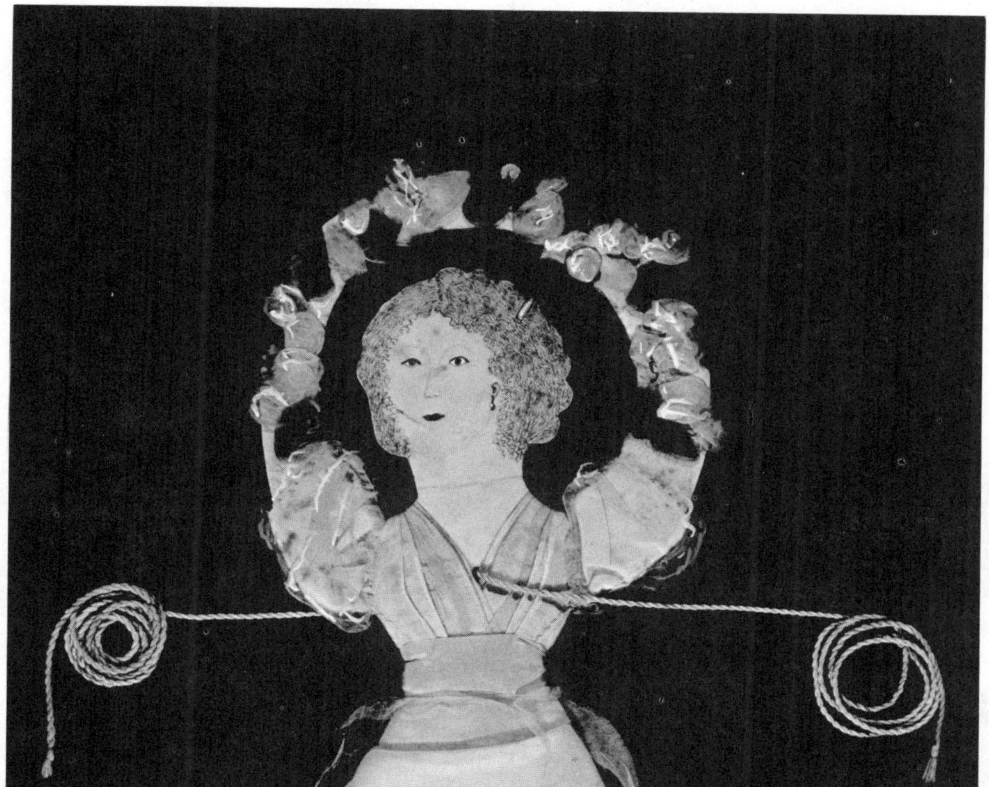

The pantine, a cardboard figure with movable arms and legs, manipulated with strings held in the hands, became a popular amusement for all ages in France during the eighteenth century and had its vogue in America as well. Examples can still be located in seaport communities. *Photo courtesy Essex Institute*

Rouse, A. R. *The Elizabethans and America.* New York: Harper, 1959.
Sears, Clara Endicott. *Early Personal Reminiscences in the Old George Peabody Mansion in Salem, Massachusetts.* Concord, N.H.: Privately printed, 1956.
Steinmetz, Rollin C. and Rice, Charles S. *Vanishing Crafts and Their Craftsmen.* New Brunswick, N. J.: Rutgers Univ. Press, 1959.
Stowe, Harriet Beecher. *The Minister's Wooing.* London: Samson, Low, Marston, 1894.
Tunis, Edwin. *Colonial Living.* New York: World Publishing Co., 1957.
Vanderbilt, Cornelius, Jr. *The Living Past of America.* New York: Crown, 1955.
Verril, A. Hyatt. *Foods America Gave the World.* Boston: Page, 1937.
Waller, Mary. *The Woodcarver of 'Lympus.* Boston: Little, Brown, 1904.
Warwick, Edward and Pitz, Henry. *Early American Costume.* New York: Century, 1929.
Wells, Frederic Palmer. *History of Barnet, Vermont.* Burlington, Vt.: Free Press Printing Co., 1923.
Wharton, Anne Hollingsworth. *Through Colonial Doorways.* Philadelphia: Lippincott, 1893.
Williamson, Scott Graham. *The American Craftsman.* New York: Bramhall House, 1960.
Willis, William. *Journals of the Rev. Thomas Smith, and the Rev. Samuel Deane, Pastors of the First Church in Portland.* Portland: Joseph J. Bailey, 1849.
Wish, Harvey. *William Bradford of Plymouth Plantation.* New York: Capricorn, 1962.
Wright, Richardson. *Grandfather Was Queer.* Philadelphia: Lippincott, 1939.
Wright, Richardson. *Hawkers and Walkers in Early America.* Philadelphia: Lippincott, 1927.
Yates, Raymond F. and Marguerite W. *Early American Crafts and Hobbies.* New York: Wilfred Funk, 1954.
Young, Alexander. *Chronicles of the First Planters of the Colony of Massachusetts Bay, from 1633 to 1636.* Boston: Little, Brown, 1846.

Wood, Wood Carving

Anonymous. *Ship Figureheads and Other Wood Carving Art in the Nautical Collection of the State Street Trust Company.* Boston: n.d.
Anonymous. *Samuel McIntire: A Bicentennial Symposium.* Salem, Mass.: Essex Institute, 1957.
Barber, Joel. *Wild Fowl Decoys.* New York: Dover, 1954.
Bjerkoe, Ethel H. and John A. *The Cabinetmakers of America.* New York: Doubleday, 1957.
Brewington, M. V. *Shipcarvers of North America.* Barre, Mass.: Barre Publishing Co., 1962.
Christensen, Erwin O. *Early American Wood Carving.* New York: World, 1952.
Cousins, Frank and Riley, Phil. *The Colonial Architecture of Salem.* Boston: Little, Brown, 1919.
Cousins, Frank and Riley, Phil. *The Woodcarver of Salem: Samuel McIntire, His Life and Work.* Boston: Little, Brown, 1916.
Gould, Mary Earle. *Early American Wooden Ware.* Springfield, Mass.: Pond-Ekberg, 1942.
Kimball, Fiske. *Mr. Samuel McIntire, Carver, the Architect of Salem.* Portland, Me.: Essex Institute, 1940.
McClinton, Catherine M. *Antique Collecting for Everyone.* New York: McGraw-Hill, 1951.
Ormsbee, Thomas H. *Early American Furniture Makers.* New York: T. Y. Crowell, 1930.
Ormsbee, Thomas H. *The Story of American Furniture.* New York: Macmillan, 1937.
Paine, Ralph D. *Ships and Sailors of Old Salem.* New York: 1919.
Pinckney, Pauline A. *American Figureheads and Their Carvers.* New York: Norton, 1940.
Pinto, Edward H. *Treen, or Small Woodenware Throughout the Ages.* London: Batsford, 1949.
Rawson, Marion N. *Handwrought Ancestors.* New York: Dutton, 1936.
Stackpole, Edouard A. *Figureheads and Ship Carvings.* Mystic, Conn.: Marine Historical Association, 1964.
Upton, John. *The Art of Wood Carving.* New York: Van Nostrand, 1958.
Webster, David S. and Kehoe, William. *Decoys at Shelburne Museum.* Shelburne, Vt.: 1961.
Wildung, Frank H. *Woodworking Tools at Shelburne Museum.* Shelburne, Vt.: 1957.

Needlework

GENERAL

Haire, Frances H. *The American Costume Book.* New York: Barnes, 1934.
Harbeson, Georgiana Brown. *American Needlework.* New York: Bonanza, 1938.
Lane, Rose Wilder. *Woman's Day Book of American Needlework.* New York: Simon, Schuster, 1963.
Spears, Ruth Wyeth. *The Work Basket Embroidery Book.* New York: Barrows, 1941.
Stearns, Martha G. *Needle in Hand.* New York: Ives Washburn, 1950.
Thomas, Mary. *Mary Thomas's Embroidery Book.* New York: Morrow, 1936.
Wheeler, Candace. *The Development of Embroidery in America.* New York: Harper, 1921.
Wright, Roxa. *Blue and White Deerfield Embroidery.* New York: Fawcett, 1962.

CREWEL

Davis, Mildred J. *The Art of Crewel Embroidery.* New York: Crown, 1962.

Hedlund, Catherine A. *A Primer of New England Crewel Embroidery.* Sturbridge, Mass.: Old Sturbridge Village, 1963.

Stearns, Martha Genung. *Homespun and Blue; a Study of American Crewel Embroidery.* New York: Scribner's, 1963.

KNITTING

Boehm, Peggy. *Knitting Without Needles.* New York: Cornerstone Library, 1963.

Thomas, Mary. *Mary Thomas's Knitting Book.* New York: Morrow.

LACE

Vanderpoel, Emily Noyes. *American Lace and Lace Makers.* New Haven: Yale Univ. Press, 1924.

Needlepoint

Hanley, Hope. *Needlepoint.* New York: Scribner's, 1964.

Quilts

Carlisle, Lillian Baker. *Pieced Work and Appliqué Quilts at Shelburne Museum.* Shelburne, Vt.: The Shelburne Museum, 1957.

Davidson, Mildred. *Early American Hand-Woven Coverlets.* Chicago: The Art Institute of Chicago, 1946.

Dunton, William Rusk, Jr., M.D. *Old Quilts.* Catonsville, Md.: Published by author, 1946.

Finley, Ruth E. *Old Patchwork Quilts and the Women Who Made Them.* Philadelphia: Lippincott, 1929.

Hall, Carrie A. and Kretsinger, Rose G. *The Romance of the Patchwork Quilt in America.* Caldwell, Idaho: Caxton Printers, 1935.

McKim, Ruby Short. *One Hundred and One Patchwork Patterns.* Independence, Mo.: McKim Studios, 1931.

Peto, Florence. *American Quilts and Coverlets.* New York: Chanticleer, 1949.

Robertson, Elizabeth Wells. *American Quilts.* New York: Studio, 1948.

Rugs

Bowles, Ella Shannon. *Handmade Rugs.* Boston: Little, Brown, 1927.

Kent, William Winthrop. *The Hooked Rug.* New York: Dodd, Mead, 1930.

Rex, Stella Hay. *Choice Hooked Rugs.* New York: Prentice-Hall, 1953.

Samplers

Christie, Mrs. Archibald. *Samplers and Stitches.* New York:

Stencils

Stephenson, Jessie Bane. *From Old Stencils to Silk Screening.* New York: Scribner's, 1953.

Textiles

Ackerman, Phyllis. *Handwoven Textiles.* Pasadena, Calif.: Esto Publishing Co.

Fennelly, Catherine. *Textiles in New England, 1790–1840.* Sturbridge, Mass.: Old Sturbridge Village, 1961.

Lewis, Ethel. *The Romance of Textiles.* New York: Macmillan, 1953.

Indian Crafts

Glubok, Shirley. *The Art of the North American Indian.* New York: Harper and Row, 1964.

Hunt, Walter Bernard. *The Golden Book of Indian Crafts and Lore.* New York: Simon and Schuster, 1954.

Hunt, W. Ben. *Indian Crafts and Lore.* New York: Golden Press, 1964.

Porter, C. Fayne. *Our Indian Heritage: Profiles of Twelve Great Leaders.* Philadelphia: Chilton, 1964.

Salomon, Julian Harris. *The Book of Indian Crafts and Indian Lore.* New York: Harper, 1928.

Jewelry

Burgess, Fred W. *Antique Jewelry and Trinkets.* New York: Putnam, 1919.

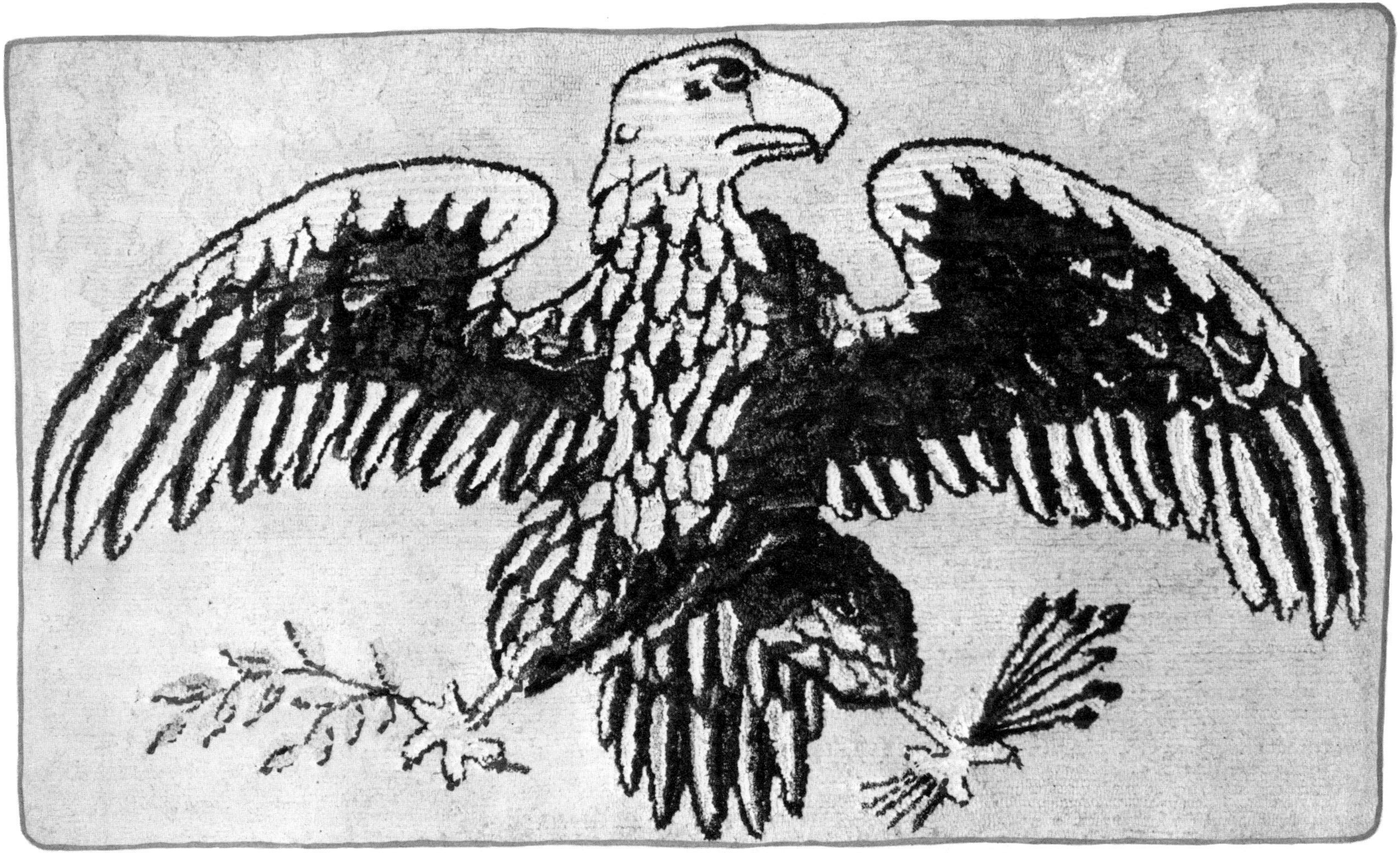

The eagle, displayed, was a favorite motif for hooked rugs and various forms of the needleworker's art. Grayish and tan wool form the background of this eagle done in black. The feather representation was made in alternating stripes of tan wool and printed cotton designs in pink, blue, yellow, and green on a tan background. A red touch was added at and above the eye, while the talons and beak were yellow. The olive branch was hooked in shades of green with the arrows in black. Seven tan cotton stars appear above the left wing, and six above the right wing. 33 x 58 inches. *Circa* 1875. *Photo Einar Mengis: courtesy Shelburne Museum*

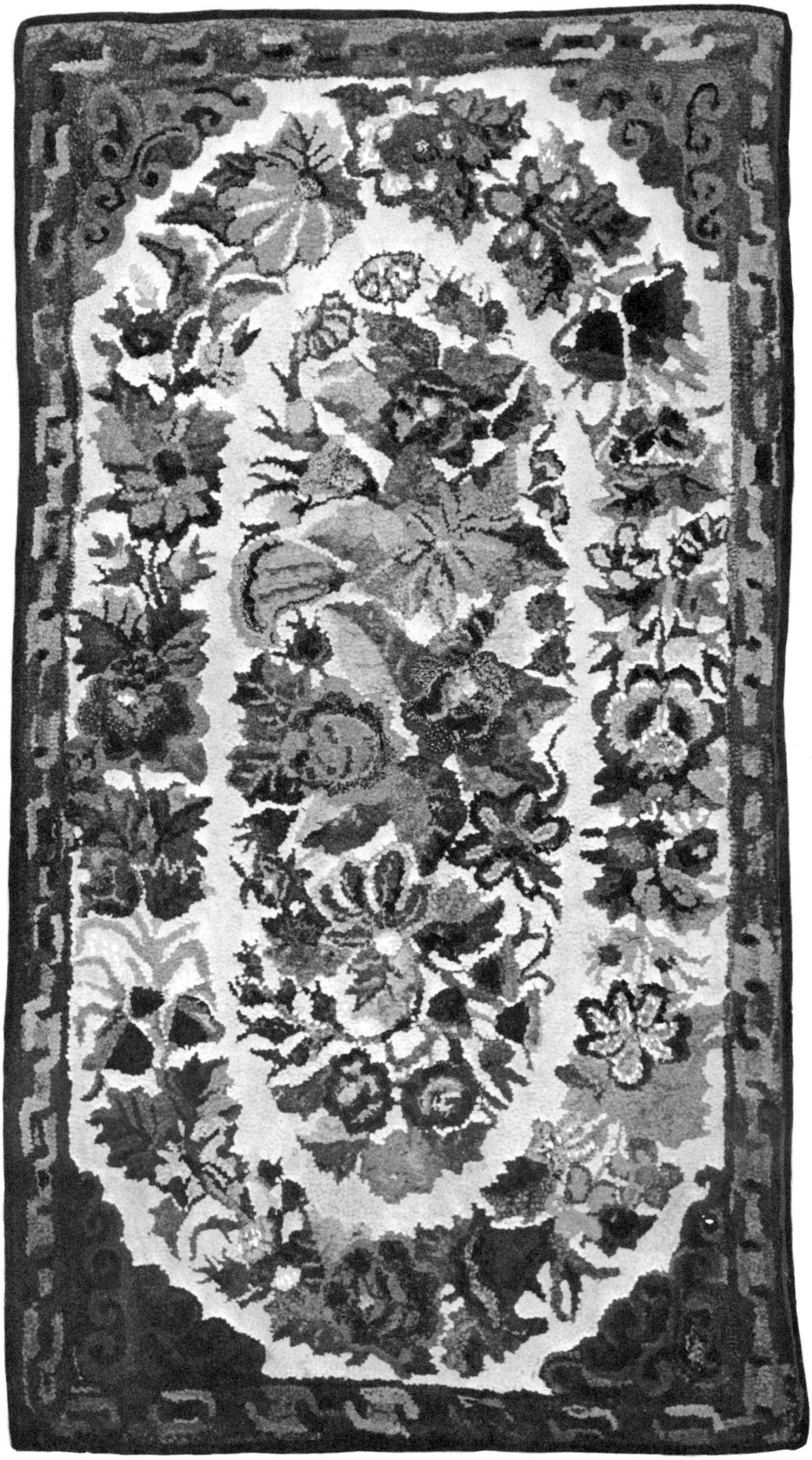

Hooked rug with floral design from *Rugs and Comfort. Photo courtesy Shelburne Museum*

Frankovich, George R. *The Jewelry Industry.* (Vocational and Professional Monographs, No. 85.) Cambridge: Bellman Publishing Co., 1955.

Kronquist, Enid F. *Metalcraft and Jewelry.* Peoria, Ill.: Manual Arts Press, 1926.

Longman, E. D. and Loch, S. *Pins and Pincushions.* New York: Longmans, Green, 1911.

Percival, MacIver. *Chats on Old Jewelry and Trinkets.* New York: Frederick A. Stokes, n.d.

Ross, Ishbel. *Grace Coolidge and Her Era: The Story of a President's Wife.* New York: Dodd, Mead, 1962.

Miniatures

O'Donnell, Georgene. *Miniaturia:The World of Tiny Things.* Chicago: Lightner Publishing, 1943.

Painting, Decoration

Anonymous. *Massachusetts Bay Colony Tercentenary Loan Exhibition of One Hundred Colonial Portraits.* Boston: Museum of Fine Arts, 1930.

Anonymous. *One Hundred and One Masterpieces of American Primitive Painting from the Collection of Edgar William and Bernice Chrysler Garbisch.* New York: American Federation of Arts, 1962.

Allen, Edward B. *Early American Wall Painting.* New Haven: Yale Univ. Press, 1926.

Burroughs, Alan. *Limners and Likenesses.* Cambridge, Mass.: 1936.

Downer, Marion. *The Story of Design.* New York: Lothrop, Lee and Shepard, 1963.

Dresser, Louisa. *Seventeenth Century Painting in New England.* Worcester, Mass.: 1935.

Dunlap, William. *History of the Rise and Progress of the Arts of Design in the United States.* 2 vols. New York: 1834.

Flexner, James Thomas. *America's Old Masters.* New York: 1939.

Flexner, James Thomas. *American Painting—First Flowers of Our Wilderness.* Boston: Houghton, Mifflin, 1947.

Flexner, James Thomas. *The Light of Distant Skies: American Painting 1760–1835.* Boston: Houghton, Mifflin, 1954.

Forbes, Esther. *Rainbow on the Road.* Boston: Houghton, Mifflin, 1954.

Ford, Alice. *Pictorial Folk Art: New England to California.* New York: Studio Publications, 1949.

Isham, Samuel. *The History of American Painting.* New York: 1905.

LaFollette, Suzanne. *Art in America.* New York: Harper, 1929.

Lee Cuthbert. *Early American Portrait Painters.* New Haven: Yale Univ. Press, 1929.

Lipman, Jean. *American Folk Art.* New York: Pantheon, 1948.

Lipman, Jean. *American Folk Decoration.* New York: Oxford Univ. Press, 1951.

Little, Nina Fletcher. *Abby Aldrich Rockefeller Folk Art Collection.* Williamsburg, Va.: 1957.

Little, Nina Fletcher. *American Decorative Wall Painting.* New York: Old Sturbridge Village in cooperation with Studio Publications, 1952.

Sears, Clara Endicott. *Some American Primitives.* Boston: Houghton, Mifflin, 1941.

Singleton, Esther. *The Furniture of Our Forefathers.* New York: Doubleday, 1901.

Waring, Janet. *Early American Stencils on Walls and Furniture.* New York: W. R. Scott, 1937.

Silhouettes

Bolton, Ethel Stanwood. *American Wax Portraits.* Boston: Houghton, Mifflin, 1929.

Bolton, Ethel Stanwood. *Wax Portraits and Silhouettes.* Boston: Mass. Society of the Colonial Dames of America, 1914.

Brown, William Henry. *Portrait Gallery of Distinguished American Citizens with Biographical Sketches.* New York: G. A. Baker, 1931.

Carrick, Alice Van Leer. *Shades of Our Ancestors.* Boston: Little, Brown, 1928.

Dunlap, William. *History of the Arts of Design in the United States.* Ed. by Bayley and Goodspeed. Boston: 1918.

Jackson, E. Nevill. *The History of Silhouettes.* London: The Connoisseur, 1911.

Lavater, John Caspar. *Essays on Physiognomy.* London: 1797.

London, Hannah R. *Shades of My Forefathers.* Springfield, Mass.: Pond-Ekberg, 1941.

Tavern and Trade Signs

Crawford, Mary C. *Old New England Inns.* Boston: Page, 1927.

Dunbar, Seymour. *History of Travel in America.* Indianapolis: Bobbs-Merrill, 1915.

Earle, Alice Morse. *Stage Coach and Tavern Days.* New York: Macmillan, 1927.

Field, Edward. *The Colonial Tavern.* Providence: Preston and Rounds, 1897.

Forbes, Allan. *Taverns and Stagecoaches of New England.* Boston: State Street Trust Co., Vol. 1, 1953, Vol. 2, 1954.

Larwood, Jacob and Hotten, John C. *The History of Signboards*. London: Hotten, n.d.
Marlowe, George Francis. *Coaching Roads of Old New England*. New York: Macmillan, 1945.
Shepard, Odell. *Connecticut Past and Present*. New York: Knopf, 1939.
Woodward, W. E. *The Way Our People Lived: An Intimate American History*. New York: Dutton, 1944.

Dyes

Schetky, Ethel Jane McD. *Dye Plants and Dyeing*. Plants & Gardens—Autumn 1964. Brooklyn, N. Y.: Brooklyn Botanic Garden.

Eagles

Adrian, Mary. *The American Eagle*. (Preserve Our Wild Life Series.) New York: Hastings House, 1963.

Pottery

Barber, E. A. *Pottery and Porcelain in the United States*. New York: Putnam's, 1903.
Barrett, Richard Carter. *Bennington Pottery and Porcelain*. New York: Bonanza Books, 1958.
Earle, Alice Morse. *China Collecting in America*. New York: Scribner's, 1892.
Kenny, John B. *Ceramic Design*. Philadelphia: Chilton Books, 1963.
Ramsay, John. *American Potters and Pottery*. Boston: Hale, Cushman & Flint, 1939.
Spargo, John. *Early American Pottery and China*. New York: Century, 1926.
Thorn, C. Jordan. *Handbook of Old Pottery and Porcelain Marks*. New York: Tudor, 1947.
Watkins, Lura Woodside. *Early New England Potters and Their Wares*. Cambridge: Harvard Univ. Press, 1950.
Watkins, Lura Woodside. *Early New England Pottery*. Sturbridge, Mass.: Sturbridge Village, 1959.
Young, Jennie J. *The Ceramic Art*. New York: Harper, 1878.

Tin

Brazer, Esther Stevens. *Early American Decoration*. Springfield, Mass.: Pond-Ekberg, 1961.
Dolan, J. R. *The Yankee Peddlers of Early America*. New York: Potter, 1964.
Gould, Mary E. *Antique Tin and Tole Ware*. Rutland, Vt.: Tuttle, 1958.
John, W. D. *Pontypool and Usk Japanned Wares*. Newport, England: Ceramic Book Co., 1953.
Kauffman, Henry J. *Early American Copper, Tin and Brass*. New York: Medill McBride Co., 1950.

Glass

Anon. *Glass From the Corning Museum of Glass*. Corning, N. Y.: Corning Glass Center, 1958.
Barbour, Harriet Buxton. *Sandwich: The Town That Glass Built*. New York: Houghton, Mifflin, 1948.
Bergstrom, Evangeline H. *Old Glass Paperweights*. New York: Crown, 1947.
Drepperd, Carl W. *The ABC's of Old Glass*. New York: Doubleday, 1949.
Fisher, Leonard Everett. *The Glassmakers*. New York: Franklin Watts, 1964.
Haynes, Williams. *Horseshoe Nails to Squeeze Bottles: A New Look at Stonington Connecticut*. Stonington, Conn.: Pequot Press, 1957.
Jarves, Deming. *Reminiscences of Glass Making*. Boston: Eastburn's Press, 1854.
Kinney, Kay. *Glass Craft: Designing, Forming, Decorating*. Philadelphia: Chilton, 1962.
Knittle, Rhea M. *Early American Glass*. New York: Century, 1927.
Lee, Ruth Webb. *The Boston and Sandwich Glass Co*. Framingham, Mass.: 1938.
Lee, Ruth Webb. *Early American Pressed Glass*. Pittsford, N. Y.: 1931.
Lee, Ruth Webb. *Sandwich Glass*. Pittsford, N. Y.: 1939.
Lee, Ruth Webb and Rose, James H. *American Glass Cup Plates*. Northborough, Mass.: Ruth Webb Lee, 1948.
McKearin, George S. and Helen. *American Glass*. New York: Crown, 1941.
VanRensselaer, Stephen. *Early American Bottles and Flasks*. Peterborough, N. H.: 1928.
Van Tassel, Valentine. *American Glass*. New York: Barrows, 1950.
Watkins, Lura Woodside. *Cambridge Glass 1818 to 1888*. Boston: Little, Brown, 1930.
Watkins, Lura Woodside. *American Glass and Glassmaking*. New York: Chanticleer Press, 1950.
Waugh, Sidney. *The Art of Glassmaking*. New York: Dodd, Mead, 1937.
Wilson, Kenneth M. *Glass in New England*. Sturbridge, Mass.: Old Sturbridge Village, 1959.
Young, Mary. *Singing Windows*. New York: Abingdon Press, 1962.

Papyrotamia, the art of cutting paper to create intricate designs, took many forms including this one featuring the greatly loved symbol of victory. *Photo courtesy Shelburne Museum*

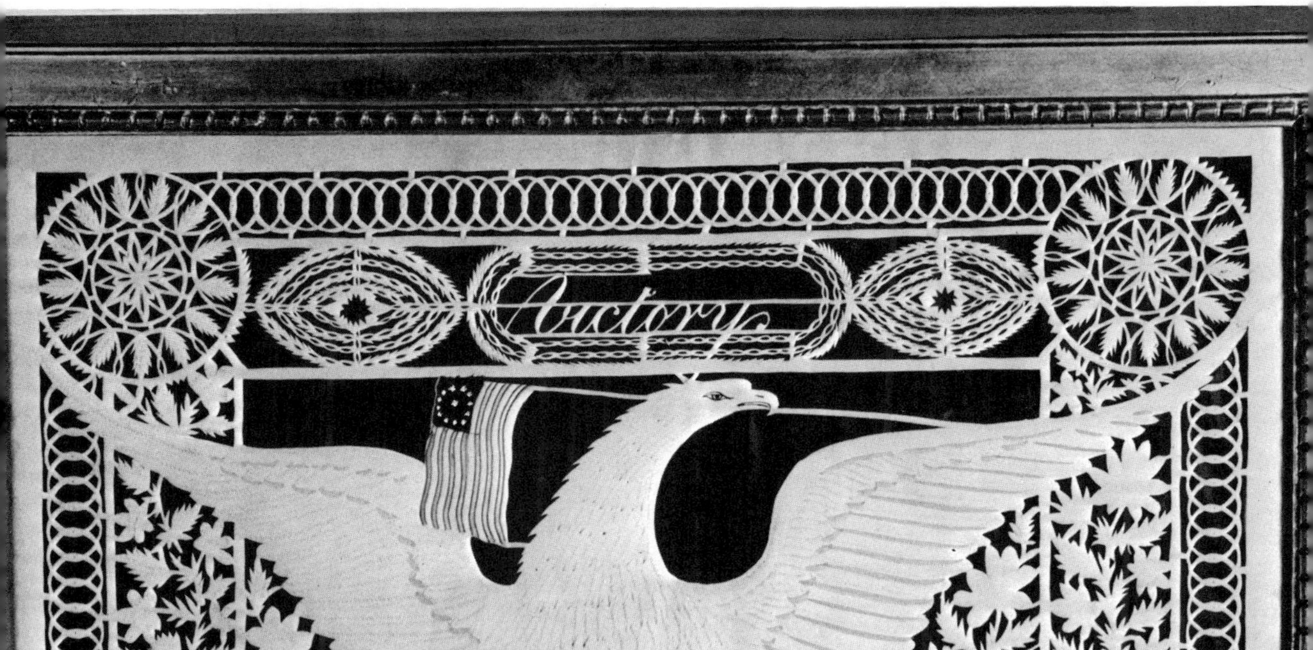

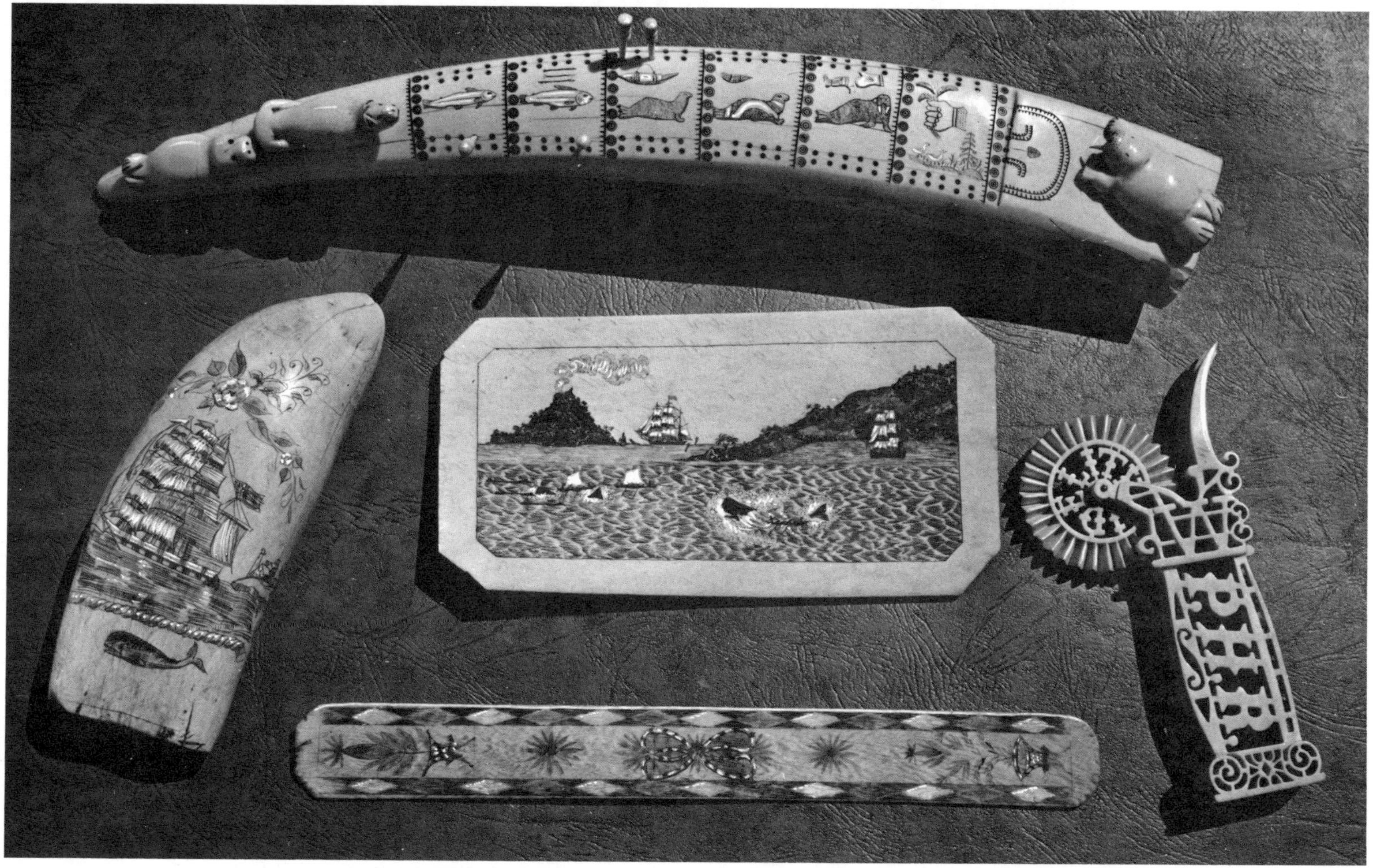

From what the sailors wrote in their letters, diaries, and logbooks, we know that their minds wandered homeward on those long voyages which took them to the Bering Sea, to the coast of Africa, to Japan, and to other distant points. A favorite piece of scrimshaw which they made was the busk (the frontal stay used in the old-fashioned corset, usually ten to twelve inches long) fashioned from the lower jawbone of the whale. These were not only elaborately engraved with sentimental designs but often contained verses phrased in a similar mood. *Photo Louis S. Martel: courtesy Mystic Seaport*

Silver and Pewter

Andrews, William Loring. *Paul Revere and His Engraving.* New York: Scribner's, 1901.
Avery, Louise C. *Early American Silver.* New York: Century, 1930.
Bigelow, F. H. *Historic Silver of the Colonies.* New York: Macmillan, 1917.
Clarke, H. F. *John Coney, Silversmith.* Boston: Houghton, Mifflin, 1932.
Fales, Martha Gandy. *American Silver in the Henry Francis DuPont Winterthur Museum.* Winterthur, Del.: 1958.
Forbes, Esther. *Paul Revere and the World He Lived In.* Boston: Houghton, Mifflin, 1942.
Kerfoot, J. B. *American Pewter.* New York: Houghton, Mifflin, 1942.
Miller, William D. *Silversmiths of Little Rest.* Boston: Merrymount Press, 1928.
Phillips, John M. *American Silver.* New York: Chanticleer Press, 1949.
Wyler, Seymour. *The Book of Old Silver.* New York: Crown, 1937.

Scrimshaw

Ashley, Clifford W. *The Yankee Whaler.* Boston: Houghton, Mifflin. 1926.
Barbeau, Marius. *All Hands Aboard Scrimshawing.* Salem, Mass.: American Neptune, 1952.
Crosby, Everett U. *Susan's Teeth.* Privately published, 1955.
Earle, Walter K. *Scrimshaw, Folk Art of the Whalers.* Coldspring Harbor, New York: Whaling Museum Society, 1957.
Melville, Herman. *Moby Dick.* New York: Harper's, 1851.
Robotti, Frances Diane. *Whaling and Old Salem.* New York: Fountainhead, 1962.
Stackpole, E. A. *Scrimshaw at Mystic Seaport.* Mystic, Conn.: 1961.

Toys

Boehn, M. Von. *Dolls and Puppets.* Boston: Branford, 1956.
Cole, Adeline P. *Notes on the Collection of Dolls and Figurines at the Wenham Museum.* Wenham (Mass.) Historical Association, 1951.
Daiken, Leslie H. *Children's Games Throughout the Year.* London: Batsford, 1949.
Daiken, Leslie H. *Children's Toys Throughout the Ages.* New York: Praeger, 1953.
Daiken, Leslie H. *Teaching Through Play.* New York: Pitman, 1953.
Earle, Alice Morse. *Child Life in Colonial Days.* New York: Macmillan, 1899.
Earle, Alice Morse. *Diary of Anna Green Winslow.* Boston: Houghton Mifflin, 1894.
Earle, Alice Morse. *The Sabbath in Puritan New England.* New York: Scribner, 1891.
Eldridge, Charlotte. *The Godey Lady Doll.* New York: Hastings, 1953.
Fawcett, Clara Evelyn (Hallard). *Dolls, A Guide for Collectors.* New York: Lindquist, 1947.
Foley, Daniel J. *Toys Through the Ages.* Philadelphia: Chilton, 1962
Freeman, Ruth. *American Dolls.* New York: Century, 1952.
Freeman, Ruth and Larry. *Cavalcade of Toys.* New York: Century, 1942.
Gordon, Lesley. *A Pageant of Dolls.* New York: Wynn, 1949.
Grober, Karl. *Children's Toys of Bygone Days.* London: Batsford, 1928.
Hertz, Louis H. *The Handbook of Old American Toys.* Wethersfield, Conn.: Mark Haber, 1947.
Hertz, Louis H. *Mechanical Toy Banks.* Wethersfield, Conn.: Mark Haber, 1947.
Hertz, Louis H. *Messrs. Ives of Bridgeport.* Wethersfield, Conn.: Mark Haber, 1950.
Hertz, Louis H. *Riding the Tinplate Rails.* Wethersfield, Conn.: Mark Haber, 1944.
Jackson, Mrs. E. Nevill. *Toys of Other Days.* London: Country Life, 1907.
Jacobs, Flora Gill. *A History of Dolls' Houses.* New York: Scribner, 1953.
Johl, J. P. *The Fascinating Story of Dolls.* New York: Lindquist, 1941.
Johl, J. P. *More About Dolls.* New York: Lindquist, 1941.
Johl, J. P. *Your Dolls and Mine.* New York: Lindquist, 1952.
McClintock, Inez and Marshall. *Toys in America.* Washington, D. C.: Public Affairs Press, 1961.
Rosenbach, A. S. W. *Early American Children's Books.* Portland, Maine: Southworth, 1933.
St. George, Eleanor. *Dolls of Three Centuries.* New York: Scribner, 1951.
St. George, Eleanor. *The Dolls of Yesterday.* New York: Scribner, 1948.
St. George, Eleanor. *Old Dolls.* New York: Barrows, 1950.
Shepard, Odell. *The Joys of Forgetting.* Boston: Houghton, Mifflin, 1929.
Sinclair, H. *Toy Manufacturing and Marketing.* Springfield: Philips, 1931.
Singleton, E. *Dolls.* New York: Payson & Clarke, 1927.
Toy Manufacturers in the U. S. A. New York: Toy Manufacturing Association, 1935.
Usher, Abbott P. *A History of Mechanical Inventions.* Cambridge: Harvard Univ. Press, 1954.

For the clipper he named for himself, Donald McKay, builder of ships in East Boston, used a Scottish Highlander for the figurehead, with a Balmoral bonnet and kilt, a red jacket, and plaid stockings. In the figurehead for the *Great Admiral*, the carver, James Anderson, portrayed a remarkable likeness of the naval hero Admiral Farragut. *Photo Louis S. Martel: courtesy Mystic Seaport*

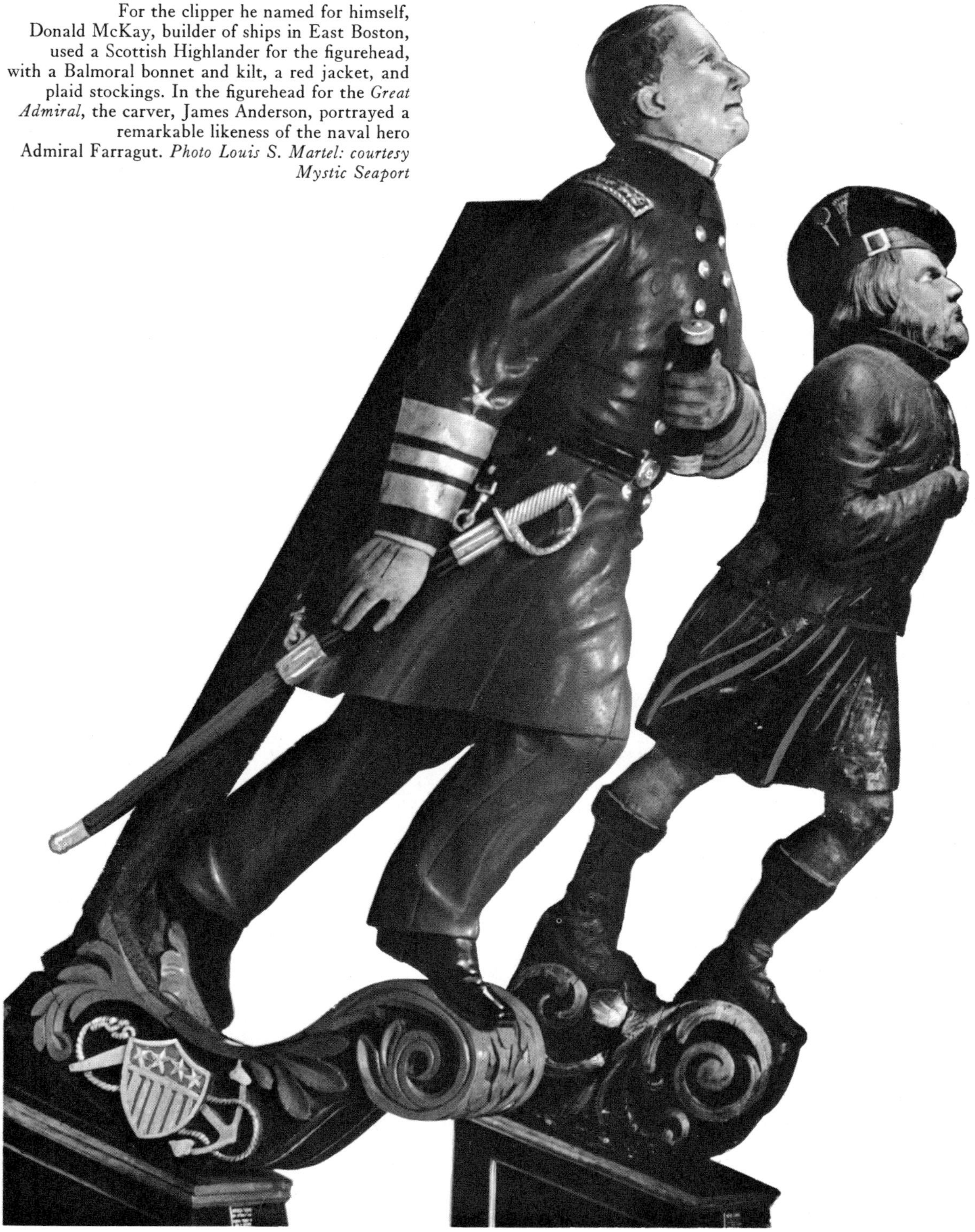

Leading Museums of New England Featuring Displays of Arts and Crafts

In the early years of this century before many of our museums and historical societies were revitalized, those who were eager to learn of the skills of the past found dusty, crowded collections, often poorly displayed and labeled. In many cases, funds were restricted limiting exhibition hours. But a new spirit prevails today which is still emerging; another decade will bring us closer to an even more workable and effective approach for the display of our artistic heritage. Art in its various forms from the great masterpieces to the thoughtfully fashioned craftsman's tool is gradually being given its appropriate niche.

Traveling exhibitions, special displays, the publication of bulletins and pamphlets, lectures, special courses, and member participation in the activities of these cultural institutions have elevated them to a significant level in the community.

Equally significant are the historical restorations where many of the older crafts are demonstrated in a vital and authentic manner. Constant reference has been made to these educational resources in the text and illustrations of this book. Each craft comes to life as techniques and details of designs are demonstrated. With few exceptions, these living museums are operated from late spring through the autumn with visiting hours seven days of the week. An inquiry by mail will provide prospective visitors with the necessary information regarding all important facilities.

Mystic Seaport, Mystic, Connecticut. Old Sturbridge Village, Sturbridge, Massachusetts. Pioneer Village, Salem, Massachusetts. Plimoth Plantation, Plymouth, Massachusetts. Saugus Iron Works, Saugus, Massachusetts. Shelburne Museum, Shelburne, Vermont. Storrowton, West Springfield, Massachusetts.

Thanks largely to the "saving" habits of New Englanders from the early days of settlement to the present, a surprisingly representative collection of artifacts has been assembled by the museums and historical societies in all six states. In nearly every community, it has remained for some individual or a small dedicated group of people, ever mindful of the significance of antiquities, to provide for their preservation. Letters, documents, journals, and diaries have been saved in similar fashion. It is these notable collections that constitute the essence of New England's heritage in the arts and crafts.

The following list, arranged by state, includes the leading museums where examples of outstanding craftsmanship may be seen and studied. In addition, practically every community, town or city, in New England has its own historical society in which are preserved countless treasures of the past. All are open to visitors during the summer months and many operate on a year-round basis.

Connecticut

Bridgeport: Museum of Art, Science and Industry *Bristol:* American Clock and Watch Museum *Farmington:* Farmington Museum *Greenwich:* Bruce Museum *Guilford:* Henry Whitefield Museum *Hartford:* Antiquarian and Landmark Society; Connecticut Historical Society; Wadsworth Atheneum *Litchfield:* Litchfield Historical Society *Middletown:* Davison Art Center *Mystic:* Mystic Seaport *New Britain:* New Britain Museum of American Art *New Haven:* New Haven Colony Historical Society; Yale University Art Gallery *New London:* Lyman Allyn Museum *New Milford:* New Milford Historical Society *Storrs:* William Benton Museum of Art *Wethersfield:* Joseph Webb House; Silas Deane House

Maine

Augusta: Fort Western Museum; Maine State Museum *Bath:* Bath Marine Museum *Brunswick:* Bowdoin College Museum of Art *Gorham:* Art Gallery, University of Maine *Kennebunk:* Brick Store Museum *Orono:* Art Gallery, University of Maine *Portland:* Maine Historical Society; Portland Museum of Art *Rockland:* Farnsworth Art Museum *Saco:* York Institute Museum *Searsport:* Penobscot Marine Museum *Waterville:* Colby College Art Museum *York:* Old York Gaol

Massachusetts

Andover: Addison Gallery of American Art *Boston:* Museum of Fine Arts; Old State House —The Bostonian Society; Society for the Preservation of New England Antiquities *Brockton:* Brockton Art Center *Concord:* Antiquarian House *Deerfield:* Historic Deerfield Inc. *Fall River:* Marine Museum of Fall River *Fitchburg:* Fitchburg Art Museum *Gloucester:* Beauport; Cape Ann Historical Society *Harvard:* Fruitlands Museum *Nantucket:* Nantucket Whaling Museum *New Bedford:* Old Whaling Museum *North Andover:* Merrimac Valley Textile Museum *Pittsfield:* Berkshire Museum; Hancock Shaker Village *Plymouth:* Pilgrim Hall Museum; Plimouth Plantation *Quincy:* Adams National Historic Site *Salem:* Essex Institute; Peabody Museum National Marine Historical Site *Sandwich:* Heritage Plantation; Sandwich Glass Museum; Yesteryears Museum *Saugus:* Saugus Ironworks *Sharon:* Kendall Whaling Museum *South Lancaster:* The Toy Cupboard *Springfield:* Connecticut Valley Historical Museum; Springfield Museum of Fine Arts; G. W. V. Smith Art Museum *Stockbridge:* Mission House: Chesterwood *Sturbridge:* Old Sturbridge Village *Williamstown:* Lawrence Art Museum; Sterling and Francine Clark Art Institute *Worcester:* American Antiquarian Society; Worcester Art Museum

New Hampshire

Canterbury: Shaker Village *Concord:* New Hampshire Historical Society *Manchester:* Currier Gallery of Art *Newport:* Newport Clock Museum *Portsmouth:* Strawberry Banke; Moffat Ladd House; Warner House *Sharon:* Sharon Arts Center

Rhode Island

Bristol: Haffenreffer Museum of Anthropology *Newport:* Newport Historical Society; Preservation Society of Newport County; Redwood Library and Athenaeum *North Kingston:* South County Museum *Pawtucket:* Old Slater Mill Museum *Providence:* Museum of Art, Rhode Island School of Design; Providence Athenaeum; Rhode Island Historical Society

Vermont

Bellows Falls: Adams Old Stone Grist Mill Museum *Burlington:* Robert Hill Fleming Museum *Fairlee:* Walker Museum *Middlebury:* Sheldon Art Museum *Montpelier:* Vermont Historical Society *Old Bennington:* Bennington Museum *Putney:* Putney Historical Museum *Rockingham:* Vermont Country Store and Museum *Shelburne:* Shelburne Museum *Springfield:* Springfield Art & Historical Society

Index